HUDSONs

HISTORIC HOUSES & GARDENS
MUSEUMS & HERITAGE SITES

Bringing Britain's Heritage to You

Published by Hudson's Media Ltd
35 Thorpe Road, Peterborough PE3 6AG
Telephone: 01733 296910
Email: info@hudsons-media.co.uk
www.hudsonsheritage.com

Front Cover: Loseley Park, Surrey, from the Walled Garden

Back Cover: Chatsworth House, Derbyshire; champagne in Blenheim Palace Gardens, Oxfordshire

2016

Discover 1,000 years of history...

- Stunning art & architecture
- Extraordinary stories
- Impressive monuments
- Amazing stained glass
- Drive, walk & cycle trails
- City, town & country locations

THE CHURCHES CONSERVATION TRUST

visitchurches.org.uk

Registered Charity No: 258612

347 historic churches across England

Welcome to HUDSONs

This is the year to get out and visit gardens. Did you know it is the Year of the English Garden? This taps into the excitement around the 300th anniversary of the birth of 'Capability' Brown, the man who shaped the ideal of English landscape and whose legacy is all around us at country houses today. It seems that Scottish gardens are determined not to be left out either; I talked to one Scottish garden owner who is not letting the grass grow under her feet. If you are more of a literary than a horticultural bent, you'll be glad to celebrate the 400th anniversary of the death of William Shakespeare and catch up with our greatest playwright on a trip to Stratford-upon-Avon. For art lovers, we've been quizzing some of today's great art collectors and meeting landscape artist, Tim Scott Bolton. We've looked at combatting theft from country houses and walked across Cornwall on one of our heritage walks.

Dan Snow is great at turning all of us into history enthusiasts and we asked him about his childhood and his hopes for his children. He should inspire you to use this book to find out where to spend your days out and get excited about the past by visiting places where history happened. We've included some useful 'Quick Guides' at the back to help you find places that suit you including, for the first time, places that welcome dogs. Have a great year visiting all our special heritage places.

Sarah

Sarah Greenwood,
Publisher

Sudeley Castle Gardens, Gloucestershire
© VISIT ENGLAND IMAGES

He Missed Out
Make Sure You Don't

If you haven't recently spoken to a renewable energy supplier, it's time you should...

The government backed RHI scheme will pay you to switch from costly fossil fuels to cost effective renewable heating. In fact, for those that make the switch early, the Renewable Heat Incentive can turn your heating requirements from a financial drain into a cash generator, whilst sustainably heating your home without the concern of running costs. Contact Ecovision to gain a free no obligation assessment.

To see how a renewable heating system can make the whole family happy, email **jeorjie.monk@ecovision.co.uk** or call **01666 501580** for more information - **www.ecovision.co.uk**

Inside

Thanks to all private owners, local authorities, Cadw, English Heritage, Historic Royal Palaces, Historic England, Historic Scotland, the National Trust, the National Trust for Scotland, the Royal Collection for their information and for keeping Hudson's accurate and up-to-date. All images are copyright to Hudson's Media Ltd or the property depicted unless otherwise stated.

Hudson's Historic Houses & Gardens team:
Editorial: Sarah Greenwood; Neil Pope
Production Manager: Deborah Coulter
Product Managers: Rebecca Owen-Fisher; Rhiannon McCluskey; Sophie Studd
Creative Team: Neil Pope; Jamieson Eley
Publishing Manager: Sarah Phillips
Advertising: James O'Rawe 01733 296913; Hall-McCartney Ltd, Baldock SG7 5SH
Web Team: Sarah Phillips; NVG www.nvg.net
Printer: Stephens & George, Merthyr Tydfil CF48 3TD
Distribution: Compass International Publishing Services, Brentford TW8 9DF
Hudson's Media Ltd, 35 Thorpe Road, Peterborough PE3 6AG 01733 296910

Pictures: Clockwise from top left: 'Capability' Brown smiles from the walls at Burghley House, Lincs in this portrait by Nathaniel Dance; magic at Duff House, Scotland; straight lines in the gardens at Renishaw Hall, Derbs; detail from one of the lost tapestries of Croome Park, Worcs; exploring the landscape at Kirkharle, Northumberland; winding the clocks at Blenheim Palace, Oxon

WHAT'S NEW

Watch out for some highlights of the heritage year in 2016.

Welbeck Treasures

The Portland Collection is one of the great private art collections in Britain. Exceptional collectors featured in several generations of the Cavendish-Bentinck family including Edward Harley, 2nd Earl of Oxford (1689-1741), whose library formed the basis of today's British Library, and the reclusive 5th Duke of Portland, whose zeal as a collector has been obscured by his reputation for subterranean building works at his home, Welbeck Abbey.

This Spring sees the opening of the Portland Collection at Welbeck, purpose built within the walls of the Victorian Tan Gallop, where racehorses were once exercised.

The Gallery will display artworks from the extensive collection of oil painted portraits, including works by van Dyck, Reynolds, Stubbs, Wootton, Sargent and de Laszlo, an exquisite collection of miniatures, books, jewellery, silver, manuscripts and the pearl earring worn by Charles I at his execution.

Previously only highlights of the collection could be seen in special exhibitions or on pre-booked tours of the State Rooms in August, now the collection should be high on everyone's list of places to visit. While you are there you can also explore the estate, the Dukeries garden centre and Welbeck Farm shop, finishing up with a bottle of Welbeck Abbey Ale.
Welbeck Abbey, Nottinghamshire (p.220)

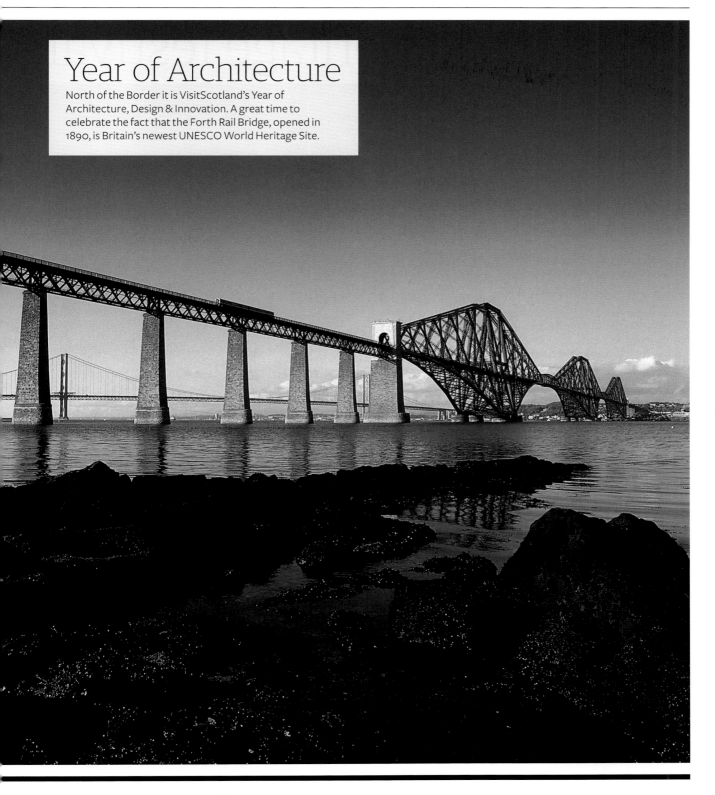

Year of Architecture

North of the Border it is VisitScotland's Year of
Architecture, Design & Innovation. A great time to
celebrate the fact that the Forth Rail Bridge, opened in
1890, is Britain's newest UNESCO World Heritage Site.

UK's largest heritage festival

heritage open days

8th to 11th
September 2016

Heritage Open Days is now the country's largest heritage festival with over 4,600 events, around 40,000 volunteers and some three million visitors taking part. Celebrating local history, architecture and culture, the four-day event offers everyone the chance to explore hidden places and experience something new completely free of charge.

If you are in Scotland and Wales, look out for Doors Open Days programmes of free openings on September weekends.

Thanks to the many private owners, National Trust, Scottish Civic Trust, Historic Scotland and Cadw and everyone who participates for making this feast of heritage adventures such a success.
www.heritageopendays.org.uk
and www.doorsopendays.org.co.uk

Doors Open Days
get into buildings!

True Blue

It is 150 years since the introduction of the Blue Plaque scheme in 1866, the first in the world, though much imitated. Blue Plaques celebrate the link between people and buildings and today English Heritage aim to install up to 12 plaques a year and a similar number of Commemorative Plaques are awarded by Historic Scotland. They continue to be founded on detailed, professional historical research but anyone can propose a plaque and all suggestions are considered.

Illuminated Turners in the North Gallery of Petworth House with
Andrew Loukes - Curator of Exhibitions.

Our latest commission: to design a new picture light for The National Trust.
Primarily for 'Mr. Turner -An Exhibition' at Petworth House and continuing to
illuminate further works in this great collection.

Queen's House celebrates 400 years

Four hundred years ago this year, the Queen's House, the first Palladian building in England, was built by Inigo Jones at Greenwich, perhaps the most influential of all buildings in Britain. Built for Anne of Denmark, queen of James I, the Queen's House is famed for its perfectly proportioned Great Hall and elegant Tulip Stairs and will reopen this July after restoration. Royal Museums Greenwich are refurbishing the sumptuous rooms and filling them with paintings not only from their own collection but also from the Royal Collection. Orazio Gentileschi's *Joseph and Potiphar's Wife* was commissioned by Charles I for the Queen's House but was removed in 1650 after the execution of Charles I, who had spent his last night here with Queen Henrietta Maria in 1642 before the Civil War parted them. Their joint portrait by Daniel Mytens is also generously loaned from the Royal Collection by Her Majesty The Queen. Above all, it is a chance for the Queen's House, in its modern role as the National Maritime Museum's prime fine-art venue, to showcase its outstanding art collection.
Queen's House, Greenwich (p.131)

All change

2016 is the first full year for the new English Heritage and Historic England and the new Historic Environment Scotland. Here's how it works:

▸ **English Heritage** is a national charity which cares for over 400 historic buildings, monuments and sites - from Dover Castle and Stonehenge to a Cold War bunker. They aim to bring the story of England to life for over 10 million visitors each year.

▸ **Historic England** is a government service championing England's heritage, maintaining the National Heritage List for England and giving expert, constructive advice. (*p.334*)

▸ **Historic Environment Scotland** is a new charity, a merger of Historic Scotland and the Royal Commission on the Ancient & Historical Monuments of Scotland, and combines care and promotion of historic sites in Scotland with statutory protection.

ENGLISH HERITAGE

Historic England

Historic Environment Scotland
Shaping our Future

Abbey Specials

The 950th anniversary of the Battle of Hastings, probably the most important battle fought on English soil, sees the opening of a new museum at Battle Abbey in Sussex. New artefacts and new ideas about the battle will be on show exactly where King Harold died, in the Great Gatehouse of the medieval abbey, one of the finest monastic gatehouses in England. And Rievaulx Abbey will also have a new museum to tell the abbey's 900-year story, shedding light on one of the most important and spectacular abbey ruins in North Yorkshire.

Scott Rail

Fans of Sir Walter Scott (and Dandie Dinmont terriers which he was the first to breed) can now get to Scott's home, Abbotsford on the new Borders Railway service between the appropriately named Waverley station in Edinburgh and Tweedbank. The journey takes less than an hour and Tweedbank is just 20 minutes walk or a quick shuttle bus ride from Abbotsford. Scott's imagination and his best selling novels helped create not just a romantic house and garden but also a vision of Scotland which endures to this day. You feel very close to Sir Walter Scott at Abbotsford by wandering through his rooms, admiring his collections and listening to the audio presentation. The modern visitor centre, open all year round, provides a fascinating introduction to Scott and his life as well as giving visitors all the modern comforts.
Abbotsford, Borders (p.299)

© VISIT SCOTLAND

Field to Fork at Holkham

Head for Holkham Hall in Norfolk this March to explore all sorts of new developments at this great Palladian house. Holkham was the crucible of the agricultural revolution, home to Coke of Norfolk, who, along with neighbours like 'Turnip' Townshend of nearby Raynham, helped to develop modern farming techniques. A new exhibition area, Field to Fork, will tell the story and explore the history of the agricultural reformers and the relationship between food, farming and the land. A new shop and café and a spacious new entertaining area for wedding receptions will add to the excitement.

Holkham Hall, Norfolk (p.209)

Transforming Hillsborough

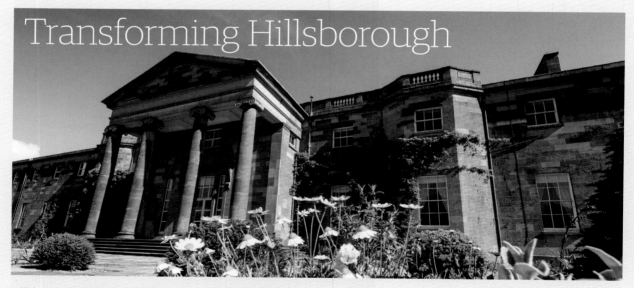

Hillsborough Castle has welcomed visitors from all corners of the globe for over three centuries. 2016 marks the second year of Historic Royal Palaces' management of the site, and plans to transform the castle are now in place to help visitors learn about its journey from family home to political stage and now a royal residence. Starting at Easter 2016, the State Entrance Hall will feature a number of newly-hung paintings including a group from Royal Collection Trust. Portraits of Charles II, William III and Mary II will hang alongside Wills Hill, the 2nd Earl of Hillsborough and Secretary of State for the Colonies (America) who built the original late Georgian mansion that is Hillsborough Castle today.

A tour of the house takes you through the elegant State Rooms, still in use today, including the Throne Room and Drawing Room. You can get outside and explore the magnificent landscaped gardens and discover the newly-created fountain on the Jubilee Parterre.

Hillsborough Castle, Northern Ireland (p.331)

PRIORY BAY
HOTEL

Priory Bay is the Isle of Wight's leading country house hotel. Set within a 60-acre estate, it's period buildings have spectacular views out to sea, with gardens and woodland running down to the seashore. Our food is fresh from the Island with a focus on local produce whether farmed, fished or foraged.

The Isle of Wight is only a couple of hours from London and a perfect escape, however you choose to arrive. Charter a RIB, fly in by helicopter or hovercraft or drive yourself via one of the three ferry routes that regularly depart Portsmouth, Southampton and Lymington in the New Forest.

Charter a classic yacht or enjoy our six-hole golf course, the estate has tennis courts, an outdoor swimming pool and enjoys access to a secluded private beach, there's even tree climbing with Goodleaf. Be as active or as laid-back as you want to be...

Photo: Available Light Photography

the Country House Hotel by the sea

TELEPHONE 01983 613146   FAX 01983 616539
ENQUIRIES@PRIORYBAY.CO.UK   WWW.PRIORYBAY.CO.UK
PRIORY DRIVE SEAVIEW ISLE OF WIGHT PO34 5BU

Year of the English Garden

Great Dixter,
East Sussex

Penshurst Place, Kent

Levens Hall, Cumbria

Adlington Hall, Cheshire

Gardening is the thing we most enjoy in Britain. It's not only a favourite hobby with readers of **Hudson's** (yes, we asked!) it is also the favourite with pretty well everyone else. We made 34 million visits to gardens in 2014 but if you were not one, 2016 is the year to start. Not only is it 'Capability' Brown's 300th birthday (if you still don't know who he is, read on) but VisitEngland have designated this year *The Year of the English Garden*.

2016 Year of the English Garden™

in association with Visit**England**

We don't know much about gardens in England before the Romans but you can explore one of those at Fishbourne Palace in Sussex. In medieval times castle gardens provided a secluded haven with turf seats and wild flowers cultivated for their scent. Visit Bolton Castle in Yorkshire for an idea of how delightful they might have been.

The first grand country houses that came after the dissolution of the monasteries and the loss of the monks' physic gardens, were intricate places of pattern: topiary, knot gardens, bowers and summerhouses. Try Kenilworth Castle, Hatfield House or Levens Hall.

Come the 18th Century and everything changed. Informality was in and landscaped gardens came right up to the walls. A taste for the classical and the picturesque brought views, clumps of trees, lakes, classical temples and follies. The movement was dominated by Lancelot 'Capability Brown' but other earlier influential designers were Charles Bridgeman and William Kent, and their legacy was taken up by landscape architects like Humphrey Repton who reintroduced flower gardens around the house.

In the 19th Century plant hunters brought back increasing numbers of exotic species, which have since become familiar garden plants, from all corners of the globe. Flowerbeds were once more used to create intricate patterns in brilliant colours laid out by Victorian gardeners in strict parterres. Holker Hall in Cumbria, Somerleyton Hall in Suffolk and Hampton Court are fine surviving examples. This rigidity was hated by William Robinson and Gertrude Jekyll at the turn of the 19th Century who proposed a wilder natural look and graduated colours. The legacy of these arts and crafts gardeners lives on at gardens like Hidcote and Great Dixter.

Mass gardening in the new suburbs of the 1920s made us all a little obsessed with gardens. The National Gardens Scheme was launched in 1927 and garden visiting became a recognisable pastime. Visiting has produced its own style of gardens for entertainment that hark back to the past at The Alnwick Garden in Northumberland or Burghley's Garden of Surprises in Lincolnshire.

Make this the year you explore plenty of gardens, whatever the weather, from the first snowdrop to the last Christmas Rose.

Iford Manor, Wiltshire

Powderham Castle, Devon

Blenheim Palace, Oxfordshire

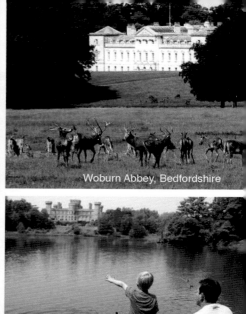

Woburn Abbey, Bedfordshire

Blair Castle, Pitlochry, Scotland

Highclere Castle, Berkshire

Eastnor Castle, Herefordshire

Arley Hall Gardens, Cheshire

Sausmarez Manor, Guernsey

Benvarden, Northern Ireland

Bolton Castle, Yorkshire

HHA

HISTORIC HOUSES ASSOCIATION

Become a Friend of the HHA and discover some of Britain's most special places

Scone Palace, Perth, Scotland

Hundreds of HHA-affiliated, privately-owned historic houses, castles and gardens open regularly to the public. Many of the properties are still lived in, often by families who have owned them for centuries, and many include exquisite gardens. Each is unique, giving you special insights into much-loved homes and their social and historical contexts.

HHA-affiliated properties welcome around 13 million visitors a year, support 26,000 jobs and are often key players in their local communities. The HHA provides practical advice and professional services to these properties, and we represent their views at local, national and European level. As a Friend, you help these properties by understanding their challenges, supporting the HHA's work and spreading the word about the special nature of privately-owned historic houses.

As an HHA Friend your membership gives you outstanding value for money:
- Free entry in normal opening hours to hundreds of historic houses, castles and gardens
- Our quarterly magazine *Historic House*
- Opportunities to join tours to visit properties not usually open to the public

Individual Friend..£45
Double Friends (same address) £72
Additional Friends
(same address, including under-16s)....................£22

Rates shown above are for payment by direct debit.
For payment by credit/debit card or cheque, see www.hha.org.uk.

Check out HHA-affiliated properties with our free app for iPhone, iPad and Android.

To join us, visit www.hha.org.uk or call 01462 896688

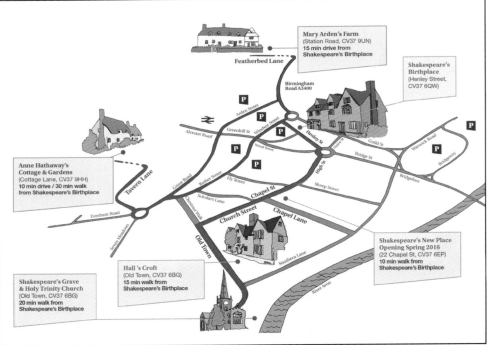

Mary Arden's Farm
(Station Road, CV37 9UN)
15 min drive from
Shakespeare's Birthplace

Shakespeare's
Birthplace
(Henley Street,
CV37 6QW)

Featherbed Lane

Birmingham
Road A3400

Arden Street

Alcester Road

Greenhill St

Windsor Street

Henley St

Wood Street

Guild St

Warwick Road

Bridge St

Bridgeway

Bridgefoot

Anne Hathaway's
Cottage & Gardens
(Cottage Lane, CV37 9HH)
10 min drive / 30 min walk
from Shakespeare's Birthplace

Tavern Lane

Grove Road

Rother Street

Ely Street

Scholars Lane

Chapel St

Sheep Street

High St

Church Street

Chapel Lane

Evesham Road

Chestnut Walk

Old Town

Severn Meadows

Southern Lane

River Avon

Shakespeare's Grave
& Holy Trinity Church
(Old Town, CV37 6BG)
20 min walk from
Shakespeare's Birthplace

Hall 's Croft
(Old Town, CV37 6BG)
15 min walk from
Shakespeare's Birthplace

Shakespeare's New Place
Opening Spring 2016
(22 Chapel St, CV37 6EP)
10 min walk from
Shakespeare's Birthplace

Mrs Hudson's Holiday

Mrs Hudson and her trusty dog Walpole can always be relied on to recommend the best places in Britain to visit. This year she's stuck on Shakespeare in Stratford-upon-Avon.

Right: Palmer's Farmhouse, neighbours to Shakespeare's grandfather, Robert Arden of Wilmcote, where today you encounter a slice of Tudor life

Willliam Shakespeare! Is there anywhere a more revered Briton? When I found out that it was the 400th anniversary of his death in 2016, I just had to go and meet him.

You have to be impressed by a man who managed not only to die on the same date he was born, 23 April (probably), but also on his country's national day, St George's Day. He chose to live in one of the prettiest English towns, Stratford-upon-Avon, which has been the centre of Shakespeare tourism since at least 1759 when the Rev. Francis Gastrell knocked down Shakespeare's house to discourage gawpers.

Friday

As soon as you arrive it is clear that there are two sides of Stratford. There's the bit for coach trippers who rush through before being bundled back to rush on somewhere else (Warwick Castle usually). And there's the bit where people wander from place to place, lapping up the atmosphere, rowing lazily in skiffs and quoting lines to each other. I'm for both, so I start amid a throng of flag-wielding Japanese tourists at **Shakespeare's Birthplace.**

Dive through the less than appealing modern entrance and head for the exhibition. You get Shakespeare in context right away, he's not Britain's bard, he's everyone's bard. Here are busts, paintings, games, street signs and souvenirs from all over the world, from Georgia, Nepal, Australia and Russia.

The Knot Garden at New Place was designed by historian and Shakespeare scholar, Ernest Law, in 1919 and will be restored to its original planting as part of the New Place Regeneration project

Above: Mock up of the entrance to New Place, which will echo the original gatehouse through which Shakespeare would have entered his house

"Nothing here is academic; it is really living"

Shakespeare's Birthplace in Henley Street which was both home and shop for the family

Straightaway, you can hear the sound of Shakespeare: rap Shakespeare, cartoon Shakespeare, recordings of Emma Watson and Leo DiCaprio doing Shakespeare and you realise that nothing here is academic; it is really living. No time to drool over early folios - move with the crowd to the heart of the shrine, the small timbered house where William Shakespeare was born. It's charming; set in a flower filled garden where every flower bed holds a label with an appropriate play reference. The house and workshop, where William grew up with his glover father and land owning mother and where he brought his new wife in 1582, feel remarkably original. It is well dressed with lots of period detail and I feel my cynicism sloughing away.

I learn lots of new facts – did you know that Tudor children slept with their parents until they were old enough to be trusted with a candle? Or that the wall hangings were coloured to confuse the devil lest he take the children away? The knowledgeable costumed interpreters look at home, the recreation is all based on careful research, sometimes from the plays themselves, to build an interior which is really right for the 1570s. Outside, it is drizzling but a costumed actor is declaiming cheerfully to a damp family on a bench. I catch up with the Japanese group in a cavernous shop jammed with Shakespeariana. The Japanese are racing for the coach stop but I have time for some Spiced Shakespeare Sausages in the café and a stroll down Henley Street to **New Place**.

Shakespeare left for London when the family was nearly bankrupt but returned in triumph in 1597 to buy the largest house in town. New Place had a street-side gatehouse, a service range and a large hall house behind with grounds running down to the river.

Thanks to Rev Gastrell, we don't know how it looked, so today's big transformation project is not going for pastiche but for atmosphere and contemplation. When I was there the site was still in the hands of the archaeologists but project manager, Julie Crawshaw, brought it all to life for me. She also took me to the very spot where Shakespeare must have written his late plays including The Tempest. Miraculously, you can still see the same view he would have seen, of the medieval Guild Chapel, the Grammar School he attended as a boy and the Tudor streetscape opposite. It gave me quite a jolt.

By the time you get here, the site will have been transformed; you'll retrace Shakespeare's steps through a gleaming bronze entrance gate into a tranquil tree lined space sheltering evocative art installations and a bronze desk, so that everyone can get the thrill of realising that he sat right here to pen a masterpiece.

An exhibition in restored **Nash's House** next door, where Shakespeare's granddaughter Elizabeth lived with her husband, will tell the family story.

→

Saturday

A stroll along the river, jostling with swans, takes me to **Holy Trinity Church**. And there he lies. Right in front of the altar, flanked by his wife and daughter, with an alarming injunction "cursed be he that moves my bones". Looking at the painted effigy above his gravestone, he is every bit the prosperous gentleman. He had made a good living from box office receipts, sales of his writings and property deals. The gaudy effigy dates to 1623, seven years after his death, but his wife and daughters must have approved it, so it may be the best likeness we have.

From the inscription on her grave, daughter Susanna was obviously quite a girl – "witty above her sex, but that's not all". Just around the corner, another appealing timbered house, **Hall's Croft**, is where she lived with her husband, respected physician, Dr John Hall. How fascinating to see the interior's domestic detail and learn that Hall and Shakespeare, only 11 years different in age, were friends. Dr Caius in The Merry Wives of Windsor is just a vehicle for a joke but after this friendship, Shakespeare's doctors are learned and wise or, like Cerimon in Pericles, even central to the plot. A hilarious steward here reports the foibles of visitors who ask for photographs of Shakespeare and want to know if Anne Hathaway is at home today. The apothecary's garden behind has an ancient mulberry tree, a feature of all the houses, laden with purple fruit. Almost as venerable as yesterday's mulberry at New Place, which is supposed to have been grown from a cutting from a tree planted by Shakespeare.

Of course I went to see the Royal Shakespeare Company perform, why would you come to Stratford and not? The original Art Deco theatre is now encased in a gleaming modern shell with a superb circular auditorium but the 1930s silvered entrance is still an architectural marvel. Going to the play is all part of the Shakespeare experience.

An Elizabethan signet ring with the initials WS found near Holy Trinity Church in 1810. Is this the ring that Shakespeare lost just before signing his will in 1616?

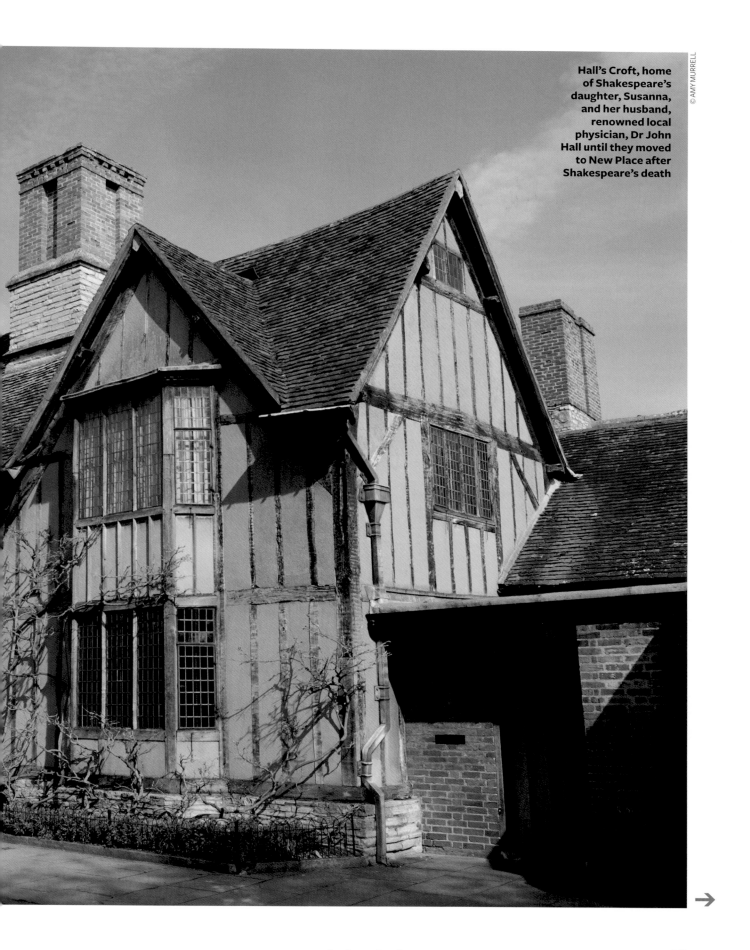

Hall's Croft, home of Shakespeare's daughter, Susanna, and her husband, renowned local physician, Dr John Hall until they moved to New Place after Shakespeare's death

© AMY MURRELL

Sunday

Next day, I'm off to **Mary Arden's Farm**, a short three miles from the centre of town, with poetry ringing in my head (or was the 'Shakesbeer'?). It's a short hop by car, take the sightseeing bus or hire a bike and peddle up the canal – the coach crowd don't make it this far. Shakespeare's mum, Mary Arden, was a country girl, growing up on a small farm before moving to Henley Street on her marriage to John Shakespeare. There are two farms, the Ardens' modest cottage and their neighbours' larger farmhouse. It's 1573 here - no really, it does begin to feel like 1573. Aside from the visitors, everyone is in costume and busy, feeding livestock, baking bread in a clay oven, tending the garden and preparing food. I learn lots more domestic detail about what and how people ate, look across a timewarp as the Tudor 'family' of volunteers has lunch – quelquechoses and pottage today – and try a bit myself in the café. A portly Tudor woman is flying a tame owl and shedding history nuggets like chaff. The crowd ducks and children squeal as the bird sails overhead. It's not perfect – there are no crops beyond garden herbs and the long drop toilet has no drop (perhaps a blessing) but as an exercise in accessing the past, it is honest, informative and fun.

"As an exercise in accessing the past, it is honest, informative and fun"

Working with leather in Shakespeare's Dad's glove shop

Authentic Tudor fun at Mary Arden's farm

Romantic An
Hathaway's Cotta

Better known is my next stop, **Anne Hathaway's Cottage**, the quintessentially romantic English country cottage, low and timbered with roses at the windows. If kitsch is to be found, surely it will be here, but the bucolic good taste of the café opposite (where I have a Tudor tart) carries over to the cottage and cottage garden. The coach crowd are here. An Indian family, disgorged just ahead of me, are at a loss to understand where they are and why. But the gardens are full of couples, catching the fragrance of the lavender maze, strolling in woods where the trees all come from the plays, relaxing in willow bowers listening to recordings of Shakespeare's love poetry. The mood is set for this visit to the childhood home of Shakespeare's wife, Anne, with whom he had three children after a shotgun marriage in 1582. Famously, he left her his 'second-best bed' in his will and the furniture in the cottage includes a Tudor bed. If not the bed in the will, legend has it that it was given to the Hathaway family by Shakespeare's daughter, so once again, there is a jolt – could he have actually slept here, or sat in this chair?

Spend three days in Shakespeareland, you can get a fresh and tantalising glimpse of his world. Not his city world of work but his intimate family world of love and children and small town life. I am amazed to leave feeling that I have genuinely been in the company of Shakespeare the man. Go now, if only to mark his death!

Unlike Shakespeare, Mrs Hudson is fictional. She is nothing to do with Sherlock Holmes, Norman Hudson or any other Hudsons we know. Her dog, Walpole, has never been let slip as a dog of war.

26

ngs gardens open for charity

OVER 3,800 GARDENS OPEN FOR CHARITY IN ENGLAND AND WALES

Rock Farm, Kent. Image: Leigh Clapp

For more information visit
our website **www.ngs.org.uk**
or telephone **01483 211535**

The National Gardens Scheme
Registered charity number 1112664

Contemporary sculpture enhances the dreamy feel of the gardens of Anne Hathaway's Cottage

The Shakespeare Houses are:
Shakespeare's Birthplace
Shakespeare's New Place
(opens April 2016)
Hall's Croft
Mary Arden's Farm
Anne Hathaway's Cottage

Also visited:
Holy Trinity Church

All photographs
©Shakespeare Birthplace Trust

"I have no doubt that heritage is a force for good. And the force is with us!"

Valuing Heritage

Sir Laurie Magnus,
Chairman of Historic England

When I arrived in my current job, two years ago, I was to help implement a demerger. This involved transferring the care of our collection of 400 properties (ranging from Stonehenge to Apsley House and archaeological humps in the ground) from an arms-length public body to a charity. The demerger became effective in 2015.

Historic England adopted its new name and retains responsibility for advising on listing, planning applications, grant making, research and guidance. It continues to be funded mainly by government and remains the owner or guardian of our property collection.

The charity, English Heritage, has received £80million from government as a one-off contribution to resolve its considerable backlog of conservation work. It is expected, within 7 years, to reach financial break-even and thereby cease to be dependent on the public purse. It is at the cutting edge of public service reform and a possible exemplar for other public bodies.

Sir Laurie Magnus explained to *Hudson's* **why he thinks heritage has a real economic value in our society.**

$\rightarrow$

The historic environment – the impact that men and women have left on our landscape – constitutes a legacy which passes through generations. I can visit a church which my father knew and which my grandfather and great-grandfather knew as well. I can get some idea of how they lived and thought from the historic fabric which they left behind, including furniture, pictures and archives.

This emotionally appealing sentimentality cuts no ice with the "History is Bunk" brigade. They argue that structural cleansing is essential for prosperity and that the UK's future depends upon new build capable of embracing new technologies. Their argument is that the root cause of the UK's poor productivity is a system of planning protection which prevents us from competing with the likes of Singapore or China in developing an infrastructure fit for the 21st Century.

I am suspicious of economic forecasts and of political predictions, mainly because they are so often wrong. I am also suspicious of "what if" arguments. What if Boadicea's revolt had driven out the Romans? Or what if Britain had lost the First World War? Arguments, therefore, that protecting heritage impedes economic growth leave me deeply unconvinced. The facts suggest otherwise.

Economic prosperity depends upon the production of goods and services that people domestically and around the world wish to buy. Some countries are blessed with capital assets which they can exploit such as oil, other minerals, agricultural commodities or gas. We have exhausted our coal, laid waste to our timber and oil is running out. Fracking is unlikely to be feasible. So what assets do we have?

Ask round the world and the answer which is most

Efficient, gleaming modern Singapore, but where is its soul?

popular is our history, represented by our castles, historic houses, churches, old towns, villages and remarkable ancient landscape. It is the reason given by most overseas visitors as to why they come here. It is also a leading reason for staying at home. A huge industry exists in this country to restore historic buildings and to adapt them for alternative use.

Heritage is a massive contributor to the building industry, reflecting a recognition by developers that historic structures provide the fabric for places where people are happier to live, work and enjoy themselves. It is generally accepted that the economic consequences of built and national heritage – through inward and domestic tourism together with construction – amounts to approximately 2% of UK GDP. It employs around 750,000 people and engages over 500,000 volunteers; the biggest contributor to the Big Society.

Diversity is not new in our population; just look at its heritage

The redevelopment of King's Cross is anchored by 20 historic buildings and will attract 300 creative and cultural businesses. Lewis Cubitt's Granary Building of 1852 is now home to Central St Martins art college

Dover Castle, just one heritage place that contributes to our booming tourism sector

There is however, a further reason why heritage in the form of our historic environment is such an important capital asset for the UK. The great driver of our economy, as evidenced over the last 5 years, has come from the creative industries. It is no surprise that many of these businesses have chosen to operate in old buildings adapted for their purposes. The Heritage Lottery Fund supplies the statistical proof for this important linkage of Britain's two great capital assets – its historic fabric and its creativity.

Our heritage does not only bring powerful economic benefits. Beautiful surroundings contribute to a sense of wellbeing and happiness. 90% of respondents to a poll conducted in areas where historic environment investment had occurred agreed that it raised pride in their local area, increased sense of place and encouraged places that promote social activities such as shopping and eating out. In 2013, there were at least 58.6 million paid for visits to historic properties in England. That is at least 15.0 million more than visits to all premier and league football matches in the same period.

The role of heritage in providing a foundation for developing a sense of community and local identity should not be under estimated. Over the last 3 years, Historic England has worked with 700 teachers in 200 primary schools in eight locations to train them in engaging their pupils in bringing local history to life. This has increased the proportion of children with good knowledge of local history and heritage in these areas from 4% to 70%.

It looks as if you may be more content in a cottage

"Beautiful surroundings contribute to a sense of wellbeing and happiness"

Every citizen has a stake in this. For example, Historic England's recent commissioned research on mosques shows an asset class little understood which forms an important component of our historic fabric. Many mosques/Buddhist temples originated in the 19th Century to accommodate citizens of the empire. This accelerated after Partition of India in 1947 and continues as Britain becomes a truly multi-racial society. We need to acknowledge the role and contribution of people from so many different ethnic groups in our national history.

I have no doubt that heritage is a force for good. And the force is with us! There is increasing evidence of popular enthusiasm for history and our historic fabric. It is not just the popularity of television programmes and the way that historians such as David Starkey, Dan Snow and Bettany Hughes have become household names. It is evidenced in social media, as people tweet and blog about places that matter to them.

England may win the World Cup once in a century, but our heritage is a winner for England every day of the year.

Good foundations for school children who enjoy their historic surroundings

The Genius of 'Capability' Brown
1716-1783

"As we passed through the entrance archway and the lovely scenery burst upon me, Randolph said with pardonable pride, 'This is the loveliest view in England'. Looking at the lake, the bridge, the miles of magnificent park studded with old oaks, I found no adequate words to express my admiration"

Lady Randolph Churchill on entering Brown's landscape at Blenheim Palace in 1874.

Mature trees in the landscape at Bowood in Wiltshire; the Lombardy Poplar *Populus nigra* (centre) was often used by Brown as a punctuation point

Facing page: Portrait of Lancelot 'Capability' Brown, c.1770-75 by Richard Cosway (1742-1821)

2016 marks the 300th anniversary of the birth of England's greatest landscape gardener, Lancelot 'Capability' Brown. Gilly Drummond is Chairman of The Capability Brown Festival which will co-ordinate celebrations throughout the year. She is also guardian of Brown's smallest surviving pleasure ground at Cadland in Hampshire. Here she explores the importance of 'Capability' Brown in British culture.

Parks, gardens and designed landscapes are creative works of art but too often go unrecognised and underappreciated as such. What does it take to create a living, dynamic work of art, much of whose form will last for over 200 years? A lively eye for topography, scale and proportion, long term vision and imagination, an understanding of the land itself and its various aspects, a broad diversity of skills in building, engineering, drainage, the management of water and of appropriate planting, all are prerequisites. Both the palette and the canvas can be immensely varied and good manners and the gift of persuasion were also vital as the wishes, taste, interests and resources of owners were as paramount in the 18th Century as they are today.

→

Lancelot 'Capability' Brown had a natural felicity and developed all the skills needed to implement his designs. His clients were influenced by their classical education and he also learnt a great deal from them. It was the era of 'mixing of mortar and moving of earth', of the Reign of Nature and of agricultural improvements which fitted seamlessly into his 'naturalistic' style. Brown was at the forefront of a landscape revolution which not only reshaped large tracts of land but helped to create an image of an idealised England which matched the romantic visions of contemporary painters like Claude Lorrain and remains with us today. He was passed around the country by recommendations from friend to friend, relation to relation and was renowned for his 'eye' and 'capable' skills, sense of humour and quiet dignity; just look at his informal portrait by Richard Cosway, painted sometime between 1770 and 1777 *(previous page)*.

'At Blenheim, Croome and Caversham we trace
Salvator's wildness, Claude's enlivening grace,
Cascades and Lakes as fine as Risdale drew
While Nature's vary'd in each charming view.
To paint his works wou'd Poussin's Powers require,
Milton's sublimity and Dryden's fire.' Anon

Brown is today associated with well over 200 designed landscapes and The Capability Brown Festival celebrates his genius in 2016. The hunt is on for every scrap of information about the man, his foremen and how he ran what was in effect the first professional major landscape practice.

Main picture: Croome in Worcestershire was Brown's first independent commission where he designed the house, church, rotunda and grotto and set all in a landscaped park. Croome is undergoing extensive restoration and replanting by the National Trust

Top: Croome Court painted by Richard Wilson in 1758, with the Capability Brown setting clearly recognisable

Above: Participants in The Croome Poetry Slam in 2015 as part of The Capability Brown Festival. The group of urban poets approached the story of the Brown landscape in new ways to attract new audiences

Volunteers from the County Gardens Trusts and NADFAS Heritage Volunteers are hard at work combing estate archives, where they have been made welcome, and Record Offices up and down the country. A volunteer in Yorkshire recently found the record of a previously unknown Brown site in Sussex. We may not always know precisely which plants and shrubs owners working with Brown selected but at Croome Park in Worcestershire we do know that his client, Lord Coventry, was an astonishingly well informed, energetic and enthusiastic plant collector. Brown worked for him for over 20 years from the 1750s so what he learned from Coventry will have informed his work elsewhere.

Assiduous research into dated bills at Croome suggests that the current introduction dates for some plants may need to be revised. At Luton Hoo in Bedfordshire, the 3rd Earl of Bute, a client of Brown's, another passionate plant collector and in effect the first Director of Kew Gardens, must have had a similar influence.

All this and much more will form part of the lasting legacy of the Festival and help to inform future conservation and management of so many special places woven into the cultural life of the country, still aesthetically beautiful as well as practical. 12 of Lancelot's parks are now public parks, others are in private ownership or cared for by the National Trust and English Heritage.

His forward-thinking designs have stood the test of time and are, what we would call today, sustainable. The Festival plans to have at least 150 'Capability' Brown sites open during 2016, the smaller sites by pre-booked tickets on designated days; many of these will be opening to the public for the first time. In addition there will be events and activities all over the country.

Capability Brown epitomised the English landscape movement of the 18th century but he was not alone. →

Early morning at Trentham, Staffordshire where the lake in Brown's landscape of c.1579 covers 50 acres

© THE TRENTHAM ESTATE

Contemporaries such as Richard Woods, whose tercentenary is also in 2016, and William Emes carried versions of his style far and wide. Brown worked from Northumberland down to Devon and over into Wales. How did he do so much work and travel the country so extensively? He had a great eye for placing buildings in a landscape, often working with great architects, such as Robert Adam and James Paine. The unsung heroes of his architectural and landscape practice were his associates or foremen who implemented his designs, not to mention his valuable architectural partnership with Henry Holland Senior and Junior. Henry Holland Junior married Brown's daughter, Bridget.

Peripatetic surveyor and draughtsman, John Spyers, drew and often painted in watercolour, several of Brown's plans. Many were later acquired by Catherine the Great and are now in The Hermitage Museum, St Petersburg. These are being lent to Historic Royal Palaces for a major exhibition at Hampton Court Palace from April to September. Catherine the Great was inspired. She wrote to Voltaire in 1772, *I am presently madly in love with English gardens, with curved lines, gentle slopes, lakes formed from swamps, and archipelagos of solid earth*. Le jardin anglais spread to Scandinavia, throughout Europe and into North America following tours by Thomas Jefferson and John Adams in 1786, who visited many Brown landscapes, including Stowe in Buckinghamshire and Caversham near Reading, which partly survives as a public park. The gardens Jefferson saw on his visit to England influenced his gardens at Monticello in Virginia.

Wedgewood dinner plate showing Trentham, part of the 952 piece *Frog Service*, commissioned in 1733 by Catherine the Great of Russia and reflecting her passion for English landscape gardens

Brown's creation, c.1746, of the naturalistic Grecian Valley at Stowe set off the existing *Temple of Concord & Victory* and allowed it to act as an eyecatcher glimpsed through trees

Magnolia grandiflora, a favourite of Brown's patron, the 6th Earl of Coventry at Croome. Among 600 bills for plants in the Croome archive, magnolias appear 48 times

'Capability' Brown recognised honest talent wherever he worked. Nathaniel Richmond, Adam Mickle, Michael Milliken, were all highly skilled levellers and plantsmen, who often engaged other subcontractors. He trusted his overseer William Ireland at Burghley, Luton and Trentham. His master carpenter was John Hobcraft, Peter Blair and Benjamin Read his reliable water engineers, all long in his employ, their loyalty handsomely repaid.

Perhaps our innate love of landscape in this country springs from the parks, gardens and designed landscapes that we visit and from those footpaths with views over farmed landscape, woodland, moorland and the coast. It was Lancelot Brown who best taught us to look up and out at the view. The ecological connectivity made by historic parks is only just being recognised.

'Capability' Brown has no better epitaph than that written by Earl Harcourt of Nuneham Courtenay after Brown's death *'exclusive of the admiration I naturally feel for true genius in every art, I respected the man's private character, & ever found him obliging, good-humoured, & accommodating in the highest degree, while I felt an affection for him and liked his company, in spite of his puns'*. So also did his King, George III and his banker and friend, the Hon. Robert Drummond, who employed Lancelot at Cadland.

The Lion Bridge at Burghley House, Lincolnshire

When Brown encountered the writer, Hannah More in 1782, he described his 'grammatical' manner in literary terms for her: *'Now there' said he, pointing his finger, 'I make a comma, and there' pointing to another spot, 'where a more decided turn is proper, I make a colon; at another part, where an interruption is desirable to break the view, a parenthesis; now a full stop, and then I begin another subject'.*

Go to www.capabilitybrown.org for details of The Capability Brown Festival 2016

The Roman Bridge designed by James Paine for 'Capability' Brown's landscape at Weston Park, Shropshire crosses the Temple Pool in a single stone span

Left: Young film makers spent a week at Stowe in 2015 learning about Brown's achievements before filming out in the landscape as part of The Capability Brown Festival

TARR ON THE ROAD

Derek Tarr walks coast to coast across Cornwall

SAINTS&
TINNERS

DEREK'S WALKS
DAY BY DAY

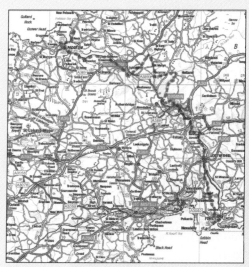

Walk 1: St Catherine's Castle to Lostwithiel
Walk 2: Lostwithiel to Helland Bridge
Walk 3: Helland Bridge to Wadebridge
Walk 4: Wadebridge to St Enodoc's Church

Photos: Nicola Burford

Ready Money Cove, near Fowey

Jutting out from England's south west corner into the wild Atlantic, Cornwall is a land of saints and myths, bridges, mines and moorlands. From the wind-swept mass of Bodmin Moor in the east to jagged Land's End in the west, it is a county with a rich and diverse landscape and history. In the native Celtic language, it is Kernow.

My coast to coast adventure took me from the English Channel in the south to the Atlantic Ocean in the north visiting heritage places along the way.

Padstow Harbour

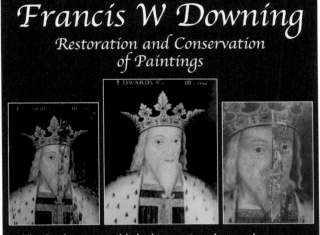

WALK 1
St Catherine's Castle to Lostwithiel
8.7 miles approx

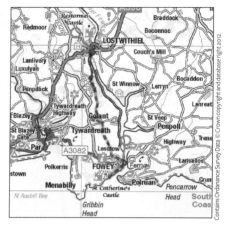

With a gentle sea breeze and the cry of gulls, I climbed to St Catherine's Castle and marvelled at the view across the River Fowey estuary to Polruan and out into the Channel. Clinging to the side of the hill this small artillery fort made an ideal starting point for the walk. Built on the order of Henry VIII in the 1530s to defend the harbour from the threat of invasion, it was last manned during the Second World War.

I followed the path down to beautiful Ready Money Cove and on to the town of Fowey. Its narrow streets led me to the bustling waterfront where little boats bobbed gently. The town has literary connections. The writer Sir Arthur Quiller-Couch, known as 'Q', best remembered for *The Oxford Book of English Verse*, was a former resident. Across the water in Bodinnick is Ferryside, once the home of Daphne Du Maurier, famous for her Cornish inspired novels *Jamaica Inn*, *Rebecca* and *Frenchman's Creek*.

The 15th Century church of St Fimbarrus, which has the second tallest tower in Cornwall, has a long and rich history and possesses a 400 year old pulpit reputedly made from the panelling of a Spanish galleon. Picking up a pasty for my journey, I headed out of town along the Saints' Way footpath which marks the ancient route taken by pilgrims and merchants travelling from Ireland to France, avoiding the treacherous sea passage around Land's End. After a couple of miles I made a detour to visit the site of Castle Dore, an Iron Age hill fort. I ate my pasty whilst savouring the panorama from this lofty position and mulled over the myth and history of this monument. Here is the setting for the legend of Tristan and Iseult, a romantic story from the Dark Ages to rival that of Lancelot and Guinevere. More recently, during The English Civil War, it was the scene of a Parliamentarian Army defeat by Charles I's forces, much to the delight of the local people as Cornwall was a Royalist stronghold.

I retraced my steps and headed towards the ancient stannary town of Lostwithiel via the railway viaduct at Milltown, a mighty symbol of the ingenuity of the Victorian engineers. Lostwithiel was at the centre of the Cornish tin mining trade in the 13th and 14th Centuries but is now a quiet and tranquil place known as the antiques capital of Cornwall. Here I was reacquainted with the River Fowey and the first of the many ancient bridges I would cross on my journey. The town is home to a fascinating museum housed in the old Corn Exchange celebrating Cornish rural life. The Poet Laureate John Betjeman claimed the town had 'history in every stone'. One stone, on a house in North Street dated 1652, confers a 3,000 year lease on one Walter Kendal.

Located on the east side of the river is the cosy 16th Century Earl of Chatham Inn. With very friendly service, homemade food and a couple of pints of St Austell beer, it made a perfect stop for the night.

Top: Sign for Lostwithiel Bridge; **above left:** Walter Kendal's lease stone, Lostwithiel; **above right:** Signpost, Ready Money Cove, near Fowey

View of the Fowey Estuary from St Catherine's Castle

Daphne Du Maurier's home 'Ferryside' from Fowey

Museum, Lostwithiel

WALK 2
Lostwithiel to Helland Bridge
12.6 miles approx

Contains Ordanance Survey Data
© Crown copyright and database right 2012

The following morning, a steady walk along a lane to Restormel Castle started a long and busy day. The castle, looking down upon The River Fowey, was built at a strategic point to protect the river crossing below. Maintained by English Heritage, all that remains is the impressive late 13th Century circular shell keep. It was once owned by the Black Prince, son of Edward III, although he only visited on a couple of occasions. Today it is a popular picnic spot with fabulous views over the surrounding countryside.

I continued with river and railway as companions until crossing the five arched medieval Respryn Bridge and entered the Lanhydrock estate. Passing Newton Lodge I followed the Avenue, rising steadily until the house appeared through the trees. It was the home of the Robartes dynasty and given to the National Trust in 1953 along with 400 acres of land. Originally a Jacobean house, most of what we see today was created after a devastating fire in 1881. From the spectacular Gallery, which survived the fire, to the servants' quarters, there are 49 rooms to explore, all giving a superb insight into Victorian living. The dressing room and bedroom of Captain Tommy Agar-Robartes are particularly moving and poignant. They contain the belongings of the heir to the estate, laid out in preparation for his departure to the Great War – a war from which he was not

to return.

The formal gardens are well worth a visit with delightful herbaceous borders and an array of magnolia trees. Set within the grounds, the Lanhydrock parish church of St Hydroc holds services every Sunday.

After lunch, I left the estate and took a footpath towards Bodmin, crossing the fast flowing A30 on yet another, if much more modern, bridge. Before the town centre, I visited the excellent Cornwall's Regimental Museum which contains many artefacts depicting the county's military history. There is a wonderful tribute to the famous 'Last Fighting Tommy' of the First World War, Harry Patch, who died in 2009 aged 111.

Passing through the town centre I arrived at the brooding Bodmin Jail, a dank and sinister group of buildings. Opened in 1779 and operational until 1927, part of the jail now houses a museum which highlights the harsh conditions of these establishments. Particularly gruesome is the UK's last remaining working execution pit.

An early meal in the jail restaurant set me up for the delightful evening walk along the Camel Trail. This disused London and South West Railway line is now a walking and cycle track linking Wenfordbridge with Padstow. I turned right and followed the trail northwards to Helland Bridge where I crossed the river and wearily ascended to my nights' stop at Tredethy House Hotel.

From the top: The Gatehouse of Restormel Castle; Cornwall's Regimental Badge, Bodmin; View of the Courtyard, Restormel

Engraved glass door, Lanhydrock; right: St Hydroc's Church, Lanhydrock

Above, Lanhydrock; above right, Captain Tommy Agar-Robartes room, Lanhydrock; right, inside Bodmin Jail

WALK 3
Helland Bridge to Wadebridge
8.5 miles approx

Contains Ordanance Survey Data © Crown copyright and database right 2012

After a continental breakfast I ventured out into the drizzle and returned to look at the early 15th Century bridge I'd crossed the night before. Here, set in lush gardens hugging the bank of the River Camel, I came across the studio of potter Paul Jackson, Chairman of the Cornwall Crafts Association. Paul uses Cornish china clay and fires his pots with wood from a nearby plantation. He draws inspiration for his vibrant ceramic designs from the local landscape. His studio is well worth a visit.

The sky started to clear as I set off towards Pencarrow House and the sun was shining brightly when I arrived about an hour later. This Georgian mansion is the private home of the Molesworth-St Aubyn family, and the visit is by guided tour only. But what a guided tour! My lady guide's knowledge of the property and family history was superb, and her presentation was entertaining and witty. The whole experience was a delight. The house itself was designed by Robert Allanson of York and completed in the 1770s. The East and South fronts were based on the Venetian style of Andrea Palladio and the roofs are of Cornish Delabole slate. The rooms contain many items of interest including family portraits by Sir Joshua Reynolds and London river scenes by Samuel Scott. However, the most fascinating of all is the Pencarrow Bowl. This large Ch'ien Lung famille rose bowl in the Ante Room is painted with a Chinese artist's interpretation of life on the Pencarrow

estate. Outside, the gardens are a pleasure to wander around, but beware of the peacock who may come and join you for lunch in the courtyard outside the café.

I left the estate and followed a lane northwards for a couple of miles before reaching the River Allen, and then headed south west towards Sladesbridge, passing the remains of the Lemail Mill on the way. This lovely stretch of water is part of the River Camel Site of Special Scientific Interest, and home to otters and kingfishers. From Sladesbridge I rejoined the Camel Trail and made my way to Wadebridge and my stop for the night.

Paul Jackson's Pottery, Helland Bridge

The gardens at Pencarrow House

The remains of the Lemail Mill on the River Allen

Prideaux Place

WALK 4
Wadebridge to St Enodoc's Church
7.6 miles approx

Contains Ordanance Survey Data © Crown copyright and database right 2012

Beneath a murky sky I continued on the Camel Trail heading towards Padstow. For six miles the path follows the side of the river where water-skiers and windsurfers were making the most of this lovely location. Eventually the town and sea came into view and as I crossed the old Iron Bridge, the obelisk on Dennis Hill, commemorating Queen Victoria's Golden Jubilee, loomed high above me.

Arriving in Padstow, the clouds cleared revealing a beautiful day. Although fishing is important for this bustling town, the major industry is now tourism. Following a bite to eat, I made my way up the hill to the Elizabethan mansion of Prideaux Place, home to the Prideaux-Brune family. Restoration of the house and gardens was started in 1988 and continues to this day. Its mix of the original Elizabethan architecture with 18th Century Strawberry Hill Gothic can be seen on a guided tour and a particular highlight was the recently uncovered ceiling in the Great Chamber.

From the garden there is a view to Brown Willy, the highest point on Bodmin Moor, in the far distance. I discovered a grotto and an unusual mirrored obelisk designed by Alex Coode, the son of a friend of the Prideaux-Brune family. A small museum in the courtyard is the home to England's earliest known wholly cast iron cannon.

Prideaux is the location for the dramatisation of a number of Rosamunde Pilcher's books for German television and both the BBC's *Antiques Roadshow and Countryfile* programmes have been recorded here. Within the estate lives one of the oldest deer herds in England and recently an extensive breeding programme has been introduced. According to legend, if the herd dies out so will the family!

Returning to Padstow harbour I boarded the ferry and crossed the estuary to Rock where I headed a short distance north to my final destination. Nestled in the sand dunes and located in the middle of a golf course is St Enodoc's church. For about 300 years until the 19th Century the church was almost completely buried by sand and was given the nickname *"Sinking Neddy"*. To maintain the 'tithes' the vicar had to hold a service once a year inside the building. He and a group of parishioners would gain access by lowering themselves through a hole in the roof! However, the sand was removed and the church restored and today it is visited not only for its wonderful setting but for the grave of the poet, Sir John Betjeman.

Cornwall showed me picturesque valleys and stunning coastal scenery in a landscape carved by miners in pursuit of tin and china clay. A vibrant tradition of song, dance, art and Cornish fare, a distinct Celtic language and warm friendly people all add up to an experience which is uniquely Kernow.

Mirrored obelisk by Alex Coode at Prideaux Place

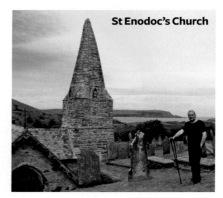

St Enodoc's Church

™ LIGHTING
BRINGING ART TO LIGHT

TM PICTURE LIGHT

LED Picture Light, gold finish, less than 3 watts of power, high colour definition, uniform light distribution, sized to fit artwork, extra long lamp life - 50,000hrs.

" We are delighted with the new picture lights supplied by TM lighting for Goodwood. We gave them a very specific brief and they worked with us to create something that was both traditional in appearance and top class in its capabilities. We would have no hesitation in recommending them."

James Peill
Curator of the Goodwood Collection, Goodwood House

APSLEY HOUSE   GOODWOOD HOUSE   HAMPTON COURT PALACE

™ LIGHTING

www.tmlighting.com | sales@tmlighting.com | +44 207 278 1600

CapabiliTeas!

Our greatest landscape gardener 'Capability' Brown probably didn't have time to stop for tea but he did live in a time when eating habits were changing. Hudson's are joining with The Capability Brown Festival to promote **CapabiliTeas!** this year, a great way to celebrate the anniversary by baking some (reasonably) authentic Georgian recipes with us and taking tea in 'Capability' Brown landscapes.

From the 1700's tea was being served in around 500 coffee houses in London alone and drinking tea was becoming a popular pastime at home too. As the century progressed, it was more likely to be accompanied by cakes and pastries for guests. Our recipes for Sally Lunns, Seed Cake, Gingerbread and Jumbles might all have been served. The 4th Earl of Sandwich enjoyed a good night out and legend has it that at an all-night gambling session in 1762 he demanded sustenance and was brought the first sandwich. Actually, he had spent time in the Eastern Mediterranean where breads filled with meat were common street food, but he certainly made sandwiches popular.

The Duchess of Bedford is credited with making a formal teatime at 4pm the go-to social event (she apparently had a 'sinking feeling' at about this time of day) but not until a whole generation after 'Capability' Brown, so don't let teatime restrict you. Have a **CapabiliTea!** at any time of day!

Sally Lunns

History leaves no evidence of a flour-dusted, apple cheeked baker named Sally Lunn, rather this English version of brioche was probably brought by Huguenots fleeing persecution in 17th Century France and the name is a corruption of Solimemne, a sweet bread from Alsace.

INGREDIENTS
1 tsp dry yeast
50ml warm water or ale
200ml milk
40g caster sugar
40g butter
1 tsp salt
2 eggs
400g strong white flour
Grated zest of 1 lemon and 1 orange
A good grating of nutmeg

METHOD
Combine yeast and warm water in a bowl and leave to stand for 5 minutes. Gently heat milk with butter, sugar and salt until the sugar is dissolved and the butter melted. Allow to cool. Mix in yeast mixture and egg. Gradually add flour, nutmeg and zests and mix gently. You will have a sticky soft dough. Cover and leave to rise in a warm place for about 1 hour until doubled in size. Knock dough back. Cover and leave to rise in a warm place for 30 minutes until doubled in size. Knead again briefly and push into a prepared tin or a ring mould. Cover and leave to rise for 20-30 minutes until doubled in size. Bake at 180°C, Gas Mark 4 for 25 to 30 minutes until golden brown. Tip out of pan to cool.

To save effort, try this bread machine version:

INGREDIENTS
1 tsp salt
175ml warm milk
75g butter
2 eggs
450g strong white flour
50g caster sugar
1/2 tsp bicarbonate of soda
Grated zest of 1 lemon and 1 orange
A good grating of nutmeg
1 tsp dried yeast

METHOD
Add the ingredients to the bread pan and set on the dough cycle. When it is mixed, divide the dough into 12 and transfer to well-buttered muffin tins. Leave in a warm place for about 1 hour until doubled in size, then bake in the oven at 180°C/Gas Mark 4 for 10 to 15 minutes. Split and serve with butter and jam.

Wigs or Whigs were similar yeasted buns but usually flavoured with caraway and coriander seeds.

Based on Eliza Smith's recipe for *A French cake to eat hot*, 1753

Seed Cake

Modern raising agents have replaced the use of yeast which was required for nearly every Georgian cake.

INGREDIENTS
175g butter
175g caster sugar
3 large eggs
225g self raising flour
50g ground almonds
2 tbsp milk
1 tsp caraway seeds

METHOD
Cream butter and sugar together until light and fluffy. Beat in 3 eggs one at a time. Fold in flour, ground almonds and caraway seeds before mixing in milk. Transfer into a prepared 2lb loaf tin and bake for 1 hour at 180°C/Gas Mark 4.

Based on Eliza Smith, *The Compleat Housewife*, 1727

Robert Adam's Tea Bridge at Audley End, Essex

Opposite page: A Tea Party by Thomas Rowlandson (1756-1827)

Gingerbread

INGREDIENTS
120g dark brown sugar
120g butter
2 tbsp black treacle
250g plain flour
2 tsp ground ginger
1/2 tsp ground nutmeg, ground cloves and ground mace
2 tbsp candied peel
1 medium egg

METHOD
Pre-heat oven to 180°C/Gas Mark 4. Melt butter with treacle and sugar over gentle heat. Mix flour, spices and candied peel in a bowl. Add melted mixture and egg. Stir together with a wooden spoon before resting in the fridge for 30 minutes. Roll out the dough, cut into shapes and lay on a lined baking tray. Bake for 15 minutes. Cool and keep in a tin.

Based on Hannah Glasse, *The Art of Cookery made Plain and Easy*, 1747

Jumbles

A popular biscuit shaped into a knot which derives its name from gemmel or twin. A gemmel ring, fashionable at the time, was a ring with two interlocking sections.

INGREDIENTS
200g plain flour
2 egg yolks
2 tbsp cream
75g caster sugar
1 tbsp aniseeds
25g butter

METHOD
Sieve the flour into a bowl and rub in the butter. Mix in the other ingredients with a wooden spoon. Roll the dough into a long sausage. Cut into 12 section. Take each section and fold over into a rough knot. Put onto a prepared baking tray and bake at 180°C/Gas Mark 4 for 10 minutes.

Adapted from Robert May's *The Accomplist Cook*, 1685

Georgian Sandwiches

The Earl of Sandwich's legendary snack was almost certainly beef and one myth for the origin of mayonnaise places it in Mahon in Menorca, an important British Mediterranean port for most of the 18th Century. Here is a delicious updating of a Georgian sandwich.

INGREDIENTS
1 small sourdough loaf
1 tbsp good mayonnaise
4 - 6 slices of frying steak
Handful of watercress
Mustard to taste

METHOD
Split the loaf lengthwise and spread the bottom half with butter and/or mustard. Flash fry the steak on both sides. Season well. Arrange the steak on the bread. Cover with watercress. Spread mayonnaise on the top half of bread and lay over. Press for 15 minutes under a weighted kitchen board. Cut into 4 to 6 slices.

To Catch

Clare Pardy is an art historian by training and has been a specialist art insurer for over 30 years. She started the Fine Art team at Ecclesiastical Insurance eight years ago where they insure a wide cross section of historic houses, museums and private collections. She went to Ripley Castle in Yorkshire to investigate The Stately Homes Hotline for **Hudson's**.

a Thief

→

Art theft always hits the headlines because it tends to evoke rather glamorous images, although the image is in fact far from reality.

There have of course been some extraordinarily daring raids over the years on historic houses. Most notably the theft of the wonderful still life by Jean-Baptiste Oudry (right), known colloquially as *The White Duck*, from Houghton Hall in Norfolk over 20 years ago, which has never surfaced, and the Leonardo da Vinci, *The Madonna of the Yardwinder*, stolen from Drumlanrig Castle in the Borders in 2003, which was luckily recovered in 2007.

Ecclesiastical Insurance was involved in a spate of porcelain thefts six years ago in which many houses were targeted and we spearheaded a campaign to recover them which ended with a remarkable recovery of many items, principally some rare 18th Century French porcelain from Firle House in Sussex.

Most thefts are directly influenced by developments in the art market. The Chinese, like every fast growing economy in history, are busy buying their heritage back and both jade and porcelain are high up on their shopping list. Taxidermy in general is enjoying a real and somewhat surprising revival, with records being broken on a regular basis, plus there is the rather sinister role it plays in Chinese medicine which in turn adds fuel to the fire.

So rather like the vogue for lead and metal of all sorts, which has caused enormous and expensive damage to church roofs and overhead cabling, the recent boom in all things Chinese has led to thefts from museums. The tragedy of these developments is not only the loss of the object but the knock-on consequences for access and display, which in turn affects every heritage visitor. In quite a few instances for example, real horns have had to be replaced with facsimiles and, where resources are stretched, the additional cost of protecting vulnerable exhibits can result in them being put away in store.

Historic houses are inevitably most vulnerable when they are open to the public as this enables criminals to do their reconnaissance. The range of many older alarms can be tested by simply monitoring the light and in this way, gaps in their coverage can be identified which enables the thief to break in at a later stage without being picked up by the alarm. The Firle theft was just such a well-planned and executed burglary by a consummate professional. Often however, criminals are opportunistic in the extreme and thefts are carried out with no more than brute force and nerve, with no plan as to where the booty might be sold at a later stage.

Whilst neither of these types of theft are necessarily easy to foil, encouraging staff to be aware and report all incidents, however seemingly inconsequential, does help to build a picture. A unique telephone network has found that it is often the indentification of a van in the wrong place at the wrong time or an individual simply displaying too much interest in the alarms or the locks that can prevent a serious burglary being committed.

The Stately Homes Hotline was started in response to a theft from Ripley Castle in 1988 and I first became aware of this wonderful initiative over 20 years ago. I am not sure that many of us who saw the first presentations would have guessed that a bigger, better and slicker version would still be operating in 2015. The Stately Homes Hotline covers a network of 1,200 heritage properties and is what creator and day-to-day operator of the Stately Homes Hotline, Sir Thomas Ingilby, of Ripley Castle in Yorkshire likes to call 'a posh Neighbourhood Watch'.

→

It has played a key strategic role in tackling theft from country houses since the 1980s and was indeed instrumental in the Firle recovery. By relying on reports from the ground and disseminating the information quickly and widely, trends can be identified and preventative measures put in place.

The Hotline is essentially an intelligence-sharing network which links castles, historic houses – some, but not all, open to the public – museums, cathedrals and historic gardens. Members are organised into regions and information is disseminated either on a local or national basis depending on seriousness and potential geographical impact. It links with heritage organisations like the National Trust and English Heritage and police constabularies. Its main thrust is to pass on intelligence about thefts, attempted thefts and burglaries and usually revolves around visitors who have been seen acting suspiciously or, very often, strange vehicles seen near premises. This intelligence can often help in the process of linking events and people across county borders, identifying vital patterns. Like the everyday Neighbourhood Watch scheme, what it does not do is investigate thefts, apprehend felons or recover stolen works of art.

Much of the Hotline's success is down to the fact that it has adapted to the changing nature of historic house operations, so whilst it continues to spot and photograph dubious visitors, it now also uncovers potentially costly scams, such as an ingenious cheque fraud identified at Balgonie Castle over a very expensive wedding booking. In this instance, a single Hotline bulletin saved its members over £135,000.

Protecting their assets has helped the Ingilbys stay at Ripley Castle since the early 14th Century. When Sir Thomas inherited at 18, he took on a massive tax bill for estate duty so that every penny of revenue for the next 7 years went to the Chancellor of the Exchequer. Today, running the estate is very much a partnership between Sir Thomas and Lady Ingilby and, with a mixture of hard work, imagination and commitment, they have created a highly successful business from this unpromising start. The Estate employed a mere 17 people when Sir Thomas inherited and the headcount is now around 130. It became one of the first historic properties to be licensed for civil wedding ceremonies back in the late 1980s and it has a very varied programme of events, ranging from fragrance launches to lakeside concerts with firework finales. In addition, in a spirit of true public mindedness, the Estate rescued the village from an imposed 'temperance' dating from 1919, by opening the Boar's Head Hotel in the centre of the village in 1990.

What strikes anyone arriving in the village of Ripley is the unchanging and traditional feel of it and this, I feel,

is the Ingilbys' crowning achievement. They have been a tremendous force for good (locally), opening a village car park, helping to revive both the village school and the village cricket ground. Over a very welcome mug of coffee on the extremely cold day of our visit, we are introduced to Jamie, who is set to take over the management of the Estate in the next few years and I am struck by the very positive way in which Sir Thomas views this, recognising that his son has different skills which will help the Estate to progress and weather whatever the future holds. Sir Thomas and his wife, meanwhile, are looking forward to an opportunity to make their own Grand Tour while continuing to run the Hotline.

'This service is completely free' is not a phrase you come across very often. When the service in question is The Stately Homes Hotline, whose network has been so effective a defence against art theft, I can only be impressed that operating the Hotline is not even Sir Thomas Ingilby's day job which, for the time being at least, continues to be responsibility for the Ripley Castle Estate.

Ripley Castle, Yorkshire (p.265)

Fire insurance marks on display in the library at Ripley Castle. Made of lead, the marks were displayed by properties that subscribed to the new fire protection companies founded after the Great Fire of London. The Sun Fire Office was founded in 1710 and still operates today; the Phoenix in 1782

All photos
© Oskar Proctor

In with the New

A major reason for building a country house has always been as a place to show off art. The art of collecting still very much alive and Britain's historic houses are some of the best places to see contemporary art in context. *Hudson's* asked a few renowned collectors to explain what they do and pick out a favourite piece.

The Devonshire family's DNA

The Duke and Duchess of Devonshire are trustees of the Chatsworth House Trust and the 17th generation of the Cavendish family to live at Chatsworth, Derbyshire

Contemporary collecting has always been intrinsic to Chatsworth. Since the 17th Century successive generations of my family have commissioned leading artists, as well as up-and-coming makers to add to the house and collection, and this is a tradition that continues today.

One of the most significant additions to the house in recent years is the site specific ceramic installation in the North Sketch Gallery, which opened in 2014. Created by ceramicist Jacob van der Beugel, the ceramic panelling on the walls of the gallery represents the present Devonshire family's DNA, in an unusual and creative take on the traditional portrait.

Outdoor sculpture has also become an important part of Chatsworth's cultural heritage. Our permanent contemporary collection featuring sculpture by Allen Jones, Barry Flanagan, Elizabeth Frink and Richard Long amongst others, sits alongside 18th Century marbles in the garden, creating a fascinating juxtaposition of old and new. In addition, each year Chatsworth hosts Sotheby's Beyond Limits, which presents a wide ranging selection of modern and contemporary monumental sculpture which encourages us and our visitors to view the landscape in new and diverse ways.

Above: Gilded leather wallcovering in the State Music Room fits well with the complex surfaces and rich interior colours of Pippa Drysdale's ceramics on the table

Right: Visitors enjoy the traditional collections alongside contemporary pieces, many in galleries which were always designed for display

Top right: The Duke and Duchess of Devonshire commissioned a series of ceramic panels from Jacob van der Beugel, a portrait of the family's DNA which demonstrates their long connection with Chatsworth and its collections

Simon Cunliffe-Lister's Mother Earth

Simon Cunliffe-Lister and his family live at Burton Agnes Hall, Yorkshire

Whilst my predecessor, Marcus Wickham-Boynton, was chastised in the 1960s for adding contemporary art into a collection otherwise dominated by old masters, I am grateful for the boldness of his taste. He brought many Impressionist and post-Impressionist treasures to Burton Agnes Hall, including pieces by Manet, Renoir, Cézanne, Gauguin, Derain and Augustus John. In my opinion, there is no better environment to appreciate the wonders of contemporary art than a well-tended historic house, which offers an assortment of aesthetic experiences and art forms. From the grand drama of Anish Kapoor's work in the baroque gardens of the Palace of Versailles, to the mercurial light sculptures of James Turrell at Georgian Houghton Hall, stately homes can mix past and present in intriguing and inspiring ways.

At Burton Agnes, contemporary work collected by my mother and myself sit happily alongside older pieces, and I feel that each benefit from the surprising juxtaposition. Many newer pieces are displayed in the Long Gallery, a magnificent room spanning the width of the house. My first commission sits here: a stunning glass sculpture by Gloucestershire-based Colin Reid incorporating an impression of Mother Earth from our Gatehouse, whose internal reflections and optical effects are enhanced by this light-flooded room. Our newest addition is a water sculpture by Giles Rayner, a thrilling commission of a huge, sinuous metal sphere in our classical pond. With its gentle, spinning movement and softly falling water, the piece delights the senses. We hope to continue the traditional role as patron of the arts, as we collect pieces for future generations to enjoy, and the house and its art evolve together.

Top right: In the Long Gallery, contemporary and traditional pieces still happily together. John Robinson's bronze *Boy and Dog* and a trio of furniture pieces by John Makepeace join important impressionist and 20th Century paintings

Left: Colin Reid's glass sculpture was inspired by the weathered medieval carved stone at Burton Agnes and perfectly combines ancient form and contemporary medium, while exploiting the light cast by Burton Agnes' windows

Right: Giles Rayner's sphere complements the formal lines of the pond and the roofline of the house

Tom Freshwater's Distant Drumbeat

Tom Freshwater is Contemporary Arts Programme Manager at the National Trust for England and Wales

The Trust New Art programme is a joint initiative between the National Trust and Arts Council England which began in 2009. We see it as a way of achieving two very distinct ambitions.

Experiencing heritage places through the lens of contemporary art can change people's perceptions of places. The art project at Fountains Abbey and Studley Royal, which runs for three years, typifies this approach. *Folly!* is a series of installations by opera designers, Gary McCann and Simon Costin, and visual artist, Irene Brown. The massive ruins of Fountains Abbey dominate the site and are the first feature that confronts visitors when they leave the visitor centre. We found that many of our visitors never got any further and failed to appreciate the wonderful 18th Century landscape garden into which the ruins are incorporated. The playful character of the installations based around the follies gives people a reason to explore the environment and for many the discovery of this ornamental landscape has been a revelation.

We also want to attract people who are not our mainstream audience. At Mottisfont in Hampshire, an important 20th Century art collection, gifted by the artist Derek Hill, was originally hung only in a congested display in a corridor. The opening of a dedicated gallery space allows for rehangs alongside a series of curated shows of contemporary works which recall the lively artistic atmosphere of Mottisfont when Maud Russell lived here. As a result, more people are visiting more regularly, either to see a new art display or taking the opportunity to approach the Mottisfont story differently.

My personal choice has to be at Lyme Park in Manchester where Sean Griffiths, formerly of FAT Architecture, created an interactive piece which framed the distant lantern folly from the lawn beside the house. *Distant Drumbeat* uses innovative computerised microwave technology to light up the top of the folly. Kids love it and our older visitors can't resist sidling up to have a go. This was an initiative of *New Expressions 3,* a publicly funded programme which encourages collaboration between contemporary artists and accredited museums.

The National Trust promises to keep special places for everyone forever, so this temporary contemporary art programme works better for us than commissioning new art for permanent exhibition. We want to inspire more people to visit and changing contemporary art exhibitions create a sense that you must visit now in case you miss it.

Above: Tom Freshwater checks out Distant Drumbeat

Lizzie Sykes' film work at Mottisfont.

Above: *Scavenger* with the artist Gary McCann at Fountains Abbey and Studley Royal

Miranda Rock's 20th Century Head

Miranda Rock is the director of The Burghley House Preservation Trust and a descendant of William Cecil, Queen Elizabeth's chief minister and the builder of Burghley House, Lincolnshire

The Sculpture Garden at Burghley was established in 1995, with just a few pieces that formed the beginnings of the core collection. In addition, we hold an annual, curated exhibition comprising loaned pieces or site-specific commissions. From quite humble beginnings, the sculpture garden has become one of the most popular elements of a visit to Burghley and along with the Garden of Surprises these annual exhibitions are the main attraction for our regular visitors.

The appeal of the country house is diverse, ranging through enthusiasm for historic buildings and interiors, general history, gardens, parkland and landscape and we must make every effort to engage with all of these audiences. For some, the enjoyment of sculpture outdoors is less challenging than a visit to the house itself, or simply provides a dynamic contrast with the historic interiors, while for others, such as our school groups, it offers a great opportunity to engage with a diverse range of materials and techniques not found inside the historic building, and to consider the relationship of contemporary art to its environment. Placing sculpture in lovely gardens and parkland is a wonderful way to make modern art available and accessible to new audiences who might not normally visit a contemporary art gallery.

My favourite piece at Burghley is probably *20th Century Head*, 2002, by Rick Kirby. It is made from mild steel quite crudely welded onto a framework that gives a ghostly outline. We actually have two slightly different versions of this piece and they have been placed in various different locations. We have one set across a gully above the cascade or outlet for the lake. It is not that easy to spot, so the first glimpse is quite a surprise, the empty eyes are a little haunting and the sparsely placed steel sections make it look as if it is quietly decaying into the landscape. It is also unreachable, which only adds to its quiet but powerful presence. I like sculpture on a big scale and this sits very well and holds its own in a mature area of planting.

Miranda Rock with the two versions of *20th Century Head*, 2002, by Rick Kirby at Burghley

Argonaut by Matthew Lane-Sanderson

Fire by David Annesley

Two Birds Heads by Armando Varela

Main picture: Diane Howse, Countess of Harewood, in the Terrace Gallery

Below: The Terrace gallery's major retrospective of Sidney Nolan in 1992 to celebrate his 75th birthday

Bottom right: Sculptor Antony Gormley in the Terrace Gallery with *Two States*

The Countess of Harewood's Terrace Gallery

The Countess of Harewood is a trustee of Harewood House Trust, a professional art curator and lives at Harewood House, West Yorkshire

We opened our contemporary art gallery here, The Terrace Gallery, in 1989. At the time it was unique, there were no other reference points then for showing contemporary art in historic locations. In some ways it was a very new and radical idea but to us it was also part of a continuum of working with contemporary artists, Turner and Girtin were young, emerging artists in their early twenties when they were commissioned to work at Harewood in the 1790s.

Over the past 26 years we've staged literally hundreds of exhibitions, projects and events here, not only in the Terrace Gallery but also throughout Harewood House, in All Saints' Church and in the gardens and landscape, all under the banner of Harewood Contemporary. The programme has been a platform for some of the most exciting and challenging artists of our time and we've worked with a very wide range of artists at different stages of their careers. It would be difficult for me to choose just one work that I feel adds most to the house as I work with so many artists and have many favourite artworks, but the Terrace Gallery space sums up all that we are continuing to achieve.

Many heritage sites have now embraced the idea of showing the work of contemporary artists alongside their historical collections and this has created a very exciting environment for the arts in this country.

→

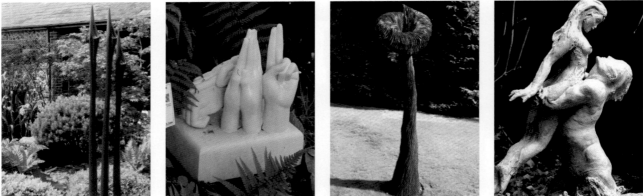

Sylph Reeds by Ginger Gilmour; *Yoga Mudra II* by Nicola Axe; *Red Villosa* by Carole Andrews; *In the Surf* by Kenneth Potts

Peter de Sausmarez' Moore Music

Peter de Sausmarez is the hereditary Seigneur of Sausmarez Manor in Guernsey and a Director of The ArtPark

Sculpture was an idea that was thrust at me by a chance remark by builder, later to become a partner in the business and friend. He said that he thought the gardens at Sausmarez Manor would make an ideal sculpture path, set amongst the jungle of the wild subtropical garden. He was mad of course, however after a lot of thought and several setbacks, I had a go. It is odd now looking back to think that this was the first sculpture park set up in the grounds of an historic house open to the public.

It was too new an idea for a lot of artists. It really wasn't until John Mills, then President of the Royal British Society of Sculptors, came out to Guernsey, that things really got under way. He pronounced that *"the bamboos would be an ideal setting"*, that he would launch the idea by loaning work and that I could quote him to doubters.

I must hasten to add that already sculptors Ev Meynell and Guy Portelli had volunteered a goodish selection, they having the advantage of having seen the gardens. They were invaluable in the way that they introduced & encouraged such artists as Philip Jackson, David Begbie, Nick Fiddian-Green, Lorne McKean, Jilly Sutton and other members of the Surrey Sculpture Society.

The sculpture park, now called The ArtPark, was always conceived as a way not only to bring sculpture to a wider audience and enhance the gardens at Sausmarez but also to be a commercial venture, finding new patrons for sculptors among the visitors to the gardens.

Now we can review some notable sales. Half a dozen sculptures have gone to a collector in New Zealand, others to collections in Kent and Hampshire and even to a council house in the south of England. We aim to make sculpture as accessible as possible and now it can be bought direct from The ArtPark and online via our website.

The opening of each year's new Sculpture Festival in May continues to be a magnet to collectors and to inspire would-be sculpture park proprietors from all over the world. Meanwhile, visitors to the subtropical gardens at Sausmarez at all times of year can enjoy sculptures in The ArtPark set off by our exotic plants.

Main image: Peter de Sausmarez with *Moore Music* by artist Rogier Ruys, who also opened the 2015 exhibition

Left: *Losing his Marbles* by Priscilla Hann

Newman Brothers Coffin Fitting Works

13–15 Fleet Street, Birmingham B3 1JP

Established in 1882 by two brothers, Alfred and Edwin, Newman Brothers began to later specialise in fittings for coffins. In 1998, having failed to modernize and unable to compete with suppliers from abroad, the factory was forced out of business. The Fitting Works is now a 'time capsule' museum, seen as though the workers have just set down their tools and left. Working machinery, costumed guides, self-guided sessions, hands-on activities and events make this a family friendly attraction.

Open: Guided tours on the hour from 12 noon Daily, Tuesday – Sunday and Bank Holiday Mondays

Heritage Open Days: Yes

Parking: On street parking nearby and NCP on Charlotte St

Disabled access: Yes

Admission charge: Yes

T: 0121 233 4790

E: newmanbrothers@coffinworks.org

W: www.coffinworks.org

Nothe Fort

Barrack Road, Weymouth DT4 8UF

Dominating the entrance to Weymouth Harbour, Nothe Fort is a labyrinth of passageways and outdoor areas with stunning views of the Jurassic Coast. It was constructed between 1860 and 1872 on three, easily accessed levels. The Fort is now filled with displays, mammoth guns and cinema areas that chart the history of this magnificent Victorian structure. Nothe Fort is now one of Weymouth's major attractions and a popular venue for events.

Open: Open daily between 25th March – 30th September, for winter opening hours please refer to website for more details.

Heritage Open Days: No

Parking: Public pay & display nearby

Disabled access: Yes

Admission charge: Yes

T: 01305 766 626

E: nothefort@uwclub.net

W: www.nothefort.org.uk

Kensal Green Cemetery

Harrow Road, London W10 4RA

The Grade I listed Kensal Green Cemetery covers 72 acres of beautiful grounds adjoining the Grand Union Canal. One of the world's first garden cemeteries it was inspired by the Père Lachaise Cemetery in Paris. Attractions include the Grade II* listed Dissenters' Chapel, Grade II North Terrace Colonnade, and the Grade II* monument to Emma and Alexis Soyer. Look out for events, exhibitions and guided tours run by the Friends of Kensal Green Cemetery.

Open: Cemetery open 1 April – 30 September: Monday – Saturday 9am – 6pm, Sunday 10am – 6pm. 1 October – 31 March: Monday – Saturday 9am – 5pm, Sunday 10am – 5pm. Bank Holidays 10am – 1pm.

London Open House: No

Parking: Roadside parking on internal cemetery roads

Disabled access: No

Admission charge: No

T: 07530 676 151

E: fokgc@hotmail.com

W: www.kensalgreen.co.uk

Bounds Walls

Ushaw College, Durham DH7 9RH

Ushaw College combines a fascinating history with some of the finest Victorian architecture in the North East. Built in 1852, the Bounds Walls were built to enclose the north and north east sides of a playing field. The games played there were peculiar to Ushaw College; they included handball and a battledore game which were regularly played by students until the 1980s. The wider site offers chapels, a children's bunny trail, beautiful gardens and a varied programme of events.

Open: Free access to the walls, approaching from the drives and car parks to the south and west. For all other parts please check website.

Heritage Open Days: Yes

Parking: Adjacent parking available

Disabled access: Partial access available

Admission charge: No

T: 0191 334 6423

E: tickets@ushaw.org

W: www.ushaw.org

Visit the places you've helped to protect

Forts and castles, mills and mausoleums, follies and parks. There are many fascinating historic places which have been repaired with the help of grants from Historic England and financed by you, the taxpayer.

Many of these places open to the public as a condition of the grant they have received and can be visited at certain times throughout the year. With over 1,600 to choose from, from the famous to lesser-known treasures – they are all worth a visit. Some of them are opening their doors to the public for the first time.

To find a site to visit today and for full details of opening arrangements, search the grant-aided places database at **HistoricEngland.org.uk**

Chatsworth, Derbyshire

A brush with Brown

Tim Scott Bolton is a landscape artist who has built a reputation for his evocative paintings of places as far apart as Argentina, Transylvania and Bhutan. Last year he was in the UK to record landscapes designed by 'Capability' Brown and capture the essence of 18th Century England. He shared his experience with **Hudson's**.

Being a large man, I have an absurd image of myself as thistle down; wherever the wind blows I am happy to go. In the unlikely location of Argentina I was introduced to the notion of having an exhibition of my paintings on 'Capability' Brown by Kitty and John Anderson, who happen to own the Kirkharle estate in Northumberland, where Brown was born 300 years ago. I embarked on this project with the enthusiasm of a badly trained Labrador but I was then sobered by the realisation of the great task I had taken on. The project meant visiting and painting a representative selection of the nearly 200 landscapes designed by 'Capability' Brown in his lifetime from Alnwick Castle in Northumberland to Burton Pynsent in Somerset and from Berrington Hall in Herefordshire to Heveningham Hall in Suffolk. For the past two years I have been out with my paint brush trying to capture the essence of Capability Brown in both watercolour and oil and in the process painting many of the most idyllic landscapes in the country. This was the perfect opportunity to write and illustrate my first book.

→

"His achievement in reshaping so many landscapes can only be appreciated by following in his footsteps and painting some aspects of them"

My wish to paint the landscapes created by Lancelot Brown seemed particularly appropriate. It was the classical landscapes of Claude Lorrain, Nicholas Poussin and their followers, collected on the Grand Tour, which inspired William Kent and later 'Capability' Brown to replace the formal gardens laid out by such as London and Wise in the early 18th Century with a 'natural' garden shaped by the landscape.

For the last 30 years I have been a full-time landscape painter. I am also an enthusiastic traveller, so have painted all over the world. Although he never left these shores, Lancelot 'Capability' Brown was also an inveterate traveller, endlessly journeying from one end of England to the other at the whim of his many employers – on horseback, by coach, and occasionally on foot. His amazing achievement in reshaping so many landscapes all over England can only be appreciated by following in his footsteps and painting some aspects of them.

Brown is traditionally associated with the park, clumps of trees, lakes and the ha-ha, but I discovered and have included other parts of his legacy. I found myself painting houses he designed such as Claremont and Croome Court – as well as their interiors notably at Corsham Court, follies as at Petworth, bridges at Audley End and walled gardens at Luton Hoo. His principal interest was, however, the landscape and, being a trustworthy and amiable man, he built up close relationships with others to whom he delegated work, including the builder Henry Holland, whose son, another Henry, married Brown's daughter and

Audley End, Essex

undertook much later building work. Berrington Hall in Herefordshire is a good example of the partnership between 'Capability' and his son-in-law. I painted here on a bitter January day but found a good view from the comfort of my car, where a pochade box enables a painting to be done in cramped circumstance.

Robert Adam was the favoured neo-classical architect and interior designer of the period and was someone Brown worked with on several occasions, as at Croome Court and Alnwick Castle. Coincidentally I had painted at Croome a few years before my involvement with Brown when a group of artists including Andrew Festing, John Wonnacott, Richard Foster and Julian Barrow were invited by the National Trust to raise money for its restoration by contributing paintings to a Sotheby's auction. The Trust's task here is immense. The house and outbuildings had been sold to a property developer who built houses in the grounds and abandoned the Grade 1 listed mansion. This was compulsorily acquired in a dilapidated state and both park and house are now being restored; even the

original white wooden bridge designed in the 1740s has been rebuilt.

Having been a land agent, I became a full-time artist in 1984 and one of my early commissions was to paint at Chatsworth. I still remember arriving at perhaps one of our greatest houses at the front door in my Citroen Deux Chevaux. At least it had two horses, unlike the single one ridden by Daniel Defoe over the 'extended moor or waste' in 1730, before he finally arrived at Chatsworth and looked down 'into the most pleasant garden and most beautiful palace in the world'. On revisiting I found Chatsworth again a stimulating and beguiling place with its wonderful collection of antiquities and paintings spiced up by contemporary art. Lucien Freud was a friend of the late Duke and when I was there this year modern sculpture revitalised the landscape and bright chairs the interior.

Brown's deft touch with interiors can be seen in the picture gallery at Corsham Court, which I painted this year. This triple cube room is of particular interest in that it houses a collection of pictures that Paul Methuen inherited

Bath House, Corsham Court, Wiltshire

from his well-travelled cousin Sir Paul Methuen (always
a common name in this family). Many of the pictures
for which the gallery was designed are still in the same
position. Interestingly the design of the ornate plasterwork
on the ceiling was originally conceived for Burton
Constable in Yorkshire. With typical frugality, 'Capability'
transferred it to Corsham when it was not needed at Burton
Constable. Another Paul Methuen was a 20th Century
Royal Academician. I spent a delightful time browsing his
work and that of his contemporaries and friends, such as
Sickert, in the attics of this great Elizabethan house. It is
this unexpected byway of exploration (both academic and
physical) that has given me so much pleasure during my
Brownian ramblings over the last two years.

I am not an academic, but my enthusiasm has enabled
me to find delight at every turn, and given me licence to
muse over anything that interests me in the properties I
have visited. I can only hope that some of that pleasure I
experienced in my encounters with 'Capability' Brown is
evident in my paintings.

The Picture Gallery, Corsham Court, Wiltshire

Hulne Abbey, Alnwick, Northumberland

Kirkharle, Northumberland

Compton Verney, Warwickshire

A Brush with Brown

THE LANDSCAPES OF 'CAPABILITY' BROWN

Tim Scott Bolton

Foreword by H.R.H. The Prince of Wales

A Brush with Brown: The Landscapes of 'Capability' Brown by Tim Scott Bolton, Foreword by H.R.H. the Prince of Wales is published in March 2016. *Hudson's* is offering a limited number of copies (which can be pre-ordered) at a special readers' price of £20 (RRP £25) available only from our eShop at www.hudsonsheritage.com

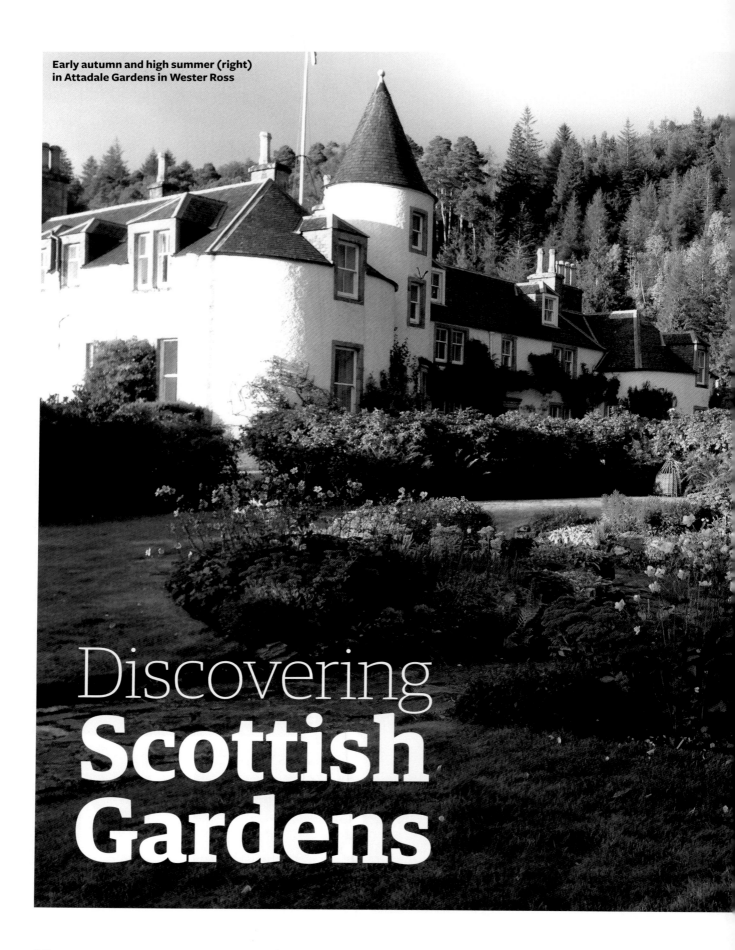

Early autumn and high summer (right) in Attadale Gardens in Wester Ross

Discovering
Scottish
Gardens

While gardens are centre stage in England in 2016, Catherine, Lady Erskine talked to Sarah Greenwood about a new initiative which is set to put gardens in Scotland in the spotlight.

Why Discover Scottish Gardens?
Scotland is so well known nationally and abroad as a land of stunning scenery, castles and whisky, that the rich heritage of its gardens tends to get overlooked. We want to help people discover them and let them see that it is more than possible to take a short tour or a long trip focussed around key seasons.

What's new about this initiative?
Visit Scotland have supported a Scotland wide snowdrop festival for the last 10 years which has been very successful but we want to do more to bring people to Scotland for its gardens at all times of year. We've tried various things. Small groups have produced leaflets, The Gardens of Perthshire, Fife, Angus and Kinross for example, but we felt we needed to do something Scotland-wide to give us an effective presence on the web and most importantly, a paid administrator, rather than depending on volunteer management. We launched at Gardening Scotland in Edinburgh last summer and we have set ourselves a target of achieving a 10% uplift in visits to Scottish gardens by 2020.

Why are Scottish gardens important?
I believe that Scotland has some of the best gardens in the world. The peculiarities of our climate have created the environment for an amazing variety of gardens so that you can travel from Himalayan plants in ferny glens on the West Coast to South African plants thriving on the drier East Coast.

→

Rich blues and purples fade into red in summer in Willowhill's South Garden in Tayside

Isn't the climate hostile to gardening?
On the contrary. I think people underestimate the climate and have the idea that it is always cold in Scotland. Wasn't it Billy Connolly who said, *"There are two seasons in Scotland: June and winter"*? Actually, Scotland has some very beneficial microclimates. The Gulf Stream runs right up along the coast in Argyll and creates a warm sheltered zone that has helped to nurture some of our greatest gardens. There are tropical and sub-tropical plants growing happily out of doors in gardens like Arduaine Gardens and Logan Botanic Gardens. Go over to the East Coast and in the counties of Fife, Angus and Aberdeenshire you are in one of the driest areas in the country, certainly drier than the Home Counties. In fact I think that Kent can have harder winters than many parts of the Highlands even as far north as the Castle of Mey in Caithness.

What about the history of gardening in Scotland?
There is reason to claim some pre-eminence for Scotland. Some very early gardens survive, like the Renaissance garden cared for by Historic Scotland at Edzell Castle in Angus. There are examples that survive from almost every period of gardening history. 17th century castle gardens at Gordon Castle and Wormiston House, 18th century landscape gardens at Hopetoun House and Paxton House, walled gardens at Rofsie and The House of Pitmuies and 20th century gardens at Cluny or Constance Spry's garden at Ard Daraich. The variety is immense from the Tibetan gardens at Cawdor Castle to the vegetable gardens at Philiphaugh.

The Rose Pergola at Rofsie Arts Gardens, Fife

The gardens at Cawdor Castle (this page) were created between 1600 and the 1960s

© DEREK HOSIE

© DEREK HOSIE

Willowhill South Garden, Tayside (this page)

© DEREK HOSIE

Is Scotland famous for unusual plants and trees?
Yes, one of the aspects of Scottish gardening we are most proud of is the plant hunters. I think that Scotland's traditions as explorers and pioneers of the British Empire made Scots particularly prominent as discoverers of new species. Some of our most familiar and important garden plants and trees were first brought back by Scots. David Douglas, after whom the lofty Douglas fir is named, started out as a gardener at Scone Palace and had a particularly eventful life collecting plants mostly in the Americas before being killed by a bull in Hawaii. Robert Fortune is famous for establishing the tea industry in India and collected many plants in China and the Himalayas. George Forrest also went to China later in the 19th century and George Sherriff was in Tibet. These characters are celebrated in the Explorers' Garden in Pitlochry. Of course there are still great gardeners in Scotland and still innovators introducing new plants. Ken Cox and his family at Glendoick Gardens has been bringing plants into Britain for generations.

→

Is it only gardens that you are promoting as part of Discover Scottish Gardens?
No, because of this history of plant collecting I think that nurseries are just as important, so several nurseries and botanic gardens are part of the group. It is the coming together of gardeners, tourist and horticultural businesses that we hope will energise the promotion of Scotland's outstanding horticultural offering. The Forestry Commission own vast tracts of land in Scotland and are the guardians of many tree species, so their participation is appreciated too. We have had fantastic support from organisations like the Royal Horticultural Society, the National Trust for Scotland and Scotland's Gardens as well as commercial sponsors, Savills, Brightwater Holidays and Alitex.

Are you planning to get involved in running training schemes?
What I would hope personally is for it to become a one stop shop for internships and practical experience. One of the things we can do is link up gardens that have the potential for training with others and run volunteer exchanges. We have a Czech garden student at the moment here at Cambo who came to us after a spell at St Andrews Botanic Gardens. With all the experience we represent we can offer advice as well. The Finnis Scott Foundation has supported Discover Scottish Gardens to help promote placements for students.

How does your own garden at Cambo fit in?
We have a walled garden and woodlands, restored over the last 20 years, and are particularly known for snowdrops. The walled garden is at its best in late summer, particularly August, so we want people to come at all times of year. We are currently involved in a big development project, part funded by the Heritage Lottery Fund. We will have facilities for training gardeners at Cambo up and running by 2017, based in the restored 18th century Stables and with a full range of new Alitex glasshouses in the walled garden.
www.discoverscottishgardens.org

Top row, left to right: Spring blossom and cottage garden flowers at Gordon Castle Gardens; *Erythonium dens canis* at Cluny House Gardens, Perthshire; Blue *Meconopsis Lingholm* in the Explorers' Garden, Pitlochry; *Echium simplex* at Lip an Cloiche on Mull

Centre: The restored Walled Garden at Gordon Castle; world famous Inverewe Gardens, Wester Ross where for the first time in 2016, the 1930s house lived in by the family of the creator, Osgood MacKenzie, will be open to visitors

Bottom: Views to Ulva from Lip Na Cloiche; rhododendrons and azaleas at Edinburgh Botanic Gardens; the team at New Hopetoun Garden Centre near Edinburgh

History's
Hotshot

The Independent called him 'the BBC's hotshot history boffin' and Dan Snow thinks that *"history is the most exciting thing that has ever happened to anyone on this planet"*. We've seen him on our screens as The One Show's history man and fronting series on the navy, railways and World War I, he is a successful author and enthusiastic advocate of new technology. He told **Hudson's** where it all began.

Cars are part of Beaulieu and Palace House's makeup where the late Lord Montagu founded the National Motor Museum to celebrate his grandfather and father's passion for the motor car

For me, picking up a copy of Hudson's invites an almost Proustian trip down memory lane. I remember Hudson's as the 'bible' in the front seat of the car, a good old fashioned book but dog eared, food encrusted, smashed and sun kissed.

My Dad* would make annotations in the margin of our copy, little notes in biro from the various trips we had made. Every Friday night we would discuss where we were going to go the following day, so that the backdrop to my very happy childhood all comes flooding back to me with the names of certain places - Ironbridge, the Tower of London, Eastnor Castle. Every single Saturday morning, the house would rock as my Dad roared and we would all pile down the stairs with our butterfly nets and teddy bears and plastic swords. Dad would load us all into the back of our terrible old family car – no car seats – it felt like about 500 kids fitted into one small hatchback, and we would tear off from Hammersmith down the A3 and the M4 into the countryside.

History comes to life inside Palace House, Beaulieu

"I'm lucky enough to live in the New Forest, so the world beating gardens of Exbury are a short bicycle ride away"

We would go to pretty much every single bit of heritage within 150 miles, taking in houses, gardens, museums and battlefields. I remember them all so well; they are like a roll call. Ham, Syon and Chiswick and a little further away, Clandon, Hatchlands and Runnymede.

Holidays were times for exciting trips further afield, the West Country or Derbyshire and the North of England with its stately piles, built by industrial revolution oligarchs, or the castles of the Scottish Marcher Lords.

I have such happy memories of scones and waxworks and octogenarian volunteers sitting on folding chairs looking angrily at us children. Dad refused to use guidebooks, giving us his own more or less true opinions on the house, the long gallery and the art. And then a hot car and long traffic jams going back into London as night came on. Streams of red lights through the front window and Radio 4 droning on as we kids dropped off to sleep. And that really was my childhood. I'm sure it was the same for many of you.

Now I am a Dad, so that's what I do with my kids. I'm lucky enough to live in the New Forest, so the world beating gardens of Exbury are a short bicycle ride away, about a mile and half down the road. Exbury is particularly special for a geek like me because in World War II it was the home of HMS Mastodon. HMS Mastodon was one of the vital planning centres of the D-Day naval operations from 1942. It was the largest naval armada ever assembled and the most successful seaboard invasion of all time – and it was all run from Exbury House. Sadly Exbury House never recovered from the experience but the gardens are absolutely beautiful and we go every day we can with the children in Spring.

The Signals Corp pictured at Exbury House, HMS Mastodon, during the build up to D-Day in the Second World War

The Middle Ages are alive at Beaulieu in the well preserved ruins of the Cistercian abbey founded by King John in 1204

Beaulieu, a real trailblazer and one of the first houses to open up in the 20th Century, is also nearby. It's a brilliantly eclectic place with a middle ages/monastic/super car/WW2/ espionage vibe. It really has got something for everybody. Each time we go to Beaulieu as a family we do one thing, we just do World War II or we just do cars.

In my professional life I am lucky enough to visit places all over Britain and it has given me a very profound sense of how lucky we are to have this treasure-trove here in Britain that I believe is unique in the world.

Heritage places are a spectacular gift from our forebears. In an increasingly busy, largely urban world, they are places for escape, for breathing the clean air, for getting away from the madding crowd or for watching Spring march across the landscape from snowdrops to daffodils to bluebells and beyond. I think that they are a great expression of the modern world. At one time they were a manifestation of an exclusive ruling class but now we all climb on the lawn and take tea in the Orangery and yet that democratisation

The past and future collide at Beaulieu, where the monorail sweeps past the historic gardens

Above, from the top: The ultimate supercars are the past holders of the British Land Speed Record set in 1965 by Donald Campbell in Bluebird; Beaulieu has an exciting story to tell of its role as a top secret training establishment for the Special Operations Executive (SOE) during World War II; Top Gear at the National Motor Museum

has taken place without violent revolution, without the pain and horror that has gripped so much of the rest of the world and that so many people assumed would be required to enter modernity. And the nature of continued ownership is that we have objects that are essential to that particular family's history, objects that were painted and designed to go into that particular house centuries ago but are still there today. That is what makes them so much richer than their equivalents in France or across East and Central Europe. So more people now go to heritage places than to football matches at weekends. It is our national pastime. We all love history here. And we love surrounding ourselves with the beautiful places of our past.

*Dan's Dad is veteran broadcaster and author, Peter Snow.

This article is an extract of a speech given by Dan at the presentation of Hudson's Heritage Awards 2015.

Celebrating the best visitor experiences

Hudson's Heritage Awards highlight the best days out in the UK. It depends what you are looking for – fun with the family, a new discovery, outstanding food or accommodation, a special place for a wedding or a gorgeous loo – we know every aspect of your visit is important. Our judges are experts in their field and the lunch we hold for the winners allows everyone a chance to be proud of what they have achieved.

The judges with the broadcaster Dan Snow who presented the awards. Below, Hudson's Heritage Award winners

2015 Winners

Special Award for Outstanding Achievement
The Tower of London

The Tower of London commissioned *Blood Swept Lands and Seas of Red*, from artists Paul Cummins and Tom Piper, to mark the anniversary of the outbreak of the First World War. The installation of 888,246 hand-made ceramic poppies (one for every soldier who died in WW1) attracted more than 4 million visitors, raised around £15 million for 6 veterans' charities and completely captured the public's imagination. It engaged local communities and volunteers, attracted different visitors and re-established the Tower at the centre of British life. The poppies went on tour and everyone was reminded that the Tower is a place every Briton must visit.
The Tower of London (p.126)

Best Family Day Out
Ironbridge Gorge Museums, Shropshire

There are 10 separate museums at Ironbridge - the true birthplace of the Industrial Revolution. Ironbridge Gorge Museums have long been applauded for introducing new ways to present the past to visitors and are a world leader in the use of living interpretation. Based on the philosophy *"to experience is to understand"*, you get an immersive experience where different generations can learn and play together. Everywhere is family friendly with children's menus, flexible family tickets, activities and retail products that appeal to all generations. With places as varied as Blist's Hill Victorian Town, the Coalport China Museum, Enginuity and the new Fab Lab it's a great day out for all.

Runner up: The Great North Museum, Hancock, Newcastle-upon-Tyne

Best Eating Out
The Alnwick Garden Treehouse, Northumberland

The Treehouse Restaurant and Café is part of the Duchess of Northumberland's extraordinary vision for The Alnwick Garden. In the largest wooden treehouse in Europe you can enjoy relaxed dining in a fairytale setting, nestled amongst a copse of lime trees. The food is local, varied and excellent with inventive cocktails – inspired by The Alnwick Garden's Poison Garden, - roaring fires and wobbly rope bridges to run around afterwards. The Potting Shed Café serves simple imaginative lunches and snacks, inside or under the canopy. Seeing the Treehouse lit at night is truly magical.
The Alnwick Garden (p.293)
Runner up: Blenheim Palace restaurants and cafés, Oxfordshire

Best Shopping
Sponsored by Jarrold Publishing

Doddington Hall, Lincolnshire

JARROLD publishing

It's worth a trip to Lincoln for a day out shopping at Elizabethan Doddington Hall. The excellent Farm Shop makes the most of produce grown on the estate. A productive walled kitchen garden and orchard supplies fruit and vegetables year round (and is open free to the public), a herd of Lincoln Red Cattle provides grass-fed beef; rare breed pigs in the woods are fed on vegetable waste from the shop and restaurant; there is plentiful game and venison as well as foraged food such as wild garlic, elderflower, blackberries and sloes. The strong environmental ethic is inspirational with captured rainwater, biomass and solar heating and recycled waste. The addition of interior, clothing, paint and a popular Christmas shop have made Doddington into a real destination for visitors.
Doddington Hall (p.226)
Runner up: Durham Cathedral, Co. Durham

Best Loos
Ballindalloch Castle, Banffshire

The public toilets at Ballindalloch Castle are probably the best outside toilets in the north of Scotland. Simple and unobtrusive from the outside, these loos are almost as magnificent as the fairytale 16th Century castle next door. There are top quality toiletries, tartan carpets, proper towels and humorous Annie Tempest prints on the walls. Add a table and chairs outside for those waiting and you will leave feeling as if you are walking on air.
Ballindalloch Castle (p.314)

Best Accommodation
Eastnor Castle, Herefordshire

There are now 12 magnificent bedrooms within this dramatic Norman Revival castle. Rising to the challenges of refurbishing a listed building, bathrooms have been squeezed into obsolete linen cupboards and the lift disguised. The addition of such posh bedrooms has significantly increased the appeal of the house, particularly for weddings. There is great attention to detail and stunning views of the Malvern Hills, lake and arboretum.
Eastnor Castle (p.238)
Runner Up: Upton Cressett Hall, Shropshire

Best New Discovery
Woburn Abbey, Bedfordshire

The discovery at Woburn of one of the earliest Chinese wallpapers in Britain sparked research into five successive decorative schemes of the 4th Duke's Private Bedchamber from 1752. One of four known early Chinese wallpapers and the earliest handpainted Chinese silk became the centrepiece of an exhibition *Peeling Back the Years* which brought visitors from China and the USA. Everyone was able to enjoy exploring Chinoiserie at Woburn with a trail through the house and gardens, where the wallpaper has inspired new planting and the purchase of white pheasants for the aviaries. The story had huge appeal, not just for interior decorators. *Woburn Abbey (p.200)*
Runner up: Burghley House, Lincolnshire: Benham & Sons Steam range, 1840

Best Innovation
Doddington Hall, Lincolnshire

At Doddington, a 30 foot pyramid has sprung up in the landscape. This attractive eyecatcher at the end of a newly planted avenue is faithful to a Kip engraving of 1707 but was designed by the owner to use recycled farm concrete. The unique 21st Century folly is a stunning focus, visible from the house and gardens. The 1km avenue and pyramid are open to the general public free of charge year round and are already proving a popular attraction. It also provides a handy home for bats.
Doddington Hall (p.226)
Runner Up: Traquair House, Peebleshire: *The Debatable Land* triptych

HUDSON'S HERITAGE AWARDS

Best Wedding Venue
Blenheim Palace, Oxfordshire

One of two equal winners, Blenheim Palace has a highly experienced team offering bespoke weddings in a range of venues. They were instrumental in establishing an International Wedding Congress held in Athens and the year was marked by a significant increase in the number of weddings held at Blenheim, including Indian and Russian couples. *Blenheim Palace (p.150)*

Best Wedding Venue
Elmore Court, Gloucestershire

Sharing the award is a new wedding venue created at the historic home of the Guise family. The Gillyflower party venue was built using entirely sustainable local materials with state of the art lighting and sound. Together with the period rooms of the 16th Century house, it provides a highly flexible wedding venue which took considerable vision to design and complete using the owners' expertise as music festival organisers and has given this house a new future.

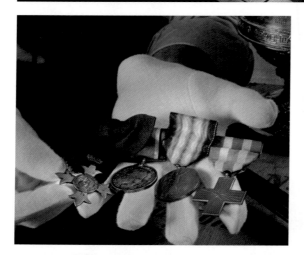

Best World War I Event
The Yorkshire Country Houses Partnership

We adapted our normal event category specifically to recognise the variety of events organised to mark the centenary of the 1914/18 War.

YCHP is a collaboration between more than a dozen historic houses in Yorkshire and the University of York. Nine houses co-operated on a series of exhibitions and events called *Duty Calls: The Country House in Time of War*. They chronicled the hardships of war experienced by the estates and surrounding communities, exploring the impact on owners, servants, tenants, and estate workers. The exhibitions are a great example of heritage attractions working together and each significantly enhanced their knowledge of their own First World War history as well as involving local people and enlightening visitors.

Runners up: South Shield Museum & Gallery, Tyne & Wear and Alford Manor House, Warwickshire

Best Hidden Gem
Sponsored by Smith & Williamson
Lady Waterford Hall, Northumberland

Lady Waterford Hall is a modest school hall of 1860, nowadays the community village hall. What makes it exceptional are the frescoes of life sized biblical scenes, painted by the celebrated pre-Raphaelite artist, Louisa, Marchioness of Waterford who commissioned the hall for the village on her estate at Ford in Northumberland. These frescoes are recognised as her greatest work but few visitors find their way to this unassuming building in the far North of England. Only an hour and a half from Edinburgh or Newcastle, in one of the most beautiful valleys in the country and near many other heritage attractions, it is well worth a trip.

Lady Waterford Hall (p.292)
Runner up: Great Witley Parish Church, Gloucestershire

Best Picnic Spot
Croome, Worcestershire

Thanks to all the members of the public who nominated their favourite picnic spots all over the country. Of five places on the shortlist, what impressed the judges about the winner was the welcome for impromptu picnickers who can fill a basket on the spot and have several options for places to picnic depending on their mobility. Here's what our winner said about Croome Park: *"I think Croome Park, Worcestershire is the best picnic spot because you can buy a complete picnic there. For £18 I had a rug to borrow, a picnic basket with all I needed – sandwiches; drinks - a great idea, because I didn't go prepared."*

Where is Britain's best heritage picnic spot?

Take a picnic to any heritage place in the UK and you could be picnicking in style with your own classic Fortnum & Mason hamper. All you need to do is nominate your favourite picnic spot. It might be a family picnic on a sunny summer afternoon or a picnic supper during a concert or theatre performance or even a place for a quick sandwich on a cycle ride. We want to know where is the best heritage picnic spot in the UK?

Send us a photograph (or up to 4) of your picnic place telling us where it is and describe why it is special to you in 150 words.

If yours is the winning entry you will win the Fortnum & Mason Piccadilly Hamper, fully equipped for 4 people, and an invitation for 2 to attend the presentation of Hudson's Heritage Awards, held each year in London. Your winning entry will also feature in next year's Hudson's Historic Houses & Gardens and you will receive a free copy of Hudson's Historic Houses & Gardens 2017.

All entries received will be judged by our independent judging panel chaired by Norman Hudson, OBE. Details can be found at www.hudsons-awards.co.uk where you can also make your nomination online. Make sure you include your name, address, email address and telephone number. You can make a nomination by post to: Hudson's Best Heritage Picnic Award, 35 Thorpe Road, Peterborough PE3 6AG.

The closing date for all entries is 30 September 2016. Winners will be advised by 1 January 2017.

in association with

FORTNUM & MASON
EST 1707

Blenheim Palace © VISIT BRITAIN IMAGES

Regional Directory

Holker Hall, Lancashire

We want to make Hudson's easy for you to use. Turn to our maps on pages 371 for all sites.
Do check opening times before you visit. Many properties are open regularly, but others only
occasionally and some may only open for weddings and special events.

Key to Symbols

i	Information
	Shop
	Plant Sales
	Corporate Hospitality / Functions
	Suitable for people with disabilities
	Refreshments / Café / Tearoom
	Restaurant
	Guided Tours
	Audio Tours
P	Parking Available
	Education - School Visits
	Suitable for Dogs
	No Dogs
	Accommodation
	Licensed for wedding ceremonies
	Open All Year
	Special Events
€	Accept Euros
	Member of the Historic Houses Association but does **not** give free access to Friends
F	Member of the HHA giving free access under the HHA Friends Scheme
	Property owned by National Trust
	Property in the care of English Heritage
	Property owned by The National Trust for Scotland
	Property in the care of Historic Scotland
	Properties in the care of Cadw, the Welsh Government's historic environment service
	2015 Hudson's Heritage Awards Winner
	2015 Hudson's Heritage Awards Highly Commended

Leighton House, Kensington

Keats House, Hampstead

London

London

London has always been the world's coolest city, so trace its history through the homes of the famous, including our kings and queens, and look for villas and country houses now swallowed by the town.

New Entries for 2016:
• Leighton House Museum

Find stylish hotels with a personal welcome and good cuisine in London. More information on page 348.

• The Mayflower Hotel
• New Linden Hotel
• San Domenico House
• Searcys Roof Garden Rooms
• Twenty Nevern Square

London - England

VISITOR INFORMATION

■ **Owner**

Chiswick House and Gardens Trust and English Heritage

■ **Address**

Chiswick House
Burlington Lane
London
W4 2RP

■ **Location**

Map 19:C8
OS Ref. TQ210 775
Burlington Lane,
London W4 2RP.
Rail: ½m NE of Chiswick Station.
Underground: Turnham Green, ¾m.
Bus: 190, E3.

■ **Contact**

Estate Office
Tel: 020 8742 3905

■ **Opening Times**

Gardens
7am - dusk all year round.
Chiswick House
April - October
Sunday - Wednesday and BHs.
10am - 6pm
(5pm Mar & Oct).
Check website for winter 2016 closure.
Café open 7 days a week from 8.30am.

■ **Admission**

Gardens:
Entry   Free

House:
Adult   £6.30
Conc.   £5.70
Child   £3.80
Family   £16.40
Discount for groups (11+).
English Heritage and National Art Pass members.
                                Free
Prices correct at time of press.

Garden & House Tours
Chiswick House
020 8995 0508.
Garden Tours and Camellia Show Group Bookings
020 8742 3905.

■ **Special Events**

Camellia Show 2016
25 February – 20 March.
(Closed Monday's).
Conservatory open daily
10am - 4pm.
There are year-round events from garden and family activities to open-air performances after dark - see www.chgt.org.uk.

Conference/Function

ROOM	Size	Max Cap
Chiswick House		150
Burlington Pavilion		350
The Conservatory		120
The Cafe		80

© Clive Boursnell

CHISWICK HOUSE AND GARDENS ⌗

www.chgt.org.uk

Chiswick House is a magnificent neo-Palladian villa set in 65 acres of beautiful historic gardens.

Chiswick House is internationally renowned as one of the first and finest English Palladian villas. Lord Burlington who designed and built the villa from 1725 – 1729, was inspired by the architecture and gardens of ancient Rome. The opulent interiors created by William Kent, display a rich collection of Old Master paintings.

The Grade 1 listed gardens surrounding Chiswick House have, at every turn, something to surprise and delight the visitor from the magnificent cedar trees to the beautiful Italianate gardens with their cascade, statues, temples, urns and obelisks. The gardens have been fully restored to their former glory, including the Conservatory, which houses the world famous Camellia collection in bloom during February and March.

There is also a children's play area and a modern café designed by award-winning architects Caruso St John. Open daily it offers seasonal breakfast and lunch menus, snacks, afternoon teas and refreshments.

Chiswick House once acted both as a gallery for Lord Burlington's fine art collection and as a glamorous party venue where he could entertain. Whether you are looking to host a wedding, exclusive private dinner, celebrate a special occasion or arrange a team building day, it is the ideal location. From a stylishly simple civil ceremony to an elaborate wedding reception, champagne celebration in the domed Conservatory, team building days in our Private Walled Gardens or a party in the Café. The House and Gardens are also popular locations for filming and photo shoots.

KEY FACTS

ℹ️ WCs. Filming, plays, photographic shoots. Weddings, corporate and private events and party hire - please call 020 8742 2762 or events@chgt.org.uk or see website.

🛍️

🍽️ Private & corporate hospitality.

♿ See website for access details.

🎫

👤 Personal guided tours must be booked in advance.

🎧 House. (Downloadable tours-Garden).

🅿️ Pay and display machines (approx. 60 bays).

📷 Contact Estate Office.

🐕 In gardens except for clearly sign-posted dog-free and short lead only areas. No dogs in house.

🔔

© Clive Boursnell

© Richard Bryant

KENSINGTON PALACE
www.hrp.org.uk/kensingtonpalace

Home to royalty for over 300 years.

Discover stories from Queen Victoria's life in her own words, as queen, wife and mother in the Victoria Revealed exhibition, told through extracts from her own letters and diaries. Follow in the footsteps of Georgian courtiers in the sumptuous King's State Apartments which show some breathtaking examples of the work of architect and painter William Kent.

Plus, don't miss Fashion Rules, featuring rare and exquisite dresses from HM Queen Elizabeth II, Princess Margaret and Diana,

Princess of Wales. This elegant exhibition will provide a feast for the eyes and a nostalgic glance back at recent decades.

Explore the beautiful gardens, inspired by the famous lawns that existed in the 18th Century and enjoy a leisurely lunch or an indulgent afternoon tea in the splendour of Queen Anne's Orangery, once the setting for the most lavish of court entertainments.

VISITOR INFORMATION

■ **Owner**
Historic Royal Palaces

■ **Address**
Kensington Gardens
London
W8 4PX

■ **Location**
Map 20:I8
OS Ref. TQ258 801
In Kensington Gardens.
Underground:
Queensway on Central Line, High Street Kensington on Circle & District Line.

■ **Contact**
Tel: 0844 482 7777
Venue Hire and Corporate Hospitality:
020 3166 6115
E-mail:
kensingtonpalace@hrp.org.uk

■ **Opening Times**
Nov-Feb:
Daily, 10am-5pm (last admission 4pm).

Mar-Oct:
Daily, 10am-6pm (last admission 5pm).
Closed 24-26 Dec.

■ **Admission**
Kids under 16 go free. Visit www.hrp.org.uk/kensingtonpalace or call 0844 482 7777 for more information.

■ **Special Events**
Special events throughout the year, see website for details.

■ **Conference/Function**
Conferences: Up to 120.
Receptions: Up to 300.
Lunches: Up to 200.
Dinners: 20 to 200.

KEY FACTS

- ℹ️
- 📷
- 🍸 Weddings, dinners, receptions and gala celebrations. Visit hrp.org.uk/hireavenue or call 020 3166 6115.
- ♿
- ☕
- 🍴
- 🏛️ Please book, 0844 482 7777.
- ✂️
- 🔔
- ❄️ Closed 24-26 Dec.
- 🐕

London - England

VISITOR INFORMATION

■ **Address**
Spencer House
27 St James's Place
London
SW1A 1NR

■ **Location**
Map 20:L8
OS Ref. TQ293 803
Central London:
off St James's Street,
overlooking Green Park.
Underground:
Green Park.

■ **Contact**
Nathan Jones, Head of
Property
Tel: 020 7514 1958
Fax: 020 7409 2952
E-mail:
tours@spencerhouse.co.uk

■ **Opening Times**
2016
Open on Sundays from:
10.30am-5.45pm.
Last tour 4.45pm.
Regular tours throughout
the day.
Max number on each tour
is 20.
Monday mornings: for
pre-booked groups only.
Group size: min 15-60.
Closed: January & August
Open for private and
corporate hospitality except
during August.

■ **Admission**
Adult: £12.00
Conc*:   £10.00
*Students, Members of the
V&A, Friends of the Royal
Academy, Tate Members
and senior citizens (only on
production of valid
identification), children
under 16.
Prices include guided tour.

**For further information
please view the website:**
www.spencerhouse.co.uk
**or telephone the Tours
Administrator:** 020 7514
1958 (Mon-Fri only).

All images are copyright of
Spencer House Limited and
may not be used without
the permission of Spencer
House Limited.

Conference/Function

ROOM	Size	Max Cap
Receptions		400
Lunches & Dinners		126
Board Meetings		40
Theatre-style Meetings		100

The Great Room

SPENCER HOUSE
www.spencerhouse.co.uk

London's most magnificent 18th Century aristocratic private palace.

Spencer House, built 1756-66 for the first Earl Spencer, an ancestor of Diana, Princess of Wales (1961-97), is London's finest surviving 18th Century town house. The magnificent private palace has regained the full splendour of its late 18th Century appearance after a painstaking ten-year restoration programme.

Designed by John Vardy and James 'Athenian' Stuart, the nine State Rooms are amongst the first neo-classical interiors in Europe. Vardy's Palm Room, with its spectacular screen of gilded palm trees and arched fronds, is a unique Palladian set-piece, while the elegant mural decorations of Stuart's Painted Room

reflect the 18th Century passion for classical Greece and Rome. Stuart's superb gilded furniture has been returned to its original location in the Painted Room by courtesy of the V&A and English Heritage. Visitors can also see a fine collection of 18th Century paintings and furniture, specially assembled for the House, including five major Benjamin West paintings, graciously lent by Her Majesty The Queen.

The State Rooms are open to the public for viewing on Sundays. They are also available on a limited number of occasions each year for private and corporate entertaining during the rest of the week.

KEY FACTS

ⓘ No photography inside House or Garden.

☂

♿ House only, ramps and lifts. WC.

🚶 Obligatory. Comprehensive colour guidebook.

🐕 Guide Dogs only.

🔔

The Palm Room

The West Facade

SYON PARK 🏛 Ⓕ
www.syonpark.co.uk

London home of the Duke of Northumberland with magnificent Robert Adam interiors, 40-acres of gardens, including the spectacular Great Conservatory.

Described by John Betjeman as the 'Grand Architectural Walk', Syon House and its 200-acre park is the London home of the Duke of Northumberland, whose family, the Percys, have lived here for 400 years. Originally the site of a late medieval monastery, excavated by Channel 4's Time Team, Syon Park has a fascinating history. Catherine Howard was imprisoned at Syon before her execution, Lady Jane Grey was offered the crown whilst staying at Syon, and the 9th Earl of Northumberland was imprisoned in the Tower of London for 15 years because of his association with the Gunpowder Plot. The present house has Tudor origins but contains some of Robert Adam's finest interiors, which were commissioned by the 1st Duke in the 1760s. The private apartments and State bedrooms are available to view.

The house can be hired for filming and photo shoots subject to availability. Within the 'Capability' Brown landscaped park are 40 acres of gardens which contain the spectacular Great Conservatory designed by Charles Fowler in the 1820s. The House and Great Conservatory are available for corporate and private hire. The Northumberland Room in Syon House is an excellent venue for conferences, meetings, lunches and dinners (max 60). The State Apartments make a sumptuous setting for dinners, concerts, receptions, launches and wedding ceremonies (max 120). Marquees can be erected on the lawn adjacent to the house for balls and corporate events. The Great Conservatory is available for summer parties, launches, filming, photoshoots and wedding receptions (max 150).

KEY FACTS

- ℹ No photography in the House.
- 🏬 Garden Centre.
- ♿ WCs. House - Limited access. Gardens and Great Conservatory - fully accessible.
- ☕ The Refectory in the Garden Centre.
- 🍴 By arrangement.
- 🅿 Free parking.
- 🐕 Assistance dogs only.
- 🔔 See website for details.

VISITOR INFORMATION

■ Owner
The Duke of Northumberland

■ Address
Syon House
Syon Park
Brentford
Middx
TW8 8JF

■ Location
Map 19:B8
OS Ref. TQ173 767
Between Brentford & Twickenham, off A4, A310 in SW London.
Sat Nav: TW7 6AZ
Public Transport:
Gunnersbury Station then bus 237 or 267. Brentford Rail, Ealing Broadway or Boston Manor Underground, then bus E8. Minicab companies available at the stations.
Air: Heathrow 8m.

■ Contact
Estate Office
Tel: 020 8560 0882
Fax: 020 8568 0936
E-mail:
info@syonpark.co.uk

■ Opening Times
Syon House:
16 Mar-30 Oct 2016
Weds, Thurs, Suns and BHs 11am-5pm, last entry 4pm.

Gardens only:
14 Mar-30 Oct 2016
Daily 10.30am-5pm, last entry at 4pm.

House, Gardens and Great Conservatory:
Closed from 2 Nov 2015- 13 Mar 2016.

■ Admission
House, Gardens & Conservatory:
Adult	£12.00
Child	£5.00
Conc.	£10.50
Family (2+2)	£27.00

Booked groups (25+)
Adult	£10.50
Conc.	£9.50
School Group	£3.00

Gardens & Great Conservatory:
Adult	£7.00
Child	£3.50
Conc.	£5.50
Family (2+2)	£15.00
School Group	£2.00

Syon House Ventures reserves the right to alter opening times. Please phone or check website for up to date details and special events.

Conference/Function

ROOM	Size	Max Cap
Great Hall	50'x30'	120
Great Conservatory	60'x40'	150
Marquee		800

London - England

VISITOR INFORMATION

■ **Owner**
Historic Royal Palaces

■ **Address**
London
EC3N 4AB

■ **Location**
Map 20:P7
OS Ref. TQ336 806
Bus: 15, 42, 78, 100, RV1.
Underground: Tower Hill on Circle/District Line. Docklands Light Railway: Tower Gateway Station.
Rail: Fenchurch Street Station and London Bridge Station.
Boat: From Embankment Pier, Westminster or Greenwich to Tower Pier. London Eye to Tower of London Express.

■ **Contact**
Tel: 0844 482 7777
Venue Hire and Corporate Hospitality: 020 3166 6226
E-mail: visitorservices.tol@hrp.org.uk

■ **Opening Times**
Summer:
Mar-Oct, Tues-Sat 9am-5.30pm (last admission 5pm).
Mons & Suns 10am-5.30pm (last admission 5pm).

Winter:
Nov-Feb, Tues-Sat 9am-4.30pm (last admission 4pm).
Mons & Suns 10am-4.30pm (last admission 4pm).
Closed 24-26 Dec and 1 Jan.

■ **Admission**
Visit www.hrp.org.uk/toweroflondon or call 0844 482 7777 for more information.

Conference/Function
Conferences: Up to 100.
Meetings: 6 to 100.
Receptions: 20 to 300.
Lunches: Up to 150.
Dinners: 6 to 240.

ENTRY TO THE TRAITORS GATE

© Historic Royal Palaces

TOWER OF LONDON ✦
www.hrp.org.uk/toweroflondon

The ancient stones reverberate with dark secrets, priceless jewels glint in fortified vaults and pampered ravens strut the grounds.

The Tower of London, founded by William the Conqueror in 1066-7, is one of the world's most famous fortresses, and one of Britain's most visited historic sites. Despite a grim reputation for being a place of torture and death, there are so many more stories to be told about the Tower and its intriguing cast of characters.

This powerful and enduring symbol of the Norman Conquest has been enjoyed as a royal palace, served as an armoury and for over 600 years even housed a menagerie! Don't miss the Crown Jewels in the famous Jewel House, unlocking the story behind the 23,578 gems in the priceless royal jewels. Marvel at the Imperial State Crown and the largest diamond ever found and see the only treasure to escape destruction in 1649, after the Civil War. For centuries, this dazzling collection has featured in royal ceremonies, and it is still in use today.

Join Yeoman Warder tours to be entertained by captivating talks of pain, passion, treachery and torture at the Tower. Visit Tower Green and see the memorial to the people who died within the Tower walls. Find out why the last execution at the Tower was in 1941 and see how instruments of torture were used to extract 'confessions' from prisoners. Explore the story of how five coins changed history in the Coins and Kings exhibition, discover what life was like in the surprisingly luxurious Medieval Palace, and explore the stories of Henry II, Edward I and their courts at work.

See one of the Tower's most famous sights, the ravens. Legend has it Charles II believed that if the ravens were ever to leave the Tower, the fortress and the kingdom would fall. Step into 1,000 years of history every day at the Tower of London.

KEY FACTS

ⓘ No photography in Jewel House.

📷 Visit www.hrp.org.uk/hireavenue or call 020 3166 6226.

♿ WCs.

🛒

🍴 Licensed.

🚶 Yeoman Warder tours are free and leave front entrance every ½ hr.

🎧

🅿 None for cars. Coach parking nearby.

🚌 To book 0844 482 7777.

✕

❄

♿

Yeoman Warders

Imperial Crown of India

© The Royal Collection © 2015, Her Majesty Queen Elizabeth II

OSTERLEY PARK AND HOUSE 🌿
JERSEY ROAD, ISLEWORTH, LONDON TW7 4RB
www.nationaltrust.org.uk/osterley

Created in the late 18th Century by architect Robert Adam, Osterley is one of the last surviving country estates in London. From the tree lined driveway, spot the Charolais cattle and ponies lazing away the day. Just around the lake the magnificent House awaits; presented as it would have been in its 1780s heyday. Three floors of rooms, from the classical grandeur of the Entrance Hall to the contrasting servants' quarters. Spot the animals in the immaculately preserved tapestries in the state apartments and imagine sleeping in the eight poster bed, reserved for visits from the monarch. The grounds are perfect for picnics or leisurely strolls. Or relax in the serenity of the restored 18th Century pleasure grounds, full of herbaceous borders, roses and ornamental vegetable beds as well as the original Robert Adam summer house with its lemon trees and highly scented shrubs. **Location:** Map 19:C7. OS Ref TQ146 780. A4 between Hammersmith and Hounslow. Main gates at Thornbury & Jersey Road junction. SatNav: TW7 4RD. **Owner:** National Trust **Tel:** 020 8232 5050 **E-mail:** osterley@nationaltrust.org.uk

Open: Gardens & Café open all year, 10-5pm (or dusk if earlier). House & Shop open 27 Feb-30 Oct, 11-5pm (or dusk if earlier). Park & car park open 7am-7pm all year. Whole property (aside from Park) closed 25 & 26 Dec.
Admission: *House & Garden: Adult £11.50, Child £5.80, Family £28.80. Groups (15+) £8.80. *Garden: Adult £6.90, Child £3.50, Family £17.30. Groups (15+) £5.20 *includes voluntary 10% Gift Aid donation. Car Park: £6.00, free to NT Members. Park and grounds: Free.
Key facts: ℹ️ No flash photography inside House. 🛍️ Wide range of goods plus second-hand bookshop. 🍴 Rooms available, contact for info. ♿ WCs. 🍽️ Seasonal menus, freshly baked cakes & cream teas. Family friendly. Kids' lunchboxes. 🎧 Audio-visual guides. 🅿️ Limited for coaches. 🏫 Schools programme, contact for info. 🐕 Guide dogs only. 💒 Civil Weddings ceremonies & receptions, contact for info. ❄️ Park, gardens & café open all year (closed 25 & 26 Dec). ⚜️

SUTTON HOUSE 🌿
2 & 4 HOMERTON HIGH STREET, HACKNEY, LONDON E9 6JQ
www.nationaltrust.org.uk/suttonhouse

A rare example of a Tudor red-brick house, built 1535 by Sir Ralph Sadleir, Principal Secretary of State for Henry VIII, with 18th Century alterations and later additions. Restoration revealed 16th Century detail, even in rooms of later periods. Notable features include original linenfold panelling and 17th Century wall paintings. Peel back the layers of time in this Hackney home and discover some unexpected occupants. Open Georgian Panels to reveal Tudor arches or see the squatters' artwork. Delve into family treasure chests or experience the sights and smells of a Tudor Kitchen. New garden, the Breaker Yard revealing the site's industrial past as a car breaker's yard with upcycled vehicles used for growing plants, play and ice-creams.
Location: Map 20:P3. OS Ref TQ352 851. At the corner of Isabella Road and Homerton High St. Closest station is Hackney Central Overground.
Owner: National Trust **Contact:** House and Gardens Manager

Tel: 020 8986 2264 **E-mail:** suttonhouse@nationaltrust.org.uk
Open: 5 Feb-20 Dec, Wed-Sun, 12pm-5pm. Open daily in Aug. Open BH Mons and Good Fri. Property regularly used by local community groups – rooms always open as advertised, but call if you would like to visit during a quiet time. Occasional 'Museum Lates' opening. **Admission:** Adults £3.90, Children £1.10.
Key facts: 🛍️ NT Gift Shop & second-hand book shop. 🍴 From lectures & talks to team building & workshops, our barn area provides you with privacy, while our adjoining café can provide you with refreshments. ♿ Ground floor only. WC. 🍽️ Open all year and everyday in summer, indulge in a cream tea served on vintage crockery in our tearoom. 🎫 Guided Tours are held at weekends. Please call ahead for times. 🏫 Wide range of school sessions. Call for details. 🐕 Assistance dogs only. 💒 Feb-Dec, whether you're looking for a ceremony only, or an all day reception, enjoy a perfect wedding day at Sutton House. ⚜️

18 STAFFORD TERRACE
18 Stafford Terrace, London W8 7BH
www.rbkc.gov.uk/museums

From 1875, 18 Stafford Terrace was the home of Punch cartoonist Edward Linley Sambourne, his wife Marion, their two children and live-in servants. Originally decorated by the Sambournes in keeping with fashionable Aesthetic principles, the interiors evolved into wonderfully eclectic artistic statements within the confines of a typical middle-class home.

Location: Map 20:I8. OS Ref TQ252 794. Parallel to Kensington High St, between Phillimore Gardens & Argyll Rd.
Owner: The Royal Borough of Kensington & Chelsea **Contact:** Curatorial staff
Tel: 020 7602 3316 **E-mail:** museums@rbkc.gov.uk
Open: Mid Sep-Mid Jun.
Admission: Visit our website for more information, opening times and prices.
Key facts: ⓘ No photography. ▣ ⓕ Obligatory.
▣ None. ▤ ▨ Guide dogs only. ✳ ☖

BANQUETING HOUSE
Whitehall, London SW1A 2ER
www.hrp.org.uk/banquetinghouse

This revolutionary structure was the first in England to be built in a Palladian style. It was designed by Inigo Jones for James I, and work finished in 1622. Intended for the splendour and exuberance of court masques, the Banqueting House is probably most famous for one real life drama: the execution of Charles I which took place here in 1649. One of Charles's last sights as he walked to his death was the magnificent ceiling painted by Peter Paul Rubens in 1630-4.

Location: Map 20:M8. OS Ref TQ302 80. Located on Whitehall in central London, a short walk from Westminster, Charing Cross and Embankment stations.
Owner: Historic Royal Palaces
Contact: Banqueting House Visitor Services **Tel:** 0844 482 7777
E-mail: banquetinghouse@hrp.org.uk
Open: Mon-Sun 10am-5pm. Closed 24, 25 and 26 Dec, 1 Jan, 4 Jan-29 Feb 2016. Before visiting, please call or visit our website to confirm we are open.
Admission: Adult £6.00, Cons £5.00, Children free.
Key facts: ⓘ ▣ ⓣ Weddings, receptions, dinners, award ceremonies. ▤ ▣ ▨
▨ ⚑ ✳ ☖

575 WANDSWORTH ROAD ❧
Lambeth, London SW8 3JD
www.nationaltrust.org.uk/575wandsworthroad

The hand-carved fretwork interior of this modest, early 19th Century, terraced house is enthralling and inspiring. Created by Khadambi Asalache, a Kenyan-born poet, novelist, philosopher of mathematics and British civil servant, who, over 20 years, turned his home into a work of art. Prompted initially by the need to disguise persistent damp he embellished almost every wall, ceiling and door in the house with fretwork patterns and motifs. The house stands as he left it, with his painted decoration on walls, doors and floors and with rooms furnished with his handmade fretwork furniture and carefully arranged collections of objects.

Location: Map 20:L12. OS Ref 176:292761. 220 yards from Wandsworth Road Overground Station **Owner:** National Trust **Contact:** Custodian
Tel: 020 7720 9459 **Telephone bookings:** 0844 249 1895.
E-mail: 575wandsworthroad@nationaltrust.org.uk
Open: March to Nov, Wed evening, Fri, Sat & Sun
Admission: Pre-booked guided tours. **Key facts:** ▣ ⓕ ▨

HOUSES OF PARLIAMENT
Westminster, London SW1A 0AA
www.parliament.uk/visiting

Inside one of London's most iconic buildings, tours of the Houses of Parliament offer visitors a unique combination of 1,000 years of history, modern day politics, and stunning art and architecture. Stylish afternoon tea in the Terrace Pavilion overlooking the River Thames can be added to many tours.

Location: Map 20:M8. OS Ref TQ303 795. Central London, 1km S of Trafalgar Square. Underground: Westminster. **Contact:** Bookings Team
Tel: 020 7219 4114 **E-mail:** visitparliament@parliament.uk
Open: Every Sat throughout the year and most weekdays during parliamentary recesses including the Summer, Christmas and Easter. **Admission:** Check website for current prices. Concessions for over 60s, students and members of the UK Armed Forces. Discounted group rates for groups of 10 plus if booked in advance.
Key facts: ▣ Jubilee Shop off Westminster Hall offers an attractive range of books, gifts and souvenirs. ▤ Tour route fully accessible. Alt route via a lift available if required. ▨ Jubilee Café - selection of light meals, and hot and cold drinks. ⓕ Approx 90 mins, available in a number of languages. ▣ Approx 60 to 75 mins, available in a number of languages. ▨ Assistance dogs only. ✳ ☖

DR JOHNSON'S HOUSE
17 Gough Square, London EC4A 3DE
www.drjohnsonshouse.org

Dr Johnson's House is a charming 300-year-old townhouse, nestled amongst a maze of courts and alleys in the historic City of London. Samuel Johnson, the writer and wit, lived and worked here during the 18th Century, compiling his great 'Dictionary' in the Garret. Today, the House is open to the public with restored interiors and a wealth of original features.

Location: Map 20:N7. OS Ref TQ313 812. North of Fleet Street.
Owner: Dr Johnson's House Trust **Contact:** The Curator
Tel: 020 7353 3745 **E-mail:** curator@drjohnsonshouse.org
Open: 11am-5pm Oct-Apr. 11am-5.30pm May-Sep.
Admission: Adults £4.50, Conc. £3.50, Child £1.50, Family £10.00. Members of the National Trust are entitled to a 50% discount on admission.
Key facts: Small shop selling books, gifts & souvenirs. Private events evenings & Suns. Many unavoidable steps. Pre-booked groups 10+. £2.00. Available in 10 languages. Disabled bays only in Gough Square & neighbouring streets. English & History workshops, tours/talks for schools, A level groups & universities. Check website for Christmas closures.

KEW PALACE
Kew Gardens, Kew, Richmond, Surrey TW9 3AB
www.hrp.org.uk/kewpalace

Kew Palace was built as a private house in 1631 but became a royal residence between 1729 and 1818. More like a home than a palace, the privacy and intimacy of this smallest of English royal palaces made it the favourite country retreat for King George III and his family in the late 18th Century. Don't miss the Royal Kitchens, the most perfectly preserved Georgian royal kitchens in existence. At weekends Queen Charlotte's Cottage is also open to visitors.

Location: Map 19:C7. OS Ref TQ188 776.193.
A307. Junc A307 & A205 (1m Chiswick roundabout M4).
Owner: Historic Royal Palaces
Tel: 0844 482 7777
E-mail: kewpalace@hrp.org.uk
Open: Apr–Sep 10am-5.30pm. Last entry 5pm.
Admission: Free of charge, but please note admission tickets to Kew Gardens must be purchased to gain access to Kew Palace. (For gardens admission prices, please visit the Kew Gardens website).
Key facts: Weddings, receptions, dinners, meetings. WCs.

KEATS HOUSE
10 Keats Grove, Hampstead, London NW3 2RR
www.cityoflondon.gov.uk/keats

Discover the beauty of poetry and place in the home of the Romantic poet John Keats. Displays of original manuscripts, artefacts and paintings tell the story of how the young poet found inspiration, friendship and love in this stunning Regency villa. Listen to Keats' famous odes and see the engagement ring he gave to Fanny Brawne, his true love. The house comes alive with regular events, from poetry performances to family fun days. Garden open all year.

Location: Map 20:K3. OS Ref TQ272 856. Hampstead Heath (London Overground); Hampstead or Belsize Park (Northern Line).
Owner: City of London Corporation **Tel:** 020 7332 3868
E-mail: keatshouse@cityoflondon.gov.uk
Open: Summer (1 Mar-31 Oct): Tue-Sun, 1pm-5pm; Winter (1 Nov-28 Feb): Fri, Sat & Sun, 1pm-5pm. Also BH Mons.
Admission: Adults £5.50, Conc. £3.50, Child 17 & under Free. Tickets allow entry for a year. **Key facts:** Books, souvenirs, vintage items & gifts. Available for private hire. Ground floor. Tactile & subtitled AV exhibits. Accessible toilet. 1.30 and 3pm - check before visiting. Disabled parking space. Learning programme. Guide dogs only.

LEIGHTON HOUSE MUSEUM
12 Holland Park Road, London W14 8LZ
www.leightonhouse.co.uk

Leighton House Museum is the former home of the Victorian artist and President of the Royal Academy, Frederic, Lord Leighton (1830-1896). The only purpose-built studio-house open to the public in the United Kingdom, it is one of the most remarkable buildings of the 19th Century, containing a fascinating collection of paintings and sculpture by Leighton and his contemporaries.

Location: Map 20:M9. OS Ref TQ 247792. High Street Kensington (10 minutes walk); Olympia (5 minutes walk); Holland Park (15 - 20 minutes walk).
Tel: 020 7602 3316 **E-mail:** museums@rbkc.gov.uk
Open: Daily 10am-5:30pm; closed Tues.
Private Museum hire available during the evening.
Admission: Adult £7.00. Concessions £5.00. National Trust 50%. National Art Pass Free.
Key facts: Free guided tours on Weds and Suns 3pm.

SOMERSET HOUSE
Strand, London WC2R 1LA
www.somersethouse.org.uk

Somerset House is an historic building where surprising and original work comes to life. A unique part of the London cultural scene with a distinctive public programme including Skate, concerts, an open-air film season, a diverse range of temporary exhibitions focusing on contemporary culture, an extensive learning programme, free guided tours and 55 fountains that dance in the courtyard in summer. Somerset House currently attracts approximately 2.5 million visitors every year.

Location: Map 20:N7. OS Ref TQ308 809. Sitting between the Strand and the north bank of the River Thames. Entrances on Strand, Embankment, Lancaster Place and Waterloo Bridge.
Owner: Somerset House Trust
Contact: Visitor Communications
Tel: 020 7845 4600 **Fax:** 020 7836 7613 **E-mail:** info@somersethouse.org.uk
Open: For opening times, please see website.
Admission: For admission prices, please see website.
Key facts: ▣ ⊤ WCs. ▥ Licensed. ‼ Licensed. ☒ By arrangement. ▣ ▨ On leads. ▲ ❋ ♥

STRAWBERRY HILL ▣ Ⓕ
268 Waldegrave Road, Twickenham TW1 4ST
www.strawberryhillhouse.org.uk

Strawberry Hill is internationally famous as Britain's finest and first example of Georgian Gothic revival architecture. With the aid of a guide book written by Horace Walpole, Strawberry Hill's creator, visitors can enjoy this 'little gothic castle's' award-winning restored interiors and a unique collection of Renaissance painted glass. **Location:** Map 19:C8. OS Ref TQ158 722. Off A310 between Twickenham and Teddington.
Owner: Strawberry Hill Trust **Contact:** Property Office
Tel: 020 8744 1241 **E-mail:** enquiry@strawberryhillhouse.org.uk
Open: Strawberry Hill is open Sat through Wed 1 Mar-1 Nov 2016. Weekends 12pm-4pm (last entry). Mon, Tue, Wed 1.40pm-4pm (last entry). Closed Thu & Fri.
Admission: Adult £12.00, Under 16s free, please visit our website for the full list of concessions and discounts.
Key facts: ▣ ⊤ ▯ WCs. ▥ Licensed. ☒ By arrangement. ▣ Limited for cars. No coaches. ▨ ▨ Guide dogs only. ▲ ❋ ♥

HONEYWOOD MUSEUM
Honeywood Walk, Carshalton SM5 3NX

Local history museum in a 17th Century listed building, next to the picturesque Carshalton Ponds, containing displays on the history of the house and local area, plus a changing programme of exhibitions and events on a wide range of subjects. Special facilities for school visits. Attractive garden at rear.
Location: Map 19:D9. OS Ref TQ279 646. A232 approximately 4m W of Croydon.
Owner: London Borough of Sutton
Contact: The Curator **Tel:** 020 8770 4297
E-mail: honeywoodmuseum@sutton.gov.uk
Website: www.sutton.gov.uk / www.friendsofhoneywood.co.uk
Open: Wed-Fri, 11am-5pm. Weekends & BH's, 10am-5pm. Guided Tours and School Visits available outside normal opening hours.
Admission: Free admission.
Key facts: ▣ ▥ WCs. ▥ Hours as museum. ☒ By arrangement. ▣ Limited. ▨ ▨ Guide dogs only. ❋ ♥

LITTLE HOLLAND HOUSE
40 Beeches Avenue, Carshalton SM5 3LW

Step back in time and visit the former home of Frank Dickinson (1874-1961) who dreamt of a house which would follow the ideals of Morris and Ruskin. Dickinson designed, built and furnished the house himself from 1902 onwards. The Grade II interior features handmade furniture, metalwork, carvings and paintings produced by Dickinson in an eclectic mix of the Arts and Crafts and Art Nouveau styles.
Location: Map 19:D9. OS Ref TQ275 634. On B278 1m S of junction with A232.
Owner: London Borough of Sutton **Contact:** Valary Murphy
Tel: 020 8770 4781 **Fax:** 020 8770 4777
E-mail: valary.murphy@sutton.gov.uk **Website:** www.sutton.gov.uk
Open: First Sun of each month & BH Suns & Mons (excluding Christmas & New Year), 1.30pm-5.30pm.
Admission: Free. Groups by arrangement, £5.50pp (inc. talk & guided tour).
Key facts: ▣ ▨ Partial. ☒ By arrangement. ▣ On-street only. ▨ Guide dogs only. ❋

WESTMINSTER CATHEDRAL
Victoria Street, London SW1P 1QW

The Roman Catholic Cathedral of the Archbishop of Westminster. Spectacular building in the Byzantine style, designed by J F Bentley, opened in 1903, famous for its mosaics, marble and music. Bell Tower viewing gallery has spectacular views across London. Exhibition displaying vestments, rare ecclesiastical objects and sacred relics. **Location:** Map 20:L9. OS Ref TQ293 791. Off Victoria Street, between Victoria Station and Westminster Abbey. **Owner:** Diocese of Westminster **Contact:** Revd Canon Christopher Tuckwell **Tel:** 020 7798 9055 **Fax:** 020 7798 9090 **Website:** www.westminstercathedral.org.uk
Open: All year: 7am-7pm. Telephone for times at Easter & Christmas.
Admission: Free. Tower lift/viewing gallery charge: Adult £6.00, Conc £3.00, Family (2+4) £12.00. Exhibition: Adult £5.00, Conc £2.50, Family (2+4) £11.00. Telephone 020 7798 9028 for Tower and Exhibition opening. Recently named a TripAdvisor 2014 Winner and awarded a Certificate of Excellence. **Key facts:** ▣ ▨ ▥ ☒ Booking required. ▨ Worksheets & tours. ▨ Except assistance dogs. ❋

WHITEHALL
1 Malden Road, Cheam SM3 8QD

A Tudor timber-framed house, c.1500, in the heart of Cheam Village. Displays include the house and Henry VIII's Nonsuch Palace - including stunning scale model. Changing exhibitions and special events. Garden with medieval well. Home-made cakes in tearoom. Please note; we will be closing for Heritage Lottery Funded refurbishment in March 2016.
Location: Map 19:C9. OS Ref TQ242638. Approx. 2m S of A3 on A2043 just N of junction with A232.
Owner: London Borough of Sutton **Contact:** The Curator
Tel: 020 8770 5670 **E-mail:** whitehallmuseum@sutton.gov.uk
Website: www.sutton.gov.uk
Open: Fri, Sat & Sun 10am-5pm. Tearoom closes 4.30pm.
Admission: Free; Groups by arrangement outside normal opening hours £4.00 pp (includes talk and tour).
Key facts: ▣ ▨ Partial. ▨ ☒ By arrangement. ▨ ▨ Guide dogs only. ❋ ♥

APSLEY HOUSE ⌗
Hyde Park Corner, London W1J 7NT
Apsley House, also known as No. 1 London, is the former residence of the first Duke of Wellington. **Location:** Map 20:L8. OS Ref TQ284 799.
Tel: 020 7499 5676 **Website:** www.english-heritage.org.uk/apsleyhouse
Open: Please visit www.english-heritage.org.uk for opening times, admission and the most up-to-date information.

BUCKINGHAM PALACE
London SW1A 1AA
Buckingham Palace serves as both the office and London residence of Her Majesty The Queen. **Location:** Map 20:L8. OS Ref TQ291 796. Underground: Green Park, Victoria, St James's Park. **Tel:** +44 (0)20 7766 7300
E-mail: bookinginfo@royalcollection.org.uk **Website:** www.royalcollection.org.uk
Open: Selected dates in the year. Contact for details or visit website.
Admission: Visit www.royalcollection.org.uk for details.

HAM HOUSE AND GARDEN ⚘
Ham Street, Richmond-upon-Thames, Surrey TW10 7RS
One of London's best kept secrets, this atmospheric Stuart mansion nestles on the banks of Richmond-upon-Thames. **Location:** Map 19:B8. OS Ref TQ172 732. On S bank of the Thames, W of A307 at Petersham between Richmond and Kingston.
Tel: 020 8940 1950 **E-mail:** hamhouse@nationaltrust.org.uk
Website: www.nationaltrust.org.uk/ham-house **Open:** Please see website.
Admission: National Trust members free. Prices vary, please see website.

KENWOOD HOUSE ⌗
Hampstead Lane, London NW3 7JR
Set in tranquil parkland in fashionable Hampstead, with panoramic views over London. **Location:** Map 20:J1. OS Ref TQ270 874. M1/J2. Signed off A1.
Tel: 020 8348 1286 **E-mail:** kenwood.house@english-heritage.org.uk
Website: www.english-heritage.org.uk/kenwoodhouse
Open: Please visit www.english-heritage.org.uk for opening times, admission prices and the most up-to-date information.

OLD ROYAL NAVAL COLLEGE
King William Walk, Greenwich, London SE10 9NN
One of the most important ensembles in European Baroque architecture and the centrepiece of the Maritime Greenwich World Heritage site.
Location: Map 19:F7. OS Ref TQ383 778.
Tel: 020 8269 4747 **E-mail:** boxoffice@ornc.org **Website:** www.ornc.org
Open: Please see website for up to date opening and admission details.

QUEEN'S HOUSE
Romney Road, Greenwich, London SE10 9NF
16th Century mansion now used to display items from the National Maritime Museum's collection. Closed for refurbishment until July 2016 when it reopens celebrating its 400th anniversary. Come back and discover the extraordinary people and events that are key to understanding this iconic building's creation, its history and its significance today. **Location:** Map 19:F7. OS Ref TQ387 776.
Tel: 020 8858 4422 **Website:** www.rmg.co.uk **Open:** Please see website.

18 FOLGATE STREET
Spitalfields, East London E1 6BX
Tel: 020 7247 4013 **E-mail:** info@dennisevershouse.co.uk

2 WILLOW ROAD ⚘
2 Willow Road, Hampstead, London NW3 1TH
Tel: 020 7435 6166 **E-mail:** 2willowroad@nationaltrust.org.uk

7 HAMMERSMITH TERRACE ▥ⓔ
London W6 9TS
Tel: 020 8741 4104 **E-mail:** admin@emerywalker.org.uk

BOSTON MANOR HOUSE
Boston Manor Road, Brentford TW8 9JX
Tel: 0845 456 2800 **E-mail:** victoria.northwood@cip.org.uk

BURGH HOUSE AND HAMPSTEAD MUSEUM
New End Square, Hampstead, London NW3 1LT
Tel: 020 7431 0144 **E-mail:** info@burghhouse.org.uk

CARLYLE'S HOUSE ⚘
24 Cheyne Row, Chelsea, London SW3 5HL
Tel: 020 7352 7087 **E-mail:** carlyleshouse@nationaltrust.org.uk

CHELSEA PHYSIC GARDEN
66 Royal Hospital Road, London SW3 4HS
Tel: 020 7352 5646 **E-mail:** enquiries@chelseaphysicgarden.co.uk

ELTHAM PALACE AND GARDENS ⌗
Eltham Palace, Court Yard, Eltham, London SE9 5QE
Tel: 020 8294 2548 **E-mail:** customers@english-heritage.org.uk

FENTON HOUSE ⚘
Hampstead Grove, London NW3 6SP
Tel: 020 7435 3471 **E-mail:** fentonhouse@nationaltrust.org.uk

FORTY HALL
Forty Hill, Enfield, Middlesex EN2 9HA
Tel: 020 8363 8196 **E-mail:** forty.hall@enfield.gov.uk

FREUD MUSEUM
20 Maresfield Gardens, London NW3 5SX
Tel: 020 7435 2002 **E-mail:** info@freud.org.uk

FULHAM PALACE & MUSEUM
Bishop's Avenue, Fulham, London SW6 6EA
Tel: 020 7736 3233 **E-mail:** admin@fulhampalace.org

HANDEL HOUSE MUSEUM
25 Brook Street, London W1K 4HB
Tel: 020 7495 1685 **E-mail:** mail@handelhouse.org

HOGARTH'S HOUSE
Hogarth Lane, Great West Road, London W4 2QN
Tel: 020 8994 6757 **E-mail:** john.collins@carillionservices.co.uk

MARBLE HILL HOUSE ⌗
Richmond Road, Twickenham TW1 2NL
Tel: 020 8892 5115 **E-mail:** customers@english-heritage.org.uk

RANGER'S HOUSE ⌗
Chesterfield Walk, Blackheath, London SE10 8QX
Tel: 020 8853 0035 **E-mail:** customers@english-heritage.org.uk

RED HOUSE ⚘
Red House Lane, Bexleyheath DA6 8JF
Tel: 0208 303 6359

SOUTHSIDE HOUSE ▥ⓔ
3 Woodhayes Road, Wimbledon, London SW19 4RJ
Tel: 020 8946 7643 **E-mail:** info@southsidehouse.com

BENJAMIN FRANKLIN HOUSE
36 Craven Street, London WC2N 5NF
Tel: 020 7925 1405

WILLIAM MORRIS GALLERY
Lloyd Park, Forest Road, Walthamstow, London E17 4PP
Tel: 020 8527 9782

Visit **www.hudsonsheritage.com** for special events and wedding venues

Riverhill Himalayan Gardens, Kent

Berkshire
Buckinghamshire
Hampshire
Kent
Oxfordshire
Surrey
Sussex
Isle of Wight

South East

Fortunes made at court were spent adorning country houses in the counties within reach of London from the earliest times so the historic places they left behind are full of treasures.

New Entries for 2016:
- Claydon House
- Harcombe House
- Loseley Park
- The Savill Garden
- Sulgrave Manor

THE SAVILL GARDEN

THE SAVILL GARDEN, WICK LANE, ENGLEFIELD GREEN, SURREY TW20 0UU

www.windsorgreatpark.co.uk

Discover a world of plants on your doorstep. The Savill Garden showcases plants from around the world, gathered by intrepid plant hunters and refined by nurserymen and breeders, these plants are arranged in stunning displays which recall their areas of origin.

Sir Eric Savill first created his woodland garden in the 1930s. Since then, many others (under the watchful eyes of Kings and Queens) have been on a tireless quest to add their own expertise and creativity. The Rose Garden, opened by H M the Queen in 2010, is a magnificent addition. Visitors can wander the swirls of rose beds and enjoy the perfume at its best from a walkway that rises into the centre of the Rose Garden.

Location: Map 3:G2. OS Ref SU976 707. Located off A30, M25 junction 13 or M4 junction 6. 15 minutes drive from Windsor town centre. Follow the brown tourist road signs. For sat navs, please use postcode TW20 0UJ and note that access to The Savill Garden is only available through public roads. 15 minutes from Heathrow Airport.

Owner: The Crown Estate **Tel:** 01784 485400
E-mail: enquiries@windsorgreatpark.co.uk
Open: Summer (Mar-Oct) 10am-6pm. Winter (Nov-Feb) 10am-4:30pm. We are closed 24 & 25 Dec only. For current open times please see website.
Admission: Mar-Nov: Adults £9.75, Seniors £8.75, Children (Under 6) Free, Children (6-16) £4.35, Family Group (2 Adults and 2 children under 16) £26.00, Groups (10+) £8.00, Carers accompanying disabled visitors Free. For current admission prices please visit our website.
Key facts: Our gift shop is ideal to pick up a treat for the family, friends, your pet or just yourself! Plants from The Royal Gardens. Enjoy a coffee and cake in our intimate gallery café. A daily selection of hot food, freshly baked cakes, sandwiches, salads and jacket potatoes. Head Gardener's Tour at £150.00 and we offer A Friend of the Savill Garden Guide at £25.00 per 25 people, both last around one hour. Guide dogs only. Closed 24 & 25 Dec.

DORNEY COURT

Nr. Windsor, Berkshire SL4 6QP

www.dorneycourt.co.uk

"One of the finest Tudor Manor Houses in England" - Country Life. Grade I Listed and noted for its outstanding architectural and historical importance. Home of the Palmers for 400 years, passing from father to son over 13 generations. Sitting in a classical setting, highlights include the magnificent Great Hall, oak and lacquer furniture and artwork which spans the lifetime of the House. The stunning Old Coach House Barn with its landscaped courtyard provides a beautiful space for events. **Location:** Map 3:G2. OS Ref SU926 791. 5 mins off M4/J7, 10mins from Windsor, 2m W of Eton. **Owner/Contact:** Mr James Palmer
Tel: 01628 604638 **Twitter:** @dorneycourt. **E-mail:** info@dorneycourt.co.uk
Open: May BHs (1 & 2 May; 29 & 30 May) and every day in Aug. 1.30pm-5pm.
Admission: Adult: £8.50, Child (10yrs+) £5.50. OAPs: £8.00. Groups (10+): £8.00 when open to public. Private group rates at other times.
Key facts: Film & photo shoots. No stiletto heels. Garden centre (www.dckg.co.uk). Events, Activity Days & Wedding receptions. Video tour of upstairs rooms. Licensed. Licensed. Obligatory. Free. Guide dogs only. By special appointment (Min numbers apply: 20+).

WINDSOR CASTLE

Windsor, Berkshire SL4 1NJ

Established in the 11th Century by William the Conqueror, Windsor Castle is the oldest and largest occupied castle in the world. **Location:** Map 3:G2. OS Ref SU969 770. M4/J6, M3/J3. 20m from central London. **Tel:** +44 (0)20 7766 7304
E-mail: bookinginfo@royalcollection.org.uk **Website:** www.royalcollection.org.uk
Open: Please see website for opening times.
Admission: Visit www.royalcollection.org.uk for details.

Garden at Dorney Court

CHENIES MANOR HOUSE 🏛Ⓕ

www.cheniesmanorhouse.co.uk

The Manor House is in the picturesque village of Chenies and lies in the beautiful Chiltern Hills.

The Manor House is approached by a gravel drive leading past the church. Home of the MacLeod Matthews family, this 15th and 16th Century manor house with fortified tower is the original home of the Earls of Bedford, visited by Henry VIII and Elizabeth I. Elizabeth was a frequent visitor, first coming as an infant in 1534 and as Queen she visited on several occasions, once staying for six weeks. The Bedford Mausoleum is in the adjacent church. The house contains tapestries and furniture mainly of the 16th and 17th Centuries, hiding places and a collection of antique dolls. Art exhibitions are held throughout the season in the restored 16th Century pavilion. The Manor is surrounded by five acres of enchanting gardens which have been featured in many publications and on television. It is famed for the Spring display of tulips. From early June there is a succession of colour in the Tudor Sunken Garden, the White Garden, herbaceous borders and Fountain Court. The Physic Garden contains a wide selection of medicinal and culinary herbs. In the Parterre is an ancient oak and a complicated yew maze while the Kitchen Garden is in Victorian style with unusual vegetables and fruit. Attractive dried and fresh flower arrangements decorate the house. Winner of the Historic Houses Association and Christie's Garden of the Year Award, 2009.

KEY FACTS

- Gardens only.
- Delicious homemade teas in the Garden Room.
- Except Guide Dogs.

VISITOR INFORMATION

■ Owner
Mrs E. MacLeod Matthews & Mr C. MacLeod Matthews

■ Address
Chenies
Buckinghamshire
WD3 6ER

■ Location
Map 7:D12
OS Ref. TQ016 984
N of A404 between Amersham & Rickmansworth M25-Ext 18, 3m.

■ Contact
Chenies Manor House
Tel: 01494 762888
E-mail:
macleodmatthews@
btinternet.com

■ Opening Times
6 April – 29 October
Wednesday & Thursday & Bank Holiday Mondays 2-5pm (last entry to the house 4.15pm).

■ Admission
House & Garden:
Adult £8.00
Child £4.50
Garden Only:
Adult £6.00
Child £4.00
Groups (20 +) by arrangement throughout the year.

■ Special Events
28 Mar - Easter BH Mon
House & Garden 2-5pm. The first mention of the distribution of eggs was at Chenies. Children's Egg & Spoon races, Egg Spotting, Homemade teas, Shop & Plants for sale.
2 May – BH Mon
House & Garden 2-5pm "Tulip Festival" Bloms Tulips throughout the house & gardens. Homemade Teas, Shop & Plants for sale.
30 May – BH Mon
House & Garden 2-5pm Homemade Teas, Shop, & Plants for sale.
17 Jul – Sun
Famous Plant & Garden Fair – Gardens 10am-5pm (House opens at 2pm) 70 specialist Nurseries from around the country. Refreshments all day.
29 Aug - BH Mon
House & Garden 2-5pm "Dahlia Festival" a display of a number of different Dahlias throughout the house and gardens.
26 & 27 Oct
House & Garden 2-5pm "Spooks & Surprises, special scary tour of the house for children, visit the difficult maze, homemade teas – shop.

CLAYDON HOUSE AND GARDENS
CLAYDON HOUSE, MIDDLE CLAYDON, BUCKINGHAMSHIRE MK18 2EY
www.nationaltrust.org.uk/claydon

Nestled in peaceful parkland, this Georgian Manor House hides a lavish interior which has been home to the Verney family since 1620. Featuring Rococo carvings, family portraits and an exquisite staircase inlaid with ebony and ivory. The riotous detail continues upstairs in the Chinese Room with a chinoiserie inspired pagoda which is truly one of a kind. To complement the grandeur of the House are Claydon Gardens - a classic example of an English country garden, being both decorative and productive. The gardens include a Kitchen Garden, Pool Garden with 19th Century greenhouse, as well as the formal Box Garden and the Florence Nightingale Centenary Garden. These beautifully tended gardens have something special to offer in any season.

Location: Map 7:C11. OS Ref SP719 253. M40 J9, signposted off A413 (Buckingham) & A41 (Waddesdon crossroads).

Owner: National Trust and Claydon Estate **Contact:** House Manager
Tel: 01296 730349 **Claydon Estate:** 01296 730252.
E-mail: claydon@nationaltrust.org.uk / info@claydonestate.co.uk
Open: House and Gardens: Sat-Wed, 11am-5pm, Mar-Oct. Please visit the website for further details.
Admission: House: Free for National Trust members. Please see website for details. Gardens: Please see website for details.
Key facts: Second-hand bookshop with huge variety of genres and authors. The ground floor of the house is accessible with a virtual tour of upstairs. Gardens have some slopes. 01296 730004. Please call for details - tours must be booked in advance. Please call for details or to book your school visit. On leads in park. House & garden.

HUGHENDEN
HIGH WYCOMBE, BUCKINGHAMSHIRE HP14 4LA
www.nationaltrust.org.uk/hughenden

Amid rolling Chilterns countryside, discover the hideaway and colourful private life of Benjamin Disraeli, the most unlikely Victorian Prime Minister. Follow in his footsteps, stroll through his German forest, relax in his elegant garden and imagine dining with Queen Victoria in the atmospheric manor. Uncover the Second World War story of Operation Hillside, for which unconventional artists painted maps for bombing missions - including the famous Dambusters raid. Discover the story of the map makers in our basement exhibition. Outdoors, get tips for growing your own vegetables in our walled garden. Don't miss our ancient woodland, where you may spot red kites soaring overhead.

Location: Map 3:F1. OS Ref SU866 955. 1½ m N of High Wycombe on the W side of the A4128.

Owner: National Trust **Contact:** The Estate Office

Tel: 01494 755573 **Fax:** 01494 474284 **Infoline:** 01494 755565
E-mail: hughenden@nationaltrust.org.uk
Open: Garden and restaurant: 1-14 Jan, daily, 10am-3:30pm, 18 Jan-28 Feb, daily, 10am-4:30pm, 29 Feb-1 Nov, 10am-5:30pm, 2 Nov-31 Dec, daily, 10am-3:30pm. Shop and Manor open at 11am. Manor closes 30 minutes before the rest of the site. Closed on 24 and 25 Dec.
Admission: House & Garden: Adult £11.50, Child £5.80, Family £28.60. Garden only: Adult £4.70, Child £2.95, Family £12.10. Groups: Adult £9.45. Child £4.45. Free for NT Members. Includes a voluntary 10% donation but visitors can choose to pay the standard prices advised at the property.
Key facts: Partial. WCs. Hughenden has a café and a tea room. Daily. Guide dogs only in the formal and walled gardens.

Register for news and special offers at www.hudsonsheritage.com

WOTTON HOUSE
Wotton Underwood, Aylesbury
Buckinghamshire HP18 0SB

The Capability Brown Pleasure Grounds at Wotton, currently undergoing restoration, are related to the Stowe gardens, both belonging to the Grenville family when Brown laid out the Wotton grounds between 1750 and 1767. A series of man-made features on the 3 mile circuit include bridges, temples and statues.
Location: Map 7:B11. OS Ref 468576, 216168. Either A41 turn off Kingswood, or M40/J7 via Thame.
Owner/Contact: David Gladstone
Tel: 01844 238363
Fax: 01844 238380
E-mail: david.gladstone@which.net
Open: 6 Apr-7 Sep: Weds only, 2-5pm. Also: 28 Mar, 30 May, 2 Jul, 6 Aug and 3 Sep: 2-5pm.
Admission: Adult £6.00, Child Free, Conc. £3.00. Groups (max 25).
Key facts: 🖼 🖼 Obligatory.
🅿 Limited parking for coaches. 🐕 On leads.

CLIVEDEN ❦
Taplow, Maidenhead SL6 0JA
Relax in grand style as you explore these stunning gardens, woodlands and Thames riverbank. Beautiful floral displays. **Location:** Map 3:F1. OS Ref SU915 851.
Tel: 01628 605069 **E-mail:** cliveden@nationaltrust.org.uk
Website: www.nationaltrust.org.uk/cliveden
Open: Please see website for up to date opening and admission details.

NATIONAL TRUST STOWE ❦
New Inn Farm, Buckingham MK18 5EQ
Picture-perfect views, winding paths, lakeside walks and temples create a timeless landscape, reflecting the changing seasons. **Location:** Map 7:B10. OS Ref SP681 364. Off A422 Buckingham - Banbury Rd. 3m NW of Buckingham.
Tel: 01280 817156 **E-mail:** stowe@nationaltrust.org.uk
Website: www.nationaltrust.org.uk/stowe
Open: Please see website for opening times. **Admission:** See website.

NETHER WINCHENDON HOUSE 🏛ⓔ
Nether Winchendon, Nr Thame, Buckinghamshire HP18 0DY
Medieval Manor Strawberry Hill Gothick. Home last Royal Governor Massachussetts. Continuous family occupation since 1559.
Location: Map 7:C11. **Tel:** 01844 290101 **Website:** www.nwhouse.co.uk
Open: 25 Apr-27 May & BHMon 2 & 30 May & 29 Aug (not Sats or Sun 1 & 29 May) 2.45, 3.45 & 4.45pm tours. **Admission:** £8.00, Art Fund £6.00, HHA Free, Conc. £5.00, not Sun or BH's. No conc to Art Fund or HHA when open for NGS.

STOWE HOUSE 🏛ⓔ
Stowe House, Stowe, Buckingham MK18 5EH
The House is known for its spectacular neo-classical interiors and the magnificent views from and towards the House. **Location:** Map 7:C10. OS Ref SP666 366. From London, M1 to Milton Keynes, 1½ hrs or Banbury 1¼ hrs, 3m NW of Buckingham. **Tel:** 01280 818002 **Fax:** 01280 818186
E-mail: Houseinfo@stowe.co.uk **Website:** www.stowehouse.org
Open: See website or telephone 01280 818166. **Admission:** See website.

WADDESDON MANOR 🏛 ❦
Waddesdon, Nr Aylesbury, Buckinghamshire HP18 0JH
Magnificent house and grounds in the style of a 19th Century French chateau. Built by Baron Ferdinand de Rothschild to display his superb collection of art treasures and entertain the fashionable world. **Location:** Map 7:C11. OS Ref SP740 169. **Tel:** 01296 653226 **Website:** www.nationaltrust.org.uk/waddesdon-manor **Open:** Please see website for up to date opening and admission details.

Rear Garden at Hughenden Manor

VISITOR INFORMATION

■ **Owner**
Lord Montagu

■ **Address**
Beaulieu
Hampshire
SO42 7ZN

■ **Location**
Map 3:C6
OS Ref. SU387 025
M27 to J2, A326, B3054
follow brown signs.
Bus: Local service within
the New Forest.
Rail: Station at
Brockenhurst 7m away.

■ **Contact**
Visitor Enquiries
Tel: 01590 612345
E-mail:
visit@beaulieu.co.uk

■ **Opening Times**
Summer Whitsun-Sep
Daily, 10am-6pm. Winter
Oct-Whitsun Daily,
10am-5pm Please check
website for exact dates.
Closed 25 Dec.

■ **Admission**
All year Individual and
group rates upon
application. Groups (15+).

■ **Special Events**
Boatjumble: 24 April
Spring Autojumble:
21-22 May
Truckmania: 29-30 May
**Hot Rod and Custom
Drive In Day:** 19 June
Supercar Showdown:
August (TBC)
**International
Autojumble:** September
(TBC)

All ticket enquiries to our
Special Events Booking
Office. Tel 01590 612888.

Conference/Function

ROOM	Size	Max Cap
Brabazon (x3)	40' x 40'	85 (x3)
Domus	69' x 27'	150
Palace House		60
Motor Museum		250

Palace House

BEAULIEU 🏛ⓕ
www.beaulieu.co.uk

Beaulieu, at the heart of the New Forest, is home to Lord Montagu and features a range of heritage attractions.

Palace House
Home of the Montagu family since 1538, Palace House was built around the Great Gatehouse of Beaulieu Abbey. Explore this fantastic gothic styled Victorian country home as costumed guides give you a flavour of life `below stairs' and share with you the fascinating history of the house and the generations who have lived there.

Beaulieu Abbey & Exhibition
Founded on land gifted by King John to Cistercian monks in 1204, Beaulieu Abbey was largely destroyed during the Reformation. The conserved ruins demonstrate the scale of what was once a vast complex. One of the surviving buildings houses an exhibition on the history of the Abbey and the monks that lived and worked here.

The National Motor Museum
Over 250 vehicles tell the story of motoring in Britain from its pioneering origins to the present day. From the earliest motor carriages to classic family saloons, displays include historic sporting motors, modern rally cars, F1 racers, a rustic 1930's country garage and Wheels – a fascinating pod ride through motoring history.

Grounds & Gardens
Explore the informal Wilderness Garden, fragrant Victorian Flower Garden and the Victorian Kitchen Garden. Enjoy the Mill Pond walk through parkland woods and look out for the Rufus Memorial Cairn – to commemorate the death of King William Rufus who, evidence suggests, was killed by an arrow whilst hunting at Beaulieu in 1100.

KEY FACTS

ⓘ Allow 4-5 hrs for visits. Helicopter landing point.

🛍 Palace House Kitchen Shop & Main Reception Shop.

🍸 Please see website.

♿ WC. Wheelchairs in Visitor Reception by prior booking.

🍴 Part of the Brabazon Restaurant-sandwiches to cooked meals and tea & cold drinks.

🍽 Seats 250.

👤 Attendants on duty.

🅿 Unlimited. Free admission for coach drivers plus voucher.

🎓 Professional staff available to assist.

🐕 In grounds, on leads only.

💒 Please see www.beaulieu.co.uk/corporate-and-weddings

❄ Closed 25 Dec.

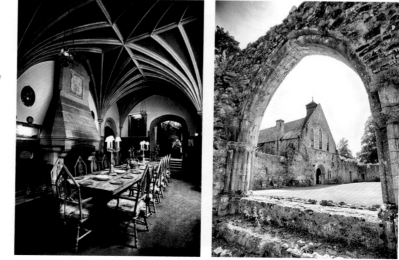

Register for news and special offers at www.hudsonsheritage.com

© Fergus Baird

AVINGTON PARK 🏛ⓕ
WINCHESTER, HAMPSHIRE SO21 1DB
www.avingtonpark.co.uk

From the wrought iron gates and long avenue of limes, approach well tended lawns, bordering the river Itchen and the elegant Palladian facade. William Cobbett wrote of Avington Park that it was 'one of the prettiest places in the County' and indeed it is true today. Dating back to the 11th Century, and enlarged in 1670, the house enjoys magnificent painted and gilded state rooms overlooking lawns and parkland. Over the years Charles II and George IV stayed at various times. St Mary's, a fine Georgian church, may also be visited.

Location: Map 3:D4. OS Ref SU534 324. 4m NE of Winchester ½m S of B3047 in Itchen Abbas.

Owner/Contact: Mrs S L Bullen **Tel:** 01962 779260
E-mail: enquiries@avingtonpark.co.uk
Open: May-Sep: Suns & BH Mons plus Mons in Aug, 2.30-5.00pm. Last tour 4.30pm. Group visits welcome by appointment all year.
Admission: Adult £8.00, Child £4.00.
Key facts: ⓘ Exclusive use for conferences, weddings, films, photoshoots, private parties, seminars and corporate events. 🖻 🖻 Partial (ground floor only) and WC. 🖻 🖻 Obligatory. 🅿 🖻 In grounds, on leads. Guide dogs only in house. 🖻 🖻 🖻 By arrangement. 🖻

© John Anderson

EXBURY GARDENS & STEAM RAILWAY
Exbury, Southampton, Hampshire SO45 1AZ
www.exbury.co.uk

A tranquil 200-acre woodland garden world-famous for dazzling displays of rhododendrons, azaleas and camellias in spring. Summer brings hydrangeas and showpiece exotics heat up the Herbaceous Borders. The extensive tree collection ensures year-round interest and stunning autumn colour. A ride on the 1¼ mile steam railway will delight visitors of all ages.

Location: Map 3:D6. OS Ref SU425 005. 20 mins Junction 2, M27 west. 11m SE of Totton (A35) via A326 & B3054 & minor road. In the New Forest.
Owner: Exbury Gardens Ltd.
Contact: Estate Office
Tel: 023 8089 1203
Fax: 023 8089 9940
E-mail: info@exbury.co.uk
Open: 12 Mar-6 Nov 2016, 10am-5.30pm last admission 4.30pm.
Admission: Please see website for up to date admission prices. Prices and opening dates subject to variations. Please visit www.exbury.co.uk.
Key facts: 🖻 🖻 🖻 🖻 🖻 🖻 Licensed. 🖻 By arrangement. 🅿 🖻 🖻 In grounds, on short leads. 🖻 🖻

HIGHCLERE CASTLE, GARDENS & EGYPTIAN EXHIBITION 🏛ⓕ
Highclere Castle, Newbury, Berkshire RG20 9RN
www.highclerecastle.co.uk

This spectacular Victorian Castle was the setting for the popular television series, Downton Abbey. Enjoy the splendid State Rooms; the masculine opulence of the Library and the lovely south facing Drawing Room. Explore the Egyptian Exhibition in the Castle Cellars; the Antiquities Room and an amazing recreation of the discovery of Tutankhamun's tomb. Visit the Gardens, inspired by Capability Brown, including: Monk's Garden, Secret Garden and new Arboretum.

Location: Map 3:D3. OS Ref SU445 587. M4/J13 - A34 south. M3/J8 - A303 - A34 north. **Owner:** Earl of Carnarvon **Contact:** The Castle Office
Tel: 01635 253210 **Fax:** 01635 255315 **E-mail:** theoffice@highclerecastle.co.uk
Open: Easter Opening: please check website. Spring/ Summer: 1-3 May; 29-31 May; 10 Jul- 6 Sep (Sun-Thu each week). (Correct at time of publication).
Admission: Groups, Concessions, Family Tickets for Castle, Exhibition & Gardens; each element available separately, please check website for prices.
Key facts: 🖻 🖻 🖻 🖻 Partial. WCs. 🖻 Licensed. 🖻 By arrangement. 🅿 Free. 🖻 🖻 Guide dogs only. 🖻 🖻

HINTON AMPNER ✤
Bramdean, Alresford, Hampshire SO24 0LA
www.nationaltrust.org.uk/hinton-ampner

This elegant country manor and tranquil garden sit so harmoniously within the landscape that one cannot exist without the other. Enjoy the exquisite collection of ceramics and art and avenues of sculptured topiary leading to breathtaking views across the South Downs. With newly opened parkland, one can experience all Hinton Ampner has to offer.

Location: Map 3:E5. OS Ref SU597 275. M3/J9 or A3 on A272, 1m W of Bramdean.
Owner: National Trust **Contact:** Property office **Tel:** 01962 771305
E-mail: hintonampner@nationaltrust.org.uk
Open: Gardens, Tearoom, Shop and Estate: 1 Jan-31 Dec, 10am-5pm. Winter exhibition: 27 Dec-7 Feb. House: 14 Feb-28 Nov, 2 Dec-19 Dec, 11am-4.30pm, Closed Christmas Eve and Christmas day.
Admission: House & garden: Adult £12.50, Child £6.25, Family £31.25, Garden only: Adult £10.00, Child £5.00, Family £25.00 Groups (15+) £8.50.
Key facts: ⬜ ⬜ ⬜ WCs. ⬜ Licensed. ⬜ By arrangement. ⬜ Limited for coaches. ⬜ Dogs are welcome on parkland, estate and tea-room courtyard. ⬜ Closed Christmas Eve and Christmas day. ⬜

HOUGHTON LODGE GARDENS ⬜ⓕ
Stockbridge, Hampshire SO20 6LQ
www.houghtonlodge.co.uk

An 18th Century Grade II* listed Gothic cottage idyllically set above the tranquil River Test. Peaceful formal and informal gardens with fine trees. Chalk Cob walls enclose traditional Kitchen Garden with espaliers, themed herb garden and orchid house. 14 acres of picturesque countryside, meadow walks, 3 charming Alpacas, topiary Peacock Garden and snorting dragon! Tea House offers light refreshments.
Location: Map 3:C4. OS Ref SU344 332. 1½m S of Stockbridge (A30) on minor road to Houghton village.
Contact: Sophie Busk **Tel:** 01264 810063
E-mail: info@houghtonlodge.co.uk
Open: Daily from 1 Mar-30 Sep, 10am-5pm.
House tours and garden tours are available to pre-booked groups.
Admission: Adult £6.50, Children £3.00, Under 3 Free.
Coach tours and groups are welcome on any day by appointment only.
Key facts: ⬜ ⬜ Tea House - light refreshments. ⬜ By arrangement. ⬜ Hard standing for 2 coaches. ⬜ On short leads. ⬜ ⬜

Exbury Gardens

KING JOHN'S HOUSE & HERITAGE CENTRE
Church Street, Romsey, Hampshire SO51 8BT
www.kingjohnshouse.org.uk

Three historic buildings on one site: Medieval King John's House, containing 14th Century graffiti and rare bone floor, Tudor Cottage complete with traditional tea room and Victorian Heritage Centre with recreated shop and parlour. Beautiful period gardens, special events/exhibitions and children's activities. Gift shop and Tourist Information Centre. Receptions and private/corporate functions.
Location: Map 3:C5. OS Ref SU353 212. M27/J3. Opposite Romsey Abbey, next to Post Office. **Owner:** King John's House & Tudor Cottage Trust Ltd
Contact: Anne James **Tel:** 01794 512200 **E-mail:** info@kingjohnshouse.org.uk
Open: Mon-Sat, 10am-4pm. Limited opening on Suns. Evenings also for pre-booked groups. Open all year except christmas week and occasional private bookings - check for details.
Admission: Adult £4.00, Child £1.00, Conc. £3.00. Family & Season tickets.
Key facts: ⬚ ⬚ Main Plant sale in May - cuttings etc on outside table all year round. ⬚ ⬚ Partial. ⬚ Traditional Tea Room with Homemade cakes, cream teas & light lunches. ⬚ By arrangement. ⬚ Off Latimer St, through King John's Garden. ⬚ Reenactment days - Stone age to WW1. ⬚ Guide dogs only. ⬚ ⬚

STRATFIELD SAYE HOUSE ⬚⬚
Stratfield Saye, Hampshire RG7 2BZ
www.stratfield-saye.co.uk

After the Duke of Wellington's victory against Napoleon at the Battle of Waterloo in 1815, the Duke chose Stratfield Saye as his country estate. The house contains many of the 1st Duke's possessions and is still occupied by his descendents being a family home rather than a museum.
Location: Map 3:E2. OS Ref SU700 615. Equidistant from Reading (M4/J11) & Basingstoke (M3/J6) 1½m W of the A33.
Owner: The Duke of Wellington
Contact: Estate Office
Tel: 01256 882694
Open: Thu 24-Mon 28 Mar. Thu 28 Jul-Mon 22 Aug.
Admission: Weekends: Adult £12.00, Child £5.00, OAP/Student £11.00. Weekdays: Adult £10.00, Child £4.00, OAP/Student £9.00. Groups by arrangement only.
Key facts: ⬚ ⬚ WC. ⬚ ⬚ Obligatory. ⬚ ⬚ Guide dogs only.

GILBERT WHITE & THE OATES COLLECTIONS
High St, Selborne, Alton GU34 3JH

Explores the lives of three explorers of the natural world. Home of the naturalist Gilbert White, and surrounded by 25 acres of garden and parkland. The Oates Collections celebrates the lives of 19th Century explorer Frank Oates, and Lawrence Oates who travelled on the ill-fated Terra Nova Expedition. **Location:** Map 3:E4. OS Ref SU741 336. Selborne is on B3006 from Alton to A3. **Tel:** 01420 511275 **E-mail:** info@gilbertwhiteshouse.org.uk
Website: www.gilbertwhiteshouse.org.uk
Open: 1 Jan-14 Feb, Fri-Sun, 10.30am-4.30pm. 15 Feb-24 Mar, Tue-Sun, 10.30am-4.30pm. 25 Mar-31 Oct, Tue-Sun, 10.30am-5.00pm. 1 Nov-20 Dec, Tue-Sun, 10.30am-4.30pm. BH Suns & Mons Jul & Aug. **Admission:** Adult £9.50, Conc £8.50, U16 £4.00, U5 Free, Family Ticket (2A+3C) £24.50. Pre-booked group of 10+ £7.50. Garden Only £7.50. **Key facts:** ⬚ Books, local produce & gifts. ⬚ Buy plants from garden. ⬚ ⬚ Suitable. Assistance provided. ⬚ Elegantly restored dining room. ⬚ In village, 2 min walk. ⬚ ⬚ In grounds only. ⬚ ⬚ ⬚

BROADLANDS
Romsey, Hampshire SO51 9ZD
Broadlands is the historic home of the Brabourne family.
Location: Map 3:C5. OS Ref SU353 202.
Tel: 01794 529750 **Website:** www.broadlandsestates.co.uk
Open: Jun-Sep. Please see our website for details.

HARCOMBE HOUSE
Park Lane, Ropley, Alresford, Hampshire SO24 0BE
House tour and grounds available for picnics.
Location: Map 3:E4. OS Ref SU636 309. **Tel:** 07796 195550
Open: 9am-6pm daily in Jun and Jul. Please call to book in advance.
Admission: Adults £9.50, Children £6.00.

MOTTISFONT ⬚
Mottisfont, Nr Romsey, Hampshire SO51 0LP
A romantic house and gallery, crafted from a medieval priory, set in beautiful riverside gardens. **Location:** Map 3:C5. OS Ref SU327 270.
Tel: 01794 340757 **E-mail:** mottisfont@nationaltrust.org.uk
Website: www.nationaltrust.org.uk/mottisfont
Open: Please see website for up to date opening and admission details.

WINCHESTER CITY MILL ⬚
Bridge Street, Winchester SO23 9BH
Winchester City Mill is a working watermill dating back to at least Saxon times.
Location: Map 3D:4. OS Ref SU486 293. M3/J9 & 10. **Tel:** 01962 870057
E-mail: winchestercitymill@nationaltrust.org.uk
Website: www.nationaltrust.org.uk/winchestercitymill **Open:** Open Daily: 1 Jan-15 Feb 10am-4pm, 16 Feb-1 Nov 10am-5pm, 2 Nov-24 Dec 10am-4pm, Closed 25-31 Dec. **Admission:** Adults £4.40, Children £2.20, Family £11.00.

Houghton Lodge Gardens

VISITOR INFORMATION

■ Owner
The Denys Eyre Bower Bequest, Registered Charitable Trust

■ Address
Chiddingstone Castle
Nr Edenbridge
Kent
TN8 7AD

■ Location
Map 19:G12
OS Ref. TQ497 452
10m from Tonbridge, Tunbridge Wells and Sevenoaks. 4m Edenbridge. Accessible from A21 and M25/J5. London 35m.
Bus: Enquiries: Tunbridge Wells TIC 01892 515675.
Rail: Tonbridge, Tunbridge Wells, Edenbridge then taxi. Penshurst then 2m walk.
Air: Gatwick 15m.

■ Contact
Tel: 01892 870347
E-mail:
events@
chiddingstonecastle.org.uk

■ Opening Times
Sunday, Monday, Tuesday, Wednesday & BH's from Good Friday until the end of October (check the website for any unforeseen alterations to this).

Times: 11am-5pm. Last entry to house 4:15pm.

■ Admission
Adults	£9.00
Children (5-13)	£4.00
Family (2 adults + 2 children or 1 adult + 3 children)	£23.50
Grounds and Tea Rooms	Free
Parking	£2.00

■ Special Events
We have a series of special event days, including the Wedding Fair in March, the inaugural Storyteller Festival in May, the Summer Vintage Fair in June, the Country Fair in September and the Christmas Fair in December. Please visit the website What's On page for more information.

CHIDDINGSTONE CASTLE 🏛Ⓕ
www.chiddingstonecastle.org.uk

Chiddingstone Castle is a hidden gem in the Garden of England; a unique house with fascinating artefacts and beautiful grounds.

Situated in an historic village in the heart of the idyllic Kentish Weald, Chiddingstone Castle has Tudor origins and delightful Victorian rooms. Lying between Sevenoaks and Tunbridge Wells, it is conveniently located close to the M25 (Junction 5 - Sevenoaks or Junction 6 - Oxted). We welcome individuals, families and groups - guided tours are available. There is ample parking available in the large car park. Delicious light lunches, homemade cakes and traditional cream teas can be enjoyed in the cosy Tea Room set in the Old Buttery or in the delightful sheltered courtyard. The Castle's Gift Shop can be found in the former Well Tower.

Set in 35 acres of informal gardens, including a lake, waterfall, rose garden and woodland, this attractive country house originates from the 1550s when High Street House, as the Castle was known, was home to the Streatfeild family. Several transformations have since taken place and the present building dates back to 1805 when Henry Streatfeild extended and remodelled his ancestral home in the 'castle style' which was then

fashionable. Rescued from creeping dereliction in 1955 by the gifted antiquary Denys Eyre Bower, the Castle became home to his amazing and varied collections - Japanese Samurai armour, swords and lacquer, Egyptian antiquities, Buddhist artefacts, Stuart paintings and Jacobite manuscripts. Visitors can also visit Bower's Study and learn of his eccentric and complicated life, which featured a notorious scandal.

Further exhibition rooms are open showing the Victorian history of the Castle - the Victorian Kitchen and Scullery and the fascinating Housekeeper's Room. From the Servants' Hall, group visitors can climb the secret back stairs and discover the Servant's Bedroom in the attic – a real 'upstairs downstairs' experience!

In 2014 the Castle created a new Ancient Egyptian garden in the grounds to complement the antiquities found indoors; the 'Fields of Eternity' is a grass maze and treasure trail full of interesting discoveries - fun for Egyptologists of all ages!

KEY FACTS

- ℹ️ Museum, scenic gardens and lake, picnics, fishing available.
- 🛍️ Well stocked gift shop.
- 🍷 Available for private and corporate functions. Licensed for Civil Ceremonies. Wedding receptions.
- ♿ WCs.
- ☕ Cream teas a speciality.
- 🍴
- 🚶 By arrangement.
- 🅿️
- 🏫 We welcome visits from schools who wish to use the collections in connection with classroom work.
- 🐕 In grounds and Tea Room courtyard on leads.
- 🔔

VISITOR INFORMATION

■ **Owner**
English Heritage

■ **Address**
Dover Castle
Castle Hill
Dover
Kent
CT16 1HU

■ **Location**
Map 4:O4
OS Ref. TR325 419
Easy access from A2 and M20. Well signposted from Dover centre and east side of Dover. 2 hrs from central London.
Bus: 0870 6082608.
Rail: London St. Pancras Intl (fast train); London Victoria; London Charing Cross.

■ **Contact**
Visitor Operations Team
Tel: 01304 211067
E-mail: customers@ english-heritage.org.uk

■ **Opening Times**
Please visit www.english-heritage.org.uk for opening times, admission prices and the most up-to-date information.

■ **Special Events**
Please visit www.english-heritage.org.uk for the most up-to-date information on our exciting days out and events.

DOVER CASTLE ⊞
www.english-heritage.org.uk/dovercastle

Explore over 2,000 years of history at Dover Castle.

Immerse yourself in the medieval world and royal court of King Henry II as you climb the stairs into the Great Tower and meet the first of the many life like projected figures which will guide you round the six great recreated rooms and several lesser chambers of the palace. On special days throughout the year interact with costumed characters as they bring to life the colour and opulence of medieval life.

Take an adventurous journey into the White Cliffs as you tour the maze of Secret Wartime Tunnels. Children will love dressing up in wartime uniforms, exploring the tunnels, the interactive displays and virtual tour. Through sight, sound and smells, re-live the wartime drama of a wounded pilot fighting for his life. Discover what life would have been like during the dark and dramatic days

of the Dunkirk evacuation with exciting audio-visual experiences. See the pivotal part the Secret Wartime Tunnels played in Operation Dynamo.

Above ground, enjoy magnificent views of the White Cliffs from Admiralty Lookout and explore the Fire Command Post, re-created as it would have appeared 90 years ago in the last days of the Great War. Also see a Roman Lighthouse and Anglo-Saxon church, as well as an intriguing network of medieval underground tunnels, fortifications and battlements.

Dover Castle was used as a film location for The Other Boleyn Girl starring Natalie Portman and Scarlett Johanssen and Zaffirelli's Hamlet amongst others.

KEY FACTS

ℹ️ WCs. No flash photography within the Great Tower.

📷 Two.

🍴 Licensed.

🚶 Tour of tunnels. Last tour 1 hr before closing.

🅿️ Ample.

🏫 Education centre. Pre-booking essential.

🐕 Dogs on leads only.

VISITOR INFORMATION

■ Owner
Hever Castle Ltd

■ Address
Hever Castle
Hever
Edenbridge
Kent
TN8 7NG

■ Location
Map 19:G12
OS Ref. TQ476 450
See website for directions.

■ Contact
Tel: 01732 865224
Fax: 01732 866796
E-mail:
info@hevercastle.co.uk

■ Opening Times
13 Feb 2016–1 Jan 2017
Gardens open at 10.30am.
Castle opens at 12 noon.
Spring Season
13 Feb–21 Feb (Daily)
24 Feb–27 Mar (Wed-Sun)
Last admission 3pm.
Final exit 4.30pm.
Main Season (Daily)
28 Mar–29 Oct
Last admission 4.30pm.
Final exit 6pm.
Winter Season
30 Oct–25 Nov (Wed-Sun)
Last admission 3.00pm.
Final exit 4.30pm.
Christmas Tickets
26 Nov–13 Dec (Wed-Sun)
14 Dec–24 Dec (Daily)
Last admission 4.30pm.
Final exit 6.00pm.
Winter Walks
27 Dec–1 Jan
Last admission 3.00pm.
Final exit 4.30pm.

■ Admission
INDIVIDUAL
Castle & Gardens

Adult	£16.50
Senior	£14.40
Student	£13.90
Child	£9.30
Family	£43.60

Gardens only

Adult	£13.90
Senior	£12.40
Student	£11.80
Child	£8.80
Family	£38.10

GROUP (15+)

Adult	£12.65
Senior	£11.65
Student	£10.00
Child	£7.00

Gardens only

Adult	£10.65
Senior	£10.15
Student	£8.60
Child	£6.70

■ Special Events
An extensive events
programme. See website.

HEVER CASTLE & GARDENS ▣ Ⓕ
www.hevercastle.co.uk

Experience 700 years of colourful history and spectacular award-winning gardens at the childhood home of Anne Boleyn.

Dating back to the 13th Century, Hever Castle was once the childhood home of Anne Boleyn, second wife of Henry VIII and mother of Elizabeth I and formed the unlikely backdrop to a sequence of tumultuous events that changed the course of Britain's history, monarchy and religion.

Its splendid panelled rooms contain fine furniture, tapestries, antiques and an important collection of Tudor portraits. Two beautifully illuminated prayer books on display in the Book of Hours Room belonged to Anne and bear her inscriptions and signature. One is believed to be the prayer book Anne took with her to her execution at the Tower.

The charming castle at Hever has a rich and varied history. Today much of what you see is the result of the remarkable efforts of a wealthy American, William Waldorf Astor, who used his fortune to restore and extend the Castle in the early 20th Century. A section of the Castle is dedicated to its more recent history, containing pictures and memorabilia relating to the Astor family and the Edwardian period.

The award-winning gardens are set in 125 acres of glorious grounds. Marvel at the Pompeiian wall and classical statuary in the Italian Garden; admire the giant topiary chess set and inhale the fragrance of over 4,000 rose bushes in the quintessential English Rose Garden. The Loggia, overlooking the 38-acre lake, is the perfect spot to relax before exploring the Tudor Garden, Blue Corner and Rhododendron Walk.

KEY FACTS

- ℹ No photography in the Castle. Accommodation, venue hire and golf.
- Gift, garden & book. Guide books.
- Seasonal variety of plants.
- Meetings, training & conferences. Team building & golf days. Parties and banqueting.
- ♿ Partial. WCs. See website.
- 🍴 Choice of restaurants. Seasonal opening.
- 🚶 Castle & Garden Guided Tours by arrangement. Min 15 persons.
- 🎧 English, French, German, Dutch, Russian & Chinese.
- 🅿 Free parking.
- Discounted rates, education room and school packs.
- 🐕 Well behaved dogs on lead in grounds.
- Luxury B&B & holiday cottage in Astor Wing of the Castle.
- Choice of venues on the estate.

Register for news and special offers at **www.hudsonsheritage.com**

© David Sellman/Penshurst Place

VISITOR INFORMATION

■ Owner
Viscount De L'Isle MBE

■ Address
Penshurst
Nr Tonbridge
Kent
TN11 8DG

■ Location
Map 19:H12
OS Ref. TQ527 438
From London M25/J5 then
A21 to Hildenborough,
B2027 via Leigh; from
Tunbridge Wells A26,
B2176. Follow brown
signs.
Metro Bus: 231, 233 from
Tunbridge Wells and
Edenbridge.
Rail: Charing Cross/
Waterloo East-
Hildenborough, Tonbridge
or Tunbridge Wells; then
bus or taxi.

■ Contact
Tel: 01892 870307
E-mail:
contactus@penshurstplace.
com

■ Opening Times
13 Feb-27 Mar:
Sats & Suns Only.
House:
12-4pm.
Grounds:
10.30-6pm or dusk if
earlier.

28 Mar-30 Oct:
Daily, 10.30am-6pm.
House:
12-4pm.
Grounds:
10.30am-6pm. Last entry
5pm.

**Shop & Porcupine
Pantry:** Open all year.
Winter: Open to Groups
by appointment only.

■ Admission
For 2016 individual prices
see website for details.
2016 Group prices:
(pre-booked 15+).
Freeflow.
Adult   £8.50
Child (5-16 yrs)   £5.00
House Tours
Adult   £10.50
Child (5-16 yrs)   £5.50
Garden Tours
(pre-booked 15+).
Adult   £10.50
Child (5-16 yrs)   £5.50
House & Garden Tours
Adult   £17.00
Child (5-16 yrs)   £10.00

■ Special Events
**Weald of Kent Craft &
Design Show:** First May
BH weekend and second
weekend in September.
Friday-Sunday.
Glorious Gardens Week:
First week in June.
Maize Maze: Open during
school Summer Holidays.

PENSHURST PLACE & GARDENS

www.penshurstplace.com

One of England's greatest family-owned historic houses with a history spanning nearly seven centuries.

In some ways time has stood still at Penshurst; the great House is still very much a medieval building with improvements and additions made over the centuries but without any substantial rebuilding. Its highlight is undoubtedly the medieval Baron's Hall, built in 1341, with its impressive 60ft-high chestnut-beamed roof. A marvellous mix of paintings, tapestries and furniture from the 15th, 16th and 17th Centuries can be seen throughout the House, including the helm carried in the state funeral procession to St Paul's Cathedral for the Elizabethan courtier and poet, Sir Philip Sidney, in 1587. This is now the family crest.

Gardens
The Gardens, first laid out in the 14th Century, have been developed over generations of the Sidney family, who first came to Penshurst in 1552. A major restoration and replanting programme undertaken by the 1st Viscount De L'Isle has been continued by his son the 2nd Viscount De L'Isle, to ensure they retain their historic splendour. The 1st Viscount De L'Isle is commemorated with an Arboretum, planted in 1991. The Gardens are divided by a mile of yew hedges into 'rooms', each planted to give a succession of colour as the seasons change, with the completion of a major redevelopment project on the Jubilee Walk and a more recent regeneration to the Blue and Yellow Border. There is also an Adventure Playground, Woodland Trail, Toy Museum and Garden Restaurant, with the Porcupine Pantry café and a Gift Shop open all year. A variety of events in the park and grounds take place throughout the year.

KEY FACTS

- [i] Guidebook available to purchase. No photography in house.
- Gift Shop outside paid perimeter.
- Small plant centre.
- Conference and private banqueting facilities.
- Partial. Contact for details.
- Porcupine Pantry outside paid perimeter.
- Garden Restaurant in the grounds.
- Guided tours available by arrangement before the House opens to the public. Garden tours available 10.30am-4.30pm.
- [P] Ample for cars and coaches.
- All year by appointment, discount rates, education room and teachers' packs.
- Guide dogs only.
- Wedding ceremonies and receptions.
- See opening times.
- See www.penshurstplace.com/whats-on

CHARTWELL ✤
MAPLETON ROAD, WESTERHAM, KENT TN16 1PS
www.nationaltrust.org.uk/chartwell

Chartwell was the much-loved Churchill family home and the place from which Sir Winston drew inspiration from 1924 until the end of his life. The house is still much as it was when the family lived here with pictures, books and personal mementoes. The studio is home to a collection of Churchill's paintings which have been saved for the nation. The gardens reflect Churchill's love of the landscape and nature. The woodland estate offers family walks, trails, den building, a Canadian Camp, dormouse dens, bomb crater and opportunites to stretch your legs and enjoy the spectacular views of Chartwell house. The Mulberry Room above the Landemare Café can be booked for meetings, conferences, lunches and dinners.

Location: Map 19:F11. OS Ref TQ455515.
2m S of Westerham, forking left off B2026.

Owner: National Trust **Contact:** Marketing & Development Manager
Tel: 01732 868381 **E-mail:** chartwell@nationaltrust.org.uk

Open: House: 27 Feb-30 Oct, Daily,11am-5pm last entry 4.15pm. Garden, Shop, Café, Exhibition & Studio, everyday 1 Jan-31 Dec, times vary please call for further details. The studio is closed in Jan, by tour only in Feb. The exhibition closes for short periods to change the display. All visitors require a timed ticket to visit the house, please obtain upon arrival at the Visitor Welcome Centre - places limited.
Admission: House, Garden & Studio: Adult £14.80, Child £7.40, Family £37.00. Garden, Exhibition, Studio & Winter season only: Adult £7.40, Child £3.70, Family £18.50. Gift Aid prices. Groups (15+) Adult £12.00, Child £6.00.
Key facts: ℹ Conference & function facilities. 🖼 The Mulberry Room can accommodate up to 80 people. Partial. There are steep slopes and steps through the garden to the house. Wheelchairs are available from the Visitor Welcome Centre. Accessible toilets. Licensed. By arrangement. £3.00 for non-members. In grounds on leads. Estate open all year except 24 & 25 Dec. House open from Mar until Oct.

LEEDS CASTLE 🏰
MAIDSTONE, KENT ME17 1PL
www.leeds-castle.com

Set in 500 acres of beautiful Kent parkland, there's something to discover every day at "the loveliest castle in the world". During its 900 year history, Leeds Castle has been a Norman stronghold, the private property of six of England's medieval Queens and a palace used by Henry VIII. In the 1930s the Castle was a playground for the rich and famous, as Lady Baillie, the last private owner, entertained high society down from London for the weekends.

During your visit discover the glorious gardens and grounds, spiraling yew maze, free-flying falconry displays, leisurely punting trips and the unique Dog Collar Museum. Children will enjoy riding on Elsie the Castle Land Train, taking a trip on the ferry boat and the adventure playgrounds.

Location: Map 4:L3. OS Ref TQ835 533. From London to A20/M20/J8, 40m, 1 hr. 7m E of Maidstone, ¼m S of A20.

Owner: Leeds Castle Foundation
Tel: 01622 765400 **Fax:** 01622 735616 **E-mail:** enquiries@leeds-castle.co.uk
Open: Summer: 1 Apr-30 Sep Daily, 10.30am-4.30pm (last adm).
Winter: 1 Oct-31 Mar Daily, 10.30am-3pm (last adm).
Admission: Annual Tickets (prices valid until 31 Mar 2016). Adults £24.00 Senior Citizens £21.00. Students £21.00 Visitors with disabilities £21.00 Children (4-15yrs) £16.00 Infants (under 4yrs) Free.
Key facts: ℹ Residential and day conferences, weddings, team building days, falconry, golf course, golf coaching, banquets, events. Banquets, meetings, seminars, presentations and conferences. WCs. Licensed. Licensed. Free parking. Guide dogs only. B&B, Holiday Cottages & Glamping. Closed to visitors on 5/6 Nov 2016 (for Fireworks) and Christmas Day 2016. €

RESTORATION HOUSE 🏛Ⓕ
17-19 CROW LANE, ROCHESTER, KENT ME1 1RF
www.restorationhouse.co.uk

Fabled city mansion deriving its name from the stay of Charles II on the eve of The Restoration. This complex ancient house has beautiful interiors with exceptional early paintwork related to decorative scheme 'run up' for Charles' visit. The house also inspired Dickens to create 'Miss Havisham' here. 'Interiors of rare historical resonance and poetry', Country Life. Fine English furniture and strong collection of English portraits (Mytens, Kneller, Dahl, Reynolds and several Gainsboroughs). Charming interlinked walled gardens and ongoing restoration of monumental Renaissance water garden. A private gem. 'There is no finer pre- Civil war town house in England than this' - Simon Jenkins, The Times. "Deserves a medal" -Jools Holland. New for 2016 - Photographers' Hour. Photography is not normally allowed inside Restoration House but for this year photography will be allowed on Friday mornings between 10 and 11. Now you can capture the beauty of these ancient interiors by natural morning light. No flash but tripods welcome. Normal entrance fee applies.

Location: Map 4:2K. OS Ref TQ744 683.
Historic centre of Rochester, off High Street, opposite the Vines Park.
Owner: R Tucker & J Wilmot
Contact: Robert Tucker
Tel: 01634 848520
E-mail: robert.tucker@restorationhouse.co.uk
Open: 26 May-30 Sep, Thu & Fri, 10am-5pm, plus Sat 28 May, 12-5pm.
Admission: Adult £8.00 (includes 36 page illustrated guidebook), Child £4.00 Conc £7.00 Booked group (8+) tours: £10.00pp.
Tea Shop: Open same days as house.
Key facts: ℹ️ No stiletto heels. No photography in house except Fri morns 10-11am. 🌿 Garden by appointment. 🍽 Open when house is open. 📷 By arrangement. 🐕 Guide dogs only.

BELMONT HOUSE & GARDENS 🏛Ⓕ
Belmont Park, Throwley, Faversham, Kent ME13 0HH
www.belmont-house.org

Belmont is an elegant 18th Century house, home to six generations of the Harris family. It contains many mementos of the family's history and travels - fine paintings, furniture, Indian silverware and perhaps the finest private clock collection in the country. The gardens contain a Pinetum complete with grotto, a walled ornamental garden, specimen trees and a large kitchen garden with Victorian greenhouses, all set in parkland.
Location: Map 4:M3. OS Ref TQ986 564. 4½m SSW of Faversham, off A251.
Owner: Harris (Belmont) Charity **Tel:** 01795 890202
E-mail: administrator@belmont-house.org
Open: Apr-Sep. Wed tours 11am & 1pm, Sat tours 2.15pm & 3.15pm, Sun & BH Mon tours 2.15pm, 3pm & 3.45pm. Gardens open daily 10am-6pm or dusk if earlier. Groups Tue & Thu by appointment. Pre-booked specialist clock tours last Sat of the month. For special events and up to date info please visit website.
Admission: House & Garden: Adult £8.00, Child (Under 12's free) £5.00, Conc. £7.00. Garden Only: Adult £5.00, Child (12-16yrs) £2.50, Conc. £4.00. Clock Tour £15.00. **Key facts:** ℹ️ No photography in house. 📷🍽🌳♿ Partial. WCs. 🍴 Tearoom open from 1pm on Sat & Sun for cream teas & cakes. Self-service Mon-Fri. 👤 The interior of the House can only be viewed by guided tour. 🅿️ Limited for coaches. 🐕 In the gardens, on lead only. 🌿 Gardens. See opening times. 🎫

THE GRANGE
St Augustine's Road, Ramsgate, Kent CT11 9NY
www.landmarktrust.org.uk

Augustus Pugin is regarded as being one of Britain's most influential architects and designers and to stay here in the home he designed for himself and his family offers a unique chance to step into his colourful and idiosyncratic world.
Location: Map 4:O2. OS Ref TR377 643.
Owner: The Landmark Trust
Tel: 01628 825925
E-mail: bookings@landmarktrust.org.uk
Open: Self-catering accommodation. Parts of house open Wed afternoons; there are eight Open Days.
Admission: Free, visits by appointment. Contact Catriona Blaker 01843 596401.
Key facts: ℹ️ This house was designed as a family home and it works as well today as it did in 1844. 👤🅿️🍽🐕♿🎫🌿

IGHTHAM MOTE ❀
Mote Road, Ivy Hatch, Sevenoaks, Kent TN15 0NT
www.nationaltrust.org.uk/ighthammote

Moated manor dating from 1320, reflecting seven centuries of history, from the medieval Crypt to a 1960s Library. Owned by knights, courtiers to Henry VIII and society Victorians. Highlights include Great Hall, Drawing Room, Tudor painted ceiling, Grade 1 listed dog kennel and apartments of US donor.
Location: Map 19:H11. OS Ref TQ584 535. 6m E of Sevenoaks off A25. 2½m S of Ightham off A227. **Owner:** National Trust **Contact:** Administrator
Tel: 01732 810378 **Fax:** 01732 811029
E-mail: ighthammote@nationaltrust.org.uk
Open: Daily all year, excl 24 & 25 Dec. 10am-5pm or dusk if earlier. House: 11am, last entry half hour before closing. Some areas may be partially open during certain times of the year. See website for full details. **Admission:** Adult £12.00, Child £6.00, Family £30.00, Group rate £9.00 (15+). Reduced rates in winter - partial house & gardens open. *Includes voluntary donation, standard prices displayed at property. **Key facts:** ⓘ No flash photography. Volunteer 8 seated electric buggy. ◩ ♿ ⊤ ⅃ WCs. 3 wheelchairs ground floor access only. Photograph album of upstairs. ▣ Licensed. Outside patio area with views of house. ⅋ House tour £3.00pp. Garden tours with Head Gardener £5.00pp. ℗ ▦ ❋ ♥

KNOLE ❀
Knole, Sevenoaks, Kent TN15 0RP
www.nationaltrust.org.uk/knole

Knole is vast, complex and full of hidden treasures. Originally an Archbishop's palace, the house passed through royal hands to the Sackville family – its inhabitants from 1603 to today. Knole is in the midst of a huge project to conserve and refurbish its remarkable rooms and collections, peeling back the layers of 600 years of history and sharing the work with visitors. This year, building works may affect some areas. Refreshments are outdoors until new Brewhouse Café opens.
Location: Map 19:H10. OS Ref TQ532 543. 25m SE of London. M25/J5 (for A21). Off A225 at S end of High Street. Opposite St Nicholas Church. Satnav: TN13 1HU.
Owner: National Trust **Contact:** Property Manager
Tel: 01732 462100 **E-mail:** knole@nationaltrust.org.uk
Open: The State Rooms are open 5 Mar-30 Oct, 11am-4pm. House is closed every Mon and car park is open 10am-6pm. Park and Green Court open all year. Please see website for full details.
Admission: Please see website.
Key facts: ▢ Bookshop also serves drinks and cake. ⅃ WCs; steps with handrail to first floor state rooms. ℗ Free to NT members. Open 10am-6pm. ▣ Contact Education Officer. ◗ In Park and Green Court only, on leads. ❋ Car park and refreshments available all year except Dec 24 & 25. ♥

TONBRIDGE CASTLE
Castle Street, Tonbridge, Kent TN9 1BG
www.tonbridgecastle.org

Standing in landscaped gardens overlooking the River Medway, Tonbridge Castle's mighty motte and bailey Gatehouse is among the finest in England. Experience the sights and sounds of the 13th Century as we bring them to life with interactive displays, dramatic special effects and personal audio tour.
Location: Map 19:H11. OS Ref TQ590 466. 5 mins walk from Tonbridge Train Station. Short drive off A21.
Owner: Tonbridge & Malling Borough Council
Contact: Tina Levett **Tel:** 01732 770929
E-mail: tonbridge.castle@tmbc.gov.uk
Open: All year: Mon-Sat, 9am-5pm last tour 4pm. Suns & BHs, 10.30am-4pm last tour 3.30pm. **Admission:** Gatehouse: Adult £8.00, Child/Conc. £4.70. Family £22.00 max 2 adults. Includes audio tour. The grounds are free. Please check website for up to date prices and availability.
Key facts: ▢ Gift Shop. ⊤ Chambers for Hire. ⅃ Some areas. ▣ Close by. ⅂⅂ Close by. ⅋ By appointment. ◈ Several Languages. ℗ Adjacent to grounds. ▩ School visits catered for with Tours and Games. ❋ Grounds only. ♨ We can cater for weddings in the Gatehouse or the Chambers. ❋ ♥

GOODNESTONE PARK GARDENS 🏠®
Goodnestone Park, Nr Wingham, Canterbury, Kent CT3 1PL
'The most perfect English garden' 14 acres of beautiful tranquillity including a woodland area, large walled garden and tearoom.
Location: Map 4:N3. OS Ref TR254 544. 8m Canterbury, 1½m E of B2046 - A2 to Wingham Road, signposted from this road. Postcode of Car Park: CT3 1PJ.
Contact: Francis Plumptre **Tel/Fax:** 01304 840107
E-mail: enquiries@goodnestoneparkgardens.co.uk
Website: www.goodnestoneparkgardens.co.uk
Open: Mar: Suns 12-4pm, Mar 23-Sep 30: Wed/Thu/Fri 11-5pm and Sun 12-5pm, Oct: Sun 12-4pm.
Admission: Adult £7.00 Concessions: £6.50 Child (6-16): £2.00 Season Ticket: £20.00 Family Season Ticket (2+2): £38.00 Groups (20+): £6.50 (out of opening hours £8.00).
Key facts: ♿ ⅃ Suitable. WCs. ▣ Licensed. ⅋ Partial. By arrangement. ℗ ❋ ♨ ♥

MOUNT EPHRAIM GARDENS 🏠®
Hernhill, Faversham, Kent ME13 9TX

In these enchanting 10 acres of Edwardian gardens, terraces of fragrant roses lead to a small lake and woodland area. A grass maze, unusual topiary, Japanese-style rock garden, arboretum, herbaceous border and many beautiful mature trees are other highlights. Peaceful, unspoilt atmosphere set in Kentish orchards with magnificent views over the Thames Estuary.
Location: Map 4:M3. OS Ref TR065 598. In Hernhill village, 1m from end of M2. Signed from A2 & A299. **Owner:** William Dawes & Family
Tel: 01227 751496 / 07516664151 **E-mail:** info@mountephraimgardens.co.uk
Website: www.mountephraimgardens.co.uk
Open: Apr-end Sep: Wed, Thu, Fri, Sat & Sun, 11am-5pm and BH Mons. Groups Mar-Oct by arrangement.
Admission: Adult £6.00, Child (4-16) £2.50. Groups (10+): £5.00.
Key facts: ▢ ♿ ⊤ ⅋ Partial. WCs. ▣ Licensed. ⅂⅂ Licensed. ⅋ By arrangement. ℗ ❋ ◗ On leads. ♨ Licensed for civil weddings inside and out. ♥

NURSTEAD COURT
Nurstead Church Lane, Meopham
Kent DA13 9AD

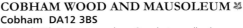

Nurstead Court is a Grade I listed manor house built in 1320 of timber-framed, crownposted construction, set in extensive gardens and parkland. The additional front part of the house was built in 1825. Licensed weddings are now held in the house with receptions and other functions in the garden marquee.
Location: Map 4:K2. OS Ref TQ642 685. Nurstead Church Lane is just off the A227 N of Meopham, 3m from Gravesend.
Owner/Contact: Mrs S Edmeades-Stearns **Tel:** 01474 812368 / 01474 812121.
E-mail: info@nursteadcourt.co.uk **Website:** www.nursteadcourt.co.uk
Open: Every Tue & Wed in Sep, and first Tue & Wed in Oct 2-5pm or all year round by arrangement.
Admission: Adult £5.00, Child £2.50, OAP/Student £4.00 Group (max 54): £4.00.
Key facts: ⬚ Weddings/Funct. ⬚ Licensed. ⬚ Obligatory, by arrangement. ⬚ Limited for coaches. ⬚ ⬚ Guide Dogs only. ⬚ 2 bed cottage. ⬚ ⬚

COBHAM HALL ⬚ⓔ
Cobham Hall, Cobham, Kent DA12 3BL

Magnificent Jacobean, Elizabethan manor house with Repton designed gardens set in 150 acres of parkland. **Location:** Map 4:K2. OS Ref TQ683 689.
Tel: 01474 823371 **Fax:** 01474 825902
E-mail: enquiries@cobhamhall.com **Website:** www.cobhamhall.com
Open: Specific days only. Check website or phone for details.
Admission: Adult £5.50, Conc. £4.50, Self-guided garden tour £2.50.

Penshurst Place & Gardens

COBHAM WOOD AND MAUSOLEUM ⬚
Cobham DA12 3BS
Restored 18th Century mausoleum & ancient woodland.
Location: Map 4:K2. OS Ref 178:TQ6946. Via the M2 and A2. Exit A2 at Shorne/ Cobham. **Tel:** 01732 810378 **E-mail:** cobham@nationaltrust.org.uk
Website: www.nationaltrust.org.uk/cobham-wood
Open: Woods open all year. Mausoleum see website for details.

DOWN HOUSE, THE HOME OF
CHARLES DARWIN ⬚
Luxted Road, Downe, Kent BR6 7JT
It was here that Charles Darwin worked on his scientific theories and wrote 'On the Origin of Species by Means of Natural Selection'. **Location:** Map 19:F9. OS Ref TQ431 611. **Tel:** 01689 859119 **Website:** www.english-heritage.org.uk/darwin
Open: Please see website for up-to-date opening and admission details.

LULLINGSTONE CASTLE & WORLD GARDEN
Eynsford, Kent DA4 0JA
Fine state rooms. Site for the World Garden of Plants. **Location:** Map 19:G9. OS Ref TQ530 644. 1m S Eynsford W side of A225. **Tel:** 01322 862114
Fax: 01322 862115 **E-mail:** info@lullingstonecastle.co.uk **Website:** www.lullingstonecastle.co.uk **Open:** Apr-Sep: Fris, Sats, Suns and BHs. Oct: Suns 12-5pm Closed Good Fri. **Admission:** Adult £8.00, Child £4.00, OAP £6.50, Family £18.00, Groups, Tours and Special Events - please see website.

OWLETTS ⬚
The Street, Cobham, Gravesend DA12 3AP
Former home of the architect Sir Herbert Baker. Highlights include an impressive Carolean staircase, plasterwork ceiling and large kitchen garden.
Location: Map 4:K2. OS Ref TQ665687. 1m south of A2 at west end of village. Limited parking at property. Parking nearby in Cobham village.
Tel: 01732 810378 **E-mail:** owletts@nationaltrust.org.uk
Website: www.nationaltrust.org.uk/owletts **Open:** See website for details.

QUEX PARK ⬚
Birchington, Kent CT7 0BH
Fine Regency country house with beautiful gardens set in the heart of an historic estate. Powell Cotton Museum houses natural history specimens and cultural objects from Africa, Asia and the Far East. **Location:** Map 4:O2. OS Ref TR309 682. **Tel:** 01843 841119 **Website:** www.quexpark.co.uk
Open: Please see website for up to date opening and admission details.

RIVERHILL HIMALAYAN GARDENS ⬚ⓔ
Sevenoaks, Kent TN15 0RR
Privately-owned historic gardens. Spectacular views, remarkable plant and tree collection, contemporary sculpture. Shop and Café. **Location:** Map 4:J3. OS Ref TQ541 522. 2m S of Sevenoaks on A225, just off A21. **Tel:** 01732 459777
E-mail: sarah@riverhillgardens.co.uk **Website:** www.riverhillgardens.co.uk
Open: 19 Mar-11 Sep. Weds-Sun & BH Mons, 10.30am-5pm.
Admission: Adult £7.75, Child £5.75.

ST JOHN'S JERUSALEM ⬚
Sutton-at-Hone, Dartford, Kent DA4 9HQ
13th Century chapel surrounded by a tranquil moated garden, once part of the former Commandery of the Knight's Hospitallers. **Location:** Map 4:J2. OS Ref TQ558703. 3 miles south of Dartford **Tel:** 01732 810378
E-mail: stjohnsjerusalem@nationaltrust.org.uk
Website: www.nationaltrust.org.uk/st-johns-jerusalem/
Open: See website for details. **Admission:** See website for details.

SISSINGHURST CASTLE ⬚
Sissinghurst, Cranbrook, Kent TN17 2AB
One of the world's most celebrated gardens and a sensory paradise of colour and beauty throughout the year.
Location: Map 4:L4. OS Ref TQ807 383. 1m E of Sissinghurst village.
Tel: 01580 710700 **E-mail:** sissinghurst@nationaltrust.org.uk
Website: www.nationaltrust.org.uk/sissinghurst
Open: Please see website for opening times and admission prices.

VISITOR INFORMATION

■ Owner
The 12th Duke and Duchess of Marlborough

■ Address
Blenheim Palace
Woodstock
OX20 1PP

■ Location
Map 7:A11
OS Ref. SO441 161
From London, M40, A44 (1.5 hrs), 8 miles North West of Oxford. London 63 miles Birmingham 54 miles.
Bus: No.S3 from Oxford Station, Gloucester Green & Cornmarket.
Coach: From London (Victoria) to Oxford.
Rail: Oxford Station.
Air: Heathrow 60 miles. Birmingham 50 miles.

■ Contact
Visitor Information
Tel: 0800 8496500
E-mail: operations@blenheimpalace.com

■ Opening Times
Open daily from 13 February - 18 December 2016.

Palace and Pleasure Gardens
Open daily from 10.30am - 17.30pm (last admission 16.45pm).
The Formal Gardens open at 10.00am.

Park
Open daily from 09.00am - 18.00pm (last admission 16.45pm).

■ Admission
Palace, Park & Gardens
Adult	£23.00
Concessions	£18.30
Child*	£12.50
Family	£60.00
*(5-16 yrs).

Park & Gardens
Adult	£13.80
Concessions	£10.40
Child*	£6.70
Family	£36.50
*(5-16 yrs).

Prices are subject to change.

Annual Pass Offer
Buy one day get 12 months free!

Discounts on group bookings (15+): contact group sales on 01993 815600 email groups@blenheimpalace.com.

BLENHEIM PALACE 🏠Ⓕ ◆ ✦
www.blenheimpalace.com

Spend an inspiring day exploring a National Treasure.

Receive a warm welcome into the home of the 12th Duke and Duchess of Marlborough and the birthplace of Sir Winston Churchill. Wonder at this masterpiece of 18th Century baroque architecture, which houses some of the finest antique collections in Europe. Take a tour of the State Rooms and admire the portraits, tapestries and exquisite furniture while learning about the 300-year history of this National Treasure.

Explore this World Heritage Site amongst over 2000 acres of 'Capability' Brown landscaped parkland. Take a stroll and admire some of the finest views in England. Discover the array of Formal Gardens, including the Rose Garden, Water Terraces and Secret Garden. A short miniature train ride away from the Palace is the Pleasure Gardens, which boast a Giant Hedge Maze, Butterfly House, Lavender Garden and 'Blenheim Bygones' exhibition.

Blenheim Palace hosts a wealth of events, exhibitions and tours throughout the year. From firm favourites to new experiences, there is something for everyone to enjoy.

Relax in one of the on-site cafés and restaurants, serving everything from informal coffee and cake to luxury afternoon teas, fine dining and more. Spend some time in the award-winning East Courtyard shop and find locally produced crafts and luxurious gifts with many ranges that are exclusive to Blenheim Palace.

Blenheim Palace is Britain's greatest Palace, and offers visitors a precious time, every time.

KEY FACTS

- ⓘ Filming and private events available.
- 🛍 Two shops.
- ⊤ Corporate Hospitality includes weddings, receptions, dinners, meetings and conferences and team building days.
- ♿ Toilet facilities & lift access to the Palace. Blue Badge Holder parking & carers go free.
- 🖥 Licensed.
- 🍴 Licensed.
- 🚶 Guided tours available from Mon-Sat.
- 🅿 Unlimited and free for cars and coaches.
- ▦ Sandford Award holder since 1982. Trails and tours for school groups available.
- 🐕 Dogs allowed in Park only and must be kept on leads. Assistant dogs welcome.
- 🔔 Call the Events Team on 01993 813874.
- ❄ The Palace and Gardens are open until 18 December. The Park is open all year round except for Christmas Day.
- ▨

VISITOR INFORMATION

■ **Owner**
Lord Saye & Sele

■ **Address**
Broughton Castle
Broughton
Nr Banbury
Oxfordshire
OX15 5EB

■ **Location**
Map 7:A10
OS Ref. SP418 382
Broughton Castle is 2½m
SW of Banbury Cross on
the B4035, Shipston-on-
Stour - Banbury Road.
Easily accessible from
Stratford-on-Avon,
Warwick, Oxford, Burford
and the Cotswolds.
M40/J11.
Rail: From London/
Birmingham to Banbury.

■ **Contact**
Manager, Mrs James
Tel: 01295 276070
E-mail:
info@broughtoncastle.com

■ **Opening Times**
Summer
Easter Sun & Mon,
1 May-15 September
Weds, Suns & BH Mons,
2-5pm. Also Thurs in July
and August, 2-5pm.
Last admission 4.30pm.
Open all year on any day,
at any time, for group
bookings - by appointment
only.

■ **Admission**
Adult	£9.00
Child (5-15yrs)	£5.00
OAP/Student	£8.00
Garden only	£5.00
Groups	
Adult	£9.00
OAP	£9.00
Child (5-10yrs)	£5.00
Child (11-15yrs)	£6.00
Garden only	£6.00

(There is a minimum
charge for groups - please
contact the manager for
details).

BROUGHTON CASTLE 🏛Ⓕ
www.broughtoncastle.com

"About the most beautiful castle in all England...for sheer loveliness of the combination of water, woods and picturesque buildings." Sir Charles Oman (1898).

Broughton Castle is essentially a family home lived in by Lord and Lady Saye & Sele and their family. The original medieval Manor House, of which much remains today, was built in about 1300 by Sir John de Broughton. It stands on an island site surrounded by a 3 acre moat. The Castle was greatly enlarged between 1550 and 1600, at which time it was embellished with magnificent plaster ceilings, splendid panelling and fine fireplaces. In the 17th Century William, 8th Lord Saye & Sele, played a leading role in national affairs. He opposed Charles I's efforts to rule without Parliament and Broughton became a secret meeting place for the King's opponents. During the Civil War William raised a regiment and he and his four sons all fought at the nearby Battle of Edgehill. After the battle the Castle was besieged and captured. Arms and armour from the Civil War and other periods are displayed in the Great Hall. Visitors may also see the gatehouse, gardens and park together with the nearby 14th Century Church of St Mary, in which there are many family tombs, memorials and hatchments.

Gardens

The garden area consists of mixed herbaceous and shrub borders containing many old roses. In addition, there is a formal walled garden with beds of roses surrounded by box hedging and lined by more mixed borders.

KEY FACTS

ℹ️ Photography allowed in house.

📷 Partial.

♿ Teas on Open Days. Groups may book morning coffee, light lunches and afternoon teas.

🚶 Available for booked groups.

🅿️ Limited.

🐕 Guide dogs only in house. On leads in grounds.

❄️ Open all year for groups.

VISITOR INFORMATION

■ **Owner**
The National Trust
(Administered on their
behalf by Lord Faringdon)

■ **Address**
Buscot Park
Faringdon
Oxfordshire
SN7 8BU

■ **Location**
Map 6:P12
OS Ref. SU239 973
Between Faringdon and
Lechlade on A417.
Bus: Stagecoach 65/66
Oxford to Swindon, alight
Faringdon; Stagecoach 64
Swindon to Carterton,
alight Lechlade.
Taxi: Faringdon or
Lechlade
Rail: Oxford or Swindon

■ **Contact**
The Estate Office
Tel: 01367 240786
Fax: 01367 241794
Info Line: 01367 240932
E-mail:
estbuscot@aol.com

■ **Opening Times**
**House, Grounds and
Tearoom:** 25 Mar-30 Sep,
Wed-Fri and BH's and
weekends as listed below,
2pm-6pm
(last entry to House 5pm,
Tearoom last orders
5.30pm).
Mar 26/27/28.
Apr 9/10, 23/24, 30.
May 1, 14/15, 28/29/30.
Jun 11/12, 25/26.
Jul 9/10, 23/24.
Aug 13/14, 27/28/29.
Sep 10/11, 24/25.
Grounds Only:
29 Mar-27 Sep, Mon-Tue,
2pm-6pm.

■ **Admission**
House & Grounds:
Adult	£10.00
Over 65s	£8.00
Child (5-15)	£5.00
Under 5 Free.	

Grounds only:
Adult	£7.00
Over 65s	£5.00
Child (5-15)	£3.50
National Trust members	Free

Groups: Advance booking
must be made with the
Estate Office.

BUSCOT PARK ❧
www.buscotpark.com

One of Oxfordshire's best kept secrets.

Buscot Park is the home of the Henderson Family and the present Lord and Lady Faringdon, with their eldest son James and his wife Lucinda. They look after the property on behalf of the National Trust as well as the family collection of pictures, furniture, ceramics and objects d'art, known as the Faringdon Collection, which is displayed in the House.

Built between 1780 and 1783 for a local landowner, Edward Lovedon Townsend, the estate was purchased in 1889 by Lord Faringdon's great-grandfather, Alexander Henderson, a financier of exceptional skill and ability, who in 1916 was created the 1st Lord Faringdon. He greatly enlarged the House, commissioned Harold Peto to design the famous Italianate water garden, and

laid the foundations of the Faringdon Collection. Among his many purchases were Rembrandt's portrait of Pieter Six, Rossetti's portrait of Pandora, and Burne-Jones's famous series, The Legend of the Briar Rose.

His grandson and heir, Gavin Henderson, added considerably to the Collection, acquiring important furniture designed by Robert Adam and Thomas Hope, and was instrumental in returning the House to its late 18th Century appearance.

The family, together with their fellow Trustees, continue to add to the Collection, to freshen its display, and to enliven the gardens and grounds for the continuing enjoyment of visitors.

KEY FACTS

- ℹ️ No photography in house.
- 🛍️ Small shop selling peppermint products, local cider and honey, along with guide books and a selection of postcards and other items showing images of the House, Grounds and the Art Collection.
- 🌿 A selection of plants and surplus kitchen garden produce available when in season.
- ♿ Partial. WCs, some ramps, motorised PMVs available – please contact Estate Office prior to visit for more information. Steps to House.
- ☕ Open the same days as the House, offering cream teas, a range of cakes and slices, cheese scones, and a selection of hot and cold drinks.
- 🅿️ Ample car parking, 2 coach spaces.
- 🐕 Guide dogs only.

The Peto Water Garden

'Pandora' by Dante Gabriel Rossetti

Register for news and special offers at **www.hudsonsheritage.com**

STONOR 🏛 Ⓕ

www.stonor.com

Stonor - a story of continuity. The same family have lived here for over 850 years and have always been Roman Catholics.

Stonor has been home to the Stonor family for over 850 years and is now home to The Lord and Lady Camoys. The history of the house inevitably contributes to the atmosphere; unpretentious yet grand. A facade of warm brick with Georgian windows conceals older buildings dating back to the 12th Century and a 14th Century Catholic Chapel sits on the south east corner. Stonor nestles in a fold of the beautiful wooded Chiltern Hills with breathtaking views of the park where Fallow deer have grazed since medieval times.

It contains many family portraits, old Master drawings and paintings, Renaissance bronzes and tapestries, along with rare furniture and a collection of modern ceramics.

St Edmund Campion sought refuge at Stonor during the Reformation and printed his famous pamphlet 'Ten Reasons', in secret, on a press installed in the roof space. A small exhibition celebrates his life and work.

Mass has been celebrated since medieval times in the Chapel. The stained glass windows were executed by Francis Eginton: installed in 1797. The Chapel decoration is that of the earliest Gothic Revival, begun in 1759, with additions in 1797. The Stations of the Cross were carved by Jozef Janas, a Polish prisoner of war in World War II and given to Stonor by Graham Greene in 1956.

The gardens offer outstanding views of the Park and valley and are especially beautiful in May and June, containing fine displays of daffodils, irises, peonies, lavenders and roses along with other herbaceous plants and shrubs.

VISITOR INFORMATION

▨ Owner
The Lord & Lady Camoys

▨ Address
Stonor Park
Henley-On-Thames
Oxfordshire
RG9 6HF

▨ Location
Map 3:E1
OS Ref. SU743 893
1 hr from London, M4/J8/9. A4130 to Henley-on-Thames. A4130/B480 to Stonor. On B480 NW of Henley. M40/J6. B4009 to Watlington. B480 to Stonor.
Bus: None
Taxi: Henley on Thames 5m
Rail: Henley on Thames 5m, or Reading 9m
Air: Heathrow

▨ Contact
Jonathan White
Tel: 01491 638587
E-mail:
administrator@stonor.com

▨ Opening Times
25 March - 25 September 2016.

House, Gardens & Chapel: For up to date open days and times please visit our website www.stonor.com or phone 01491 638587

Private Groups:
20+ by arrangement.

▨ Admission
For up to date admission prices to the House, Gardens and Chapel and for private group visits, please visit our website www.stonor.com or phone 01491 638587.

▨ Special Events
26-29 August 2016
Chilterns Craft & Design Show.

KEY FACTS

- ⓘ No photography in house.
- 🛍 Small gift shop with local crafts and honey from the estate.
- 🍷 Please contact the Administrator for further details.
- ♿ Partial.
- 🍽 Stonor Pantry serves a selection of hot and cold lunches and delicious homemade cakes and scones. Group visits - all refreshments must be prebooked.
- 🚶 By arrangement. Minimum 20, maximum 55.
- 🅿 100yds away.
- ▨ Please contact the Administrator for further details.
- 🐕 On leads in park at all times. Assistance dogs only in House & Gardens.
- 💍
- 🎥

KINGSTON BAGPUIZE HOUSE 🏠Ⓕ
KINGSTON BAGPUIZE, ABINGDON, OXFORDSHIRE OX13 5AX
www.kbhevents.uk

This lovely family home circa 1660 was remodelled in the early 1700's for the Blandy family. With English and French furniture in the elegant panelled rooms the entrance hall is dominated by a handsome cantilevered staircase. The house is surrounded by mature parkland and gardens notable for an interesting collection of cultivated plants which give year round interest including snowdrops & Magnolia in spring, flowering trees & shrubs in summer and autumn colour from September. A raised terrace leads to the 18th Century panelled pavilion which looks over the gardens and towards the house. Available for filming. The house featured in Series 5 of Downton Abbey. Venue for weddings and small conferences.

Location: Map 7:A12. OS Ref SU408 981. In Kingston Bagpuize village, off A415 Abingdon to Witney road S of A415/A420 intersection. Abingdon 5m, Oxford 9m.

Owner: Mrs Francis Grant **Contact:** Virginia Grant

Tel: 01865 820259 **E-mail:** info@kbhevents.uk
Open: Gardens Only (Snowdrops): 7, 14, 21 & 28 Feb. House & Gardens: 6, 7, 20 & 21 Mar. 3, 4, 17 & 18 Apr. 8, 9, 29 & 30 May.12, 13, 26 & 27 Jun. 10-12 & 24-26 Jul. 7-9 & 21-23 Aug. 11, 12, 18 & 19 Sep. All days 2-5pm. (Last entry to house 4pm). Free flow visits to ground floor of house.
Admission: House & Garden: Adult £7.50, Child (4-16) £4.50, Family (2+3) £20.00. Gardens: Adult £5.00, Child (4-16) £3.00. Season tickets available. Group rates 20+ by appointment weekdays throughout the year. NB: Please visit website to confirm before travelling as dates & times may be subject to change.
Key facts: ⓘ No photography in house on open days. 🛍 Cards & pottery in tea room. 🌿 Rare Plant Fair 29 May 2016 www.rareplantfair.co.uk 🗓 See website. ♿ WCs. 🍴 Homemade teas. 🎦 Free flow visits to ground floor only on advertised open days. Guided tours for pre-booked groups only. 🅿 🐕 Guide dogs only. 🎩 See website. ❄ ⚭

MAPLEDURHAM HOUSE AND WATERMILL
MAPLEDURHAM, READING RG4 7TR
www.mapledurham.co.uk

Late 16th Century Elizabethan home of the Blount family. Original plaster ceilings, great oak staircase, fine collection of paintings and a private chapel in Strawberry Hill Gothick added in 1797. 15th Century watermill fully restored producing flour, semolina and bran. Hydro powered turbine producing green electricity added in 2011. Visitors may visit the Old Manor tearoom where sandwiches, cream teas and cakes are served. A passenger boat service from nearby Caversham runs on open days.

Location: Map 3:E2. OS Ref SU670 767. N of River Thames. 4m NW of Reading, 1½ m W of A4074.

Owner: The Mapledurham Trust **Contact:** Mrs Lola Andrews

Tel: 0118 9723350 **E-mail:** enquiries@mapledurham.co.uk
Open: Easter-Sep: Sats, Suns & BHs, 2-5.30pm. Last admission 5pm. Midweek parties by arrangement only. Also Sun afternoons in Oct.
Admission: Please call 0118 9723350 for details. Mapledurham Trust reserves the right to alter or amend opening times or prices without prior notification.
Key facts: 🛍 Gift shop located in the watermill. 🗓 Ideal venue for fairs, shows and wedding receptions. ♿ Partial. 🍴 Tearoom serving sandwiches, cream teas and cakes. 🎦 Guided tours for midweek party visits. 🅿 🚌 School visits welcome at the watermill. 🐕 Dogs welcome on leads in the grounds only. Guide dogs only in the house, watermill or tearooms. ⚭

ROUSHAM HOUSE
NR STEEPLE ASTON, BICESTER, OXFORDSHIRE OX25 4QX
www.rousham.org

Rousham represents the first stage of English landscape design and remains almost as William Kent (1685-1748) left it. One of the few gardens of this date to have escaped alteration. Includes Venus' Vale, Townesend's Building, seven-arched Praeneste, the Temple of the Mill and a sham ruin known as the 'Eyecatcher'. The house was built in 1635 by Sir Robert Dormer. Dont miss the walled garden with their herbaceous borders, small parterre, pigeon house and espalier apple trees. A fine herd of Longhorn cattle are to be seen in the park.
Excellent location for fashion, advertising, photography etc.
Location: Map 7:A10. OS Ref SP477 242. E of A4260, 12m N of Oxford, S of B4030, 7m W of Bicester.
Owner/Contact: Charles Cottrell-Dormer Esq

Tel: 01869 347110 / 07860 360407 **E-mail:** ccd@rousham.org
Open: Garden: All year: daily, 10am-4.30pm (last adm). House: Pre-booked groups, May-Sep (Mon-Thu).
Admission: Garden: £5.00. No children under 15yrs.
Key facts: ⓘ Rousham is an ideal Oxfordshire venue for wedding receptions, offering a site to pitch a marquee together with acres of landscape and formal gardens that can be used for photographs and pre-reception drinks. We have also held some car rallies, The Bentley, MG and Aston Martin owners clubs have all held rallies at Rousham. These events are held in the park, immediately next to the house. Open access to the house and garden can be arranged. ⓢ Partial. ⓟ ⓧ ⓧ ⓥ

MILTON MANOR HOUSE
Milton, Abingdon, Oxfordshire OX14 4EN

Dreamily beautiful mellow brick house, traditionally designed by Inigo Jones. Celebrated Gothick library and Catholic chapel. Lived in by family; pleasant relaxed and informal atmosphere. Park with fine old trees, stables, walled garden and woodland walk. Picknickers welcome. Free parking, refreshments and pony rides usually available.
Location: Map 3:D1. OS Ref SU485 924. Just off A34, village and house signposted, 9m S of Oxford, 15m N of Newbury. 3m from Abingdon & Didcot.
Owner: Anthony Mockler-Barrett Esq **Contact:** By email for weddings, special events etc. florentinagifts@hotmail.co.uk or 020 899 32580. Please write to The Administrator for group visits giving contact details & proposed dates & numbers.
Tel: 01235 831287 **Fax:** 01235 862321
Open: Easter Sun & BH Mon, 27/28 Mar; Sun 1 May & BH Mon; Sun 15 May - 31 May; Sun 14 Aug - Wed 31 Aug.
Admission: House and Gardens: Adult £8.00; Child (under 14) £2.00. Gardens and grounds only: Adult £4.00, Child (under 14) £1.00.
Key facts: ⓢ Grounds. ⓕ Obligatory. ⓟ Free. ⓧ Guide dogs only. ⓧ ⓥ

SULGRAVE MANOR
Manor Road, Sulgrave, Nr Banbury, Oxfordshire OX17 2SD
www.sulgravemanor.org.uk

Ancestral Home of George Washington, The manor house was built by Lawrence Washington in the middle of the 16th Century and has a later 18th Century wing. With three acres of beautiful gardens, designed by the renowned architect Sir Reginald Blomfield, the Manor is open to the public between April and October but will take bookings for small private parties and larger groups all year round.
Location: Map 7:B10. OS Ref SP560 455.
Contact: Cymon Snow **Tel:** 01295 760205
E-mail: enquiries@sulgravemanor.org.uk
Open: Please see website for details.
Admission: Adults £7.90, Concs £7.40, Children (4-15yrs) £3.60, Family (2 Adults and up to 3 children) £21.00. Garden only £3.60, Infants (under 4yrs) Free. Prices are valid until 31 Mar 2016.
Key facts: ⓘ Picnic site, Coach parties/groups welcomed, Credit cards accepted. ⓟ ⓣ ⓢ Partial. ⓦ Light Refreshments. ⓣ Entertaining and informative tours. ⓟ Free. ⓧ ⓧ In grounds only. ⓐ ⓧ Small private parties and larger groups by appointment. ⓥ

VISITOR INFORMATION

■ Owner
Historic Royal Palaces

■ Address
Hampton Court Palace
Surrey
KT8 9AU

■ Location
Map 19:B9
OS Ref. TQ155 686
From M25/J15 or M25/J12
or M25/J10.
Rail: 30 minutes from
Waterloo, zone 6
travelcard
Boat: From Richmond,
Kingston or Runnymede

■ Contact
Historic Royal Palaces
Tel: 0844 482 7777
**Venue Hire and
Corporate Hospitailty:**
hrp.org.uk/hireavenue,
020 3166 6507.
E-mail:
hamptoncourt@hrp.org.uk

■ Opening Times
Mar-Oct:
Daily, 10am-6pm.
(last admission 5pm).

Nov-Feb:
Daily, 10am-4.30pm.
(last admission 3.30pm).

Closed 24-26 Dec.
Please always check
website before visiting for
full details.

■ Admission
Visit www.hrp.org.uk for
admission prices, or call
0844 482 7777.

■ Special Events
Special events year round,
visit website for details.

Conference/Function
Conferences: Up to 250.
Receptions: Up to 400.
Lunches: Up to 220.
Dinners: Up to 270.
Marquees: Up to 3000.

HAMPTON COURT PALACE
www.hrp.org.uk/hamptoncourtpalace

Discover the magnificence of this former royal residence, once home to the flamboyant King Henry VIII.

Marvel at the two distinct and contrasting Tudor and Baroque architectural styles and soak up the atmosphere in 60 acres of stunning gardens. Extended and developed in grand style in the 1520s by Henry VIII, the present day elegance and romance of the palace owes much to the Christopher Wren designed baroque buildings commissioned by William and Mary at the end of the 17th Century.

At the palace you are able to step back in time and relive some of the extraordinary moments in the life of Henry VIII and the Glorious Georgians. Try on a courtier gown and explore the majestic environment where kings have entertained, celebrated and mourned. Marvel at the grandeur of the magnificent Great Hall and Great Watching Chamber, see the stunning vaulted ceiling of the Chapel Royal and explore the enormous kitchens, the most extensive surviving 16th Century kitchens in Europe today.

The palace is surrounded by formal gardens and sits in 60 acres of parkland gardens, including the 18th Century Privy Garden and world famous maze.

KEY FACTS

ℹ️ Information Centre.

📷 Weddings, dinners, receptions.

♿ WCs.

☕ Licensed.

🎧

🅿️ Ample for cars, coach parking nearby.

🏫 Rates on request 0844 482 7777.

🐕 Guide dogs only.

🔔

❄️ Closed 24-26 Dec.

POLESDEN LACEY 🌰

www.nationaltrust.org.uk/polesdenlacey

Polesden Lacey is an Edwardian party house set in an area of Outstanding Natural Beauty overlooking the Surrey Hills. Explore the house or stroll through the grounds enjoying the view and leave feeling revitalised.

'This is a delicious house...' remarked Queen Elizabeth, the Queen Mother on her honeymoon at Polesden Lacey. This country retreat, with glorious views across the rolling Surrey Hills, was home to famous Edwardian hostess Mrs Greville, who entertained royalty and the celebrities of her time. The house has stunning interiors and contains a fabulous collection of art and ceramics. The gardens offer something for every season, including climbing roses, herbaceous borders and a winter garden. There are four waymarked countryside walks around the estate.

Margaret Greville bought Polesden Lacey in 1906, and left it to the National Trust in 1942. She inherited a fortune from her father, William McEwan, and she mixed with royalty and politicians. She was loved by many, but not all, mainly because she liked to gossip and wasn't afraid to speak her mind.

Mrs Greville was renowned for being a wonderful hostess as well as generous to those less fortunate than her.

'Tea is at 5 o'clock, and at Polesden 5 o'clock means 5 o'clock and not 5 minutes past. Which in its turn means the Spanish ambassador, who has gone for a walk down the yew avenue, hastily retraces his steps, and the Chancellor of the Exchequer, whoever he may be, hurries down the great staircase, followed by several members of the House of Lords, and that the various ladies belonging to these gentlemen rise from their chaise-longues on which they have been resting in their bedrooms.' Down the Kitchen Sink by Beverley Nichols.

KEY FACTS

The gift shop stocks homeware, luxury gifts, books and delicious nibbles and drinks.

Accessible WC, catering & retail. Courtesy shuttle. Grounds mostly accessible. Free wheelchairs & powered mobility vehicles. Hearing loops available.

Hot and cold food, home-made cakes and drinks.

House tours weekday mornings Mar-Nov, weekends in winter. Free garden tours.

Gardens only.

In the grounds (excluding formal gardens). Assistance dogs welcome.

Grounds only.

Discover Mrs Greville's rags to riches story

Enjoy the splendour of the Edwardian formal garden

VISITOR INFORMATION

■ Owner
National Trust

■ Address
Great Bookham
Nr Dorking
Surrey
RH5 6BD

■ Location
Map 19:B10
OS Ref. TQ136 522
5m NW of Dorking, 2m S of Great Bookham, off A246.

■ Contact
Tel: 01372 452048
E-mail:
polesdenlacey@ nationaltrust.org.uk

■ Opening Times
Gardens, table service cafe, coffee shop and gift shop: daily from 10am-5pm (4pm in winter). Closed 24 and 25 Dec.

House: Jan-20 Mar, access by guided tour only. 25 Mar-30 Oct, daily 11am-5pm (weekday mornings entry by guided tour only). Nov and Dec access to house via guided tour 11-12:30pm then free flow. Special Christmas event at additional charge for all visitors (inc NT members).

■ Admission
Group admission prices:
House and grounds:
Adults: £12.20
Child: £6.10
Grounds only:
Adult: £7.60
Child: £3.80

A group constitutes 12+ people.

■ Special Events
Throughout Easter, the house is decorated with stunning displays of seasonal flowers.

Polesden Lacey will host a season of outdoor theatre in the summer 2016, in particular a Shakespeare production led by the Polesden Lacey Shakespeare Company.

At Christmas, the house and grounds are dressed to impress in keeping with Edwardian traditions and evoking the warming spirit of Christmas. An 18ft Christmas tree welcomes guests into the hall of the house, Christmas music floats through the air and our room guides can answer any questions dressed in full period costume.

HATCHLANDS PARK ✣
East Clandon, Guildford, Surrey GU4 7RT
www.nationaltrust.org.uk/hatchlands-park

Hatchlands Park was built in 1756 for Admiral Boscawen. The house is set in a beautiful 430-acre Repton park, with a variety of way-marked walks and there is a stunning bluebell wood in the spring. The house contains the Cobbe Collection of Old Master paintings and also the Cobbe Collection of keyboard instruments, the world's largest group of early keyboard instruments owned or played by famous composers such as Purcell, J C Bach, Mozart and Elgar.

Location: Map 19:A10. OS Ref TQ065 518. Off the A246. Follow brown signs.
Owner: National Trust
Tel: 01483 222482 **E-mail:** hatchlands@nationaltrust.org.uk
Open: Parkland, café and shop open daily (except Christmas Eve and Christmas Day). 10.30-5.30pm or dusk if earlier.
House: 1 Apr-30 Oct Tue-Thu, Sun & BH Mon, plus Fris in Aug, 2-5.30pm.
Admission: House £10.00, Park walks £6.00, Groups £7.00. (includes voluntary donation - visitors can pay standard prices shown at property and on website).
Key facts: ⓘ No photography inside the house. 🅿 Please call for details. Open as shop. 🗓 Thurs. 🅿 Free parking. 🐕 Under close control in designated areas of parkland. ✣

LOSELEY PARK 🏠Ⓕ
Guildford, Surrey GU3 1HS
www.loseleypark.co.uk

Loseley Park, built in 1562 by Sir William More, is a fine example of Elizabethan architecture. The rooms contain fascinating works of art, furniture from the 17th Century and many unique features. The Walled Garden is compared favourably to gardens of national renown.

Location: Map 3:G3. OS Ref SU976 471. 30m SW of London, leave A3 S of Guildford on to B3000. Signposted.
Owner: Mr Michael More-Molyneux **Contact:** Sue Grant
Tel: 01483 304440 / 01483 405119/120.
Wisteria Tea Room bookings: 01483-457103
E-mail: enquiries@loseleypark.co.uk
Open: House: May-Aug Mon-Thur 12pm-4pm. Sun: 1pm-5pm & BHs.
Gardens & Grounds: May-Sep: Sun-Thu: 11am-5pm.
Admission: House & Gardens Adult £9.00. Child (5-16yrs) £4.50. Conc. £8.00. Child (under 5yrs) Free. Family (2 + 3) £23.50. Gardens & Grounds only: Adult £5.00. Child (5-16yrs) £2.50. Conc. £4.50. Please contact for Group bookings.
Key facts: ⓘ Lunches and teas. Fully licensed.
Obligatory: 40 mins. Prebooked Garden tours available.
🅿 150 cars, 6 coaches.
For weddings, private and corporate functions.

PAINSHILL LANDSCAPE GARDEN 🏠Ⓕ
Portsmouth Road, Cobham, Surrey KT11 1JE
www.painshill.co.uk

Painshill is a beautiful 18th Century landscape garden. The 158 acre wonderland has something for everyone. Discover magical follies, including the restored crystal Grotto (limited opening times), historic plantings, the John Bartram Heritage Collection of North American trees and shrubs (Plant Heritage) and spectacular vistas. Visitor entrance is off Between Streets, Cobham.

Location: Map 19:B9. OS Ref TQ 10228 6. M25/J10/A3 to London. W of Cobham on A245. Signposted. Closest Sat Nav ref KT11 1AA.
Owner: Painshill Park Trust **Contact:** Visitor Operations Team
Tel: 01932 868113 **Fax:** 01932 868001 **E-mail:** info@painshill.co.uk
Open: All Year (Closed 25-26 Dec). Mar-Oct 10.30am-6pm or dusk (last entry 4.30pm). Nov-Feb 10.30am to 4pm or dusk (last entry 3pm).
Admission: Adult £8.00 Concessions £7.00, Child (5-16 yrs) £4.50, Family (2 Adults & 4 Children) £27.00, U5's & Disabled Carer: Free. Group rates available.
Key facts: ⓘ Books, gifts, Painshill Sparkling Wine & Painshill Honey. 🚻 WCs. Accessible route. Free pre-booked wheelchair loan. Pre-booked guided buggy tours. Licensed. Picnic area. Pre-book 10+ groups. 🅿 Free. Coaches must book. Pre-book via Education Dept. On short fixed leads. Closed 25-26 Dec

---

GREAT FOSTERS
Stroude Road, Egham, Surrey TW20 9UR

Set in 50 acres of stunning gardens and parkland Great Fosters is a fine example of Elizabethan architecture and is now a luxury hotel with two restaurants, The Estate Grill and The Tudor Room. Open to non-residents for lunch, dinner and afternoon tea, its past is evident in the mullioned windows, chimneys and brick finials, whilst the gardens include a Saxon moat, Japanese bridge, amphitheatre, lake and knot garden designed by WH Romaine-Walker and Gilbert Jenkins.

Location: Map 3:G2. OS Ref TQ015 694. M25 J/13, follow signs to Egham and then brown historic signs for Great Fosters.
Owner: The Sutcliffe family **Contact:** Amanda Dougans **Tel:** 01784 433822
E-mail: reception@greatfosters.co.uk **Website:** www.greatfosters.co.uk
Open: All year. **Admission:** No charge.
Key facts: ⓘ 🚻 WC. Licensed. 🅿 Guide dogs only.

CLAREMONT LANDSCAPE GARDEN ✣
Portsmouth Road, Esher, Surrey KT10 9JG

One of the earliest surviving English landscape gardens, restored to its former glory. Features include a lake, island with pavilion, grotto, turf amphitheatre, viewpoints and avenues. **Location:** Map 19:B9. OS Ref TQ128 632.
Tel: 01372 467806 **E-mail:** claremont@nationaltrust.org.uk **Website:** www.nationaltrust.org.uk/claremont **Open:** Please see website or telephone for details. **Admission:** See website or telephone for details.

VISITOR INFORMATION

■ Owner
Arundel Castle Trustees Ltd

■ Address
Arundel Castle
Arundel
West Sussex
BN18 9AB

■ Location
Map 3:G6
OS Ref. TQ018 072
Central Arundel, N of A27.
Brighton 40 mins,
Worthing 15 mins,
Chichester 15 mins. From
London A3 or A24, 1½ hrs.
M25 motorway, 30m.
Bus: Bus stop 100 yds.
Rail: Station 1½m.
Air: Gatwick 25m.

■ Contact
Bryan McDonald,
Castle Manager
Tel: 01903 882173
E-mail: bryan.mcdonald@
arundelcastle.org

■ Opening Times
25 Mar to 30 Oct 2016:
Tuesdays to Sundays,
BH Mondays, and
Mondays in August.

**Fitzalan Chapel,
Gardens & Grounds, Gift
Shop:**
10am-5pm
**Castle Keep, Restaurant
& Coffee Shop:**
10am-4.30pm.
Main Castle Rooms:
12 noon-5pm.
Last entry 4pm.

■ Admission
Please contact us or see
website for up-to-date
admissions rates.
Group rates available.

ARUNDEL CASTLE & GARDENS 🏛
www.arundelcastle.org

Ancient Castle, Stately Home, Gardens & The Collector Earl's Garden.

A thousand years of history is waiting to be discovered at Arundel Castle in West Sussex. Dating from the 11th Century, the Castle is both ancient fortification and stately home of the Dukes of Norfolk and Earls of Arundel.

Set high on a hill, this magnificent Castle commands stunning views across the River Arun and out to sea. Climb the Keep, explore the battlements, wander in the grounds and recently restored Victorian gardens and relax in the garden of the 14th Century Fitzalan Chapel.

In the 17th Century during the English Civil War the Castle suffered extensive damage. The process of structural restoration began in earnest in the 18th Century and continued up until 1900. The Castle was one of the first private residences to have electricity and central heating and had its own fire engine.

Inside the Castle over 20 sumptuously furnished rooms may be visited including the breathtaking Barons' Hall with 16th Century furniture; the Armoury with its fine collection of armour and weaponry, and the magnificent Gothic library entirely fitted out in carved Honduras mahogany. There are works of art by Van Dyck, Gainsborough, Canaletto and Mytens; tapestries; clocks; and personal possessions of Mary Queen of Scots including the gold rosary that she carried to her execution.

There are special event days throughout the season, including, Shakespeare in The Collector Earl's Garden, Arundel International Jousting & Medieval Tournament, and medieval re-enactments.

Do not miss the magnificent Collector Earl's Garden based on early 17th Century classical designs.

KEY FACTS

- ℹ️ No photography or video recording inside the Castle.
- 🛍 Distinctive and exclusive gifts.
- ♿ WCs.
- 🍷 Licensed.
- 🍴 Licensed.
- 👤 By prior arrangement. Tour time 1½-2 hrs. Tours available in various languages - please enquire.
- 🅿 Ample car and coach parking in town car park. Free admission and refreshment voucher for coach driver.
- 🏰 Norman Motte & Keep, Armoury & Victorian bedrooms. Special rates for schoolchildren (aged 5-16) and teachers.
- 🐕 Registered Assistance dogs only.
- 🎫 On special event days admission prices may vary.

VISITOR INFORMATION

■ Owner
The Goodwood Estate Co.Ltd. (Earl of March and Kinrara).

■ Address
Goodwood House
Goodwood
Chichester
West Sussex
PO18 0PX

■ Location
Map 3:F6
OS Ref. SU888 088
3½m NE of Chichester. A3 from London then A286 or A285. M27/A27 from Portsmouth or Brighton.
Rail: Chichester 3½m Arundel 9m.
Air: Heathrow 1½ hrs Gatwick ¾hr.

■ Contact
Assistant to the Curator
Tel: 01243 755012
Fax: 01243 755005
Recorded Info:
01243 755040.
Weddings:
01243 775537.
E-mail: curator@goodwood.com or curators.assistant@goodwood.com

■ Opening Times
House
13 Mar-24 Oct: Most Suns and Mons, 1-5pm (last entry 4pm).
1-31 Aug: Sun-Thu, 1-5pm.
Please note these dates are provisional. Please always check the website or call Recorded Info 01243 755040 before visiting. Special tours for booked groups of 20+ only.
Closures
Closed for some special events and around Members Meeting, the Festival of Speed and Revival Meeting.

■ Admission
House
Adult	£9.50
Young Person (12-18yrs)	£4.00
Child (under 12yrs)	Free
Family	£22.00

Booked Groups (20-60)
Open Day (am - by request only)	£12.00
Open Day (pm)	£9.00

Please note these rates are provisional.

■ Special Events
74th Members' Meeting
Festival of Speed
Glorious Goodwood
Goodwood Revival Meeting
Please visit our website.

Conference/Function
ROOM	Size	Max Cap
Ballroom	79' x 23'	180

GOODWOOD HOUSE 🏠Ⓕ
www.goodwood.com

Goodwood House, ancestral home of the Dukes of Richmond and Gordon with magnificent art collection.

Goodwood is one of England's finest sporting estates. At its heart lies Goodwood House, the ancestral home of the Dukes of Richmond and Gordon, direct descendants of King Charles II. Today, it is lived in by the present Duke's son and heir, the Earl of March and Kinrara, with his wife and family. Their home is open to the public on at least 60 days a year.

The art collection includes a magnificent group of British paintings from the 17th and 18th Centuries, such as the celebrated views of London by Canaletto and superb sporting scenes by George Stubbs. The rooms are filled with fine English and French furniture, Gobelins tapestries and Sèvres Porcelain. Special works of art are regularly rotated and displayed and the books can be viewed by written application to the Curator (there is a special charge for these viewings). Each Summer there is an exhibition focusing on items in the collection and the family history.

Goodwood is also renowned for its entertaining, enjoying a reputation for excellence. Goodwood's own organic farm provides food for the table in the various restaurants on the estate. With internationally renowned horseracing and motor sport events, the finest downland golf course in the UK, its own aerodrome and hotel, Goodwood offers an extraordinarily rich sporting experience.

KEY FACTS

ℹ️ Conference and wedding facilities. No photography. Very well informed guides. Shell House optional extra on Connoisseurs' Days.

♿ WCs.

🚶 Obligatory.

🅿️ Ample.

🐕 Guide dogs only.

🏨 Goodwood Hotel.

💒 Civil Wedding Licence. Call Wedding Line or email estatesalesofficenquiries@goodwood.com.

GREAT DIXTER HOUSE & GARDENS 🏠Ⓕ
www.greatdixter.co.uk

A very special garden with a great deal of character, planted with flair, always something to see, whatever the season.

Great Dixter, built c1450, is the birthplace of the late Christopher Lloyd, gardening author. Its Great Hall is the largest medieval timberframed hall in the country, restored and enlarged for Christopher's father (1910-12). The house was largely designed by the architect, Sir Edwin Lutyens, who added a 16th Century house (moved from elsewhere) knitting the buildings together as a family home. The house retains much of the collections of furniture and other items put together by the Lloyds early in the 20th Century, with some notable modern additions by Christopher. The gardens feature a variety of topiary, ponds, wild meadow areas and the famous Long Border and Exotic Garden. Featured regularly in 'Country Life' from 1963, Christopher was asked to contribute a series of weekly articles as a practical

gardener - he never missed an issue in 42 years. There is a specialist nursery which offers an array of unusual plants of the highest quality, many of which can be seen in the fabric of the gardens. Light refreshments are available in the gift shop as well as tools, books and gifts. The whole estate is 57 acres which includes ancient woodlands, meadows and ponds which have been consistently managed on a traditional basis. Coppicing the woodlands, for example, has provided pea sticks for plant supports and timber for fencing and repairs to the buildings. There is a Friends programme available throughout the year. Friends enjoy invitations to events and educational courses as well as regular newsletters.

VISITOR INFORMATION

■ **Owner**
The Great Dixter Charitable Trust

■ **Address**
Northiam
Rye
East Sussex
TN31 6PH

■ **Location**
Map 4:L5
OS Ref. TQ817 251
Signposted off the A28 in Northiam.

■ **Contact**
Perry Rodriguez
Tel: 01797 252878
E-mail: office@ greatdixter.co.uk

■ **Opening Times**
25 March-30 October:
Tue-Sun, House 2-5pm.
Garden 11am-5pm.

Specialist Nursery Opening times:
April-October
Mon-Fri, 9am-5pm.
Sat 9am-5pm.
Sun 10am-5pm.

November-End of March
Mon-Fri, 9am-12.30pm,
1.30-4.30pm.
Sat 9am-12.30pm.
Sun Closed.

■ **Admission**
House & Garden:
Adult   £10.50
Child   £4.00

Garden only:
Adult   £8.50
Child   £3.00
A Gift Aid on admission scheme is in place.

■ **Special Events**
Study days on a wide range of subjects available. Please check the website for details.

KEY FACTS

ℹ️ No photography in House.

📷

🍴

🚶 Obligatory.

🅿️ Limited for coaches.

♿

🐕 Guide dogs only.

🛡️

VISITOR INFORMATION

■ Owner
Lancing College Chapel Trust

■ Address
Lancing
West Sussex
BN15 0RW

■ Location
Map 3:H6
OS Ref. TQ 196 067
North of the A27 between Shoreham-by-Sea and Lancing at the Coombes Road/Shoreham Airport traffic lights. Filter right if coming from the east. Turn off Coombes Road at sign for Lancing College and proceed to the top of Lancing College drive. It is usually possible to park outside the Chapel.
Rail: Train to Shoreham-by-Sea or Lancing on the London-Littlehampton and Portsmouth line and take a taxi.
Bus: The nearest bus routes are Brighton and Hove Buses 2A, Compass Buses, 106 and Coastliner 700.

■ Contact
The Verger
Tel: 01273 465949
Fax: 01273 464720
Enquiries may also be made at Reception, Lancing College on 01273 452213.
E-mail:
verger@lancing.org.uk

■ Opening Times
10am-4pm Mon-Sat.
12 noon-4pm on Sun.
Every day of the year except for Christmas Day, Boxing Day and New Year's Day.

■ Admission
Admission Free.
Donations are requested for the Friends of Lancing Chapel.
Visitors are asked to sign in for security purposes as they enter the Chapel.
The other College buildings are not open to the public.

■ Special Events
Visitors can reserve seats for Public Carol Services by applying in writing to Lancing College Chapel, Lancing, West Sussex, BN15 0RW with a stamped, self-addressed envelope.
Visitors wishing to attend other services should contact the Verger.

The glorious gothic architecture of Lancing College Chapel

LANCING COLLEGE CHAPEL
www.lancingcollege.co.uk

'I know of no more spectacular post-Reformation ecclesiastical building in the kingdom.' Evelyn Waugh, former pupil.

Lancing College Chapel is the place of worship for the community of Lancing College, the Central Minster of the Woodard Schools and a well-loved Sussex landmark. The Chapel stands prominently on the South Downs. The exterior, with its pinnacles and flying buttresses, is a testament to Victorian structural bravado. Designed by Herbert Carpenter in the 13th Century French gothic style, it is the fourth tallest ecclesiastical building in England.

The foundations were laid in 1868 and the atmospheric crypt came into use in 1875. The upper chapel was dedicated in 1911 but the west wall and rose window were added in the 1970s. There is now a plan to complete the building with a west porch. A beautiful war memorial cloister was built in the 1920s.

The interior is breathtaking. Soaring columns branch out into fan vaulting, perfectly proportioned arches and vast clerestory windows. There are stained glass windows by Comper and Dykes Bower and one commemorating former pupil Fr Trevor Huddleston made by Mel Howse in 2007. Behind the high altar are superb tapestries woven on the William Morris looms in the 1920s. The oak stall canopies are by Gilbert Scott. There are two organs (Walker 1914 and Frobenius 1986) with intricately carved oak cases.

The Chapel has a fascinating history which is still unfolding and it is a treasure house of ecclesiastical art. Lancing Chapel welcomes visitors both as an important heritage landmark and as a place of quiet reflection and prayer.

KEY FACTS

- 🛈 Guide books, information leaflets and a DVD.
- Stall with guide books and postcards at entrance to the Chapel.
- The upper chapel (but not the crypt) is easily accessible for the disabled.
- Guided tours and brief talks about the Chapel can be booked with the Verger. Groups should be booked in advance.
- 🅿 It is usually possible to park very near the entrance to the Chapel.
- School and other educational groups are welcome and may request guided tours and other information.
- Guide dogs only in Chapel. Dogs on leads welcome in College grounds.
- ❄ Open all year except Christmas Day, Boxing Day and New Year's Day.

Interior of Lancing College Chapel looking East

The splendid rose window and Walker organ

© National Trust Images / John Miller

© Geoffrey Frosh

BATEMAN'S

BURWASH, ETCHINGHAM, EAST SUSSEX TN19 7DS

www.nationaltrust.org.uk/batemans

"A good and peaceable place" was how Rudyard Kipling described Bateman's, a beautiful Sussex sandstone manor house and garden where the Kiplings lived from 1902-1936. Originally built in 1634 this mellow house, with its little watermill, was a sanctuary to the most famous writer in the English speaking world. Set in the glorious landscape of the Sussex Weald, the house and gardens are kept much as they were in Kipling's time and visitors can discover a fascinating collection of mementos of Kipling's time in India.

Location: Map 4:K5. OS Ref TQ671 238.
0.5 m S of Burwash off A265.

Owner: National Trust

Contact: The Administrator **Tel:** 01435 882302

E-mail: batemans@nationaltrust.org.uk

Open: House/Shop/Tearoom/Garden: Open all year (closed Christmas Eve and Christmas Day) Please call 01435 882302 or visit our website for details of seasonal opening times.

Admission: For 2016 prices please call 01435 882302 or visit our website. Group discount available (15+ pre-booked).

Key facts: Garden available for wedding receptions and functions. The shop has a large selection of new and second-hand Kipling books. Partial. WC. Ground floor access only. Virtual tour of upstairs. Licensed. Our tearoom offers a selection of snacks, hot and cold meals as well as delicious cakes. Limited for coaches. Closed Christmas Eve and Christmas Day.

FIRLE PLACE

FIRLE, LEWES, EAST SUSSEX BN8 6LP

www.firle.com

Firle Place has been the home of the Gage family for over 500 years. Set at the foot of the Sussex Downs within its own parkland, this unique house of Tudor origin was built of Caen stone by Sir John Gage, friend of Henry VIII. Remodelled in the 18th Century, the house contains a magnificent collection of Old Master paintings, fine English and European furniture and an impressive collection of Sèvres porcelain. Events and wedding receptions can be held in the parkland throughout the year or in the Georgian Riding School from April to October. The Great Hall can, on occasion, be used for private dinners, with drinks on the Terrace or in the Billiard Room. Please contact the Estate Office for all event and wedding reception enquiries.

Location: Map 4:J6. OS Ref TQ473 071.
4m SE of Lewes on A27 Brighton/Eastbourne Road.

Owner: The Rt Hon Viscount Gage

Tel: 01273 858567

Events: 01273 858567

E-mail: enquiries@firle.com

Open: Jun-Sep, Sun-Thu, 2.00-4.30pm. Last admission 4.15pm. (Dates and times subject to change. Please check before your visit). Tearoom open on House opening days only, from 12.00-4.30pm. Garden Show 22-24 Apr 2016. Vintage Fair: 13-14 Aug 2016.

Admission: Adult £9.00, Child £4.50, Conc. £8.00

Private Tours: Private group tours can be arranged by prior appointment. Please telephone 01273 858307 for details or visit the website.

Key facts: No photography in house. Available for private hire. Ground floor & tearoom. Licensed. In grounds on leads.

NYMANS ✤
HANDCROSS, HAYWARDS HEATH, WEST SUSSEX RH17 6EB
www.nationaltrust.org.uk/nymans

One of the National Trust's premier gardens, Nymans was a country retreat for the creative Messel family, and has views stretching out across the Sussex Weald. From vibrantly colourful summer borders to the tranquillity of ancient woodland, Nymans is a place of experimentation with constantly evolving planting designs and a rare and unusual plant collection. The comfortable yet elegant house, a partial ruin, reflects the personalities and stories of the talented Messel family, from the Countess of Rosse to Oliver Messel and photographer Lord Snowdon.

Location: Map 4:I4. OS Ref SU187:TQ265 294. At Handcross on B2114, 12 miles south of Gatwick, just off London-Brighton M23.

Owner: National Trust **Contact:** Nymans

Tel: 01444 405250 **E-mail:** nymans@nationaltrust.org.uk

Open: Garden, woods, café, shop and garden centre, gallery in the House, and second hand bookshop: 1 Jan-29 Feb, daily, 10am-4pm. 1 Mar-31 Oct, daily, 10am-5pm. 1 Nov-31 Dec, daily, 10am-4pm. House open for special events only from 1 Nov-29 Feb. Closed 25 & 26 Dec. Last admission to Gallery 30mins before closing and for short periods during the year to change exhibitions. For more information and any other changes please check the website.

Admission: Please see website.

Key facts: ⬚ ▨ ▧ WC, some level paths. ▨ Licensed. ▨ Daily, free. Special interest tours for groups £2.50pp booked in advance. ▣ ▨ ▨ Guide dogs only. No dogs in garden. ▨ ✳ Closed 25 & 26 Dec. ▨

PARHAM HOUSE & GARDENS 🏠ⓕ
PARHAM PARK, PULBOROUGH, WEST SUSSEX RH20 4HS
www.parhaminsussex.co.uk

One of the top twenty in Simon Jenkins's book 'England's Thousand Best Houses'. Idyllically set in the heart of an ancient deer park, below the South Downs, the Elizabethan house contains an important collection of needlework, paintings and furniture. The spectacular Long Gallery is the third longest in England. The gardens include a four-acre Walled Garden with stunning herbaceous borders, plus Pleasure Grounds. Parham has always been a well-loved family home, and only three families have lived here since its foundation stone was laid in 1577. Its tranquillity and timeless beauty have changed little over the years. Now owned by a charitable trust, the house is lived in by Lady Emma Barnard, her husband James and their family.

Location: Map 3:G5. OS Ref TQ060 143. Midway between Pulborough & Storrington on A283. Equidistant from A24 & A29. SatNav: RH20 4HR.

Owner: Parham Park Trust **Contact:** Parham Estate Office

Tel: 01903 742021 **Facebook:** ParhamHouseAndGardens

Twitter: @parhaminsussex **E-mail:** enquiries@parhaminsussex.co.uk

Open: Easter Sun-end of Sep on Wed, Thur, Fri and Sun plus BH's. In Oct Sun only. Gardens open 12 noon, House at 2pm. Please see website for up-to-date information and additional events.

Admission: House & Gardens: Adult £10.50, Senior £9.50, Child £5.50, Family £30. Gardens only: Adult £8.50, Senior £7.50, Child £4.50, Family £24.00.

Key facts: ⓘ No flash photography in house. ◎ Gifts including Parham's own jams and preserves. ▨ Plants grown by our own Garden Team. ▾ Exclusive packages by arrangement, on Mons and Tues during the open season. ▨ Disabled access in the gardens and ground floor of the house. Please see website for full accessibility statement. ▨ Open on House & Garden open days only. ▨ Licensed. ▨ House & Garden tours are available by arrangement, led by professional guides. ◎ ▣ There is ample free parking in the Park. Designated parking for coaches and disabled visitors is within 50 metres of the House entrance. ▨ Tailored programmes by arrangement, please enquire. ▨ In gardens only, on leads. ▨

PETWORTH HOUSE & PARK 🦌
CHURCH STREET, PETWORTH, WEST SUSSEX GU28 0AE
www.nationaltrust.org.uk/petworth

Magnificent country house and park with an internationally important art collection. The vast late 17th Century mansion is set in a beautiful 283-hectare (700-acre) deer park, landscaped by 'Capability' Brown and immortalised in Turner's paintings. Inside, the house contains the National Trust's finest collection of pictures, with numerous works by Turner, Van Dyck, Reynolds and Blake, ancient and Neo-classical sculpture, fine furniture and carvings by Grinling Gibbons. The servants' quarters contain fascinating kitchens (including a copper batterie de cuisine of more than 1,000 pieces) and other service rooms.
Location: Map 3:G5. OS Ref SU976 218. Both house and park car parks located on A283; Follow signs from centre of Petworth (A272/A283). Sat-Nav: GU28 9LR
Owner: National Trust

Contact: The Administration Office
Tel: 01798 342207
E-mail: petworth@nationaltrust.org.uk
Open: House: 19 Mar-6 Nov, Sat-Wed, 11am-5pm last admission 4:30pm, partially open on Thu-Fri, please check website before visiting. Pleasure Grounds, Restaurant, Coffee Shop & Gift Shop: 10am-5pm daily. (closed 24 & 25 Dec).
Admission: House and Grounds Adult £15.00, Child (5-17yrs) £7.50, Family £37.00, Groups (pre-booked) £12.00.
Key facts: ⬛ ⬛ ⬛ WCs. ⬛ Licensed. ⬛ Licensed. ⬛ By arrangement. ⬛ Multi-media House Tours. ⬛ 700 meters from house. Parking charge for non-members (£4.00), NT Members parking Free. ⬛ ⬛ Guide dogs only. ⬛ ⬛

ST MARY'S HOUSE & GARDENS 🏠Ⓕ
BRAMBER, WEST SUSSEX BN44 3WE
www.stmarysbramber.co.uk

Enchanting medieval house, winner of Hudsons Heritage 'Best Restoration' award in 2011. Features in Simon Jenkins' book 'England's Thousand Best Houses'. Fine panelled interiors, including unique Elizabethan 'Painted Room'. Interesting family memorabilia and other collections including English costume dolls.
Traditional cottage-style tea room. Five acres of grounds include formal gardens with amusing topiary, and an exceptional example of the prehistoric tree Ginkgo biloba. 'Secret' Garden, with Victorian fruit-wall and rare pineapple pits, Rural Museum, Jubilee Rose Garden, Terracotta Garden, King's Garden, unusual circular Poetry Garden, woodland walk and Landscape Water Garden with its island and waterfall. In the heart of the South Downs National Park, St. Mary's is a house of fascination, charm and friendliness.

Location: Map 3:H6. OS Ref TQ189 105. Bramber village off A283. From London 56m via M23/A23 or A24. Buses from Brighton, Shoreham and Worthing.
Owner: Mr Peter Thorogood MBE and Mr Roger Linton MBE
Tel: 01903 816205 **E-mail:** info@stmarysbramber.co.uk
Open: May-end Sep: Suns, Thus & BH Mons, 2-6pm. Last entry 5pm. Groups at other days and times by arrangement.
Admission: House & Gardens: Adult £9.00, Conc. £8.50, Child £4.00. Groups (25+) £9.00. Gardens only: Adult £6.00, Child £2.00, Groups £6.00.
Key facts: ⬛ No photography in house. ⬛ ⬛ ⬛ ⬛ Partial. ⬛
⬛ Obligatory for groups (max 55).Visit time 2½-3 hrs. ⬛ 20 cars or 2 coaches.
⬛ ⬛ ⬛ ⬛

SHEFFIELD PARK AND GARDEN 🍃
SHEFFIELD PARK, UCKFIELD, EAST SUSSEX TN22 3QX
www.nationaltrust.org.uk/sheffield-park-and-garden

The garden is a horticultural work of art formed through centuries of landscape design, with influences of 'Capability' Brown and Humphry Repton. Four lakes form the heart of the garden, with paths circulating through the glades and wooded areas surrounding them. Each owner has left their impression, which can still be seen today in the layout of the lakes, the construction of Pulham Falls, the planting of Palm Walk and the many different tree and shrub species from around the world. Our historic parkland forms a larger footprint for the Sheffield Park estate. Dating back several centuries, it has had many uses including a deer park and WWII camp, and is now grazed with livestock. (Please note house is privately owned). **Location:** Map 4:I5. OS Ref TQ415 240. Midway between East Grinstead and Lewes, 5m NW of Uckfield on E side of A275.

Owner: National Trust **Contact:** Property Office
Tel: 01825 790231 **Fax:** 01825 791264 **Alt tel:** 01825 790302

E-mail: sheffieldpark@nationaltrust.org.uk
Open: Garden/Shop/Tearoom: Open all year (closed Christmas Day). Please call 01825 790231 or visit our website for details of seasonal opening times. Parkland: Open all year, dawn to dusk.
Admission: For 2016 prices, please call 01825 790231 or visit our website. Groups discount available (15+ prebooked) NT, RHS Individual Members and Great British Heritage Pass holders Free. Discounts available in conjunction with the Bluebell Railway for groups. **Key facts:** ℹ️ Garden: Dogs after 2.30pm only. Parkland: Dogs allowed under close control. 🎁 Gifts, condiments, books, gardening accessories & outdoor wear. 🌱 Extensive, well-stocked plant sales area. ♿ Accessible route in garden. WCs in tearoom & reception. Mobility scooters & wheelchairs. ☕ Coach House tearoom. 🎟️ Tues & Thus 11am-12pm. 🅿️ Coach parking area & accessible spaces. 🖼️ 🐕 ❄️ ☑️

STANDEN 🍃
WEST HOATHLY ROAD, EAST GRINSTEAD, WEST SUSSEX RH19 4NE
www.nationaltrust.org.uk/standen

Designed by Philip Webb in the 1890s for wealthy solicitor, James Beale, and his family, Standen is a family home with nationally important Arts & Crafts interiors, most famous for its Morris & Co. designs.

The 12 acre hillside garden, is part of a 5 year project to restore lost features and conserve the historic plant collection. A licensed café serves seasonal dishes and Arts & Crafts inspired gifts are available in the shop.
Location: Map 4:I4. OS Ref TQ389 356.
2m S of East Grinstead, signposted from B2110.
Owner: National Trust **Contact:** Property Office
Tel: 01342 323029
Twitter & Facebook: Search for StandenNT.
E-mail: standen@nationaltrust.org.uk

Open: Garden, Café and shop open all year 10am-5pm. (Closes at dusk if earlier). House opens at 11am daily*
* Access by guided tour only at certain times.
Last entry to house one hour before closing time. House closing time varies depending on season, please check website for full details. Closed 24 and 25 Dec.
Admission: Admission is free for National Trust members. For admission prices for non-members, please check the website or call us on 01342 323029.
Key facts: ℹ️ Year round events programme. 🎁 🌱
♿ WCs. Wheelchairs available to borrow. 🍴 Licensed. 🍴 Licensed.
🎟️ Guided tours available at certain times, check website for details. 🅿️ 🖼️
🐕 Dogs welcome in the gardens on short leads. 🏠 Morris Apartment (Self-catering, sleeps 2+2) available to hire. ❄️ Closed 24 & 25 Dec. ☑️

BORDE HILL GARDEN 🏛ⓕ
Borde Hill Lane, Haywards Heath, West Sussex RH16 1XP
www.bordehill.co.uk

Botanical heritage and stunning landscapes make Borde Hill the perfect day out for horticulture enthusiasts, country lovers, and families. The Elizabethan House nestles in the centre of the formal garden which is set as outdoor 'rooms', including the Azalea, Rhododendron, Rose and Italian gardens. Themed events, gift shop, café, tea garden, restaurant, and gallery. Dog friendly.

Location: Map 4:15. OS Ref TQ323265. 1½ miles north of Haywards Heath, 20 mins N. of Brighton, or S. of Gatwick on A23 taking exit 10a via Balcombe & Cuckfield.
Contact: Joanna Stewart
Tel: 01444 450326
E-mail: info@bordehill.co.uk
Open: Please see website or call for details.
Admission: Adults £8.20, Conc. £7.80, Group £7.00, Child £5.50. Season Tickets.
Key facts: ▣ 📷 🎭 👜 WCs. Maps. 🍴 Homemade food. 🎖 Award-winning. 🎟 Garden & House. 🅿 Free parking. 🐕 On leads. 🎗

CHARLESTON
Firle, Nr Lewes, East Sussex BN8 6LL
www.charleston.org.uk

Charleston, with its unique interiors and beautiful walled garden, was the home of artists Vanessa Bell and Duncan Grant from 1916 and the country meeting place of the Bloomsbury group. They decorated the house, painting walls, doors and furniture and filling the rooms with their own paintings and works by artists they admired, such as Picasso, Derain and Sickert.

Location: Map 4:J6. OS Ref TQ490 069. 7 miles east of Lewes on A27 between Firle and Selmeston **Owner:** The Charleston Trust
Tel: 01323 811626 **E-mail:** info@charleston.org.uk
Open: Apr-Oct: Wed-Sat, guided tours from 1pm (12pm Jul-Sep) Last entry 5pm. Sun & BH Mon open 1-5.30pm.
Admission: Please check website for full details of admission costs.
Key facts: ⓘ ▣ 🎭 🎟 👜 ◻ 🍴 🎟 Obligatory, except Sunday. 🅿 ▣ 🎗

Parham House

CHICHESTER CATHEDRAL
Chichester, West Sussex PO19 1PX
www.chichestercathedral.org.uk

Ancient and modern, this magnificent 900 year old Cathedral has treasures from every age, from medieval stone carvings to world famous contemporary artworks. Open every day and all year with free entry. Free guided tours and special trails for children. Regular exhibitions, free weekly lunchtime concerts and a superb Cloisters Café and Shop. A fascinating place to visit.

Location: Map 3:F6. OS Ref SU860 047. West Street, Chichester.
Contact: Visitor Services Officer
Tel: 01243 782595 **Fax:** 01243 812499
E-mail: visitors@chichestercathedral.org.uk
Open: Summer: 7.15am-7pm, Winter: 7.15am-6pm. Choral Evensong daily (except Wed).
Admission: Free entry. Donations greatly appreciated.
Key facts: ▣ 🎭 ◻ 👜 🍴 🎟 🎟 🅿 ❄

CLINTON LODGE GARDEN
Fletching, E Sussex TN22 3ST
www.clintonlodgegardens.co.uk

A formal but romantic garden around a Caroline and Georgian house, reflecting the gardening fashions throughout its history, particularly since the time of Sir Henry Clinton, one of Wellington's generals at Waterloo. Lawn and parkland, double blue and white herbaceous borders between yew and box hedges, a cloister walk swathed in white roses, clematis and geraniums, a Herb Garden where hedges of box envelop herbs, seats are of turf, paths of camomile. A Pear Walk bursts with alliums or lilies, a Potager of flowers for cutting, old roses surround a magnificent water feature by William Pye, and much more. Private groups by appointment - Lunches can be arranged for groups of 10-30.
Location: Map 4:I5. OS Ref TQ428 238. In centre of village behind tall yew and holly hedge. **Owner/Contact:** Lady Collum **Tel/Fax:** 01825 722952
E-mail: garden@clintonlodge.com
Open: NGS Open Days: Sun 24 Apr, Mon 13 Jun, Mon 27 Jun & Mon 8 Aug. Other days by appointment. **Admission:** NGS Entrance £5.00, Children Free.
Key facts: ⓘ WCs. ⬛ ♿ Partial. ⬛ ⓕ By arrangement. 🅿 Limited. 🐕 Guide dogs only.

HAMMERWOOD PARK
East Grinstead, Sussex RH19 3QE
www.hammerwoodpark.co.uk

The best kept secret in Sussex, "untouched by a corporate plan". Built by White House architect Latrobe in Greek Revival style in 1792, left derelict by Led Zeppelin, painstakingly restored by the Pinnegar family over the last 30 years and brought to life with guided tours, concerts and filming.
Location: Map 4:J4. OS Ref TQ442 390. 3.5 m E of East Grinstead on A264 to Tunbridge Wells, 1m W of Holtye.
Owner: David and Anne-Noelle Pinnegar
Tel: 01342 850594 **E-mail:** antespam@gmail.com
Open: 1 Jun-end Sep: Wed, Sat & BH Mon, 2-5pm. Guided tour starts 2.05pm. Private groups: Easter-Jun. Coaches strictly by appointment. Small groups any time throughout the year by appointment.
Admission: House & Park: Adult £8.00, Child £2.00. Private viewing by arrangement.
Key facts: ⓘ Conferences. Helipad (see Pooley's - prior permission required). 🅣 ⬛ ⓕ Obligatory. ⬛ 🐕 In grounds. ⬛ B&B. ⬛ ♿ €

GLYNDE PLACE 🏠ⓕ
Glynde, East Sussex BN8 6SX
www.glyndeplace.co.uk

Glynde Place is a magnificent example of Elizabethan architecture commanding exceptionally fine views of the South Downs. Amongst the collections of 400 years of family living can be seen 17th and 18th Century portraits of the Trevors, furniture, embroidery and silver.
Location: Map 4:J5. OS Ref TQ456 092. Signposted off the A27, 4m SE of Lewes at top of village. Rail: Glynde is on the London/Eastbourne and Brighton/Eastbourne mainline railway. London 1½ hours by car, Gatwick 35 mins by car.
Contact: The Estate Office **Tel:** 01273 858224 **E-mail:** info@glynde.co.uk
Open: May–Jun: Wed, Thu & Sun & BHs from 1-5pm. Aug: BH and preceding Sun from 1-5pm. Visits to the House are by guided tours only starting at 2pm, 3pm and 4pm. Group bookings by prior arrangement only.
Admission: House & Grounds: Adult £5.00, Children over 12yrs & Students £3.00, Children under 12 yrs free. **Key facts:** 🅣 House & parkland available for corporate events. ⬛ ⓕ All visits to the House by guided tours only. 🅿 Limited parking for coaches. 🐕 Guide dogs only. ⬛ A range of wedding options are available. Please contact the Estate Office for more information. ⬛

HIGH BEECHES WOODLAND & WATER GARDEN 🏠ⓕ
High Beeches Lane, Handcross RH17 6HQ
www.highbeeches.com

A hidden gem in the High Weald of Sussex. There is much to see and appreciate throughout the seasons. Camellias, magnificent magnolias and hosts of daffodils in spring. In summer wander through glades carpeted with bluebells and surrounded by the colour of many azaleas and rhododendrons. The wildflower meadow is at its best in June and autumn brings a display of glorious autumn colour.
Location: Map 4:I4. OS Ref TQ275 308. S side of B2110. 1m NE of Handcross
Owner: High Beeches Gardens Conservation Trust (Reg. Charity 299134)
Contact: Sarah Bray
Tel: 01444 400589 **E-mail:** gardens@highbeeches.com
Open: Apr-1 Nov: daily except Weds, 1-5pm (last adm. 4.30pm). Coaches/guided tours anytime, by appointment only.
Admission: Adult £7.50, Child (under 14yrs) Free. Group concessions (20+). Guided tours for groups £10.00pp.
Key facts: 🅿 Partial. WCs. Tearoom fully accessible. ⬛ 🍴 Licensed. ⓕ By arrangement. 🅿 🐕 Guide dogs only. ⬛

SACKVILLE COLLEGE
High Street, East Grinstead, West Sussex RH19 3BX
www.sackvillecollege.org.uk

Built in 1609 for Robert Sackville, Earl of Dorset, as an almshouse and overnight accommodation for the Sackville family. Feel the Jacobean period come alive in the enchanting quadrangle, the chapel, banqueting hall with its fine hammerbeam roof and minstrels' gallery, the old common room and Warden's study where the carol "Good King Wenceslas" was composed. Chapel weddings by arrangement.

Location: Map 4:I4. OS Ref TQ397 380. A22 to East Grinstead, College in High Street (town centre).

Owner: Board of Trustees **Contact:** The Warden

Tel: 01342 323414

E-mail: admin@sackvillecollege.org.uk

Open: Mid Jun-Mid Sep, Wed to Sun afternoons, 2-5pm. Groups all year round, by arrangement. Pre-booked school visits welcome.

Admission: Adult £4.50, Child £1.00. Groups: (10-60) no discount.

Key facts: ℹ️ Large public car park adjacent to entrance. 📷 📺 ♿ Partial. 📷 Obligatory. 🅿️ Chequer Mead car park nearby. 🏫 Pre-booked school groups welcome. 🐕 Guide dogs only.

STANSTED PARK 🏠ⓕ
Rowlands Castle, Hampshire PO9 6DX
www.stanstedpark.co.uk

Stansted House and its Chapel stands in 1700 acres of parkland and ancient forest within the South Downs National Park.The state rooms are furnished as though the 10th Earl was still at home giving the visitor a real sense of a bygone era, the extensive servants' quarters below stairs are filled with historic artefacts that are brought to life by the very knowledgeable and friendly stewards who will guide you through the vibrant history of Stansted Park.

Location: Map 3:F5. OS Ref SU761 103. Follow brown heritage signs from A3(M) J2 Emsworth or A27 Havant **Owner:** Stansted Park Foundation

Contact: Reception **Tel:** 023 9241 2265 **Fax:** 023 9241 3773

E-mail: enquiry@stanstedpark.co.uk

Open: House & Chapel: Easter Sun-end Sep; Sun, Mon, Tues & Wed 1-5pm (last adm. 4pm). Tearoom, Farm Shop & Garden Centre: open every day. Maze: weekends and school holidays 11-4pm (Feb-Oct). Light Railway: weekends and Weds. **Admission:** House & Chapel: Adult £8.00, Child (5-15yrs) £4.00, Conc. £7.00, Family (2+3) £20.00. Groups/educational visits by arrangement.

Key facts: 🎁 📺 Private & corporate hire. ♿ Suitable. WCs. 🍴 Licensed. 📷 By arrangement. 🅿️ 🏫 By arrangement. 🐕 Guide dogs only. 🏠 ❄️ Grounds. 🛏️

Clinton Lodge Garden

UPPARK HOUSE & GARDEN 🌿
South Harting, Petersfield, West Sussex GU31 5QR
www.nationaltrust.org.uk/uppark

Admire the Georgian grandeur of Uppark from its stunning hilltop location on the South Downs. Discover the fascinating world of Sir Harry Fetherstonhaugh, Lady Emma Hamilton and the dairymaid who married her master. See the famous doll's house, Victorian servants' quarters, lovely garden and breathtaking views.

Location: Map 3:F5. OS Ref 197 SU775 177.
In Between Petersfield & Chichester on B2146.

Owner: National Trust **Contact:** The Property Office

Tel: 01730 825415 **Fax:** 01730 825873 **E-mail:** uppark@nationaltrust.org.uk

Open: Garden, café, shop: All year 10am-5pm. House: all year 1am-4pm*, Closed Christmas Eve and Christmas Day. *Ground floor 5 Mar-31 Oct 12.30-4.00pm. Print room first Wed of each month Mar-Oct.

Admission: Adult £11.00, Child (5-17yrs) £5.50, Family (2+3) £27.50. Garden only: Adult £6.60, Child £3.30. Gift Aid prices.

Key facts: ℹ️ No photography in the house. 📷 🎁 ♿ WCs at carpark, in shop and in house. Lift to basement of house. 🍴 📷 Available for hire. 🅿️ 🐕 Guide dogs only. 🛏️

WILMINGTON PRIORY
Wilmington, Nr Eastbourne, East Sussex BN26 5SW
www.landmarktrust.org.uk

The Priory is part of an outstanding now mostly ruinous monastic site in the South Downs, combined with the comfort of rooms improved by the Georgians. This area was beloved by the Bloomsbury set whose influential houses are nearby; it's close to Glyndebourne and a few miles from the sea.

Location: Map 3:F5. OS Ref TQ544 042.
Owner: Leased to The Landmark Trust by Sussex Archaeological Society
Tel: 01628 825925
E-mail: bookings@landmarktrust.org.uk
Open: Self-catering accommodation. 30 days Apr-Oct, contact for details.
Admission: Free on Open Days, visits by appointment.
Key facts: ℹ A vaulted medieval entrance porch leading off the large farmhouse kitchen makes an atmospheric summer dining room and the monastic ruins are yours to wander.

ARUNDEL CATHEDRAL
London Road, Arundel, West Sussex BN18 9AY
French Gothic Cathedral, church of the RC Diocese of Arundel and Brighton built by Henry, 15th Duke of Norfolk and opened 1873.
Location: Map 3:G6. OS Ref TQ015 072. Above junction of A27 and A284.
Contact: Rev. Canon T. Madeley
Tel: 01903 882297
Fax: 01903 885335
E-mail: aruncath1@aol.com
Website: www.arundelcathedral.org
Open: Summer: 9am-6pm. Winter: 9am-dusk. Tue, Wed, Fri, Sat: Mass 10am; Mon and Thu: Mass 8.30am (at Convent of Poor Clares, Crossbush); Sat: Vigil Mass 6.15pm (at Convent of Poor Clares, Crossbush); Sun: Masses 9.30am and 11.15am. Shop open in the summer, Mon-Fri, 10am-4pm and after services and on special occasions and otherwise on request.
Admission: Free.
Key facts: ♿ ℹ By arrangement. ❄

COWDRAY HERITAGE TRUST ♿ⓟ
River Ground Stables, Midhurst, West Sussex GU29 9AL

Cowdray is one of the most important survivals of a Tudor nobleman's house. Set within the stunning landscape of Cowdray Park, the house was partially destroyed by fire in 1793. Explore the Tudor Kitchen, Buck Hall, Chapel, Gatehouse, Vaulted Storeroom and Cellars, Visitor Centre and Shop.
Location: Map 3:F5. OS Ref TQ891 216. On the outskirts of Midhurst on A272.
Owner: Cowdray Heritage Trust **Contact:** The Manager
Tel: 01730 812423 **Visitor Centre Tel:** 01730 810781 (during opening hours only). **E-mail:** heritage@cowdray.co.uk **Website:** www.cowdray.co.uk
Open: Please check our website for opening times.
Groups all year round by arrangement. **Admission:** Check website for details.
Key facts: ♿ ♿ Full level access, WCs, wheelchair available, limited disabled parking. ⓘ Free audio guides. Children's tour available. Ⓟ In Midhurst by bus stand, a short walk along causeway. ❄ Well behaved dogs on leads welcome.

1066 BATTLE OF HASTINGS ⌗
Battle, Sussex TN33 0AD
Founded in penance by William the Conqueror following the Norman defeat of the English in 1066, the site of the high altar is traditionally believed to be the spot where King Harold of England fell. **Location:** Map 4:K5. OS Ref TQ749 157. Top of Battle High St. **Tel:** 01424 775705 **E-mail:** customers@english-heritage.org.uk **Website:** www.english-heritage.org.uk/1066 **Open:** Please see website for up to date opening times and admission prices.

BODIAM CASTLE ⚜
Bodiam, Nr Robertsbridge, East Sussex TN32 5UA
Built in 1385 to defend the surrounding countryside and as a comfortable dwelling for a rich nobleman. One of the finest examples of medieval architecture.
Location: Map 4:K5. OS Ref TQ785 256. 3m S of Hawkhurst, 2m E of A21 Hurst Green. **Tel:** 01580 830196 **E-mail:** bodiamcastle@nationaltrust.org.uk
Website: www.nationaltrust.org.uk/bodiam-castle
Open: Please see website for opening times and admisson prices.

DENMANS GARDEN
Denmans Lane, Fontwell, Denmans Lane BN18 0SU
Unique 4 acre garden, home of renowned garden designer John Brookes MBE. Plant centre and café. **Location:** Map 3:G6. OS Ref SU944 070.
Tel: 01243 542808 **E-mail:** denmans@denmans-garden.co.uk
Website: www.denmans-garden.co.uk **Open:** 10am-4pm daily all year - check website for winter opening times. **Admission:** Adults £4.95, OAP £4.75.

THE ROYAL PAVILION
Brighton, East Sussex BN1 1EE
Universally acclaimed as one of the most exotically beautiful buildings in the British Isles, the Royal Pavilion is the former seaside residence of King George IV.
Location: Map 4:I6. OS Ref TQ312 041. **Tel:** 03000 290900 **E-mail:** visitor.services@brighton-hove.gov.uk **Website:** www.royalpavilion.org.uk
Open: Please see website for up to date opening and admission details.

Bodiam Castle

VISITOR INFORMATION

■ **Owner**
English Heritage

■ **Address**
Osborne House
East Cowes
Isle of Wight
PO32 6JX

■ **Location**
Map 3:D6
OS Ref. SZ516 948
1 mile SE of East Cowes.
Ferry: Isle of Wight ferry terminals. Red Funnel, East Cowes 1½ miles Tel: 02380 334010. Wightlink, Fishbourne 4 miles Tel: 0870 582 7744

■ **Contact**
The House Administrator
Tel: 01983 200022
Venue Hire and Hospitality Tel: 01983 203055
E-mail:
customers@english-heritage.org.uk

■ **Opening Times**
Please visit www.english-heritage.org.uk for opening times and prices and the most up-to-date information.

■ **Special Events**
There is an exciting events programme available throughout the year, for further details please contact the property or visit the website.

Conference/Function

ROOM	Max Cap
Duchess of Kent Suite	Standing 70 Seated 30
Durbar Hall	Standing/Seated 40
Marquee	Large scale events possible
Upper Terrace	Standing 250
Victoria Hall	Standing 120 Seated 80

OSBORNE HOUSE ⌗

www.english-heritage.org.uk/osborne

Take an intimate glimpse into the family life of Britain's longest reigning monarch and the house Queen Victoria loved to call home.

Osborne House was a peaceful, seaside retreat of Queen Victoria, Prince Albert and their family. Step inside and marvel at the richness of the State Apartments including the lavish Indian Durbar Room.

The Queen died at the house in 1901 and many of the rooms have been preserved almost unaltered ever since. The nursery bedroom remains just as it was in the 1870s when Queen Victoria's first grandchildren came to stay.

Don't miss the Swiss Cottage, a charming chalet in the grounds built for teaching the royal children domestic skills. Enjoy the beautiful gardens with their stunning views over the Solent, the fruit and flower Victorian Walled Garden and Queen Victoria's private beach – now open to visitors for the first time.

Osborne hosts events throughout the year, and Queen Victoria's palace-by-the-sea offers both the superb coastal location and facilities for those who want to entertain on a grand scale in style.

KEY FACTS

ℹ️ Available for corporate and private hire. Suitable for filming, concerts, drama. No photography in the house.

📷

⭐ Private and corporate hire.

♿ WCs.

🍴 Nov-Mar for pre-booked guided tours only. Tours allow visitors to see the Royal Apartments and private rooms.

🅿️ Ample.

🚌 Please book. Education room.

BASILDON PARK 🍂
Lower Basildon, Reading, Berkshire RG8 9NR
Tel: 0118 984 3040 **E-mail:** basildonpark@nationaltrust.org.uk

SHAW HOUSE
Church Road, Shaw, Newbury, Berkshire RG14 2DR
Tel: 01635 279279 **E-mail:** shawhouse@westberks.gov.uk

ASCOTT 🍂
Wing, Leighton Buzzard, Buckinghamshire LU7 0PR
Tel: 01296 688242 **E-mail:** info@ascottestate.co.uk

WEST WYCOMBE PARK 🍂
West Wycombe, High Wycombe, Buckinghamshire HP14 3AJ
Tel: 01494 513569

HASTINGS CASTLE
Castle Hill Road, West Hill, Hastings, East Sussex TN34 3AR
Tel: 01424 444412 **E-mail:** bookings@discoverhastings.co.uk

LEWES PRIORY
Town Hall, High Street, Lewes, East Sussex BN7 2QS
Tel: 01273 486185 **E-mail:** enquiries@lewespriory.org.uk

BREAMORE HOUSE & MUSEUM 🏠®
Breamore, Fordingbridge, Hampshire SP6 2DF
Tel: 01725 512858 **E-mail:** breamore@btinternet.com

JANE AUSTEN'S HOUSE MUSEUM
Chawton, Alton, Hampshire GU34 1SD
Tel: 01420 83262 **E-mail:** enquiries@jahmusm.org.uk

PORTCHESTER CASTLE ⌗
Portsmouth, Hampshire PO16 9QW
Tel: 02392 378291 **E-mail:** customers@english-heritage.org.uk

SIR HAROLD HILLIER GARDENS
Jermyns Lane, Ampfield, Romsey, Hampshire SO51 0QA
Tel: 01794 369318 **E-mail:** info@hilliergardens.org.uk

THE VYNE 🍂
Sherborne St John, Basingstoke RG24 9HL
Tel: 01256 883858 **E-mail:** thevyne@nationaltrust.org.uk

WINCHESTER CATHEDRAL
9 The Close, Winchester SO23 9LS
Tel: 01962 857200 **E-mail:** visits@winchester-cathedral.org.uk

CARISBROOKE CASTLE ⌗
Newport, Isle Of Wight PO30 1XY
Tel: 01983 522107 **E-mail:** customers@english-heritage.org.uk

NUNWELL HOUSE & GARDENS 🏠
Coach Lane, Brading, Isle Of Wight PO36 0JQ
Tel: 01983 407240 **E-mail:** info@nunwellhouse.co.uk

BOUGHTON MONCHELSEA PLACE
Boughton Monchelsea, Nr Maidstone, Kent ME17 4BU
Tel: 01622 743120 **E-mail:** mk@boughtonplace.co.uk

CHILHAM CASTLE
Canterbury, Kent CT4 8DB
Tel: 01227 733100 **E-mail:** chilhamcastleinfo@gmail.com

DEAL CASTLE ⌗
Victoria Road, Deal, Kent CT14 7BA
Tel: 01304 372762 **E-mail:** customers@english-heritage.org.uk

EMMETTS GARDEN 🍂
Ide Hill, Sevenoaks, Kent TN14 6BA
Tel: 01732 750367 **E-mail:** emmetts@nationaltrust.org.uk

FINCHCOCKS MUSICAL MUSEUM 🏠
Goudhurst, Kent TN17 1HH
Tel: 01580 211702 **E-mail:** info@finchcocks.co.uk

GODINTON HOUSE AND GARDENS
Godinton Lane, Ashford, Kent TN23 3BP
Tel: 01233 620773 **E-mail:** info@godinton-house-gardens.co.uk

GREAT COMP GARDEN
Comp Lane, Platt, Borough Green, Kent TN15 8QS
Tel: 01732 886154 **E-mail:** info@greatcompgarden.co.uk

GROOMBRIDGE PLACE GARDENS
Groombridge, Tunbridge Wells, Kent TN3 9QG
Tel: 01892 861 444 **E-mail:** carrie@groombridge.co.uk

HALL PLACE & GARDENS 🏠
Bourne Road, Bexley, Kent DA5 1PQ
Tel: 01322 526574 **E-mail:** info@hallplace.org.uk

LULLINGSTONE ROMAN VILLA ⌗
Lullingstone Lane, Eynsford, Kent DA4 0JA
Tel: 01322 863467 **E-mail:** customers@english-heritage.org.uk

Portchester Castle

QUEBEC HOUSE 🍂
Westerham, Kent TN16 1TD
Tel: 01732 868381

SCOTNEY CASTLE 🍂
Lamberhurst, Tunbridge Wells, Kent TN3 8JN
Tel: 01892 893820 **E-mail:** scotneycastle@nationaltrust.org.uk

SMALLHYTHE PLACE 🍂
Smallhythe, Tenterden, Kent TN30 7NG
Tel: 01580 762334

ST AUGUSTINE'S ABBEY ⌗
Longport, Canterbury, Kent CT1 1TF
Tel: 01227 767345 **E-mail:** customers@english-heritage.org.uk

TUDOR HOUSE
King Street, Margate, Kent CT9 1QE
Tel: 01843 577577 **E-mail:** visitorinformation@thanet.gov.uk

WALMER CASTLE AND GARDENS ⌗
Deal, Kent CT14 7LJ
Tel: 01304 364288 **E-mail:** customers@english-heritage.org.uk

ARDINGTON HOUSE 🏚ⓟ
Wantage, Oxfordshire OX12 8QA
Tel: 01235 821566 **E-mail:** info@ardingtonhouse.com

CHASTLETON HOUSE 🍂
Chastleton, Nr Moreton-In-Marsh, Oxfordshire
Tel: 01608 674981 **E-mail:** chastleton@nationaltrust.org.uk

GREYS COURT 🍂
Rotherfield Greys, Henley-On-Thames, Oxfordshire RG9 4PG
Tel: 01491 628529 **E-mail:** greyscourt@nationaltrust.org.uk

NUFFIELD PLACE 🍂
Huntercombe, Henley on Thames RG9 5RY
Tel: 01491 641224 **E-mail:** nuffieldplace@nationaltrust.org.uk

WATERPERRY GARDENS
Waterperry, Nr Wheatley,
Oxfordshire OX33 1JZ

GODDARDS
Abinger Common, Dorking, Surrey RH5 6TH
Tel: 01628 825925 **E-mail:** bookings@landmarktrust.org.uk

RHS GARDEN WISLEY
Nr Woking, Surrey GU23 6QB
Tel: 0845 260 9000

VANN
Hambledon, Godalming GU8 4EF
E-mail: vann@caroe.com

ANNE OF CLEVES HOUSE
52 Southover High Street, Lewes, East Sussex BN7 1JA
Tel: 01273 474610 **E-mail:** Anne@sussexpast.co.uk

MICHELHAM PRIORY 🏚
Upper Dicker, Hailsham, East Sussex BN27 3QS
Tel: 01323 844224 **E-mail:** adminmich@sussexpast.co.uk

Waterperry Gardens

PALLANT HOUSE GALLERY
9 North Pallant, Chichester, West Sussex PO19 1TJ
Tel: 01243 774557 **E-mail:** info@pallant.org.uk

PASHLEY MANOR GARDENS 🏚ⓟ
Pashley Manor, Ticehurst, Wadhurst, East Sussex TN5 7HE
Tel: 01580 200888 **E-mail:** info@pashleymanorgardens.com

PEVENSEY CASTLE ⌗
Pevensey, Sussex BN24 5LE
Tel: 01323 762604 **E-mail:** customers@english-heritage.org.uk

PRESTON MANOR
Preston Drove, Brighton, East Sussex BN1 6SD
Tel: 03000 290900 **E-mail:** visitor.services@brighton-hove.gov.uk

WAKEHURST PLACE
Ardingly Road (B2028), North of Ardingly,
West Sussex RH17 6TN

WEALD AND DOWNLAND OPEN AIR MUSEUM
Singleton, Chichester, West Sussex PO18 0EU
Tel: 01243 811019

WEST DEAN COLLEGE & GARDENS 🏚
West Dean, Chichester, West Sussex PO18 0RX
Tel: Gardens: 01243 818210 **E-mail:** enquiries@westdean.org.uk

WOOLBEDING GARDENS 🍂
Midhurst, West Sussex GU29 9RR
Tel: 0844 249 1895 **E-mail:** woolbedinggardens@nationaltrust.org.uk

Iford Manor Gardens, Wiltshire

©VISITBRITAIN / BRITAIN ON VIEW

Channel Islands
Cornwall
Devon
Dorset
Gloucestershire
Somerset
Wiltshire

South West

Gloucester-shire

Wiltshire

Somerset

Devon

Dorset

Cornwall

Channel Islands

Drawn to the West Country by the promise of sunshine and coast, holidaymakers should not overlook the fine country houses and gardens that have thrived here for generations.

New Entries for 2016:
- Ablington Manor
- Kilworthy Farm

SAUSMAREZ MANOR 🏛ⓕ
SAINT MARTIN, GUERNSEY, CHANNEL ISLANDS GY4 6SG
www.sausmarezmanor.co.uk www.artparks.co.uk

A delightful Manor to tour, crammed with history of the family since c1220 with the façade built at the bequest of one of the first Governors of New York. It is regarded as the finest example of Queen Anne Colonial Architecture, voted the Best private Attraction in 2013 by the Visitors to Guernsey. The Wild Subtropical Garden, with its collection of Exotica, Bamboos, Lilies, Brugmansias, Camellias, Banana & Palm trees and Tree Ferns & tender plants draws people worldwide as does the changing selection of sculptures spread throughout. Also the ride on train, 9 hole Par 3, the Copper Smithy Tearoom, Craft shop & Saturday Farmers' Country Market.

Location: Map 2:O11. 2m S of St Peter Port, clearly signposted.
Owner/Contact: Peter de Sausmarez
Tel: 01481 235571 / 01481 235655.
E-mail: sausmarezmanor@cwgsy.net
Open: Daily Apr-Oct, 10am-5pm.
Admission: House £7.00, Subtropical Gardens/Sculpture Park £6.00, P&P £6.00, Train £2.00, everything else free. Check website for concessions.
Key facts: 🔲 🔲 🔲 🔲 🔲 Guided tours of House Easter-Oct. 🅿 🔲 🔲 Guide dogs only. 🔲 2 holiday flats available. 🔲 🔲 🔲 €

© EHPL / Skyscan

TINTAGEL CASTLE ⊞

www.english-heritage.org.uk/tintagel

Tintagel Castle is a magical day with its wonderful location, set high on the rugged North Cornwall coast.

Steeped in legend and mystery; said to be the birthplace of King Arthur, you can still visit the nearby Merlin's Cave. The castle also features in the tale of Tristan and Isolde.

Joined to the mainland by a narrow neck of land, Tintagel Island faces the full force of the Atlantic. On the mainland, the remains of the medieval castle represent only one phase in a long history of occupation.

The remains of the 13th Century castle are breathtaking. Steep stone steps, stout walls and rugged windswept cliff edges encircle the Great Hall, where Richard Earl of Cornwall once feasted.

KEY FACTS

ℹ️ WC. Video film shown about the Legend of Arthur.

🅿️ No vehicles. Parking (not EH) in village only.

🐕 Dogs on leads only.

BOCONNOC
THE ESTATE OFFICE, BOCONNOC, LOSTWITHIEL, CORNWALL PL22 0RG
www.boconnoc.com

Boconnoc House, the winner of the 2012 HHA/Sotheby's Award for Restoration and the Georgian Group Award, was bought with the proceeds of the Pitt Diamond in 1717. Three Prime Ministers, a history of duels and the architect Sir John Soane play a part in the story of this unique estate. The beautiful woodland garden, the Georgian Bath House, Soane Stable Yard, 15th Century Church and naturesque landscape tempt the explorer. The Boconnoc Music Award for ensembles from the Royal College of Music, the Cornwall Spring Flower Show and fairytale weddings are part of Boconnoc today, in between filming, fashion shoots, corporate days and private parties. Groups by appointment (15-150).
Location: Map 1:G8. OS Ref 148 605. A38 from Plymouth, Liskeard or from Bodmin to Dobwalls, then A390 to East Taphouse and follow signs.
Owner: Anthony Fortescue Esq. **Contact:** Sam Cox

Tel: 01208 872507 **Fax:** 01208 873836 **E-mail:** info@boconnoc.com
Open: Garden: 1, 8, 15, 22 May. 2-5pm. Private Tours 2016: 10 May, 24 May, 14 Jun, 5 Jul, 13 Sep. Special Events: Cornwall Garden Society Spring Flower Show: 2/3 Apr, Botanical Art Course 12-14 Apr, Boconnoc Music Award concerts with the Royal College of Music 19 & 21 Jul, Steam Fair at Boconnoc 29-31 Jul, Motorsport Carnival 14 Aug, Landscape Art Course 20-23 Sep, Glow in the Park Night Run 22 Oct. Group bookings daily by appointment.
Admission: House: £5.00, Garden: £5.00. Children under 12yrs free.
Key facts: ◩ ⊤ Conferences. ◲ Partial. ⚑ Licensed.
🖾 By arrangement. 🅿 ⛽ ⛽ In grounds, on leads.
⊞ 18 doubles (9 en suite). Holiday and residential houses to let.
⛪ Church or Civil ceremony. ❀ ⚈

CAERHAYS CASTLE & GARDEN
CAERHAYS, GORRAN, ST AUSTELL, CORNWALL PL26 6LY
www.caerhays.co.uk

One of the very few Nash built castles still left standing - situated within approximately 140 acres of informal woodland gardens created by J C Williams, who sponsored plant hunting expeditions to China at the turn of the century.
As well as guided tours of the house from March to June visitors will see some of the magnificent selection of plants brought back by the intrepid plant hunters of the early 1900s these include not only a national collection of magnolias but a wide range of rhododendrons and the camellias which Caerhays and the Williams family are associated with worldwide.
Location: Map 1:F9. OS Ref SW972 415. S coast of Cornwall - between Mevagissey and Portloe. 9m SW of St Austell.
Owner: F J Williams Esq **Contact:** Lucinda Rimmington
Tel: 01872 501310 **Fax:** 01872 501870 **E-mail:** enquiries@caerhays.co.uk
Bookings and Enquiries: Sophie Hodge

Open: House: 21 Mar-17 Jun: Mon-Fri only (including BHs), tours 11.30am, 1.00pm and 2.30pm, booking recommended. Gardens: 22 Feb-19 Jun: daily (including BHs), 10am-5pm (last admission 4pm).
Admission: House: £8.50. Gardens: £8.50. House & Gardens: £13.50. Group tours: by arrangement. Groups please contact Estate Office.
Key facts: ⓘ No photography in house. ◙ Selling a range of Caerhays products & many other garden orientated gifts. 🖾 Located beside entrance point.
⊤ The Georgian Hall is available for hire for meetings. ◩
◨ The Magnolia Tearooms serve a wide range of foods using locally sourced produce. 🖾 Obligatory. By arrangement. 🅿 Limited for large coaches.
⛽ ⛽ On leads. ◨ Caerhays has a selection of 5* properties available for hire for self-catering holidays. ❀ Weddings can be held at The Vean or the Coastguard's Lookout. Please visit www.caerhays.co.uk for more information. ⚈

PRIDEAUX PLACE ⓘⒻ
PADSTOW, CORNWALL PL28 8RP
www.prideauxplace.co.uk

Tucked away above the busy port of Padstow, the home of the Prideaux family for over 400 years, is surrounded by gardens and wooded grounds overlooking a deer park and the Camel estuary to the moors beyond. The house still retains its 'E' shape Elizabethan front and contains fine paintings and furniture. Now a major international film location, this family home is one of the brightest jewels in Cornwall's crown. The historic garden is undergoing major restoration work and offers some of the best views in the county. A cornucopia of Cornish history under one roof.

Location: Map 1:E8. OS Ref SW913 756. 5m from A39 Newquay/Wadebridge link road. Signposted by Historic House signs.

Owner/Contact: Peter Prideaux-Brune Esq
Tel: 01841 532411 **Fax:** 01841 532945 **E-mail:** office@prideauxplace.co.uk
Open: Easter Sun 27 Mar-Thur 31 Mar. Sun 8 May-Thur 6 Oct.
Grounds & Tearoom: 12.30-5pm. House Tours: 1.30-4pm (last tour).
Admission: House & Grounds: Adult £9.00, Children U12 free.
Grounds only: Adult £4.00, Children U12 free. Groups (15+) discounts apply.
Key facts: ⓘ Open air theatre, open air concerts, car rallies, art exhibitions, charity events. ⓒ ⓣ By arrangement. Ⓢ Partial. Ground floor & grounds. ● Fully licensed. Ⓣ Obligatory. Ⓟ ■ By arrangement. ⛌ On leads. ⊞ By arrangement. ♥

ST MICHAEL'S MOUNT ❧
MARAZION, NR PENZANCE, CORNWALL TR17 0EL
www.stmichaelsmount.co.uk / www.nationaltrust.org.uk

This beautiful island has become an icon for Cornwall and has magnificent views of Mount's Bay from its summit. There the church and castle, whose origins date from the 12th Century, have at various times acted as a Benedictine priory, a place of pilgrimage, a fortress, a mansion house and now a magnet for visitors from all over the world.

Location: Map 1:C10. OS Ref SW515 300. 3 miles East of Penzance.
Owner: National Trust **Contact:** St Aubyn Estates
Tel: 01736 710507
Tide Information: 01736 710265
E-mail: enquiries@stmichaelsmount.co.uk
Open: Castle:13 Mar-3 Jul 10.30am-5.00pm, 4 Jul-2 Sep 10.30am-5.30pm, 4 Sep-30 Oct 10.30am-5.00pm. Check website for garden dates.

Admission: Castle: Adult £9.00, Child (Under 5) Free, Child (5-16) £4.50, Family (2 adults and up to 3 children) £22.50, Single Adult Family (up to 3 children) £13.50. Check website for garden prices.
Key facts: ⓘ For a full events calendar throughout the season, please check the website. ⓒ ⓣ Ⓢ Partial. WCs. ● Our Island Café offers expansive sea views from its garden. Opt for a light bite from the good value menu which includes pasties, coffees, freshly prepared sandwiches and cake. ⑪ Our licensed café serves a wide selection of light lunches, home-made breads and cakes plus fresh fish specials, using the best local, seasonal and sustainable ingredients. Ⓣ By arrangement. Ⓟ On mainland, including coach parking (not NT.) ■ ⛌ Guide dogs only. ⊞ ♥

PENCARROW 🏚Ⓕ
Washaway, Bodmin, Cornwall PL30 3AG
www.pencarrow.co.uk

Owned, loved and lived in by the family. Georgian house and Grade II* listed gardens. Superb collection of portraits, furniture and porcelain. Marked walks through 50 acres of beautiful formal and woodland gardens, Victorian rockery, Italian garden, over 700 different varieties of rhododendrons, lake, Iron Age hill fort and icehouse. **Location:** Map 1:F8. OS Ref SX040 711. Between Bodmin and Wadebridge. 4m NW of Bodmin off A389 & B3266 at Washaway. **Owner:** Molesworth-St Aubyn family **Contact:** Administrator **Tel:** 01208 841369 **E-mail:** info@pencarrow.co.uk
Open: House: 20 Mar-29 Sep, 11am-4pm (guided tour only - the last tour of the House is at 3.00pm). Café & Shop are open same dates and days as the house. Shop 10.00am-5.00pm. Café 11.00am-5.00pm (House, Café and shop closed Fris and Sats.) Gardens: 1 Mar-31 Oct, Daily, 10am-5.30pm.
Admission: House and Gardens: Adult £10.75, Concession £9.75, Child £5.00, under 5's free. Gardens: Adult £5.75, Concession £5.25, Child £2.50, under 5's free. Discounted family tickets and group rates available.
Key facts: ℹ️ Café, Gift and plant shop, small children's play area. 🖼🚫♿️🚻📷 ⓘ Obligatory. 🅿️ Free. 🐕🚆 In grounds. 🔺☂️

PORT ELIOT HOUSE & GARDENS 🏚Ⓕ
St. Germans, Saltash, Cornwall PL12 5ND
www.porteliot.co.uk

Port Eliot is an ancient, hidden gem, set in stunning fairytale grounds which nestle beside a secret estuary in South East Cornwall. It has the rare distinction of being a Grade I Listed house, park and gardens. This is due in part to the work of Sir John Soane, who worked his magic on the house and Humphrey Repton, who created the park and garden. Explore the treasures in the house. Gaze at masterpieces by Reynolds and Van Dyck. Decipher the Lenkiewicz Round Room Riddle Mural. Still a family home, you will be beguiled by the warm atmosphere.
Location: Map 1:H8. OS Ref SX359 578. Situated in the village of St Germans on B3249 in SE Cornwall. **Owner:** The Earl of St Germans
Contact: Port Eliot Estate Office **Tel:** 01503 230211 **E-mail:** info@porteliot.co.uk
Open: 29 Feb-26 Jun every day except Sats (also closed 3-5 Jun). 2pm-5.30pm last admission 5pm. From 29 Feb-24 March by guided tour only: 2.15pm and 3.15pm. Basement tours available on Mons.
Admission: House & Garden: Adult £8.00, Student/Senior/Group £7.00, Children £4.00, Family £20.00. Gardens only: Adult £5.00, Children £2.00.
Key facts: ℹ️ No photography. 🚫🖼♿️ⓘ🅿️🐕🚆 In gardens. 🔺☂️

TREWITHEN GARDENS 🏚Ⓕ
Grampound Rd, Nr Truro, Cornwall TR2 4DD

Trewithen is an historic estate near Truro, Cornwall that has been lived in by the same family for 300 years. The Woodland Gardens are outstanding with 22 Champion Trees, rare and highly prized plants and Trewithen is 1 of 39 gardens internationally recognised as a Camellia Society Garden of Excellence (1 of only 5 in the UK). The House is open for guided tours on Monday and Tuesday afternoons (booking advisable). **Location:** Map 1:E9. OS Ref SW914 524. Grampound Road, near Truro, Cornwall on the A390. **Owner:** A M J Galsworthy
Contact: The Estate Office (Liz White) **Tel:** 01726 883647 **Fax:** 01726 882301
Liz White: secretary@trewithenestate.co.uk.
E-mail: info@trewithengardens.co.uk **Website:** www.trewithengardens.co.uk
Open: House & Gardens: Mar-Jun 10am-4pm. House: Mon & Tue afternoons 2-4pm inc Aug BH Mon (guided tour only-booking advisable). **Admission:** Adult £8.50, Child U12 Free. Combined entry & group rates available. Contact us or visit website. **Key facts:** ℹ️ No inside pics. 🖼🚫♿️ WCs. 📷ⓘ🅿️🚆 On leads.

LANHYDROCK 🌿
Lanhydrock, Bodmin, Cornwall PL30 5AD

Lanhydrock is the grandest house in Cornwall, set in a glorious landscape of gardens, parkland and woods overlooking the valley of the River Fowey.
Location: Map 1:F8. OS Ref SX085 636. **Tel:** 01208 265950
E-mail: lanhydrock@nationaltrust.org.uk **Website:** www.nationaltrust.org.uk/lanhydrock **Open:** Please see website for most up-to-date times and prices.

RESTORMEL CASTLE ⚜
Lostwithiel, Cornwall PL22 0EE

Hilltop Norman castle, with remains of circular keep, deep moat, keep gate and Great Hall visible. **Location:** Map 1:F8. OS Ref OS200, SX104 614. 1½m N of Lostwithiel off A390. **Tel:** 01208 872687 **E-mail:** customers@english-heritage.org.uk **Website:** www.english-heritage.org.uk/restormel
Open: Please visit www.english-heritage.org.uk for opening times, admission prices and the most up-to-date information.

ST CATHERINE'S CASTLE ⚜
St Catherine's Cove, Fowey, Cornwall PL23 1JH

One of a pair of small artillery forts built by Henry VIII in the 1530s to defend Fowey Harbour, consisting of two storeys with gun ports at ground level.
Location: Map 1:F9. OS Ref SX118 509.
Tel: 0370 333 1181
Website: www.english-heritage.org.uk
Open: Open any reasonable time during daylight hours. **Admission:** Free.

Gardens at Boconnoc

GREAT FULFORD
DUNSFORD, NR. EXETER, DEVON EX6 7AJ
www.greatfulford.co.uk

On a hill overlooking a lake and set in a landscaped park Great Fulford has been the home of the Fulford family since at least the 12th Century. The current house reflects the financial ups and downs of the family over the centuries, with a major rebuilding and enlargement taking place in 1530 and again in 1580 while in 1690 the house, which had been badly damaged in the Civil War, was fully restored. Internally then there is a stunning suite of Great Rooms which include a superb Great Hall replete with some of the finest surviving examples of early Tudor carved panelling as well as a William & Mary period Great Staircase which leads to the recently restored Great Drawing Room or Ballroom. Other rooms in the house are in the 'gothic' taste having been remodelled, as was the exterior, by James Wyatt in 1805.

Location: Map 2:J7. OS Ref SX790 917. In centre of Devon. 10m W of Exeter. South of A30 between villages of Cheriton Bishop and Dunsford.
Owner/Contact: Francis Fulford
Tel: 01647 24205 **Fax:** 01647 24401
E-mail: francis@greatfulford.co.uk
Open: All year by appointment for parties of any size but with a minimum fee of £150. Alternatively individuals can book tours on prearranged dates via www.invitationtoview.co.uk.
Admission: £9.00 per person.
Key facts: ⊤ ☎ 🏠 Obligatory.
🅿 🍴 🚃 🎫 🛅 ✳

HARTLAND ABBEY 🏠Ⓕ
NR BIDEFORD, NORTH DEVON EX39 6DT
www.hartlandabbey.com

Built in 1160, Hartland Abbey is a hidden gem on the stunning North Devon coast. Passing down generations from the Dissolution to this day it remains a friendly, family home full of interest: architecture from 1160 to 1850 by Meadows and Sir George Gilbert Scott; murals, important paintings and furniture, porcelain, early photographs, documents, family memorabilia and changing exhibitions. Family links to characters such as Sir Walter Raleigh, Rev William Stukeley, Pocohontas, Haile Sellasie. Woodland gardens and walks lead to the Jekyll designed Bog Garden and Fernery, restored 18th Century Walled Gardens full of flowers, fruit and vegetables, the Summerhouse, Gazebo and the beach at Blackpool Mill, film location for BBC's 'Sense and Sensibility' and recently 'The Night Manager'. Beautiful daffodils, bluebells and tulips in spring. Delicious homemade food in The Old Kitchens. 1 mile from Hartland Quay. Special Events - see website. **Location:** Map 1:G5. OS Ref SS240 249. 15m W of Bideford, 15m N of Bude off A39 between Hartland and Hartland Quay on B3248.

Owner: Sir Hugh Stucley Bt **Contact:** Theresa Seligmann
Tel: 01237441496/234 / 01884 860225 **E-mail:** ha_admin@btconnect.com
Open: House, Gardens, Grounds & Beachwalk: Good Fri 25 Mar-2 Oct, Sun-Thu 11-5pm. (House 2-5pm - last admission 4.15pm).
Tearoom, Light lunches and cream teas. 11am-5pm.
Admission: House, Gardens, Grounds & Beachwalk: Adult £12.00, OAP £11.00, Child (5-15ys) £5.00, Under 5 Free, Registered disabled £8.50, Family (2+2) £29.00. Gardens, Grounds, Beachwalk & Exhibition: Adult £8.00, OAP £7.50, Child (5-15ys) £4.00, Under 5 Free, Registered disabled £4.50, Family (2+2) £21.00. Groups & coaches: Concs 20+. Open at other dates and times. Booking essential. Large car park adjacent to the house.
Key facts: 📷 🎁 ⊤ Wedding receptions. 🖼 Partial. WC. ☎ 🎫 By arrangement. 🅿 🚃 In grounds, on leads. 🛅 🎭

POWDERHAM CASTLE 🏰ⓕ
KENTON, NR EXETER, DEVON EX6 8JQ
www.powderham.co.uk

Powderham Castle is the magnificent 600 year old family home of the 18th Earl of Devon. The Castle is grade 1 listed. It sits within an ancient Deer Park and enjoys breathtaking views across the Exe Estuary. Powderham Castle and its extensive woods and gardens are open to visitors from April to October and are available all year for private functions. Visitors enjoy the unique architecture, fascinating history and exquisite interiors, furniture and artwork of the Castle on entertaining guided tours which run frequently each day. The Courtenay Café offers a selection of home cooked food. The gift shop, walled garden, animal and play area and an extensive calendar of events create a wonderful day out.
Location: Map 2:K7. OS Ref SX965 832. 6m SW of Exeter, 4m S M5/J30. Access from A379 in Kenton village.
Owner: The Earl of Devon **Contact:** Lord and Lady Courtenay

Tel: 01626 890243
E-mail: castle@powderham.co.uk
Open: Apr-Oct 2016. Please visit our website for specific dates and times. Woodland Garden and Belvedere close on 1 Aug 2016.
Admission: Please visit www.powderham.co.uk for admission prices.
Key facts: ℹ️ Available for private hire, including corporate events, all year. Powderham Castle is licenced for Marriages and Civil Partnerships and offers a bridal suite and extensive accommodation. 🖥️ 🖼️ 🇹 🔲 Partial. WCs. 🍽️ Licensed. 🍴 Licensed. 🎫 Obligatory. Included. 1hr. 🅿️ Free. 🎭 Victorian Learning Programme - suitable for Key Stage 1 and 2 - An excellent learning resource to supplement children's learning outside of the classroom. 🦮 Guide Dogs Only. 🛏️ 🏠 🎗️

CADHAY 🏰ⓕ
Ottery St Mary, Devon EX11 1QT
www.cadhay.org.uk

Cadhay is approached by an avenue of lime-trees, and stands in an extensive garden, with herbaceous borders and yew hedges, with excellent views over the original medieval fish ponds. The main part of the house was built in about 1550 by John Haydon who had married the de Cadhay heiress. He retained the Great Hall of an earlier house, of which the fine timber roof (about 1420-1460) can be seen. An Elizabethan Long Gallery was added by John's successor at the end of the 16th Century, forming a unique courtyard with statues of Sovereigns on each side, described by Sir Simon Jenkins as one of the 'Treasures of Devon'.
Location: Map 2:L6. OS Ref SY090 962. 1m NW of Ottery St Mary. From W take A30 and exit at Pattesons Cross, follow signs for Fairmile and then Cadhay. From E, exit at the Iron Bridge and follow signs as above.
Owner: Mr R Thistlethwayte **Contact:** Jayne Covell **Tel:** 01404 813511
Open: May-Sep, Fri 2pm-5pm. Also: late May + Summer BH Sat-Sun-Mon. Last tour 4pm. **Admission:** House (Guided tour) and Gardens: Adult £7.00, Child £3.00. Gardens Only: Adults £3.00, Child £1.00. Parties of 15+ by prior arrangement. **Key facts:** 🖼️ 🔲 Ground floor & grounds. 🍽️ 🎫 Obligatory. 🅿️ 🦮 Guide dogs only. 🏠

CASTLE HILL GARDENS 🏰
Castle Hill, Filleigh, Barnstaple, Devon EX32 0RQ
www.castlehilldevon.co.uk

Set in the rolling hills of Devon, Castle Hill Gardens provides a tranquil and beautiful setting. Stroll through the spectacular gardens, dotted with mystical temples, follies, statues, vistas and a sham castle. The path through the Woodland Gardens, filled with flowering shrubs, leads you down to the river, the magical Satyr's temple and Ugley Bridge. Newly restored 18th Century Kennel dedicated to Lady Margaret Fortescue.
Location: Map 2:I14. OS Ref SS661 362. A361, take B3226 to South Molton. Follow brown signs to Castle Hill.
Owner: The Earl and Countess of Arran **Contact:** Marie Tippet
Tel: 01598 760421 / 01598 760336 Ext 1 **Fax:** 01598 760457
E-mail: gardens@castlehill-devon.com
Open: Daily except Sats Apr-Sep 11am-5pm. Oct-Mar 11am-dusk. Refreshments are only available outside from Apr-Sep. Groups and coach parties are welcome at all times by prior arrangement.
Admission: Adults £6.00, Senior citizens £5.50, Family £15.00, Children 5-15 £2.50, Under 5's Free, Groups (20+) £5.00. **Key facts:** 🇹 🔲 Partial. WCs. 🎫 By arrangement. 🅿️ Free parking. 🐕 🦮 On leads. 🏠 🎗️ Daily except Sats. 🎗️

FURSDON HOUSE AND GARDENS 🏠ⓕ
Cadbury, Nr Thorverton, Exeter, Devon EX5 5JS
www.fursdon.co.uk

Fursdon House is at the heart of a small estate where the family has lived for over 750 years. Set within a hilly and wooded landscape the gardens and grounds are attractive with walled and open areas with far reaching views. Family memorabilia with fine costume and textiles are displayed on informal guided tours. Two spacious apartments and a restored Victorian cottage offer stylish holiday accommodation. **Location:** Map 2:K6. OS Ref SS922 046. By car- Off A3072 between Bickleigh & Crediton. 9m N of Exeter signposted through Thorverton from A396 Exeter to Tiverton road **Owner:** Mr E D Fursdon **Contact:** Mrs C Fursdon
Tel: 01392 860860 **Fax:** 01392 860126 **E-mail:** admin@fursdon.co.uk
Open: Garden & Tearoom, Wed, Sun and BH Mons from Easter to end Sep 2pm-5pm; House open for tours BH Mons & Wed & Sun in Jun, Jul & Aug 2.30pm & 3.30pm. Group Tours at other times by arrangement.
Admission: House and Garden Adult £8.00, Child Free. Garden only £4.00.
Key facts: ℹ️ Conferences. No photography or video. 🎫 Coach Hall suitable for small meetings and conferences. Max 40 seated. ■ Coach Hall Tearoom serving cream teas and selection of cakes. 🎫 Obligatory. 🅿️ Limited for coaches.
🐕 Dogs on leads are allowed in the gardens 🏠 Self-catering.

HEMERDON HOUSE 🏠ⓕ
Plympton, Devon PL7 5BZ

Built in the late 18th Century by the current owners' ancestors, Hemerdon House is a trove of local history, containing naval and military mementos, paintings, furniture, china and silver collected through many generations. Family members offer tours of the interior on certain days of the year and visitors are welcome to explore the grounds on those days. **Location:** Map 2:I9. OS Ref SX573 574. SatNav instructions may be misleading so please see website for directions.
Tel: 07704 708416 **E-mail:** hemerdon.house@gmail.com
Website: www.hemerdonhouse.co.uk **Open:** See website for 2016 dates.
Admission: £7.50, HHA members and children under 12 no charge.
Key facts: ℹ️ Parties of 6 or more please contact us in advance; parties of 10 or more by prior arrangement only. 🔽 Partial access. 🎫 Two tours of approximately 1 hour 15 minutes each, starting at 2.15pm and 4pm - last entry at 4pm. 🅿️ Free parking. 🐕 Dogs on leads are permitted in the grounds while the house is open.

SAND 🏠ⓕ
Sidbury, Sidmouth EX10 0QN

Sand is one of East Devon's hidden gems. The beautiful valley garden extends to six acres and is the setting for the lived-in Tudor house, the 15th Century Hall House, and the 16th Century Summer House. The family, under whose unbroken ownership the property has remained since 1560, provide guided house tours.
Location: Map 2:L7. OS Ref SY146 925. Well signed, 400 yards off A375 between Honiton and Sidmouth. **Contact:** Mr & Mrs Huyshe-Shires
Tel: 01395 597230 **E-mail:** info@SandSidbury.co.uk
Website: www.SandSidbury.co.uk
Open: Suns & Mons in Jun and BH Suns & Mons. Other dates see website. Open 2-6pm. Groups by appointment.
Admission: House & Garden: Adult £7.00, Child/Student £1.00. Garden only: Adult £3.00, accompanied Child (under 16) Free.
Key facts: ℹ️ No photography 🔽 Partial. 🎫 Obligatory.
🅿️ 🐕 On leads. ♿

TIVERTON CASTLE 🏠ⓕ
Park Hill, Tiverton EX16 6RP

Part Grade I Listed, part Scheduled Ancient Monument, few buildings evoke such immediate feeling of history. Originally built 1106, later alterations. Home of medieval Earls of Devon & Princess Katherine Plantagenet. Fun for children, try on Civil War armour; ghost stories, secret passages, medieval loos, beautiful walled gardens. Interesting furniture, pictures. Comfortable holiday accommodation.
Location: Map 2:K5. OS Ref SS954 130. Just N of Tiverton town centre.
Owner: Mr and Mrs A K Gordon **Contact:** Mrs A Gordon
Tel: 01884 253200 **Fax:** 01884 254200 **Alt tel:** 01884 255200.
E-mail: info@tivertoncastle.com **Website:** www.tivertoncastle.com
Open: Easter-end Oct: Sun, Thu, BH Mon, 2.30-5.30pm. Last admission 5pm. Open to groups (12+) by prior arrangement at any time.
Admission: Adult £7.00; Child 7-16yrs £3.00, under 7 Free; Garden only £2.00.
Key facts: 🅿️ 🎫 🔽 Partial. 🎫 By arrangement. 🅿️ Limited for coaches. ■
🐕 Guide dogs only. 🏠 5 properties

A LA RONDE 🌿
Summer Lane, Exmouth, Devon EX8 5BD

A unique 16 sided house, completed c1796. Built for two spinster cousins, Jane and Mary Parminter, on their return from a grand tour of Europe.
Location: Map 2:L7. OS Ref SY004 834. 2m N of Exmouth on A376.
Tel: 01395 265514 **E-mail:** alaronde@nationaltrust.org.uk
Website: www.nationaltrust.org.uk/a-la-ronde
Open: Please see website for up to date opening and admission details.

CASTLE DROGO 🌿
Drewsteignton, Nr Exeter EX6 6PB

Extraordinary granite and oak castle which combines the comforts of the 20th Century with the grandeur of a Baronial castle. **Location:** Map 2:J7. OS Ref SX724 902. **Tel:** 01647 433306 **E-mail:** castledrogo@nationaltrust.org.uk
Website: www.nationaltrust.org.uk/castle-drogo
Open: Please see website for up to date opening and admission details.

GREENWAY 🌿
Greenway Road, Galmpton, nr Brixham, Devon TQ5 0ES

Greenway house and garden: 'the loveliest place in the world'. Take this extraordinary glimpse into the beloved holiday home of the famous author Agatha Christie. **Location:** Map 2:K8. OS Ref SX876 548. **Tel:** 01803 842382
E-mail: greenway@nationaltrust.org.uk **Website:** www.nationaltrust.org.uk/greenway **Open:** Please see website for up to date opening and admission details.

KILWORTHY FARM
Tavistock, Devon PL19 0JN

Described as one of Devon's Hidden Gems, and is well known for its range of Victorian farm buildings built in 1851-1853 by Francis, the 7th Duke of Bedford.
Location: Map 2:I7. OS Ref SX481 769. **Tel:** 01822 618042
E-mail: info@kilworthyfarm.co.uk **Website:** www.kilworthyfarm.co.uk
Open: 25, 26 & 28 Mar, 30 Apr, 1, 28, 29, 30 May, 1 - 31 Aug excluding Thurs.
Admission: Free

Castle Hill Gardens

■ VISITOR INFORMATION

■ Owner
Mr & Mrs Patrick Cooke

■ Address
Athelhampton
Dorchester
Dorset
DT2 7LG

■ Location
Map 2:P6
OS Ref. SY771 942
Athelhampton House is located just 5 miles East of Dorchester, between the villages of Puddletown and Tolpuddle.
Follow the brown tourist signs for Athelhampton from the A35.

■ Contact
Owen Davies or Laura Pitman
Tel: 01305 848363
E-mail:
enquiry@athelhampton.co.uk

■ Opening Times
1 Mar-1 Nov, Sun-Thurs, 10am-5pm. Closed every Fri & Sat (also open every Sunday throughout the Winter months).

■ Admission
House & Gardens:
Adult/Senior   £13.50
Child (under 16)   £3.00
Disabled/Student   £8.00
Gardens Only Ticket   £9.00
Please contact us for group booking rates and hospitality.
Some Fridays may be available by appointment.

■ Special Events
Flower Festival.
Spring Plant Sale.
MG Car Rally.
Quarterly Car Auctions.
Christmas Food Fair.
Outdoor Theatre.
Traditional Village Fete.
Autumn Plant Sale.

Athelhampton has a thriving Conference and Wedding business and offers exclusive use for Wedding parties and private functions on Fridays and Saturdays throughout the year.

Please see contact us by phone or visit our website for more information.

Conference/Function

ROOM	Size	Max Cap
Long Hall	13mx6m	80
Conservatory	16mx11m	120
Media Suite/ Cinema	fixed seating	75
Great Hall	12mx8m	82

ATHELHAMPTON HOUSE ⓗⒻ & GARDENS
www.athelhampton.co.uk

One of the finest 15th Century Houses in England nestled in the heart of the picturesque Piddle Valley in the famous Hardy county of rural Dorset.

Home to the Cooke family, this House dates from 1485 and is a magnificent example of early Tudor architecture. Sir William Martyn was granted a license by Henry VII to enclose 160 acres of deer park and to build the fortified manor. His great hall, with a roof of curved brace timbers and an oriel window with fine heraldic glass is now one of the finest examples from this period. In 1891 Alfred Carte de Lafontaine (the then owner of Athelhampton) commissioned the building of the formal gardens.

The Grade 1 listed gardens which have won the HHA 'Garden of the Year' award surround the main house, with Elizabethan style ham stone courts. The famous 30 foot high yew pyramids dominate the Great Court and the 15th Century Dovecote is still home to a colony of beautiful white fantail doves. Water forms a recurring theme with pools, fountains and the River Piddle. The House has an array of fine furniture from Jacobean to Victorian periods. The west wing gallery hosts an exhibition of paintings and sketches by the Russian Artist, Marevna (1892 - 1984). The collection of her works, painted mainly in the cubist style, includes pieces painted throughout her lifetime including her travels, life in Paris, her time whilst she lived at Athelhampton during the 1940's and 50's and her final years in Ealing.

In 2015, the kitchen garden was opened for the first time in a generation. The garden had been lost to the wild and over the next few years it will be lovingly restored to its former glory, providing our thriving restaurant and pub with fresh and seasonal produce, as well as enhancing our visitor experience.

KEY FACTS

- ℹ www.athelhampton.co.uk
- 📕 Books, food, DVDs, gifts & souvenirs.
- 🌷 Plants for sale from the gift shop.
- 🍽 By arrangement, for a range of activities and catering please contact us.
- ♿ Limited access to upper floors.
- ☕ Morning coffee, lunches & afternoon tea.
- 🍴 The Coach House: Home-cooked lunches and a Sunday Carvery.
- 🚶 Guided tours by arrangement.
- 🅿 Free car and coach parking.
- 📖 Educational staff to assist available.
- 🐕 On leads, grounds only.
- 🏠 Delightful holiday cottage on the estate, sleeps 6 in 3 en suite bedrooms.
- 🔔 Civil wedding ceremonies indoor and outdoor locations.
- ❄ Open all year round on a Sunday.

CLAVELL TOWER
Kimmeridge, near Wareham, Dorset BH20 5PE
www.landmarktrust.org.uk

This four storey, circular tower stands high on the cliff overlooking one of the most striking bays on the Dorset coast. Built in 1830 its location has captivated many including writers like Hardy and PD James.

Location: Map 2:A7. OS Ref SY915 796.
Owner: The Landmark Trust
Tel: 01628 825925
E-mail: bookings@landmarktrust.org.uk
Open: Self-catering accommodation. Two Open Days per year. Other visits by appointment. **Admission:** Free on Open Days and visits by appointment.
Key facts: A four storey tower with each room on a different floor. The bedroom, on the first floor, has a door onto a balcony that encircles the whole building.

LULWORTH CASTLE & PARK
East Lulworth, Wareham, Dorset BH20 5QS
www.lulworth.com

Impressive 17th Century Castle & historically important 18th Century Chapel set in extensive parkland; with views towards the Jurassic Coast. Built as a hunting lodge to entertain Royalty, the Castle was destroyed by fire in 1929. Since then it has been externally restored and internally consolidated by English Heritage. The Castle provides informative displays & exhibitions on its history.
Location: Map 3:A7. OS Ref ST853 822. In E Lulworth off B3070, 3m NE of Lulworth Cove. **Owner:** The Weld Estate **Tel:** 0845 4501054
Fax: 01929 40563 **E-mail:** enquiries@lulworth.com
Open: Castle & Park: All year, Sun-Fri. Opening dates & times may vary throughout the year, check website or call before visiting. Last admission to Castle is 1hr before closing. **Admission:** Pay & Display parking £3.00, allowing access to Park walks, Play & Picnic areas. Admission applies for Castle & Chapel - please see website www.lulworth.com. EH & HHA members Free. **Key facts:** Concerts, corporate & private hire/events, weddings by arrangement. WCs. Lift access to Upper Ground floor. Obligatory. By arrangement. Guide dogs only.

HIGHCLIFFE CASTLE
Highcliffe-On-Sea, Christchurch BH23 4LE
www.highcliffecastle.co.uk

Built in the 1830s in the Romantic/Picturesque style. Once home of Gordon Selfridge and host to many royal visits, it's idyllic cliff top location provides a stunning setting. Although no longer with its rich interiors, the magnificent Castle now houses a Heritage Centre & Gift Shop providing a unique location for exhibitions and events. Licenced for civil weddings. Available for ceremonies, receptions, banquets and corporate use. Access to Christchurch Coastal Path and beach. **Location:** Map 3:B6. OS Ref SZ200 930. Off the A337 Lymington Road, between Christchurch and Highcliffe-on-Sea.
Owner: Christchurch Borough Council **Contact:** David Hopkins
Tel: 01425 278807 **Fax:** 01425 280423 **E-mail:** enquiries@highcliffecastle.co.uk
Open: 1 Feb-23 Dec: daily, 11am-5pm. Last adm 4.30pm (4pm Fri/Sat). Grounds: All year: daily from 7am. Tearooms daily (except Christmas Day). Coaches by appointment. **Admission:** Adult £3.50, accompanied U16 free. Group (10+) rates available. Guided tour (non-public areas): Adult £6.00. Grounds: Free *Prices correct at time of going to press.
Key facts: Public Tours 11am Sun. 2pm Tue & Thu. Private tours any day (by arrangement). Limited. In grounds. Romantic & Picturesque, just perfect. Check for room closures before visiting.

MAPPERTON
Beaminster, Dorset DT8 3NR
www.mapperton.com

Voted 'The Nation's Finest Manor House' by Country Life and principal location of 2015 film 'Far from the Madding Crowd'. Glorious Jacobean manor with Sandwich family collection overlooking 10 acre Italianate garden, with orangery, topiary and borders, descending to ponds and arboretum. Outstanding views of Dorset hills and woodlands.
Location: Map 2:N6. OS Ref SY503 997. 2m southeast of Beaminster, follow brown signs on B3163. **Owner/Contact:** The Earl & Countess of Sandwich
Tel: 01308 862645 **Fax:** 01308 861082 **E-mail:** office@mapperton.com
Open: House: 1 Apr-31 Oct daily (exc. Fri & Sat) 12pm-4pm. Gardens: 1 Mar-31 Oct: daily (exc. Sat) 11am-5pm. Café: 1 Apr-31 Oct: daily (exc. Sat) 11am-5pm.
Admission: House & Gardens: Adult £12.00, Child (under 15yrs) free. Gardens only: Adult £9.00, Child (under 15yrs) free. Gardens in March only £4.50. House & Gardens £10.00 per person for groups over 20, by appointment only.
Key facts: Partial. WCs. Licensed. By arrangement. Limited for coaches. Guide dogs only.

MINTERNE GARDENS 🏛Ⓕ
Minterne Magna, Nr Dorchester, Dorset DT2 7AU
www.minterne.co.uk

Landscaped in the manner of 'Capability' Brown, Minterne's unique garden has been described by Simon Jenkins as 'a corner of paradise'. 20 wild, woodland acres of magnolias, rhododendrons and azaleas providing new vistas at each turn, with small lakes, streams and cascades. Private House tours, dinners, corporate seminars, wedding and events. As seen on BBC Gardeners' World. Voted one of the ten Prettiest Gardens in England by The Times.

Location: Map 2:O6. OS Ref ST660 042. On A352 Dorchester/Sherborne Rd, 2m N of Cerne Abbas.
Owner/Contact: The Hon Mr & Mrs Henry Digby
Tel: 01300 341370 **Fax:** 01300 341747 **E-mail:** enquiries@minterne.co.uk
Open: Mid Feb-9 Nov: daily, 10am-6pm.
Admission: Adult £5.00, accompanied children free. Free to RHS members.
Key facts: ⊞ Seminars/Team Building/Away Days. ⬜ Unsuitable. ⊞ By arrangement. Tours personally guided by Lord Digby. 🅿 Free. Picnic tables in car park. ⛯ In grounds on leads. ⬛ 4 rooms licenced for Civil Ceremonies. Capacity between 60-160.

ST GILES HOUSE 🏛
Wimborne St Giles, Dorset BH21 5NA
www.shaftesburyestates.com

Beautiful secluded setting in unspoilt Dorset, famous for the Grand Tri Run in May. Home of the Earls of Shaftesbury, the 17th Century house, gardens and landscape are under restoration. Events held in the parkland, designed by Henry Flitcroft, in the summer months; the house is available for bespoke events.

Location: Map 3:A5. OS Ref SU031119.
In Wimborne St Giles, 4mls SE of A354, past almshouses and church.
Owner: The Earl of Shaftesbury
Tel: 01725 517214
E-mail: office@shaftesburyestates.com

Open: By appointment for groups and for bespoke events.
Key facts: ⊞ ⛯ ⬛ ☒

SHERBORNE CASTLE & GARDENS 🏛Ⓕ
New Road, Sherborne, Dorset DT9 5NR
www.sherbornecastle.com

Discover the historic Digby stately home built by Sir Walter Raleigh in 1594. View magnificent staterooms besides Raleigh's kitchen and a museum in the castle's cellars. Explore acres of impressive lakeside gardens in a stunning setting forming one of 'Capability' Brown's finest landscapes in the south west.

Location: Map 2:O5. OS Ref ST649 164. 4m SE of Sherborne town centre. Follow brown signs from A30 or A352. ½m S of the Old Castle.
Owner: Mr & Mrs Wingfield Digby
Contact: Robert B. Smith
Tel: 01935 812072 Ext 2 **Fax:** 01935 816727
E-mail: enquiries@sherbornecastle.com
Open: Castle, Gardens, Gift Shop & Tearooms: Open daily except Mon & Fri. 25 Mar-30 Oct 2016; Gardens & Tearooms at 10am, Castle at 11am.
Admission: Castle & Gardens: Adult £11.00, Senior £10.00, Child Free (max 4 per full paying adult). Gardens only: Adult/Senior £6.00, Child Free (max of 4 per adult). Groups +15 discount options available on application.
Key facts: ⬛ ⊞ ⬜ WCs. ☒ ⊞ ⊞ By arrangement. 🅿 ⬛ ⛯ On leads. ⬛ ☒

Sherborne Castle Gardens

WOLFETON HOUSE 🏛Ⓕ
Nr Dorchester, Dorset DT2 9QN

A fine medieval and Elizabethan manor house lying in the water-meadows near the confluence of the rivers Cerne and Frome. It was embellished around 1580 and has splendid plaster ceilings, fireplaces and panelling. To be seen are the Great Hall, Stairs and Chamber, Parlour, Dining Room, Chapel and Cyder House.
Location: Map 2:O6. OS Ref SY678 921. 1½m from Dorchester on the A37 towards Yeovil. Indicated by Historic House signs.
Owner: Capt N T L L T Thimbleby
Contact: The Steward
Tel: 01305 263500
E-mail: kthimbleby.wolfeton@gmail.com
Open: Jun-end Sep: Mon, Wed & Thu, 2-5pm. Groups by appointment throughout the year.
Admission: £8.00
Key facts: ⓘ Catering for groups by prior arrangement. ⓣ By arrangement. 🅰 ⓕ By arrangement. Ⓟ Limited for coaches.
▣ ✖ ❋

CHURCH OF OUR LADY & ST IGNATIUS
North Chideock, Bridport, Dorset DT6 6LF

Built by Charles Weld of Chideock Manor in 1872 in Italian Romanesque style, it is a gem of English Catholicism and the Shrine of the Dorset Martyrs. Early 19th Century wall paintings in original barn-chapel (priest's sacristy) can be seen by arrangement. A museum of local history & village life displayed in adjoining cloister.
Location: Map 2:A7. OS Ref SY090 786. A35 to Chideock, turn into N Rd & ¼mile on right.
Owner: The Weld Family Trust **Contact:** Mrs G Martelli
Tel: 01308 488348 **E-mail:** amyasmartelli40@hotmail.com
Website: www.chideockmartyrschurch.org.uk
Open: All year: 10am-4pm.
Admission: Donations welcome.
Key facts: 🅰 Partial. Ⓟ Limited for coaches. ▣ ✖ Guide dogs only. ❋

EDMONDSHAM HOUSE & GARDENS 🏛Ⓕ
Cranborne, Wimborne, Dorset BH21 5RE

Charming blend of Tudor and Georgian architecture with interesting contents. Organic walled garden, six acre garden with unusual trees and spring bulbs. 12th Century church nearby.
Location: Map 3:A5. OS Ref SU062 116. Off B3081 between Cranborne and Verwood, NW from Ringwood 9m, Wimborne 9m.
Owner/Contact: Mrs Julia E Smith
Tel: 01725 517207
Open: House & Gardens all BH Mons, Weds in Apr & Oct only, 2-5pm. Gardens Apr-Oct Suns & Weds 2-5pm. Groups by arrangement (max 50).
Admission: House & Garden: Adult £5.00, Child £1.00 (under 5yrs free). Garden only: Adult £2.50, Child 50p (under 5yrs free).
Key facts: 🈂 🅰 Partial. WCs. ▣ Only Weds Apr & Oct. ⓕ Obligatory. Ⓟ Limited. ▣ ✖ Guide dogs only. 🅰

SANDFORD ORCAS MANOR HOUSE
Sandford Orcas, Sherborne, Dorset DT9 4SB

Tudor manor house with gatehouse, fine panelling, furniture, pictures. Terraced gardens with topiary and herb garden. Personal conducted tour by owner.
Location: Map 2:O5. OS Ref ST623 210. 2½m N of Sherborne, Dorset 4m S of A303 at Sparkford. Entrance next to church.
Owner/Contact: Sir Mervyn Medlycott Bt
Tel: 01963 220206
Open: Easter Mon, 10am-5pm. May & Jul-Sep: Suns & Mons, 2-5pm.
Admission: Adult £5.00, Child £2.50. Groups (10+): Adult £4.00, Child £2.00.
Key facts: 🅰 Unsuitable. ⓕ Obligatory. Ⓟ Parking available. ✖ In grounds, on leads.

STOCK GAYLARD HOUSE 🏛Ⓕ
Nr Sturminster Newton, Dorset DT10 2BG

A Georgian family house overlooking an ancient parkland with the parish church of St. Barnabas in the garden. Events include the Stock Gaylard Oak Fair on August Bank Holiday weekend (please see website for details).
Location: Map 2:P5. OS Ref ST722 130. 1m S junction A357 & A3030 Lydlinch Common.
Owner/Contact: Mrs J Langmead
Tel: 01963 23511
E-mail: Office@stockgaylard.com
Website: www.stockgaylard.com
Open: 23 Apr-2 May; 22-30 Jun; 22-30 Sep. 2-5pm. Groups by appointment.
Admission: Adult £5.00.
Key facts: ⓕ Ⓟ ✖ Guide dogs only. 🅰

KINGSTON LACY 🦌
Wimborne Minster, Dorset BH21 4EA

Explore this elegant country mansion, built to resemble an Italian Palace, and discover an outstanding collection of fine works of art.
Location: Map 3:A6. OS Ref ST980 019. **Tel:** 01202 883402
E-mail: kingstonlacy@nationaltrust.org.uk **Website:** www.nationaltrust.org.uk/kingston-lacy **Open:** Please see website for up-to-date opening and admission.

Athelhampton House

■ Owner
Mr David Lowsley-Williams

■ Address
Chavenage House
Chavenage
Tetbury
Gloucestershire
GL8 8XP

■ Location
Map 3:A1
OS Ref. ST872 952
Less than 20m from M4/
J16/17 or 18. 1¾m NW of
Tetbury between the
B4014 & A4135. Signed
from Tetbury. Less than
15m from M5/J13 or 14.
Signed from A46 (Stroud-
Bath road). Coaches -
access the site through the
Coach Entrance.
Taxi: The Pink Cab 07960
036003
Rail: Kemble Station 7m.
Air: Bristol 35m.
Birmingham 70m. Grass
airstrip on farm.

■ Contact
Caroline Lowsley-Williams
Tel: 01666 502329
Fax: 01666 504696
E-mail:
info@chavenage.com

■ Opening Times
Summer
May-September
Thur, Sun, 2-5pm. Last
admission 4pm. Also Easter
Sun, Mon & BH Mons.

NB. Will open on any day
and at other times by prior
arrangement for groups.

Winter
October-March
By appointment only for
groups.

■ Admission
Guided Tours are inclusive
in the following prices.
Summer
Adult   £8.00
Child (5-16 yrs)   £4.00
Winter
Groups only (any date or
time) Rates by
arrangement.

Conference/Function

ROOM	Size	Max Cap
Ballroom	70' x 30'	120
Oak Room	25' x 20'	30

CHAVENAGE HOUSE 🏠Ⓕ
www.chavenage.com

The Elizabethan Manor Chavenage House, a TV/Film location, is still a family home, offers unique experiences, with history, ghosts and more.

Chavenage is a wonderful Elizabethan house of mellow grey Cotswold stone and tiles which contains much of interest for the discerning visitor. The approach aspect of Chavenage is virtually as it was left by Edward Stephens in 1576. Only two families have owned Chavenage; the present owners since 1891 and the Stephens family before them. A Colonel Nathaniel Stephens, MP for Gloucestershire during the Civil War was cursed for supporting Cromwell, giving rise to legends of weird happenings at Chavenage since that time.

There are many interesting rooms housing tapestries, fine furniture, pictures and relics of the Cromwellian period. Of particular note are the Main Hall, where a contemporary screen forms a minstrels' gallery and two tapestry rooms where it is said Cromwell was lodged.

Recently Chavenage has been used as a location for TV and film productions: credits include, Barry Lyndon, the Hercule Poirot story The Mysterious Affair at Styles, The House of Elliot, Casualty, Cider with Rosie, Jeremy Musson's The Curious House Guest; Dracula, Lark Rise to Candleford; Bonekickers; Tess of the D'Urbervilles and New Worlds. Scenes from critically acclaimed 'Wolf Hall' were shot at Chavenage. For televisual purposes Chavenage was moved to Cornwall as it features as Trenwith House in 'Poldark' . Chavenage is the ideal attraction for those wishing a personal tour, usually conducted by the owner or his family, or for groups wanting a change from large establishments. Meals for pre-arranged groups have proved hugely popular. It also provides a charming venue for wedding receptions, conferences, seminars and other functions.

KEY FACTS

ℹ️ Suitable for filming, photography, corporate entertainment, activity days, seminars, receptions & product launches. No photography inside house.

👥 Occasional.

🍽️ Corporate entertaining. Private drinks parties, lunches, dinners, anniversary parties & wedding receptions.

♿ Partial. WCs.

🚶 By owner. Large groups given a talk prior to viewing. Couriers/group leaders should arrange tour format prior to visit.

🅿️ Up to 100 cars. 2-3 coaches (by appointment). Coaches access from A46 (signposted) or from Tetbury via B4014, enter back gates for parking area.

▪️ Chairs can be arranged for lecturing.

🐕 Assistance Dogs Only.

❄️ Out of season - only by appointment.

Aiden Turner as Ross Poldark

The tapestried 'Oliver Cromwell Room'.

SUDELEY CASTLE & GARDENS 🏛

www.sudeleycastle.co.uk

A must-see on any visit to The Cotswolds, Sudeley Castle & Gardens is the only private castle in England to have a queen – Katherine Parr – buried within the grounds.

Located only eight miles from the picturesque Broadway, Sudeley Castle & Gardens has played an important role in England's history, boasting royal connections that stretch back over 1,000 years - and is now a much-loved family home with award-winning gardens.

Inside, the castle contains many fascinating treasures from ancient Roman times to the present day. Outside, the castle is surrounded by award-winning gardens and a breathtaking 1,200 acre estate.

It is also the only private castle in England to have a queen buried within the grounds. The last of Henry VIII's six wives, Katherine Parr lived and died in the castle. She is now entombed in a beautiful 15th Century church found within the award-winning gardens.

Sudeley Castle's magnificent gardens are world-renowned, providing variety and colour from spring through to autumn. The centerpiece is the Queens Garden, so named because four of England's queens – Anne Boleyn, Katherine Parr, Lady Jane Grey and Elizabeth I – once admired the hundreds of varieties of roses found in the garden.

A pheasantry, adventure playground with picnic area, gift shop and Terrace Café in the banqueting hall complete the perfect day out.

KEY FACTS

- ℹ️ www.sudeleycastle.co.uk 01242 604244.
- 🏛 Open daily from Monday 7 March until Sunday 30 October 2016.
- ⚊ Weddings & Events.
- ♿ Partial. WCs.
- 🍴 Light lunches, afternoon tea, cakes, snacks, tea, coffee & soft drinks.
- 🍴 Licensed.
- 🚶 By arrangement. Call the Estate Office.
- 🅿 Ample parking.
- 📷 Contact Estate Office for schools materials.
- 🐕 Guide dogs only.
- 🏠 Country Cottages.
- 📖 The family's Private Library situated within the family's apartments is available for civil ceremonies & civil partnerships.
- 📺 See website.

VISITOR INFORMATION

■ Owner
Elizabeth, Lady Ashcombe and family

■ Address
Sudeley Castle & Gardens
The Cotswolds
Gloucestershire
GL54 5JD

■ Location
Map 6:O10
OS Ref. SP032 277
8m NE of Cheltenham, at Winchcombe off B4632. From Bristol or Birmingham M5/J9. Take A46 then B4077 towards Stow-on-the-Wold.
Coaches: Marchants Coaches
Rail: Cheltenham Station 8m.
Air: Birmingham or Bristol 45m.

■ Contact
Visitor Centre
Tel: 01242 604 244
Fax: 01242 602 959
Estate Office:
01242 602 308.
E-mail:
enquiries@sudeley.org.uk

■ Opening Times
Sudeley Castle & Gardens is open daily from Monday 7 March until Sunday 30 October 2016; 10am-5pm. Events planned throughout the season - check the website or call for details.

■ Admission
2016 Admission Prices:

Adult	£14.50
Concessions	£13.50
Child (5-15yrs)	£5.50
Family (2 adults and up to 3 children)	£37.50
Children under 5	Free

HHA & CPRE members 50% discount

12 Month Pass:

Adult	£26.00
Child (5–15 years)	£11.00
Family (2 adults and up to 3 children)	£65.00

■ Special Events
Special events throughout the season. See www.sudeleycastle.co.uk, Facebook.com/SudeleyCastle and Twitter @SudeleyCastle.

Conference/Function

ROOM	Size	Max Cap
Chandos Hall		60
Banqueting Hall + Pavilion		100
Marquee		Unlimited
Long Room		80
Library		50

RODMARTON MANOR 🏠ⓕ
CIRENCESTER, GLOUCESTERSHIRE GL7 6PF
www.rodmarton-manor.co.uk

A Cotswold Arts and Crafts house, one of the last great country houses to be built in the traditional way, containing beautiful furniture, ironwork, china and needlework specially made for the house. The large garden complements the architecture and contains many areas of great beauty and character including the magnificent herbaceous borders, topiary, roses, rockery and kitchen garden. Available as a film location and for small functions.

Location: Map 6:N12. OS Ref ST934 977.
Off A433 between Cirencester and Tetbury.
Owner: Mr Simon Biddulph
Contact: John & Sarah Biddulph

Tel: 01285 841442
E-mail: enquiries@rodmarton-manor.co.uk
Open: For 2016 opening details please see website. (www.rodmarton-manor.co.uk) or telephone 01285 841442.
Admission: House & Garden: £8.00, Child (5-15yrs) £4.00. Garden only: £5.00, Child (5-15yrs) £1.00. Guided tour of Garden: Entry fee plus £40.00 per group.
Key facts: ⓘ Colour guidebook & postcards on sale. Available for filming. No photography in house. WCs in garden. ♿ Garden & ground floor. ▣ Open days & groups by appointment. ⓘ By arrangement. 🅿 ▣ 🐕 Guide dogs only. ❋

STANWAY HOUSE & WATER GARDEN 🏠ⓕ
STANWAY, CHELTENHAM, GLOS GL54 5PQ
www.stanwayfountain.co.uk

'As perfect and pretty a Cotswold manor house as anyone is likely to see' (Fodor's Great Britain 1998 guidebook). Stanway's beautiful architecture, furniture, parkland and village are complemented by the restored 18th Century water garden and the magnificent fountain, 300 feet, making it the tallest garden and gravity fountain in the world. Teas available. Beer for sale. Wedding reception venue.
The Watermill in Church Stanway, now fully restored as a working flour mill, was recently re-opened by HRH The Prince of Wales. Its massive 24-foot overshot waterwheel, 8th largest waterwheel in England, drives traditional machinery, to produce stoneground Cotswold flour.
Location: Map 6:O10. OS Ref SP061 323. N of Winchcombe, just off B4077.

Owner: The Earl of Wemyss and March
Contact: Debbie Lewis
Tel: 01386 584528
Fax: 01386 584688
E-mail: stanwayhse@btconnect.com
Open: House & Garden: Jun-Aug: Tue & Thu, 2-5pm. Private tours by arrangement at other times.
Admission: Please see website for up to date admission prices.
Key facts: ⓘ Film & photographic location. 📷 ⊤ Wedding receptions. ▣ ⓘ By arrangement. 🅿 🐕 In grounds on leads. ❋

Register for news and special offers at **www.hudsonsheritage.com**

FRAMPTON COURT, THE ORANGERY AND FRAMPTON MANOR 🏠
Frampton on Severn, Gloucestershire GL2 7EP
www.framptoncourtestate.co.uk

Built in 1731 & now run as a luxury B&B, Frampton Court has a superb panelled interior, antique furniture & 'Frampton Flora' watercolours. The 18th Century 'Strawberry Hill' gothic Orangery sits, breath-takingly, at the end of a Dutch ornamental canal in The Court grounds & is a self-catering holiday house. Frampton Manor is said to be the birthplace of 'Fair Rosamund' Clifford mistress of Henry II & has an impressive 16th Century Wool Barn; its walled garden is a plantsman's delight.

Location: Map 6:M12. OS Ref SO 748080. 2 miles from M5 J13 via A38 & B4071. **Owner:** Mr & Mrs Rollo Clifford **Contact:** Janie Clifford **Tel:** 01452 740698 **E-mail:** events@framptoncourtestate.co.uk **Open:** Frampton Court & Manor by appointment for groups (10+). Manor Garden: Mon & Fri 2.30-5pm, 25 Apr to 1 Aug. **Admission:** Frampton Court: House & Garden £10.00. Frampton Manor: House, Garden & Wool Barn £10.00. Garden only £5.00. Wool Barn only £3.00. **Key facts:** ⓘ Filming, Parkland for hire. 🌿 Pan-Global Plants. 🎎 Wedding receptions. ♿ Partial. 🍽 For pre-booked groups. 🐕 🅿 ✈ 🛏 B&B at The Court: 01452 740267 Self-catering at The Orangery: 01452 740698 ❋ By arrangement.

KIFTSGATE COURT GARDENS 🏠ⓕ
Chipping Campden, Gloucestershire GL55 6LN
www.kiftsgate.co.uk

Magnificently situated garden on the edge of the Cotswold escarpment with views towards the Malvern Hills. Many unusual shrubs and plants including tree peonies, abutilons, specie and old-fashioned roses.
Winner HHA/Christie's Garden of the Year Award 2003.

Location: Map 6:O9. OS Ref SP173 430. 4m NE of Chipping Campden. ¼ m W of Hidcote Garden. **Owner:** Mr and Mrs J G Chambers **Contact:** Mr J G Chambers **Tel:** 01386 438777 **E-mail:** info@kiftsgate.co.uk **Open:** May, Jun, Jul, Sat-Wed, 12 noon-6pm. Aug, Sat-Wed, 2pm-6pm. Apr & Sep, Sun, Mon & Wed, 2pm-6pm. **Admission:** Adult £8.00, Child £2.50. Groups (20+) £7.00. **Key facts:** ◻ 🎎 ♿ Partial. 🍽 🅿 Limited for coaches. 🐕 Guide dogs only.

NEWARK PARK 🌿
Ozleworth, Wotton-Under-Edge Gloucestershire GL12 7PZ
www.nationaltrust.org.uk/newark-park

Newark Park is a 750 acre estate on the Cotswold escarpment with at its heart Newark House. Originally a Tudor hunting lodge, the house has been extended and restored over 450 years into a fascinating home with eclectic collections and exhibitions. The Newark estate offers a choice of woodland walks and the gardens provide space to play, explore and contemplate with spectacular views.

Location: Map 2:P1. OS Ref 172. ST786 934. Approx. 10 minutes' drive from M5 jcts 13 & 14. Off A4135 Tetbury/Dursley, follow signs for Newark Park. **Owner:** National Trust **Tel:** 01453 842644 **E-mail:** newarkpark@nationaltrust.org.uk **Open:** Wed-Mon (closed Tues). 13-29 Feb, 3-4 Dec and 10-11 Dec: 11am-4pm. 1 Mar-1 Nov: 11am-5pm. Last entry 30 mins before closing. **Admission:** Adult £8.70, Child £4.35, Family £21.75. **Key facts:** ⓘ ◻ 🎎 ♿ Ground floor ramp access. 🍽 Offering light lunches, drinks, cakes and ice creams. 🐕 Contact us for availability. 🅿 🐕 On leads in gardens and estate (guide dogs only in Newark House). 🛏 Holiday cottage. ♿

OWLPEN MANOR
Uley, Nr Dursley, Gloucestershire GL11 5BZ
www.owlpen.com

The romantic Tudor manor house stands in a picturesque valley setting with church, courthouse and mill. Stuart terraced gardens with magnificent yew topiary. Unique painted cloths, and family and Arts and Crafts collections. "By far the finest small manor house in all of England"— Prof Francis Comstock. "Owlpen, in Gloucestershire: ah, what a dream is there!"— Vita Sackville-West.

Location: Map 6:M12. OS Ref ST800 983. One mile east of Uley, off the B4066. **Owner:** Sir Nicholas and Lady Mander **Contact:** Bella Wadsworth **Tel:** 01453 860261 **E-mail:** sales@owlpen.com **Open:** The house will be open by appointment only for groups of 15 people or more. Apr-Oct, Mon-Fri. **Admission:** Cream tea £26.00 per person including a tour of the house and gardens. Or, a two course lunch for £36.00 per person including a tour of the house and gardens. **Key facts:** ⓘ Accessible by coach only via Uley Village. 🐕 Usually by owner. 🅿 At top of drive. 🛏 🏠 9 Self catering holiday cottages. ♿

SEZINCOTE 🏠ⓕ
Moreton-In-Marsh, Gloucestershire GL56 9AW
www.sezincote.co.uk

Exotic oriental water garden by Repton and Daniell. Large semi-circular orangery. House by S P Cockerell in Indian style was the inspiration for Brighton Pavilion.
Location: Map 6:P10. OS Ref SP183 324. 2 miles west of Moreton-in-Marsh on the A44 opposite entrance to Batsford Arboretum.
Contact: Dr E Peake
Tel: 01386 700444
E-mail: enquiries@sezincote.co.uk
Open: Garden: Thus, Fris & BH Mons, 2-6pm except Dec. House: As above May-Sep. Teas in Orangery when house open.
Admission: House: Adult £10.00 (guided tour). Garden: Adult £5.00, Child £1.50 (under 5yrs Free). Groups welcomed weekdays, please contact for details.
Key facts: ⓘ Please see our website for up to date events and special openings.
🔄 For full information for disabled visitors please email enquiries@sezincote.co.uk.
📷 🎥 Obligatory. 🐕 Except assistance dogs.
🏛 Weddings. ❄ ⚰

ABLINGTON MANOR
Bibury, Cirencester, Gloucestershire GL7 5NY
Ablington Manor is a grade I, 16th Century manor house with a 4 acre garden through which the River Coln runs. **Location:** Map 6: O12. OS Ref SP102 075. Ablington is situated off the B4425 Cirencester to Burford road.
Tel: 01285 740363 **E-mail:** prue@ablingtonmanor.com
Open: Please contact for opening times.
Admission: Please contact for admission prices.

CHEDWORTH ROMAN VILLA 🌿
Yanworth, Cheltenham, Gloucestershire GL54 3LJ
One of the best preserved Roman sites in Britain set in beautiful Cotswold countryside. **Location:** Map 6:N11. OS Ref SP05 6136.
Tel: 01242 890256 **E-mail:** chedworth@nationaltrust.org.uk
Website: www.nationaltrust.org.uk/chedworth
Open: Daily 13 Feb- 27 Nov. Café and gift shop. **Admission:** NT Members & under 5's go free. Please see website for admission rates.

HIDCOTE MANOR GARDEN 🌿
Hidcote Bartrim, Nr Chipping Campden, Gloucs GL55 6LR
One of the most delightful gardens in England, created in the early 20th Century by the great horticulturist Major Lawrence Johnston.
Location: Map 6:O10. OS Ref SP176 429. **Tel:** 01386 438333
E-mail: hidcote@nationaltrust.org.uk **Website:** www.nationaltrust.org.uk/hidcote
Open: Please see website for up to date opening and admission details.

WHITTINGTON COURT 🏠ⓕ
Cheltenham, Gloucestershire GL54 4HF
Elizabethan & Jacobean manor house with church.
Location: Map 6:N11. OS Ref SP014 206. 4m E of Cheltenham on N side of A40.
Tel: 01242 820556 **E-mail:** jstringer@whittingtoncourt.co.uk
Open: 26 Mar-10 Apr & 13-29 Aug: 2-5pm.
Admission: Adult £5.00/Child £1.00/OAP £4.00.

Sudeley Castle

Register for news and special offers at **www.hudsonsheritage.com**

GLASTONBURY ABBEY
Magdalene Street, Glastonbury BA6 9EL
www.glastonburyabbey.com

A hidden jewel in the heart of Somerset, Glastonbury Abbey is traditionally associated with the earliest days of Christianity in Britain. It is also the resting place for the legendary King Arthur. Open 364 days a year. Events held throughout the year - check out the website or follow on Twitter @glastonburyabbe.
Location: Map 2:N4. OS Ref ST499 388. 50 yds from the Market Cross, in centre of Glastonbury. M5/J23, A39, follow signs to Glastonbury; M4/J18 to Bath, A367 to Shepton Mallet and A361 to Glastonbury; M3/J8 A303 and head for Glastonbury. **Owner:** Glastonbury Abbey Estate
Tel: 01458 832267 **Fax:** 01458 836117 **E-mail:** info@glastonburyabbey.com
Open: Daily except 25 Dec. Nov-Feb 9am-4pm. Mar-May 9am-6pm. Jun-Aug 9am-8pm. Sep-Oct 9am-6pm.
Admission: Adult £7.60*, Child (5-15) £4.75, Conc £6.60*, Family (2+3) £19.60*. *Gift Aid admission price.
Key facts: ⊡ ⧄ ⊡ Summer. ⬛ Mar-Oct (groups pre-book Nov-Feb). 🅿 Pay & display car parks nearby. ⬛ Primary to University, RE, History, tailormade workshops & activities 01458 8361103. ⬛ On leads. ⬛ Except Christmas Day. ⬛

FAIRFIELD
Stogursey, Bridgwater, Somerset TA5 1PU

Elizabethan and medieval house. Occupied by the same family (Acland-Hoods and their ancestors) for over 800 years. Woodland garden. Views of Quantocks and the sea. House described in Simon Jenkins' book 'England's Thousand Best Houses'.
Location: Map 2:L4. OS Ref ST187 430. 11m W Bridgwater, 8m E Williton. From A39 Bridgwater/Minehead turn North. House 1m W Stogursey.
Tel: 01278 732251
Open: 13 Apr-30 May, 8-17 Jun Wed, Thu, Fri & BH Mon. Guided house tours at 2.30 & 3.30pm. Garden also open.
Admission: £6.00 in aid of Stogursey Church. Advisable to contact to confirm dates.
Key facts: ⓘ No inside photography. ⧄ ⬛ Obligatory. 🅿 No coach parking. ⬛ Guide dogs only.

DODINGTON HALL
Nr Nether Stowey, Bridgwater, Somerset TA5 1LF

Small Tudor manor house on the lower slopes of the Quantocks. Great Hall with oak roof. Semi-formal garden with roses and shrubs.
Location: Map 2:L4. OS Ref ST172 405. ½m from A39, 11m W of Bridgwater, 7m E of Williton. **Tel:** 01278 741400 **Open:** 4-17 Jun, 2-5pm.
Admission: Donations to Dodington Church. No coach parking.

HESTERCOMBE GARDENS ⬛ⓔ
Cheddon Fitzpaine, Taunton, Somerset TA2 8LG

Exquisite Georgian landscape garden designed by Coplestone Warre Bampfylde, Victorian terrace/shrubbery, and Edwardian Lutyens/Jekyll formal gardens.
Location: Map 2:M5. OS Ref ST241 287. 4m NE from Taunton, 1m NW of Cheddon Fitzpaine. **Tel:** 01823 413923 **E-mail:** info@hestercombe.com
Website: www.hestercombe.com **Open:** All year except Christmas Day. See website for full opening times. **Admission:** See website for admission prices.

KENTSFORD
Washford, Watchet, Somerset TA23 0JD
Location: Map 2:L4. OS Ref ST058 426.
Tel: 01984 632309 **E-mail:** wyndhamest@btconnect.com
Open: Please contact for details.
Admission: Please contact for details.

MONTACUTE HOUSE ⬛
Montacute, Somerset TA15 6XP

A glittering Elizabethan house, adorned with elegant chimneys, carved parapets and other Renaissance features. **Location:** Map 2:N5. OS Ref ST499 172.
Tel: 01935 823289 **E-mail:** montacute@nationaltrust.org.uk
Website: www.nationaltrust.org.uk/montacute-house
Open: Please see website for most up to date times and prices.

ORCHARD WYNDHAM ⬛
Williton, Taunton, Somerset TA4 4HH

English manor house. Family home for 700 years encapsulating continuous building and alteration from the 14th to the 20th Century. **Location:** Map 2:L4. OS Ref ST072 400. 1m from A39 at Williton. **Tel:** 01984 632309
E-mail: wyndhamest@btconnect.com **Website:** www.orchardwyndham.com
Open: Please telephone for details. **Admission:** Please telephone for details.

PRIOR PARK LANDSCAPE GARDEN ⬛
Ralph Allen Drive, Bath BA2 5AH

Beautiful and intimate 18th Century landscape garden created by Bath entrepreneur Ralph Allen with advice from Alexander Pope and 'Capability' Brown.
Location: Map 2:P3. OS Ref ST762 628. **Tel:** 01225 833422
E-mail: priorpark@nationaltrust.org.uk **Website:** www.nationaltrust.org.uk/prior-park **Open:** Please see website for up-to-date opening and admission details.

TYNTESFIELD ⬛
Wraxall, North Somerset BS48 1NX

Extraordinary Victorian Estate. The House is a Gothic revival extravaganza with surrounding formal gardens, kitchen garden and extensive woodland.
Location: Map 2:N2. OS Ref ST506715. **Tel:** 0844 800 4966
E-mail: tyntesfield@nationaltrust.org.uk **Website:** www.nationaltrust.org.uk/tyntesfield **Open:** Please see website for up-to-date opening and admission.

Montacute House

WILTON HOUSE 🏛Ⓕ
WILTON, SALISBURY SP2 0BJ
www.wiltonhouse.com

Wilton House has been the Earl of Pembroke's ancestral home for 460 years. Inigo Jones and John Webb rebuilt the house in the Palladian style after the 1647 fire whilst further alterations were made by James Wyatt from 1801. Recipient of the 2010 HHA/Sotheby's Restoration Award, the chief architectural features are the 17th Century state apartments (Single and Double Cube rooms), and the 19th Century cloisters. The House contains one of the finest art collections in Europe and is set in magnificent landscaped parkland featuring the Palladian Bridge. A large adventure playground provides hours of fun for younger visitors.
Location: Map 3:B4. OS Ref SU099 311. 3m W of Salisbury along the A36.
Owner: The Earl of Pembroke **Contact:** The Estate Office
Tel: 01722 746714 **Fax:** 01722 744447 **E-mail:** tourism@wiltonhouse.com
Open: House: 25-28 Mar inclusive; 30 Apr-1 Sep Sun-Thur plus BH Sats, 11.30am-5.00pm, last admission 4.30pm. *Please check website for up to date information. Grounds: 25 Mar-10 Apr; 30 Apr-18 Sep Sun-Thur plus BH Sats, 11.00am-5.30pm. Private groups at other times by arrangement.
Admission: House & Grounds*: Adult £15.00, Child (5-15) £7.75, Concession £11.75, Family £37.00 *includes admission to Dining & South Ante Rooms when open. Grounds: Adult £6.25, Child (5-15) £4.75, Concession £5.75, Family £17.50. Group Admission: Adult £12.75, Child £6.25, Concession £9.75. Guided Tour: £8.00. Exhibitions: "Cecil Beaton at Wilton". An exhibition of photographs from The Cecil Beaton Studio Archive at Sotheby's: Lord Pembroke's Classic Car Collection, in the Old Riding School.
Key facts: ⓘ Film location, equestrian events, antiques fairs, vehicle rallies. No photography in house. ⏲ Open 5 days a week during the season. ♿ WCs. 🍽 Licensed. 🍴 Licensed. 🎧 By arrangement. £8.00. French and German. 🅿 200 cars & 12 coaches. Free coach parking. Group rates (min 15), drivers' meal voucher. 📚 National Curriculum KS1/2. Sandford Award Winner 2002 & 2008. 🐕 Guide dogs only. ♿

IFORD MANOR: THE PETO GARDEN 🏛Ⓕ
Lower Westwood, Bradford-on-Avon, Wiltshire BA15 2BA
www.ifordmanor.co.uk

Unique Grade 1 Italian-style garden set on a romantic hillside above the River Frome. Designed by Edwardian architect Harold Peto, who lived at Iford from 1899-1933, the garden features terraces, colonnades, cloisters, casita, statuary, evergreen planting and magnificent rural views. Winner of the 1998 HHA/Christie's Garden of the Year Award. 2016 is year four of a five year historic replant in the rose garden and Great Terrace. **Location:** Map 2:P3. OS Ref ST800 589. 7m SE of Bath. Coaches must call in advance for directions.
Owner: Mrs E A J Cartwright-Hignett **Contact:** Mr William Cartwright-Hignett
Tel: 01225 863146 **E-mail:** info@ifordmanor.co.uk
Open: Apr 1-Sep 30: Tue-Thu, Sat, Sun & BH Mons, 2-5pm. Oct: Suns only, 2-5pm. Tearoom at weekends May-Sep, closed May 7 & 8.
Admission: Adult £5.50, Conc. £5.00. Groups (10+) welcome for exclusive use outside normal opening hours, strictly by appointment.
Key facts: ⓘ No professional photography without permission. Children under 10yrs preferred on weekdays for safety reasons. 📷 ♿ Partial. WCs. 🍽 Tearoom open at weekends 2:30-5.00pm 🎧 Subject to availability for groups booked in advance. 🅿 Limited for coaches. 🐕 On leads. ♿

LYDIARD PARK 🏛
Lydiard Tregoze, Swindon, Wiltshire SN5 3PA
www.lydiardpark.org.uk

Lydiard Park is the ancestral home of the Viscounts Bolingbroke. The Palladian house contains original family furnishings and portraits, exceptional plasterwork and rare 17th Century window. The Georgian ornamental Walled Garden has beautiful seasonal displays of flowers and unique garden features. Exceptional monuments, including the Golden Cavalier, in the church.
Location: Map 3:B1. OS Ref SU104 848. 4m W of Swindon, 1½m N M4/J16.
Owner: Swindon Borough Council **Contact:** Lydiard Park Manager
Tel: 01793 466664 **E-mail:** lydiardpark@swindon.gov.uk
Open: House & Walled Garden: Tue to Sun 11am-5pm (Feb-Nov). Tue to Sun 11am-4pm (Dec-Mar). Open BH Mons. Grounds: All day, closing at dusk.
Admission: House and Garden: Adult £6.50, Child (3-16 yrs) £3.50, Senior £6.00, Student £6.00, Family (2 Adults + 1 Child) £15.00, (2 Adults + 2 Children) £18.00, (2 Adults + 3 Children) £21.00, Under 3 yrs Free. **Key facts:** ⓘ No photography in house. 🛍 Small gift shop. 🌱 Seasonal plants available. ♿ Designated parking. WCs. 🍽 Forest Café open all year, Coach House Tearooms closed winter. 🎧 By arrangement. 🅿 Free, parking for coaches. 📚 Full programme of sessions linked to National Curriculum. 🐕 In grounds only. ♿ ♿

MOMPESSON HOUSE ✕
Cathedral Close, Salisbury, Wiltshire SP1 2EL
www.nationaltrust.org.uk

Elegant, spacious house in the Cathedral Close, built 1701. Featured in award-winning film Sense and Sensibility. Magnificent plasterwork and fine oak staircase. Good period furniture and the Turnbull collection of 18th Century drinking glasses. The delightful walled garden has a pergola and traditional herbaceous borders. Garden Tearoom serves light refreshments. For 2016, an exciting new exhibition featuring work by renowned artist and printmaker, Rena Gardiner (1929-1999).
Location: Map 3:B4. OS Ref SU142 297. On N side of Choristers' Green in Cathedral Close, near High Street Gate.
Owner: National Trust **Contact:** The House Steward
Tel: 01722 335659 **Fax:** 01722 321559 **Infoline:** 01722 420980
E-mail: mompessonhouse@nationaltrust.org.uk
Open: 12 Mar-30 Oct: Sat-Wed, 11am-5pm. Last admission 4.30pm. Open more during summer holidays. Open Good Fri and Christmas, see website for dates.
Admission: Please see website for full admission price details. Groups £5.50. Garden only: £1.00. Tearoom vouchers when arriving by public transport.
Key facts: ▣ ▧ WCs. ▦ ▣ ▣ Guide dogs only. ▣

The Peto Garden at Ilford Manor

CORSHAM COURT ▣◉
Corsham, Wiltshire SN13 0BZ
Historic collection of paintings and furniture. Extensive gardens. Tours by arrangement.
Location: Map 3:A2. OS Ref ST874 706. Sign-posted from the A4, approx. 4m W of Chippenham. **Owner:** Lord Methuen
Contact: The Curator
Tel: 01249 712214 \ 01249 701610.
E-mail: staterooms@corsham-court.co.uk **Website:** www.corsham-court.co.uk
Open: Tues, Weds, Thurs, Sat, Sun 20 Mar-30 Sept 2-5.30pm. Weekends only: 1 Oct-19 Mar 2-4.30pm (Closed Dec).
Admission: House & gardens: Adult £10.00 Child £5.00. Gardens only: Adult £5.00 Child £2.50. **Key facts:** ⓘ No photography in house. ▣ Guide books, postcards, etc at cash desk. ▧ Platform lift & WC. ▣ Max 45. If requested the owner may meet the group. Morning tours preferred. ▣ 120yds from house. Coaches may park in Church Square. Coach parties must book in advance. ▣ Available: rate negotiable. A guide will be provided. ▦ ▣

BOWOOD HOUSE & GARDENS ▣◉
Calne, Wiltshire SN11 0LZ
The House is set in one of the most beautiful parks in England. Over 2,000 acres of gardens and grounds were landscaped by 'Capability' Brown between 1762 and 1768. **Location:** Map 3:A2. OS Ref ST974 700. **Tel:** 01249 812102
E-mail: houseandgardens@bowood.org **Website:** www.bowood.org
Open: Please see website for up-to-date opening and admission details.

LACOCK ABBEY ✕
Lacock, Nr Chippenham, Wiltshire SN15 2LG
Founded in 1232 and coverted to a country house in c1540, once home to William Henry Fox Talbot. **Location:** Map 3:A2. OS Ref ST919 684. **Tel:** 01249 730459
E-mail: lacockabbey@nationaltrust.org.uk
Website: www.nationaltrust.org.uk/lacock
Open: Please see website for up-to-date opening and admission details.

LONGLEAT ▣◉
Longleat, Warminster, Wiltshire BA12 7NW
Longleat House is widely regarded as one of the best examples of high Elizabethan architecture in Britain. **Location:** Map 2:P4. OS Ref ST809 430.
Tel: 01985 844328 **E-mail:** sales@longleat.co.uk
Website: www.longleat.co.uk **Open:** Please see www.longleat.co.uk to confirm opening dates and times.

NEWHOUSE ▣◉
Redlynch, Salisbury, Wiltshire SP5 2NX
A brick, Jacobean 'Trinity' House, c1609, with two Georgian wings and a basically Georgian interior. **Location:** Map 3:B5. OS Ref SU218 214. 9m S of Salisbury between A36 & A338. **Tel:** 01725 510055
E-mail: events@newhouseestate.co.uk **Website:** www.newhouseestate.co.uk
Open: 1 Mar-7 Apr, Mon-Fri & 29 Aug: 2-5pm. **Admission:** Adult £5.00, Child £3.00, Conc. £5.00. Groups (15+): Adult £4.00, Child £3.00, Conc. £4.00.

NORRINGTON MANOR
Alvediston, Salisbury, Wiltshire SP5 5LL
Built in 1377 it has been altered and added to in every century since, with the exception of the 18th Century. **Location:** Map 3:AS. OS Ref ST966 237. Signposted to N of Berwick St John and Alvediston road (half way between the two villages). **Tel:** 01722 780 259 **Open:** By appointment in writing.
Admission: A donation to the local churches is asked for.

STOURHEAD ✕
Stourton, Nr Warminster BA12 6QD
Explore the world-famous landscape garden, experience the Grand Tour in the Palladian mansion and enjoy fresh air with a walk in the woods or on the chalkdowns. **Location:** Map 2:P4. OS Ref ST776 340. At Stourton off the B3092, 3m NW of A303 (Mere), 8m S of A361 (Frome). **Tel:** 01747 841152 **E-mail:** stourhead@nationaltrust.org.uk **Website:** www.nationaltrust.org.uk
Open: Please call us for opening times and admission prices.

ANTONY HOUSE & GARDEN ⚘
Torpoint, Cornwall PL11 2QA
Tel: 01752 812191 **E-mail:** antony@nationaltrust.org.uk

CHYSAUSTER ANCIENT VILLAGE ⌗
Nr Newmill, Penzance, Cornwall TR20 8XA
Tel: 07831 757934 **E-mail:** customers@english-heritage.org.uk

COTEHELE ⚘
Saint Dominick, Saltash, Cornwall PL12 6TA
Tel: 01579 351346 **E-mail:** cothele@nationaltrust.org.uk

LAUNCESTON CASTLE ⌗
Castle Lodge, Launceston, Cornwall PL15 7DR
Tel: 01566 772365 **E-mail:** customers@english-heritage.org.uk

LAWRENCE HOUSE MUSEUM ⚘
9 Castle Street, Launceston, Cornwall PL15 8BA
Tel: 01566 773277 **E-mail:** lawrencehousemuseum@yahoo.co.uk

MOUNT EDGCUMBE HOUSE & COUNTRY PARK
Cremyll, Torpoint, Cornwall PL10 1HZ
Tel: 01752 822236

PENDENNIS CASTLE ⌗
Falmouth, Cornwall TR11 4LP
Tel: 01326 316594 **E-mail:** pendennis.castle@english-heritage.org.uk

PENTILLIE CASTLE & ESTATE
Paynters Cross, St Mellion, Saltash, Cornwall PL12 6QD
Tel: 01579 350044 **E-mail:** contact@pentillie.co.uk

ST MAWES CASTLE ⌗
St Mawes, Cornwall TR2 5DE
Tel: 01326 270526 **E-mail:** stmawes.castle@english-heritage.org.uk

THE LOST GARDENS OF HELIGAN
Pentewan, St Austall, Cornwall PL26 6EN
Tel: 01726 845100 **E-mail:** info@heligan.com

TREBAH GARDEN ▥
Mawnan Smith, Nr Falmouth, Cornwall TR11 5JZ
Tel: 01326 252200 **E-mail:** mail@trebah-garden.co.uk

TRELISSICK GARDEN ⚘
Feock, Truro, Cornwall TR3 6QL
Tel: 01872 862090 **E-mail:** trelissick@nationaltrust.org.uk

TRERICE ⚘
Kestle Mill, Nr Newquay, Cornwall TR8 4PG
Tel: 01637 875404 **E-mail:** trerice@

ARLINGTON COURT ⚘
Nr Barnstaple, North Devon EX31 4LP
Tel: 01271 850296 **E-mail:** arlingtoncourt@nationaltrust.org.uk

BERRY POMEROY CASTLE ⌗
Totnes, Devon TQ9 6LJ
Tel: 01803 866618 **E-mail:** customers@english-heritage.org.uk

BUCKLAND ABBEY ⚘
The National Trust, Yelverton, Devon PL20 6EY
Tel: 01822 853607 **E-mail:** bucklandabbey@nationaltrust.org.uk

CHAMBERCOMBE MANOR ▥®
Ilfracombe, Devon EX34 9RJ
Tel: 01271 862624

CLOVELLY
Clovelly, Nr Bideford, N Devon EX39 5TA
Tel: 01237 431781 **E-mail:** visitorcentre@

COLETON FISHACRE ⚘
Brownstone Road, Kingswear, Dartmouth TQ6 0EQ
Tel: 01803 842382 **E-mail:** coletonfishacre@nationaltrust.org.uk

COMPTON CASTLE ⚘
Marldon, Paighton TQ3 1TA
Tel: 01803 843235 **E-mail:** compton@nationaltrust.org.uk

DARTMOUTH CASTLE ⌗
Castle Road, Dartmouth, Devon TQ6 0JN
Tel: 01803 833588 **E-mail:** dartmouth.castle@english-heritage.org.uk

DOWNES ▥
Crediton, Devon EX17 3PL
Tel: 01363 775142 **E-mail:** darren@downesestate.co.uk

KILLERTON ⚘
Broadclyst, Exeter EX5 3LE
Tel: 01392 881345 **E-mail:** killerton@nationaltrust.org.uk

KNIGHTSHAYES ⚘
Bolham, Tiverton, Devon EX16 7RQ
Tel: 01884 254665 **E-mail:** knightshayes@nationaltrust.org.uk

Dartmouth Castle

Register for news and special offers at **www.hudsonsheritage.com**

RHS GARDEN ROSEMOOR
Great Torrington, Devon EX38 8PH
Tel: 01805 624067 **E-mail:** rosemooradmin@rhs.org.uk

SALTRAM 🌿
Plympton, Plymouth, Devon PL7 1UH
Tel: 01752 333500 **E-mail:** saltram@nationaltrust.org.uk

SHILSTONE ▥
Modbury, Devon PL21 0TW
Tel: 01548830888 **E-mail:** abi@shilstonedevon.co.uk

THE GARDEN HOUSE
Buckland Monachorum, Yelverton PL20 7LQ
Tel: 01822 854769 **E-mail:** office@the gardenhouse.org.uk

TOTNES CASTLE ⌗
Castle Street, Totnes, Devon TQ9 5NU
Tel: 01803 864406 **E-mail:** customers@english-heritage.org.uk

ABBOTSBURY SUBTROPICAL GARDENS ▥ⓔ
Abbotsbury, Weymouth, Dorset DT3 4LA
Tel: 01305 871387 **E-mail:** info@abbotsbury- tourism.co.uk

CORFE CASTLE 🌿
Wareham, Dorset BH20 5EZ
Tel: 01929 477 062 **E-mail:** corfecastle@nationaltrust.org.uk

FORDE ABBEY & GARDENS ▥ⓔ
Forde Abbey, Chard, Somerset TA20 4LU
Tel: 01460 221290 **E-mail:** info@fordeabbey.co.uk

HIGHER MELCOMBE ▥
**Melcombe Bingham, Dorchester,
Dorset DT2 7PB**

PORTLAND CASTLE ⌗
Castletown, Portland, Weymouth, Dorset DT5 1AZ
Tel: 01305 820539 **E-mail:** customers@english-heritage.org.uk

BATSFORD ARBORETUM
Batsford, Moreton-in-Marsh, Gloucestershire GL56 9QB
Tel: 01386 701441 **E-mail:** arboretum@batsfordfoundation.co.uk

BERKELEY CASTLE ▥ⓔ
Berkeley Castle, Berkeley, Gloucestershire GL13 9BQ
Tel: 01453 810303 **E-mail:** info@berkeley-castle.com

BOURTON HOUSE GARDEN
Bourton-on-the-Hill, Gloucestershire GL56 9AE
Tel: 01386 700754 **E-mail:** info@bourtonhouse.com

CIRENCESTER PARK GARDENS ▥ⓔ
Cirencester, Glocestershire GL7 2BU
Tel: 01285 653135

DYRHAM PARK 🌿
Dyrham, Nr Bath, Gloucestershire SN14 8ER
Tel: 0117 937 2501 **E-mail:** dyrhampark@nationaltrust.org.uk

HIGHGROVE GARDENS
**The Garden Tours Office, The Barn, Close Farm,
Gloucestershire GL8 8PH**

KELMSCOTT MANOR ▥ⓔ
Kelmscott, Nr Lechlade, Gloucestershire GL7 3HJ
Tel: 01367 252486 **E-mail:** admin@kelmscottmanor.org.uk

PAINSWICK ROCOCO GARDEN ▥ⓔ
Painswick, Gloucestershire GL6 6TH
Tel: 01452 813204 **E-mail:** info@rococogarden.org.uk

WOODCHESTER MANSION ▥ⓔ
Stonehouse, Gloucestershire GL10 3TS
Tel: 01453 861541 **E-mail:** ray.canham@woodchestermansion.org.uk

ACTON COURT ▥ⓔ
Latteridge Road, Iton Acton, Bristol, Gloucestershire BS37 9TL
Tel: 01454 228 224 **E-mail:** info@actoncourt.com

ASSEMBLY ROOMS
Bennett Street, Bath BA1 2QH
Tel: 01225 477785 **E-mail:** costume_enquiries@bathnes.gov.uk

COTHAY MANOR & GARDENS
Greenham, Wellington, Somerset TA21 0JR
Tel: 01823 672283 **E-mail:** cothaymanor@btinternet.com

DUNSTER CASTLE 🌿
Dunster, Nr Minehead, Somerset TA24 6SL
Tel: 01643 821314 **E-mail:** dunstercastle@nationaltrust.org.uk

FARLEIGH HUNGERFORD CASTLE ⌗
Farleigh Hungerford, Bath, Somerset BA2 7RS
Tel: 01225 754026 **E-mail:** customers@english-heritage.org.uk

ROMAN BATHS
Roman Baths, Abbey Church Yard, Bath BA1 1LZ
Tel: 01225 477785 **E-mail:** romanbaths_bookings@bathnes.gov.uk

THE AMERICAN MUSEUM & GARDENS
Claverton Manor, Bath BA2 7BD
Tel: 01225 460503 **E-mail:** info@americanmuseum.org

OLD SARUM ⌗
Castle Road, Salisbury, Wiltshire SP1 3SD
Tel: 01722 335398 **E-mail:** customers@english-heritage.org.uk

OLD WARDOUR CASTLE ⌗
Nr Tisbury, Wiltshire SP3 6RR
Tel: 01747 870487 **E-mail:** customers@english-heritage.org.uk

STONEHENGE
Wiltshire SP4 7DE
Tel: 0870 333 1181 **E-mail:** customers@english-heritage.org.uk

THE MERCHANT'S HOUSE
132 High Street, Marlborough, Wiltshire SN8 1HN
Tel: 01672 511491 **E-mail:** admin@merchantshousetrust.co.uk

Woburn Abbey, Bedfordshire

Helmingham Hall, Suffolk

Bedfordshire
Cambridgeshire
Essex
Hertfordshire
Norfolk
Suffolk

East of England

Norfolk

Cambridgeshire

Suffolk

Bedford-
shire

Hertford-
shire

Essex

Ambitious medieval noblemen, agricultural reformers, great landowners and art collectors have all left their mark on the open lands of East Anglia.

New Entries for 2016:
• Bourne Mill
• Mannington Gardens

VISITOR INFORMATION

■ Owner
The Duke and Duchess of Bedford & The Trustees of the Bedford Estates

■ Address
Woburn
Bedfordshire
MK17 9WA

■ Location
Map 7:D10
OS Ref. SP965 325
Signposted from M1 J12/J13 and A4012. Easy access from A5 via Hockliffe, follow signs to Woburn village.

■ Contact
Woburn Abbey
Tel: 01525 290333
E-mail:
admissions@woburn.co.uk

■ Opening Times
Woburn Abbey, Gardens and Deer Park.
Please telephone or visit our website for details.

■ Admission
Please telephone or visit our website for details. Group rates available.

WOBURN ABBEY AND GARDENS 🏛️Ⓕ ✦
www.woburnabbey.co.uk

Explore the 28 acres of gardens and enjoy elegant horticultural designs, woodland glades, ponds and architectural features.

Set in a 3,000 acre deer park with nine free roaming species of deer, Woburn Abbey has been the home of the Russell Family for nearly 400 years, and is now home to the 15th Duke of Bedford and his family.

Visiting the house reveals centuries of the family's stories and English history over three floors including the State Rooms, gold and silver vaults and porcelain display in the crypt. The stunning art collection includes over 250 pictures by artists such as Rembrandt, Gainsborough, Reynolds, Van Dyck and even Queen Victoria.

The Abbey also houses the largest private collection of Venetian views by Canaletto (pictured). The English tradition of Afternoon Tea was reportedly popularised by Duchess Anna Maria, wife of the 7th Duke, who entertained her friends in the Abbey.

Explore the 28 acres of gardens and enjoy elegant horticultural designs, woodland glades, ponds and architectural features; much of which were the inspiration of Humphry Repton who contributed to their design. The restoration of Repton's original Pleasure Grounds from 200 years ago continues today with the rockery and Children's Garden recently recreated.

Woburn Abbey provides a magnificent backdrop for a myriad of events throughout the year, including the annual Woburn Abbey Garden Show (25th and 26th June 2016).

KEY FACTS

- ℹ️ Suitable for tv/film location, fashion shows, product launches, company 'days out'. No photography in House.
- 🏪 Gift and souvenir shop.
- 🌱 Plants available to buy throughout the main season.
- 🍽️ Conferences, exhibitions, banqueting, luncheons, dinners.
- ♿ Very limited access in the house. Good access in the gardens.
- 🍴 Licensed Tearoom. Serves food, hot and cold drinks, and afternoon tea.
- 🚶 By arrangement.
- 🅿️ Free parking.
- 📷 Please telephone for details.
- 🐕 Except assistance dogs in Gardens only.
- 🏛️ Weddings are held in the Sculpture Gallery, visit website or call for more information.

Register for news and special offers at **www.hudsonsheritage.com**

QUEEN ANNE'S SUMMERHOUSE
Shuttleworth, Old Warden, Bedfordshire SG18 9DU
www.landmarktrust.org.uk

Hidden in a pine wood on the edge of the Shuttleworth estate is this intriguing folly with high quality 18th Century brickwork. Inside is the most elegant bedsit and a staircase in which one of the turrets winds up to the roof terrace or down to the vaulted basement, now a bathroom, where the servants once prepared refreshments. Surrounded by the flora and fauna of beautiful woodland, this is a magical spot.

Location: Map 7:E10. OS Ref TL154 444.
Owner: The Landmark Trust
Tel: 01628 825925
E-mail: bookings@landmarktrust.org.uk
Open: Self-catering accommodation. Visits by appointment.
Admission: Free for visits by appointment.
Key facts: ⓘ A bedsit with kitchen, dining, sitting and sleeping on the ground floor. A spiral staircase leads down to the bathroom.

TURVEY HOUSE 🏠ⓖ
Turvey, Bedfordshire MK43 8EL
A neo-classical house set in picturesque parkland bordering the River Great Ouse. The principal rooms contain a fine collection of 18th and 19th Century English and Continental furniture, pictures, porcelain, objets d'art and books. Walled Garden.
Location: Map 7:D9. OS Ref SP939 528.
Between Bedford and Northampton on A428.
Owner: The Hanbury Family
Contact: Daniel Hanbury
Tel: 01234 881244
E-mail: danielhanbury@hotmail.com
Open: 2016 opening times are to be confirmed. Please visit the Turvey House Website www.turveyhouse.co.uk
Admission: Adult £6.00, Child £3.00.
Key facts: ⓘ No photography in house. 🖼 🎦 Obligatory.
🅿 Ample for cars, none for coaches. ✉

SWISS GARDEN
Old Warden Park, Bedfordshire SG18 9EP
The Swiss Garden is a late Regency garden created between 1820 and 1835 by the third Lord Ongley and is an outstanding example of the Swiss picturesque.
Location: Map 7:E10. OS Ref TL150 447.
Tel: 01767 627927 **Website:** www.theswissgarden.org
Open: Please see website for up-to-date opening and admission details.

WREST PARK ⌗
Silsoe, Luton, Bedfordshire MK45 4HS
Take a stroll through three centuries of landscape design at Wrest Park.
Location: Map 7:E10. OS Ref 153. TL093 356.
Tel: 01525 860000 **E-mail:** customers@english-heritage.org.uk
Website: www.english-heritage.org.uk/wrest
Open: Please see website for up-to-date opening and admission details.

FANCY A WALK WITH YOUR DOG?
SEE OUR DOG FRIENDLY QUICK GUIDE SECTION AT THE BACK OF THIS BOOK

ELTON HALL ⓕ
ELTON HALL AND GARDENS, ELTON, CAMBRIDGESHIRE PE8 6SH
www.eltonhall.com

Elton Hall is a fascinating mixture of styles and has evolved as a family house since the late 15th Century. The house contains wonderful furniture, porcelain and magnificent paintings. Artists represented in the collection include Gainsborough, Constable, Reynolds and Old Masters from the early Italian Renaissance. The library is one of the largest in private ownership and contains such treasures as Henry VIII's prayer book.

The formal gardens have been restored during the last 30 years and include a Gothic Orangery, a Flower Garden with spectacular fountain, Shrub Garden and Box Walk. Billowing borders surround the lily pond, while topiary parterres and immaculately kept lawns and paths give structure to the many unusual plants.

Location: Map 7:E7. OS Ref TL091 930. Close to A1 in the village of Elton, off A605 Peterborough - Oundle Road.

Owner: Sir William Proby Bt, CBE **Contact:** Marion Bauer
Tel: 01832 280468 **E-mail:** events@eltonhall.com
Open: 2pm-5pm: May: Last May BH, Sun & Mon. Jun & Jul: Wed, Thu. Aug: Wed, Thu, Sun & BH Mon. Private groups by arrangement daily May-Sep.
Admission: House & Garden: Adult £9.50, Garden only: Adult £7.00. Accompanied children under 16 free.
Groups (minimum 20): £9.50 (organiser free).
Key facts: ⓘ No photography in house. Walled Garden Plant Centre and Tearoom. For meetings and dinners, Parkland for outdoor activities. Garden suitable. Obligatory. P At Walled Garden Plant Centre, adjacent to Elton Hall. Contact events@eltonhall.com No dogs in Hall and Formal Gardens. Guide dogs in gardens only.

ISLAND HALL 🏠
Godmanchester, Cambridgeshire PE29 2BA
www.islandhall.com

An important mid 18th Century mansion of great charm, owned and restored by an award-winning interior designer. This family home has lovely Georgian rooms, with fine period detail, and interesting possessions relating to the owners' ancestors since their first occupation of the house in 1800. A tranquil riverside setting with formal gardens and ornamental island forming part of the grounds in an area of Best Landscape. Octavia Hill wrote 'This is the loveliest, dearest old house, I never was in such a one before'.

Location: Map 7:F8. OS Ref TL244 706. Centre of Godmanchester, Post Street next to free car park. 1m S of Huntingdon, 15m NW of Cambridge A14.
Owner: Mr Christopher & Lady Linda Vane Percy **Contact:** Mr C Vane Percy
Tel: Groups 01480 459676. Individuals via Invitation to View 01206 573948.
E-mail: enquire@islandhall.com
Open: Groups by arrangement: All year round. Individuals via Invitation to View.
Admission: Groups (40+) £8.00 per person, (30+) £8.50 and Parties under 20 a minimum charge of £180.00.
Key facts: See website for more details. Homemade teas.

KIMBOLTON CASTLE
Kimbolton, Huntingdon, Cambridgeshire
PE28 0EA
www.kimbolton.cambs.sch.uk/thecastle

Vanbrugh and Hawksmoor's 18th Century adaptation of 13th Century fortified house. Katherine of Aragon's last residence. Tudor remains still visible. Courtyard by Henry Bell of Kings Lynn. Outstanding Pellegrini murals. Gatehouse by Robert Adam. Home of Earls and Dukes of Manchester, 1615-1950. Family portraits in State Rooms. Now Kimbolton School.

Location: Map 7:E8. OS Ref TL101 676. 7m NW of St Neots on B645.
Owner: Governors of Kimbolton School
Contact: Mrs N Butler
Tel: 01480 860505 **Fax:** 01480 861763
Open: 6 Mar & 6 Nov 2016, 1-4pm.
Admission: Adult £5.00, Child £2.50, OAP £4.00. Groups by arrangement throughout the year, including evenings, special rates apply.
Key facts: Unsuitable. By arrangement. P On leads. In grounds only.

HUDSONs

NOTHING BEATS STAYING IN AN HISTORIC HOUSE OR A TRADITIONAL COTTAGE ON AN HISTORIC ESTATE.

GO TO THE QUICK GUIDE SECTION AT THE BACK OF THIS BOOK TO FIND GREAT PLACES TO STAY

THE MANOR, HEMINGFORD GREY 🏠
Norman Court, High Street, Hemingford Grey, Cambridgeshire PE28 9BN
www.greenknowe.co.uk

Built about 1130 and one of the oldest continuously inhabited houses in Britain. Made famous as 'Green Knowe' by the author Lucy M. Boston. The internationally known patchwork collection sewn by Lucy Boston is also shown. Four acre garden, laid out by Lucy Boston, surrounded by moat, with topiary, old roses, award-winning irises and herbaceous borders. **Location:** Map 7:F8. OS Ref TL290 706. A14, 3m SE of Huntingdon. 12m NW of Cambridge. Access via small gate on riverside. **Owner:** Mrs D S Boston **Contact:** Diana Boston
Tel: 01480 463134 **E-mail:** diana_boston@hotmail.com
Open: House: All year to individuals or groups by prior arrangement. Also in May guided tours daily at 2pm (booking advisable). Garden: All year, daily, 11am-5pm (4pm in winter). **Admission:** House & Garden: Adult £8.00, Concessions £6.50, Child £3.00, Family £22.00. Garden only: see website.
Key facts: 🛈 No photography in house. 💷 Cash and cheque payments only. 🅿
♿ Partial. Access to hall and dining room only. Garden has some gravel areas. 🅵
Obligatory. 🅿 Cars: Disabled plus a few spaces if none in High Street. Coaches: Nearby. 📷 Particularly suitable for children. 🐕 Guide dogs only. ❄🐾🎄

PECKOVER HOUSE & GARDEN 🌿
North Brink, Wisbech, Cambridgeshire PE13 1JR
www.nationaltrust.org.uk/peckover

Peckover House is an oasis hidden away in an urban environment. A classic Georgian merchant's townhouse, it was lived in by the Peckover family for 150 years and reflects their Quaker lifestyle. The house is open over three floors, including the basement service area and our Banking Wing. The gardens are outstanding - two acres of sensory delight, complete with summerhouses, Orangery, over 60 varieties of rose and specimen trees.
Location: Map 7:G6. OS Ref TF458 097. N bank of River Nene, Wisbech B1441.
Owner: National Trust **Contact:** The Property Secretary
Tel: 01945 583463 **Fax:** 01945 587904 **E-mail:** peckover@nationaltrust.org.uk
Open: We are open on varying days throughout the year. See website or call for full opening information. **Admission:** NT members free. Groups discount: (min 15 people) book in advance with Property Secretary. See website for full admission prices. **Key facts:** 🛈 PMV available for loan in grounds. Free garden tours & Behind the Scenes tours on selected days. 📷🐾🅣♿ Partial. WCs. 🍽 Licensed.
🅵 By arrangement. 🅿 Signposted. 📷🐕 Guide dogs only.
🏠 www.nationaltrustcottages.co.uk 🏠🐾

ANGLESEY ABBEY, GARDENS & LODE MILL 🌿
Quy Road, Lode, Cambridgeshire CB25 9EJ
A passion for tradition and style inspired one man to transform a run-down country house and desolate landscape.
Location: Map 7:G9. OS Ref TL533 622. 6m NE of Cambridge on B1102, signs from A14 jct35. **Tel:** 01223 810080 **E-mail:** angleseyabbey@nationaltrust.org.uk
Website: www.nationaltrust.org.uk/angleseyabbey
Open: Please see website for up-to-date opening and admission details.

WIMPOLE ESTATE 🌿
Arrington, Royston, Cambridgeshire SG8 0BW
A unique working estate still guided by the seasons, an impressive mansion at its heart with beautiful interiors by Gibbs, Flitcroft and Soane.
Location: Map 7:F9. OS Ref 154, TL336 510. **Tel:** 01223 206000
E-mail: wimpolehall@nationaltrust.org.uk **Website:** www.nationaltrust.org.uk/wimpole-estate **Open:** Please see website for up-to-date details.

Peckover House Gardens

East of England

VISITOR INFORMATION

■ Owner
English Heritage

■ Address
Audley End House
Audley End
Saffron Walden
Essex
CB11 4JF

■ Location
Map 7:G10
OS Ref. TL525 382
1m W of Saffron Walden
on B1383, M11/J8 & J10.
Rail: Audley End 1¼ m.

■ Contact
Visitor Operations Team
Tel: 01799 522842
E-mail: customers@
english-heritage.org.uk

■ Opening Times
Please visit www.english-heritage.org.uk for opening times, admission prices and the most up-to-date information.

■ Special Events
There is an exciting events programme available throughout the year, for further details please contact the property or visit the website.

AUDLEY END ⌗
www.english-heritage.org.uk/audleyend

One of England's finest country houses, Audley End is also a mansion with a difference. Enjoy a great day out.

Experience the daily routine of a Victorian stable yard as it is brought to life. Complete with resident horses and a costumed groom, the stables experience includes an exhibition where you can find out about the workers who lived on the estate in the 1880s, the tack house and the Audley End fire engine. There is also a children's play area and Café which are ideal for family visitors.

Every great house needed an army of servants and the restored Victorian Service Wing shows a world 'below stairs' that was never intended to be seen. Immerse yourself in the past as you visit the kitchen, scullery, pantry and laundries with film projections, introductory wall displays and even original food from the era.

The cook, Mrs Crocombe, and her staff can regularly be seen trying out new recipes and going about their chores.

Audley End House is itself a magnificent house, built to entertain royalty. Among the highlights is a stunning art collection including works by Masters Holbein, Lely and Canaletto. Its pastoral parkland is designed by 'Capability' Brown and there is an impressive formal garden to discover. Don't miss the working Organic Kitchen Garden with its glasshouses and vinery growing original Victorian varieties of fruit and vegetables. Audley End also boasts Cambridge Lodge a two storey detached holiday cottage. The sitting room enjoys magnificent views of the grounds of Audley End House.

KEY FACTS

- ℹ️ Open air concerts and other events. WCs.
- 🏬 Service Yard and Coach House Shops.
- 🧑 By arrangement for groups.
- 🅿️ Coaches to book in advance. Free entry for coach drivers and tour guides.
- 🐕 Dogs on leads only.

Register for news and special offers at **www.hudsonsheritage.com**

PAYCOCKE'S HOUSE & GARDEN 🌿

www.nationaltrust.org.uk/paycockes

"One of the most attractive half-timbered houses of England" - Nikolaus Pevsner

A magnificent half-timbered Tudor wool merchant's house with a beautiful and tranquil arts-and-crafts style cottage garden. Visitors can follow the changing fortunes of the house over its five hundred year history as it went from riches to rags and discover how it was saved from demolition and restored to its former glory as one of the earliest buildings saved by the National Trust.

Thomas Paycocke was an affluent merchant whose home reflected the wealth of the wool industry in Coggeshall. The House passed to the Buxton family, descendents of Paycocke but after the decline of the wool trade it saw harder times passing through different hands and uses and by the 19th Century was used as tenements and a haulier's store and office and threatened with

dereliction. In 1904 it was bought by Noel Buxton, a descendent of the family who owned the House from the late 16th Century. He began a 20 year renovation of the building to restore it to how he thought it might have looked in 1509 when it was built. During this time it was lived in by friends and relatives of Buxton including Conrad Noel the 'red' vicar of Thaxted and composer Gustav Holst. Buxton bequeathed Paycocke's to the National Trust on his death in 1924.

The House has a charming Coffee Shop and relaxing garden. The House has recently benefited from a substantial investment in interpretation and hosts changing exhibitions of art; in 2016 this is planned to be of work from the Fry Gallery in Saffron Walden.

VISITOR INFORMATION

■ **Owner**
National Trust

■ **Address**
25 West Street
Coggeshall
Essex
C06 1NS

■ **Location**
Map 8:I11
OS Ref. TL848 225
On West Street parking available nearby or at The Grange Barn (also NT), a five minute walk away.

■ **Contact**
The Manager
Tel: 01376 561305
E-mail: paycockes@nationaltrust.org.uk

■ **Opening Times**
16 March–30 October:
Wed-Sun and BH Mon, 11am-5pm (last admission 4.30pm), Garden opens at 10.30am

■ **Admission**
Adults £5.50
Children £2.50
National Trust Members Free

Joint discount tickets available with The Grange Barn £6.50

KEY FACTS

- ℹ️
- 📷
- 🚻
- 🍴
- ☕ Cream tea, coffee and cake offer.
- 🚶
- 🅿️ At The Coggeshall Grange Barn.
- ♿
- 🐕 Guide dogs only in Garden.
- 🎪 Events through the year.

Coffee Shop

Study

BOURNE MILL ❧
BOURNE ROAD, COLCHESTER, ESSEX CO2 8RT
www.nationaltrust.org.uk/bourne-mill/

In 1591 Sir Thomas Lucas built Bourne Mill, an ornate building that served as both a genteel fishing lodge for him to entertain guests and for milling grain. In around 1640 it was converted for 'fulling' wool-cloth but after the collapse of the wool trade in Colchester in the 1840s it was converted back into a grain mill; it continued producing flour until 1935. Bourne Mill is set in tranquil grounds, next to a millpond and babbling stream. The waterwheel and cog wheels still turn and the grounds hold woodlands and wetlands and a Tudor Physic Garden, a good place for a tea or coffee by the pond. One can follow the Bourne stream to see the sites of two lower mills further down its course. **Location:** Map 8:J11. OS Ref 168:TM0062. 1 mile south of centre of Colchester, on Bourne Road, off Mersea Road (B1025) **Owner:** National Trust **Contact:** The House Manager **Tel:** 01206 549799 **E-mail:** bournemill@nationaltrust.org.uk
Open: Weds to Suns and BH Mons from 16 Mar-30 Oct, 11am-5pm, closes at 4pm in Oct.
Admission: Adults £3.75, Children £1.90, free for National Trust Members.
Key facts: ⓘ Info point. 🖻 Gift shop. 🌱 Plant sales. ⊤ Hire the Mill. 🔾 Limited access to some areas - please call. ☕ Teas, coffees, cakes and cold drinks. 🎤 Welcome talk for groups. 🅿 Limited parking; undesignated parking on surrounding streets. 🎒 Schools by appointment. 🐕 Well behaved dogs allowed on a lead in the grounds.

COPPED HALL
Crown Hill, Epping, Essex CM16 5HS
www.coppedhalltrust.org.uk

Mid 18th Century Palladian mansion under restoration. Situated on ridge overlooking landscaped park. Ancillary buildings including stables and racquets court. Former elaborate gardens being rescued from abandonment. Large 18th Century walled kitchen garden - adjacent to site of 16th Century mansion where 'A Midsummer Night's Dream' was first performed. Ideal film location.
Location: Map 7:G12. OS Ref TL433 016. 4m SW of Epping, N of M25.
Owner: The Copped Hall Trust
Contact: Alan Cox
Tel: 020 7267 1679
E-mail: coxalan1@aol.com
Open: Ticketed events and special open days. See website for dates. Private tours by appointment.
Admission: Open Days £8.00. Guided Tour Days £8.00. Gardens Only £5.00.
Key facts: 🖻 🌱 🔾 Partial. ☕ 🎤 🅿 🎒 🐕 In grounds on leads. ❋ ♨

INGATESTONE HALL 🏛ⓕ
Hall Lane, Ingatestone, Essex CM4 9NR
www.ingatestonehall.com

16th Century mansion, with 11 acres of grounds (formal garden and wild walk), built by Sir William Petre, Secretary of State to four Tudor monarchs, which has remained in his family ever since. Furniture, portraits and memorabilia accumulated over the centuries - and two Priests' hiding places.
Location: Map 7:H12. OS Ref TQ654 986. Off A12 between Brentwood & Chelmsford. From London end of Ingatetone High St., take Station Lane, cross level crossing and continue for ½ mile.
Owner/Contact: The Lord Petre
Tel/Fax: 01277 353010 **Additional Contact:** Mrs Gina Cordwell.
E-mail: house@ingatestonehall.co.uk
Open: 27 Mar-28 Sep: Wed, Suns & BH Mons, 12noon-5pm.
Admission: Adult £7.00, Child £3.00 (under 5yrs Free), Conc. £6.00. (Groups of 20+ booked in advance: Adult £6.00, Child £2.00, Conc. £5.00).
Key facts: ⓘ No photography in house. 🖻 ⊤ Capacity for receptions - 100. Capacity for dinners - 65. 🔾 Partial. WCs. ☕ 🎤 Available out of normal hours by arrangement. 🅿 Free parking. 🎒 🐕 Guide dogs only. 🏛 ♨

HATFIELD HOUSE
www.hatfield-house.co.uk

Over 400 years of culture, history and entertainment.

Hatfield House is the home of the 7th Marquess and Marchioness of Salisbury and their family. The Estate has been in the Cecil family for over 400 years. Superb examples of Jacobean craftsmanship can be seen throughout the House.

In 1611, Robert Cecil, 1st Earl of Salisbury built his fine Jacobean House adjoining the site of the Old Palace of Hatfield. The House was splendidly decorated for entertaining the Royal Court, with State Rooms rich in paintings, fine furniture and tapestries.

Superb examples of Jacobean craftsmanship can be seen throughout Hatfield House such as the Grand Staircase with its fine carving and the rare stained glass window in the private chapel. Displayed throughout the House are many historic mementos collected over the centuries by the Cecils, one of England's foremost political families.

The garden at Hatfield House dates from the early 17th Century when Robert Cecil employed John Tradescant the Elder to collect plants for his new home. Tradescant was sent to Europe where he found and brought back trees, bulbs, plants and fruit trees, which had never previously been grown in England.

In the Park, an oak tree marks the place where the young Princess Elizabeth first heard of her accession to the throne. Visitors can enjoy extensive walks in the park, following trails through the woods and along the Broadwater. The Veteran Tree Trail also provides the opportunity to learn more about our ancient oaks.

KEY FACTS

- ℹ️ No flash photography in house. Tours of Old Palace when building is not in use.
- 🏛️ Newly refurbished Stable Yard home to variety of independent retailers & Hatfield House Gift Shop.
- 🍸 Weddings, Banquets & Conferences venue & catering. Tel 01707 262055.
- ♿ All floors of House accessible via lift.
- ☕ The Coach House Restaurant. Morning coffee, afternoon tea, cakes, hot & cold lunches. Tel: 01707 262030.
- 🚶 Group tours by arrangement, please call 07107 287052.
- 🎧 Audio tours of House.
- 🅿️ Free.
- 🏫 Living History Schools programme.
- 🐕 On leads. Park only.

VISITOR INFORMATION

■ Owner
The 7th Marquess of Salisbury

■ Address
Hatfield House
Hatfield
Hertfordshire
AL9 5NQ

■ Location
Map 7:F11
OS Ref. TL237 084
21 miles north of London, M25 Jct 23, A1(M) Jct 4. Pedestrian Entrance directly opposide Hatfield Railway Station.
Bus: Nearest stop at Hatfield Station, also regular buses from surrounding towns.
Rail: Kings Cross to Hatfield 22mins. Station is opposite entrance to Park. Underground links to main line at Finsbury Park.

■ Contact
Visitors Department
Tel: 01707 287010
E-mail: visitors@hatfield-house.co.uk

■ Opening Times
House:
26 March-30 September 2016 Wed-Sun & BH 11-5pm (last admission 4pm).

Garden, Park, Farm, Shops and Restaurant:
Tues-Sun & BH 10am to 5.30pm.

■ Admission
House, Park and West Garden:
Adults   £16.00
Seniors   £15.00
Children   £8.00
Group rates available.

East Garden:
(Wednesday only) £4.00 per person.

West Garden and Park only:
Adults   £10.00
Seniors   £9.00
Children   £6.00
Group rates available.

■ Special Events
There are a number of events held throughout the year, pleasee see the website for more details.

Conference/Function

ROOM	Size	Max Cap
The Old Palace	112' x 33'	280
Riding School Conference Centre	100' x 40'	170

East of England

KNEBWORTH HOUSE 🏛ⓕ
Knebworth, Hertfordshire SG1 2AX
www.knebworthhouse.com

Home of the Lytton family since 1490, Knebworth's romantic gothic exterior hides a much earlier Tudor house. A fantastic day out for all the family. Explore the historic formal gardens with dinosaur trail, wilderness and walled garden. Adventure playground. Events programme throughout the year. Knebworth is well known for its rock concerts and as a popular TV/feature film location.

Location: Map 7:E11. Direct access off the A1(M) J7 Stevenage, SG1 2AX, 28m N of London, 15m N of M25/J23

Contact: The Estate Office

Tel: 01438 812661 **E-mail:** info@knebworthhouse.com

Open: Mar-Sep, Please check website for open dates and times. Open all year for events, corporate and social functions.

Admission: See website for current prices. Children under 3 admitted free of charge. HHA members free on non-event days. RHS Partner Garden.

Key facts: ⓘ 📷 ♿ 🚂 ♿ See Access statement online. 🐕 ⓕ Admission generally by guided tour. 🅿 Free of charge. 🎓 See Education section of Website. 🐕 In Park on leads only. ▲ ♿ ✿

BENINGTON LORDSHIP GARDENS 🏛ⓕ
Stevenage, Hertfordshire SG2 7BS

7 acre garden overlooking lakes in a timeless setting. Features include Norman keep and moat, Queen Anne manor house, James Pulham folly, formal rose garden, renowned herbaceous borders, walled vegetable garden, grass tennis court and verandah. Spectacular display of snowdrops in February. Location work welcome. **Location:** Map 7:F11. OS Ref TL296 236. In village of Benington next to the church. 4m E of Stevenage.

Owner: Mr R R A Bott **Contact:** Mr or Mrs R R A Bott **Tel:** 01438 869668

E-mail: garden@beningtonlordship.co.uk

Website: www.beningtonlordship.co.uk

Open: Snowdrops 6-28 Feb 2016 daily 12-4pm, Easter and May BH Suns & Mons 12-4pm, Chilli Festival Aug BH weekend 10-5pm (admission £7.50).

Admission: Adult £5.00, Conc £4.00, Child under 12 Free.

Key facts: ♿ Feb only. ♿ Partial. 🐕 ⓕ By arrangement. 🅿 Limited. 🐕 ✿

GORHAMBURY 🏛ⓕ
St Albans, Hertfordshire AL3 6AH

Late 18th Century house by Sir Robert Taylor. Family portraits from 15th-21st Centuries.

Location: Map 7:E11. 2m W of St Albans. Access via private drive off A4147 at St Albans. For SatNav please enter AL3 6AE for unlocked entrance to estate at Roman Theatre.

Owner: Gorhambury Estates Co Ltd

Contact: The Administrator

Tel: 01727 854051

Website: www.gorhamburyestate.co.uk

Open: May-Sep: Thurs, 2-5pm (last entry 4pm).

Admission: House: Adult £8.00, Senior £7.00, Child £5.00 including guided tour. Special groups by arrangement (Thu am preferred).

Key facts: ⓘ No photography. ♿ Partial. ⓕ Obligatory. 🅿 🐕

Knebworth House in Winter

HOLKHAM HALL ⓐⒻ
www.holkham.co.uk

A breathtaking Palladian house with an outstanding art collection, panoramic landscapes and the best beach in England.

Holkham is a special place where a stunning coastal landscape meets one of England's great agricultural estates. At the heart of this thriving, privately-owned, 25,000 acre estate stands Holkham Hall, an elegant 18th Century Palladian-style mansion, based on designs by William Kent and built by Thomas Coke, 1st Earl of Leicester. The Marble Hall, with its 50ft domed ceiling, is a spectacular entrance with stairs leading to the magnificent state rooms displaying superb collections of ancient statuary, original furniture, tapestries and paintings.

Following a major redevelopment, new visitor facilities for 2016 will include an exhibition entitled 'Field to Fork - Food and Farming on the Holkham Estate Past and Present'. The exhibition tells the story of Holkham's unique farming heritage through interactive displays and conveys the fascinating and interwoven stories of crop production, gamekeeping and conservation and how this all contributes to produce the food on your fork. There will also be a new café and gift shop to showcase the work and produce of local artisans and suppliers.

Discover the wildlife and landscape of Holkham park with walks and cycle or boat hire. To the west of the hall, visitors can enjoy the tranquillity and colourful plantings of the 18th Century walled gardens which are undergoing an extensive project to restore the six acres of gardens to their former glory. At the north entrance to the park lies Holkham village with the estate-owned inn, The Victoria, several shops and the entrance to the award-winning Holkham beach and National Nature Reserve, with its golden sands and panoramic vista.

KEY FACTS

- ℹ️ 2016 will see opening of new visitor facilities. Photography allowed. Stair climbing machine in hall offers access for most manual wheelchairs.
- 🏪 Gift shop. Local produce.
- 🍴 Hall, Lady Elizabeth Wing and grounds.
- ♿ WC in courtyard. Full access statement on Holkham website.
- ☕ Courtyard café. Licensed. Local produce.
- 🍴 Licensed. The Victoria, Holkham village.
- 🚶 Private guided tours by arrangement.
- 🅿️ Ample. Parking charge.
- 🏛️ Comprehensive education programme.
- 🐕 On leads in park. Guide dogs only in hall.
- 🛏️ Victoria Inn, Holkham village.
- 💒 Civil ceremonies and partnerships.
- ❄️ Open for events and functions outside of main visitor season.
- 🎪 Outdoor and indoor events.

HOUGHTON HALL 🏛ⓕ
HOUGHTON, KING'S LYNN, NORFOLK PE31 6UE
www.houghtonhall.com

Houghton Hall is one of the finest examples of Palladian architecture in England. Built in the 18th Century by Sir Robert Walpole, Britain's first prime minister. Original designs by James Gibbs & Colen Campbell, interior decoration by William Kent. The House has been restored to its former grandeur, containing many of its original furnishings. Award-winning 5-acre walled garden divided into themed areas.

Stunning 120 yard double-sided herbaceous borders, formal rose garden with over 150 varieties, mixed kitchen garden, fountains and statues. Unique Model Soldier Collection, over 20,000 models arranged in various battle formations. Contemporary Sculptures in the Gardens.

Location: Map 8:15. OS Ref TF792 287.
13m E of King's Lynn, 10m W of Fakenham 1½m N of A148.
Owner: The Marquess of Cholmondeley
Contact: Susan Cleaver
Tel: 01485 528569 **Fax:** 01485 528167
E-mail: info@houghtonhall.com
Open: See website www.houghtonhall.com
Admission: See website for opening times/prices/booking details. www.houghtonhall.com.
Key facts: 📷 🚻 ♿ WCs. Allocated parking near the House. 🍽 Licensed. 🍴 Licensed. ⓕ By arrangement. 🅿 🐕 On leads.

Holkham Hall

Oxburgh Hall

HINDRINGHAM HALL AND GARDENS 🏠ⓕ
Blacksmiths Lane, Hindringham, Norfolk NR21 0QA
www.hindringhamhall.org

House: Beautiful Tudor Manor House surrounded by 12th Century moat. A scheduled Ancient Monument, along with the adjacent 3 acres of fishponds. Gardens: Four acres of peaceful gardens within and without the moat surrounding the house. Working walled vegetable garden, herb parterre, daffodil walk, bluebell and cyclamen copse, stream garden, bog garden, herbaceous borders, Autumn border, Victorian nut tunnel, rose and clematis pergolas.
Location: Map 8:J4. Turn off the A148 halfway between Fakenham & Holt signposted Hindringham & follow brown signs.
Owner/Contact: Mr & Mrs Charles Tucker **Tel:** 01328 878226
E-mail: info@hindringhamhall.org **Open:** House: 5 times a year for a 2 hr guided history tour. Groups on other days by arrangement. Gardens & tearoom: Sun afternoons and Wed mornings Apr-Sep inclusive. See website for dates and times.
Admission: House: Tour £17.50 inc refreshments. Garden: Adults £6.50, Children under 15 Free. **Key facts:** 🌱 Many plants for sale from seeds & cuttings from the gardens. 🚶 No hills or steps but some gravel paths.
🍴 Teas, coffee and other beverages and cakes. 🅸 🅿 ✕ 🔲 3 detached holiday cottages within the grounds each with their own garden- sleep 2 and 4.

CASTLE RISING CASTLE
Castle Rising, King's Lynn, Norfolk PE31 6AH
www.castlerising.co.uk

Possibly the finest mid-12th Century Keep in England: it was built as a grand and elaborate palace. It was home to Queen Isabella, grandmother of the Black Prince. Still in good condition, the Keep is surrounded by massive ramparts up to 120 feet high. Picnic area, adjacent tearoom. Audio tour.
Location: Map 7:H5. OS Ref TF666 246.
Located 4m NE of King's Lynn off A149.
Owner: Lord Howard **Contact:** The Custodian
Tel: 01553 631330
Fax: 01553 631724
Open: 1 Apr-1 Nov: daily, 10am-6pm (closes at dusk if earlier in Oct). 2 Nov-31 Mar: Wed-Sun, 10am-4pm. Closed 24-26 Dec.
Admission: Adult £4.00, Child £2.50, Conc. £3.30, Family £12.00. 15% discount for groups (11+). Opening times and prices are subject to change.
Key facts: 🅸 Picnic area. 🔲 🚶 Suitable. 🔲 🅿 ✳

OXBURGH HALL 🦋
Oxborough, King's Lynn, Norfolk PE33 9PS
www.nationaltrust.org.uk/oxburgh-hall

Explore 500 years of history including hidden doors, rooftop views, a secret priest's hole and embroideries worked by Mary, Queen of Scots. The moated Hall is surrounded by 70 acres of gardens and woodland.
Location: Map 8:I6. OS Ref TF742 012.
7m SW of Swaffham on S side of Stoke Ferry road.
Owner: National Trust
Tel: 01366 328258
E-mail: oxburghhall@nationaltrust.org.uk
Open: Whole property open every day during school holidays, 11am-5pm. Open 6 days a week (excluding Thurs) from Mar-Oct, 11am-5pm. Garden, shop & tearoom open on weekends only from, Nov-mid Feb, 11am-4pm.
Admission: House & Garden: (Gift Aid in brackets) Adult £9.60 (£10.60), Child £4.80 (£5.30), Family £24.00 (£26.50). For full list of prices/group bookings please refer to website. **Key facts:** 🅸 Free garden tours daily. 🔲 Gift shop & secondhand bookshop 🔲 🔲 🚶 🔲 Light lunches, hot and cold drinks. 🅸 By arrangement. 🅿 Limited for coaches. 🔲 ✕ Assistance dogs only. 🔲 ✳ 🔲

Blickling Estate

RAVENINGHAM GARDENS ⬛ℱ
Raveningham, Norwich, Norfolk NR14 6NS
www.raveningham.com

Superb herbaceous borders, 19th Century walled kitchen garden, Victorian glasshouse, herb garden, rose garden, time garden, contemporary sculptures, Millennium lake, arboretum with newly created stumpery,14th Century church, all in a glorious parkland setting surrounding Raveningham Hall. Tearoom serving homemade cake and refreshments.

Location: Map 8:L7. OS Ref TM399 965. Between Norwich & Lowestoft off A146 then B1136.
Owner: Sir Nicholas Bacon Bt
Contact: Barbara Linsley
Tel: 01508 548480 **Fax:** 01508 548958
E-mail: barbara@raveningham.com
Open: Apr-Aug, Mon-Fri, 11am-4pm. See website for full details.
Admission: Adult £5.00, Child (under 16yrs) Free, Concessions £4.50. Groups welcome by prior arrangement.
Key facts: 🚻 ♿ Disabled toilet, gardens accessible via gravel paths. ☕ Tearoom, drinks and cakes only. 🅿 🐕 Well behaved dogs on leads welcome. ♿

SANDRINGHAM
The Estate Office, Sandringham, Norfolk PE35 6EN
Sandringham House, the Norfolk retreat of Her Majesty The Queen, is set in 60 acres of beautiful gardens. The main ground floor rooms used by The Royal Family, still maintained in the Edwardian style, are open to the public, as well as the fascinating Museum and the charming parish church.

Location: Map 7:H5. OS Ref TF695 287. 8m NE of King's Lynn on B1440 off A148. **Owner:** H M The Queen
Contact: The Public Enterprises Manager
Tel: 01485 545408 **Fax:** 01485 541571 **E-mail:** visits@sandringhamestate.co.uk
Website: www.sandringhamestate.co.uk
Open: 26 Mar-late Jul & early Aug-16 Oct.
Admission: House, Museum & Gardens, Adult £14.00, Child £7.00, Conc. £12.00. Museum & Gardens, Adult £9.00, Child £4.50, Conc. £8.00.
Key facts: ℹ No photography in house. 📷 🍴 Plant Centre. 🎫 Visitor Centre only. ♿ WCs. ☕ Licensed. 🍴 Licensed. 🎓 By arrangement. Private evening tours. 🅿 Ample. 🦮 Guide dogs only. ♿

WALSINGHAM ABBEY GROUNDS & THE SHIREHALL MUSEUM ⬛ℱ
Common Place, Walsingham, Norfolk NR22 6BP

Ruins of the medieval Augustinian Priory and place of pilgrimage. Peaceful gardens, woodland and river walks open all year, with spectacular naturalised snowdrops throughout in February. Visitor entry is at The Shirehall Museum, a preserved Georgian Courthouse, where you can discover Walsingham's unique history since 1061. **Location:** Map 8:J4. OS Ref TF934 367. 4 miles N of Fakenham, on B1105. **Owner:** Walsingham Estate
Tel: 01328 820510 **E-mail:** museum@walsinghamabbey.com
Website: www.walsinghamabbey.com
Open: Snowdrop walks: 30 Jan-6 Mar, Mon-Sun, 10am-4pm. 7 Mar: Sat & Suns, 11am-4pm. Mar weekdays, Mon-Fri 11-1pm & 2-4pm. 21 Mar-6 Nov, Mon-Sun 11am-4pm. 7 Nov to end Jan 2017, Mon-Fri, 11am-1pm & 2pm-4pm.
Admission: Adult £5.00, Child 6-16 £2.50. Under 6 free.
Key facts: ℹ Coaches please follow route marked. 📷 Gift shop. 🎫 Feb snowdrops. ♿ Partial access. 🎓 By arrangement. 🐕 Dogs on leads. ✲ ♿

BLICKLING ESTATE 🍃
Blickling, Norwich, Norfolk NR11 6NF
Built in the early 17th Century, Blickling boasts one of England's finest Jacobean houses, famed for its important book collection and spectacular 55 acre gardens.
Location: Map 8:K5. OS Ref TG176 285. See website for directions.
Tel: 01263 738030 **E-mail:** blickling@nationaltrust.org.uk **Website:** www.nationaltrust.org.uk/blickling **Open:** See website for opening times.
Admission: NT members free. See website for up-to-date admission prices.

MANNINGTON GARDENS & COUNTRYSIDE ⬛ℱ
Mannington Hall, Norwich NR11 7BB
The gardens around this medieval moated manor house feature thousands of roses, especially classic varieties. **Location:** Map 8:K5. OS Ref TG144 320.
Tel: 01263 584175 **E-mail:** admin@walpoleestate.co.uk
Website: www.manningtongardens.co.uk
Open: Please contact us for 2016 opening times and admission prices.

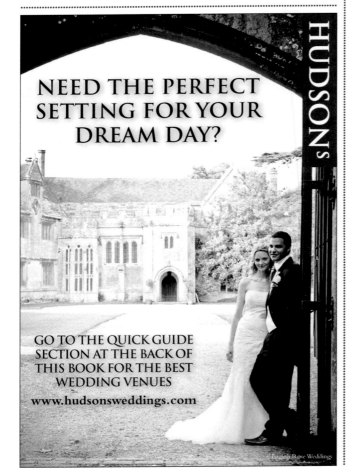

LAVENHAM: THE GUILDHALL OF CORPUS CHRISTI ❧
THE MARKET PLACE, LAVENHAM, SUDBURY CO10 9QZ
www.nationaltrust.org.uk/lavenham

Once one of the wealthiest towns in Tudor England, Lavenham oozes charm and character. The rich clothiers who thrived here left a legacy of buildings that now make up the streets of crooked timber-framed houses that are so beloved of visitors today. With its timber-framed houses and magnificent church, a visit to picturesque Lavenham is a step back in time. The 16th Century Guildhall is the ideal place to begin with its exhibitions on local history bringing to life the fascinating stories behind this remarkable village.

Once you have explored the Guildhall and sampled some homemade fare in our tearoom, why not visit some of the unique shops and galleries in the village. Lavenham truly has something for everyone.

Location: Map 8:J9. OS Ref OS155, TL915 942. 6m NNE of Sudbury. Village centre. A1141 & B1071.

Owner: National Trust **Contact:** Jane Gosling
Tel: 01787 247646
E-mail: lavenhamguildhall@nationaltrust.org.uk
Open: Guildhall, shop & tearoom: 9 Jan-6 Mar, Sat & Sun, 11am-4pm. 7 Mar-30 Oct, Mon-Sun, 11am-5pm. 3 Nov-23 Dec, Thu-Sun, 11am-4pm.
Parts of the building may be closed occasionally for community use.
Admission: Adult £6.90, Child £3.45, Family £17.25, Groups £5.25.
School parties by arrangement.
Key facts: ⬜ 🚻 ♿ Access to ground floor, shop and tearoom. Photo albums and large print guides available. ☕ Tearoom serving homemade fare, light lunches and cream teas. 🎫 By arrangement. 🅿 Free parking in Lavenham village. ⬛ ✖ ♨

FRESTON TOWER
Nr Ipswich, Suffolk IP9 1AD
www.landmarktrust.org.uk

Freston Tower is a six-storey Tudor folly that looks out over the River Orwell. There is a single room on each floor with the sitting room at the top to take advantage of the unrivalled views.

Location: Map 8:K9. OS Ref TM177 397.
Owner: The Landmark Trust
Tel: 01628 825925
E-mail: bookings@landmarktrust.org.uk
Open: Self-catering accommodation. Open Days on 8 days per year, other visits by appointment.
Admission: Free on Open Days and visits by appointment.
Key facts: ⓘ Six storeys joined by a steep spiral staircase. There is a room on each floor and a roof terrace. 🅿 ⬛ ⬛ ✖ ♨

GAINSBOROUGH'S HOUSE
46 Gainsborough St, Sudbury, Suffolk CO10 2EU
www.gainsborough.org

Gainsborough's House is the childhood home of Thomas Gainsborough RA (1727-1788) and displays an outstanding collection of his paintings, drawings and prints. A varied programme of temporary exhibitions is also shown throughout the year. The historic house dates back to the 16th Century and has an attractive walled garden. **Location:** Map 8:I10. OS Ref TL872 413. Sudbury town centre.
Owner: Gainsborough's House Society
Contact: Liz Cooper **Tel:** 01787 372958 **Fax:** 01787 376991
E-mail: mail@gainsborough.org
Open: All year: Mon-Sat, 10am-5pm; Sun 11am-5pm.
Closed: Good Fri & Christmas to New Year.
Admission: Please phone for details of admission charges or see website.
Key facts: ⓘ No photography in the Exhibition Gallery. ⬜ The new shop offers a range of themes based on the heritage of Gainsborough and the Georgian period. 🌱 A small selection of plants from Gainsborough's Garden are available for sale. ♿ Suitable WCs. 🎫 By arrangement. ⬛ ✖ Guide dogs only. ♨

HELMINGHAM HALL GARDENS ⓐⒻ
Helmingham, Stowmarket, Suffolk IP14 6EF
www.helmingham.com

Grade 1 listed gardens, redesigned by Lady Tollemache (a Chelsea Gold Medallist) set in a 400 acre deer park surrounding a moated Tudor Hall.

Visitors are enchanted by the stunning herbaceous borders, the walled kitchen garden, herb, knot, rose and wild gardens. A delicious range of local food is served in the Coach House Tearooms and the Stable Shops offer a wide range of local produce, plants, garden accessories and local crafts.

Coach bookings warmly welcomed. There are a variety of events throughout the season including The Festival of Classic & Sports Cars and Suffolk Dog Day.

Location: Map 8:K9. OS Ref TM190 578. B1077, 9m N of Ipswich, 5m S of Debenham.
Owner: The Lord & Lady Tollemache **Contact:** Events Office
Tel: 01473 890799 **E-mail:** events@helmingham.com
Open: Gardens only: 1 May-18 Sep 2016. 12-5pm Tue, Wed, Thu, Sun & all BH's.
Admission: Adults £7.00, Child (5-15yrs) £3.50. Groups (30+) £6.00.
Key facts: ⓐ ⓕ ⓣ ⓖ WCs. ⓛ Licenced. Ⓕ By arrangement. Ⓟ
ⓜ Pre-booking required. ⓗ Dogs on leads only. ⓐ ⓦ

ICKWORTH HOUSE, PARKLAND, WOODLAND & GARDENS ⚘
Horringer, Bury St Edmunds, Suffolk IP29 5QE
www.nationaltrust.org.uk/ickworth

A touch of classical Italy brought to Suffolk. Enjoy an entertaining day at this idiosyncratic and beautiful country estate. The grand Rotunda is filled with treasures collected by the Hervey family and sits in tranquil, landscaped parkland with waymarked walks and cycle routes. Discover one of the earliest Italianate gardens in England. Experience 1930's life in the newly restored Servants' basement. **Location:** Map 8:19. OS Ref TL816 611. In Horringer, 3m SW of Bury St Edmunds on W side of A143. **Owner:** The National Trust **Contact:** Property Administrator **Tel:** 01284 735270 **E-mail:** ickworth@nationaltrust.org.uk
Open: House: 5 Mar-30 Oct, Thu-Tue, 11am-4pm (Tours only 11-12 & 4- 5pm, last entry 4pm). Parkland & Gardens: Daily 9.00am-5.30pm all year. Shop & Café: Daily 10.30am-5pm. Closed Christmas Day. **Admission:** Gift Aid Admission: House, Park & Gardens £14.00, Child £7.00, Family £35.00. Groups (15+) £11.00pp. **Key facts:** ⓐ ⓕ Mar-Oct. Weekends only Nov & Dec. ⓖ Lift in main house. Mobility scooters available. West Wing drop off point. ⓦ ⓘ Ⓕ Ⓟ Car park with parking for coaches. ⓗ Assistance dogs only in Italianate gardens. All dogs on leads on the Estate. ⓑ 5 Holiday cottages. ⓐ ⓦ

Gardens at Somerleyton Hall

OTLEY HALL
Hall Lane, Otley, Suffolk IP6 9PA
www.otleyhall.co.uk

The outstanding late medieval house in East Suffolk. Stunning medieval Moated Hall (Grade I) frequently described as 'one of England's loveliest houses'. Noted for its richly carved beams, superb linenfold panelling and 16th Century wall paintings. The unique 10 acre gardens include historically accurate Tudor re-creations and voted among the top 10 gardens to visit in Great Britain.
Location: Map 8:K9. OS Ref TM207 563. 7m N of Ipswich, off the B1079.
Owner: Dr Ian & Reverend Catherine Beaumont **Contact:** Bronyia Tebenham
Tel: 01473 890264 **Fax:** 01473 890803
Facebook: facebook.com/otleyhallsuffolk. **Twitter:** @OtleyHall
E-mail: events@otleyhall.co.uk
Open: Gardens and café every Wed May-Sep. 11am-5pm. £3.00 entrance, café serving light lunches and afternoon tea. The House and grounds are available for wedding ceremonies and receptions where we offer exclusive access to the venue on the wedding day. Tours by appointment all year round. For more info please visit our website. **Admission:** By appointment only. No commercial photography.
Key facts: ⓘ 🚂 ♿ Partial. 🍴 Licensed. 🎬 By arrangement. 🅿 🐕 In grounds only and on a short lead. 🔔 ✳ ♨

SOMERLEYTON HALL & GARDENS 🏠Ⓕ
Somerleyton, Lowestoft, Suffolk NR32 5QQ
www.somerleyton.co.uk

Originally Jacobean, re-modelled in 1844 to a magnificent Anglo-Italian styled stately home. 12 acres of beautiful gardens include the famous yew hedge maze, 300ft pergola, Vulliamy tower clock, Paxton glasshouses, restored Nesfield's parterre and new white sunken garden. Please see website for special events.
Location: Map 8:M7. OS Ref TM493 977. 5m NW of Lowestoft on B1074, 7m SW of Great Yarmouth off A143. **Owner:** Lord and Lady Somerleyton.
Contact: Clare **Tel:** 08712 224244 (office) **Twitter:** @SomerleytonHall
Facebook: SomerleytonHall. **E-mail:** info@somerleyton.co.uk
Open: Times vary throughout the season - please check website for details.
Admission: Please visit website for prices & special events.
Key facts: ⓘ No photography in house. 🛍 Selling books, postcards and gifts. ✳ Kitchen garden produce available and Peter Beales roses. 🚂 Available for receptions, conferences, weddings and exclusive Private Hire of the entire Hall. ♿ Suitable. WCs. Partial disabled access. 🍴 Kitchen Garden Café. 🎬 Obligatory. 🅿 🏛 Available by pre-arrangement. 🐕 Guide dogs only. 🏨 The Fritton Arms. 🔔 ♨ ♨

FLATFORD 🌿
Bridge Cottage, East Bergholt, Suffolk CO7 6UL
In the heart of the beautiful Dedham Vale, the hamlet of Flatford is the location for some of John Constable's most famous paintings. Discover more about the work of John Constable in our exhibition, explore Bridge Cottage then relax in our riverside tearoom and gift shop. Note: No public entry inside Flatford Mill.
Location: Map 8:J10. OS Ref TM076 332. On N bank of Stour, 1m S of East Bergholt B1070.
Owner: National Trust **Contact:** Visitor Services
Tel: 01206 298260 **E-mail:** flatfordbridgecottage@nationaltrust.org.uk
Website: www.nationaltrust.org.uk/Flatford
Open: Please see website for details. Jan-Feb: weekends only. Mar: Wed-Sun. Apr-Oct: open every day. Nov-Dec: Wed-Sun (closed Christmas).
Key facts: ⓘ Parking free for NT members. 🛍 ✳ ♿ WCs. 🍴 Licensed. 🎬 🅿 Charge applies. 🐕 ♨

HAUGHLEY PARK 🏠Ⓕ
Stowmarket, Suffolk IP14 3JY
Grade 1 listed red-brick manor house of 1620 set in gardens, park and woodland. Original five-gabled east front, north wing rebuilt in Georgian style, 1820. Varied six acre gardens including walled kitchen garden. Way-marked woodland walks. 17th Century barn bookable for weddings, meetings etc.
Location: Map 8:J8. OS Ref TM005 618. Signed from J47a and J48 on A14.
Owner: Mr & Mrs Robert Williams
Contact: Barn Office
Tel: 01359 240701 **E-mail:** info@haughleypark.co.uk
Website: www.haughleypark.co.uk
Open: Garden only: May-Sep: Tues, 2-5.30pm. For Bluebell Sunday and Weird & Wonderful Wood dates, see website.
Admission: Garden: £4.00 Child under 16 Free.
Key facts: ⓘ Picnics allowed. ✳ Bluebell Sun. 🚂 ♿ WCs. 🎬 By arrangement. 🅿 Limited for coaches. 🐕 On leads. 🔔 ♨

ST EDMUNDSBURY CATHEDRAL
Angel Hill, Bury St Edmunds, Suffolk IP33 1LS
The striking Millennium Tower, completed in 2005, is the crowning glory of St Edmundsbury Cathedral. Further enhanced with the stunning vaulted ceiling in 2010, the 150ft Lantern Tower, along with new chapels, cloisters and North Transept, completes nearly fifty years of development in a style never likely to be repeated. The Cathedral is open daily for visiting, worship, events and exhibitions.
Location: Map 8:I8. OS Ref TL857 642. Bury St Edmunds town centre.
Owner: The Church of England **Contact:** Sarah Friswell
Tel: 01284 748720 **E-mail:** pr.manager@stedscathedral.org
Website: www.stedscathedral.co.uk
Open: All year: daily 8.30am-6pm.
Admission: Donations invited.
Key facts: 🛍 Open daily. 🍴 🍽 Open Mon-Sat. 🎬 11.00am. 🏛 🐕 ♨

St Edmundsbury Cathedral

CECIL HIGGINS ART GALLERY
Castle Lane, Bedford MK40 3RP
Tel: 01234 718618 E-mail: thehiggins@bedford.gov.uk

MOGGERHANGER PARK 🏠ⓔ
Park Road, Moggerhanger, Bedfordshire MK44 3RW
Tel: 01767 641007 E-mail: enquiries@moggerhangerpark.com

THE LUTON HOO WALLED GARDEN
Luton Hoo Estate, Luton, Bedfordshire LU1 3TQ
Tel: 01582 879089 E-mail: office@lhwg.org.uk

ELY CATHEDRAL
The Chapter House, The College, Ely, Cambridgeshire CB7 4DL
Tel: 01353 667735 ext.261

HILL HALL
Theydon Mount, Essex CM16 7QQ
Tel: 01799 522842

HYLANDS ESTATE
Hylands Park, London Road, Chelmsford CM2 8WQ
Tel: 01245 605500 E-mail: hylands@chelmsford.gov.uk

LAYER MARNEY TOWER 🏠ⓔ
Nr Colchester, Essex CO5 9US
Tel: 01206 330784 E-mail: info@

RHS HYDE HALL
Creephedge Lane, Rettendon, Chelmsford, Essex CM3 8ET
Tel: 0845 265 8071 E-mail: hydehall@rhs.org.uk

THE MUNNINGS ART MUSEUM 🏠ⓔ
Castle House, Castle Hill, Dedham, Essex CO7 6AZ
Tel: 01206 322127 E-mail: enquiries@munningsmuseum.org.uk

ASHRIDGE GARDENS 🏠ⓔ
Berkhamsted, Hertfordshire HP4 1NS
Tel: 01442 843491 E-mail: reception@

BACONSTHORPE CASTLE
Baconsthorpe, Norfolk
Tel: 01223 582700 E-mail: customers@english-heritage.org.uk

CASTLE ACRE PRIORY ⌗
Stocks Green, Castle Acre, King's Lynn, Norfolk PE32 2XD
Tel: 01760 755394 E-mail: customers@english-heritage.org.uk

CLIFTON HOUSE
Queen Street, King's Lynn PE30 1HT
E-mail: anna@kingstaithe.com

DRAGON HALL
115-123 King Street, Norwich, Norfolk NR1 1QE
Tel: 01603 663922 E-mail: info@dragonhall.org

FAIRHAVEN WOODLAND AND WATER GARDEN
School Road, South Walsham, Norfolk NR13 6DZ
Tel: 01603 270449 E-mail: fairhavengarden@btconnect.com

FELBRIGG HALL 🌿
Felbrigg, Norwich, Norfolk NR11 8PR
Tel: 01263 837444 E-mail: felbrigg@nationaltrust.org.uk

KIMBERLEY HALL
Wymondham, Norfolk NR18 0RT
Tel: 01603 759447 E-mail: events@kimberleyhall.co.uk

NORWICH CASTLE MUSEUM & ART GALLERY
Norwich, Norfolk NR1 3JU
Tel: 01603 493625 E-mail: museums@norfolk.gov.uk

SHERINGHAM PARK 🌿
Upper Sheringham, Norfolk NR26 8TL
Tel: 01263 820550 E-mail: sheringhampark@nationaltrust.org.uk

BELCHAMP HALL
Belchamp Walter, Sudbury, Suffolk CO10 7AT
Tel: 01787 881961

BRUISYARD HALL
Bruisyard Hall, Bruisyard, Saxmundham, Woodbridge IP17 2EJ
Tel: 01728 639000 E-mail: info@

FRAMLINGHAM CASTLE ⌗
Framlingham, Suffolk IP13 9BP
Tel: 01728 724189 E-mail: customers@english-heritage.org.uk

GLEMHAM HALL 🏠ⓔ
Little Glemham, Woodbridge, Suffolk IP13 0BT
Tel: 01728 746704 E-mail: events@glemhamhall.co.uk

KENTWELL HALL & GARDENS 🏠ⓔ
Long Melford, Suffolk CO10 9BA
Tel: 01787 310207 E-mail: info@kentwell.co.uk

LANDGUARD FORT ⌗
Felixstowe, Suffolk IP11 3TX
Tel: 01394 675900 E-mail: customers@english-heritage.org.uk

MELFORD HALL 🌿
Long Melford, Sudbury, Suffolk CO10 9AA
Tel: 01787 379228 E-mail: melford@nationaltrust.org.uk

ORFORD CASTLE ⌗
Orford, Woodbridge, Suffolk IP12 2ND
Tel: 01394 450472 E-mail: customers@english-heritage.org.uk

SUTTON HOO 🌿
Woodbridge, Suffolk IP12 3DJ
Tel: 01394 389700 E-mail: suttonhoo@nationaltrust.org.uk

THE RED HOUSE - ALDEBURGH
Golf Lane, Aldeburgh, Suffolk IP15 5PZ
Tel: 01728 452615 E-mail: enquiries@brittenpears.org

WYKEN HALL GARDENS
Stanton, Bury St Edmunds, Suffolk IP31 2DW
Tel: 01359 250287

Houghton Hall, Norfolk

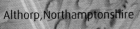
Althorp, Northamptonshire

Renishaw Hall Gardens, Derbyshire

Derbyshire
Leicestershire &
Rutland
Lincolnshire
Northamptonshire
Nottinghamshire

East Midlands

At the centre of wars, agriculture and trade routes, the East Midlands cradles castles and historic estates that vie with our national museums for the quality of their collections.

New Entries for 2016:
• Carlton Hall

Find stylish hotels with a personal welcome and good cuisine in the East Midlands.
More information on page 348.

- Barnsdale Lodge Hotel
- Biggin Hall Hotel
- The Cavendish Hotel
- The Dower House
- East Bridgford Hill
- Langar Hall
- Losehill House Hotel & Spa
- The Manners Arms
- Rushton Hall
- Washingborough Hall Hotel
- Whittlebury Hall Hotel & Spa

SIGNPOST
RECOMMENDING THE UK'S FINEST HOTELS SINCE 1935

www.signpost.co.uk

219

East Midlands - England

■ VISITOR INFORMATION

■ Owner
Welbeck Estates
Company Limited

■ Address
Welbeck Abbey
Welbeck
Worksop
Nottinghamshire
S80 3LL

■ Location
Map 7:B2
OS Ref. SK 56328 74286
From the M1 – leave the
motorway at Junction 30
and follow brown signs
for Welbeck.
From the A1 – leave the A1
at Worksop and follow
brown signs to Welbeck.

The car park entrance is
marked on the A60 with a
brown sign for The Harley
Gallery.

■ Contact
The Harley Gallery
Tel: 01909 501700
E-mail:
info@harleygallery.co.uk

■ Opening Times
Tours run during the
summer.
Please always check the
website before visiting for
full details.

■ Admission
£16.50 per person.

Welbeck Abbey

WELBECK ABBEY 🏛
www.welbeck.co.uk

Home of the Cavendish-Bentinck family since 1607.

The Welbeck Estate covers some 15,000 acres, nestled between Sherwood Forest & Clumber Park. At its heart lies Welbeck Abbey, a stately home which dates back to 1153 when it was founded as a Premonstratensian monastery.

Welbeck was acquired by Charles Cavendish, Bess of Hardwick's third son, in 1607. Over the next four centuries, the family at Welbeck would collect artworks, commission architecture and combine family names, with, unusually, three females in succession inheriting the Estate. This line of descent includes marriages with the Dukedom of Newcastle, Earldom of Oxford and the Dukedom of Portland, each bringing additional wealth, status and power to Welbeck.

Welbeck Abbey's architecture has evolved as it has passed through the generations. Visitors can see some of these additions, including the Countess of Oxford's soaring plasterwork ceiling in the Gothic Hall, and the Duchess of Portland's State Rooms

remodelled by Sir Ernest George, c1905. The State Rooms are decorated with objects and artworks from The Portland Collection; an internationally significant collection which includes one of the largest privately owned collections of British portraits. Works on show at Welbeck Abbey include pieces by Sir Peter Lely, John Wootton and Sir Joshua Reynolds.

Welbeck Abbey's State Rooms are open to the public during August for guided tours, which depart from The Harley Gallery by mini bus. Tours last approximately an hour and a half. Toilets, refreshments, shopping and exhibitions can be found at The Harley Gallery.

The Harley Foundation and Gallery was set up by Ivy, Duchess of Portland in 1977, to 'encourage creativity in all of us'. The Harley Gallery shows a programme of contemporary exhibitions, alongside displays from The Portland Collection.

KEY FACTS

- ℹ No photography.
- 🏬 The Harley Shop.
- ♿ By prior arrangement. Ground floor only.
- ☕ The Harley Café.
- 👤 Obligatory.
- 🅿 Free parking. Please park at The Harley Gallery.

The Swan Drawing Room

The Gobelin Tapestries

HADDON HALL 🏛ⓕ
ESTATE OFFICE, HADDON HALL, BAKEWELL, DERBYSHIRE DE45 1LA
www.haddonhall.co.uk

There has been a dwelling here since the 11th Century but the house we see today dates mainly from the late 14th Century with alterations in the 16th & 17th Centuries. Haddon was the home of the Vernon family until the late 16th Century when the estate passed by marriage to the Manners family, who still live in the hall today. When the Dukedom of Rutland was conferred on the Manners family in 1703 they moved to Belvoir Castle, and Haddon was left deserted for 200 years. The 9th Duke returned in the 20th Century and began restoring the hall and estate. Haddon Hall is a popular location for film and television productions, featuring as Thornfield Hall in several renditions of 'Jane Eyre', as well as appearing in 'The Princess Bride'.
Location: Map 6:P2. OS Ref SK234 663. From London 3 hrs, Sheffield ½hr, Manchester 1 hr. Haddon is on E side of A6 1½m S of Bakewell. M1/J29.
Owner: Lord Edward Manners **Contact:** Vikki Kastenbauer Stronge

Tel: 01629 812855 **E-mail:** info@haddonhall.co.uk
Open: Easter: 23 Mar-4 Apr 12-5pm. Apr: Sat, Sun & Mon. May-Sep: Open daily (except 21 & 22 May). Oct: Sat, Sun & Mon. Opening times: 12-5 pm (last admission 4 pm). Christmas: 1-18 Dec. (10.30 am-4 pm (last admission 3.30pm). Haddon Hall is closed during Jan, Feb & Nov. **Admission:** Please see website.
Key facts: ⓘ Ideal film location due to authentic & genuine architecture requiring little alteration. Suitable locations also on Estate. 🛍 Gatehouse Gift Shop, local & specially selected souvenirs, gifts, cards & plants. 🚻 ♿ WCs. Further accessibility information can also be found on our website. 🍴 Licensed. 🎟 Special tours - Minimum charges apply. 🅿 Ample. 450yds from house. Parking charge applies. 🎭 Tours of the house bring alive Haddon Hall of old. Costume room also available, very popular! 🐕 Assistance dogs only. 💒 Licensed for civil ceremonies. 💷 💍

RENISHAW HALL AND GARDENS 🏛ⓕ
RENISHAW, NR SHEFFIELD, DERBYSHIRE S21 3WB
www.renishaw-hall.co.uk

Renishaw Hall and Gardens have been home to the Sitwell family for over 400 years. Its present owner, Alexandra, welcomes you. Renishaw Hall is set in eight acres of Italianate gardens, designed by Sir George Sitwell featuring statues, yew hedges, beautiful herbaceous borders and ornamental ponds. Mature woodlands and lakes offer wonderful walks. The hall offers an intriguing insight into the Sitwell family's history, with a fascinating collection of paintings including work by John Piper. The hall & gardens are open for group and public tours, see website for details. The Gallery Café, shop and museum are in the stables. Tours of the vineyard are available throughout the season. The hall & gardens can be hired for film and photo shoots. **Location:** Map 7:A2. OS Ref SK435 786. On A6135, 3m from M1/J30, located between Sheffield and Chesterfield.
Owner: Mrs Hayward **Contact:** The Hall & Visitor Manager **Tel:** 01246 432310
Fax: 01246 430760 **E-mail:** enquiries@renishaw-hall.co.uk

Open: 23 Mar-30 Sep. Gardens open Wed-Sun & BH Mons, 10.30am-4.30pm. Hall open to public on Fris throughout season 1pm or 2.30pm & weekends in Aug, pre-booking advisable for guided tours. Hall, garden & vineyard tours available throughout year for private groups & coach tours, by appointment only.
Admission: HHA /RHS members free entry to Gardens. Guided Hall Tours £6.50. Discounts for coach/group bookings over 25 people. Parking £1.00. Non member entry Gardens Adults £6.50, Concessions £5.50, Children £3.25, under 5s free. Non member Guided Hall Tour Adults £12.75, Concessions £11.75.
Key facts: ⓘ Café, Gift Shop, WC available during garden opening. 🛍 🌱 Plant sales by Handley Rose Nursery available at the visitor centre. 🇹 ♿ Partial. WCs. 🍴 Licensed. 🎟 By arrangement throughout season for groups & on Fridays to public. 🅿 £1.00 per car for the day. 🎭 🐕 On leads. 💒 The Red Dining Room can be hired for up to 70 guests for a civil ceremony. 💷

CHATSWORTH
Bakewell, Derbyshire DE45 1PP
www.chatsworth.org

Chatsworth, home of the Duke and Duchess of Devonshire, is set in the heart of the Peak District in Derbyshire. You can explore the historic house for fascinating stories and one of Europe's most significant art collections, in the garden you'll discover water features, giant sculptures and beautiful flowers. Or come face to face with our farm animals in our working farmyard and adventure playground.

Location: Map 6:P2. OS Ref SK260 703. From London 3 hrs M1/J29, signposted via Chesterfield. 3m E of Bakewell, off B6012,10m W of Chesterfield.
Rail: Chesterfield Station, 11m. Bus: Chesterfield - Baslow 1½m.
Owner: Chatsworth House Trust **Contact:** The Booking Office
Tel: 01246 565430 **Fax:** 01246 583536
E-mail: visit@chatsworth.org
Open: The house, garden and farmyard are open daily from 19 Mar 2016. The Stables gift shops, restaurants and the Chatsworth Estate Farm Shop are open every day from 2 Jan 2016.
Admission: Visit www.chatsworth.org for details.
Key facts: ▢ ▢ ▢ ▢ ▢ ▢ ▢ ▢ ▢ ▢ ▢ ▢ ▢ ▢ ▢

Chatsworth

MELBOURNE HALL & GARDENS ▢
Melbourne, Derbyshire DE73 8EN
www.melbournehall.com

This beautiful house of history, in its picturesque poolside setting, was once the home of Victorian Prime Minister William Lamb. The fine gardens, in the French formal style, contain Robert Bakewell's intricate wrought iron arbour and a fascinating yew tunnel. Upstairs rooms available to view by appointment.
Location: Map 7:A5. OS Ref SK389 249. 8m S of Derby.
From London, exit M1/J24.
Owner: Lord & Lady Ralph Kerr **Contact:** Mrs Gill Weston
Tel: 01332 862502 **Fax:** 01332 862263 **E-mail:** melbhall@globalnet.co.uk
Open: Hall: Aug only (not first 3 Mons) 2-5pm. Last admission 4.15pm.
Gardens: 1 Apr-30 Sep: Weds, Sats, Suns, BH Mons, 1.30-5.30pm. Additional open days possible in Aug. Additional days in Aug whenever the Hall is open.
Admission: Please see website or telephone for up-to-date admission charges.
Key facts: ▢ No photography in house. ▢ Visitor centre shops, hospice shop, gift shop, antiques, jewellery, cakes, furniture restorer.
▢ Partial. WCs. ▢ Melbourne Hall Tearoom. ▢ Obligatory in house Tue-Sat.
▢ Limited. No coach parking. ▢ Guide dogs only.

CATTON HALL ▢
**Catton, Walton-On-Trent,
South Derbyshire DE12 8LN**

Catton, built in 1745, has been in the hands of the same family since 1405 and is still lived in by the Neilsons as their private home. This gives the house a unique, relaxed and friendly atmosphere, with its spacious reception rooms, comfortable bedrooms and delicious food and wine. The acres of parkland alongside the River Trent are ideal for all types of corporate and public events.
Location: Map 6:P5. OS Ref SK20 6153. Birmingham NEC 20m.
Owner/Contact: Robin & Katie Neilson
Tel: 01283 716311 **E-mail:** estateoffice@catton-hall.com
Website: www.catton-hall.com
Open: By prior arrangement all year, for corporate hospitality, shooting parties, or private groups. Guided tours at 2pm BH Mons, and all Mons in Aug.
Key facts: ▢ ▢ By arrangement. ▢ ▢ By arrangement.
▢ 4 x four posters, 5 twin, all En suite. ▢

BOLSOVER CASTLE ▢
Castle Street, Bolsover, Derbyshire S44 6PR
An enchanting and romantic spectacle, situated high on a wooded hilltop dominating the surrounding landscape. **Location:** Map 7:A2. OS Ref OS120, SK471 707. **Tel:** 01246 822844 **E-mail:** customers@english-heritage.org.uk
Website: www.english-heritage.org.uk/bolsover
Open: Please visit wesbite for opening times and the most up-to-date information.

HARDWICK ESTATE ▢
Doe Lea, Chesterfield, Derbyshire S44 5QJ
One of the most splendid houses in England. Built by the extraordinary Bess of Hardwick in the 1590's, and unaltered. Rich tapestries, plaster friezes, alabaster fireplaces, fine gardens and parkland. **Location:** Map 7:A3. OS Ref SK456 651.
See website for directions. **Tel:** 01246 850430 **Fax:** 01246 858424 **E-mail:** hardwickhall@nationaltrust.org.uk **Website:** www.nationaltrust.org.uk/hardwick
Open: Please see website or contact us for up-to-date opening and prices.

KEDLESTON HALL ▢
Kedleston Hall, Derby DE22 5JH
Kedleston Hall boasts the most complete and least altered sequence of Robert Adam interiors in England. Take in the 18th Century pleasure grounds and 800 acre park. **Location:** Map 6:P4. OS Ref SK312 403. **Tel:** 01332 842191
E-mail: kedlestonhall@nationaltrust.org.uk **Website:** www.nationaltrust.org.uk/kedleston **Open:** Please see website for up-to-date opening and admission details.

STANFORD HALL 🏛ⓕ
LUTTERWORTH, LEICESTERSHIRE LE17 6DH
www.stanfordhall.co.uk

Stanford has been the home of the Cave family, ancestors of the present owner since 1430. In the 1690s, Sir Roger Cave commissioned the Smiths of Warwick to pull down the old Manor House and build the present Hall. Throughout the house are portraits of the family and examples of furtniture and objects which they collected over the centuries. There is also a collection of Royal Stuart portraits. The Hall and Stables are set in an attractive Park on the banks of Shakespeare's Avon. There is a walled Rose Garden and an early ha-ha.

Location: Map 7:B7. OS Ref SP587 793. M1/J18 6m, M1/J19 (from/to the N only) 2m, M6 exit/access at A14/M1(N)J19 2m, A14 2m. Historic House signs.
Owner: Mr & Mrs N Fothergill **Contact:** Nick Fothergill
Tel: 01788 860250 **E-mail:** enquiries@stanfordhall.co.uk
Open: Special 3 week Easter opening – Mon 14 Mar-Sun 3 Apr 2016. Open other days in conjunction with park events and bank holidays.

See our website or telephone for details. House open any weekday or weekday evening for pre-booked groups.
Admission: House & Grounds: Adult £8.00, Child (5-15 yrs) £2.50. Private group tours (20+): Adult £8.00, Child £2.50.
Special admission prices will apply on event days.
Key facts: ⓘ Craft centre (event days and Bank Hols). Corporate days, clay pigeon shoots, filming, photography, small conferences, accommodation. Parkland, helicopter landing area, lecture room, Stables Tearoom. Caravan site. ⬜ 🍽 Lunches, dinners & wedding receptions. ♿ Partial. WCs. ♿ Stables Tearoom. 🎦 Tour time: ¾ hr in groups of approx 25.
🅿 1,000 cars and 6-8 coaches. Coach parking on gravel in front of house. 🎓
🐕 Dogs on leads only. ⓦ

BELVOIR CASTLE 🏛ⓕ
Belvoir, Grantham, Leicestershire NG32 1PE
Belvoir Castle stands high on a hill overlooking 16,000 acres of woodland and farmland. Events in the park, weddings, world famous pheasant and partridge shoot, tours of the Castle, art collection and renovated gardens.
Location: Map 7:C4. OS Ref SK820 337. A1 from London 110m. Leicester 30m. Grantham 7m. **Tel:** 01476 871001 **Website:** www.belvoircastle.co.uk
Open: Please see website for details. **Admission:** Please see website for details.

Stanford Hall

VISITOR INFORMATION

■ **Owner**
Burghley House
Preservation Trust Ltd

■ **Address**
House Manager
Stamford
Lincolnshire
PE9 3JY

■ **Location**
Map 7:E7
OS Ref. TF048 062
Burghley House is 1m SE of
Stamford. From London,
A1 2hrs. Visitors entrance
is on B1443.
Rail: London -
Peterborough 1hr (East
Coast mainline). Stamford
Station 12mins, regular
service from Peterborough.
Taxi: Direct line 01780
481481

■ **Contact**
The House Manager
Tel: 01780 752451
Fax: 01780 480125
E-mail:
burghley@burghley.co.uk

■ **Opening Times**
House & Gardens:
19 March-30 October
(closed 1-4 September).
Open daily (House closed
on Fridays), 11am-5pm,
(last admission 4.30pm).

■ **Admission**
House & Gardens
Adult	£15.50
Child (3-15 yrs)	£8.00
Conc.	£14.00
Family	£44.00

Groups (20+)
Adult	£13.50
School (up to 14 yrs)	£8.00

Gardens Only
Adult	£9.50
Child (3-15 yrs)	£6.00
Conc.	£8.00
Family	£29.00

■ **Special Events**
South Gardens Opening
19 March-10 April.
Burghley Horse Trials
1-4 September.
Battle Proms
9 July.
Flower Festival
1-9 October.

Conference/Function
ROOM	Size	Max Cap
Great Hall	70' x 30'	160
Orangery	100' x 20'	120
Summer House	17.5' x 17.5'	25

BURGHLEY HOUSE 🏠 Ⓕ ◆
www.burghley.co.uk

Burghley House, home of the Cecil family for over 400 years is one of England's Greatest Elizabethan Houses.

Burghley was built between 1555 and 1587 by William Cecil, later Lord Burghley, principal adviser and Lord High Treasurer to Queen Elizabeth. During the 17th and 18th Centuries, the House was transformed by John 5th Earl of Exeter and Brownlow, the 9th Earl; travelling to the cultural centres of Europe and employing many of the foremost craftsmen of their day. Burghley contains one of the largest private collections of Italian art, unique examples of Chinese and Japanese porcelain and superb items of 18th Century furniture. Principal artists and craftsmen of the period are to be found at Burghley: Antonio Verrio, Grinling Gibbons and Louis Laguerre all made major contributions to the beautiful interiors.

Park and Gardens
The house is set in a 300-acre deer park landscaped by 'Capability' Brown and is one of the finest examples of his work. A lake was created by him and delightful avenues of mature trees feature largely in his design. Brown also carried out alterations to the architecture of the House and added a summerhouse in the South Gardens. The park is home to a large herd of Fallow deer, established in the 16th Century. The Garden of Surprises is a modern oasis of flowing water and fountains, statues, and obelisks. The contemporary Sculpture Garden was reclaimed from 'Capability' Brown's lost lower gardens in 1994 and is dedicated to exhibiting innovative sculptures. The private gardens around the house are open from mid-March to mid-April for the display of spring bulbs.

KEY FACTS

ⓘ Suitable for a variety of events, large park, golf course, helicopter landing area, cricket pitch. No photography in house.

🏛️

🎁

🍷

♿ WCs.

☕ Licensed.

🍴 Licensed.

🎫 By Arrangement.

🎧

🅿 Ample. Free refreshments for coach drivers.

🚌 Welcome. Guide provided.

🦮 Guide dogs only.

💒 Civil Wedding Licence.

GRIMSTHORPE CASTLE, PARK AND GARDENS 🏛ⓕ
GRIMSTHORPE, BOURNE, LINCOLNSHIRE PE10 0LZ
www.grimsthorpe.co.uk

Building styles from 13th Century. North Front is Vanbrugh's last major work. State Rooms and picture galleries including tapestries, furniture and paintings. Interesting collection of thrones, fabrics and objects from the old House of Lords, associated with the family's hereditary Office of Lord Great Chamberlain. 3,000 acre park with lakes, ancient woods, walking and cycle trail, cycle hire shop. Extensive gardens including unusual ornamental kitchen garden. Groups can explore the park in their own coach by booking a one-hour, escorted park tour. Tailor-made group visits available on request including Head Gardener tour and 'How Grimsthorpe Works' day. **Location:** Map 7:D5. OS Ref TF040 230. 4m NW of Bourne on A151, 8m E of Colsterworth Junction of A1.
Owner: Grimsthorpe & Drummond Castle Trust Ltd. A Charity registered in England, Wales & Scotland SCO39364.

Contact: Ray Biggs
Tel: 01778 591205 **E-mail:** ray@grimsthorpe.co.uk
Open: Castle - Apr & May: Sun, Thu & BH Mons. Jun-Sep: Sun-Thu inclusive. 12-4pm (last admission 3pm). Park & Gardens - same days as Castle, 11am-6pm (last admission 5pm). Groups: Apr-Sep: by arrangement.
Admission: Castle, Park & Garden: Adult £10.50, Child £4.00, Conc. £9.50, Family (2+3) £25.00. Park & Gardens: Adult £5.50, Child £2.00, Conc. £4.50, Family (2+3) £13.00. Group rates on application.
Key facts: ℹ No photography in house. ▣ ⒯ Conferences (up to 40), inc catering. ♿ WCs. ▣ Light lunches 12-2.30. Afternoon tea service. Closes 5pm. Ⓕ Obligatory except Suns & BH Mons. Ⓟ Ample. ▣ ▣ Dogs on leads only. Please avoid formal gardens & adventure playground. ▣

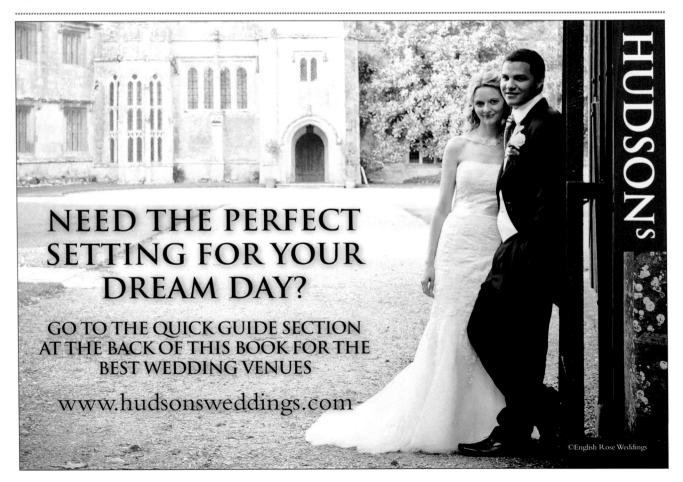

AUBOURN HALL
Lincoln LN5 9DZ
www.aubournhall.co.uk

Nine acres of lawns and floral borders surround this homely Jacobean manor house. The Rose and Prairie Gardens and the Turf Maze, Dell Garden and Stumpery all add to the fascination of this much loved family home. Guided tours are available throughout the season. Aubourn Hall Gardens is also available for Marquee Wedding Receptions, we can provide a stunning setting for your bespoke marquee wedding and other celebrations.
Location: Map 7:D3. OS Ref SK928 628. 6m SW of Lincoln. 2m SE of A46.
Owner: Mr & Mrs Christopher Nevile **Contact:** Paula Dawson, Estate Office
Tel: 01522 788224 **Fax:** 01522 788199
E-mail: estate.office@aubournhall.co.uk
Open: Garden open for Events, Groups and Garden visits from May-Sep. Please contact the Estate Office or go to our website www.aubournhall.co.uk for details.
Admission: Adults £4.50. Children Free.
Key facts: ⊞ ⊠ Partial. WCs. ▣
⊮ By arrangement. ℙ Limited for coaches. ⊠ Guide dogs only.

AYSCOUGHFEE HALL MUSEUM & GARDENS
Churchgate, Spalding, Lincolnshire PE11 2RA
www.ayscoughfee.org

Ayscoughfee Hall, a magnificent grade I listed building, was built in the 1450s. The Hall is set in five acres of extensive landscaped grounds which include amongst other features a memorial designed by Edwin Lutyens. The Museum features the history of the Hall, the people who lived there and the surrounding Fens.
Location: Map 7:F5. OS Ref TF249 223. E bank of the River Welland, 5 mins walk from Spalding town centre.
Owner: South Holland District Council **Contact:** Museum Officer
Tel: 01775 764555 **E-mail:** museum@sholland.gov.uk
Open: Hall 10.30am-4pm Wed-Sun (open on BH Mon), closed over Christmas period. Gardens 8am until dusk every day (except Christmas Day).
Admission: Free.
Key facts: ⊞ Photography allowed, apart from in temporary exhibition Gallery. ⊡ Small shop in Hall. ⊤ Email for info. ⊠ WCs, lift. ▣ Open 7 days a week. ⊮ By arrangement. ⊡ ▣ Email for info. ⊠ Guide dogs only in Hall, all dogs allowed in Gardens (on lead). ▣ Email for info. ⊞ Closed at Christmas. ▣

DODDINGTON HALL & GARDENS
Lincoln LN6 4RU
www.doddingtonhall.com

Romantic Smythson house standing today as it was built in 1595. Still a family home. Georgian interior with fascinating collection of porcelain, paintings and textiles. Five acres of wild and walled formal gardens plus kitchen garden provide colour and interest year-round. Award-winning Farm Shop, Café & Restaurant. Country Clothing, Large Bicycle Shop, Farrow & Ball and India Jane Interiors Store.
Location: Map 7:D2. OS Ref SK900 710. 5m W of Lincoln on the B1190, signposted off the A46 and B1190.
Owner: Mr & Mrs J J C Birch **Contact:** The Estate Office **Tel:** 01522 812510
E-mail: info@doddingtonhall.com **Open:** Gardens Only: 14 Feb-20 Mar & Oct, Suns only, 11am-4.30pm. Last admission 4pm. House & Gardens: 27 Mar-28 Sep, Suns, Weds & BH Mons. 12.00-4.30pm (Gardens from 11am) Last admission 4pm.
Admission: Gardens only: Adult £6.50, Child £3.50, Family £18.00 (2 adults + up to 4 children). House & Gardens: Adult £10.50, Child £4.75, Family £28.00. Group visits (guided tours for 20+) £11.00pp. **Key facts:** ⊞ Photography permitted, no flash. No stilettos. ⊡ Farm Shop - Doddington & local produce. ⊛ Seasonal. ⊤ ⊠ Virtual tour. Garden accessible - mixed surface. ▣ Open 7 days. Breakfast, lunches and teas. No booking. ⊞ Open 7 days and Fri/Sat eve. ⊮ By arrangement. ⊡ ℙ ▣ Workshops for KS1/2. ⊠ Guide dogs only. ▣ ▣ ▣ ⊞ ▣

Grimsthorpe Castle & Gardens

LINCOLN CASTLE
Castle Hill, Lincoln LN1 3AA
www.lincolncastle.com

Discover Lincoln Castle, home to one of the four surviving Magna Cartas, the attraction has undergone a £22m refurbishment. Bringing 1,000 years of history to life – right where it happened.
Location: Map 7:D2. OS Ref SK976 718. Set next to Lincoln Cathedral in the Historic Quarter of the city. Follow signs from A1 Newark or A15 North and South.
Owner: Lincolnshire County Council **Contact:** Lincoln Castle
Tel: 01522 554559 **E-mail:** lincoln_castle@lincolnshire.gov.uk
Open: Apr-Sep 10am–5pm, Oct-Mar 10am–4pm.
Admission: Adults £12.00, Conc £9.60, Child 5 & over £7.20, Under 5's free. Walk, Prison and Vault included. Entry to Castle grounds, shop and café are free.
Key facts: ℹ️ Events through the year. Some events will have seperate admission prices. 📷 Set within the Prison with a range to suit all pockets. 🍽 Tailor made packages. ♿ Accessible including part of the Medieval Wall. 🍷 Set within the Prison and licenced. 🎫 A variety of tours available. 🎧 Audio tour inlcuded in admission price. ✏️ Please contact us for education visits. 🐕 Assistance dogs only. ✻ Closed 24-26 Dec & 31 Dec-1 Jan.

FULBECK MANOR 🏚
Fulbeck, Grantham, Lincolnshire NG32 3JN
Built c1580. 400 years of Fane family portraits. Open by written appointment. Guided tours by owner approximately 1¼ hours. Tearooms at Craft Centre, 100 yards, for light lunches and teas.
Location: Map 7:D3. OS Ref SK947 505. 11m N of Grantham. 15m S of Lincoln on A607. Brown signs to Craft Centre & Tearooms and Stables.
Owner/Contact: Mr Julian Francis Fane
Tel: 01400 272231
E-mail: fane@fulbeck.co.uk
Open: By written appointment.
Admission: Adult £7.00. Groups (10+) £6.00.
Key facts: ℹ️ No photography. ♿ Partial. WCs. 🍷 🍽 🎫 Obligatory. 🅿 Ample for cars. Limited for coaches. 🐕 Except assistance dogs. ✻

MARSTON HALL 🏚
Marston, Grantham NG32 2HQ
The ancient home of the Thorold family. The building contains Norman, Plantaganet, Tudor and Georgian elements through to the modern day. Marston Hall is undergoing continuous restoration some of which may be disruptive. Please telephone in advance of intended visits.
Location: Map 7:D4. OS Ref SK893 437. 5m N of Grantham and 1m E of A1.
Owner/Contact: J R Thorold
Tel: 07812 356237
Fax: 0208 7892 857
E-mail: johnthorold@aol.com
Open: Feb 16-21, Mar 23-30, Apr 30, May 1-4 & 27-31, Aug 26-30.
Admission: Adult £4.00, Child £1.50. Groups must book.
Key facts: ℹ️ No photography.

ARABELLA AUFRERE TEMPLE
Brocklesby Park, Grimsby, Lincolnshire DN41 8PN
Garden Temple of ashlar and red brick with coupled doric columns.
Location: Map 11:E12. OS Ref TA139 112. Off A18 in Great Limber Village.
Tel: 01469 560214 **E-mail:** office@brocklesby.co.uk
Open: 1 Apr–31 Aug: viewable from permissive paths through Mausoleum Woods at all reasonable times. **Admission:** None.

BELTON HOUSE 🏚
Grantham, Lincolnshire NG32 2LS
Begun for Sir John Brownlow in 1685, Belton was certainly designed to impress and across its 300 year history, each generation of the Brownlows left their creative mark. **Location:** Map 7:D4. OS Ref SK929 395.
Tel: 01476 566116 **E-mail:** belton@nationaltrust.org.uk
Website: www.nationaltrust.org.uk/belton-house
Open: Please see website for up-to-date opening and admission details.

BROCKLESBY MAUSOLEUM
Brocklesby Park, Grimsby, Lincolnshire DN41 8PN
Family Mausoleum designed by James Wyatt and built between 1787 and 1794.
Location: Map 11:E12. OS Ref TA139 112. Off A18 in Great Limber Village.
Tel: 01469 560214 **E-mail:** office@brocklesby.co.uk
Open: By prior arrangement with Estate Office.
Admission: Modest admission charge for interior.

LEADENHAM HOUSE
Lincolnshire LN5 0PU
Late 18th Century house in park setting. **Location:** Map 7:D3. OS Ref SK949 518. Entrance on A17 Leadenham bypass (between Newark and Sleaford).
Tel: 01400 273256 **E-mail:** leadenhamhouse@googlemail.com
Open: 29-31 Mar; 4-8; 11-15; 18-22 Apr; 9-13; 16-18 May; Spring & Aug BHs.
Admission: £5.00. Please ring door bell.
Groups by prior arrangement only.

SCAWBY HALL 🏚
Brigg, N. Lincolnshire DN20 9LX
Early Jacobean manor house. WW1 Centenary exhibit.
Location: Map 11:D12. OS Ref SE966 058. **Tel:** 01652 654 272
E-mail: info@scawbyhall.com **Website:** www.scawbyhall.com
Open: 29-31 May, 1-4 Jun & 24-30 Jun, 1-2 Jul & 14-18 Jul, 21-29 Aug.
Admission: Adults: £8.00, Concessions: £6.50, Child (under 16): £4.00, Child (under 5): Free, Family: £18.50.

Burghley House

VISITOR INFORMATION

■ Owner
Mr and Mrs Robert Brudenell

■ Address
Deene Park
Corby
Northamptonshire
NN17 3EW

■ Location
Map 7:D7
OS Ref. SP950 929
6m NE of Corby off A43.
From London via M1/J15
then A43, or via A1, A14,
A43 - 2 hrs. From
Birmingham via M6, A14,
A43, 90 mins.
Rail: Corby Station 10 mins
and Kettering Station
20mins.

■ Contact
The Administrator
Tel: 01780 450278
Fax: 01780 450282
E-mail:
admin@deenepark.com

■ Opening Times
Mar: Sun 27 & BH Mon 28
Apr: Sun 24.
May: Suns 1, 8, 15, 22, 20, BH Mons 2, 30.
Jun: Suns 5, 12, 19, 26.
Jul: Suns 3, 10, 17, 24, 31.

Aug: Suns 7, 14, 21, 28, BH Mon 29.
Sep: Weds 7, 14, 21, 28.

Gardens & Tearoom:
12pm-5pm. House 2-5pm,
last adm 4pm. Tearoom
open for light lunches until
2pm and afternoon tea
from 2pm-5pm.

■ Admission
Public Open Days
House & Gardens
Adult	£9.00
Conc.	£8.00
Child (5-16yrs)	£5.00
Under 5 free with an adult.	

Gardens only:
Adult & Conc.	£6.00
Child (5-16yrs)	£3.00
Under 5 free with an adult.	

Groups (20+)
by arrangement:
Tue-Thu, Suns	£9.00
(Min 20	£180.00)
Under 5 free with an adult.	

■ Special Events
Please visit our website for
full details of our special
events.

DEENE PARK 🏛Ⓕ
www.deenepark.com

Home of the Brudenell family since 1514, this 16th Century house incorporates a medieval manor with important Georgian additions.

Seat of the 7th Earl of Cardigan who led the charge of the Light Brigade at Balaklava in 1854, today the house is the home of Mr and Mrs Robert Brudenell and their son William. The rooms on show are regularly used by their family and friends. It has grown in size as generations have made their own mark through the years, providing the visitor with an interesting yet complementary mixture of styles. There is a considerable collection of family portraits and possessions, including memorabilia from the Crimean War.

The gardens are mainly to the south and west of the house and include long borders, old-fashioned roses and specimen trees. Close to the house there is a parterre designed by David Hicks in the 1990s. The topiary teapots, inspired by the finial on the Millenium obelisk, form a fine feature as they mature.

Open parkland lies across the water from the terraced gardens providing enchanting vistas in many directions. The more energetic visitor can discover these during a rewarding walk in the tranquil surroundings. As well as the flora, there is also a diversity of bird life ranging from red kites to kingfishers and black swans to little grebes. On public open days homemade scones and cakes are available in the Old Kitchen and souvenirs can be found in the Courtyard Gift Shop. Group visits are available at between April and the end of September by prior arrangement, with booked lunch and dinners available.

KEY FACTS

ℹ️	No photography in house. No large bags.
🏬	Shop.
🌱	A vairety of plants are available for sale through May, June & July.
🍽	Including buffets, lunches and dinners by arrangement.
♿	Partial. Visitors may alight at the entrance, access to ground floor & garden.
🎫	Special rates for groups, bookings can be made in advance, menus on request.
🍴	In house dining by arrangement.
🚶	Available for group visits by arrangement (approx 90 mins).
🅿️	Unlimited for cars, space for 2 coaches 10 yds from house.
🐾	In car park only.
🎪	Conference facilities by arrangement.
🎬	Suitable for events, filming and lectures.

Register for news and special offers at **www.hudsonsheritage.com**

ALTHORP 🏛ⓕ
NORTHAMPTON NN7 4HQ
www.spencerofalthorp.com

Althorp House was built in 1508, by the Spencers, for the Spencers, and that is how it has remained for over 500 years. Today, Althorp contains one of the finest private collections of art, furniture and ceramics in the world, including numerous paintings by Rubens, Reynolds, Stubbs, Gainsborough and Van Dyck. Visitors can enjoy the extensive Grounds and the Arboretum, the new Spencer Exhibition and Café in the Stables, as well as viewing the House by guided tour.

Location: Map 7:C9. OS Ref SP682 652. From the M1, 7m from J16 and 10m from J18. Situated on A428 Northampton - Rugby. Rail: 5m from Northampton station and 14m from Rugby station. Sat nav postcode: NN7 4HQ.

Owner: The Rt Hon The 9th Earl Spencer

Contact: Althorp

Tel: 01604 770107

E-mail: mail@althorp.com

Open: House open 1st July to 31st August.
The Althorp Literary Festival will be held on Fri 1-Sun 3 Jul.
Please see website for other events in 2016.

Admission: Grounds, Exhibition and guided tour. Adults £18.50, Conc £16.00, 5-16 years £11.00, 0-4 years and HHA Friends free entry. Please call 01604 770107 or email groups@althorp.com to pre-book coach parties & group visits.

Key facts: ⓘ No indoor photography with still or video cameras. 📷 🍴 ♿ House and Estate accessible to wheelchairs, except the first floor of the House. 🍽 The Stables Café serves a wide selection of drinks, cakes, sandwiches and snacks. 🎫 Althorp is available to view by guided tour only, departing frequently throughout afternoon. 🅿 Free parking with a 5/10 minute walk to the House. Disabled parking available. 🐕 Guide dogs only. ♿ ♿

COTTESBROOKE HALL & GARDENS 🏛ⓕ
COTTESBROOKE, NORTHAMPTONSHIRE NN6 8PF
www.cottesbrooke.co.uk

Dating from 1702 the Hall's beauty is matched by the magnificence of the gardens and the excellence of the picture, furniture and porcelain collections. The Woolavington collection of sporting pictures is possibly the finest of its type in Europe and includes paintings by Stubbs, Ben Marshall and artists renowned for works of this genre. Portraits, bronzes, 18th Century English and French furniture and fine porcelain are among the treasures.

The formal gardens are continually being updated and developed by influential designers. The Wild Gardens, a short walk across the Park, are planted along the course of a stream.

Location: Map 7:B8. OS Ref SP711 739. 10m N of Northampton near Creaton on A5199 (formerly A50). Signed from Junction 1 on the A14.

Owner: Mr & Mrs A R Macdonald-Buchanan

Contact: The Administrator

Tel: 01604 505808

E-mail: welcome@cottesbrooke.co.uk

Open: May-end of Sep. May & Jun: Wed & Thu, 2-5.30pm. Jul-Sep: Thu, 2-5.30pm. Open BH Mons (May-Sep), 2-5.30pm.
The first open day is Mon 2 May 2016.

Admission: House & Gardens: Adult £8.00, Child £4.50, Conc £7.00. Gardens only: Adult £6.00, Child £4.00, Conc £5.50. Group & private bookings by arrangement.

Key facts: ⓘ No large bags or photography in house. Filming & outside events. 🍴 ♿ Partial. WCs. 🍽 🎫 Hall guided tours obligatory. 🅿 🔲 🐕 Guide dogs only. ♿

HOLDENBY HOUSE
NORTHAMPTON NN6 8DJ
www.holdenby.com

Once the largest private house in England and subsequently the palace of James I and prison of Charles I, Holdenby has recently been seen in the BBC's acclaimed adaptation of 'Great Expectations'. Its suite of elegant state rooms overlooking beautiful Grade I listed gardens and rolling countryside make it an enchanting and ever popular venue for weddings. Its combination of grandeur and intimacy make it a magnificent location for corporate dinners, parties and meetings, while the spacious grounds have accommodated many large events, from Civil War battles and concerts to The Northamptonshire Food Show. Ask about visiting Holdenby's remarkable Falconry Centre and special interest days in the Garden in addition to the normal Sunday openings.

Location: Map 7:B8. OS Ref SP693 681. M1/J15a.
7m NW of Northampton off A428 & A5199.

Owner: James Lowther
Contact: Commercial Manager
Tel: 01604 770074
Fax: 01604 770962
E-mail: office@holdenby.com
Open: Gardens and Tearoom open: Apr-Sep; Suns & BH Mons; 1-5pm.
Admission: Adult £5.00, Child £3.50, Conc. £4.50, Family (2+2) £15.00; Different prices on event days. Groups must book.
Key facts: ⓘ Children's play area. ◻ ⛾ ◻ ◻ Victorian Kitchen Tearoom serving homemade Cream Teas and cakes. ⓕ Obligatory, by arrangement. Ⓟ Limited for coaches. ◼ 7 times Sandford Award Winner. ◻ On leads. ⛾ ⛾

KELMARSH HALL AND GARDENS
KELMARSH, NORTHAMPTON NN6 9LY
www.kelmarsh.com

Built in the Palladian style to a James Gibbs design, 18th Century Kelmarsh Hall is set in beautiful gardens with views over the surrounding parkland. The former home of society decorator, Nancy Lancaster, Kelmarsh still reflects the essence of her panache and flair. The Great Hall has recently undergone sensitive re-decoration work to bring this magnificent room back to its former glory. Other preservation works include the restoration of the 18th Century Orangery. The award-winning gardens include a formal terrace, horse chestnut avenues, rose gardens and the historic walled kitchen garden. Kelmarsh Hall, gardens and parkland can be hired exclusively for weddings, corporate events and private parties.

Location: Map 7:C8. OS Ref SP736 795. 1/3 m N of A14-A508 jct 2.
Rail & Bus: Mkt Harborough.
Owner: The Kelmarsh Trust **Tel/Fax:** 01604 686543
E-mail: enquiries@kelmarsh.com
Open: Please refer to website for exact opening times. Season Apr-Sep.
Admission: House tour with garden admission: Adult £8.00, Concessions available. Gardens only: Adult £6.00, Concessions and Family tickets available. Garden season tickets available. Visit website for all pricing details.
Key facts: ◻ ⛾ ⛾ Suitable for corporate events & functions. ◻ WCs. ◻ Licensed. ⛾ ⓕ Obligatory. Ⓟ ◻ ◻ On leads. ⛾ ⛾ €

LAMPORT HALL & GARDENS 🏛ⓕ
LAMPORT HALL, NORTHAMPTONSHIRE NN6 9HD
www.lamporthall.co.uk

Lamport Hall contains an outstanding collection of furniture and paintings accumulated over 400 years by the Isham family, including works acquired on the Grand Tour in the 1670s. The west front is by John Webb and the Smiths of Warwick. Surrounded by parkland, the delightful 10-acre gardens are famous as the home of the first garden gnome, and there are fascinating examples of changes in garden design across the centuries. 2016 sees a major new exhibition in the Edwardian stable block, with the Museum of Rural Life an added attraction. Group visits to the Hall and gardens are very welcome, and for 2016 a range of themed tours are available for groups.

Location: Map 7:C8. OS Ref SP759 745. Entrance on A508. Midway between Northampton and Market Harborough, 3m S of A14 J2.
Owner: Lamport Hall Preservation Trust
Contact: Executive Director

Tel: 01604 686272 **Fax:** 01604 686224
E-mail: admin@lamporthall.co.uk
Open: Every Wed & Thu from Easter Sun to 16 Oct (guided house tours at 2.15 and 3pm; free-flow around gardens). Also open most BH Sun/Mon (free-flow). Private tours at other times by arrangement. Please check website for opening times and prices.
Admission: House & Garden: Adult £8.50, Senior £8.00, Child (11-18) £3.00. Gardens Only: Adult £5.00, Senior £4.50, Child (11-18) £2.50. Private groups: House and gardens £8.50, Gardens only £5.00. Minimum charges apply.
Key facts: ⓘ No photography in house. Available for filming. 🅣 🔍 Partial. WCs. 🍽 Licensed. ⓕ Group visits welcome by prior arrangement. 🅿 Limited for coaches. 🔲 🔳 Guide dogs only in the Hall, but all dogs welcome on leads in the gardens. 🔺 ❋ Groups only. 🔔

Rockingham Castle

ROCKINGHAM CASTLE 🏛Ⓕ
ROCKINGHAM, MARKET HARBOROUGH, LEICESTERSHIRE LE16 8TH
www.rockinghamcastle.com

Rockingham Castle stands on the edge of an escarpment giving dramatic views over five counties and the Welland Valley below. Built by William the Conqueror, the Castle was a royal residence for 450 years. In the 16th Century Henry VIII granted it to Edward Watson and for 450 years it has remained a family home. The predominantly Tudor building, within Norman walls, has architecture, furniture and works of art from practically every century. Surrounding the Castle are 18 acres of gardens following the foot print of the medieval castle. The 400 year old 'Elephant Hedge' bisects the formal terraced gardens.

Location: Map 7:D7. OS Ref SP867 913. 1m N of Corby on A6003.
9m E of Market Harborough. 14m SW of Stamford on A427.
Owner: James Saunders Watson
Contact: Laurie Prashad, Operations Manager
Tel: 01536 770240 **E-mail:** estateoffice@rockinghamcastle.com

Open: Easter Sun, 27 Mar-end of May, Suns & BH Mons. Jun-Sep, Tues, Suns & BH Mons. Open 12.00-5.00pm. Grounds open at noon. Castle opens at 1.00pm. Last entry 4.30pm.
Admission: House & Gardens: Adults £10.50, Children (5-16 years) £6.00, Family (2+2) £27.00. Grounds only: (Incl. Gardens, Salvin's Tower, Gift Shop & Licensed Tea Room) Adult or Child £6.00 (Not when special events held in grounds).
Groups: (min 20) Adults £10.50 (on open days), Adults £12.00 (private guided tour), Children (5-16 years) £5.00. School groups: (min 20) Adult £10.50, Children £5.00 (1 Adult free with 15 Children).
Groups/school parties on most days by arrangement.
Key facts: ⓘ No photography in Castle. ⬚ Ⓣ ♿ Partial. WCs. ☕ Licensed.
🍴 Licensed. Ⓕ By arrangement. ⬚ Ⓟ Limited for coaches. ⬚
🐕 On leads. ⬚ ⬚

HADDONSTONE SHOW GARDENS
The Forge House, Church Lane, East Haddon
Northampton NN6 8DB
www.haddonstone.com

See Haddonstone's classic garden ornaments and architectural stonework in the beautiful walled manor gardens including: planters, fountains, statues, bird baths, sundials and balustrades - even an orangery, gothic grotto and other follies. As featured on BBC TV. New features include a statue walk, contemporary garden and a new reception area with replicas of Soane Museum designs. Gastro pub nearby.
Location: Map 7:B8. OS Ref SP667 682. 7m NW of Northampton off A428. Located in village centre opposite school. Signposted.
Owner: Haddonstone Ltd **Contact:** Simon Scott, Marketing Director
Tel: 01604 770711 **E-mail:** info@haddonstone.co.uk
Open: Mon-Fri, 9am-5.30pm. Closed weekends, BHs and Christmas period. Check Haddonstone website for details of NGS weekend opening and Sat openings in Summer. **Admission:** Free (except NGS). Groups by appt only. No coach parties.
Key facts: ⓘ No photography without permission. ⬚ Haddonstone designs can be ordered for delivery to addresses worldwide. ♿ Almost all areas of garden accessible. Ⓕ By arrangement. Ⓟ Limited. 🐾 Except assistance dogs. ⬚ ⬚ €

SOUTHWICK HALL

Southwick, Nr Oundle, Peterborough PE8 5BL

Well off the beaten track, Southwick Hall - a family home for 700 years - offers a friendly and informal welcome. Featuring an unusual variety of family and local village artefacts and with building additions throughout its history, the house vividly illustrates the development of the English Manor House, with medieval towers, Elizabethan hall and Georgian and Victorian alterations.

Location: Map 7:E7. OS Ref TL022 921. 3m N of Oundle, 4m E of Bulwick.
Owner: Christopher Capron **Contact:** G Bucknill
Tel: 01832 274064 **E-mail:** southwickhall@hotmail.co.uk
Website: www.southwickhall.co.uk
Open: Please see Southwick Hall website for open days and times.
Admission: Please see Southwick Hall website for admission prices.
Key facts: Partial. Groups welcome. Dogs on leads in the grounds only. No dogs permitted inside.

BOUGHTON HOUSE

Kettering, Northamptonshire NN14 1BJ

Boughton is a Tudor manor house transformed into a vision of Louis XIV's Versailles. The house displays a staggering collection of fine art.
Location: Map 7:D8. OS Ref SP900 815.
Tel: 01536 515731 **E-mail:** blht@boughtonhouse.co.uk
Website: www.boughtonhouse.co.uk
Open: Please see website for up-to-date opening and admission details.

STOKE PARK PAVILIONS

Stoke Bruerne, Towcester, Northamptonshire NN12 7RZ

The two pavilions, dated c1630 and attributed to Inigo Jones, formed part of one of the first Palladian country houses built in England. They have extensive gardens and overlook parkland. **Location:** Map 7:C10. OS Ref SP740 488. 7m S of Northampton. **Tel:** 01604 862329 **Open:** Aug: daily, 3-6pm. Other times by appointment only. **Admission:** Adult £3.00, Child - free.

WAKEFIELD LODGE

Potterspury, Northamptonshire NN12 7QX

Georgian hunting lodge with deer park. **Location:** Map 7:C10. OS Ref SP739 425. 4m S of Towcester on A5. Take signs to farm shop for directions. **Tel:** 01327 811395 **Open:** House: 16 Apr-29 May: Mon-Fri (closed BHs), 12 noon-4pm. Appointments by telephone. Access walk open Apr & May. **Admission:** £5.00.

WESTON HALL

Towcester, Northamptonshire NN12 8PU

A Queen Anne Northamptonshire manor house with an interesting collection associated with the literary Sitwell family.
Location: Map 7:B10. OS Ref SP592 469. 5 miles W of Towcester.
Tel: 07710 523879 **E-mail:** george@crossovercapital.co.uk
Open: Most weekends by appointment. **Admission:** £8.00. Free on Open Days.

Gardens at Kelmarsh Hall

Haddonstone Show Gardens

CARLTON HALL

Carlton-On-Trent, Nottingham NG23 6LP

Carlton Hall is a grade II* listed building built in 1765. Typical of period with pedimented central block flanked by lower wings. Contains its original collection of fine family portraits, as well as 17th/18th Century paintings and antique continental furniture. The ornamental stable block completed in 1769 is possibly by John Carr of York.
Location: Map 7:C3. OS Ref SK799 639.
Owner/Contact: George Vere-Laurie
Tel: 07775 785344
E-mail: carltonhallnotts@gmail.com
Open: 1 Apr-30 Sep, Wed only. 2pm-5pm. 24 hour notice required for tours only. Other dates and times by appointment.
Admission: £10.00pp, inc. tour and tea.
Key facts: Saddlery shop in stable block. 24 hour notice required.

PAPPLEWICK HALL

Papplewick, Nottinghamshire NG15 8FE

A beautiful classic Georgian house, built of Mansfield stone, set in parkland, with woodland garden laid out in the 18th Century. The house is notable for its very fine plasterwork, and elegant staircase. Grade I listed.
Location: Map 7:B4. OS Ref SK548 518. Halfway between Nottingham & Mansfield, 3m E of M1/J27. A608 & A611 towards Hucknall. Then A6011 to Papplewick and B683 N for ½m.
Owner/Contact: Mr J R Godwin-Austen **Tel:** 0115 9632623
E-mail: mail@papplewickhall.co.uk
Website: www.papplewickhall.co.uk
Open: 1st, 3rd & 5th Wed in each month 2-5pm, and by appointment.
Admission: Adults: £5.00 each. Groups (10+): £4.00 per head.
Key facts: No photography. Obligatory. Limited for coaches.

CALKE ABBEY ❧
Ticknall, Derbyshire DE73 7LE
Tel: 01332 863822 **E-mail:** calkeabbey@nationaltrust.org.uk

HARDWICK OLD HALL ⊞
Doe Lea, Nr Chesterfield, Derbyshire S44 5QJ
Tel: 01246 850431 **E-mail:** customers@english-heritage.org.uk

PEVERIL CASTLE ⊞
Market Place, Castleton, Hope Valley S33 8WQ
Tel: 01433 620613 **E-mail:** customers@english-heritage.org.uk

SUDBURY HALL & MUSEUM OF CHILDHOOD ❧
Ashbourne, Derbyshire DE6 5HT
Tel: 01283 585337 **E-mail:** sudburyhall@nationaltrust.org.uk

SUTTON SCARSDALE HALL ⊞
Hall Drive, Sutton Scarsdale, Chesterfield, Derbyshire S44 5UR
Tel: 01246 822844 **E-mail:** bolsover.castle@english-heritage.org.uk

THE PAVILION GARDENS
St John's Road, Buxton, Derbyshire SK17 6XN
Tel: 01298 23114 **E-mail:** terry.crawford@highpeak.gov.uk

TISSINGTON HALL 🏠ⓔ
Ashbourne, Derbyshire DE6 1RA
Tel: 01335 352200 **E-mail:** events@tissingtonhall.co.uk

ASHBY DE LA ZOUCH CASTLE ⊞
South Street, Ashby De La Zouch LE65 1BR
Tel: 01530 413343 **E-mail:** customers@english-heritage.org.uk

DONINGTON LE HEATH MANOR HOUSE
Manor Road, Heath, Coalville, Leicestershire LE67 2FW
Tel: 01530 831 259 **E-mail:** richard.knox@leics.gov.uk

KIRBY MUXLOE CASTLE ⊞
Kirby Muxloe, Leicestershire LE9 2DH
Tel: 01162 386886 **E-mail:** customers@english-heritage.org.uk

OAKHAM CASTLE
Castle Lane (Off Market Place), Oakham, Rutland LE15 6DF
Tel: 01572 758440

QUENBY HALL
Hungarton, Leicestershire LE7 9JF
Tel: 0116 2595224 **E-mail:** enquiries@quenbyhall.co.uk

STAUNTON HAROLD HALL 🏠
Staunton Harold, Ashby de la Zouch, Leicestershire LE65 1RT
Tel: 01332 862 599 **E-mail:** rowan@stauntonharoldhall.co.uk

EASTON WALLED GARDENS 🏠ⓔ
Easton, Grantham, Lincolnshire NG33 5AP
Tel: 01476 530063 **E-mail:** info@eastonwalledgardens.co.uk

ELSHAM HALL GARDENS & COUNTRY PARK 🏠ⓔ
Elsham Hall, Brigg, Lincolnshire DN20 0QZ
Tel: 01652 688698 **E-mail:** enquiries@elshamhall.co.uk

GAINSBOROUGH OLD HALL
Parnell Street, Gainsborough, Lincolnshire DN21 2NB
Tel: 01427 677348 / **E-mail:** gainsboroughholdhall@lincolnshire.gov.uk

GUNBY HALL ❧
Gunby Hall, Spilsby, Lincolnshire PE23 5SL
Tel: 01754 890102 **E-mail:** gunbyhall@nationaltrust.org.uk

NORMANBY HALL COUNTRY PARK
Normanby, Scunthorpe DN15 9HU
Tel: 01724 720588 **E-mail:** normanby.hall@northlincs.gov.uk

TATTERSHALL CASTLE ❧
Sleaford Road, Tattershall, Lincolnshire LN4 4LR
Tel: 01526 342543 **E-mail:** tattershallcastle@nationaltrust.org.uk

WOOLSTHORPE MANOR ❧
Water Lane, Woolsthorpe by Colsterworth NG33 5PD
Tel: 01476 862823 **E-mail:** woolsthorpemanor@nationaltrust.org.uk

78 DERNGATE: THE CHARLES RENNIE MACKINTOSH HOUSE & GALLERIES
Tel: 01604 603407 **E-mail:** info@78derngate.org.uk

CANONS ASHBY ❧
Canons Ashby, Daventry, Northamptonshire NN11 3SD
Tel: 01327 861900 **E-mail:** canonsashby@nationaltrust.org.uk

COTON MANOR GARDEN
Nr Guilsborough, Northamptonshire NN6 8RQ
Tel: 01604 740219 **E-mail:** pasleytyler@cotonmanor.co.uk

KIRBY HALL ⊞
Deene, Corby, Northamptonshire NN17 5EN
Tel: 01536 203230 **E-mail:** customers@english-heritage.org.uk

RUSHTON TRIANGULAR LODGE ⊞
Rushton, Kettering, Northamptonshire NN14 1RP
Tel: 01536 710761

HODSOCK PRIORY GARDENS 🏠ⓔ
Blyth, Nr Worksop, Blyth S81 0TY
Tel: 01909 591204

HOLME PIERREPONT HALL 🏠ⓔ
Holme Pierrepont, Nr Nottingham NG12 2LD
Tel: 0115 933 2371

KELHAM HALL 🏠ⓔ
Newark, Nottinghamshire NG23 5QX
Tel: 01636 650000 **E-mail:** info@kelham-hall.com

MR STRAW'S HOUSE ❧
5-7 Blyth Grove, Worksop S81 0JG
Tel: 01909 482380 **E-mail:** mrstrawshouse@nationaltrust.org.uk

NEWSTEAD ABBEY
Ravenshead, Nottingham, Nottinghamshire NG15 8GE
Tel: 01623 455900 **E-mail:** sallyl@newsteadabbey.org.uk

NOTTINGHAM CASTLE AND ART GALLERY
Lenton Road, Nottingham NG1 6EZ
Tel: 0115 876 1400 **E-mail:** nottingham.castle@nottinghamcity.gov.uk

WOLLATON HALL AND PARK
Wollaton Park, Nottingham, Unitary Authority NG8 2AE
Tel: 0115 915 3900 **E-mail:** maria.narducci@nottinghamcity.gov.uk

Lincoln Castle, Lincolnshire

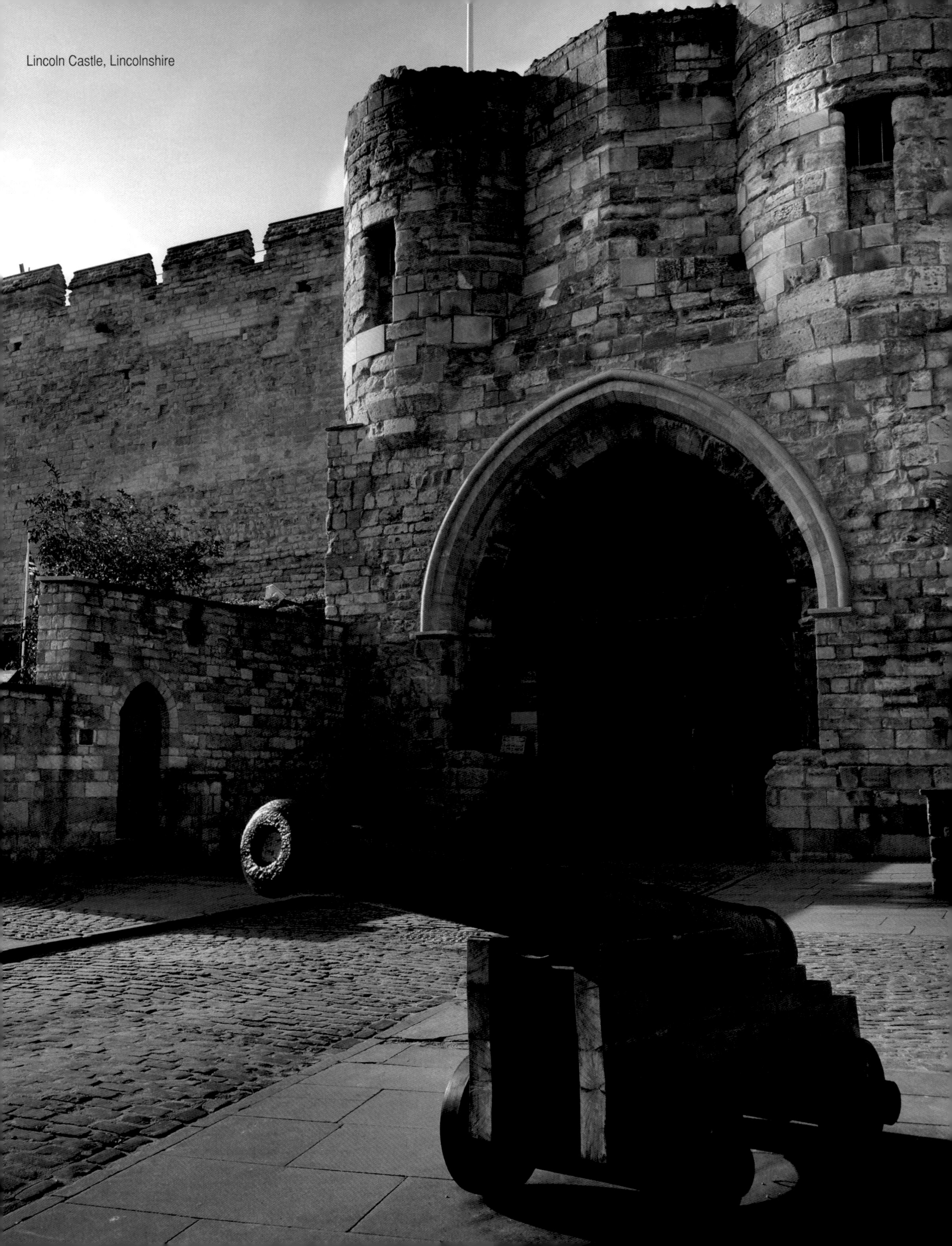

Lord Leycester Hospital, Warwickshire
©VISITBRITAIN/LEE BEEL

Winterbourne House & Garden, Birmingham

Herefordshire
Shropshire
Staffordshire
Warwickshire
West Midlands
Worcestershire

Heart of England

Truly the centre of the country, geographically and historically, the Heart of England boasts historic places large and small within easy reach of Birmingham.

New Entries for 2016:
- Aston Hall
- Birmingham Museum & Art Gallery
- Blakesley Hall
- Museum of the Jewellery Quarter
- Sarehole Mill
- Sinai Park House
- Soho House

EASTNOR CASTLE Ⓜ Ⓕ ◆
NR LEDBURY, HEREFORDSHIRE HR8 1RL
www.eastnorcastle.com

Eastnor Castle was built 200 years ago by John, 1st Earl Somers, and is an example of Norman Revival. Standing at the southern end of the Malvern Hills, the castle is still a family home. The inside is dramatic: a 60' high Hall leads to the State Rooms, including the Pugin Gothic Drawing Room and an Italian-style Library, each with a view of the lake. There is a collection of mature specimen trees in the grounds, with a maze, tree trail, children's adventure playground, Burma Bridge tree top walkway, junior assault course and full-size play Land Rover. Exclusive use offered for weddings, private and corporate events.

Location: Map 6:M10. OS Ref SO735 368. 2m SE of Ledbury on A438 Tewkesbury road. M50/J2 & from Ledbury take the A449/A438. Tewkesbury 20 mins, Malvern 20 mins, Hereford 25 mins, Cheltenham 30 mins, B'ham 1 hr.

Owner: Mr J Hervey-Bathurst **Contact:** Castle Office

Tel: 01531 633160 **Fax:** 01531 631776 **E-mail:** enquiries@eastnorcastle.com

Open: Easter Weekend Fri 25-Mon 28 Mar. May BH Weekends Sun 1, Mon 2 & Sun 29, Mon 30 May. 5 Jun-17 Jul-Every Sun. 24 Jul-25 Aug - Sun to Thu. Aug BH Weekend Sun 28 & Mon 29 Aug. Sep-Every Sun.

Admission: Castle & Grounds: Adult £10.50, Child (3-15yrs) £7.00, Family (2+3) £28.00. Grounds Only: Adult £7.00, Child (3-15yrs) £5.00, Family (2+3) £19.00, Groups (20+) Guided £11.50, Self-guided £9.50, Schools £7.50 Groups (40+) Guided £11.00, Self-guided £9.00.

Key facts: ⓘ Corporate events - off-road driving, team building, private dinners, exclusive hire, visitor events. ⬚ Gift shop open on visitor open days. Ⓣ Product launches, TV & feature films, concerts & charities. ♿ Wheelchair stairclimber to main state rooms. 🍽 Licensed. Ⓕ Pre-booked on Mons & Tues all year, Self-Guided on normal opening hours. Ⓟ Ample 10-200 yds from Castle. ▣ Guides available. ⬚ Dogs on leads. ⬚ Exclusive use accommodation. ▣ ⬚

HERGEST CROFT GARDENS 🏛ⓕ
Kington, Herefordshire HR5 3EG
www.hergest.co.uk

Garden for all seasons; from bulbs to spectacular autumn colour, including spring and summer borders, roses, azaleas and an old-fashioned kitchen garden growing unusual vegetables. Brightly coloured rhododendrons 30ft high grow in Park Wood. Over 60 champion trees set in 70 acres of spectacular countryside of the Welsh Marches. **Location:** Map 6:J9. OS Ref SO281 565. Follow brown tourist signs along A44 to Rhayader. **Owner:** Mr E J Banks **Contact:** Mrs Melanie Lloyd **Tel:** 01544 230160 **E-mail:** gardens@hergest.co.uk
Open: Mar. Sats & Suns. Daily from 22 Mar-6 Nov, 12 noon-5.30pm. Season tickets and groups by arrangement throughout year. Flower Fair 2 May, 10am-5.30pm. Plant Fair 16 Oct 10.30am-4.30pm. See website for all other events. **Admission:** Adult £6.50, Child (under 16yrs) Free. Pre-booked groups (20 +) £5.50 per person. Pre-booked group with guided tour (20+) £7.50 per person. Season ticket £25.00 each.
Key facts: ⬜ Containing interesting gifts. 🌿 Rare & unusual plants. ♿ Limited disabled access, special disabled route & WC. ⬛ 🍴 Ridgeway Catering supply homemade light lunches, cakes and teas in the old dining room. ⓕ Pre-booked. 🅿 🐕 On leads. 🏠 Haywood Cabin - available through website. ✳ ⬜

KINNERSLEY CASTLE
Kinnersley, Herefordshire HR3 6QF

Marches castle renovated around 1580. Still a family home. Available for fashion shoots, small scale weddings/celebrations. Fine plasterwork solar ceiling. Organic gardens with specimen trees including one of Britain's largest gingkos.
Location: Map 6:K9. OS Ref SO3460 4950. A4112 Leominster to Brecon Road, castle drive behind Kinnersley village sign on left.
Owner/Contact: Katherina Garratt-Adams
Tel: 01544 327407
E-mail: katherina@kinnersley.com
Website: www.kinnersleycastle.co.uk
Open: See website for dates and wedding information.
Admission: Adult £7.50. Child £2.00. Concs. & Groups over 8: £6.50.
Key facts: ⓘ No indoor photography. Coach parties by arrangement throughout year. ♿ Unsuitable. ⓕ Obligatory. 🅿

OLD SUFTON
Mordiford, Hereford HR1 4EJ

A 16th Century manor house which was altered and remodelled in the 18th and 19th Centuries and again in this Century. The original home of the Hereford family (see Sufton Court) who have held the manor since the 12th Century.
Location: Map 6:L10. OS Ref SO575 384. Mordiford, off B4224 Mordiford - Dormington road.
Owner: Trustees of Sufton Heritage Trust
Contact: Mr & Mrs J N Hereford
Tel: 01432 870268/01432 850328.
E-mail: james@sufton.co.uk
Open: By Appointment to: james@sufton.co.uk
Key facts: ♿ Partial. ⓕ Obligatory. 🅿
⬛ Small school groups. No special facilities. 🐕 ✳

SUFTON COURT 🏛ⓕ
Mordiford, Hereford HR1 4LU
Sufton Court is a small Palladian mansion house. Built in 1788 by James Wyatt for James Hereford. The park was laid out by Humphry Repton whose 'red book' still survives. The house stands above the rivers Wye and Lugg giving impressive views towards the mountains of Wales.
Location: Map 6:L10. OS Ref SO574 379. Mordiford, off B4224 on Mordiford-Dormington road.
Owner: J N Hereford **Contact:** Mr & Mrs J N Hereford
Tel: 01432 870268/01432 850328
E-mail: james@sufton.co.uk
Open: 17-30 May & 16-29 Aug: 2-5pm. Guided tours: 2, 3 and 4pm.
Admission: Adult £5.00, Child 50p.
Key facts: ⓕ Obligatory. 🅿 Only small coaches.
⬛ Small school groups. No special facilities. 🐕 In grounds, on leads.

BERRINGTON HALL 🌿
Nr Leominster, Herefordshire HR6 0DW
The creation of Thomas Harley, the 3rd Earl of Oxford's remarkable son, who made a fortune from supplying pay and clothing to the British Army in America and became Lord Mayor of London in 1767 at the age of 37. **Location:** Map 6:L8. OS Ref SO509 636. 3m N of Leominster, 7m S of Ludlow. **Tel:** 01568 615721 **E-mail:** berrington@nationaltrust.org.uk **Website:** www.nationaltrust.org.uk/berrington
Open: Please see website for up-to-date opening times and admission prices.

LANGSTONE COURT 🏛
Llangarron, Ross on Wye, Herefordshire HR9 6NR
Mostly late 17th Century house with older parts. Interesting staircases, panelling and ceilings. **Location:** Map 6:L11. OS Ref SO534 221. Ross on Wye 5m, Llangarron 1m. **Tel:** 01989 770254 **E-mail:** richard.jones@langstone-court.org.uk **Website:** www.langstone-court.org.uk **Open:** 2nd Mon & Tue Jan-Dec, 1st Mon & Tue in Jun: 11am-2.30pm, also spring & summer BHs. **Admission:** Free.

Eastnor Castle

VISITOR INFORMATION

■ Owner
The Weston Park Foundation

■ Address
Weston Park
Weston-Under-Lizard
Nr Shifnal
Shropshire
TF11 8LE

■ Location
Map 6:N6
OS Ref. SJ808 107
Birmingham 40 mins.
Manchester 1 hr 30 mins.
Motorway access M6/J12
or M54/J3 and via the M6
Toll road J12. House
situated on A5 at Weston-
under-Lizard.
Rail: Nearest Railway
Stations: Wolverhampton,
Stafford or Telford.
Air: Birmingham, East
Midlands, Manchester.

■ Contact
Andrea Webster
Tel: 01952 852100
E-mail: enquiries@weston-
park.com

■ Opening Times
Open daily from Saturday
28 May-Sunday 4
September (Except 17-24
August inc.) House is
closed on Saturdays.
Granary Deli & Café and
Art Gallery. Free entry and
open all year round (Deli is
closed on Mondays).
Granary Grill open daily all
year round for lunch.
Dates are correct at the
time of going to print.

■ Admission
Park & Gardens:
Adult   £6.50
Child (3-14yrs)   £3.50
Family (2+3/1+4)   £25.00
OAP   £6.00
House admission +   £3.00

Groups (House, Park & Gardens):
Adult   £6.00
OAP   £6.00

Granary Deli & Café and Art Gallery:
Free entry and open all year
round.

Granary Grill:
Open daily, all year round,
for lunch.
Prices are correct at the
time of going to print.

Conference/Function

ROOM	Size	Max Cap
Dining Rm	52' x 23'	90
Orangery	56'1'x 22'4'	120
Music Rm	55' x 17'	60

WESTON PARK
weston-park.com

Weston Park is a magnificent Stately Home and Parkland situated on the Shropshire/Staffordshire border.

The former home of the Earls of Bradford, the House, Park and Gardens is now owned and maintained by the Weston Park Foundation, an independent charitable trust. Built in 1671, by Lady Elizabeth Wilbraham, this warm and welcoming house is home to internationally important paintings including works by Van Dyck, Gainsborough and Stubbs; furniture and objets d'art, providing enjoyment for all visitors.

Step outside to enjoy the 1,000 acres of glorious Parkland, take one of a variety of woodland and wildlife walks, all landscaped by the legendary 'Capability' Brown in the 18th Century. In 2016 Weston Park will be marking the 300th anniversary of Lancelot 'Capability' Brown's birth. What makes Weston so significant are the pleasure grounds; Temple Wood and Shrewsbury Walk which

are one of only five remaining such examples. Celebratory events include themed guided walks and exhibitions inspired by Brown.

With the exciting Woodland Adventure Playground, Walled Garden, Deer Park and Miniature Railway, there is plenty of fun to be had for all the family.

Over in the Granary Grill & Deli you can enjoy home-cooked seasonal dishes, light bites, freshly brewed coffee and homemade cakes and pastries. The Deli's shelves are stocked with an excellent range of delicious food and drink. Upstairs the Granary Art Gallery stages a series of exciting changing exhibitions throughout the year. (The Granary Grill & Deli and Art Gallery are open all year round. Free Entry).

KEY FACTS

i Interior photography by prior arrangement only.

Granary Deli & Café is open all year round. (Closed on Mondays).

Full event organisation service. Residential parties, special dinners, wedding receptions.

The Granary Deli & Café serves coffee, homemade cakes and light bites.

¶ Granary Grill. Licensed.

By arrangement.

P Ample free parking.

Award-winning educational programme available during all academic terms. Private themed visits aligned with both National Curriculum and QCA targets.

In grounds. On leads.

Weston Park offers 28 delightful bedrooms with bathrooms. Exclusive use accommodation.

Register for news and special offers at **www.hudsonsheritage.com**

LUDLOW CASTLE
CASTLE SQUARE, LUDLOW, SHROPSHIRE SY8 1AY
www.ludlowcastle.com

Ludlow Castle is one of the country's finest medieval ruins set in the glorious Shropshire countryside at the heart of the bustling black and white town of Ludlow. The castle was a Norman fortress extended over the centuries to become a fortified Royal Palace. Castle House has been restored and now has Gift Shops, Tearoom & terrace, three beautifully appointed self-catering apartments and is also a unique wedding venue.

Location: Map 6:L8. OS Ref SO509 745.
Owner: The Earl of Powis & The Trustees of the Powis Estates
Contact: Sonja Belchere (The Custodian)
Tel/Fax: 01584 874465 **Facebook:** Ludlow Castle **Twitter:** @LudlowCastle1
E-mail: info@ludlowcastle.com

Open: Weekends Only: Jan-3rd Mon in Feb. 7 Days a week: Oct-Mar 10am-4pm. Apr-Sep 10am-5pm. Visit the website for Closure details.
Admission: Visit the website for up-to-date admission charges.
Key facts: ⬚ There are 3 gift shops around the Castle - Castle Gift Shop, Castle Gallery & Picture Framing, The Art Room. ⬚ The grounds are accessible but uneven in places. We provide WCs. ⬚ Traditional tea rooms with waiting staff. Licensed. ⬚ By arrangement. ⬚ £3.00 each. ⬚ ⬚ Welcome throughout Castle, Tea Room and the Sir Henry Sidney Apartment. ⬚ Three 4-5* self-catering apartments. ⬚ Civil ceremonies & receptions in The Round Chapel and Castle House function rooms. There is also an option for a marquee. ⬚ The Castle is closed for events set ups. Always check website before visiting. ⬚

UPTON CRESSETT HALL AND GATEHOUSE ⬚ ◆
BRIDGNORTH, SHROPSHIRE WV16 6UH
www.uptoncressetthall.co.uk

Moated Grade 1 Elizabethan manor and romantic turreted Gatehouse set in unspoilt Shropshire countryside near Bridgnorth and Ludlow. Group Tours all year and weekend opening in the summer. The Gatehouse offers luxury award-winning accommodation on separate floors (B&B or self-catering) with sumptuous poster beds in either the Prince Rupert Bedroom or Thatcher Suite. Runner-up last year for Best Accommodation at Hudson's awards and a previous winner of Best Hidden Gem. The Gatehouse is perfect for romantic honeymoons and mini-breaks, standing in the middle of expansive moated topiary gardens. In 'The Thousand Best Houses of Britain', Simon Jenkins describes Upton Cressett as as an 'Elizabethan gem'. Country Life says the Hall is 'a splendid example of the English manor house at its most evocative' whilst John Betjeman describes our hamlet as a 'remote and beautiful place', The Hall was the historic home of the royalist Cressett family before Sir Bill Cash MP renovated the Hall in the early

1970s. The young king Edward V - the Prince in the Tower - stayed in 1483 and Prince Rupert stayed in the Gatehouse in the Civil War.
Location: Map 6:M7. OS Ref OS506 592. Bridgnorth 4 miles. Ludlow 17 miles. Brown tourist signs to Hall are located two miles from A 458 Bridgnorth-Shrewsbury road. **Owner:** William and Lady Laura Cash **Contact:** Laura Cash
Tel: 01746 714616 **E-mail:** laura@uptoncressett.co.uk **Open:** Group tours all year. For summer public opening days see website. **Admission:** Adults £12.50 (including entry to gardens, Hall tour and homemade scones and tea). Gardens and tearoom entry, including scones/tea £7.50. No concessions. Group tours min 10, max 45. Group lunches and private dining in Great Hall, prices on request.
Key facts: ⬚ No photography in the house. ⬚ Millinery Tearoom on all open days, 'Bosworth Tea Pavilion' tea tent open in good weather.
⬚ Free with admission. ⬚ On leads only. ⬚

STOKESAY COURT 🏠
Onibury, Craven Arms, Shropshire SY7 9BD
www.stokesaycourt.com

Unspoilt and secluded, Stokesay Court is an imposing late Victorian mansion with Jacobean style façade, magnificent interiors and extensive grounds containing a grotto, woodland and interconnected pools. Set in the rolling green landscape of South Shropshire near Ludlow, the house and grounds featured as the Tallis Estate in award-winning film 'Atonement'. During WW1 Stokesay Court played an important role as a military hospital and additional rooms and displays bring this history to life. **Location:** Map 6:K7. OS Ref SO444 786. A49 Between Ludlow and Craven Arms. **Owner/Contact:** Ms Caroline Magnus
Tel: 01584 856238 **E-mail:** info@stokesaycourt.com
Open: Guided tours Apr-Oct for booked groups (20+). Groups (up to 60) can be accommodated by arrangement. Tours for individuals take place on dates advertised on website. Booking essential.
Admission: Please check website for up-to-date admission prices.
Key facts: ℹ️ No stilettos. No photography in house. 🚽 ♿ Partial. WCs. 🍽 Tea & home baked refreshments included in ticket price. 🎫 Obligatory. 🅿️ 🚌 🐕 Dogs on leads - gardens only. 🈵

HODNET HALL GARDENS 🏠
Hodnet, Market Drayton, Shropshire TF9 3NN
Over 60 acres of brilliant coloured flowers, magnificent forest trees, sweeping lawns and a chain of ornamental pools which run tranquilly along the cultivated garden valley to provide a natural habitat for waterfowl and other wildlife. No matter what the season, visitors will always find something fresh and interesting to ensure an enjoyable outing.
Location: Map 6:L5. OS Ref SJ613 286. 12m NE of Shrewsbury on A53; M6/J15, M54/J3. **Owner:** Sir Algernon and the Hon Lady-Percy
Contact: Secretary **Tel:** 01630 685786 **Fax:** 01630 685853
E-mail: secretary@heber-percy.freeserve.co.uk
Website: www.hodnethallgardens.org
Open: Every Sun and BH Mon from Sun 28 Mar-Sun 25 Sep. Also the following Weds: 11 May, 15 Jun, 20 Jul. 12pm-5pm. Please see our website and Facebook page for details of our up and coming special days and events.
Admission: Adult £6.50. Children (aged 5-15) £3.00. Under 5's free.
Key facts: ♿ Partial. WCs. 🍽 🍴 🅿️ 🚌 On leads.

Entrance Hall at Weston Park

Great Hall at Stokesay Court

LONGNER HALL 🏠Ⓔ
Uffington, Shrewsbury, Shropshire SY4 4TG
Designed by John Nash in 1803, Longner Hall is a Tudor Gothic style house set in a park landscaped by Humphry Repton. The home of one family for over 700 years. Longner's principal rooms are adorned with plaster fan vaulting and stained glass.
Location: Map 6:L6. OS Ref SJ529 110. 4m SE of Shrewsbury on Uffington road, ¼m off B4380, Atcham.
Owner: Mr R L Burton **Contact:** Sara Watts
Tel: 07903 842235
Open: Weekdays from Mon 30 May-Fri 1 Jul & BH Mons: 28 Mar, 2 May & 29 Aug. Tours at 2pm & 3.30pm. Groups at any time by arrangement.
Admission: Adult £5.00, Child/OAP £3.00.
Key facts: ℹ️ No photography in house. ♿ Partial. 🎫 Obligatory. 🅿️ Limited for coaches. 🍽 By arrangement. 🐕 Guide dogs only.

COUND HALL
Cound, Shropshire SY5 6AH
Queen Anne red brick Hall.
Location: Map 6:L6. OS Ref ST560 053.
Tel: 01743 761721 **Fax:** 01743 761722
Open: Mon 15 Feb–Fri 19 Feb 2016, 10am-4pm.
Admission: Adult £4.50, Child £2.30, Conc. £3.40, Family £11.30.

DUDMASTON ESTATE 🌿
Quatt, Bridgnorth, Shropshire WV15 6QN
Enchanted wooded parkland, sweeping gardens and a house with a surprise, Dudmaston is something unexpected in the Shropshire countryside.
Location: Map 6:M7. OS Ref SO748 888. **Tel:** 01746 780866
E-mail: dudmaston@nationaltrust.org.uk **Website:** www.nationaltrust.org.uk/dudmaston-estate **Open:** Please see website for up-to-date details.

SHIPTON HALL 🏠Ⓔ
Much Wenlock, Shropshire TF13 6JZ
Elizabethan house with Georgian extensions. Fine plasterwork and panelling. Gardens, church and dovecote. **Location:** Map 6:L7. OS Ref SO563 918. 6 miles from Much Wenlock on B4378 towards Craven Arms, close to junction with B4368
Tel: 01746 785225 **E-mail:** mjanebishop@hotmail.co.uk **Open:** Easter-end Sep: Thu, 2.30-5.30pm. BH Suns/Mons, 2.30-5.30pm. Groups 20+ by arrangement.
Admission: Adult £6.00, Child (under 14yrs) £3.00.

CHILLINGTON HALL

Codsall Wood, Wolverhampton, Staffordshire WV8 1RE

www.chillingtonhall.co.uk

Home of the Giffards since 1178, the present house dates from the 18th Century, firstly by the architect Francis Smith of Warwick in 1724 and completed by John Soane in 1786. Parkland laid out by 'Capability' Brown in the 1760s with additional work by James Paine. Chillington was the winner of the HHA/Sotheby's Restoration Award 2009 for work done on Soane's magnificent Saloon. The Georgian Model Farm has undergone major renovation over the past 8 years and has an educational/meeting area. **Location:** Map 6:N6. OS Ref SJ864 067. 2m S of Brewood off A449. 4m NW of M54/J2.
Owner: Mr & Mrs J W Giffard **Contact:** Estate Office
Tel: 01902 850236 **E-mail:** info@chillingtonhall.com
Open: House: 2pm-4pm (last entry 3.30pm). 27-31 Mar; 1-5 May; 29-31 May; 6-8 Jun; 1-4 Aug; 8-11 Aug; 15-18 Aug. Grounds: as house. Parties at other times by prior arrangement. **Admission:** Adult £8.00, Child £4.00. Grounds only: half price. **Key facts:** Available for Civil Ceremonies, meetings, filming and events. WCs. Obligatory. In grounds. Licensed for up to 130 guests for the ceremony in the Grand Saloon.

WHITMORE HALL

Whitmore, Newcastle-Under-Lyme ST5 5HW

Whitmore Hall is a Grade I listed building, designated as a house of outstanding architectural and historical interest. Parts of the hall date back to a much earlier period and for 900 years has been the seat of the Cavenagh-Mainwarings, who are direct descendants of the original Norman owners. The hall has beautifully proportioned light rooms and has recently been refurbished; it is in fine order. There are good family portraits to be seen with a continuous line dating from 1624 to the present day. The park encompasses an early Victorian summer house and the outstanding and rare Elizabethan stables.
Location: Map 6:M4. OS Ref SJ811 413. On A53 Newcastle-Market Drayton Road, 3m from M6/J15.
Owner/Contact: Mr Guy Cavenagh-Mainwaring
Tel: 01782 680 478 **E-mail:** whitmore.hall@yahoo.com
Open: 1 May-31 Aug: Tues and Weds, 2pm-5pm (last tour 4.30pm).
Admission: Adult £5.00, Child 50p.
Key facts: Ground floor and grounds.
Afternoon teas for booked groups (15+), May-Aug. Ample. Except assistance dogs. Please contact us for information on Weddings at Whitmore.

SINAI PARK HOUSE

Shobnall Road, Burton upon Trent, Staffordshire DE13 0QJ

Built in the 15th, 16th, 17th and 18th Centuries, Grade II* listed Sinai Park House is a timber-framed building. Situated on a hilltop overlooking the Trent Valley, between Burton, Derby and Lichfield, this intriguing historic house is surrounded by a 13th Century moat, itself an Ancient Monument.
Location: Map 6:O6. OS Ref SK221 230.
Contact: Kate Murphy **Tel:** 01889 598600
E-mail: kate@brookesandco.net
Website: www.sinaiparkhouse.co.uk
Open: Guided tours only, booking in advance needed. Please contact.
Admission: Please see website.
Key facts: Must book in advance. Must book in advance. Guide Dogs only. Subject to booking.

BIDDULPH GRANGE GARDEN

Grange Road, Biddulph, Staffordshire ST8 7SD

This amazing Victorian garden was created by James Bateman for his collection of plants from around the world. **Location:** Map 6:N3. OS Ref SJ891 592.
Tel: 01782 517999 **E-mail:** biddulphgrange@nationaltrust.org.uk
Website: www.nationaltrust.org.uk/biddulph-grange-garden
Open: Please see website for up-to-date opening and admission details.

THE HEATH HOUSE

Tean, Stoke-On-Trent, Staffordshire ST10 4HA

Set in rolling parkland with fine formal gardens, Heath House is an early Victorian mansion built 1836-1840 in the Tudor style. **Location:** Map 6:O4. OS Ref SK030 392. **Tel:** 01538 722212 **E-mail:** info@theheathhouse.co.uk
Website: www.theheathhouse.co.uk **Open:** See our website for details. Please phone in advance. **Admission:** £6.50pp. No concessions.

SHUGBOROUGH ESTATE

Milford, Stafford, Staffordshire ST17 0XB

Rare survival of a complete estate, with all major buildings including mansion house, servants' quarters, model farm and walled garden. **Location:** Map 6:N5. OS Ref SJ990 215. **Tel:** 0845 459 8900 **E-mail:** shugborough@nationaltrust.org.uk **Website:** www.nationaltrust.org.uk/shugborough-estate
Open: Please see website for up-to-date opening and admission details.

Whitmore Hall

VISITOR INFORMATION

■ **Owner**
The Viscount Daventry

■ **Address**
Arbury Hall
Nuneaton
Warwickshire
CV10 7PT

■ **Location**
Map 6:P7
OS Ref. SP335 893
London, M1, M6/J3 (A444 to Nuneaton), 2m SW of Nuneaton. 1m W of A444. Nuneaton 5 mins. Birmingham City Centre 20 mins. London 2 hrs, Coventry 20 mins.
Bus/Coach: Nuneaton Station 3m.
Air: Birmingham International 17m.

■ **Contact**
Events Secretary
Tel: 024 7638 2804
Fax: 024 7664 1147
E-mail:
info@arburyestate.co.uk

■ **Opening Times**
Hall & Gardens open on BH weekends only (Sunday & Monday). Easter-August from 1pm-6pm. Last guided tour of the Hall 4.30pm.
Groups/Parties (25+) by arrangement.

■ **Admission**
Hall & Gardens
Adult	£8.50
Child (up to 14 yrs)	£4.50
Family (2+2)	£20.00

Gardens Only
Adult	£5.50
Child (up to 14 yrs.)	£4.00

Conference/Function

ROOM	Size	Max Cap
Dining Room	35' x 28'	120
Saloon	35' x 30'	70
Room 3	48' x 11'	40
Stables Tearooms	31' x 18'	80

ARBURY HALL 🏠Ⓕ
www.arburyestate.co.uk

Arbury Hall, original Elizabethan mansion house, Gothicised in the 18th Century surrounded by stunning gardens and parkland.

Arbury Hall has been the seat of the Newdegate family for over 450 years and is the ancestral home of Viscount Daventry. This Tudor/Elizabethan House was Gothicised by Sir Roger Newdegate in the 18th Century and is regarded as the 'Gothic Gem' of the Midlands. The principal rooms, with their soaring fan vaulted ceilings and plunging pendants and filigree tracery, stand as a most breathtaking and complete example of early Gothic Revival architecture and provide a unique and fascinating venue for corporate entertaining, product launches, fashion shoots and activity days. Exclusive use of this historic Hall, its gardens and parkland is offered to clients. The Hall stands in the middle of beautiful parkland with landscaped gardens of rolling lawns, lakes and winding wooded walks. Spring flowers are profuse and in June rhododendrons, azaleas and giant wisteria provide a beautiful environment for the visitor. George Eliot, the novelist, was born on the estate and Arbury Hall and Sir Roger Newdegate were immortalised in her book 'Scenes of Clerical Life'.

KEY FACTS

ℹ️ Corporate hospitality, film location, small conferences, product launches and promotions, marquee functions, let day shooting. No cameras or video recorders indoors.

🎁 Small selection of souvenir gifts.

🍽️ Exclusive lunches and dinners for corporate parties in dining room, max. 50, buffets 80.

♿ Partial, WCs.

☕ Stables Tearooms (on first floor) open from 1pm.

🚶 Obligatory. Tour time: 50min.

🅿️ 200 cars and 3 coaches 250 yards from house. Follow tourist signs. Approach map available for coach drivers.

🐕 Dogs on leads in garden. Guide dogs only in house.

SHAKESPEARE'S FAMILY HOMES
www.shakespeare.org.uk

Discover Shakespeare's Homes, farm and gardens in Stratford-upon-Avon, with Shakespeare's New Place reopening Spring 2016.

Shakespeare's Birthplace - Where the story began
Explore the extraordinary story of William and the house he was born and grew up in. Our fascinating guides will captivate you with tales of his father's business ventures. Take centre stage with our costumed troupe, Shakespeare Aloud!

Mary Arden's Farm - A working Tudor farm
Visit the family farm where Shakespeare's mother grew up. Experience the sights, sounds and smells of a working Tudor farm and follow our resident Tudors as they work. Meet rare breed animals, enjoy archery and falconry, or explore the nature trails and playground. Don't miss our free events throughout the school holidays.

Anne Hathaway's Cottage - Love and marriage
Follow young Shakespeare's footsteps to the Cottage where he courted an older woman. Our guides will bring this Tudor love story to life in its original setting with nine acres of beautiful cottage gardens, woodland walks and sculpture trail to explore. Enjoy refreshments in the delightful Cottage Garden Café.

Harvard House - Stratford's hidden gem
Built by the wealthy Thomas Rogers it is one of Stratford-upon-Avon's most striking Elizabethan houses. Closing Spring 2016.

Shakespeare's New Place - His family home
The only home Shakespeare ever bought and where he lived for 19 years. Due to reopen in Spring 2016 for the 400th anniversary of Shakespeare's death, walk in his footsteps and trace the footprint of his family home in a contemporary landscape setting.

Hall's Croft - Daughter and Granddaughter
The elegant Tudor home of Shakespeare's daughter Susanna and her husband Dr John Hall. Stroll round the walled garden planted with fragrant herbs used in his remedies. Unwind in the Café or browse hand crafted local gifts in The Arter gift shop.

KEY FACTS

- ℹ️ City Sightseeing bus tour connecting town houses with Anne Hathaway's Cottage and Mary Arden's Farm. No photography inside houses.
- 🛍️ Gifts available.
- 🍴 Available, tel for details.
- ♿ Partial. WCs.
- ☕ Shakespeare's Birthplace, Mary Arden's Farm, Anne Hathaway's Cottage, Hall's Croft.
- 🚶 By special arrangement.
- 🅿️ Free coach terminal for groups drop off and pick up at Birthplace. Max stay 15 mins. Parking at Mary Arden's Farm. Pay & display parking at Anne Hathaway's Cottage.
- 🏛️ Available for all houses. For information 01789 201806.
- 🐕 Guide dogs only.
- ✳️ Please check for full details.
- ♿ Please check website for details.

CHARLECOTE PARK 🦌
WELLESBOURNE, WARWICK, WARWICKSHIRE CV35 9ER
www.nationaltrust.org.uk/charlecote-park

Protected by the Rivers Dene & Avon and by its distinctive cleft-oak paling fencing Charlecote Park presents a picture of peace and repose. Generations of the Lucy family have left their mark on the property. The house holds surprising treasures from early editions of Shakespeare to an impressive Beckford table. The Tudor Gatehouse draws visitors from park to court walking in the same processional footsteps as Queen Elizabeth 1. The outbuildings consist of a Laundry, Brew House, Carriage House & Stables. The gardens present a riot of colour throughout the year. The family's continued presence adds an intriguing dimension for visitors as they picnic, play and wander through the parkland watched by the Jacob sheep & fallow deer.

Location: Map 6:P9. OS Ref OS151, SP263 564. 1m W of Wellesbourne, 5m E of Stratford-upon-Avon. Exit 15 from M40 (Take A429 marked Stow & follow brown NT signs). **Owner:** National Trust **Contact:** Property Office

Tel: 01789 470277 **Fax:** 01789 470544
E-mail: charlecotepark@nationaltrust.org.uk
Open: Park, gardens, outbuildings, shop & tearoom open daily throughout the year 10.30am-5.30pm (Closing at 4pm in winter) House 13 Feb-25 Mar, 11.30am-4pm (Closed Wed), 26 Mar-30 Oct, 11am-4.30pm (Closed Wed), 5 Nov-18 Dec 11.30am-3.30pm Sat and Sun only. Hidden Charlecote Tours available daily 1 Jan-12 Feb & 31 Oct-31 Dec, also on Weds 17 Feb-26 Oct. Whole property closed 27 & 28 Jan and 24 & 25 Dec.
Admission: House, Garden & Park Gift Aid (Standard): Adult £11.50 (£10.45), Child £5.70 (£5.15), Family £28.70 (£26.05). Garden and Park only: Adult £7.80 (£7.05), Child £3.90 (£3.50), Family £19.50 (£17.70). House, Garden & Park Winter: Adult £7.80 (£7.05), Child £3.90 (£3.50) Family £19.50 (£17.70).
Key facts: ℹ️ ⬛ ♿ 📷 🎫 🅿️ ⬛ ✕ Holiday Flat (Sleeps 6) ❄️ ⬛

Charlecote Park

LORD LEYCESTER HOSPITAL
HIGH STREET, WARWICK CV34 4BH
www.lordleycester.com

This magnificent range of 14th and 15th Century half-timbered buildings was adapted into almshouses by Robert Dudley, Earl of Leycester, in 1571. The Hospital still provides homes for ex-Servicemen and their wives. The Guildhall, Great Hall, chantry Chapel, Brethren's Kitchen and galleried Courtyard are still in everyday use. The regimental museum of the Queen's Own Hussars is housed here. The historic Master's Garden was featured in BBC TV's 'Gardener's World', and the Hospital buildings in many productions including, most recently, 'Dr Who' and David Dimbleby's 'How We Built Britain'.

Location: Map 6:P8. OS Ref 280 468. 1m N of M40/J15 on the A429 in town centre. Rail: 10 minutes walk from Warwick Station.

Owner: The Governors
Contact: The Master
Tel: 01926 491422
Open: All year: Tue-Sun & BHs (except Good Fri & 25 Dec), 10am-5pm (4pm in winter). Garden: Apr-Sep: 10am-4.30pm.
Admission: Adult £5.90, Child £4.90, Conc. £5.40. Garden only £2.00.
Key facts: ⬚ 🅵 🅃 ♿ Partial. WCs.
🍴 🕍 𝑓 By arrangement.
🅿 Limited for cars. No coaches.
🚫 🐕 Except assistance dogs. ⬛ ❋

ASTLEY CASTLE
Nuneaton, Warwickshire CV10 7QS
www.landmarktrust.org.uk

Groundbreaking modern accommodation has been inserted within the ruined walls of this ancient moated site to combine the thrill of modern architecture with the atmosphere of an ancient place. Large glass walls now frame views of medieval stonework and the adjacent church and surrounding countryside.

Location: Map 7:A7. OS Ref SP310 894.
Owner: The Landmark Trust
Tel: 01628 825925
E-mail: bookings@landmarktrust.org.uk
Open: Self-catering accommodation. Part of grounds open Mon and Fri, 8 Open Days per year, contact office.
Admission: Free on Open Days and visits by appointment.
Key facts: ⓘ The living accommodation is on the first floor and the bedrooms and bathrooms on the ground floor. A lift enables easy access for all.
♿ 🅿 🚫 🐕 ❋ 🍴

COMPTON VERNEY
Warwickshire CV35 9HZ
www.comptonverney.org.uk

Set within a Grade I listed mansion remodelled by Robert Adam in the 1760s, Compton Verney offers a unique art gallery experience. Relax and explore the 120 acres of 'Capability' Brown landscaped parkland, discover a collection of internationally significant art, enjoy free tours and a programme of popular events.

Location: Map 7:A9. OS Ref SP312 529. 9m E of Stratford-upon-Avon, 10 mins from M40/J12, on B4086 between Wellesbourne and Kineton. Rail: Nearest station is Banbury or Leamington Spa. Air: Nearest airport Birmingham International.

Owner: Compton Verney House Trust **Contact:** Ticketing Desk
Tel: 01926 645500 **Fax:** 01926 645501 **Ticket Desk Hours:** 11am-4.30pm Tue-Sun. **E-mail:** info@comptonverney.org.uk
Open: 19 Mar-10 Dec 2016; Tue-Sun and BH Mons, 11am-5pm.
Last entry to Gallery 4.30pm. Groups welcome, please book in advance.
Admission: Please call for details. Group discounts are available.
Key facts: ⓘ Photography is not permitted in some areas of the Gallery.
⬚ 🅃 ♿ WCs. and access throughout the building on all floors. 🍴 Licensed.
🕍 Licensed and waitress service. 𝑓 By arrangement. 🅿 Ample. 🍴
🐕 Guide dogs only. ⬛ 🍴

HILL CLOSE GARDENS TRUST
Bread and Meat Close, Warwick, Warwickshire CV34 6HF
www.hillclosegardens.com

16 hedged Victorian gardens overlooking Warwick racecourse with delightful listed brick summerhouses. Created by tradespeople to escape the congestion and pollution of the town. Spring bulbs, old varieties of soft fruit and vegetables, unusual fruit trees and extensive herbaceous borders. Glasshouse for tender plants. Plant, produce and gift sales. Café serving lunches and teas at weekends and Bank Holidays in summer. Teas and snacks all year. Events throughout the year listed on website. **Location:** Map 6:P8. M40 Junction 15 Follow A429 & signs for racecourse, enter main racecourse gate off Friars Street. Bear right to entrance to Gardens. **Owner:** Hill Close Gardens Trust **Contact:** Centre Manager
Tel: 01926 493 339 **E-mail:** centremanager@hcgt.org.uk
Open: Apr-Oct Gardens every day 11am-5pm. Café Sat & Sun & BH Mons. Nov-Mar Gardens Mon-Fri 11am-4pm. Teas & snacks available during all opening times. Closed Xmas-New Year. Check website for details.
Admission: Adults £4.00, Child £1.00 (to include garden trail). Under 5s free Members free. **Key facts:** 🎁 Gifts, cards, jam. 🌱 Garden produce sales. 🍴 Corporate, party, informal. ♿ Access, toilet & parking. ☕ Hot and cold drinks, cakes. Quiche, soup, teacakes, scones, snacks. 🎫 On request. Min 10 max 48. 🅿 2 hours free. 📷 On request. 🐕 Assistance only. ♿

Kenilworth Castle

HONINGTON HALL 🏛
Shipston-On-Stour, Warwickshire CV36 5AA

This fine Caroline manor house was built in the early 1680s for Henry Parker in mellow brickwork, stone quoins and window dressings. Modified in 1751 when an octagonal saloon was inserted. The interior was also lavishly restored around this time and contains exceptional mid-Georgian plasterwork. Set in 15 acres of grounds.
Location: Map 6:P9. OS Ref SP261 427. 10m S of Stratford-upon-Avon. 1½m N of Shipston-on-Stour. Take A3400 towards Stratford, then signed right to Honington.
Owner/Contact: Benjamin Wiggin Esq
Tel: 01608 661434 **Fax:** 01608 663717
E-mail: bhew@honingtonhall.plus.com
Open: By appointment for groups (10+).
Admission: Email for details.
Key facts: 🎫 Obligatory. 🐕

KENILWORTH CASTLE & GARDEN ⊞
Kenilworth, Warwickshire CV8 1NE

Kenilworth's varied buildings and architectural styles reflect its long connection with successive English monarchs. Magnificent garden and fascinating exhibitions in the Gatehouse and castle stables. **Location:** Map 6:P8. OS Ref OS140, SP278 723. In Kenilworth off A46, W end of town. **Tel:** 01926 852 078 **E-mail:** customers@english-heritage.org.uk **Website:** www.english-heritage.org.uk/kenilworth **Open:** Please see website. **Admission:** See website.

STONELEIGH ABBEY
Kenilworth, Warwickshire CV8 2LF

A Cistercian monastery converted into a stately home. Stoneleigh hosted Jane Austen and Queen Victoria. **Location:** Map 6:P8. OS Ref SP320 712. Off B4115 Ashow Road. **Tel:** 01926 858535 **E-mail:** enquire@stoneleighabbey.org
Website: www.stoneleighabbey.org
Open: Good Fri-31 Oct. Guided tour only - times on website. Grounds 11am-5pm.
Admission: Adults £8.50, Child £4.50.

WARWICK CASTLE
Warwick CV34 4QU

Over 1000 years of jaw-dropping history, where ancient myths and spell-binding tales will set your imagination alight. Meet history face to face and be prepared to participate fully in Castle life. **Location:** Map 6:P8. OS Ref SP283 647.
Tel: 01926 495 421 **E-mail:** customer.information@warwick-castle.com
Website: www.warwick-castle.com **Open:** Please visit our website for details.

© Birmingham Museums Trust

BIRMINGHAM MUSEUMS
www.birminghammuseums.org.uk

Take a journey back into Birmingham's rich and vibrant past.

Birmingham Museum & Art Gallery - Free Entry
From Renaissance masterpieces to Egyptian mummies and the Staffordshire Hoard, Birmingham Museum & Art Gallery showcases a world class collection that offers fascinating glimpses into Birmingham's vibrant past.

Aston Hall
Experience the splendour of this 17th Century Jacobean mansion. Take a tour through majestic state rooms, including the imposing Long Gallery, and the beautiful Lady Holte's Garden. Display rooms illustrate the part Aston Hall played in the English Civil War, and how it prepared to receive royalty on more than one occasion.

Blakesley Hall
Visit one of Birmingham's finest timber-framed houses, built in 1590. With a herb garden and orchard within its grounds, Blakesley Hall is a peaceful haven set in an urban location.

Museum of the Jewellery Quarter
Enjoy a lively guided tour of the perfectly preserved Smith & Pepper jewellery factory, which reveals Birmingham's jewellery heritage and offers a unique glimpse of working life in the city's famous Jewellery Quarter.

Sarehole Mill
Discover the idyllic childhood haunt of J.R.R.Tolkien. One of only two surviving working watermills in Birmingham, gain a unique insight into the lives of the millers who once worked there. Today, the mill retains its tranquil atmosphere and the millpond provides a peaceful haven for kingfishers, moorhens and herons.

Soho House
Discover the elegant Georgian home of the pre-eminent industrialist and entrepreneur Matthew Boulton. Soho House was also the meeting place of the leading 18th Century intellectuals of the Lunar Society.

KEY FACTS

- Gift shops located at all sites.
- Available for corporate hire and special events. See Birmingham Museums website for full details.
- Wheelchair access across sites.
- Tearooms located at all sites.
- Expert-led Heritage Tours are available across all heritage sites. See Birmingham Museums website for full details.
- Parking available across sites. See Birmingham Museums website for full details.
- School visits are welcome. See Birmingham Museums for full details of our educational programme.
- Guide dogs only.
- Weddings and receptions available at some sites. See Birmingham Museums website for full details.

© Birmingham Museums Trust

VISITOR INFORMATION

■ Owner
Birmingham Museums Trust

■ Address
Registered address:
Birmingham Museums Trust
Birmingham Museum & Art Gallery
Birmingham
B3 3DH

■ Location
Map 6:O7
OS Ref. SP066 869

■ Contact
Birmingham Museums Trust
Tel: 0121 348 8000 (General Enquiries)
Tel: 0121 348 8001 (Group Bookings)
E-mail:
enquiries@ birminghammuseums.org. uk

■ Opening Times
Opening times vary throughout the year. See Birmingham Museums website for up-to-date information.

■ Admission
See Birmingham Museums website for up-to-date admission prices.

Entry into grounds, gardens, visitor centres and tearooms at our heritage sites is free.

You can enjoy 12 months unlimited entry across all Birmingham Museums heritage sites, and exhibitions at Birmingham Museum & Art Gallery with an annual membership. Adult membership starts at £25.00, with concession, joint, family and life options available.

With Membership Plus, you can enjoy all of these benefits plus unlimited admission into Thinktank, Birmingham Science Museum.

Thinktank, Birmingham Science Museum
Journey to the stars in the Planetarium, discover Birmingham's Spitfire Story in the new Spitfire Gallery, and get hands-on with the giant-sized exhibits in the outdoor Science Garden. Plus, with four floors of interactive exhibits dedicated to science, technology and industry, Thinktank offers mind-boggling days out for all the family.

© Birmingham Museums Trust

WINTERBOURNE HOUSE AND GARDEN 🏛️ⓕ
University of Birmingham, 58 Edgbaston Park Road, Birmingham B15 2RT
www.winterbourne.org.uk

Winterbourne is set in 7 acres of botanic garden, just minutes from Birmingham city centre. Ground and first floor exhibition spaces tell the history of the previous owners and the garden has a beautiful Japanese bridge, tea house and walled garden, all designed in the Arts and Crafts style. A terrace tearoom overlooks the garden where afternoon tea, hot lunches and refreshments are served every day. **Location:** Map 6:O7. OS Ref SP052 839. Just off the A38 in Selly Oak, Birmingham. **Owner:** The University of Birmingham **Tel:** 0121 414 3003 **E-mail:** enquiries@winterbourne.org.uk **Open:** Jan-Mar/Nov-Dec 10am-4pm weekdays, 11am-4pm weekends Apr-Oct 10am-5.30pm weekdays, 11am-5.30pm weekends. Closed over Christmas period. **Admission:** Adult £5.45, Conc £4.45, Family £16.00. Group prices on request. **Key facts:** ℹ️ Organised professional photography must be notified to management & will incur a charge. 📷 Garden-inspired gifts, guidebooks, secondhand books & greetings cards. 🌱 Quality plants for sale, many home-grown species. ☎ Conference facilities on site. 🚻 WCs. 🍽 Licensed. 🍴 Licensed. 🎟 Pre-booked. 🅿 🚹 🚗 Guide dogs only. ❄ ♿

Birmingham Botanical Gardens

BIRMINGHAM BOTANICAL GARDENS
Westbourne Road, Edgbaston, Birmingham B15 3TR
15 acres of beautiful historic landscaped gardens with 7000 shrubs, plants and trees. Four glasshouses, Roses and Alpines, Woodland and Rhododendron Walks, Rock Pool, Herbaceous Borders, Japanese Garden. Children's playground, aviaries, gallery, bandstand, tearoom giftshop, parking. **Location:** Map 6:O7. OS Ref SP048 855. 2m W of city centre. Follow signs to Edgbaston then brown tourist signs. **Owner:** Birmingham Botanical & Horticultural Society **Contact:** Kim Hill **Tel:** 0121 454 1860 **Fax:** 0121 454 7835 **E-mail:** Kim@birminghambotanicalgardens.org.uk **Website:** www.birminghambotanicalgardens.org.uk **Open:** Daily: 10am-dusk. Closed Christmas Day and Boxing Day. Refer to website for details. **Admission:** Adult £7.00, Family £22.00. Groups, Conc. £4.75, Children U5 free. **Key facts:** 📷 🌱 ☎ 🚻 🍽 🍴 On application. 🅿 🚹 🚗 Guide dogs only. 🏛 ❄ Closed 25/26 Dec. ♿

CASTLE BROMWICH HALL GARDENS TRUST
Chester Road, Castle Bromwich, Birmingham B36 9BT

10 acres of historic walled gardens, rescued by volunteers, and restored to 17/18th Century formal English style, pre-'Capability' Brown. Formal walks, espaliered fruit and holly maze contrasts with informal wildlife areas beyond the walls. **Location:** Map 6:O6. OS Ref SP141 899. Off B4114, 5m E of Birmingham City Centre, 1 mile from M6/J5 exit N only. **Owner:** Castle Bromwich Hall & Gardens Trust **Contact:** Sue Brain **Tel:** 0121 749 4100 **Twitter:** @cbhallgardens. **E-mail:** admin@cbhgt.org.uk **Website:** www.cbhgt.org.uk **Open:** 1 Apr-31 Oct: Tues-Thurs, 11 am-4 pm. Sat, Sun BH Mon 12.30-4.30 pm. 1 Nov-31 Mar: Tues-Thur 11 am-3 pm. **Admission:** Summer: Adults £4.50/£4.00, Child £1.00. Winter: All Adults £4.00, Child £1.00. **Key facts:** ℹ️ Guide and books. 📷 🌱 🚻 WCs, wheelchairs. 🍽 🎟 By arrangement. 🅿 Limited for coaches. 🚹 🚗 On leads. ❄ ♿

BADDESLEY CLINTON 🌿
Rising Lane, Baddesley Clinton, Warwickshire B93 0DQ
A 500 year old moated medieval manor house with hidden secrets! **Location:** Map 6:P8. OS Ref SP199 715. **Tel:** 01564 783294 **E-mail:** baddesleyclinton@nationaltrust.org.uk **Website:** www.nationaltrust.org.uk/baddesley-clinton **Open:** Please see website for up-to-date opening and admission details.

WIGHTWICK MANOR & GARDENS 🌿
Wightwick Bank, Wolverhampton, West Midlands WV6 8EE
Wightwick is in every way an idyllic time capsule of Victorian nostalgia for medieval England. Step back in time and visit the family home that's also the world's most unlikely art gallery. **Location:** Map 6:N6. OS Ref SO869 985. **Tel:** 01902 761400 **E-mail:** wightwickmanor@nationaltrust.org.uk **Website:** www.nationaltrust.org.uk/wightwickmanor **Open:** Please see website.

© Arnhel de Serra

© David Noton

CROOME

NEAR HIGH GREEN, WORCESTERSHIRE WR8 9DW

www.nationaltrust.org.uk/croome

There's more than meets the eye at Croome. A secret wartime airbase, now a visitor centre, was once a hub of activity for thousands of people. Outside is the grandest of English landscapes, 'Capability' Brown's masterful first commission, with commanding views over the Malverns. The parkland was nearly lost, but is now great for walks and adventures with a surprise around every corner. At the heart of the park lies Croome Court, once home to the Earls of Coventry. The 6th Earl was an 18th Century trend-setter, and today Croome follows his lead using artists and craftspeople to tell the story of its eclectic past in inventive ways. Explore four floors of the mansion, perfect for making new discoveries.

Location: Map 6:N9. OS Ref SO878 448. Approximately 10 miles south of Worcester. Leave M5 motorway at Junction 7 and follow B4084 towards Pershore. Alternatively, access from the A38. Follow Brown Signs.

Owner: National Trust **Contact:** House Manager

Tel: 01905 371006 **Fax:** 01905 371090

E-mail: croome@nationaltrust.org.uk

Open: See National Trust website for full opening times. Park, Restaurant & Shop open every day except 24 & 25 Dec. House open most days throughout the year.

Admission: See National Trust website for full prices.

Key facts: WCs. Licensed. Licensed. By arrangement. On leads.

HARVINGTON HALL

HARVINGTON, KIDDERMINSTER, WORCESTERSHIRE DY10 4LR

www.harvingtonhall.com

Harvington Hall is a moated, medieval and Elizabethan manor house. Many of the rooms have their original Elizabethan wall paintings and the Hall contains the finest series of priest hides in the country. During the 19th Century it was stripped of furniture and panelling and the shell was left almost derelict but is now restored. The Hall has walled gardens surrounded by a moat, a gift shop and a tearoom serving morning coffees, light lunches and afternoon teas. A programme of events throughout the year including outdoor plays and music, candlelight tours and a pilgrimage is available.

On many weekends the Hall is enhanced by Living History events when the Hall's re-enactment group depict one of the many significant periods throughout its long history. **Location:** Map 6:N8. OS Ref SO877 745. On minor road, ½m NE of A450/A448 crossroads at Mustow Green. 3m SE of Kidderminster.

Owner: Roman Catholic Archdiocese of Birmingham

Contact: The Hall Manager **Tel:** 01562 777846 **Fax:** 01562 777190

E-mail: harvingtonhall@btconnect.com

Open: Mar-Oct, Wed-Sun and BH Mons; 11.30am (closing times vary, check website). Also open throughout the year for pre-booked groups and schools. Occasionally the Hall may be closed for a private function, please check the website. **Admission:** Adult £8.50, Child (5-16) £5.50, OAP £7.50, Family (2 adults & 3 children) £24.00, Garden and Malt House Visitor Centre: £3.50.

Key facts: Partial. WCs. Limited for coaches. Guide dogs only.

BEWDLEY MUSEUM
12 Load Street, Bewdley, Worcestershire DY12 2AE
www.bewdleymuseum.co.uk

Situated in the delightful Georgian town of Bewdley this unique museum can be enjoyed by the whole family. Beautiful gardens, imaginative displays, a café with fresh local produce. Exhibitions, events and plenty of activities for children. The Tourist Information Centre is based on site at the entrance to the museum.
Location: Map 6:M8. OS Ref SO786 753. 4 miles to the west of Kidderminster on the B1490 in the centre of Bewdley. Two public car parks are within walking distance. **Owner:** Wyre Forest District Council **Contact:** Alison Bakr
Tel: 0845 603 5699 **E-mail:** Alison.bakr@wyreforestdc.gov.uk
Open: Mar-Oct 10am-4.30pm. Nov and Dec 11am-3pm. Fri, Sat and Sun. Café and access to the gardens Mar-Dec. **Admission:** Free.
Key facts: Situation at the entrance to the museum. Situated in the herb garden. Private events and functions are held on site. Full access on site. Shambles café set in the museum. Serving hot and cold drinks, snacks, lightbites, hot meals and alcohol. Guided tours and walks. Blitz and evacuation, river and rail plus bespoke programmes. Welcome on site. Wedding receptions and parties held in the museum and gardens.

H DOWNLOAD OUR HANDY APP HUDSON'S UK
TO FIND OUT WHERE TO GO & WHERE TO STAY ON THE MOVE

LITTLE MALVERN COURT
Nr Malvern, Worcestershire WR14 4JN

Prior's Hall, associated rooms and cells, c1489. Former Benedictine Monastery. Oak-framed roof, five bays. Library, collection of religious vestments and relics. Embroideries and paintings. Gardens: 10 acres of former monastic grounds with spring bulbs, blossom, old fashioned roses and shrubs. Access to Hall only by flight of steps. **Location:** Map 6:M9. OS Ref SO769 403. 3m S of Great Malvern on Upton-on-Severn Road (A4104).
Owner: Trustees of the late T M Berington **Contact:** Mrs T M Berington
Tel: 01684 892988 **Fax:** 01684 893057
E-mail: littlemalverncourt@hotmail.com **Website:** www.littlemalverncourt.co.uk
Open: 13 Apr-14 Jul, Weds & Thus, 2.15-5pm, last admission 4.00pm. Open for NGS Sunday 20 Mar & Mon 2 May.
Admission: House & Garden: Adult £8.00, Child £3.00. Garden only: Adult £7.00, Child £2.00. Groups by prior arrangement.
Key facts: Garden (partial). House only.

MADRESFIELD COURT
Madresfield, Malvern WR13 5AJ

Moated family home with mainly Victorian architecture and fine collection of furniture and art. Extensive gardens and arboretum.
Location: Map 6:M9. OS Ref SO808 472. 6m SW of Worcester. 1½ m SE of A449. 2m NE of Malvern.
Owner: The Trustees of Madresfield Estate
Contact: Mrs Cheryl Stone
Tel: 01684 573614 **E-mail:** madresfield@btconnect.com
Open: Guided tours of about 1.5 hours on specified dates and times between Apr and Sep. Numbers are restricted and prior booking is essential to avoid disappointment. We have no refreshment facilities.
Admission: £12.00. No concessions and no Under 16s.
Key facts: Guide books. WCs. Obligatory.

Witley Court

THE TUDOR HOUSE MUSEUM
16 Church Street, Upton-upon-Severn, Worcestershire WR8 0HT

Exhibits of Upton past and present, local pottery and "Staffordshire Blue".
Location: Map 6:N10. OS Ref SO852 406. Centre of Upton-upon-Severn, 7miles SE of Malvern by B4211.
Owner: Tudor House Museum Trust
Tel: 01684 438820 **E-mail:** lavendertudor@talktalk.net
Website: www.tudorhousemuseum.org
Open: Apr-Oct. Tue-Sun and BH afternoons. 1.30pm-4.30pm.
Key facts: Garden and ground floor only. Prebooked.

BROCKHAMPTON ESTATE
Bringsty, Nr Bromyard WR6 5TB
Tel: 01885 488099 **E-mail:** brockhampton@nationaltrust.org.uk

CROFT CASTLE
Aymestrey, Nr Leominster, Herefordshire HR9 9PW
Tel: 01568 780246 **E-mail:** croftcastle@nationaltrust.org.uk

GOODRICH CASTLE
Ross-On-Wye, Herefordshire HR9 6HY
Tel: 01600 890538 **E-mail:** customers@english-heritage.org.uk

ACTON BURNELL CASTLE
Acton Burnell, Shrewsbury, Shropshire UK
Tel: 0121 625 6832 **E-mail:** andrea.fox@english-heritage.org.uk

ATTINGHAM PARK
Atcham, Shrewsbury, Shropshire SY4 4TP
Tel: 01743 708170/162 **E-mail:** attingham@nationaltrust.org.uk

BENTHALL HALL
Benthall Hall, Broseley, Shropshire TF12 5RX
Tel: 01746 780838 **E-mail:** wendy.barton@nationaltrust.org.uk

HAWKSTONE HALL & GARDENS
Marchamley, Shrewsbury, Shropshire SY4 5LG
Tel: 01630 685242 **E-mail:** hawkhall@aol.com

MAWLEY HALL
Cleobury Mortimer DY14 8PN
Tel: 0208 298 0429 **E-mail:** rsharp@mawley.com

MUCH WENLOCK PRIORY
Much Wenlock, Shropshire TF13 6HS
Tel: 01952 727466 **E-mail:** customers@english-heritage.org.uk

STOKESAY CASTLE
Nr Craven Arms, Shropshire SY7 9AH
Tel: 01588 672544 **E-mail:** customers@english-heritage.org.uk

WROXETER ROMAN CITY
Wroxeter, Shrewsbury, Shropshire SY5 6PH
Tel: 01743 761330 **E-mail:** customers@english-heritage.org.uk

BOSCOBEL HOUSE & THE ROYAL OAK
Bishop's Wood, Brewood, Staffordshire ST19 9AR
Tel: 01902 850244 **E-mail:** customers@english-heritage.org.uk

CASTERNE HALL
Ilam, Nr Ashbourne, Derbyshire DE6 2BA
Tel: 01335 310489 **E-mail:** mail@casterne.co.uk

ERASMUS DARWIN HOUSE
Beacon Street, Lichfield, Staffordshire WS13 7AD
Tel: 01543 306260 **E-mail:** enquiries@erasmusdarwin.org

MOSELEY OLD HALL
Moseley Old Hall Lane, Wolverhampton WV10 7HY
Tel: 01902 782808 **E-mail:** moseleyoldhall@nationaltrust.org.uk

SANDON HALL
Sandon, Staffordshire ST18 OBZ
Tel: 01889 508004 **E-mail:** info@sandonhall.co.uk

THE TRENTHAM ESTATE
Stone Road, Trentham, Staffordshire ST4 8AX
Tel: 01782 646646 **E-mail:** enquiry@trentham.co.uk

BAGOTS CASTLE
Bagots Castle, Church Road, Baginton CV8 3AR
Tel: 07786 438711 **E-mail:** delia@bagotscastle.org.uk

COUGHTON COURT
Alcester, Warwickshire B49 5JA
Tel: 01789 400777 **E-mail:** office@throckmortons.co.uk

FARNBOROUGH HALL
Banbury OX17 1DU
Tel: 01295 690002 **E-mail:** farnboroughhall@nationaltrust.org.uk

PACKWOOD HOUSE
Packwood Lane, Lapworth, Warwickshire B94 6AT
Tel: 01564 783294 **E-mail:** packwood@nationaltrust.org.uk

UPTON HOUSE & GARDENS
Upton, Near Banbury, Warwickshire OX15 6HT
Tel: 01295 670266 **E-mail:** uptonhouse@nationaltrust.org.uk

BACK TO BACKS
55-63 Hurst Street, Birmingham, West Midlands B5 4TE
E-mail: backtobacks@nationaltrust.org.uk

HAGLEY HALL
Hall Lane, Hagley, Nr. Stourbridge, Worcestershire DY9 9LG
Tel: 01562 882408 **E-mail:** joycepurnell@hagleyhall.com

KINVER EDGE AND THE ROCK HOUSES
Compton Road, Kinver, Nr Stourbridge, Staffordshire DY7 6DL
Tel: 01384 872553

BROADWAY TOWER
Middle Hill, Broadway, Worcestershire WR12 7LB
Tel: 01386 852390 **E-mail:** info@broadwaytower.co.uk

HANBURY HALL
Droitwich, Worcestershire WR9 7EA
Tel: 01527 821214 **E-mail:** hanburyhall@nationaltrust.org.uk

SNOWSHILL MANOR
Snowshill, Broadway WR12 7JU
Tel: 01386 852410 **E-mail:** snowshillmanor@nationaltrust.org.uk

SPETCHLEY PARK GARDENS
Spetchley Park, Worcester WR5 1RS
Tel: 01453 810303 **E-mail:** hb@spetchleygardens.co.uk

WITLEY COURT & GARDENS
Great Witley, Worcestershire WR6 6JT
Tel: 01299 896636 **E-mail:** customers@english-heritage.org.uk

Newman Brothers Coffin Fitting Works

13–15 Fleet Street, Birmingham B3 1JP

Established in 1882 by two brothers, Alfred and Edwin, Newman Brothers began to later specialise in fittings for coffins. In 1998, having failed to modernize and unable to compete with suppliers from abroad, the factory was forced out of business. The Fitting Works is now a 'time capsule' museum, seen as though the workers have just set down their tools and left. Working machinery, costumed guides, self-guided sessions, hands-on activities and events make this a family friendly attraction.

Open: Guided tours on the hour from 12 noon Daily, Tuesday – Sunday and Bank Holiday Mondays

Heritage Open Days: Yes

Parking: On street parking nearby and NCP on Charlotte St

Disabled access: Yes

Admission charge: Yes

T: 0121 233 4790

E: newmanbrothers@coffinworks.org

W: www.coffinworks.org

Nothe Fort

Barrack Road, Weymouth DT4 8UF

Dominating the entrance to Weymouth Harbour, Nothe Fort is a labyrinth of passageways and outdoor areas with stunning views of the Jurassic Coast. It was constructed between 1860 and 1872 on three, easily accessed levels. The Fort is now filled with displays, mammoth guns and cinema areas that chart the history of this magnificent Victorian structure. Nothe Fort is now one of Weymouth's major attractions and a popular venue for events.

Open: Open daily between 25th March – 30th September, for winter opening hours please refer to website for more details.

Heritage Open Days: No

Parking: Public pay & display nearby

Disabled access: Yes

Admission charge: Yes

T: 01305 766 626

E: nothefort@uwclub.net

W: www.nothefort.org.uk

Kensal Green Cemetery

Harrow Road, London W10 4RA

The Grade I listed Kensal Green Cemetery covers 72 acres of beautiful grounds adjoining the Grand Union Canal. One of the world's first garden cemeteries it was inspired by the Père Lachaise Cemetery in Paris. Attractions include the Grade II* listed Dissenters' Chapel, Grade II North Terrace Colonnade, and the Grade II* monument to Emma and Alexis Soyer. Look out for events, exhibitions and guided tours run by the Friends of Kensal Green Cemetery.

Open: Cemetery open 1 April – 30 September: Monday – Saturday 9am – 6pm, Sunday 10am – 6pm. 1 October – 31 March: Monday – Saturday 9am – 5pm, Sunday 10am – 5pm. Bank Holidays 10am – 1pm.

London Open House: No

Parking: Roadside parking on internal cemetery roads

Disabled access: No

Admission charge: No

T: 07530 676 151

E: fokgc@hotmail.com

W: www.kensalgreen.co.uk

Bounds Walls

Ushaw College, Durham DH7 9RH

Ushaw College combines a fascinating history with some of the finest Victorian architecture in the North East. Built in 1852, the Bounds Walls were built to enclose the north and north east sides of a playing field. The games played there were peculiar to Ushaw College; they included handball and a battledore game which were regularly played by students until the 1980s. The wider site offers chapels, a children's bunny trail, beautiful gardens and a varied programme of events.

Open: Free access to the walls, approaching from the drives and car parks to the south and west. For all other parts please check website.

Heritage Open Days: Yes

Parking: Adjacent parking available

Disabled access: Partial access available

Admission charge: No

T: 0191 334 6423

E: tickets@ushaw.org

W: www.ushaw.org

Historic England

Visit the places you've helped to protect

Forts and castles, mills and mausoleums, follies and parks. There are many fascinating historic places which have been repaired with the help of grants from Historic England and financed by you, the taxpayer.

Many of these places open to the public as a condition of the grant they have received and can be visited at certain times throughout the year. With over 1,600 to choose from, from the famous to lesser-known treasures – they are all worth a visit. Some of them are opening their doors to the public for the first time.

To find a site to visit today and for full details of opening arrangements, search the grant-aided places database at **HistoricEngland.org.uk**

Castle Howard, North Yorkshire

Sion Hill Hall, North Yorkshire

East Yorkshire
North Yorkshire
South Yorkshire
West Yorkshire

Yorkshire & The Humber

Yorkshire

No county has more important country houses than Yorkshire, where established medieval powerbases have been joined by the stately homes of enlightenment gentry through the centuries.

New Entries for 2016:
• Wentworth Woodhouse
• Ripley Castle

Find stylish hotels with a personal welcome and good cuisine in Yorkshire & The Humber. More information on page 348.

- The Blue Bell Inn
- The Coniston Hotel & Country Estate
- The Feversham Arms Hotel & Verbena Spa
- Lastingham Grange
- Sportsmans Arms Hotel
- The Traddock

SIGNPOST
RECOMMENDING THE UK'S FINEST HOTELS SINCE 1935

www.signpost.co.uk

257

WASSAND HALL
SEATON, HULL, EAST YORKSHIRE HU11 5RJ
www.wassand.co.uk

Fine Regency house 1815 by Thomas Cundy the Elder. Beautifully restored walled gardens, woodland walks, Parks and vistas over Hornsea Mere, part of the Estate since 1580. The Estate was purchased circa 1520 by Dame Jane Constable and has remained in the family to the present day, Mr Rupert Russell being the great nephew of the late Lady Strickland-Constable.

The house contains a fine collection of 18/19th Century paintings, English and Continental silver, furniture and porcelain. Wassand is very much a family home and retains a very friendly atmosphere. Homemade afternoon teas are served in the conservatory on Open Days.

Location: Map 11:F9. OS Ref TA174 460. On the B1244 Seaton-Hornsea Road. Approximately 2m from Hornsea.

Owner/Contact: R E O Russell - Resident Trustee
Tel/Fax: 01964 534488 **E-mail:** rupert@reorussell.co.uk
Open: 27-30 May (May 30 Vintage Car Rally), 10-13 & 24-28 Jun, 8-10 Jul (10 Jul - East Yorkshire Youth Wind Band Concert, Hall closed), 29-31 Jul; 1 & 2, 5-9 (Sat 6 closed), 26-29 Aug.
Admission: Hall & Gardens: Adult £6.00, OAP £5.50, Child (11-15yrs) £3.00, Child (under 10) Free. Hall: Adult £4.00, OAP £3.50, Child (11-15yrs) £1.50, Child (under 10) Free. Grounds & Garden: Adult £4.00, OAP £3.50, Child (11-15yrs) £1.50, Child (under 10) Free.
Key facts: ⓘ Group Bookings - Guided Tours, contact Shirley Power 01964-537474. ⬛ Limited. ⬛ ⬛ By arrangement. ⬛ Ample for cars, limited for coaches. ⬛ In grounds, on leads.

BURTON CONSTABLE ⓕ
Skirlaugh, Hull, East Yorks HU11 4LN
www.burtonconstable.com

East Yorkshire's 'hidden gem'. Meander upstairs and downstairs through 30 evocative grand rooms filled with fine art and furniture, visit the stable lad's bedchamber, blacksmith's shop, tack rooms and the restored workings of the 18th Century stable clock and of course see the skeleton of a 60' sea monster. Explore the historic grounds, with their woodland and parkland walks, follow the wildlife trail or just find a favourite spot to relax in this glorious setting.
Location: Map 11:E10. OS Ref TA 193 369. Beverley 14m, Hull 10m. Signed from Skirlaugh. **Owner:** Burton Constable Foundation **Contact:** Mrs Helen Dewson
Tel: 01964 562400 **E-mail:** enquiries@burtonconstable.com
Open: Easter Sat-23 Oct: Sat-Thu inclusive (every day in Jul & Aug). Hall: 12noon-5pm (last admission 1 hour before closing). Tearoom, Grounds, Stables & Gift Shop 11am-5pm. Christmas Opening 19 Nov-11 Dec. (tbc) Hall, 11am-4pm (last admission 1 hour before closing). Tearoom, Gift Shop, Stables and Grounds 11am to approx. 4.30pm. **Admission:** Adult £8.75, Child £4.50, OAP £8.25. Family £22.00 (2 adults & 4 children). Prices include 10% Gift Aid.
Key facts: ⓘ Photography. ⬛ Small gift shop. ⬛ Seminars/meetings. ⬛ Mostly accessible. ⬛ Stables Tearoom. ⬛ A variety of tours can be arranged in advance of your visit. ⬛ Ample free parking.

BURTON AGNES HALL & GARDENS ⓕ
Driffield, East Yorkshire YO25 4NB
Elizabethan house with award winning gardens.
Location: Map 11:E9. OS Ref TA103 633. Off A614 between Driffield and Bridlington. **Tel:** 01262 490324
Fax: 01262 490513 **E-mail:** office@burtonagnes.com
Website: www.burtonagnes.com **Open:** 1 Apr-31 Oct & 14 Nov-23 Dec 11am-5pm. **Admission:** See website.

SLEDMERE HOUSE ⓕ
Sledmere, Driffield, East Yorkshire YO25 3XG
At the heart of the Yorkshire Wolds, Sledmere House exudes 18th Century elegance with each room containing decorative plasterwork by Joseph Rose Junior.
Location: Map 11:D9. OS Ref SE931 648. **Tel:** 01377 236637
E-mail: info@sledmerehouse.com **Website:** www.sledmerehouse.com
Open: Please see website for up-to-date opening and admission details.

Sledmere House

CASTLE HOWARD 🏛Ⓕ
www.castlehoward.co.uk

Designed by Sir John Vanbrugh in 1699 Castle Howard is undoubtedly one of Britain's finest private residences.

Built for Charles Howard the 3rd Earl of Carlisle and taking over 100 years to complete, today Castle Howard remains home to the Howard family. Discover the rich and varied history, dramatic interiors and sweeping parklands of this magnificent house.

Free flowing tours of the house allow you to explore at your leisure, with friendly and knowledgeable guides throughout happy to share stories. From decadent bedrooms and lavish drawing rooms to the stunning Great Hall and vast Long Gallery there are architectural wonders and world renowned collections in every room.

The house façade bristles with carvings and the gold topped dome reaches skyward giving Castle Howard its iconic silhouette.

Spend a day exploring the beautiful gardens; with meandering woodland paths, lakeside terraces and sweeping vistas dotted with temples, statues and follies. The walled garden is the perfect place to relax with a stunning collection of roses, herbaceous borders and a formal potager. Seasonal highlights include daffodils, rhododendrons, bluebells, roses and striking autumnal hues.

Enjoy a changing programme of exhibitions and events, including Christmas opening when the house is decorated for the festive season. Plus free outdoor tours, illustrated children's trail, adventure playground and summer boat trips on the Great Lake (weather permitting). Treat yourself at a range of cafés and shops, including garden centre, farm shop and gift shops.

KEY FACTS

- ℹ️ Photography allowed.
- 🏪 Gift shops, farm shop and garden centre.
- 🍽 Available for private events.
- ♿ Access to all areas except High South, Exhibition Wing and Chapel.
- ☕ Choice of four Cafés.
- 🚶 Guides in each room.
- 🅿 Free parking.
- 🏫 School parties welcome.
- 🐕 Dogs on leads welcome in gardens only. Assistance dogs welcome in house.
- ⛺ Camping and caravanning.
- 🔔 Great Hall licensed for weddings.
- ❄️ Gardens, shops and cafés open all year.
- 👪 Full programme for all the family.

VISITOR INFORMATION

■ Owner
Castle Howard Estate Ltd

■ Address
Castle Howard
York
North Yorkshire
YO60 7DA

■ Location
Map 11:C8
OS Ref. SE716 701
From the North: From the A1 take the A61 to Thirsk then the A170 to Helmsley. Before Helmsley turn right onto the B1257 and follow the brown signs.
From the South: Take the A1M to Junction 44 and follow the A64 east to York. Continue past York and follow the brown signs.
Bus: Service from York.
Rail: London Kings Cross to York 1hr. 50 mins. York to Malton Station 30 mins.

■ Contact
Visitor Services
Tel: 01653 648333
E-mail: house@castlehoward.co.uk

■ Opening Times
House:
19 March-30 October & 19 November-23 December. Open daily from 11am.

Grounds:
Open all year except Christmas Day, from 10am-5.30pm (dusk in winter).

Stable Courtyard Shops, Café & Garden Centre:
Open daily all year except Christmas Day from 10am-5pm (4pm in winter).

For more information please contact Castle Howard Estate Office on 01653 648444.

■ Admission
Visit www.castlehoward.co.uk for details of admission prices.

Conference/Function

ROOM	Size	Max Cap
Long Gallery	197' x 24'	200
Grecian Hall	40' x 40'	70

Yorkshire & The Humber - England

VISITOR INFORMATION

■ Address
Skipton Castle
Skipton
North Yorkshire
BD23 1AW

■ Location
Map 10:09
OS Ref. SD992 520
In the centre of Skipton, at the N end of High Street. Skipton is 20m W of Harrogate on the A59 and 26m NW of Leeds on A65.
Rail: Regular services from Leeds & Bradford.

■ Contact
Penny Cannon
Tel: 01756 792442
Fax: 01756 796100
E-mail:
info@skiptoncastle.co.uk

■ Opening Times
All year
(Closed 23-25 December)
Mon-Sat 10am-5pm
Sun 11am-5pm
(October-March 4pm).

■ Admission
Adult	£7.80
Child (0-4yrs)	Free
Child (5-17yrs)	£4.90
OAP	£6.80
Student (with ID)	£6.80
Family (2+3)	£24.90
Groups (15+)	
Adult	£6.70
Child (0-17yrs)	£4.90

Includes illustrated tour sheet in a choice of ten languages, plus free badge for children.

Groups welcome - Coach parking and guides available for pre-booked groups at no extra charge.

■ Special Events
Historical Re-enactments. Plays. Art Exhibitions. For up-to-date information and events, visit our website www.skiptoncastle.co.uk.

Conference/Function

Room	Size	Max Cap
Oak Room		30
Granary		100

SKIPTON CASTLE
www.skiptoncastle.co.uk

Skipton Castle, over 900 years old, one of the best preserved, most complete medieval castles in England.

Guardian of the gateway to the Yorkshire Dales for over 900 years, this unique fortress is one of the most complete, well-preserved medieval castles in England. Standing on a 40-metre high crag, fully-roofed Skipton Castle was founded around 1090 by Robert de Romille, one of William the Conqueror's Barons, as a fortress in the dangerous northern reaches of the kingdom.

Owned by King Edward I and Edward II, from 1310 it became the stronghold of the Clifford Lords withstanding successive raids by marauding Scots. During the Civil War it was the last Royalist bastion in the North, yielding only after a three-year siege in 1645. 'Slighted' under the orders of Cromwell, the Castle was skillfully restored by the redoubtable Lady Anne Clifford and today visitors can climb from the depths of the Dungeon to the top of the Watch Tower, explore the Banqueting Hall, Kitchens, the Bedchamber and even the Privy!

Every period has left its mark, from the Norman entrance and the medieval towers, to the beautiful Tudor courtyard with the great yew tree planted by Lady Anne in 1659.

In the grounds visitors can see the Tudor wing built as a royal wedding present for Lady Eleanor Brandon, niece of Henry VIII, the beautiful Shell Room decorated in the 1620s with shells and Jamaican coral and the ancient medieval chapel of St. John the Evangelist. The Chapel Terrace, with its delightful picnic area, has fine views over the woods and Skipton's lively market town.

KEY FACTS

- ℹ Fully roofed. Photography allowed for personal use only.
- 🏪 Specialist books, cards, gifts. Online shop.
- 🌱 Unusual plants grown in grounds.
- 🍸 Corporate hospitality. Wedding ceremonies. Champagne receptions.
- ♿ Unsuitable.
- 🍴 Licensed. Open all year.
- 🍽 Licensed. Open all year.
- 👥 By arrangement.
- 🅿 Large public coach and car park nearby.
- 🚶 Tour guides, educational rooms and teachers packs available.
- 🐕 Dogs on leads only.
- 💒 Civil Wedding Licence. Max 80 guests.
- ❄ Open all year except 23-25 December.

Register for news and special offers at **www.hudsonsheritage.com**

FOUNTAINS ABBEY & STUDLEY ROYAL
RIPON, NORTH YORKSHIRE HG4 3DY
www.nationaltrust.org.uk/fountainsabbey

Come and discover for yourself why Fountains Abbey & Studley Royal is a World Heritage Site. Experience the beauty, history and tranquillity of this inspirational place in the heart of the beautiful North Yorkshire countryside. Explore the spectacular ruin of a 12th Century Cistercian Abbey, one of the best surviving examples of a Georgian Water Garden, Elizabethan Manor House, Monastic Watermill and Medieval Deer Park home to over 500 wild deer. Enjoy exhibitions, guided tours, family activities and wildlife walks throughout the year.

Location: Map 10:P8. OS Ref SE275 700.
Abbey entrance: 4m W of Ripon off B6265. 8m W of A1.
Owner: National Trust
Contact: The National Trust
Tel: 01765 608888
E-mail: fountainsabbey@nationaltrust.org.uk
Open: Apr-Sep Daily: 10am-5pm. Oct-Mar Daily: 10am-4pm or dusk if earlier. Closed 24 & 25 Dec, & Fri's from Nov-Jan.
Deer Park: All year, daily during daylight. Closed 24 & 25 Dec.

Admission: Adult £13.00, Child (5-16yrs) £6.50, Family £32.50, Groups (15+) Adult £10.60, Groups (31+) Adult £10.30. Group discount applicable with prior booking. Telephone in advance, 01765 643197. NT, EH Members & Under 5s Free. Group visits and disabled visitors, please telephone in advance. Includes voluntary donation, visitors can choose to pay standard prices displayed at property and website. Does not apply to group prices.
Key facts: ⓘ Events held throughout the year. Exhibitions. Seminar facilities. The Abbey is owned by English Heritage. St Mary's Church is owned by English Heritage and managed by the National Trust. ⬚ Two shops. ✿ Plant sales available at the Visitor Centre. ☎ Dinners. ⬚ WCs. ✦ Licensed. ⁙ Licensed. ✦ Free, but seasonal. Groups (please book on 01765 643197), please use Visitor Centre entrance. ⬚ Audio tour free (limited number available at the Visitor Centre). ⓟ Drivers must book groups. ■ ✉ Dogs on leads only. ✦ Fountains Hall, an Elizabethan Mansion is an ideal setting for weddings. For details or a Wedding pack tel: 01765 643198. ✦ Closed 24/25 Dec. ✿

KIPLIN HALL AND GARDENS ⓕ
NR SCORTON, RICHMOND, NORTH YORKSHIRE DL10 6AT
www.kiplinhall.co.uk

This award-winning house & garden was the Jacobean country seat of founder of Maryland, George Calvert. 'Gothic' wing added in 1820s & redesigned in 1887 by W.E. Nesfield. This intriguing property is now furnished as a comfortable Victorian home with an eclectic mix of previous owners' furniture, paintings, portraits & personalia, including Arts & Crafts items. Many original paintings from 16th–19th Centuries include works by Beuckelaer, Carlevarijs, Kauffman & Watts. Attractive Gardens, productive Walled Garden, woodland/lakeside walks. Tearoom serving homemade scones, cakes & lunches. Children's Play Ship, garden games, dipping-pond, archaeology 'trench'.
2016 Exhibition: 'My Darling Sally: Sarah Carpenter of Kiplin & Stoke Rochford'.
Location: Map 11:A7. OS Ref SE274 976. Midway between Richmond & Northallerton, 5 miles east of A1, on B6271 Scorton - Northallerton road.
Owner: Kiplin Hall CIO **Tel:** 01748 818178 **E-mail:** info@kiplinhall.co.uk

Open: Gardens and Tearoom: Sun, Mon, Tue & Wed from 7 Feb-26 Oct, 10am-5pm (4pm Feb & Mar). Also Good Fri & Easter Sat.
Hall: Good Fri & Easter Sat 25 & 26 Mar, and then Sun, Mon, Tue & Wed from 27 Mar-26 Oct, 2-5pm. Christmas: Fri–Sun 2-4 and 9-11 Dec, 10am-4pm.
Admission: Hall/Gardens/Grounds: Adult £8.50, Conc. £7.50, Child £4.50, Family (2+3) £25.50. Gardens/Grounds only: Adult £5.50, Conc. £4.50, Child £2.50, Family (2+3) £15.50.
Key facts: ⓘ Special Events, incl. Christmas - see website. ⬚ Small, but well-stocked, shop. ✿ Fruit, Veg & Plants from Walled Garden in season. ☎ Please telephone to discuss. ⬚ Wheelchair access to ground floor & gardens. Accessible W.C. ✦ Home cooking using Walled Garden produce. ✦ Pre-booked for groups of 18 or more. ⓟ ■ ✉ In gardens only. Assistance dogs are welcome in Hall. ✿

MARKENFIELD HALL 🏛Ⓕ
NR RIPON, NORTH YORKSHIRE HG4 3AD
www.markenfield.com

"This wonderfully little-altered building is the most complete surviving example of the medium-sized 14th Century country house in England" John Martin Robinson 'The Architecture of Northern England'. Tucked privately away down a mile-long winding drive, Markenfield is one of the most astonishing and romantic of Yorkshire's medieval houses: fortified, completely moated, and still privately owned. Winner of the HHA and Sotheby's Finest Restoration Award 2008.
Location: Map 10:P8. OS Ref SE294 672. Access from W side of A61. 2½ miles S of the Ripon bypass.

Owner: Mr Ian & Lady Deirdre Curteis **Contact:** The Administrator
Tel: 01765 692303 **Fax:** 01765 607195 **E-mail:** info@markenfield.com
Open: 30 Apr-15 May and 11-26 Jun daily 2pm-5pm. Last entry 4:30pm. Groups bookings can be accepted all year round by appointment.
Admission: Prices £5.00 Adult, £4.00 conc. Booked groups £6.00 per person for a guided tour (min charge £100.00).
Key facts: ⓘ 🖻 🎦 🗊 🖳 Partial. Wheelchair access to the ground floor only. Ⓕ 🅿 🖻 🐾 Dogs in grounds only. 🅰 🎫 🎗

© Peter Packer   © Jerry Hardman Jones

NEWBY HALL & GARDENS 🏛Ⓕ
NEWBY HALL, RIPON, NORTH YORKSHIRE HG4 5AE
www.newbyhall.com

Designed under the guidance of Sir Christopher Wren, this graceful country house, home to the Compton family, epitomises the Georgian 'Age of Elegance'. Its beautifully restored interior presents Robert Adam at his best and houses rare Gobelins tapestries and one of the UK's largest private collections of classical statuary. The award-winning gardens, created in the early 1920s boast one of Europe's longest double herbaceous borders and are of interest to specialist and amateur gardeners alike. Newby also offers a large, thoughtfully designed Adventure Garden for children, a miniature railway, excellent restaurant, shop and plant centre and stunning new Dollshouse Exhibition. Events: 8 May-Spring Plant Fair, 11 & 12 Jun-Tractor Fest, 17 Jul-Historic Vehicle Rally.
Location: Map 11:A8. OS Ref SE348 675. Midway between London and Edinburgh, 4m W of A1(M), towards Ripon. From north use J49, from south use J48 and follow brown tourist signs. 40 mins from York, 30 mins from Harrogate.
Owner: Mr Richard Compton **Contact:** The Administrator
Tel: 01423 322583 opt 3 **Fax:** 01423 324452 **E-mail:** info@newbyhall.com

Open: Summer- House*, 25 Mar-25 Sep. Apr, May, Jun & Sep: Tue-Sun & BH Mons; Jul-Aug: Daily. See website for tour times. *Areas of the House can be closed to the public from time to time, please check website for details. Garden, dates as House, 11am-5.30pm. last admission 5pm. Winter, Oct-end Mar closed.
Admission: See website for 2016 prices.
Key facts: ⓘ Allow a full day for viewing house and gardens. Suitable for filming and for special events. No indoor photography. 🖻 'The Shop @ Newby Hall' - Modern British Art and Craftsmanship. Quality toys. 🎦 Quality plants available, reflecting the contents of the garden. 🗊 Wedding receptions & special functions. Licensed for civil ceremonies. 🖳 Suitable. WCs. Parking. Electric and manual wheelchairs available - booking essential. 🖻 Licensed. 🍴 Licensed. Ⓕ Obligatory. 🅿 Ample. Hard standing for coaches. 🖻 Welcome. Rates on request. Woodland discovery walk, adventure gardens and train rides. 🐾 Guide/hearing dogs only in Gardens/Woodland. Dog exercise area for other dogs not permitted into gardens or woodland walk. 🅰 House licensed. 🎫 🎗

NUNNINGTON HALL 🦋
NUNNINGTON, NORTH YORKSHIRE YO62 5UY
www.nationaltrust.org.uk/nunnington-hall

Picturesque Yorkshire manor house with organic garden and exciting exhibitions. Enjoy the atmosphere of this beautiful Yorkshire manor house, nestled on the quiet banks of the River Rye. Explore the period rooms whilst hearing the Hall's many tales and discover one of the world's finest collections of miniature rooms in the attic. Famed for its picturesque location, organic walled garden with spring-flowering meadows, flamboyant resident peacocks and a changing programme of exclusive and high profile art and photography exhibitions, Nunnington Hall offers something for everyone to enjoy.

Location: Map 11:C8. OS Ref SE669 793. In Ryedale, 4½ m SE of Helmsley, 1½ m N of B1257. **Owner:** National Trust **Contact:** The Property Manager

Tel: 01439 748283 **E-mail:** nunningtonhall@nationaltrust.org.uk
Open: 13 Feb-30 Oct, daily except Mons, 11am-5pm. 5 Nov-11 Dec, Sats & Suns, 11am-4pm. Last adm. 30min before closing. BH Mons & Mons in school holidays.
Admission: Adult £8.25, Child (under 17) £4.15, Family £20.65, Groups (15+) £6.75. National Trust Members Free. *includes voluntary donation but visitors can choose to pay standard prices displayed at the property and on website.
Key facts: 🏬 An expanded shop with an array of souvenirs, plants and gifts. 🍽 🚻 Ground floor and grounds. WC. 🍴 Waitress service in our beautiful tearoom, serving local and seasonal produce. 🅿 🐕 Guide dogs only in the hall. Dogs on a lead in the gardens. 🐕

BROUGHTON HALL ESTATE 🏛
Skipton, Yorkshire BD23 3AE
www.broughtonhall.co.uk

Broughton Estate has been nurtured by the Tempest Family for over 900 years. Guests can exclusively hire any one of the five exquisite venues from contemporary Utopia, luxury holiday retreats Eden, Higher Scarcliffe, Yellison and the historic Hall itself. Properties are available year round for residential stays, celebrations and corporate events.

Location: Map 10:N9. OS Ref SD943 507. On A59, 2m W of Skipton.
Owner: The Tempest Family **Contact:** The Estate Office
Tel: 01756 799608 **Fax:** 01756 700357 **Email:** info@broughtonhall.co.uk
E-mail: tempest@broughtonhall.co.uk
Open: Utopia is open for Breakfast and Lunch, Mon-Fri.
Viewings of other properties are by prior arrangement only. Contact Estate Office.
Admission: Please contact for prices.
Key facts: 🗣 Meetings & Events space available. 🖼 🍽 🍴 Breakfast & Lunch - Licensed. 🎦 By arrangement. 🅿 Ample car parking. 🍽 Must be pre-booked. 🛏 29 luxury bedrooms. ⛪ Chapel on site for Catholic services. ❋ 🐕

CONSTABLE BURTON HALL GARDENS 🏛ⓕ
Leyburn, North Yorkshire DL8 5LJ
www.constableburton.com

A delightful terraced woodland garden of lilies, ferns, hardy shrubs, roses and wild flowers surrounds this beautiful Palladian house designed by John Carr. Garden trails and herbaceous borders and stream garden with large architectural plants and reflection ponds. Stunning seasonal displays of snowdrops and daffodils. An annual Tulip Festival takes place over the early May Bank Holiday weekend. Group tours of the House and Gardens are invited by prior arrangement.

Location: Map 10:P7. OS Ref SE164 913. 3m E of Leyburn off the A684.
Owner/Contact: D'Arcy Wyvill **Tel:** 01677 450428 **Fax:** 01677 450622
E-mail: gardens@constableburton.com
Open: Garden open season 2016: Sat 19 Mar-Sun 25 Sep. Tulip Festival: Sat 30 Apr-Mon 2 May. Please consult website for exceptional closures for private events. House closed to the public. Private tours and venue for classic car rallies available by arrangement through the estate office.
Admission: Adult £4.00, Child (5-16yrs) 50p, OAP £3.00.
Key facts: 🚶 Woodland walks. 🗣 🚻 Partial. 🎦 🅿 Limited for coaches. 🐕 On leads only. 🐕 🐕

DUNCOMBE PARK 🏛ⓕ
Helmsley, North Yorkshire YO62 5EB
www.duncombepark.com

The sweeping grass terraces, towering veteran trees, and classical temples are described by historian Christopher Hussey as 'the most spectacularly beautiful among English landscape conceptions of the 18th Century'. Beside superb views over the Rye valley, visitors will discover woodland walks, ornamental parterres, and a 'secret garden' at the Conservatory.

Location: Map 11:B7. OS Ref SE604 830. Entrance just off Helmsley Market Square, signed off A170 Thirsk-Scarborough road.
Owner/Contact: Hon Jake Duncombe
Tel: 01439 770213 **Fax:** 01439 771114 **E-mail:** info@duncombepark.com
Open: Garden Only: 29 Mar-31 Aug, Sun-Fri, 10:30am-5pm. The garden may close for private events and functions - please check website for information.
Admission: Gardens & Parkland: Adult £5.00, Conc £4.50, Child (5-16yrs) £3.00, Child (0-5yrs) Free, Groups (15+) £4.00, Group guided tour £5.00.
Parkland: Adult £1.00, Child (0-16yrs) Free.
Key facts: ⓘ Wedding receptions, conferences, corporate hospitality, country walks, nature reserve, orienteering, film location, product launches, vehicle rallies. Ⓣ Banqueting facilities. ⓕ For 15+ groups only. 🅿 ▣ 🔺 ♿

FAIRFAX HOUSE 🏛ⓕ
Castlegate, York, North Yorkshire YO1 9RN
www.fairfaxhouse.co.uk

Come and unlock the splendour within one of the finest Georgian townhouses in England. A classical architectural masterpiece with superb period interiors, incomparable stucco ceilings and the outstanding Noel Terry collection of furniture, Fairfax House transports you to the grandeur of 18th Century city living. Don't miss a programme of special events and exhibitions.

Location: Map 11:B9. Centrally located, close to Clifford's Tower & Jorvik Centre. Park & Ride 2 mins away. **Tel:** 01904 655543 **E-mail:** info@fairfaxhouse.co.uk
Open: 5 Feb-31 Dec (closed 24-26 Dec). Tue-Sat & BHs: 10am-5pm.
Sun: 11am-4pm. Mon: Guided tours at 11am and 2pm.
Admission: Adult £6.00, Conc. £5.00, Children Free. Daytime and exclusive access evening group tours available, plus catering package options.
Key facts: ⓘ Suitable for filming. ▣ Ⓣ Stunning venue for private dining & drinks receptions. ♿ ⓕ Audio guides in French, German, Italian, Spanish, Polish, Japanese, Chinese 🅿 Parking in adjacent Clifford's Tower car park. ▣ ✖ Guide dogs only. ❄ ♿

THE FORBIDDEN CORNER LTD
Tupgill Park Estate, Coverham, Nr Middleham
North Yorkshire DL8 4TJ
www.theforbiddencorner.co.uk

A unique labyrinth of tunnels, chambers, follies and surprises created in a four acre garden in the heart of the Yorkshire dales. The Temple of the Underworld, The Eye of the Needle, a large pyramid made of translucent glass paths and passageways that lead nowhere. Extraordinary statues at every turn. A day out with a difference that will challenge and delight children and adults of all ages.

Location: Map 10:07. OS Ref SE094 866. A6108 to Middleham, situated 2½ miles west of Middleham on the Coverham Lane.
Owner: Colin R Armstrong CMG, OBE **Contact:** John or Wendy Reeves
Tel: 01969 640638 **E-mail:** forbiddencorner@gmail.com
Open: 1 Apr-31 Oct daily, then every Sun until Christmas. Mon-Sat 12-6pm. Suns & BH's 10am-6pm (or dusk if earlier). **Admission:** Please see website for up-to-date info & prices. **Key facts:** ⓘ ▣ Gifts & branded mementoes. ♿ WCs. Ramps into shop and café. and limited access in gardens. ▣ Own blend of barrista served coffee, locally sourced food & award-winning pies & teas. 🅿 large free parking area. Limited spaces for coaches. ▣ Special rates (see our website). ✖ Guide dogs only. ⌂ Self-catering cottages all year. Free day pass with all stays over 2 days. ♿

HOVINGHAM HALL 🏛ⓕ
Hovingham, York, North Yorkshire YO62 4LU
www.hovingham.co.uk

Attractive Palladian family home, designed and built by Thomas Worsley. The childhood home of Katharine Worsley, Duchess of Kent. It is entered through a huge riding school and has beautiful rooms with collections of pictures and furniture. The house has attractive gardens with magnificent Yew hedges and cricket ground.

Location: Map 11:C8. OS Ref SE666 756. 18m N of York on Malton/Helmsley Road (B1257).
Owner: Sir William Worsley
Contact: The Estate Office
Tel: 01653 628771 **Fax:** 01653 628668
E-mail: office@hovingham.co.uk
Open: 1-28 Jun inclusive 12.30pm-4.30pm; Guided tours only (last tour at 3.30pm); Tearoom open daily 1pm-4pm.
Admission: Adult £9.50, Concessions £9.00, Child £4.00, Gardens only £5.00.
Key facts: ⓘ No photography permitted in the Hall. Ⓣ ♿ Ground floor only. ▣ Tearoom open daily 1pm-4pm, 1 Jun-28 Jun inc. ⓕ Obligatory. 🅿 Limited.

NEWBURGH PRIORY
Coxwold, York, North Yorkshire YO61 4AS
www.newburghpriory.co.uk

Home to the Earls of Fauconberg and the Wombwell family the house was built in 1145 with alterations in 1538 and 1720 and contains the tomb of Oliver Cromwell. The beautiful grounds contain a lake, water garden, walled garden, amazing topiary yews and woodland walks set against the White Horse. The Tearooms set in the old kitchens sell a range of delicious teas and homemade cakes. **Location:** Map 11:B8. OS Ref SE541 764.
4m E of A19, 18m N of York, ½ m E of Coxwold.
Owner/Contact: Stephen Wombwell **Tel:** 01347 868372
E-mail: estateoffice@newburghpriory.co.uk
Open: 3 Apr-29 Jun, Wed & Sun. BH Mon 30 May & 29 Aug. Gardens 2-6pm, House 2.30-4.45pm. Tours every ½ hour. Bus parties by prior arrangement. Special tours of private apartments Wed 6, 13, 20, 27 Apr & 4 May, £5.00pp.
Admission: House & Gardens: Adult £6.00, Child £2.00.
Gardens only: Adult £3.00, Child Free.
Key facts: ⓘ No photography in house. ⊤ ⑤ Partial. ⬛ Ⓕ Obligatory. ⓟ Limited for coaches. ⬛ In grounds, on leads. ⬛ And wedding receptions. ⬛ ⬛

SION HILL HALL ⬛
Kirby Wiske, Thirsk, North Yorkshire YO7 4EU
www.sionhillhall.co.uk

A tree lined sweeping driveway leads to the elegant Hall, set in 5 acres of inspiring gardens. 'A Masterpiece in the Neo-Georgian Style' designed in 1912 by the renowned York architect Walter H Brierley 'the Lutyens of the North'. The Hall is exquisitely furnished and hosts a fine collection of art and antiques. Graceful gardens include a formal parterre with clipped box and hornbeam, Long Walk with bountiful herbaceous borders, charming woodland Lower Walk, and a traditional Kitchen Garden.
Location: Map 11:A7. OS Ref SE373 844. 7m E of A1. 6m S of Northallerton off A167. 4m W of Thirsk.
Owner: H W Mawer Trust **Contact:** R M Mallaby - Trustee
Tel: 01845 587206 **E-mail:** sionhill@btconnect.com
Open: All year by appointment only. Please contact hall to book.
Admission: £12.00 per person. Includes guided tour of the hall and gardens, with tea/coffee and biscuits served in the original Edwardian kitchens.
Key facts: ⓘ No photography in the hall. ⑤ Partial. WC. Ⓕ By arrangement. Minimum of 12 people. ⓟ Ample for cars and coaches. ⬛ Guide dogs only. ⬛

RIPLEY CASTLE ⬛Ⓕ
Ripley, Harrogate, North Yorkshire HG3 3AY
www.ripleycastle.co.uk

Home to the Ingilby Family, Ripley Castle dates from the 1555 Tudor Tower and Priests Hole to elegant Georgian rooms. A unique collection of objects and paintings reflecting the family's 700 year history. Guided tours are informative and amusing with themed and family tours available. Extensive Gardens, Parkland and Lakes, Garden tours and family activities. **Location:** Map 10:P9. OS Ref SE283 605. W edge of village. Just off A61 between Harrogate and Ripon.
Owner: Sir Thomas Ingilby Bt **Contact:** Estate & Events Admin Team
Tel: 01423 770152 **Fax:** 01423 771745 **E-mail:** enquiries@ripleycastle.co.uk
Open: Gardens open daily. Castle by guided tour. Please see website for times.
Admission: Castle & Gardens: Adult £11.00, Conc £9.00 Child (5-16yrs) £7.50, Child under 5yrs Free. Gardens: Adult £7.50, Concession £6.50, Child (5-16yrs) £5.00 Groups (20+): Adult £6.00, Child (5-16yrs) £4.50, Child under 5yrs Free.
Key facts: ⓘ No photography in Castle unless by prior written consent. Parkland for outdoor activities & concerts. Check website for event details. ⬛ ⬛ ⊤ Dinners, Weddings, all types of corporate event, 12-120 guests. ⑤ Hearing Loop system. ⬛ Licensed. ⑪ Licensed. Ⓕ Tour time 60 mins. ⓟ 290 cars - 300 yards from Castle entrance. Coach park 50 yards. Free. ⬛ By prior arrangement. ⬛ Guide dogs only. ⬛ 100 yards from the Castle with 25 bedrooms. ⬛ ⬛ ⬛

STOCKELD PARK ⬛
Off the A661, Wetherby, North Yorkshire LS22 4AN
www.stockeldpark.co.uk

A gracious Palladian mansion by James Paine (1763), featuring a magnificent cantilevered staircase in the central oval hall. Surrounded by beautiful gardens and set in 18th Century landscaped parkland at the heart of a 2000 acre estate. Popular for filming and photography. In 2012 Stockeld Park was winner of Hudsons Best Family Day Out for its Adventure attraction, with interactive, imaginative play indoor and out and famous Enchanted forest.
Location: Map 11:A9. OS Ref SE376 497. York 12m, Harrogate 5m, Leeds 12m.
Owner: Mr and Mrs P G F Grant **Contact:** Mr P Grant
Tel: 01937 586101 **Fax:** 01937 580084 **E-mail:** office@stockeldpark.co.uk
Open: House: Privately booked events and tours only. Contact Estate Office 01937 586101. Please see website for further opening of the adventure site and special events www.stockeldpark.co.uk. Please note we are open throughout all the local school holidays. **Admission:** Prices on application.
Key facts: ⬛ Fantastic seasonal gift emporium filled with gift ideas. ⊤ Private event & Wedding enquiries welcome. ⬛ Homemade & Local, Fully Licensed. Ⓕ Groups, Tours and Groups welcome by appointment. ⓟ Free Parking. ⬛ Schools welcome by appointment. ⬛ ⬛

Yorkshire & The Humber - England

ASKE HALL

Richmond, North Yorkshire DL10 5HJ

A predominantly Georgian collection of paintings, furniture and porcelain in house which has been the seat of the Dundas family since 1763. Tours limited to 15 people per tour. Booking advisable and ID will be required (passport, driving licence etc). For further details contact Mandy Blenkiron.
Location: Map 10:P6. OS Ref NZ179 035. 4m SW of A1 at Scotch Corner, 2m from the A66, on the B6274.
Owner: Earl of Ronaldshay
Contact: Mandy Blenkiron
Tel: 01748 822000
E-mail: mandy.blenkiron@aske.co.uk
Website: www.aske.co.uk
Open: 8 & 9 Sep 2016 (Heritage Open Days). Tours at 10.00, 11.00 & 12.00.
Admission: Free.
Key facts: Partial. Obligatory. Limited.

BROCKFIELD HALL

Warthill, York YO19 5XJ

Georgian house (1804) by Peter Atkinson for Benjamin Agar Esq. Mrs. Wood's father was Lord Martin Fitzalan Howard, son of Lady Beaumont of Carlton Towers, Selby. Brockfield has portraits of her Stapleton family. There is a permanent exhibition of paintings by Staithes Group artists, by appointment outside August.
Location: Map 11:C9. OS Ref SE664 550. 5m E of York off A166 or A64.
Owner: Mr & Mrs Simon Wood **Contact:** Simon Wood **Tel:** 01904 489362
E-mail: simon@brockfieldhall.co.uk **Website:** www.brockfieldhall.co.uk
Open: Spring BH Mon (30 May). Daily in Aug from 1pm to 5pm except Mons but including BH Mon. On all the above days there will be three conducted tours by the owner at 1pm, 2.30pm and 4pm.
Admission: Adult £7.00.
Key facts: No photography inside house. By arrangement. In grounds, on leads.

NORTON CONYERS

Nr Ripon, North Yorkshire HG4 5EQ

Visited by Charlotte Brontë and an original of 'Thornfield Hall'. Has belonged to the Grahams since 1624. Family pictures and furniture. Outstanding mid-18th Century walled garden. House won the 2014 HHA/Sotheby's Restoration Award.
Location: Map 11:A8. OS Ref SF319 763. 4m NW of Ripon. 3 ½ m from the A1.
Owner: Sir James and Lady Graham **Contact:** The Administrator
Tel: 01765 640333 **E-mail:** info@nortonconyers.org.uk
Website: www.nortonconyers.org.uk/www.weddingsatnortonconyers.co.uk
Open: House: 25-28 Mar, 1-4 & 27-30 May, 14-18 & 27-31 Jul, 18-21 & 26-29 Aug. Garden: as house, also Suns 5 Jun-31 Jul and Mons & Thurs throughout the year (Please check during winter months). Times: 2-5pm; garden closes 4pm in winter. Wedding receptions by arrangement. **Admission:** House: £15.00 (Numbers limited - see website). Garden: free, except for charity days & group bookings. **Key facts:** Orangery and garden for hire. Partial. WC. By arrangement. On leads in garden only.

PLUMPTON ROCKS

**Plumpton, Knaresborough
North Yorkshire HG5 8NA**

Grade II* listed garden extending to over 30 acres including an idyllic lake, dramatic millstone grit rock formation, romantic woodland walks winding through bluebells and rhododendrons. Declared by English Heritage to be of outstanding interest. Painted by Turner. Described by Queen Mary as 'Heaven on earth'.
Location: Map 11:A9. OS Ref SE353 535. Between Harrogate and Wetherby on A661, 1m SE of A661 junction with Harrogate southern bypass.
Owner/Contact: Robert de Plumpton Hunter
Tel: 01289 382322
Website: www.plumptonrocks.com
Open: May-Oct: Sat, Sun & BHs, 11am-6pm.
Admission: Adult £3.50, Child/OAP £2.50. (Prices subject to change).
Key facts: Unsuitable. Limited for coaches. In grounds, on leads.

SUTTON PARK

Sutton-On-The-Forest, N. Yorkshire YO61 1DP

The Yorkshire home of Sir Reginald and Lady Sheffield. Early Georgian architecture. Magnificent plasterwork by Cortese. Rich collection of 18th Century furniture. Award-winning gardens attract enthusiasts from home and abroad. Tranquil Caravan and Camping Club CL Site also available for Rallies. Woodland Walk. Tearooms. **Location:** Map 11:B9. OS Ref SE583 646. 8 miles N of York on B1363 York-Helmsley Road follow brown signs **Contact:** Administrator
Tel: 01347 810249 **Fax:** 01347 811251 **E-mail:** suttonpark@statelyhome.co.uk
Website: www.statelyhome.co.uk **Open:** Private parties all year by appointment (min. charge for 15). Gardens: 11am-4pm 1 May-28 Jun inc. House: 30 May Spring BH Mon, Wed 1 Jun-Tues 28 Jun inc. 29 Aug Summer BH Mon. Heritage Days in Sep. For House tour times & admission prices see website for details.
Key facts: No photography. Flower Power Fairs www.flowerpowerfairs.co.uk Partial. WCs. Obligatory. Limited for coaches. Woodland Walk only.

RIEVAULX TERRACE & TEMPLES

The National Trust, Rievaulx, North Yorkshire YO62 5LJ

One of Yorkshire's finest 18th Century landscape gardens, containing two temples. Take in views from the terrace over the Cistercian ruin of Rievaulx Abbey.
Location: Map 11:B7. OS Ref SE579 848. **Tel:** 01723 870423
E-mail: nunningtonhall@nationaltrust.org.uk **Website:** www.nationaltrust.org.uk/rievaulx-terrace **Open:** Please see website for up-to-date details.

SCAMPSTON WALLED GARDEN

Scampston Hall, Malton, North Yorkshire YO17 8NG

A contemporary garden with striking perennial meadow planting that explodes with colour in the summer. Created by acclaimed designer and plantsman, Piet Oudolf. **Location:** Map 11:D8. OS Ref SE865 755. 5m E of Malton, off A64.
Tel: 01944 759111
E-mail: info@scampston.co.uk **Website:** www.scampston.co.uk/gardens
Open: Please see website for up-to-date opening times and admission prices.

TREASURER'S HOUSE

Minster Yard, York, North Yorkshire YO1 7JL

Named after the Treasurer of York Minster, the house is not all that it first seems! The size and splendour and contents of the house are a constant surprise.
Location: Map 11:B9. OS Ref SE604 523. **Tel:** 01904 624247
Website: www.nationaltrust.org.uk/treasurers-house-york
Open: Please see website for up-to-date opening and admission details.

BRODSWORTH HALL & GARDENS

Brodsworth, Nr Doncaster, Yorkshire DN5 7XJ

Inside this beautiful Victorian country house almost everything has been left exactly as it was when it was still a family home. **Location:** Map 11:B12. OS Ref SE506 070. In Brodsworth, 5m NW of Doncaster off A635. Use A1(M)/J37.
Tel: 01302 722598 **E-mail:** customers@english-heritage.org.uk
Website: www.english-heritage.org.uk/brodsworthhall **Open:** Please visit www.english-heritage.org.uk for the most up-to-date times and admission prices.

WENTWORTH WOODHOUSE

Wentworth Woodhouse, Wentworth, Rotherham S62 7TQ

A grand Georgian house with two distinct facades. **Location:** Map 7:A1. OS Ref SK393 978. Enter by driveway on Cortworth Lane, (opp Clayfields Lane), ignore Private Signs. **Tel:** 01226 351161 **E-mail:** tours@wentworthwoodhouse.co.uk
Website: www.wentworthwoodhouse.co.uk **Open:** Throughout the year for pre-booked guided tours. For availability/dates consult our website.
Admission: Consult the website.

Harewood House from the North

HAREWOOD HOUSE & GARDENS

www.harewood.org

Harewood is one of the finest Treasure Houses of England, set in one of Yorkshire's most beautiful landscapes.

From the moment you arrive, Harewood captures your imagination and feeds your curiosity. It's a place filled with culture and heritage, which continues to develop and thrive today.

Built 1759-1772, Harewood House is the seat of the Earl and Countess of Harewood. The magnificent Georgian building has remained within the Lascelles family since its construction and has retained much of its original splendour. Designed by renowned Georgian architect John Carr, furnished by Thomas Chippendale and with interiors by Robert Adam, Harewood House offers visitors the chance to unearth striking, original features and experience the grandeur of one of Yorkshire's finest country houses.

In each room, our friendly guides are on hand to offer insights into the history and detail of the House, including the extensive art collections. From El Greco, JMW Turner and Joshua Reynolds to Epstein, Sidney Nolan and Gaudier-Brzeska, there is a diverse range on offer, spanning centuries of patronage.

Like the building, the landscape was painstakingly created by the finest craftsman. Representing one of 'Capability' Brown's most important designs, the Grade 1 listed parkland has remained unchanged since it was created in the late 18th Century. With a 32 acre lake, soft rolling hills and mature, established tree lines, visitors can experience the idyllic, picturesque views Brown imagined for Harewood in the 1760's. Wander through rows of neat box hedging on the Terrace, filled with perfumed flowers, and gaze across the landscape.

2016 sees a celebration of this eminent designer and landscape artist in the new Art of Landscape series. Enjoy exhibitions, guided walks or indulge in afternoon tea on the Terrace as part of your 'Capability' Brown experience.

With over 100 acres of grounds and gardens to explore, from the informal Himalayan Garden which bursts into life in May, to the traditional south facing borders which are at their best in October, visitors won't be disappointed. The gardens are a wonderful place to while-away a lazy afternoon.

VISITOR INFORMATION

■ Owner
The Earl and Countess of Harewood

■ Address
Harewood House
Harewood
Leeds
West Yorkshire
LS17 9LG

■ Location
Map 10:P10
OS Ref. SE311 446
A1 N or S to Wetherby. A659 via Collingham, Harewood is on A61 between Leeds and Harrogate. Easily reached from A1, M1, M62 and M18. 40 mins from York, 20 mins from centre of Leeds or Harrogate.
Bus: No. 36 from Leeds or Harrogate.
Rail: London Kings Cross to Leeds/Harrogate 2hrs 20 mins. Leeds/Harrogate Station 7m.
Air: Leeds Bradford Airport 9m.

■ Contact
Harewood House
Tel: 0113 2181010
E-mail: info@harewood.org

■ Opening Times
House, Gardens, Grounds, Bird Garden, Courtyard and Bookshop open from April to November 2016. Please see website or call our team for details.

■ Admission
Please see website.

Conference/Function
Private venue hire available.

KEY FACTS

- Please see website for further information.
- Homeware, gifts, souvenirs, postcards and publications.
- Fine Dining in House & private venue hire available.
- WCs. No access to State Rooms for electric wheelchairs. Courtesy wheelchair.
- Terrace Café. Licensed.
- Courtyard Café & Restaurant. Licensed.
- Guided tours by prior arrangement.
- Free. Designated for blue badge holders.
- Sandford Award for Education. School parties welcome.
- On leads. Service dogs welcome except in Bird Garden.

The Gallery, Harewood House

The Terrace

OAKWELL HALL & RED HOUSE
NUTTER LANE, BIRSTALL WF17 9LG / OXFORD RD, GOMERSAL BD19 4JP
www.kirklees.gov.uk/museums

Visit two stunning West Yorkshire Historic Houses less than a mile apart! Both have unique Brontë connections and featured in Charlotte Brontë's novel 'Shirley'. Both have gorgeous award-winning period gardens to explore.

Oakwell Hall is an atmospheric Elizabethan manor house with important Civil War connections, displayed as the 17th Century home of the Batt family. Wander through the fine oak panelled Great Hall, decorative Parlours and evocative Kitchens. Surrounded by award-winning Country Park and 17th Century gardens; Café, Play Area, Nature Trail, Arboretum & Shop.

Red House is a delightful former woollen cloth merchant's home set in enchanting 1830s gardens. From elegant Parlour to stone-flagged Kitchens, each room brings you closer to the 1830s, when Charlotte Brontë visited her friend, early feminist Mary Taylor, here. Restored Garden with scented old roses, period flowers and tree shaded lawns. Bronte & local history exhibitions. Shop.

Pre-booked Group Visits; Weddings & Venue Hire; Events & Schools programme.
Location: Map 10:P11. M62 Jct 26 take A58 towards Leeds, turn right on A651. M62 Jct 27 take A62 towards Huddersfield. Follow brown tourist signs.
Owner: Kirklees Council **Contact:** Oakwell Hall
Oakwell: 01924 326240 / 324761 **Red House:** 01274 335056
E-mail: oakwell.hall@kirklees.gov.uk / red.house@kirklees.gov.uk
Open: Summer opening: 1 Mar-31 Oct: Tue-Thu 11am-5pm; Sat & Sun 12noon-5 pm. Winter opening: 1 Nov-end Feb: Tue-Thu 11am-4pm Sat-Sun 12noon-4pm Closed Mon & Fri.
Admission: At each house: Adult £2.50, Child £1.00, Family £6.00 (2 adults+4 children). 'Annual Tickets' also available.
Key facts: ⓘ ⌾ ⊤ ⬢ Tel for access details. 🍴 🅿 🎁 ⚔ ⬆ ❄ ♿

LOTHERTON HALL
Aberford, Leeds, West Yorkshire LS25 3EB
www.leeds.gov.uk/lothertonhall

Explore this Edwardian country estate with extensive grounds, historic house, deer park, gardens and children's playgrounds. Discover the stories of this fantastic country home, once the home of the Gascoigne family; housing a wonderful collection of fine and decorative arts, as well as a dedicated Fashion Gallery opened in 2015. From the bird garden, to the woodland play area, to stunning nature trails, this historic estate really has got something for everyone.
Location: Map 11:B10. OS Ref SE450 360.
Owner: Leeds City Council
Contact: Visitor Services
Tel: 0113 3782959
E-mail: lotherton.hall@leeds.gov.uk
Open: Please check the website or call for seasonal opening dates.
Admission: Please check the website for current admission prices.
Key facts: ⓘ We welcome group visits, please call to arrange your day out. ⌾ ⬢ Recently installed passenger lift in the House. 🍴 🅵 🅿 🎁 ⚔ ♿

Harewood House

© VisitBritain / Simon Kreitem

WANT A GREEN SOUVENIR?
SEE OUR PLANT SALES QUICK GUIDE SECTION
AT THE BACK OF THIS BOOK

YORK GATE GARDEN
Back Church Lane, Adel, Leeds LS16 8DW
www.yorkgate.org.uk

Inspirational one acre garden widely recognised as one of Britain's finest small gardens. A series of smaller gardens with different themes and in contrasting styles are linked by a succession of delightful vistas. Striking architectural features play a key role throughout the garden which is noted for its exquisite planting details and Arts and Crafts features.

Location: Map 10:P10. OS Ref 275 403. 2¼m SE of Bramhope, just off A660.
Owner: Perennial **Contact:** Garden Co-ordinator
Tel: 0113 267 8240 **E-mail:** yorkgate@perennial.org.uk
Open: 27 Mar-30 Sep, Sun to Thu and BH Mons, 1:30pm-4:30pm. Evening openings every Weds in Jun.
Admission: Standard £5.00. Gift Aid £5.50. Child (16 & under) and Carers Free. Annual Friends Membership £25.00 per annum. POA for groups.
Key facts: ℹ Groups welcome by appointment. ◻ Wide selection of locally sourced items, garden gear, cards and gifts. ⚘ Seasonal plants available from greenhouse and garden selected by Head Gardener. ☕ Newly renovated tearoom. Serves tea or coffee and delicious homemade cake. 🎟 By arrangement. Ⓟ Local parking by the church on Church Lane. ⊠ Guide dogs only.

TEMPLE NEWSAM
Temple Newsam Road, Leeds LS15 0AE
www.leeds.gov.uk/templenewsam

Discover 500 years of history in this beautiful country mansion set within 1500 acres of parkland. Explore rooms filled with fine and decorative art treasures and uncover the secrets of past residents. One of the great country houses of England, this Tudor-Jacobean mansion was the birthplace of Lord Darnley, husband of Mary Queen of Scots. Rich in beautifully restored interiors, the House includes a wealth of paintings, Chippendale furniture, textiles, silver and ceramics.

Location: Map 10:P10. OS Ref SE358 321. 4m E of city centre B6159 or 2m from M1 junction 46. 4 miles from city centre.
Owner: Leeds City Council **Contact:** Visitor Services
Tel: 0113 3367460 **E-mail:** temple.newsam.house@leeds.gov.uk
Open: Please check the website or call 0113 3367460 for seasonal opening times.
Admission: Please check the website or call 0113 3367460 for admission prices.
Key facts: ℹ We welcome group visits, please call to arrange your day out.
◻ 🍴 ⚘ ☕ 🎟 ◻ Ⓟ ■ ◻ ⊠

York Gate Garden

LEDSTON HALL 🏛
Hall Lane, Ledston, Castleford, West Yorkshire WF10 2BB
17th Century mansion with some earlier work, lawned grounds.
Location: Map 11:A11. OS Ref SE437 289. 2m N of Castleford, off A656.
Tel: 01423 707838 **E-mail:** victoria.walton@carterjonas.co.uk
Website: www.whelerfoundation.co.uk **Open:** Exterior only: May-Aug: Mon-Fri, 9am-4pm. Other days by appointment. **Admission:** Free.

NOSTELL PRIORY & PARKLAND ⚘
Doncaster Road, Wakefield, West Yorkshire WF4 1QE
One of Yorkshire's jewels, an architectural treasure by James Paine with later additions by Robert Adam. **Location:** Map 11:A11. OS Ref SE403 175.
Tel: 01924 863892 **E-mail:** nostellpriory@nationaltrust.org.uk
Website: www.nationaltrust.org.uk/nostell-priory
Open: Please see website for up-to-date opening and admission details.

SEWERBY HALL AND GARDENS
Church Lane, Sewerby, Bridlington YO15 1EA
Tel: 01262 673769 E-mail: sewerby.hall@eastriding.gov.uk

ALLERTON PARK
Allerton Park, Knaresborough, North Yorkshire HG5 0SE
Tel: 01423 330927

BARLEY HALL
2 Coffee Yard, Off Stonegate, York YO1 8AR
Tel: 01904 610275 E-mail: dscott@yorkat.co.uk

BENINGBROUGH HALL & GARDENS
Beningbrough, North Yorkshire YO30 1DD
Tel: 01904 472027 E-mail: beningbrough@nationaltrust.org.uk

BOLTON ABBEY
Skipton, North Yorkshire BD23 6EX
Tel: 01756 718009 E-mail: tourism@boltonabbey.com

BOLTON CASTLE
Bolton Castle, Nr Leyburn, North Yorkshire DL8 4ET
Tel: 01969 623981 E-mail: info@boltoncastle.co.uk

CLIFFORD'S TOWER
Tower Street, York YO1 9SA
Tel: 01904 646940 E-mail: customers@english-heritage.org.uk

HELMSLEY CASTLE
Castlegate, Helmsley, York YO62 5AB
Tel: 01904 601946 E-mail: caroline.topps@english-heritage.org.uk

HELMSLEY WALLED GARDEN
Cleveland Way, Helmsley, North Yorkshire YO62 5AH
Tel: 01439 771427 E-mail: info@helmsleywalledgarden.org.uk

JERVAULX ABBEY
Ripon, North Yorkshire HG4 4PH
Tel: 01677 460226

MIDDLEHAM CASTLE
Castle Hill, Middleham, Leyburn, North Yorkshire DL8 4QR
Tel: 01969 623899

ORMESBY HALL
Ladgate Lane, Ormesby, Middlesbrough TS7 9AS
Tel: 01642 324188 E-mail: ormesbyhall@nationaltrust.org.uk

PARCEVALL HALL GARDENS
Skyreholme, Nr Appletreewick, North Yorkshire BD23 6DE
Tel: 01756 720311 E-mail: parcevallhall@btconnect.com

RHS GARDEN HARLOW CARR
Crag Lane, Harrogate, North Yorkshire HG3 1QB
Tel: 01423 565418 E-mail: harlowcarr@rhs.org.uk

RICHMOND CASTLE
Richmond Castle, Richmond, North Yorkshire DL10 4QW
Tel: 01904 601946 E-mail: caroline.topps@english-heritage.org.uk

RIPON CATHEDRAL
Ripon, North Yorkshire HG4 1QR
Tel: 01765 602072

SCARBOROUGH CASTLE
Castle Road, Scarborough, North Yorkshire YO11 1HY
Tel: 01723 372451 E-mail: scarborough.castle@english-heritage.org.uk

SHANDY HALL
Coxwold, Thirsk, North Yorkshire YO61 4AD
Tel: 01347 868465 E-mail: shandyhall@dial.pipex.com

THE GEORGIAN THEATRE ROYAL
Victoria Road, Richmond, North Yorkshire DL10 4DW
Tel: 01748 823710 E-mail: admin@georgiantheatreroyal.co.uk

THORP PERROW ARBORETUM
Bedale, North Yorkshire DL8 2PR
Tel: 01677 425323 E-mail: enquiries@thorpperrow.com

WHITBY ABBEY
Whitby, North Yorkshire YO22 4JT
Tel: 01947 603568 E-mail: customers@english-heritage.org.uk

CANNON HALL MUSEUM, PARK & GARDENS
Cawthorne, Barnsley, South Yorkshire S75 4AT
Tel: 01226 790270 E-mail: cannonhall@barnsley.gov.uk

WENTWORTH CASTLE GARDENS
Lowe Lane, Stainborough, Barnsley, South Yorkshire S75 3ET
Tel: 01226 776040 E-mail: heritagetrust@wentworthcastle.org

BRAMHAM PARK
The Estate Office, Bramham Park, Bramham LS23 6ND
Tel: 01937 846000 E-mail: enquiries@bramhampark.co.uk

BRONTE PARSONAGE MUSEUM
Church Street, Haworth BD22 8DR
Tel: 01535 642323 E-mail: lauren.livesey@bronte.org.uk

CLIFFE CASTLE MUSEUM
Spring Gardens Lane, Keighley BD20 6LH
Tel: 01274 431212 E-mail: cartwright.hall@bradford.gov.uk

EAST RIDDLESDEN HALL
Bradford Road, Riddlesden, Keighley, W. Yorkshire BD20 5EL
Tel: 01535 607075 E-mail: eastriddlesden@nationaltrust.org.uk

PONTEFRACT CASTLE
Castle Chain, Pontefract, West Yorkshire WF8 1QH
Tel: 01977 723 440 E-mail: castles@wakefield.gov.uk

SHIBDEN HALL
Lister's Road, Halifax, West Yorkshire HX3 6XG
Tel: 01422 352246 E-mail: shibden.hall@calderdale.gov.uk

Helmsley Castle

Register for news and special offers at **www.hudsonsheritage.com**

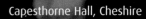
Capesthorne Hall, Cheshire

Holker Hall, Cumbria

Cheshire
Cumbria
Lancashire
Manchester
Merseyside

North West

Cumbria and Lancashire preserve some of Britain's most spectacular landscapes and a startling range of castles, small country houses and lush gardens.

New Entries for 2016:
• Combermere Abbey

ADLINGTON HALL 🏛F
MACCLESFIELD, CHESHIRE SK10 4LF
www.adlingtonhall.com

Adlington Hall, home of the Leghs from 1315 built on the site of a Hunting Lodge in the Forest of Macclesfield in 1040. Two oaks, part of the original building, remain rooted in the ground supporting the east end of the Great Hall. Between the trees in the Great Hall stands an organ built by 'Father' Bernard Smith. Played on by Handel.

The Gardens laid out over many centuries include a Lime walk planted 1688, Regency rockery surrounding the Shell Cottage. The Wilderness, a Rococo styled landscape garden containing the chinoserie T'Ing House, Pagoda bridge and classical Temple to Diana. **Location:** Map 6:N2. OS Ref SJ905 804. 5m N of Macclesfield, A523,13m S of Manchester. London 178m.

Owner: Mrs C J C Legh

Tel: 01625 827595 **Fax:** 01625 820797

E-mail: enquiries@adlingtonhall.com

Open: Apr 3, 10, 17, 24. May 1, 2, 8, 15, 22, 30. Jun 4, 5, 12, 19, 26. Jul 3, 10, 17, 24, 31. Aug 7, 14, 21, 28. Sep 4, 11, 18, 25.

Admission: House & Gardens: Adult £9.00, Child £5.00, Student £5.00, Gardens only: Adult £6.00, Child Free, Student Free, Groups of 20+ £8.50.

Key facts: ⅈ Suitable for corporate events, product launches, business meetings, conferences, concerts, fashion shows, garden parties, rallies, filming and weddings. ⊤ The Great Hall and Dining Room are available for corporate entertaining. Catering can be arranged. ♿ WCs. ☕ Tearoom open on Hall open days. ⅉ By arrangement. Ⓟ For 100 cars and 4 coaches, 100 yds from Hall. ▪ 🐾 On leads. ▲ ❋ ♿

CAPESTHORNE HALL 🏛F
SIDDINGTON, MACCLESFIELD, CHESHIRE SK11 9JY
www.capesthorne.com

Capesthorne Hall, built between 1719 and 1732 and set in 100 acres of picturesque Cheshire parkland, has been touched by nearly 1,000 years of history. The Hall has a fascinating collection of fine art, marble sculptures, furniture and tapestries. In the grounds enjoy the family Chapel, the 18th Century Italian Milanese Gates, the beautiful lakeside gardens and woodland walks.

The hall can be hired for civil weddings and corporate events.

Location: Map 6:N2. OS Ref SJ840 727. 5m W of Macclesfield. 30 mins S of Manchester on A34. Near M6, M60 and M62.

Owner: Sir William and Lady Bromley-Davenport **Contact:** Christine Mountney

Tel: 01625 861221 **E-mail:** info@capesthorne.com

Open: Apr-Oct Suns\Mons & BHs. Hall: 1.30-4.00pm. Last admission 3.30pm. Gardens & Chapel: 12.00-5.00pm. Groups welcome by appointment.

Admission: Suns & BHs - Hall, Gardens & Chapel: Adult £9.00, Child (5-16 yrs) £5.00, Senior £8.00, Family £25.00. Suns - Gardens & Chapel only: Adult £6.50, Child (5-16 yrs) £3.00 Senior £5.50. Mons Only- Park, Gardens & Chapel: Per Car £10.00. Hall Entrance: Per person £3.00. Group discounts available.

Key facts: ⅈ Available for civil weddings, filming, corporate functions, festivals, activity days, garden parties. Caravan Park 4* AA Rated, open Mar-Oct inclusive. ⊤ Catering can be provided for groups (full menus on request). ♿ Partial. WC. ☕ The Butler's Pantry offers light refreshments including afternoon teas. ⅉ Guided tours available for pre-booked parties (except Suns). Ⓟ 100 cars/20 coaches on hard-standing and unlimited in park. ▪ Pre-booked educational visits available. ▲ Licensed for civil weddings. ♿

CHOLMONDELEY CASTLE GARDEN ⓜⒻ
MALPAS, CHESHIRE SY14 8AH
www.cholmondeleycastle.com

Cholmondeley Castle Garden is said by many to be among the most romantically beautiful gardens they have seen. Even the wild orchids, daisies and buttercups take on an aura of glamour in this beautifully landscaped setting with extensive ornamental gardens dominated by a romantic Castle built in 1801 of local sandstone. Visitors can enjoy the tranquil Temple Water Garden, Ruin Water Garden, memorial mosaic designed by Maggy Howarth, newly planted "Lavinia Walk", Rose garden and many mixed borders. Lakeside walk, picnic area, children's play areas and adventure den, farm animals including llamas and alpacas. Tearoom.

Location: Map 6:L3. OS Ref SJ540 515. Off A41 Chester/Whitchurch Rd. & A49 Whitchurch/ Tarporley Road. 7m N of Whitchurch.

Owner: Lavinia, Dowager Marchioness of Cholmondeley.
Contact: The Secretary **Tel:** 01829 720383 **Fax:** 01829 720877
E-mail: dilys@cholmondeleycastle.co.uk
Open: 25 Mar-29 Sep 2016 Wed, Thurs, Sun & BH's 11.00 am-5.00 pm (last entry 4.30pm). Also open Fridays in Aug. Oct: Sun only for Autumn Tints. (Castle open for groups only, by pre-arrangement, on limited days).
Admission: Adult £7.00, Child £4.00 under 5's free. (reduction for groups to gardens of 25+). For special events and variations to opening dates please refer to our website www.cholmondeleycastle.com.
Key facts: ⓘ ♿ Partial. WCs. 🍽 🅿 🖼 On leads. ♥

LYME 🍂
DISLEY, STOCKPORT, CHESHIRE SK12 2NX
www.nationaltrust.org.uk/lymepark

Much-loved home of the Legh family for more than 600 years, Lyme sits in 570 hectares (1,400 acres) of parkland, with glorious views across Manchester and the Cheshire Plain. Its lavish interiors reflect the life of a great estate, from its earliest beginnings to its Edwardian 'Golden Era' – the heyday of aristocratic life, with its social whirl of parties, all of which ended with the start of the First World War. You may recognise Lyme as 'Pemberley' from the BBC adaptation of Pride and Prejudice, starring Colin Firth, and the 'Big House' in series two of The Village. Lyme's ever-changing gardens with the Reflection Lake, Orangery and Rose Garden, are an ideal place to relax and stroll.

Location: Map 6:N2. OS Ref SJ965 825. Off the A6 at Disley. 6½m SE of Stockport. M60 J1.

Owner: National Trust **Contact:** The Visitor Experience Manager
Tel: 01663 762023 **Fax:** 01663 765035 **E-mail:** lymepark@nationaltrust.org.uk
Open: House: 15 Feb-30 Oct, 11am-5pm (last entry 4pm), Mon, Tue, Fri-Sun. House also open Thurs, 25 Jul-4 Sept. Garden: 15 Feb-30 Oct, 11am-5pm (last entry 4.30pm), Mon-Sun. Please call for winter opening times.
Admission: Please visit the website for ticket prices. NT members free.
Key facts: ⓘ No flash photography in the house. 📷 ♿ 🚻 Licensed. 🍴 Licensed. 🅿 Limited for coaches. 🖼 Guide dogs only. East Lodge. A beautiful Edwardian cottage built in 1904, with two bedrooms, sleeps 4 (one double, one twin), dogs welcome. Enjoy spectacular views of Manchester and the Peak District. Closed Christmas Day. ♥

PEOVER HALL & GARDENS ⓜⒻ
OVER PEOVER, KNUTSFORD WA16 9HW
www.peoverhall.com

A Grade 2* listed Elizabethan family house dating from 1585. Situated within some 500 acres of landscaped 18th Century parkland with formal gardens designed between 1890-1900 that include a series of "garden rooms" filled with clipped box, lily ponds, Romanesque loggia, warm brick walls, unusual doors, secret passageways, beautiful topiary work, herb and walled gardens. The grounds of the Hall house working stables, estate cottages and the parish church of St Laurence which, contains two Mainwaring Chapels. The architectural jewel Grade I listed Carolean stables built in 1654, with richly carved stalls and original Tuscan columns and strap work.
Location: Map 6:M2. OS Ref SJ772 734. 4m S of Knutsford off A50 at Whipping

Stocks Inn. Further directions on website, satnav leads down an unsuitable road.
Owner: Mr R Brooks **Contact:** David Young
General Enquiries: via Rostherne Estate Office - 01565 830395
E-mail: bookings@peoverhall.com
Open: 2015 May-Aug, Tue & Thu afternoons. Stables & Gardens open between 2-5pm. Tours of Peover Hall at 2.30pm & 3.30pm.
The Church is open 2.00pm-4.00pm.
Admission: House, Stables & Gardens £6.00, Stables & Gardens only £4.00. Children under 16 years free of charge.
Key facts: 🅿 🚻 Obligatory. 🐕

TABLEY HOUSE
TABLEY LANE, KNUTSFORD, CHESHIRE WA16 0HB
www.tableyhouse.co.uk

The finest Palladian House in the North West, Tabley a Grade I listing, was designed by John Carr of York for the Leicester family. It contains one of the first collections of English paintings, including works of art by Turner, Reynolds, Lawrence, Lely and Dobson. Furniture by Chippendale, Bullock and Gillow and fascinating family memorabilia adorn the rooms. Fine plasterwork by Thomas Oliver and carving by Daniel Shillito and Mathew Bertram. Interesting Tearoom and 17th Century Chapel adjoin, including Burne-Jones window.
Location: Map 6:M2. OS Ref SJ725 777. M6/J19, A556 S on to A5033. 2m W of Knutsford. **Owner:** The University of Manchester **Contact:** The Administrator
Tel: 01565 750151
E-mail: tableyhouse@btconnect.com

Open: House: Apr-end Oct: Thu-Sun & BHs, 1-5pm.
Last admission at 4.30pm. Tea Room open from 12-5pm.
Admission: Adult £5.00. Child/Student £1.50. Groups by arrangement.
Key facts: ⓘ No photography in galleries. No stiletto heels. Heel guards can be provided. 🅣 Suitable for drinks receptions and presentations for up to 100 people. ♿ Call the office before arriving to arrange for lift entrance to be opened. 🍽 Serving light lunches, afternoon teas, refreshments and homemade cakes. 🅕 By arrangement, also available outside normal opening hours, guides provided at no extra charge. 🅿 Free. 🏫 Suitable for post 16 students. 🐕 Guide dogs only. 💍 Civil Wedding and Partnerships Licence. Naming Ceremonies & Renewal of Vows. 🎗

ARLEY HALL & GARDENS 🏛️Ⓕ
Northwich, Cheshire CW9 6NA
www.arleyhallandgardens.com

Arley has been a cherished family home owned for over 550 years. Renowned features include the double herbaceous border, pleached Lime Avenues, Ilex Columns, Cruck Barn and Chapel. The Hall (Grade II*) built in the Victorian Jacobean style, with elaborate ceilings & oak panelling, impressive fireplaces, intricate stained glass and beautiful contents.

Location: Map 6:M2. OS Ref SJ675 809.
Owner: Viscount & Viscountess Ashbrook **Contact:** Helen Begent - Marketing
Tel: 01565 777353 **E-mail:** reception@arleyhallandgardens.com
Open: Gardens: Mar-Oct, Mon-Sun 11am-5pm. The Hall: Mar-Oct, Sun, Tues & BHs 12noon-5pm. Parts of the Gardens are also open Nov-Feb 11am-dusk.
Admission: Gardens Mar-Oct: Adult £8.50, Children (5-12yrs) £3.50, Senior £8.00, Family (2+2) £20.00. Hall & Gardens March-Oct: Adult £11.00, Child (5-12yrs) £4.50, Senior £10.00, Family (2+2) £25.00. Group rates are available please visit the website.
Key facts: ⓘ Weddings & corporate events. WCs. Licensed. Ⓟ Free. All dogs on a lead. See website for details.

COMBERMERE ABBEY 🏛️
Whitchurch, Shropshire SY13 4AJ
www.combermereabbey.co.uk

Combermere Abbey, its large mere and 1000 acre parkland celebrates almost 900 years of history. The Cistercian monastery est.in 1133 was dissolved in 1536. New for 2016! The restored North Wing opens for public tours. Group tours incl. the restored Walled Gardens, unique Fruit Tree Maze and Glasshouse. The estate offers luxury accommodation and is licensed for weddings.

Location: Map 6:L4. OS Ref SJ599 434. 5m E of Whitchurch, off A530.
Owner: Mrs S Callander Beckett **Contact:** Administrator
Tel: 01948 662880 **E-mail:** estate@combermereabbey.co.uk
Open: 5 Apr-7 Jul for public tours - advance booking essential. Group visits (20-50) by arrangement (Apr-Oct). Bluebell Walk - Sun 24 Apr 2016 1-4pm. Garden Open Afternoons - Wed - 25 May, 29 Jun, 20 Jul, 24 Aug, 21 Sep 2016 - 1-4pm. **Admission:** Open days: Adult £6.00, Child (U16) £4.00. Group tours: £12.00 pp incl of refreshments. Bluebell Walk & Garden Open Afternoons: Adult £5.00
Key facts: ⓘ No photography in the house.

DORFOLD HALL 🏛️Ⓕ
Acton, Nr Nantwich, Cheshire CW5 8LD
www.dorfoldhall.com

Jacobean country house built in 1616 for Ralph Wilbraham. Family home of the Roundells. Beautiful plaster ceilings and oak panelling. Attractive woodland gardens and summer herbaceous borders.

Location: Map 6:L3. OS Ref SJ634 525. 1m W of Nantwich on the A534 Nantwich-Wrexham road.
Owner/Contact: Charles Roundell
Tel: 01270 625245
Fax: 01270 628723
E-mail: info@dorfold.com
Open: Apr-Oct: Tue only and BH Mons, 2-5pm.
Admission: Adult £7.00, Child £3.00.
Key facts: Obligatory.
Ⓟ Limited. Narrow gates with low arch prevent coaches. Access for coaches from a different entrance. Please contact the hall.

CHESHIRE

DUNHAM MASSEY ❧
Altrincham, Cheshire WA14 4SJ
www.nationaltrust.org.uk/dunhammassey

In 1856 Victorian carriages rolled along the avenues of Dunham's deer-park laden with the family's most treasured possessions. Having suffered the rejection of Cheshire society, Catherine, a former circus performer, and her husband, the 7th Earl, left Dunham and never returned. We take you on Catherine and George Harry's journey to consider what it might be like to leave this home. The newly-opened historic stable buildings tell the story of horses and the motor car at Dunham. **Location:** Map 6:M1. OS Ref SJ735 874. 3m SW of Altrincham off A56. M6/J19. M56/J7. Station Altrincham (Train & Metro) 3m. **Owner:** National Trust **Contact:** Visitor Experience **Tel:** 0161 941 1025
E-mail: dunhammassey@nationaltrust.org.uk **Open:** Please see website.
Admission: House & Garden: £14.00, Child £7.00, Family £35.00. Groups (15+) £11.50, Child £5.70. Garden only: £8.80, Child £4.40, Family £22.00 Groups (15+) £7.00, Child £3.50. Parking: Cars £6.00, Motorbikes £1.50, Coaches £20.
Key facts: ℹ️ Photography permitted, no flash or tripods. 🏬 Large gift shop selling homewares & local produce. ❀ Plant sales area; seasonal bulbs & ornamental plants. ♿ Good access to most of property. Access to house is limited. ● Indoor & outdoor seating, range of light meals & snacks. 🍴 Licensed. 🅿 £6.00 Free to NT members. ● ● Dedicated walking area in North Park. ❀ Park, garden, shop & café. ♿

GAWSWORTH HALL
Macclesfield, Cheshire SK11 9RN
www.gawsworthhall.com

Fully lived-in Tudor half-timbered manor house with Tilting Ground. Former home of Mary Fitton, Maid of Honour at the Court of Queen Elizabeth I, and the supposed 'Dark Lady' of Shakespeare's sonnets. Fine pictures, sculpture, furniture and beautiful grounds adjoining a medieval church. Garden Theatre performances take place in the Hall courtyard in July and August.
Location: Map 6:N2. OS Ref SJ892 697. 3m S of Macclesfield on the A536 Congleton to Macclesfield road.
Owner: Mr and Mrs T Richards **Contact:** Mr J Richards
Tel: 01260 223456
E-mail: gawsworthhall@btinternet.com
Open: See www.gawsworthhall.com.
Admission: Adult £7.50, Child £3.50. Groups (20+) £6.00.
Key facts: 🏬 ♿ Partial. WCs. ● Licensed. 🍴 Licensed. 🎫 Guided tours by arrangement. 🅿 ● In grounds. ▲ ♿

RODE HALL 🏠Ⓕ
Church Lane, Scholar Green, Cheshire ST7 3QP
www.rodehall.co.uk

Rode Hall stands in a Repton landscape and the extensive gardens include a woodland garden, formal rose garden designed by Nesfield in 1860 and a stunning two acre walled kitchen garden. Rode Pool also has its own herony on Birthday Island and the icehouse in the park is well worth a visit.
Location: Map 6:M3. OS Ref SJ819 573. 5m SW of Congleton between the A34 and A50. Kidsgrove railway station 2m NW of Kidsgrove.
Owner/Contact: Sir Richard Baker Wilbraham Bt
Tel: 01270 873237 **E-mail:** enquiries@rodehall.co.uk
Open: 1 Apr-30 Sep, Wed & BH Mons. Gardens 11-5pm, House 2-5pm. The gardens are also open alongside the monthly farmers' market on the first Sat of every month, (exc Jan) 9.00am-1pm. Snowdrop Walks 30 Jan-6 Mar, Tues-Sun 11am-4pm (Closed Mons). Groups welcome by appointment on alternative days.
Admission: House & Garden: Adult £8.00, Conc £7.00 Children £1.00 Garden only & Snowdrop Walks: Adult £5.00. Children £1.00
Key facts: 🏬 ❀ ● Light lunches & Cream teas. Homemade cakes & refreshments. 🎫 🅿 ● On leads.

BEESTON CASTLE ⊞
Chapel Lane, Beeston, Tarporley, Cheshire CW6 9TX

Standing majestically on a sheer rocky crag, Beeston offers perhaps the most stunning views of any castle in England. **Location:** Map 6:L3. OS Ref SJ537 593.
Tel: 01829 260464 **Website:** www.english-heritage.org.uk/beeston
Open: Please visit www.english-heritage.org.uk/beeston for opening times, admission prices and the most up-to-date information.

TATTON PARK ❧
Knutsford, Cheshire WA16 6QN

A complete historic estate with 1,000 acres of deer park, 200 year old 50 acre gardens and Tudor Old Hall. **Location:** Map 6:M2. OS Ref SJ745 815. From M56/J7 follow signs. From M6/J19, signed on A56 & A50.
Tel: 01625 374400/01625 374435 **E-mail:** tatton@cheshireeast.gov.uk
Website: www.tattonpark.org.uk **Open:** See website or call 01625 374400 for all opening times. **Admission:** See website or call 01625 374400.

Gardens at Rode Hall

KIRKLINTON HALL AND GARDENS 🏛ⓕ
KIRKLINTON, CARLISLE CA6 6BB
www.kirklintonhall.co.uk

Adjacent to the 12th Century de Boyville stronghold, Kirklinton Hall is said to have been built from its stone. Begun in the 1670's, extended in the 1870's and ruined in the 1970's, the Hall has been a Restoration Great House, an RAF base, a school, a gangsters' gambling den and worse. Walk in the footsteps of Norman Knights, Cavalier Commanders, Victorian Plutocrats and the Kray twins. Now, Kirklinton Hall and its Gardens are being restored by the Boyle family to its former glory, a painstaking and fascinating process. It is also the official home of SlowFood Cumbria and is available for weddings and events.
'Spectacularly sinister ruin' - Pevsners Buildings of England.
Location: Map 10:K3. OS Ref NY433672. 6 miles north east of M6 junction 44, follow A7 towards Longtown. At Blackford turn right following sign to Kirklinton 5 miles. Stay on road and follow Brown Signs.

Owner: Mr and Mrs Christopher Boyle **Contact:** The Administrator
Tel: 01697 748850 **Fax:** 01697 748472 **Facebook:** Kirklinton Hall.
Twitter: @kirklintonhall. **E-mail:** info@kirklintonhall.co.uk
Open: 1 Apr-30 Sep, 12-5pm weekdays and Suns.
Sats for Public or Private Events. Available for Wedding Receptions.
Admission: Admission £4.00 Adults, £1.00 Children under 16.
Free to HHA and MyCumbria Card Holders.
Key facts: ⬛ Postcards, David Austen Roses Books & Hudson's Heritage. ⬛ Specialising in David Austin Roses & Rare Rhododendrons. ⬛ Disabled WC, contact property for more information. ⬛ Tea, coffee, cake, ice cream biscuits & soft drinks. ⬛ By arrangement for groups. ⬛ Free Car parking. ⬛ Contact property. ⬛ On leads. ⬛

LEVENS HALL 🏛ⓕ
KENDAL, CUMBRIA LA8 0PD
www.levenshall.co.uk

Levens Hall is an Elizabethan mansion built around a 13th Century pele tower. The much loved home of the Bagot family, with fine panelling, plasterwork, Cordova leather wall coverings, paintings by Rubens, Lely and Cuyp, the earliest English patchwork and Wellingtoniana combine with other beautiful objects to form a fascinating collection. The world famous Topiary Gardens were laid out by Monsieur Beaumont from 1694 and his design has remained largely unchanged to this day. Over 90 individual pieces of topiary, some over nine metres high, massive beech hedges and colourful seasonal bedding provide a magnificent visual impact.
Location: Map 10:L7. OS Ref SD495 851. 5m S of Kendal on the A6. Exit M6/J36.

Owner: C H Bagot **Contact:** The Administrator **Tel:** 015395 60321
Fax: 015395 60669 **E-mail:** houseopening@levenshall.co.uk
Open: 17 Apr- 6 Oct Sun-Thu (closed Fri & Sat). Garden, Tearoom, Gift Shop & Plant Centre: 10am-5pm. House: 12 noon-4.30pm (last entry 4pm). Groups (20+) please book.
Admission: House & Gardens or Gardens Only. Please see www.levenshall.co.uk for full details, special offers & current events. Group Rates on application.
Key facts: ⓘ No indoor photography. ⬛ Gift shop. ⬛ Partial. WCs. ⬛ Licensed. ⬛ Licensed. ⬛ By arrangement. ⬛ Free on-site parking. ⬛ ⬛ Assistance dogs only. ⬛

ABBOT HALL ART GALLERY
Abbot Hall, Kendal, Cumbria LA9 5AL
www.abbothall.org.uk

Abbot Hall Art Gallery is housed in one of Kendal's most important buildings, a Grade I listed villa, on the banks of the River Kent. The galleries offer two floors of light-filled spaces in which to see art. The Gallery holds an impressive collection of 18th, 19th and 20th Century British art. The Gallery also hosts an ambitious temporary exhibition programme. **Location:** Map 10:L7. OS Ref SD517921. 10 min drive from M6 J36. Follow signs to south Kendal & then for Abbot Hall. Nearest train stations: main line, Oxenholme, the Lake District, local line, Kendal.
Owner/Contact: Lakeland Arts
Tel: 01539 722464 **E-mail:** info@abbothall.org.uk
Open: Mon-Sat, 10.30am-5pm (4pm Nov-Feb). Jan - Dec 2016.
Admission: Adult £7.00 (without donation £6.35). Adult during Canaletto exhibition (until 14 Feb 2016) £9.00 (without donation £8.15). Children & students free, 50% discount for National Art Pass.
Key facts: ▣ The Gallery Shop is packed with books on art & culture, artists' prints & materials. ▣ Serving a menu of freshly prepared sandwiches, soups & cakes. ▣ Pay & display parking on site. ▣ See our website for details. ✳ See our website for details.

ASKHAM HALL AND GARDENS ▥
Askham, Penrith, Cumbria CA10 2PF
www.askhamhall.co.uk

Meander through the beautiful gardens, visit the animals and enjoy lunch in the Kitchen Garden Café. Askham Hall is grade I listed, dating back to the late 1200s. It has recently been transformed from a stately family home into a stylish retreat also with a restaurant, 15 bedrooms and a wedding barn.
Location: Map 10:L5. OS Ref NY514 237. Askham Hall in Cumbria is situated in a quiet and picturesque village within easy access (about ten minutes drive) from Penrith and junction 40 of the M6. Follow the brown tourist signs.
Owner: Charles Lowther **Contact:** Marie-Louisa Raeburn
Tel: 01931 712350
E-mail: enquiries@askhamhall.co.uk
Open: Gardens and café: Every day except Sat. 10am-5pm in high season, reduced hours and times in low season. Restaurant and accommodation: Tue-Sat for dinner and overnight stays.
Admission: Entry to the gardens and animals: Adult £4.00, children are free.
Key facts: ℹ www.askhamhall.co.uk/gardens-and-cafe ▣ ⬓ ▣ Free to enter. ▥ 𝑓 Groups, by arrangement. ▣ Free. ▣ Permitted in café but not gardens. ▣ ▣ ▣

Register for news and special offers at **www.hudsonsheritage.com**

BLACKWELL, THE ARTS & CRAFTS HOUSE
Bowness-on-Windermere, Cumbria LA23 3JT
www.blackwell.org.uk

Blackwell, completed in 1900, is the largest and most important surviving example of work by architect Mackay Hugh Baillie Scott. Designed as a holiday retreat for Sir Edward Holt, the house survives in a truly remarkable state of preservation retaining many original decorative features. Visitors are encouraged to sit and soak up the atmosphere in Blackwell's fireplace inglenooks and are free to enjoy the house as it was originally intended, without roped-off areas. The period rooms are furnished with Arts & Crafts furniture and decorative arts, which are complemented by exhibitions of historical applied arts and contemporary craft.
Location: Map 10:K7. OS Ref SD401945. 1.5 m S of Bowness just off the A5074 on the B5360. **Owner:** Lakeland Arts **Contact:** Blackwell **Tel:** 015394 46139 **E-mail:** info@blackwell.org.uk **Open:** Daily 10.30am-5pm (4pm Nov-Feb). Jan-Dec 2016. **Admission:** Adult £8.50 (without donation £7.70), Children & Students free, 50% discount for National Art Pass.
Key facts: ⬚ Shop stocks contemporary craft by leading craft-makers selected for its quality & beauty. ⬚ WCs. ⬚ Café menu emphasises quality & the handmade, reflecting the philosophy of Arts & Crafts Movement. ⬚ Free for cars, coaches by appointment. ⬚ See website. ⬚ Guide dogs only. ⬚ See website.

DALEMAIN MANSION & GARDENS ⬚
Penrith, Cumbria CA11 0HB
www.dalemain.com

A fine mixture of Medieval, Tudor & early Georgian architecture. Lived in by the same family since 1679 and home to the International Marmalade Festival. Award-winning gardens, richly planted with unusual combinations of flowers and shrubs. Highlights include the Rose Walk, Ancient Apple Trees, Tudor Knot Garden, Blue Himalayan Poppies, Earth Sculpture and Stumpery.
Location: Map 10:L5. OS Ref NY477 269. On A592 1m S of A66. 4m SW of Penrith. London, M1, M6/J40. Edinburgh, A73, M74, M6/J40.
Owner: Robert Hasell-McCosh Esq **Contact:** Claire Hexter - Marketing
Tel: 017684 86450 **Fax:** 017684 86223 **E-mail:** marketing@dalemain.com
Open: 20 Mar-27 Oct: Gardens, Tearoom & Gift Shop: Sun-Thu 10.15am-5pm (4pm in Oct). House 11.00am-4pm (3pm in Oct). Groups (12+) please book.
Admission: House & Gardens or Gardens Only. Please see website for details. Group Prices on application. Bespoke Guided Tours available.
Key facts: ⬚ No photography in house. Phone for event enquiries. ⬚ Gift Shop. ⬚ Plant Sales. ⬚ ⬚ Partial. WCs. ⬚ Licensed Tearoom. ⬚ 1hr tours. German and French translations. Garden tours available. Guided tour details on website. ⬚ 50 yds. Free. ⬚ ⬚ Guide dogs only. ⬚

HOLKER HALL & GARDENS ⬚ⓕ
Cark-In-Cartmel, Grange-Over-Sands, Cumbria LA11 7PL
www.holker.co.uk

Holker is the family home of the Cavendish family, set amongst beautiful countryside surrounding the Lake District. Steeped in history, this magnificent Victorian Mansion of neo-Elizabethan Gothic style was largely re-built in the 1870's following a fire, but origins date back to the 1600's. The glorious gardens, café, food hall & gift shop complete the visitor experience.
Location: Map 10:K8. From Motorway M6/J36, Signed Barrow A590.
Owner: Cavendish Family **Contact:** Jillian Rouse
Tel: 015395 58328 **Fax:** 015395 58378 **E-mail:** info@holker.co.uk
Open: 20 Mar-30 Oct, Wed-Sun & BH Mons (closed Mon & Tue), Hall: 11-4pm. Gardens: 10.30-5pm. Café, Food Hall & Gift Shop: 4-19 Mar, Fri, Sat & Sun, 10.30-4pm and from 20 Mar-30 Oct, Wed-Sun (& BH Mons), 10.30-5pm.
Admission: Hall & Gardens: Adult £12.00, Child FOC. Gardens only: Adult £8.00, Child FOC. Hall only: Adults £7.50, Child FOC. Group Rates (10+) Hall & Gardens: Adult £8.00 Gardens only: Adult £5.50.
Key facts: ⓘ No photography in house. ⬚ Food Hall & Gift Shop. ⬚ ⬚ ⬚ ⬚ ⬚ ⬚ For groups, by arrangement. ⬚ ⬚ ⬚ Dogs on leads (in park). ⬚

MIREHOUSE ⬚ⓕ
Keswick, Cumbria CA12 4QE

Melvyn Bragg described Mirehouse as 'Manor from Heaven'. Set in stunning landscape, Mirehouse is a literary house linked with Tennyson and Wordsworth. Live piano music and children's history trail in house. Natural playgrounds, serene bee garden and lakeside walk.
Location: Map 10:J5. OS Ref NY235 284. Beside A591, 3½m N of Keswick.
Owner: James Fryer-Spedding
Contact: Janaki Spedding
Tel: 017687 72287
E-mail: info@mirehouse.com
Website: www.mirehouse.com
Open: Please see website for open dates.
Admission: Please see website for admission rates.
Key facts: ⓘ No photography in house. Good bus service to property. ⬚ ⬚ ⬚ By arrangement. ⬚ ⬚ ⬚ On leads in grounds.

CARLISLE CASTLE ⬚
Carlisle, Cumbria CA3 8UR

Standing proudly in the city it has dominated for nine centuries, Carlisle Castle was a constantly updated working fortress until well within living memory.
Location: Map 10:K3. OS Ref NY396 562. **Tel:** 01228 591922 **E-mail:** customers@english-heritage.org.uk **Website:** www.english-heritage.org.uk/carlisle **Open:** Please see website for up-to-date opening and admission details.

LANERCOST PRIORY ⬚
Lanercost, Brampton, Cumbria CA8 2HQ

This Augustian Priory was founded c1166. The east end of the noble 13th Century church survives to its full height. **Location:** Map 10:L3. OS Ref NY556 637.
Tel: 01697 73030 **E-mail:** customers@english-heritage.org.uk
Website: www.english-heritage.org.uk/lanercost
Open: Please see website for up-to-date opening and admission details.

LEIGHTON HALL 🏛Ⓕ
CARNFORTH, LANCASHIRE LA5 9ST
www.leightonhall.co.uk

Leighton Hall's setting, in a bowl of parkland against a backdrop of the Lakeland Fells, can deservedly be described as spectacular. Nestled in 1,550 acres of lush grounds, this romantic, Gothic house is the lived-in home of the famous Gillow furniture making family. Boasting priceless pieces of Gillow furniture, pictures, clocks, silver and objéts d'art, Leightons' informal guided tours appeal to all ages. Outside the Hall are woodland walks, an abundant 19th Century walled garden, herbaceous borders and roses, a fragrant herb patch and an ornamental vegetable plot. Birds of prey are flown every day at 3:30pm (weather permitting). Finally, visit the charming tearooms for a quintessential English afternoon tea.

Location: Map 10:L8. OS Ref SD494 744. 9m N of Lancaster, 10m S of Kendal, 3m N of Carnforth. 1½ m W of A6. 3m from M6/A6/J35, signed from J35

Owner: Richard Gillow Reynolds Esq

Contact: Mrs C S Reynolds

Tel: 01524 734474 **Fax:** 01524 720357

Additional Contact: Mrs Lucy Arthurs

E-mail: info@leightonhall.co.uk

Open: May-Sep, Tue-Fri (also BH Sun and Mon, Sun in Aug) 2-5pm. Pre-booked groups (25+) all year by arrangement. Group rates.

Admission: Adult £7.95, OAP/Student £7.25, Child (5-12 years) £4.95, Family (2 adults and up to 3 children) £24.95, Grounds only £4.75.

Key facts: ⓘ No photography in house. ◻ ⓕ Ⓣ ⬟ Partial. WCs. Regrettably the halls first floor is inaccessible for unaccompanied wheelchair users. ◼ Ⓚ Child friendly, enthusiastic guides bring Leighton's history to life. Informal, relaxed tours. Ⓟ Free and ample parking. ◼ 3 themed packages available covering the new cross curriculum. 🐾 On leads, on the parkland only. ▣ ⊡

Browsholme Hall

BROWSHOLME HALL 🏛
Clitheroe, Lancashire BB7 3DE
www.browsholme.com

Browsholme Hall has been the ancestral home of the Parkers, Bowbearers of the Forest of Bowland since the time Tudor times. Today it is still the family's home and Robert and Amanda Parker invite visitors to enjoy its magnificent architecture, fabulous interiors, antique furnishings and lovely gardens set in the beautiful landscape of the Forest of Bowland. Superb oak chests, Gillow furniture, portraits, porcelain, Civil War arms and many unique relics including mementos of Bonnie Prince Charlie and even a fragment of a Zeppelin reflect the continuous occupation of the Hall by the Parkers for over 500 years.

Location: Map 10:M10. OS Ref SD683 452. 5m NW of Clitheroe off B6243.
Owner: The Parker Family **Contact:** Catherine Turner - Administrator
Tel: 01254 827160 **E-mail:** info@browsholme.com
Open: Gardens and Tearoom 11.00-4.30pm. Hall Tours from 12.00pm. May-Sep every Weds and 1st Sun in the month. Spring & August BH Mon. Booked parties and groups welcome at other times, including Christmas (28 Nov-9 Dec), by prior arrangement.
Admission: See website for full details.
Key facts: 🔲 💼 🅿 🔳 ✖ Guide dogs only. 🔲 ♿

HOGHTON TOWER
PRESERVATION TRUST 🏛Ⓕ
Hoghton, nr Preston, Lancashire PR5 0SH
www.hoghtontower.co.uk

A Tudor fortified Manor House, the ancestral home of the de Hoghton family. Join a tour of the staterooms to learn about the history of the house. Stroll through the stunning walled gardens. Browse the gift shop and finish with an afternoon tea in our Vaio Tearoom. Self-catering accommodation is available in your very own tower. Private and school tours welcome by pre-booking. Wedding Venue.

Location: Map 10:L11. OS Ref SD622 264. M65/J3. Midway between Preston & Blackburn on A675. **Owner:** Hoghton Tower Preservation Trust
Contact: mail@hoghtontower.co.uk **Tel:** 01254 852986
E-mail: mail@hoghtontower.co.uk
Open: May-Sep (Sun-Thur), BHs (except Christmas & New Year) and every 3rd Sun of the Month. Mon-Thu 11:00am-5:00pm, Sun 10:00am-5:00pm (First Tour 11:30am, last tour 3:30pm). Tearoom Mon-Thu 11:00am-5:00pm, Sun 10:00am-5:00pm. Group visits by appointment all year round. Please see our website for variations. **Admission:** Please check website.
Key facts: 🔲 Gift ideas. 🔳 Conferences. 💼 Tearoom. 🎥 Obligatory. 🅿 🔳 Prebook only. ✖ Assistance dogs only. 🛏 Self-catering. 🔲 ♿

Bedroom at Leighton Hall

ASTLEY HALL, COACH HOUSE AND PARK 🏛
Astley Park, Off Hallgate, Chorley PR7 1NP
Astley Hall "the most exhilarating house in Lancashire" (Simon Jenkins).
Location: Map 10:L11. OS Ref SD574 183. Jct 8 on M61. Signposted from A6.
Sat Nav is PR7 1XA **Tel:** 01257 515151 **E-mail:** astley.hall@chorley.gov.uk
Website: www.chorley.gov.uk/astleyhall
Open: See website. **Admission:** Free admission.

MANCHESTER CATHEDRAL
Victoria Street, Manchester M3 1SX
Manchester Cathedral Grade I listed masterpiece. **Location:** Map 6:N1. OS Ref SJ838 988. **Tel:** 0161 833 2220 **Fax:** 0161 839 6218
E-mail: office@manchestercathedral.org
Website: www.manchestercathedral.org **Open:** Every day. Times vary, please check website for up-to-date information. **Admission:** Donations welcome.

MEOLS HALL 🏛Ⓕ
Churchtown, Southport, Merseyside PR9 7LZ
17th Century house with subsequent additions. Interesting collection of pictures and furniture. Tithe Barn available for wedding ceremonies and receptions all year.
Location: Map 10:K11. OS Ref SD365 184. 3m NE of Southport town centre in Churchtown. SE of A565.
Owner: The Hesketh Family
Contact: Pamela Whelan
Tel: 01704 228326 **Fax:** 01704 507185
E-mail: events@meolshall.com **Website:** www.meolshall.com
Open: May BH Mon: 2 & 30 May. 20 Aug-14 Sep. 1.30-5.30pm.
Admission: Adult £4.00, Child £1.00. Groups welcome but Afternoon Tea is only available for bookings of 25+.
Key facts: 🔳 Wedding ceremonies and receptions available in the Tithe Barn. 🔲 🅿 🔳 🔲 ♿

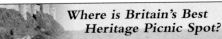

LITTLE MORETON HALL
Congleton, Cheshire CW12 4SD
Tel: 01260 272018 **E-mail:** littlemoretonhall@nationaltrust.org.uk

NESS BOTANIC GARDENS
Neston Road, Ness, Cheshire CH64 4AY
Tel: 0845 030 4063 **E-mail:** nessgdns@liv.ac.uk

ALLAN BANK
Grasmere, Cumbria LA22 9QZ
Tel: 015394 35143 **E-mail:** allanbank@nationaltrust.org.uk

BRANTWOOD
Coniston, Cumbria LA21 8AD
Tel: 01539 441396 **E-mail:** enquiries@brantwood.org.uk

BROUGHAM CASTLE
Penrith, Cumbria CA10 2AA
Tel: 01768 862488 **E-mail:** customers@english-heritage.org.uk

CARLISLE CATHEDRAL
Carlisle, Cumbria CA3 8TZ
Tel: 01228 548151

DOVE COTTAGE & WORDSWORTH MUSEUM
Grasmere, Cumbria LA22 9SH
Tel: 01539 435544 **E-mail:** enquiries@wordsworth.org.uk

HALECAT GARDEN NURSERY & GARDENS
Halecat House, Witherslack, Grange-over-Sands, Cumbria
LA11 6RT

HILL TOP
Near Sawrey, Hawkshead, Ambleside, Cumbria LA22 0LF
Tel: 015394 36269 **E-mail:** hilltop@nationaltrust.org.uk

HOLEHIRD GARDENS
Patterdale Road, Windermere, Cumbria LA23 1NP
Tel: 015394 46008 **E-mail:** maggie.mees@btinternet.com

HUTTON-IN-THE-FOREST
Hutton-in-the-Forest, Penrith, Cumbria CA11 9TH
Tel: 017684 84449 **E-mail:** info@hutton-in-the-forest.co.uk

LOWTHER CASTLE & GARDENS TRUST
Lowther Castle, Penrith, Cumbria CA10 2HG
Tel: 01931 712192

MUNCASTER CASTLE GARDENS
Muncaster Castle, Ravenglass, Cumbria CA18 1RQ
Tel: 01229 717614 **E-mail:** info@muncaster.co.uk

NAWORTH CASTLE
Naworth Castle Estate, Brampton, Cumbria CA8 2HF
Tel: 016977 3229. **E-mail:** office@naworth.co.uk

RYDAL MOUNT & GARDENS
Rydal, Cumbria LA22 9LU
Tel: 01539 433002 **E-mail:** info@rydalmount.co.uk

SIZERGH CASTLE AND GARDEN
Sizergh, Kendal, Cumbria LA8 8AE
Tel: 015395 60951 **E-mail:** sizergh@nationaltrust.org.uk

STOTT PARK BOBBIN MILL
Colton, Ulverston, Cumbria LA12 8AX
Tel: 01539 531087 **E-mail:** stott.park@english-heritage.org.uk

SWARTHMOOR HALL
Swarthmoor Hall Lane, Ulverston, Cumbria LA12 0JQ
Tel: 01229 583204 **E-mail:** info@swarthmoorhall.co.uk

TOWNEND
Troutbeck, Windermere, Cumbria LA23 1LB
Tel: 015394 32628 **E-mail:** townend@nationaltrust.org.uk

TULLIE HOUSE MUSEUM & ART GALLERY
Castle Street, Carlisle, Cumbria CA3 8TP
Tel: 01228 618718 **E-mail:** enquiries@tulliehouse.org

WINDERWATH GARDENS
Winderwath, Temple Sowerby, Penrith, Cumbria CA10 2AG
Tel: 01768 88250

WORDSWORTH HOUSE AND GARDEN
Main Street, Cockermouth, Cumbria CA13 9RX
Tel: 01900 820884 **E-mail:** wordsworthhouse@nationaltrust.org.uk

GAWTHORPE HALL
Padiham, Nr Burnley, Lancashire BB12 8UA
Tel: 01282 771004 **E-mail:** gawthorpehall@nationaltrust.org.uk

LANCASTER CASTLE
Shire Hall, Castle Parade, Lancaster, Lancashire LA1 1YJ
Tel: 01524 64998 **E-mail:** lancastercastle

LYTHAM HALL
Lytham Hall, Ballam Road, Lytham FY8 4JX
Tel: 01253 736652 **E-mail:** lytham.hall@htnw.co.uk

RUFFORD OLD HALL
Rufford, Nr Ormskirk, Lancashire L40 1SG
Tel: 01704 821254 **E-mail:** ruffordoldhall@nationaltrust.org.uk

SAMLESBURY HALL
Preston New Road, Samlesbury, Preston PR5 0UP
Tel: 01254 812010 **E-mail:** info@samlesburyhall.co.uk

SMITHILLS HALL
Smithills Dean Road, Bolton BL7 7NP
Tel: 01204 332377 **E-mail:** historichalls@bolton.gov.uk

TOWNELEY HALL ART GALLERY & MUSEUMS
Burnley BB11 3RQ
Tel: 01282 447130

HEATON HALL
Heaton Park, Prestwich, Manchester M25 9WL
Tel: 0161 235 8815

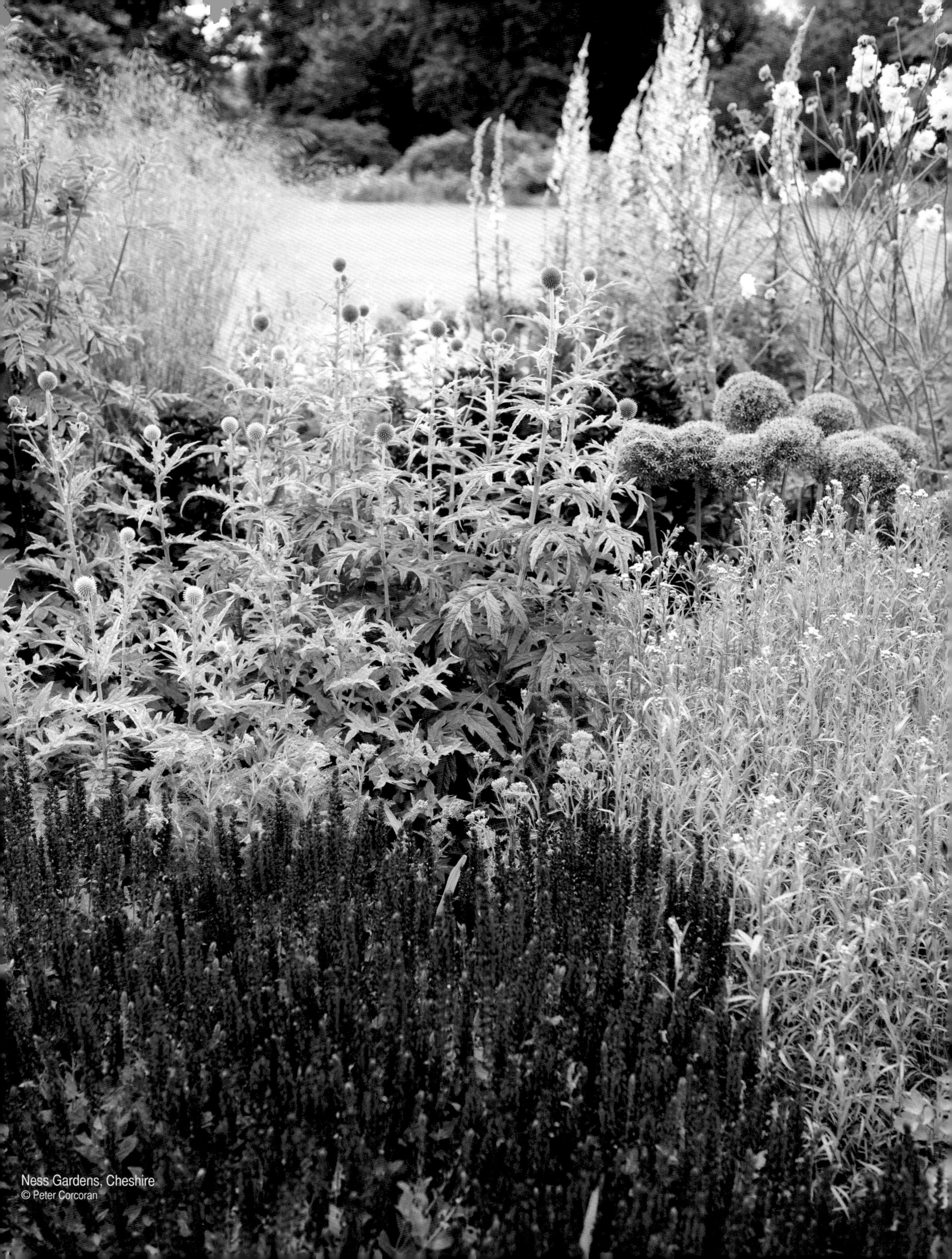

Ness Gardens, Cheshire

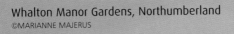

Raby Castle, County Durham

©VISITBRITAIN / CO DURHAM TOURISM PARTNERSHIP

Co. Durham
Northumberland
Tyne & Wear

North East

Northumberland

Tyne &
Wear

Co. Durham

A long tradition of independence has given the North East a style all its own and helped it retain its castles, fortified manors and fascinating stories.

New Entries for 2016:
• Whalton Manor Gardens

Find stylish hotels with a personal welcome and good cuisine in the North East. More information on page 348.

• Waren House Hotel

SIGNPOST
RECOMMENDING THE UK'S FINEST HOTELS SINCE 1935

www.signpost.co.uk

RABY CASTLE ⓗⒻ
STAINDROP, DARLINGTON, CO. DURHAM DL2 3AH
www.rabycastle.com

Raby Castle is surrounded by a large deer park, with two lakes and a beautiful walled garden with formal lawns, yew hedges and an ornamental pond. It was built by the mighty Nevill family in the 14th Century, and has been home to Lord Barnard's family since 1626. Highlights include the vast Barons' Hall, where it is reputed 700 knights gathered to plot the doomed 'Rising of the North' rebellion, and the stunning Octagon Drawing Room. With Meissen porcelain, fine furniture and paintings by Munnings, Reynolds, Van Dyck, Batoni, Teniers, Amigoni and Vernet. Also in the grounds is the 18th Century Stable block with impressive horse-drawn carriage collection, and a delightfully converted Gift Shop and Tearooms, and woodland play area.

Location: Map 10:O5. OS Ref NZ129 218. On A688, 1m N of Staindrop. 8m NE of Barnard Castle, 12m WNW of Darlington.
Owner: The Lord Barnard **Contact:** Castle Admin Office
Tel: 01833 660202 **E-mail:** admin@rabycastle.com

Open: Castle: Easter weekend Sat, Sun, Mon. May & Jun, Sun-Wed. Jul & Aug, Daily except Sats, Sep Sun-Wed. 1pm-4.30pm.
Park & Gardens: As Castle, 11am-5.00pm.
Admission: Castle, Park & Gardens: Adult £10.00, Child (5-15yrs) £4.50, Conc. £9.00, Family discounts available. Groups (12+): Adult £8.00. Park & Gardens: Adult £6.00, Child £2.50, Conc. £5.00. Groups (12+) Adult £4.50. Season Tickets available. Private Group Guided Tours (20+)* Adult £9.00 *Please book in advance. **Key facts:** ⓘ No photography or video filming is permitted inside. Colour guidebook on sale. ⓖ Gift Shop. ⓛ Limited access to Castle interior. Accessible WCs, designated parking, free wheelchair loan. ⓣ Tearoom.
ⓧ Castle Tours available on certain dates. ⓟ Ample car parking on grass and coach parking on hard standing. ⓢ Schools by arrangement, £4.00pp
ⓓ Dogs welcome on leads in deer park only. No dogs are allowed in the Walled Gardens or inside buildings. ⓦ ⓦ

St Peter's Chapel at Auckland Castle

AUCKLAND CASTLE 🏛

Market Place, Bishop Auckland, County Durham DL14 7NR

www.aucklandcastle.org

900 years of history to discover in a palace fit for kings, built for Prince Bishops. Enjoy St Peter's Chapel, State Rooms and Spanish masterpieces; fascinating Exhibitions, Gardens and Parkland. Family activities 12-3pm weekends and School holidays. **Location:** Map 10:P5. OS Ref NZ213 302. See website for directions. **Owner:** Auckland Castle Trust **Contact:** Visitor Services 01388 743797 opening, admissions, group bookings etc. **Tel:** General enquiries 01388 743750 **E-mail:** enquiries@aucklandcastle.org **Open:** 14 Feb-20 Dec, Boxing Day and New Year's Day. Open daily (except Tues) from 10am until last admission 4pm. **Admission:** Adults £6.00, Annual Pass £15.00, Children under 16 Free. **Key facts:** 🛍 We stock a range of locally sourced items in our gift shop. 🎟 Available for private hire. 🍴 Tearoom serves light lunches, afternoon teas and a range of hot and cold beverages. 🎫 Daily guided tours at 11.30 and 2.30. 🎓 We have an active education programme and work with many schools across County Durham. 🐕 Guide Dogs Only. Dog walkers welcome in Bishop's Park. ♿

DURHAM CATHEDRAL ✦

Durham DH1 3EH

www.durhamcathedral.co.uk

One of the finest examples of Romanesque architecture in Europe, located at the heart of a UNESCO World Heritage Site. Burial place of St Cuthbert and the Venerable Bede. Climb the Cathedral Tower for spectacular views, explore the heritage woodlands and riverbanks, and discover the most intact surviving set of monastic buildings in the British Isles. Exhibition galleries showcasing the Cathedral's internationally renowned collections, open in 2016. **Location:** Map 10:P4. OS Ref NZ274 422. Durham City Centre. **Contact:** The Cathedral Office **Tel:** 0191 3864266 **E-mail:** enquiries@durhamcathedral.co.uk **Open:** Daily 7.30am-6pm (8pm Summer), with Services three times daily. **Admission:** Free, donations welcome. Admission applies to guided tours, exhibition galleries and the Tower. Groups contact visits@durhamcathedral.co.uk **Key facts:** ℹ 🛍 Souvenirs and gifts. Mon-Sat 9.00-5.30, Sun 12.00-5.00. 🎟 events@durhamcathedral.co.uk ♿ Partial. 🍴 Locally-sourced food and drink served daily, 10.00-4.30. 🍽 Restaurant available for hire. 🎫 Adults £5.00, Conc. £4.50. Children free (U16). 🅿 Limited disabled, public parking nearby. 🎓 education@durhamcathedral.co.uk 🐕 Guide dogs only. ♿

THE BOWES MUSEUM

Barnard Castle, County Durham DL12 8NP

www.thebowesmuseum.org.uk

The recently transformed Museum houses fine art, fashion & textiles, silver & metals, ceramics, furniture and the iconic Silver Swan musical automation. A rolling exhibition programme is complemented by varied indoor and outdoor events. The acclaimed Café Bowes, a high quality gift shop, tranquil gardens and woodland walks add to the enjoyment. **Location:** Map 10:O6. OS Ref NZ055 163. Situated on Newgate in Barnard Castle. Just off the A66 in the heart of the North Pennines. **Tel:** 01833 690606 **Fax:** 01833 637163 **E-mail:** info@thebowesmuseum.org.uk **Open:** 10.00-5.00 daily. Closed only 25 & 26 Dec & 1 Jan. **Admission:** Adults £10.50, Conc. £9.50, 6 month pass £16.00. Admission to all exhibitions included. Accompanied children Free (U16). Accompanying carers Free. Free access to Café Bowes, Shop & Grounds. **Key facts:** 🛍 Souvenirs & gifts. Open daily 10.00-4.45. 🎟 hire@thebowes museum.org.uk. ♿ Access to all areas. 🍴 Locally produced seasonal menu, speciality teas, coffees & wines. Mon-Sat 9.00-4.30, Sun 10.00-4.30. 🎫 Available via group visits or selected days in Summer. 🎧 Children's Audio available. 🅿 Ample free parking & coach & accessible parking bays. 🎓 education@thebowes museum.org.uk. 🐕 Except guide dogs. 🎟 hire@thebowesmuseum.org.uk. ♿ ♿

Durham Cathedral

VISITOR INFORMATION

■ Owner
His Grace The Duke of Northumberland

■ Address
Alnwick Castle
Alnwick
Northumberland
NE66 1NQ

■ Location
Map 14:11M
OS Ref. NU187 135
Well signposted less than a mile off A1; 35 miles north of Newcastle and 80 miles south of Edinburgh.
Bus: Regular bus services to Alnwick from around the region
Rail: 4 miles from Alnmouth Station (3.5 hours from London King's Cross)
Air: 34 miles from Newcastle Airport
Sea: 37 miles from North Sea ferry terminal

■ Contact
Tel: 01665 511100
Group bookings:
01665 511184.
Media & filming:
01665 511794.
E-mail:
info@alnwickcastle.com

■ Opening Times
24 March - 25 October 2016
10.00am-5.30pm (last admission 3.45pm).

State Rooms are open 11.00am-5.00pm (last admission 4.00pm, Chapel closes at 2.30pm). Check alnwickcastle.com for up-to-date opening dates and times.

■ Admission
Adult:	£14.75
Concession:	£12.00
Child (5-16yrs):	£7.60
Family (2+up to 4):	£39.00

(2015 prices shown, subject to change).
Tickets can be validated for unlimited free visits for 12 months, at no extra cost (see website for T&Cs)
Discounted rates available for groups of 14 or more.

■ Special Events
Daily events include guided tours of the State Rooms and grounds, Knight's Quest activities, and broomstick training. Seasonal events include knights tournaments, falconry displays, jester performances, and visits from skilled artisans. See website for details.

Conference/Function
Venue	Size	Max cap
Guest Hall	100' x 30'	300
Hulne Abbey	varies	500

ALNWICK CASTLE 🏰ⓕ
www.alnwickcastle.com

Home to the Duke of Northumberland's family, the Percys, for over 700 years; Alnwick Castle offers history on a grand scale.

Alnwick Castle's remarkable history is brimming with drama, intrigue, and extraordinary people; from a gunpowder plotter and visionary collectors, to decadent hosts and medieval England's most celebrated knight: Harry Hotspur.

Combining magnificent medieval architecture with sumptuous Italianate State Rooms, Alnwick Castle is one of the UK's most significant heritage destinations. In recent years it has also taken starring roles in a number of film and television productions, featuring as a location for ITV's Downton Abbey and as Hogwarts School of Witchcraft and Wizardry in the Harry Potter films.

With a history beginning in the Norman Age, Alnwick Castle was originally built as a border defence, before eventually being transformed from a fortification into a family home for the first Duke and Duchess of Northumberland in the 1760s.

The castle's State Rooms were later recreated by the 4th Duke in the lavish Italian Renaissance style that we see today, now boasting one of the country's finest private collections of art and furniture.

This remarkable collection includes works by Canaletto, Titian, Van Dyck, Turner, and Dobson; an extensive gallery of Meissen, Chelsea, and Paris porcelain; and the priceless Cucci cabinets, originally created for Louis XIV of France.

Alnwick Castle aims to create a vibrant and engaging heritage experience for families, with opportunities aplenty for children to get hands-on with history in the Knight's Quest arena, with dressing up, swordplay, medieval crafts and games.

KEY FACTS

- ⓘ Storage available for suitcases. Photography is not permitted in the State Rooms.
- 🛍 Gift Shop open daily.
- 🍽 Team-building, banqueting, dinner dances. Call 01665 511086.
- ♿ Accessible WCs. Free wheelchair and mobility scooter hire available. Limited access in areas.
- Licensed.
- 🚶 Free daily tours of the State Rooms and grounds.
- 🅿 Coach parking also available.
- Workshops, activities and discounted admission available. Call 01665 511184.
- 🐕 Assistance dogs only.
- Wedding ceremonies and receptions. Call 01665 511086.
- See website for details.

CHILLINGHAM CASTLE 🏛ⓕ
www.chillingham-castle.com

20 Minutes from seaside or mountains. 4 stars in Simon Jenkins' 'Thousand Best Houses' and the very first of The Independent's '50 Best Castles in Britain & Ireland'.

This remarkable and very private castle has been continuously owned by just one family line since the 1200's. A visit from Edward I in 1298 was followed by many other Royal visits right down through this century. See Chillingham's alarming dungeons as well as active restoration in the Great Halls and State Rooms which are gradually brought back to life with tapestries, arms and armour. We even have a very real torture chamber.

The 1100s stronghold became a fortified castle in 1344, see the original Royal Licence to Crenellate on view. Wrapped in the nation's history Chillingham also occupied a strategic position during Northumberland's bloody border feuds being a resting place to many royal visitors. Tudor days saw additions but the underlying medievalism remains. 18th and 19th Centuries saw decorative extravagances including 'Capability' Brown lakes and grounds with gardens laid out by Sir Jeffrey Wyatville, fresh from his triumphs at Windsor Castle. Prehistoric Wild Cattle roam the park beyond more rare than mountain gorilla (a separate tour) and never miss the family tomb in the church.

Gardens
With romantic grounds, the castle commands breathtaking views of the surrounding countryside. As you walk to the lake you will see, according to season, drifts of snowdrops, daffodils or bluebells and an astonishing display of rhododendrons. This emphasises the restrained formality of the Elizabethan topiary garden, with its intricately clipped hedges of box and yew. Lawns, the formal gardens and woodland walks are all fully open to the public.

VISITOR INFORMATION

■ **Owner**
Sir Humphry Wakefield Bt

■ **Address**
Chillingham Castle
Northumberland
NE66 5NJ

■ **Location**
Map 14:L11
OS Ref. NU062 258
45m N of Newcastle
between A697 & A1.
2m S of B6348 at Chatton.
6m SE of Wooler.
Rail: Alnmouth or Berwick.

■ **Contact**
The Administrator
Tel: 01668 215359
E-mail:
enquiries@chillingham-castle.com

■ **Opening Times**
Summer
Castle, Garden & Tearoom
Easter-31 October. Closed
Sats, 12 noon-5pm.

Winter
October-April. Groups &
Coach Tours any time by
appointment.
All function activities
available.

■ **Admission**
Adult   £9.50
Children   £5.50
Conc.   £8.50
Family Ticket   £23.00
(2 adults and 3 children
under 15).

KEY FACTS

🖥 Corporate entertainment, lunches, drinks, dinners, wedding ceremonies and receptions.

By arrangement.

🅿 Avoid Lilburn route, coach parties welcome by prior arrangement. Limited for coaches.

Guide dogs only.

Self-catering apartments.

BAMBURGH CASTLE 🏛ⓕ
Bamburgh, Northumberland NE69 7DF
www.bamburghcastle.com

These formidable stone walls have witnessed dark tales of royal rebellion, bloody battles, spellbinding legends and millionaire benefactors. With 14 public rooms and over 3000 artefacts, including arms and armour, porcelain, furniture and artwork. The Armstrong and Aviation artefacts Museum houses artefacts spanning both World Wars as well as others relating to Lord Armstrongs ship building empire on the Tyne.

Location: Map 14:M10. OS Ref NU184 351. 42m N of Newcastle-upon-Tyne. 20m S of Berwick-upon-Tweed. 6m E of Belford by B1342 from A1 at Belford.
Owner: Francis Watson-Armstrong **Contact:** Chris Calvert, Director
Tel: 01668 214208 **E-mail:** administrator@bamburghcastle.com
Open: 13 Feb-30 Oct 2016, 10am-5pm. Last admission 4pm. 31 Oct 2016-10 Feb 2017, Weekends only, 11am-4.30pm. Last admission 3.30pm.
Admission: Adult £10.75, Senior £10.50, Child (5-16 yrs) £5.00, Family (2 adults and up to 3 dependants under 18) £25.00. For groups please contact.
Key facts: ℹ No flash photography in the State Rooms. 📷 🖼 WCs. 🍽 Licensed. 🎬 By arrangement at any time, min charge out of hours £150. 🏠 🅿 100 cars, coaches park on tarmac drive at entrance. 🎫 Welcome. Guide provided if requested. 🐕 Guide dogs only. ♿ ⚘

LADY WATERFORD HALL & GALLERY ◆
Ford, Berwick-Upon-Tweed, Northumberland TD15 2QA
www.ford-and-etal.co.uk

At the heart of Ford & Etal Estates in rural North Northumberland, this 'must see venue' is a real hidden gem. Built as a school in 1860, the building houses a unique collection of magnificent watercolour murals (1861-1883) and smaller original paintings & sketches by Louisa Waterford, one of the most gifted female artists of the 19th Century. The fascinating story of Louisa's life & work is depicted through interpretation & film. Quizzes & games available for children to enjoy.
Location: Map 14:K10. OS Ref NT945 374. Midway between Edinburgh & Newcastle-upon-Tyne. Signed from A1 Berwick-upon-Tweed/A687 Cornhill-on-Tweed **Owner:** Ford & Etal Estates / Lady Waterford Hall Trust
Contact: Dorien Irving **Tel:** 07790 457580 / 07971 326177 / 01890 820338.
E-mail: tourism@ford-and-etal.co.uk **Open:** 10am-4pm daily (times may vary slightly early & late season), late Mar-early Nov. Last entry 45 minutes before closing. **Admission:** 2015 prices: Adult £3.00, Conc/Child £2.70, Family £8.00. U-5's Free. Discounts for pre-booked groups & joint venue tickets. **Key facts:** ℹ Occasionally closed for private functions - please phone before travelling. 📷 🖼 Level access. 🍽 Tearoom nearby. 🅿 Free. 🎫 🐕 Guide dogs only.

The Alnwick Garden

THE ALNWICK GARDEN

Denwick Lane, Alnwick, Northumberland NE66 1YU

One of the world's most contemporary gardens, The Alnwick Garden combines provocative and traditional landscapes in the heart of Northumberland. Featuring Europe's largest wooden treehouse, a Poison Garden and Bamboo Labyrinth, The Garden also offers an expansive rose garden, climbing clematis and honeysuckle, as well as interactive water features and stunning ornamental garden.

Location: Map 14:M11. OS Ref NU192 132.
Just off the A1 at Alnwick, Northumberland.
Owner: The Alnwick Garden Trust **Tel:** 01665 511350
E-mail: info@alnwickgarden.com **Website:** www.alnwickgarden.com
Open: Apr-Oct 10am-6pm. Nov-Mar 11-5pm.
Admission: Please check website for details.
Key facts: ▢ ▦ ▭ ▣ WCs. ▣ ▥ Licensed. ▨ By arrangement. ▣ Cars & coaches. ▣ ▨ Assistance dogs only. ▣ ▣ ▣

WHALTON MANOR GARDENS

Whalton, Morpeth, Northumberland NE61 3UT

Historically significant, this 17th Century house with its three-acre garden is bursting with inspirational planting and magnificent architectural structures. The charming Italianate summerhouse, game larder, pergolas and vast stone-paved courtyard were designed by Sir Edward Lutyens and strongly influenced by Gertrude Jekyll. The garden is available for group visits, weddings and events.
Location: Map 10:O2. OS Ref NZ132 814.
Owner/Contact: Penny Norton **Tel:** 01670 775205
E-mail: Garden Visits - gardens@whaltonmanor.co.uk
Weddings and Events - events@signatureone.co.uk
Website: www.whaltonmanor.co.uk **Open:** Apr-Oct. By appointment only.
Admission: The gardens can be enjoyed by individuals or groups of up to 50 people and entry to the gardens start from £7.00 per person. Tours must be booked in advance.
Key facts: ▦ ▭ ▣ ▨ ▣ ▥ ▧ ▨ ▣ ▣

Belsay Hall, Castle & Gardens

BELSAY HALL, CASTLE & GARDENS ▦

Belsay, Nr Morpeth, Northumberland NE20 0DX

Belsay has something for everyone. A fine medieval castle, which was later extended to include a magnificent Jacobean mansion.
Location: Map 10:O2. OS Ref OS87, NZ086 785.
Tel: 01661 881636 **Website:** www.english-heritage.org.uk/belsay
Open: Please visit www.english-heritage.org.uk/belsay for opening times, admission prices and the most up-to-date information.

CHIPCHASE CASTLE ▣ⓔ

Wark, Hexham, Northumberland NE48 3NT

The Castle overlooks the River North Tyne and is set in formal and informal gardens. **Location:** Map 10:N2. 10m NW of Hexham via A6079 to Chollerton. 2m SE of Wark. **Tel:** 01434 230203 **E-mail:** info@chipchasecastle.com
Website: www.chipchasecastle.com **Open:** Castle: 1-28 Jun, 2-5pm daily. Gardens & Nursery: Easter-31 Aug, Thu-Sun Incl. & BH Mon, 10am-5pm.
Admission: Castle £6.00, Garden £4.00, concessions available. Nursery Free.

CRAGSIDE ▨

Rothbury, Morpeth, Northumberland NE65 7PX

Revolutionary home of Lord Armstrong, Victorian inventor and landscape genius, Cragside sits on a rocky crag high above the Debdon Burn.
Location: Map 14:L12. OS Ref NU073 022. ½m NE of Rothbury on B6341.
Tel: 01669 620333 **E-mail:** cragside@nationaltrust.org.uk
Website: www.nationaltrust.org.uk/cragside
Open: Please see website for opening times and admission prices.

DUNSTANBURGH CASTLE ▨ ▦

Dunstanburgh Road, Craster, Northumberland NE66 3TT

Reached by a beautiful coastal walk, this 14th Century castle rivals any castle of its day. **Location:** Map 14:M11. OS Ref NU257 200. 8m NE of Alnwick.
Tel: 01665 576231 **Website:** www.english-heritage.org.uk/dunstanburghcastle
Open: Please visit www.english-heritage.org.uk for opening times, admission prices and the most up-to-date information.

LINDISFARNE CASTLE ▨

Holy Island, Berwick-Upon-Tweed, Northumberland TD15 2SH

Built in 1550 to protect Holy Island harbour from attack, the castle was restored and converted into a private house for Edward Hudson in 1903.
Location: Map 14:L10. OS Ref NU136 417. **Tel:** 01289 389244
E-mail: lindisfarne@nationaltrust.org.uk **Website:** www.nationaltrust.org.uk/lindisfarne-castle **Open:** Please see website for most up-to-date details.

PRESTON TOWER ▣ⓔ

Chathill, Northumberland NE67 5DH

Built by Sir Robert Harbottle in 1392. **Location:** Map 14:M11. OS Ref NU185 253. Follow Historic Property signs on A1 7m N of Alnwick.
Tel: 01665 589227 / 07966 150216 **Website:** www.prestontower.co.uk
Open: All year daily, 10am-6pm, or dusk, whichever is earlier.
Admission: Adult £2.00, Child 50p, Concessions £1.50. Groups £1.50.

WALLINGTON ▨

Cambo, Morpeth, Northumberland NE61 4AR

Impressive, yet friendly, house with a magnificent interior and fine collections. Home to many generations of the unconventional Trevelyan family.
Location: Map 10:O2. OS Ref NZ030 843. **Tel:** 01670 773600
E-mail: wallington@nationaltrust.org.uk **Website:** www.nationaltrust.org.uk/wallington **Open:** Please see website for up-to-date details.

GIBSIDE ▨

Nr Rowlands Gill, Burnopfield, Newcastle upon Tyne NE16 6BG

Gibside is an 18th Century 'forest' landscape garden, created by wealthy coal baron George Bowes. **Location:** Map 10:P3. OS Ref NZ172 584. **Tel:** 01207 541820
E-mail: gibside@nationaltrust.org.uk **Website:** www.nationaltrust.org.uk/gibside
Open: Please see website for up-to-date opening and admission details.

BARNARD CASTLE ⌗
Nr Galgate, Barnard Castle, Durham DL12 8PR
Tel: 01833 638212 **E-mail:** barnard.castle@english-heritage.org.uk

BEAMISH, THE LIVING MUSEUM
Beamish Museum, Beamish, County Durham DH9 0RG
Tel: 0191 370 4000 **E-mail:** museum@beamish.org.uk

CROOK HALL & GARDENS
Sidegate, Durham DH1 5SZ
Tel: 0191 3848028

DURHAM CASTLE
Palace Green, Durham DH1 3RW
Tel: 0191 3343800

ROKEBY PARK 🏚ⓒ
Barnard Castle, County Durham DL12 9RZ
Tel: 01609 748612 **E-mail:** admin@rokebypark.com

AYDON CASTLE ⌗
Corbridge, Northumberland NE45 5PJ
Tel: 01434 632450 **E-mail:** customers@english-heritage.org.uk

BRINKBURN PRIORY ⌗
Long Framlington, Morpeth, Northumberland NE65 8AR
Tel: 01665 570628 **E-mail:** customers@english-heritage.org.uk

CHERRYBURN ⌘
Station Bank, Mickley, Stocksfield, Northumberland NE43 7DD
Tel: 01661 843276 **E-mail:** cherryburn@nationaltrust.org.uk

CHESTERS ROMAN FORT ⌗
Chollerford, Hexham, Northumberland NE46 4EU
Tel: 01434 681379 **E-mail:** customers@english-heritage.org.uk

CORBRIDGE ROMAN TOWN ⌗
Corchester Lane, Corbridge, Northumberland NE45 5NT
Tel: 01434 632349 **E-mail:** customers@english-heritage.org.uk

EDLINGHAM CASTLE
Edlingham Castle, Edlingham, Alnwick NE66 2BW
Tel: 0191 269 1200

Corbridge Roman Town

ETAL CASTLE ⌗
Cornhill-On-Tweed, Northumberland TD12 4TN
Tel: 01890 820332 **E-mail:** customers@english-heritage.org.uk

HERTERTON HOUSE GARDENS
Hartington, Cambo, Morpeth, Northumberland NE61 4BN
Tel: 01670 774278

HOUSESTEADS ROMAN FORT ⌗
Haydon Bridge, Hexham, Northumberland NE47 6NN
Tel: 01434 344363 **E-mail:** customers@english-heritage.org.uk

HOWICK HALL GARDENS & ARBORETUM
Alnwick, Northumberland NE66 3LB
Tel: 01665 577285 **E-mail:** estateoffice@howickuk.com

LINDISFARNE PRIORY ⌗
Holy Island, Berwick-Upon-Tweed, Northumberland TD15 2RX
Tel: 01289 389200 **E-mail:** lindisfarne.priory@english-heritage.org.uk

MELDON PARK
Morpeth, Northumberland NE61 3SW
Tel: 01670 772341 **E-mail:** michelle@flyingfox.co.uk/james@flying-fox.co.uk

NORHAM CASTLE ⌗
Norham, Northumberland TD15 2JY
Tel: 01289 304493 **E-mail:** customers@english-heritage.org.uk

PRUDHOE CASTLE ⌗
Prudhoe, Northumberland NE42 6NA
Tel: 01661 833459 **E-mail:** customers@english-heritage.org.uk

SEATON DELAVAL HALL ⌘
The Avenue, Seaton Sluice, Northumberland NE26 4QR
Tel: 0191 237 9100 **E-mail:** seatondelavalhall@nationaltrust.org.uk

WARKWORTH CASTLE ⌗
Warkworth, Alnwick, Northumberland NE65 0UJ
Tel: 01665 711423 **E-mail:** warkworth.castle@english-heritage.org.uk

BESSIE SURTEES HOUSE ⌗
41-44 Sandhill, Newcastle, Tyne & Wear NE1 3JF
Tel: 0191 269 1200 **E-mail:** customers@english-heritage.org.uk

HYLTON CASTLE ⌗
Craigavon Road, Sunderland, Tyne and Wear SR5 3PB
Tel: 01912 611585

NEWCASTLE CASTLE
Castle Garth, Newcastle, Tyne & Wear NE1 1RQ
Tel: 0191 230 6300 **E-mail:** info@newcastlecastle.co.uk

SOUTER LIGHTHOUSE ⌘
Coast Road, Whitburn, Sunderland, Tyne & Wear SR6 7NH
Tel: 0191 529 3161 **E-mail:** souter@nationaltrust.org.uk

TYNEMOUTH CASTLE AND PRIORY ⌗
Tynemouth, Tyne & Wear NE30 4BZ
Tel: 01912 691215 **E-mail:** customers@english-heritage.org.uk

WASHINGTON OLD HALL ⌘
The Avenue, Washington Village, Tyne & Wear NE38 7LE
Tel: 0191 416 6879 **E-mail:** washington.oldhall@nationaltrust.org.uk

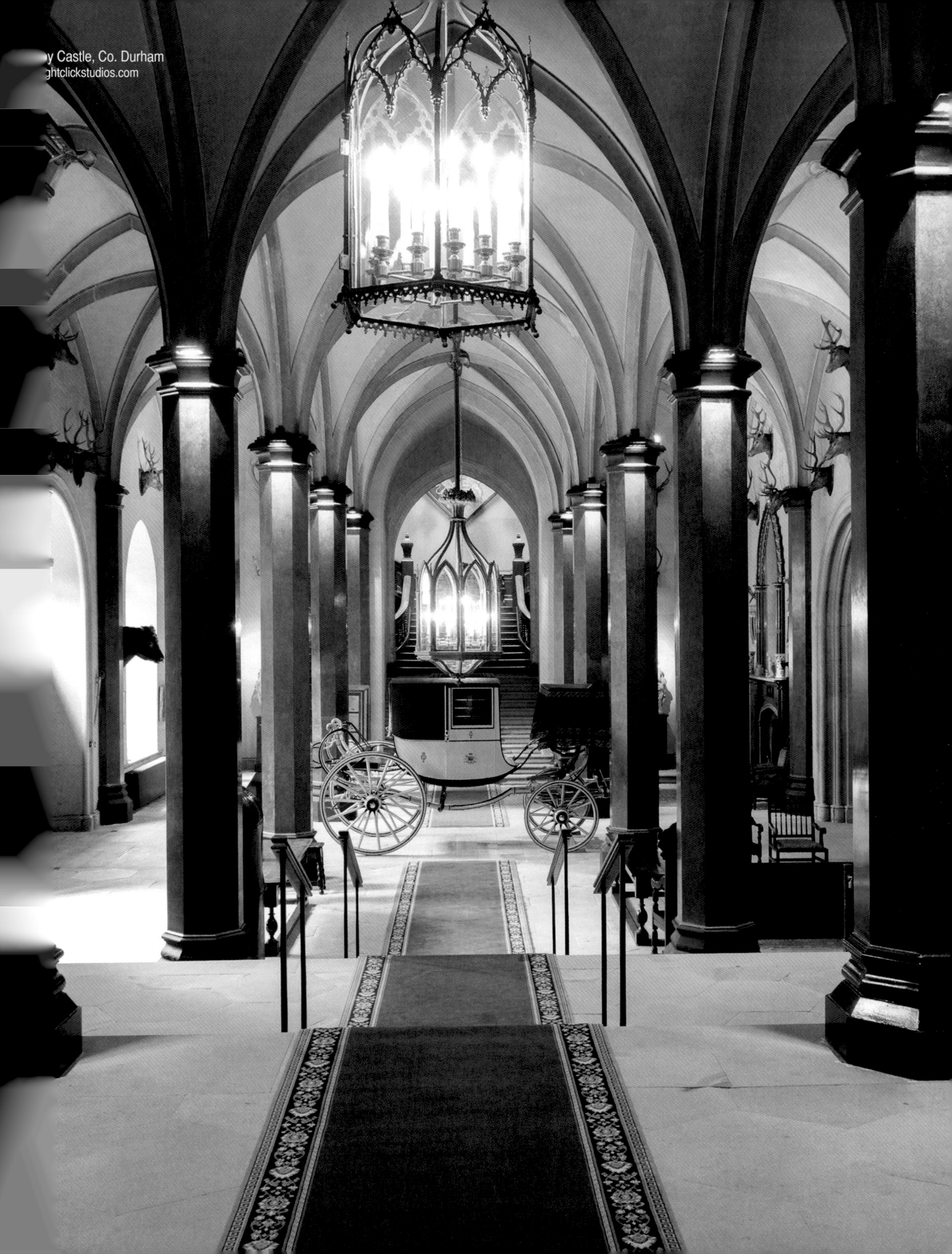

y Castle, Co. Durham
ghtclickstudios.com

Duart Castle, Isle of Mull

Scotland

A land with a rich culture, a turbulent history and a reputation for fine food, also offers visitors an extraordinary wealth of castles, country houses and gardens.

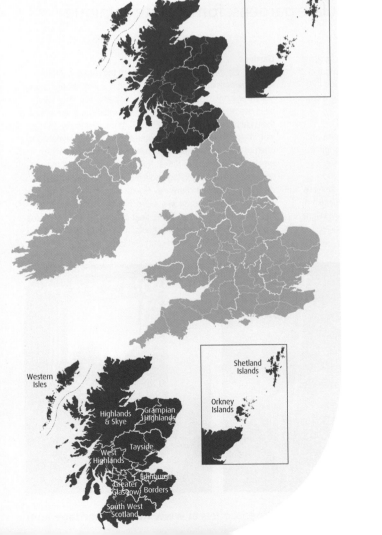

Find stylish hotels with a personal welcome and good cuisine in Scotland. More information on page 348.

- Atholl Palace Hotel
- Blackaddie Country House Hotel
- Coul House Hotel
- Craigadam House
- Eddrachilles Hotel
- The Four Seasons Hotel
- Roman Camp Country House & Restaurant
- Viewfield House

SIGNPOST
RECOMMENDING THE UK'S FINEST HOTELS SINCE 1935

www.signpost.co.uk

VISITOR INFORMATION

■ Owner
The Lord Palmer

■ Address
Manderston
Duns
Berwickshire
Scotland
TD11 3PP

■ Location
Map 14:K9
OS Ref. NT810 544
From Edinburgh 47m, 1hr.
1½m E of Duns on A6105.
Bus: 400yds.
Rail: Berwick Station 12m.
Airport: Edinburgh or
Newcastle both 60m or
80mins.

■ Contact
The Lord Palmer
Tel: 01361 883450
Fax: 01361 882010
Secretary: 01361 882636
E-mail:
palmer@manderston.co.uk

■ Opening Times
Summer 2016
5 May-25 September,
Thurs and Sun only.
Gardens and tearoom
open 11.30am.
House opens 1.30–5pm;
last entry 4.15pm. BH
Mons, late May and late
August. Groups welcome
all year by appointment.

Winter
Group visits welcome by
appointment.

■ Admission
House & Grounds
(Open Days)
Adult	£10.00
Child (under 12yrs)	Free
Groups (15+)	£9.50
Grounds only	£6.00

Open any other day by
appointment.

Conference/Function
ROOM	Size	Max Cap
Dining Rm	22' x 35'	100
Ballroom	34' x 21'	150
Drawing Rm	35' x 21'	150

MANDERSTON 🏛Ⓕ
www.manderston.co.uk

Manderston, together with its magnificent stables, stunning marble dairy and 56 acres of immaculate gardens, forms quite a unique ensemble.

Manderston is the supreme country house of Edwardian Scotland: the swansong of its era. Manderston, as it is today, is a product of the best craftsmanship and highest domestic sophistication the Edwardian era had to offer and was completely rebuilt between 1903 and 1905.

Visitors are able to see not only the sumptuous State Rooms and bedrooms, decorated in the Adam manner, but also all original domestic offices, in a truly 'upstairs downstairs' atmosphere.

Manderston boasts a unique and recently restored silver staircase. There is a special museum with a nostalgic display of valuable tins made by Huntly and Palmer from 1868 to the present day. Winner of the AA/NPI Bronze Award UK 1994.

Gardens

Outside, the magnificence continues and the combination of formal gardens and picturesque landscapes is a major attraction unique amongst Scottish houses. The stables, still in use, have been described by Horse and Hound as 'probably the finest in all the wide world'. The Marble Dairy and its unusual tower, built to look like a Border Keep, enjoys commanding views. Manderston is often used as a film location but can also cater for corporate events. It is also an ideal retreat for business groups and think-tank weekends. Manderston also lends itself very well to fashion shows, air displays, archery, clay pigeon shooting, equestrian events, garden parties, shows, rallies, filming, product launches and marathons. Two airstrips for light aircraft, approx. 5m, grand piano, billiard table, pheasant shoots, sea angling, salmon fishing, stabling, cricket pitch, tennis court and lake.

KEY FACTS

ℹ️ No photography in house.

📷

🍽 Available. Buffets, lunches and dinners. Wedding receptions.

♿ Special parking available outside the house.

☕ Snaffles Tearoom - homemade lunches, teas, cakes and tray bakes. Can be booked in advance, menus on request.

🚶 Included. Available in French. Guides in rooms. If requested, the owner may meet groups. Tour time 1¼ hrs.

🅿️ 400 cars 125yds from house, 30 coaches 5yds from house. Appreciated if group fees are paid by one person.

🎒 Welcome. Guide can be provided. Biscuit Tin Museum of particular interest.

🐕 Grounds only, on leads.

🛏 6 twin, 4 double.

❄️

ABBOTSFORD, HOME OF SIR WALTER SCOTT 🏛Ⓕ
The Abbotsford Trust, Abbotsford, Melrose, Roxburghshire TD6 9BQ
www.scottsabbotsford.com

Abbotsford, the home world renowned author & poet Sir Walter Scott built on the banks of the River Tweed within the beautiful landscape of the Scottish Borders. Stunning state of the art visitor centre with restaurant, gift shop & free to access Exhibition on the Life & Legacy of Sir Walter Scott. Luxury accommodation in the Hope Scott Wing, beautiful gardens, woodland play trail, riverside & estate walks.

Location: Map 14:I10. OS Ref NT508 342. 2 miles from Melrose & Galashiels. Edinburgh 35 miles, Glasgow & Newcastle approx 70 miles. Major routes: A1, A68 and A7. **Owner:** The Abbotsford Trust **Tel:** 01896 752043 **Fax:** 01896 752916 **E-mail:** enquiries@scottsabbotsford.co.uk

Open: Visitors Centre: 1 Apr-30 Sep, 10am-5pm. 1 Oct-31 Mar, 10am-4pm. House & Gardens: 1-31 Mar 10am-4pm, 1 Apr-30 Sep 10am-5pm, 1 Oct-30 Nov, 10am-4pm.

Admission: House & Gardens: £8.95, £7.70 Conc, £4.50 U17 (free for 5 yrs and under). Gardens only: £3.60, £2.60 Conc & U17, Group rates available.

Key facts: ⓘ 📷 📋 ♿ 🍴 Licensed. 🎫 House only for groups. ⚐ In house. 🅿 🚌 🐕 Except in walled gardens. 🛏 Hope Scott Wing, self-catering accommodation. 🎈 ❋ Visitor Centre & wider Estate only. ♥

FLOORS CASTLE 🏛Ⓕ
Kelso, The Scottish Borders TD5 7SF
www.floorscastle.com

Explore the spectacular State Rooms with outstanding collections of paintings, tapestries and furniture. Find hidden treasures like the collections of porcelain and oriental ceramics. Enjoy the picturesque grounds and gardens including the beautiful walled gardens. Stop at the Courtyard Café and enjoy a morning coffee or delicious lunch. For special events, please check our website.

Location: Map 14:J10. OS Ref NT711 347. From South A68, A698. From North A68, A697/9 In Kelso follow signs.

Owner: His Grace the Duke of Roxburghe **Contact:** Beverley Rutherford

Tel: 01573 223333 **Fax:** 01573 226056

E-mail: brutherford@floorscastle.com **Open:** 25 Mar-30 Oct 2016.

Admission: Adult £8.50, Child (5–16yrs) £4.50, OAP/Student £7.50, Family £22.50, Under 5yrs Free.

Key facts: ⓘ Dogs must be kept on leads and under control at all times. Photography is not permitted within the Castle. 📷 We have 3 delightful gift shops to browse and shop. ❋ Visit our Plant Centre within the Walled Garden. 🍴 Exclusive lunches and dinners. ♿ Partial. WCs. 🚌 Licensed. 🎫 🎟 By arrangement. ⚐ Audio App on a tablet can be hired for £2.99 or download to your own device. 🅿 Cars and coaches. 🛏 🐕 Dogs on leads only. 🎈 ♥

Manderston

MELLERSTAIN HOUSE & GARDENS 🏛Ⓕ
Mellerstain, Gordon, Berwickshire TD3 6LG
www.mellerstain.com

One of Scotland's finest stately homes, this outstanding Georgian mansion house is a unique example of Adam design, begun in 1725 by Scottish architect William Adam and completed in 1778 by his more famous son, Robert. Some say this is one of Robert Adam's finest works, complemented by the fine art, period furniture, china and embroidery collections within. Its idyllic location does not disappoint, with acres of stunning parkland, formal gardens, lakeside walks, playground and holiday cottages.

Location: Map 14:J10. OS Ref NT648 392. From Edinburgh A68 to Earlston, turn left 5m, signed.
Owner: The Mellerstain Trust
Contact: The Trust Administrator
Tel: 01573 410225 **Fax:** 01573 410636 **E-mail:** enquiries@mellerstain.com
Open: Easter weekend (4 days), May-Sep on Fri - Mon. House: 12.30-5pm. Last ticket 4.15pm. Coffee shop and gardens: 11.30am-5pm.
Admission: Please see our website or call us.
Key facts: ⓘ No photography/ filming in the house. 🗐 🗐 🗐 🗐 Ⓘ By arrangement. Ⓟ Free onsite parking. 🗐 🗐 Dogs on leads only. Guide dogs only in the house. 🗐 🗐

TRAQUAIR HOUSE 🏛Ⓕ ✦
Innerleithen, Peeblesshire EH44 6PW
www.traquair.co.uk

Dating back to 1107, Traquair was originally a hunting lodge for the kings and queens of Scotland. Later a refuge for Catholic priests in times of terror the Stuarts of Traquair supported Mary Queen of Scots and the Jacobite cause. Today, Traquair is a unique piece of living history.
Location: Map 13:H10. OS Ref NY330 354. On B709 near junction with A72. Edinburgh 1hr, Glasgow 1½ hrs, Carlisle 1½ hrs.
Owner/Contact: Catherine Maxwell Stuart, 21st Lady of Traquair
Tel: 01896 830323 **Fax:** 01896 830639 **E-mail:** enquiries@traquair.co.uk
Open: 25 Mar-31 Oct (11am-5pm & 11am-4pm in Oct).
Weekends only in Nov (11am-3pm).
Admission: House & Grounds: Adult £8.70; Child £4.40; Senior £7.70, Family £24.00 (2+3). Groups (20+): Adult £7.70; Child £3.70; Senior £6.70. Grounds only: Adults £4.00; Conc £3.00. Guide Book £4.50.
Key facts: 🗐 Brewery & Gift Shops. Craft shops on site. 🗐 🗐 Tours, Ale Tastings & Dinners available. 🗐 Ground floor accessible with video available to highlight rest of house. 🗐 Licensed. 🗐 Ⓟ Coaches; please book. 🗐 🗐 In grounds only, on leads. 🗐 Three double en suite bedrooms with antique furniture. 🗐 🗐

MERTOUN GARDENS 🏛Ⓕ
St. Boswells, Melrose, Roxburghshire TD6 0EA
26 acres of beautiful grounds. Walled garden and well preserved circular dovecot.
Location: Map 14:J10. OS Ref NT617 318. **Tel:** 01835 823236
Fax: 01835 822474 **E-mail:** mertoun@live.co.uk
Website: www.mertoungardens.co.uk **Open:** Apr-Sep, Fri-Mon 2-6pm. Last Admission 5.30pm. **Admission:** Adults £5.00, Children Free.

THIRLESTANE CASTLE 🏛
Lauder, Berwickshire TD2 6RU
www.thirlestanecastle.co.uk

Set in the Scottish Borders at Lauder, Thirlestane Castle has its origins in the 13th Century. It was rebuilt as the Maitland's family home in 1590 and greatly enhanced by The Duke of Lauderdale in the 1670s. In 1840 it was extended and refurbished with the edition of two new wings. Thirlestane has exquisite 17th Century plasterwork ceilings, a fine portrait collection and historic toy collection. Facilities include free parking, café, children's playground, and woodland picnic area.
Location: Map 14:I9. OS Ref NT540 473. Off A68 at Lauder, 28m S of Edinburgh.
Owner: Thirlestane Castle Trust
Tel: 01578 722430
E-mail: enquiries@thirlestanecastle.co.uk
Open: Please check website for 2016 opening program.
Admission: Castle and Grounds: Adults: £8.00, Children: £3.50, Senior Citizens: £6.50, Family: 2+3 £20. Grounds Only: Adults: £3.50, Children: £1.50
Key facts: ⓘ Woodland walk, children's adventure playground. 🗐 🗐 🗐 Suitable. 🗐 🗐 By arrangement. Ⓟ Cars and coaches. 🗐 🗐 🗐 Double, en suite. 🗐

Mellerstain

DUMFRIES HOUSE 🏛Ⓕ
www.dumfries-house.org.uk

A Georgian Gem, nesting within 2,000 acres of scenic Ayrshire countryside in south-west Scotland.

Commissioned by William Crichton Dalrymple, the 5th Earl of Dumfries, the House was designed by renowned 18th Century architect brothers John, Robert and James Adam and built between 1754 and 1759.

Recognised as one of the Adam brothers' masterpieces it remained unseen by the public since it was built 250 years ago until it opened its doors as a visitor attraction in June 2008. The former home of the Marquesses of Bute, it was saved for the nation at the eleventh hour by a consortium of organisations and individuals brought together by HRH The Prince Charles, Duke of Rothesay.

The house holds the most important collection of works from Thomas Chippendale's 'Director' period. It is widely recognised that Scotland was a testing ground for Thomas Chippendale's early rococo furniture and the Dumfries House collection is regarded as his key project in this area.

Dumfries House also holds the most comprehensive range of pieces by Edinburgh furniture makers Alexander Peter, William Mathie and Francis Brodie. Indeed, the Scottish furniture together with the Chippendale collection is of outstanding worldwide historical significance.

KEY FACTS

- ℹ️ Prebooking of Tours is recommended.
- 🏪 Visitor Centre and Gift Shop.
- 🦽 Stairlift. WCs. 1 wheelchair per tour.
- 🍴 Hot and cold food throughout the day.
- 🍽️ Thur-Sat evenings and Sunday Lunch.
- 🚶 Obligatory.
- 🅿️
- 🐕 On leads in grounds only. Guide dogs only in the house.
- 🛏️ Exclusive 5 star country Guest House accommodation.
- 💒 Licensed for weddings.
- ❄️ Grounds only.
- ⚙️ Check website for information - www.dumfries-house.org.uk.

AUCHINLECK
Ochiltree, Ayrshire KA18 2LR
www.landmarktrust.org.uk

Once diarist James Boswell's family seat, this grand 18th Century country house has its own grounds, river, ice-house and grotto. The large dining room and its elaborate plasterwork makes any meal special while the library lends itself to conversation and contemplation, just as it did for James Boswell and Dr Johnson.

Location: Map 13:C11. OS Ref NS510 226.

Owner: The Landmark Trust

Tel: 01628 825925

E-mail: bookings@landmarktrust.org.uk

Open: Self-catering accommodation. Parts of house open Easter-Oct, Wed afternoons. The Grounds are open dawn-dusk Spring and Summer.

Admission: Free on Open Days and visits by appointment.

Key facts: ℹ This building has grand, elegant rooms, a sweeping staircase, large dining and sitting rooms and plenty of open fires.

P 🖿 🖿 ❄ ♿

CASTLE KENNEDY GARDENS
Castle Kennedy, Stranraer
Dumfries and Galloway DG9 8SJ
www.castlekennedygardens.com

Famous 75-acre gardens situated between two large natural lochs. Ruined Castle Kennedy at one end overlooking beautiful herbaceous walled garden; Lochinch Castle at the other. Proximity to the gulf-stream provides an impressive collection of rare trees, including 20 Champion Trees, magnolias, and spectacular rhododendron displays. Guided walks, children's activities, regular ranger activities, open air theatre, bird hide, gift shop, plant centre and charming tearoom - a 'must-visit'. **Location:** Map 9:D3. OS Ref NX109 610. 3m E of Stranraer on A75.

Owner: The Earl and Countess of Stair **Contact:** Stair Estates

Tel: 01776 702024 / 01581 400225 **E-mail:** info@castlekennedygardens.com

Open: Gardens and Tearoom: 1 Apr-31 Oct: daily 10am-5pm.
Feb & Mar: Weekends only.

Admission: Adult £5.50, Child £2.00, Conc. £4.50, Family (2+2) £12.00. Groups of 20 or more 10% discount.

Key facts: ℹ 🖿 🖿 T ♿ WCs 🖿 🖿 P 🖿 On leads only. 🖿 🖿 ❄ ♿

Gardens at Dumfries House

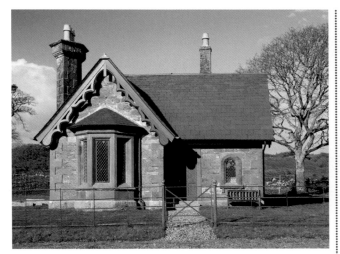

GLENMALLOCH LODGE
Newton Stewart, Dumfries And Galloway DG8 6AG
www.landmarktrust.org.uk

A fairytale cottage in a wild and beautiful glen, this diminutive former schoolroom makes a perfect hideaway or writing retreat for two, or even one.

Location: Map 9:F3.
Owner: The Landmark Trust
Tel: 01628 825925
E-mail: bookings@landmarktrust.org.uk
Open: Self-catering accommodation. Visits by appointment.
Admission: Free for visits by appointment.
Key facts: ℹ Although not far from Newton Stewart, the Lodge feels remote and looks out over the unspoilt and geologically interesting Galloway landscape.
🅿 🐕 🏠 ✳ ♿

KELBURN CASTLE & COUNTRY CENTRE 🏚Ⓕ
Fairlie, By Largs, Ayrshire KA29 0BE
www.kelburnestate.com

Kelburn is the home of the Earls of Glasgow and has been in the Boyle family for over 800 years. It is notable for its waterfalls, historic gardens, romantic glen and unique trees. The castle continues to be the venue of a major graffiti art installation, now considered to be in the top 10 graffiti installations in the world.

Location: Map 13:B9. OS Ref NS210 580. A78 to Largs, 2m S of Largs.
Owner: The Earl of Glasgow **Tel:** 01475 568685/568595
Fax: 01475 568121 **E-mail:** admin@kelburncountrycentre.com
Open: Country Centre: Easter-Oct: daily. Castle: Jul and Aug. Open by arrangement for groups at other times of the year.
Now available for Weddings and Special Events.
Admission: Country Centre: Adult £8.50, Child/Conc. £6.00, Under 3s Free, Family £28.00. Groups (10+): Adult, £4.50, Conc. £3.50. Castle: £2.00 extra pp.
Key facts: 🏚 🅃 🖾 Partial. 🖃 🍽 Licensed. 🎭 Jul and Aug. By arrangement at other times of the year. 🅿 🔳 🐕 In grounds, on leads. ✳

Kelburn Castle

CRAIGDARROCH HOUSE 🏚Ⓕ
Moniaive, Dumfriesshire DG3 4JB
Built by William Adam in 1729, over the old house dating from 14th Century (earliest records). The marriage home of Annie Laurie, the heroine of 'the world's greatest lovesong', who married Alexander Fergusson, 14th Laird of Craigdarroch, in 1710 and lived in the house for 33 years.
Location: Map 9:G1. OS Ref NX741 909.
S side of B729, 2m W of Moniaive, 19m WNW of Dumfries.
Owner/Contact: Mrs Carin Sykes
Tel: 01848 200202
Open: Jul: daily except Mons, 2-4pm.
Admission: £3.00.

CULZEAN CASTLE & COUNTRY PARK ⚘
Maybole, Ayrshire KA19 8LE
Robert Adam's 18th Century masterpiece - a real 'castle in the air' - is perched on a cliff high above the crashing waves of the Firth of Clyde.
Location: Map 13:B11. OS Ref NS232 103. On A719, 4m west of Maybole and 12m south of Ayr. KA19 8LE **Tel:** 0844 493 2149 **E-mail:** culzean@nts.org.uk
Website: www.nts.org.uk **Open:** Please see our website or call us for up-to-date opening times and admission prices.

RAMMERSCALES 🏚Ⓕ
Lockerbie, Dumfriesshire DG11 1LD
Fine Georgian house with views over Annan valley
Location: Map 10:I2. OS Ref NY080 780. Directions available on Rammerscales.co.uk **Tel:** 01387 810229 **E-mail:** malcolm@rammerscales.co.uk
Website: www.rammerscales.co.uk **Open:** May & Jun. Tues,Thurs,Sat 1pm-4pm. Bus parties by appointment. **Admission:** Adult £5.00.

VISITOR INFORMATION

■ **Owner**
The Earl of Rosebery

■ **Address**
Dalmeny House
South Queensferry
Edinburgh
EH30 9TQ

■ **Location**
Map 13:G8
OS Ref. NT167 779
From Edinburgh A90,
B924, 7m N, A90 ½m.
On south shore of Firth of
Forth.
Bus: From St Andrew
Square to Chapel Gate 1m
from House.
Taxi: Hawes Cars
0131 331 1077.
Rail: Dalmeny station 3m.

■ **Contact**
The Administrator
Tel: 0131 331 1888
Fax: 0131 331 1788
E-mail:
events@dalmeny.co.uk

■ **Opening Times**
June and July Sundays-
Wednesdays 2pm-5pm.
Entry is by guided tour only
and tours are 2.15pm and
3.30pm.

Open at other times by
appointment only for
groups (20+).

■ **Admission**
Summer
Adult	£10.00
Child (14-16yrs)	£6.50
OAP	£9.00
Student	£9.00
Groups (20+)	£9.00

DALMENY HOUSE
www.dalmeny.co.uk

Welcome to a family home which contains Scotland's finest French treasurers. Dine in splendor, and enjoy sea-views over superb parkland.

Dalmeny House rejoices in one of the most beautiful and unspoilt settings in Great Britain, yet it is only seven miles from Scotland's capital, Edinburgh, 15 minutes from Edinburgh airport and less than an hour's drive from Glasgow. It is an eminently suitable venue for group visits, business functions, and special events, including product launches. Outdoor activities, such as off-road driving, can be arranged.

Dalmeny House, the family home of the Earls of Rosebery for over 300 years, boasts superb collections of porcelain and tapestries, fine paintings by Gainsborough, Raeburn, Reynolds and Lawrence, together with the exquisite Mentmore Rothschild collection of 18th Century French furniture. There is also the Napoleonic collection, assembled by the 5th Earl of Rosebery, Prime Minister, historian and owner of three Derby winners.

The Hall, Library and Dining Room will lend a memorable sense of occasion to corporate receptions, luncheons and dinners. A wide range of entertainment can also be provided, from a clarsach player to a floodlit pipe band Beating the Retreat.

KEY FACTS

ⓘ Fashion shows, product launches, archery, clay pigeon shooting, shows, filming, background photography, and special events. Lectures on House, contents and family history. Helicopter landing area.

Ⓣ Conferences and functions, buffets, lunches, dinners.

Ⓚ WCs.

Ⓚ Obligatory. Special interest tours can be arranged outside normal opening hours.

Ⓟ 60 cars, 3 coaches. Parking for functions in front of house.

Ⓓ Dogs on leads in grounds only.

Register for news and special offers at **www.hudsonsheritage.com**

HOPETOUN HOUSE ⓐⓕ
SOUTH QUEENSFERRY, EDINBURGH, WEST LOTHIAN EH30 9SL
www.hopetoun.co.uk

As you approach Hopetoun House the impressive panoramic view of the main façade is breathtakingly revealed. Designed by William Bruce and then altered and extended by William Adam, Hopetoun House is one of the finest examples of 18th Century architecture in Britain. Hopetoun House is filled with stunning collections and has been home to the Hope Family since the late 1600s, with the present Lord Hopetoun and his family still living in the House. As a five star Visitor Attraction, Hopetoun offers something for everyone with daily tours, 100 acres of majestic grounds with nature trails and scenic walks. The Stables Tearoom is also a must see, with traditional afternoon teas served in stunning surroundings.
Location: Map 13:F7. OS Ref NT089 790. Exit A90 at A904, Follow Brown Signs.
Owner: Hopetoun House Preservation Trust **Contact:** Reception
Tel: 0131 331 2451 **E-mail:** enquiries@hopetoun.co.uk

Open: Daily From Easter - last weekend Sep; 10.30am-5pm. Last admission 4pm. Groups (20+) welcome out of season by appointment.
Admission: House and Grounds: Adult £9.20; Child (5-16yrs)* £4.90; Conc/Student £8.00; Family (2+2) £25.00. Grounds only: Adult £4.25; Child (5-16yrs)* £2.50; Conc/Student £3.70; Family (2+2) £11.50. *Under 5yrs Free. Winter group rates on request. Tearoom only admission is free.
Key facts: ⓘ Visit www.hopetoun.co.uk/events to see our calendar of events. ▣ ⓣ Private functions, wedding celebrations, banquets & gala evenings, meetings, conferences, exhibitions, incentive groups, outdoor activities, media & filming location. ⓛ Lift to 1st floor, Virtual access to upper floors. WCs. ⓦ Licensed. ⓕ Daily tour at 2pm. Groups by arrangement. ⓟ Cars & coaches welcome. ▣ ▣ Dogs permitted (on leads) in grounds. ▣ ▣ ▣ €

GOSFORD HOUSE ⓐⓕ
Longniddry, East Lothian EH32 0PX
www.gosfordhouse.co.uk

1791 the 7th Earl of Wemyss, aided by Robert Adam, built one of the grandest houses in Scotland, with a 'paradise' of lakes and pleasure grounds. New wings, including the celebrated Marble Hall were added in 1891 by William Young. The house has a fine collection of paintings and furniture.
Location: Map 14:17. OS Ref NT453 786. Off A198 2m NE of Longniddry.
Owner/Contact: The Earl of Wemyss
Tel: 01875 870201
Open: Please check our website for most up-to-date opening times/days.
Admission: Adult £6.00, Child under 16 Free.
Key facts: ⓣ
ⓕ By arrangement.
ⓟ Limited for coaches. ▣

Staircase at Hopetoun House

Edinburgh City, Coast & Countryside

AMISFIELD MAINS
Nr Haddington, East Lothian EH41 3SA
Georgian farmhouse with gothic barn and cottage. **Location:** Map 14:I8. OS Ref NT526 755. Between Haddington and East Linton on A199.
Tel: 01875 870201 **Fax:** 01875 870620
Open: Exterior only: By appointment, Wemyss and March Estates Office, Longniddry, East Lothian EH32 0PY. **Admission:** Please contact for details.

ARNISTON HOUSE 🏛ⓡ
Gorebridge, Midlothian EH23 4RY
Magnificent William Adam mansion started in 1726. Beautiful country setting beloved by Sir Walter Scott. **Location:** Map 13:H9. OS Ref NT326 595. 1 mile from A7 at Gorebridge **Tel:** 01875 830515 **E-mail:** info@arniston-house.co.uk
Website: www.arniston-house.co.uk **Open:** May & Jun: Tue & Wed; Jul-11 Sep: Tue, Wed & Sun, guided tours at 2pm & 3.30pm. Pre-arranged groups.
Admission: Adult £6.00, Child £3.00.

BEANSTON
Nr Haddington, East Lothian EH41 3SB
Georgian farmhouse with Georgian orangery.
Location: Map 14:I8. OS Ref NT450 766. Between Haddington and East Linton on A199. **Tel:** 01875 870201 **Open:** Exterior only: By appointment, Wemyss and March Estates Office, Longniddry, East Lothian EH32 0PY.
Admission: Please contact for details.

HARELAW FARMHOUSE
Nr Longniddry, East Lothian EH32 0PH
Early 19th Century 2-storey farmhouse built as an integral part of the steading. Dovecote over entrance arch. **Location:** Map 14:I8. OS Ref NT450 766. Between Longniddry and Drem on B1377. **Tel:** 01875 870201
Open: Exteriors only: By appointment, Wemyss and March Estates Office, Longniddry, East Lothian EH32 0PY. **Admission:** Please contact for details.

LINLITHGOW PALACE ♿
Linlithgow, West Lothian EH49 7AL
The royal pleasure palace was the birthplace of Mary Queen of Scots. Visit the great hall where Monarchs hosted banquets. **Location:** Map 13:F8. OS Ref NS 996774. **Tel:** 01506 842896 **E-mail:** hs.explorer@scotland.gsi.gov.uk
Website: www.historic-scotland.gov.uk
Open: Please see website for up-to-date opening and admission details.

NEWLISTON 🏛ⓡ
Kirkliston, West Lothian EH29 9EB
Late Robert Adam house. 18th Century designed landscape, rhododendrons, azaleas and water features.
Location: Map 13:G8. OS Ref NT110 735. 9miles W of Edinburgh, 4miles S of Forth Road Bridge, off B800. **Tel:** 0131 333 3231
Open: 1 May–4 Jun: Wed–Sun, 2–6pm. Also by appointment.
Admission: Adult: £4.00, Children under 12: Free of charge.

PALACE OF HOLYROODHOUSE
Edinburgh EH8 8DX
The Palace of Holyroodhouse, the official residence of Her Majesty The Queen, stands at the end of the Royal Mile against the spectacular backdrop of Arthur's Seat. **Location:** Map 13:G8. OS Ref NT110 735. Central Edinburgh.
Tel: +44 (0)131 556 5100 **E-mail:** bookinginfo@royalcollection.org.uk
Website: www.royalcollection.org.uk
Open: Please see website for opening times and admission rates.

RED ROW
Aberlady, East Lothian EH32 0DE
Terraced Cottages.
Location: Map 14:I7. OS Ref NT464 798. Main Street, Aberlady, East Lothian.
Tel: 01875 870201 **Fax:** 01875 870620
Open: Exterior only. By appointment, Wemyss and March Estates Office, Longniddry, East Lothian EH32 0PY. **Admission:** Please contact for details.

ROSSLYN CHAPEL
Chapel Loan, Roslin, Midlothian EH25 9PU
One of Scotland's most beautiful heritage attractions, Rosslyn Chapel is a medieval treasure in stone. Open daily to visitors, admission includes guided tours.
Location: Map 13:H8. OS Ref NT274 630. **Tel:** 0131 440 2159
E-mail: mail@rosslynchapel.com **Website:** www.rosslynchapel.com
Open: Every day of the year except 24, 25 and 31 Dec and 1 Jan. Please see website for times. **Admission:** Please see website for admission prices.

NEW LANARK WORLD HERITAGE SITE
New Lanark Mills, Lanark, South Lanarkshire ML11 9DB
www.newlanark.org
Close to the famous Falls of Clyde, this cotton mill village c1785 became famous as the site of Robert Owen's radical reforms. Beautifully restored as a living community and attraction, the fascinating history of the village has been interpreted in New Lanark Visitor Centre.
Location: Map 13:E9. Sat Nav code ML11 9BY. Nearest train station is Lanark. Glasgow > Lanark Bus from Buchanan Bus Station.
Owner: New Lanark Trust **Contact:** Trust Office
Tel: 01555 661345 **E-mail:** trust@newlanark.org
Open: Daily, 10-5pm Apr-Oct, 10-4pm Nov-Mar. Shops/catering open until 5pm daily. Closed 25 Dec and 1 Jan. **Admission:** Visitor Centre: Adult £8.50, Conc. (senior/student) £7.00, Child £6.00. Family (2+2) £25.00, Family (2+4) £35.00. Groups: 1 free/10 booked. **Key facts:** 🛍 Mill Shop. 🏨 New Lanark Mill Hotel. ♿ Suitable. WC 🍽 Mill Café. 🍴 Mill One Restaurant. 🎫 Book guided tours in advance. 🅿 Cars & coaches. 5 min walk. ☎ Contact for information. 🐕 Only service dogs inside buildings. 🏨 Hotel, Self-catering & Hostel. 🏛 ❄ ☀

COREHOUSE 🏛ⓡ
Lanark ML11 9TQ
Designed by Sir Edward Blore and built in the 1820s, Corehouse is a pioneering example of the Tudor Architectural Revival in Scotland.
Location: Map 13:E9. OS Ref NS882 416. On S bank of the Clyde above village of Kirkfieldbank. **Tel:** 01555 663126 **Open:** 2-29 May & 30 Jul-3 Aug: Sat–Wed. Tours: weekdays: 1 & 2pm, weekends: 2 & 3pm. Closed Thu & Fri.
Admission: Adult £7.00, Child (under 16yrs)/OAP £4.00.

Palace of Holyroodhouse

GLAMIS CASTLE & GARDENS 🏠ⓕ
GLAMIS, FORFAR, ANGUS DD8 1RJ
www.glamis-castle.co.uk

Ancestral home of the Earls of Strathmore and Kinghorne. Childhood home of the Queen Mother. A fairytale castle of both history and mystery, also renowned as the most haunted castle in Scotland. Ghost stories abound on the 10 room guided tour which takes approximately one hour. Hear about the card playing earls, the Grey Lady and the ghostly servant boy in the Royal Apartments as well as seeing a snapshot of one family's contribution to Scottish history. Extend your visit to include a walk round our Italian and walled gardens or have lunch in our Victorian Kitchen Restaurant. We have special admission rates for groups and can offer group lunches to be booked in advance.

Location: Map 13:H4. OS Ref NO386 480. 15 min from Dundee. 35 min from Perth, one hour from Aberdeen and 1 hr 30min from Edinburgh and Glasgow. Turn off the A90 at Forfar and take the A94 to Glamis approx 5 miles.

Owner: The Earl of Strathmore & Kinghorne

Contact: Thomas Baxter, General Manager
Tel: 01307 840393
Fax: 01307 840733
E-mail: enquiries@glamis-castle.co.uk
Open: Daily 27 Mar-31 Oct 12.00pm. Coaches and private parties by arrangement from 9am daily.
Admission: Please see website for admission rates.
Key facts: ℹ️ No photography in castle. 🖥️🍴🎪 Gala corporate dinners and weddings a speciality. ♿ Limited disabled access in castle, free mobile scooter can be reserved. 🍽️🍴🎬🅿️📷 Schools are very welcome and Guided Tours of the castle are tailored for all ages and interests. 🐕 On lead, in grounds only. 🔺 ❄️ By appointment out of season. ♿

DRUMMOND GARDENS 🏠ⓕ
Muthill, Crieff, Perthshire PH7 4HN
www.drummondcastlegardens.co.uk

Scotland's most important formal gardens. The Italianate parterre is revealed from a viewpoint at the top of the terrace. First laid out in the 17th Century and renewed in the 1950s. The perfect setting to stroll amongst the manicured plantings and absorb the atmosphere of this special place.

Location: Map 13:E5. OS Ref NN844 181. 2m S of Crieff off the A822.
Owner: Grimsthorpe & Drummond Castle Trust, a registered charity SC03964
Contact: The Caretaker
Tel: 01764 681433 **Fax:** 01764 681642
E-mail: thegardens@drummondcastle.sol.co.uk
Open: Easter weekend, 1 May-31 Oct: Daily, 1-6pm. Last admission 5pm.
Admission: Adult £5.00, Child £2.00 Conc. £4.00, Groups (20+) £4.00 Special rates available for out of hours visits and guided garden tours.
Key facts: 🖥️🍴♿ Partial. WCs. Viewing platform. Special vehicle access, ask on arrival. 🎬 By arrangement. 🅿️🐕 Dogs on leads. ♿

BALCARRES
Colinsburgh, Fife KY9 1HN

16th Century tower house with 19th Century additions by Burn and Bryce. Woodland and terraced gardens.
Location: Map 14:I6. OS Ref NO475 044. ½m N of Colinsburgh.
Owner: Balcarres Heritage Trust
Contact: Lord Balniel
Tel: 01333 340520
Open: Woodland & Gardens: 1 Mar-30 Sep, 2-5pm. House not open except by written appointment and 1-30 Apr, excluding Sun.
Admission: House £6.00, Garden £6.00. House & Garden £10.00.
Key facts: ♿ Partial. 🎬 By arrangement. 🐕 Dogs on leads only.

CORTACHY ESTATE
Cortachy, Kirriemuir, Angus DD8 4LX

Countryside walks including access through woodlands to Airlie Monument on Tulloch Hill with spectacular views of the Angus Glens and Vale of Strathmore. Footpaths are waymarked and colour coded. **Location:** Map 13:H3. OS Ref NO394 596. Off the B955 Glens Road from Kirriemuir. **Owner:** Trustees of Airlie Estates
Contact: Estate Office **Tel:** 01575 570108 **Fax:** 01575 540400
E-mail: office@airlieestates.com **Website:** www.airlieestates.com
Open: Walks all year. Gardens 25-28 Mar; 2 & 16 May – 5 Jun inclusive; 1 & 29 Aug. Last admission 3.30pm.
Admission: Please contact estate office for details.
Key facts: ℹ️ The estate network of walks are open all year round. The gardens and grounds can be hired for the location and setting of wedding ceremonies and photographs. 🎪♿ Unsuitable. 🎬 By arrangement. 🅿️ Limited. 🐕 Dogs on leads only. 🔺 Licensed to hold Civil Weddings and can offer wedding receptions, either a marquee in the grounds or a reception within the Castle. ♿

BLAIR CASTLE & GARDENS 🏛®
Blair Atholl, Pitlochry, Perthshire PH18 5TL
Blair Castle has a centuries old history as a strategic stonghold at the gateway to the Grampians and the route North to Inverness.
Location: Map 13:E3. OS Ref NN880 660.
Tel: 01796 481207 **E-mail:** bookings@blair-castle.co.uk
Website: www.blair-castle.co.uk
Open: Please see website for up-to-date opening and admission details.

CAMBO GARDENS
Cambo Estate, Kingsbarns, St. Andrews, Fife KY16 8QD
This iconic Victorian walled garden with a modern twist offers woodland walks by a sparkling burn leading to the sea. **Location:** Map 14:J6. OS Ref NO603 112.
Tel: 01333 450054 **E-mail:** cambo@camboestate.com
Website: www.camboestate.com **Open:** Daily from 10am-5pm.
Admission: Please see website.

CHARLETON HOUSE
Colinsburgh, Leven, Fife KY9 1HG
Location: Map 14:I6. OS Ref NO464 036. Off A917. 1m NW of Colinsburgh. 3m NW of Elie. **Tel:** 01333 340249
Open: 1 Sep-2 Oct: daily, 12 noon-3pm.
Guided tours obligatory, admission every ½hr. **Admission:** £12.00.

GLENEAGLES 🏛
Auchterarder, Perthshire PH3 1PJ
Gleneagles has been the home of the Haldane family since the 12th Century. The 18th Century pavilion is open to the public by written appointment.
Location: Map 13:F6. OS Ref NS931 088. 0.75 miles S of A9 on A823. 2.5m S of Auchterarder. **Tel:** 01764 682388 **Fax:** 01764 682535
E-mail: jmhaldane@gleneagles.org **Open:** By written appointment only.

Scone Palace

Hill of Tarvit Mansion House

HILL OF TARVIT MANSION HOUSE ♛
Cupar, Fife KY15 5PB
Hill of Tarvit is one of Scotland's finest Edwardian mansion houses, replete with a splendid collection of antiques, furniture, Chinese porcelain and superb paintings.
Location: Map 13:H5. OS Ref NO379 118. **Tel:** 0844 493 2185
E-mail: hilloftarvit@nts.org.uk **Website:** www.nts.org.uk
Open: Please see website for up-to-date opening and admission details.

HOUSE OF DUN ♛
Montrose, Angus DD10 9LQ
The house features fine furniture, a wonderful art collection and superb plasterwork, a particular and memorable feature.
Location: Map 14:J3. OS Ref NO670 599. **Tel:** 0844 493 2144
E-mail: houseofdun@nts.org.uk **Website:** www.nts.org.uk
Open: Please see website for up-to-date opening and admission details.

MONZIE CASTLE 🏛®
Crieff, Perthshire PH7 4HD
Built in 1791. Destroyed by fire in 1908 and rebuilt and furnished by Sir Robert Lorimer. **Location:** Map 13:E5. OS Ref NN873 244. 2miles NE of Crieff.
Tel: 01764 653110 **Open:** 14 May- 12 Jun: daily, 2-4.30pm. By appointment at other times. **Admission:** Adult £5.00, Child £1.00. Group rates available, contact property for details.

SCONE PALACE & GROUNDS 🏛®
Scone Palace, Perth PH2 6BD
1500 years ago it was the capital of the Picts. In the intervening centuries, it has been the seat of parliaments and the crowning place of the Kings of Scots.
Location: Map 13:G5. OS Ref NO114 266. **Tel:** 01738 552300
E-mail: visits@scone-palace.co.uk **Website:** www.scone-palace.co.uk
Open: Please see website for up-to-date opening and admission details.

STRATHTYRUM HOUSE & GARDENS 🏛
St Andrews, Fife KY16 9SF
Location: Map 14:I5. OS Ref NO490 172. Entrance from the St Andrews/ Guardbridge Road which is signposted when open. **Tel:** 01334 473600
E-mail: info@strathtyrumhouse.com **Open:** Mon-Thu weeks beginning 4, 11, 18, 25 April, 2, 9 & 16 May: Guided tours at 2pm and 3pm.
Admission: Adult £5.00, Child + Concessions £2.50.

TULLIBOLE CASTLE
Crook Of Devon, Kinross KY13 0QN
Scottish tower house c1608 with ornamental fishponds, a roofless lectarn doocot, 9th Century graveyard. **Location:** Map 13:F6. OS Ref NO540 888. B9097 1m E of Crook of Devon. **Tel:** 01577 840236 **E-mail:** visit@tulbol.demon.co.uk **Website:** www.tulbol.demon.co.uk **Open:** Last week in Aug-30 Sep: Tue-Sun, 1-4pm.
Admission: Adult £5.50, Child/Conc. £3.50. Free for Doors Open weekend.

INVERARAY CASTLE & GARDENS
www.inveraray-castle.com

Inveraray Castle & Gardens - Home to the Duke & Duchess of Argyll and ancestral home of the Clan Campbell.

The ancient Royal Burgh of Inveraray lies about 60 miles north west of Glasgow by Loch Fyne in an area of spectacular natural beauty. The ruggedness of the highland scenery combines with the sheltered tidal loch, beside which nestles the present Castle built between 1745 and 1790. The Castle is home to the Duke and Duchess of Argyll. The Duke is head of the Clan Campbell and his family have lived in Inveraray since the early 15th Century. Designed by Roger Morris and decorated by Robert Mylne, the fairytale exterior belies the grandeur of its gracious interior. The Clerk of Works, William Adam, father of Robert and John, did much of the laying out of the present Royal Burgh, which is an unrivalled example of an early planned town. Visitors enter the famous Armoury Hall containing some 1,300 pieces including

Brown Bess muskets, Lochaber axes, 18th Century Scottish broadswords, and can see preserved swords from the Battle of Culloden. The fine State Dining Room and Tapestry Drawing Room contain magnificent French tapestries made especially for the Castle, fabulous examples of Scottish, English and French furniture and a wealth of other works of art. The unique collection of china, silver and family artifacts spans the generations which are identified by a genealogical display in the Clan Room.

The castle's private garden which was opened to the public in 2010 for the first time is also not to be missed, especially in springtime with its stunning displays of rhododendrons and azaleas.

KEY FACTS

- No flash photography. Guide books in French and German translations.
- A wide range of Scottish gifts, books and Clan Campbell memorabilia.
- A varied selection of plants & shrubs available for purchase.
- Inveraray Castle provides the perfect location for corporate events of all sizes.
- Partial. Disabled Toilets inside the Castle.
- Licenced Tearoom serving lunches, tea/ coffee, soft drinks and homebaking.
- Available for up to 46 people per group. Tour time: approx 1 hr.
- 100 cars. Car/coach park close to Castle.
- £4.00 per child. Areas of interest include a woodland walk.
- Guide dogs only.

MOUNT STUART 🏠 ⓕ
ISLE OF BUTE PA20 9LR
www.mountstuart.com

One of the world's finest houses - Mount Stuart, ancestral home of the Marquess of Bute, is a stupendous example of Victorian Gothic architecture set amidst 300 acres of gloriously landscaped gardens. Spectacular interiors include the stunning white Marble Chapel and magnificent Marble Hall complete with kaleidoscopic stained glass. A Fine Art Collection and astounding architectural detail presents both stately opulence and unrivalled imagination. With something for all the family, this award-winning visitor attraction offers facilities including way-marked walks, Tearoom, Gift Shop, picnic areas, Adventure Play Area and Contemporary Visual Arts Exhibition.

Location: Map 13:A9. OS Ref NS100 600. SW coast of Scotland, 5 miles S of Rothesay.

Owner: Mount Stuart Trust
Contact: Mount Stuart Office
Tel: 01700 503877 **Fax:** 01700 505313
E-mail: contactus@mountstuart.com
Open: Seasonal opening. Easter and May-Sep. May be closed occasionally for private functions, please check website before travelling.
Admission: Please see our website for up-to-date information.
Key facts: ⓘ No photography. 🅿 🚻 ♿ Gardens - Partial disabled access. 🚌 ✗ 🅿 Ample. 🍽 ⓧ Grounds only. Assistance dogs only in House. 🏠 Exclusive - House/Self-Catering - Grounds. ⬛ ⬛

DUART CASTLE 🏠 ⓕ
Isle Of Mull, Argyll PA64 6AP
www.duartcastle.com

The 13th Century Castle of the Clan Maclean proudly guards the sea cliffs of the Isle of Mull. Explore the ancient island fortress with dungeons, keep, state rooms, Great Hall, museum & battlements. Discover the tearoom & gift shop, cottage garden, Millennium Wood & coastal walks around Duart Point. The set for 1999 film "Entrapment" with Sean Connery.

Location: Map 12:O4. OS Ref NM750 350. Off A849, 3.5 miles from Craignure Ferry Terminal. The Duart Coach operates between the Ferry and the Castle.
Owner/Contact: Sir Lachlan Maclean Bt
Tel: 01680 812309
E-mail: guide@duartcastle.com
Open: 3-30 April, Sun-Thurs 11am-4pm. 1 May-18 Oct. Open daily 10:30am-5pm.
Admission: Adult: £6.00, Child (4-15) £3.00, Conc £5.40, Family (2+2) £15.00.
Key facts: ⓘ Summer events calendar. 🅿 Duart gift shop. 🍽 Duart tearoom. ✗ Guided tours. 🅿 50m away. 🏫 Schools welcome. 🐕 Dogs welcome. 🏠 Duart cottage (self-catering). ⬛ Weddings. ⬛

ARDTORNISH ESTATE & GARDENS
Morvern, Nr Oban, Argyll & Bute PA80 5UZ
30 acres of garden including over 200 species of rhododendron, extensive planting for year round interest. **Location:** Map 12:O4. OS Ref NM702 472. In Ardtornish (Highland region, nr Loch Aline) - just off the A884 to Mull. **Tel:** 01967 421 288 **E-mail:** stay@ardtornish.co.uk **Website:** www.ardtornishgardens.co.uk
Open: Mar-Nov, Mon-Sun, 9am-6pm. **Admission:** £4.00 per person.

ARDUAINE GARDEN 🌱
Arduaine, Oban PA34 4XQ
This tranquil garden oasis can surprise and delight visitors all year. In spring and summer, the renowned rhododendrons attract enthusiasts from far and wide.
Location: Map 12:O6. OS Ref NM794103. Off A816, 20 miles south of Oban.
Tel: 0844 493 2216 **E-mail:** information@nts.org.uk **Website:** www.nts.org.uk
Open: Please visit our website or call us for opening times and admission prices.

CASTLE STALKER
Portnacroish, Appin, Argyll PA38 4BL
Early 15th Century tower house and seat of the Stewarts of Appin. Set on an islet 400 yds off the shore of Loch Linnhe. **Location:** Map 12:P3. OS Ref NM930 480.
Tel: 01631 730354 **E-mail:** rossallward@madasafish.com
Website: www.castlestalker.com **Open:** May 2-6, May 16-20, Jun 27-Jul 1, Jul 25-29, Aug 8-12. Phone for app. **Admission:** Adult £20.00, Child £10.00.

CRAIGSTON CASTLE 🏰
Turriff, Aberdeenshire AB53 5PX
www.craigston-castle.co.uk

Built between 1604 and 1607 by John Urquhart Tutor of Cromarty. Two wings were added in the early 1700s. The beautiful sculpted balcony, unique in Scottish architecture, depicts a piper, two grinning knights and David and Goliath. Remarkable carved oak, panels of Scottish kings' biblical heroes, originally from the family seat at Cromarty castle were mounted in doors and shutters in the early 17th Century. The house is a private home and is still owned and lived in by the Urquhart family.

Location: Map 17:D8. OS Ref NJ762 550. On B9105, 4.5m NE of Turriff.
Owner: William Pratesi Urquhart **Contact:** Claus Perch
Tel: 01888551707 **E-mail:** info@craigston.co.uk
Open: 16 - 24 Apr, 8 - 23 Oct. Plus throughout the year by appointment.
Admission: Adult £6.00, Child £2.00, Conc. £4.00. Groups: Adult £5.00, Child/School £1.00.
Key facts: ℹ️ 🍽 Bespoke events can be organised with partner organisations. ♿ Very limited wheelchair access. 📷 Obligatory. 🅿️ 🚌 🛏 ♿ 🏠 In process of being applied for Craigston, an ideal venue for your special day.

DELGATIE CASTLE
Turriff, Aberdeenshire AB53 5TD
www.delgatiecastle.com

'Best Visitor Experience' Award Winner. Dating from 1030 the Castle is steeped in Scottish history yet still has the atmosphere of a lived in home. It has some of the finest painted ceilings in Scotland, Mary Queen of Scots' bed-chamber. Clan Hay Centre. Scottish Home Baking Award Winner. Victorian Christmas Fayre held the last weekend in November and first weekend December. The castle is decorated throughout this period with decorations, Christmas trees and much more. Santa is here for the children with a pre-christmas present, crafters in many of the rooms throughout the Castle and staff in period costume.

Location: Map 17:D9. OS Ref NJ754 506. Off A947 Aberdeen to Banff Road.
Owner: Delgatie Castle Trust
Contact: Mrs Joan Johnson
Tel: 01888 563479 **E-mail:** joan@delgatiecastle.com
Open: Daily 15 Jan-20 Dec. 1 Apr-30 Sep, 10am-5pm. 1 Oct-31 Mar, 10am-4pm.
Admission: Adult £8.00, Child/Conc. £5.00, Family £21.00 (2 Adults & 2 Children), Groups (10+): £5.00. B&B in Symbister Suite £60.00 pppn.
Key facts: ℹ️ No photography. 📷 🍽 ♿ WCs. 🏠 🍴 📷 By arrangement. 🅿️ 🚌 Guide dogs only. 🛏 2 self-catering apartments in Castle. 🎯 🏠

Crathes Castle, Garden & Estate

CRIMONMOGATE
Lonmay, Fraserburgh, Aberdeenshire AB43 8SE

Situated in Aberdeenshire, Crimonmogate is a Grade A listed mansion house and one of the most easterly stately homes in Scotland, it is now owned by William and Candida, Viscount and Viscountess Petersham. Pronounced 'Crimmon-moggat', this exclusive country house stands within beautiful and seasonally-changing parkland and offers one of Aberdeenshire's most outstanding and unusual venues for corporate events, parties, dinners and weddings.

Location: Map 17:F8. OS Ref NK043 588.
Owner/Contact: Viscount Petersham **Tel:** 01346 532401
E-mail: naomi@cmg-events.co.uk
Open: 1-8 May, 18-30 June, Aug 27-1 Sep. Tours at 10.30am, 11.30am, and 12.30pm, or by appointment.
Admission: Adult £7.00, Conc. £6.00, Child £5.00. Max of 12 at any one time, guided tours only.
Key facts: 🍽 Weddings & special events: max 60 in hall & up to 200 in Marquee. 📷 Only the principal rooms are part of the tour. 🅿️ 🚫 No dogs. 🏠 🛏

BALFLUIG CASTLE
Alford, Aberdeenshire AB33 8EJ

Small 16th Century tower house, restored in 1967. Its garden and wooded park are surrounded by farmland.

Location: Map 17:D11. OS Ref NJ586 151. Alford, Aberdeenshire.
Tel: 020 7624 3200
Open: Please write to M I Tennant Esq, 30 Abbey Gardens, London NW8 9AT.

CRATHES CASTLE, GARDEN & ESTATE ♛
Banchory, Aberdeenshire AB31 3QJ

Fairytale-like turrets, gargoyles of fantastic design and the ancient Horn of Leys given in 1323 by Robert the Bruce are just a few features of this historic castle.

Location: Map 17:D12. OS Ref NO735 967. On A93, 3m E of Banchory.
Tel: 0844 493 2166 **E-mail:** crathes@nts.org.uk **Website:** www.nts.org.uk
Open: Please see website for opening times.
Admission: Please see our website or call us for up-to-date prices.

DRUMMUIR CASTLE
Drummuir, By Keith, Banffshire AB55 5JE

Castellated Victorian Gothic-style castle built in 1847 by Admiral Duff. 60ft high lantern tower with fine plasterwork, family portraits and interesting artefacts.

Location: Map 17:B9. OS Ref NJ372 442. Between Keith and Dufftown, off the B9014. **Tel:** 01542 810332 **Open:** Sat 27 Aug-Sun 25 Sep: daily, 2-5pm (last tour 4.15pm). **Admission:** Adult £4.00, Child £2.50. Groups by arrangement.

LICKLEYHEAD CASTLE
Auchleven, Insch, Aberdeenshire AB52 6PN

Beautifully restored Laird's Castle, built by the Leslies c1450, renovated in 1629 by John Forbes of Leslie. Boasts many interesting architectural features.

Location: Map 17:C10. OS Ref NJ628 237. 2m S of Insch on B992.
Tel: 01464 820200. **Open:** 10am-12noon. May 2-22 inclusive and June 11,12, 18,19 and 25. **Admission:** Free.

Dunvegan Castle

VISITOR INFORMATION

■ **Owner**
Hugh Macleod of Macleod

■ **Address**
Dunvegan Castle
Dunvegan
Isle of Skye
Scotland
IV55 8WF

■ **Location**
Map 15:F9
OS Ref. NG250 480
1m N of village. NW corner
of Skye. Kyle of Lochalsh to
Dunvegan via Skye Bridge.
Rail: Inverness to Kyle of
Lochalsh
Ferry: Maillaig to
Armadale

■ **Contact**
Lynne Leslie, Office
Manager
Tel: 01470 521206
Fax: 01470 521205
E-mail:
info@dunvegancastle.com

■ **Opening Times**
1 April - 15 October
Daily 10am-5.30pm
Last admission 5pm
16 October - 31 March
Open by appointment for
groups only on weekdays.
Castle and Gardens closed
Christmas and New Year.

■ **Admission**
Castle & Gardens
Adult	£12.00
Child (5-15yrs)	£9.00
Senior/Student/Group (Group min. 10 adults)	£10.00
Family Ticket (2 Adults, 4 Children)	£31.00

Gardens only
Adult	£10.00
Child (5-15yrs)	£7.00
Senior/Student/ Group	£8.00

Seal Boat Trips (Prices valid with a Castle or Garden Ticket)
Adult	£7.50
Child (5-15yrs)	£5.50
Senior/Student/ Group	£6.50
Infant (under 3yrs)	Free

Wildlife Loch Cruises (1 hour)
Adult from	£18.00
Child (5-15yrs) from	£13.00

Fishing Trips (2 hours)
Adult	£45.00
Child	£35.00

■ **Special Events**
A unique location for film,
TV or advertising. Check
website for details.

DUNVEGAN CASTLE & GARDENS 🏰Ⓕ
www.dunvegancastle.com

Experience living history at Dunvegan Castle, the ancestral home of the Chiefs of Clan MacLeod for 800 years.

Any visit to the Isle of Skye is incomplete without savouring the wealth of history on offer at Dunvegan Castle & Gardens, the ancestral home of the Chiefs of Clan MacLeod for 800 years. Originally designed to keep people out, it was first opened to visitors in 1933 and is one of Skye's most famous landmarks. On display are many fine oil paintings and Clan treasures, the most famous of which is the Fairy Flag. Legend has it that this sacred Banner has miraculous powers and when unfurled in battle, the Clan MacLeod will defeat their enemies. Another of the castle's great treasures is the Dunvegan Cup, a unique 'mazer' dating back to the Middle Ages. It was gifted by the O'Neils of Ulster as a token of thanks to one of the Clan's most celebrated Chiefs, Sir Rory Mor, for his support of their cause against the marauding forces of Queen Elizabeth I of England in 1596.

Today visitors can enjoy tours of an extraordinary castle and Highland estate steeped in history and clan legend, delight in the beauty of its formal gardens, take a boat trip onto Loch Dunvegan to see the seal colony, enjoy an appetising meal at the MacLeods Table Café or browse in one of its four shops offering a wide choice to suit everyone. Over time, we have given a warm Highland welcome to visitors including Sir Walter Scott, Dr Johnson and Queen Elizabeth II and we look forward to welcoming you.

KEY FACTS

ℹ️ Boat trips to seal colony. Fishing trips & loch cruises. Boat trips dependent upon weather. No photography in castle.

🛍️ Our gift shops sell a wide range of quality items, Harris Tweed products, knitwear, jewellery & small gifts.

♿ Partial. WCs. Laptop tour of Castle available.

☕ MacLeod Table Café (seats 76).

🚶 By appointment. Self Guided.

🅿️ 120 cars & 10 coaches. Coaches please book if possible.

🏫 Welcome by arrangement. Guide available on request.

🐕 Dogs on leads in Gardens only.

🏠 Self-catering holiday cottages.

Dunvegan Castle Gardens

Boat Trips to Seal Colony

© Derek Hoare

CAWDOR CASTLE AND GARDENS ⓘⒻ
CAWDOR CASTLE, NAIRN, SCOTLAND IV12 5RD
www.cawdorcastle.com

This splendid romantic castle, dating from the late 14th Century, was built as a private fortress by the Thanes of Cawdor, and remains the home of the Cawdor family to this day. The ancient medieval tower was built around the legendary holly tree. Although the house has evolved over 600 years, later additions, mainly of the 17th Century, were all built in the Scottish vernacular style. It has three gardens to enjoy: the earliest dating from the 16th Century with the symbolic gardens and maze: an 18th Century flower garden, and a 19th Century wild garden with rhododendrons and spring bulbs as well as splendid trees. Two further gardens, the Tibetan Garden and the Traditional Scottish Vegetable Garden, are at the Dower House at Auchindoune.

Location: Map 16:O9. OS Ref NH850 500. From Edinburgh A9, 3.5 hrs, Inverness 20 mins, Nairn 10 mins. Main road - A9, 14m.

Owner: The Dowager Countess Cawdor **Contact:** Ian Whitaker
Tel: 01667 404401 **Fax:** 01667 404674 **E-mail:** info@cawdorcastle.com
Open: 1 May-2 Oct 2016 Daily 10am-5.30pm. Last adm 4.45pm. Groups by appointment. Limited private tours can be arranged out of season.
Admission: Adult £10.70, Child (5-15 yrs) £6.70, Conc. £9.70, Family (2 + up to 5) £31.00. Gardens, Grounds and Nature Trails £6.00. Adult Groups (12+) £9.20, Child Groups (12+ children, 1 adult free per 12) £6.00. Auchindoune Gardens (May-Jul only) £3.70.
Key facts: ⓘ 9 hole golf course, whisky tasting. No flash photography in the castle. ⓐ Gift, Highland & Wool shops. ⓣ ⓰ WC. Parts of ground floor & gardens accessible. ⓑ Courtyard Café, May-Oct & Coffee House May-Oct. ⓕ By arrangement. ⓟ 250 cars & 25 coaches. ⓘ £6.00 per child.

Gardens at Cawdor Castle

ARMADALE CASTLE & GARDENS
Armadale, Sleat, Isle of Skye IV45 8RS
www.clandonald.com

The romantic ruin of Armadale Castle is a stunning backdrop to the most amazing views across the Sound of Sleat. With beautiful historic gardens and walks through 40 acres of ancient woodland, this iconic building sits at the heart of the 22,000 acres estate. Home to Museum of the Isles with 7 galleries & audio guides. Wildlife trips across the estate in all terrain vehicle with picnic and Guide. Castle Ruin will undergo Conservation in Action in 2016.
Location: Map 15:H11. OS Ref NG633036. From Skye Bridge, 16 miles south of Broadford on the A851; or, take ferry from Mallaig to Amadale and follow signs.
Owner: Clan Donald Lands Trust **Contact:** Jan Wallwork Clarke
Tel: 01471 844305 **Fax:** 01471 844275 **E-mail:** office@clandonald.com
Open: Apr-Oct, 9:30am-5:30pm. Nov-Mar, gardens open dawn to dusk. Check website for updates.
Admission: Adults £8.50, Children & Conc. £6.50, Family (2 adults & 3 children) £25.00. Groups (10 or more) £6.50 per person. Children under 5 free.
Key facts: ▣ ▣ ▣ Mobility scooters available. Pre-booking advisable. ▣ ▣ ▣ ▣ Various languages & visually impaired. ▣ ▣ ▣ ▣ ▣ ▣

CASTLE & GARDENS OF MEY ▣
Thurso, Caithness, Scotland KW14 8XH
www.castleofmey.org.uk

The home of The Queen Mother in Caithness. She bought the Castle in 1952, developed the gardens and it became her holiday home because of the beautiful surroundings and the privacy she was always afforded. There is a Visitor Centre with shop and tearoom and an Animal Centre for children. There is also a wonderful walled garden.
Location: Map 17:B2. OS Ref ND290 739. On A836 between Thurso and John O'Groats, just outside the village of Mey.
Owner: The Queen Elizabeth Castle of Mey Trust **Contact:** Shirley Farquhar
Tel: 01847 851473 **Fax:** 01847 851475 **E-mail:** enquiries@castleofmey.org.uk
Open: 18 May-30 Sep 2016. Closed 25 Jul-8 Aug inclusive. Check website or please telephone for details.
Admission: Adult £11.00, Child (5-16yrs) £6.50, Concession £9.75. Family £29.00. Booked groups (15+): £9.75. Gardens and Grounds only: Adult £6.50. Garden and Grounds family ticket £19.00.
Key facts: ▣ No photography in the Castle. ▣ ▣ ▣ ▣ Limited disabled access, please phone ahead for advice. ▣ Licensed. ▣ ▣ ▣ ▣ Guide dogs only. ▣ ▣

BALLINDALLOCH CASTLE ▣▣▣
Ballindalloch, Banffshire AB37 9AX
Ballindalloch Castle has been occupied by its original family, the Macpherson-Grants, since 1546. You'll enjoy this beautiful home, its decor, paintings, china, furniture and family photographs. Beautiful rock and rose gardens, children's play area, a grass labyrinth and river walks. The estate is home to the famous Aberdeen-Angus cattle breed. A superb family day out. **Location:** Map 17:A9. OS Ref NJ178 366. 14m NE of Grantown-on-Spey on A95. 22m S of Elgin on A95.
Owner: Mr & Mrs Guy Macpherson-Grant **Contact:** Fenella Corr
Tel: 01807 500205 **E-mail:** enquiries@ballindallochcastle.co.uk
Website: www.ballindallochcastle.co.uk
Open: Good Fri-30 Sep: 10.00am-5.00pm (last entry 4.00pm). Closed on Sats (with the exception of Easter Sat).
Admission: Castle & Grounds: Adults £11.00, Senior Citizens £9.00, Children (6-16) £5.00, Family (2+3) £27.00, Individual Season Ticket £35.00.
Key facts: ▣ ▣ Please enquire. ▣ Partial. ▣ ▣ Short film. ▣ Cars & coaches. ▣ Designated areas only.

DUNROBIN CASTLE & GARDENS ▣▣
Golspie, Sutherland KW10 6SF

Dating from the 13th Century with later additions. Wonderful furniture, paintings & Victorian museum set in woodlands overlooking the sea. Magnificent formal gardens, featuring French/Scottish formal parterres. And Falconry displays.
Location: Map 16:O6. OS Ref NC850 010. 50m N of Inverness on A9.
Owner: The Sutherland Dunrobin Trust **Contact:** Scott Morrison
Tel: 01408 633177 **Fax:** 01408 634081 **E-mail:** info@dunrobincastle.co.uk
Website: www.dunrobincastle.co.uk
Open: 1 Apr-15 Oct: Apr, May, Sep and Oct, Mon-Sat, 10.30am-4.30pm, Sun, 12noon-4.30pm. Jun, Jul and Aug, daily, 10.00am-5.00pm. Falconry displays at 11.30am and 2pm.
Admission: Adult £11.00, Child £6.50, OAP/Student. £9.00, Family (2+3) £32.00. Groups (minimum 10): Rates on request. Rates include falconry display, museum and gardens.
Key facts: ▣ ▣ Unsuitable for wheelchairs. ▣ ▣ ▣ By arrangement. ▣ ▣

EILEAN DONAN CASTLE ▣
Dornie, Kyle Of Lochalsh, Wester Ross IV40 8DX

A fortified site for eight hundred years, Eilean Donan now represents one of Scotland's most iconic images. Located at the point where three great sea lochs meet amidst stunning highland scenery on the main road to Skye. Spiritual home of Clan Macrae with century old links to Clan Mackenzie.
Location: Map 16:J10. OS Ref NG880 260. On A87 8m E of Skye Bridge.
Contact: David Win - Castle Keeper
Tel: 01599 555202
E-mail: eileandonan@btconnect.com
Website: www.eileandonancastle.com
Open: Please see our website for 2016 opening dates and times.
Admission: Please see our website for up-to-date admission prices.
Key facts: ▣ ▣ ▣ ▣ For groups 20+. ▣ Free. ▣ ▣ Holiday cottage. ▣

THE DOUNE OF ROTHIEMURCHUS
By Aviemore PH22 1QP
The family home of the Grants of Rothiemurchus since 1560.
Location: Map 16:P11. OS Ref NH900 100. 2m S of Aviemore. On B970 to Feshiebridge. **Tel:** 01479 812345 **E-mail:** info@rothie.net
Website: www.rothiemurchus.net **Open:** Please see website for open dates.
Admission: Please see website for admission rates.

Pitmedden Garden

BRECHIN CASTLE 🏠ⓔ
Brechin, Angus DD9 6SG
Tel: 01356 624566 **E-mail:** enquiries@dalhousieestates.co.uk

BEMERSYDE GARDENS 🏠ⓔ
Melrose, Roxburghshire, Scotland TD6 9DP
Tel: 01968 678465

BOWHILL HOUSE & COUNTRY ESTATE 🏠ⓔ
Bowhill, Selkirk TD7 5ET
Tel: 01750 22204

BUGHTRIG GARDEN 🏠ⓔ
Bughtrig, Coldstream TD12 4JP

DUNS CASTLE
Duns, Berwickshire TD11 3NW
Tel: 01361 883211

FERNIEHIRST CASTLE
Jedburgh, Roxburghshire, Scottish Borders TD8 6NX
Tel: 01450 870051 **E-mail:** curator@clankerr.co.uk

HERMITAGE CASTLE 🏛
Scottish Borders TD9 0LU
Tel: 01387 376 222

HIRSEL ESTATE 🏠ⓔ
Coldstream TD12 4LP
Tel: 01555 851536 **E-mail:** joy.hitchcock@daestates.co.uk

NEIDPATH CASTLE
Peebles, Scotland EH45 8NW
Tel: 01721 720 333

PAXTON HOUSE, GALLERY & COUNTRY PARK 🏠ⓔ
Berwick-Upon-Tweed TD15 1SZ
Tel: 01289 386291 **E-mail:** info@paxtonhouse.com

SMAILHOLM TOWER 🏛
Smailholm, Kelso TD5 7PG
Tel: 01573 460365

DIRLETON CASTLE 🏛
North Berwick EH39 5ER
Tel: 01620 850 330

EDINBURGH CASTLE 🏛
Castle Hill, Edinburgh EH1 2NG
Tel: 0131 225 9846 **E-mail:** hs.explorer@scotland.gsi.gov.uk

LENNOXLOVE HOUSE 🏠ⓔ
Haddington, East Lothian EH41 4NZ
Tel: 01620 828614 **E-mail:** ken-buchanan@lennoxlove.com

BLACKNESS CASTLE 🏛
Blackness Castle, Blackness, Linlithgow EH49 7NH
Tel: 01506 834807

CASTLE FRASER & GARDEN 🏛
Sauchen, Inverurie AB51 7LD
Tel: 0131 243 9300

CRAIG CASTLE
Rhynie, Huntly, Aberdeenshire AB54 4LP
Tel: 01464 861705

DRUM CASTLE & GARDEN ♛
Drumoak, By Banchory, Aberdeenshire AB31 3EY
Tel: 0844 493 2161 **E-mail:** information@nts.org.uk

DUFF HOUSE 🏛
Banff AB45 3SX
Tel: 01261 818181 **E-mail:** hs.explorer@scotland.gsi.gov.uk

DUNOTTAR CASTLE 🏠ⓔ
Stonehaven, Aberdeenshire AB39 2TL
Tel: 01569 762173 **E-mail:** dunottarcastle@btconnect.com

FORT GEORGE 🏛
Grampian Highlands IV2 7TD
Tel: 01667 460232

FYVIE CASTLE & GARDEN ♛
Turriff, Aberdeenshire AB53 8JS
Tel: 0844 493 2182 **E-mail:** information@nts.org.uk

GORDON CASTLE 🏠ⓔ
Estate Office, Fochabers, Morayshire IV32 7PQ
Tel: 01343 820244

HADDO HOUSE ♛
Tarves, Ellon, Aberdeenshire AB41 0ER
Tel: 0844 493 2179 **E-mail:** information@nts.org.uk

HUNTLY CASTLE 🏛
Huntly, North and Grampian, Scotland AB54 4SH
Tel: 01466 793191

KILDRUMMY CASTLE 🏛
Alford, Aberdeenshire AB33 8RA
Tel: 01975 571 331

PITMEDDEN GARDEN ♛
Pitmedden Garden, Ellon, Aberdeenshire AB41 7PD
Tel: 01651 842352 **E-mail:** information@nts.org.uk

SPYNIE PALACE 🏛
Spynie Palace, Elgin IV30 5QG
Tel: 01343 546358

POLLOK HOUSE ♛
2060 Pollokshaws Road, Glasgow G43 1AT
Tel: 0844 4932202 **E-mail:** information@nts.org.uk

THE HILL HOUSE ♚
Upper Colquhoun Street, Helensburgh G84 9AJ
Tel: 0844 493 2208 **E-mail:** thehillhouse@nts.org.uk

SKAILL HOUSE
Breckness Estate, Sandwick, Orkney, Scotland KW16 3LR
Tel: 01856 841 501

URQUHART CASTLE ♨
Drumnadrochit, Loch Ness, Inverness-shire IV63 6XJ
Tel: 01456 450551 **E-mail:** hs.explorer@scotland.gsi.gov.uk

ARDWELL GARDENS ⛓ℹ
Ardwell House, Ardwell, Stranraer, Wigtownshire DG9 9LY
Tel: 01776 860227 **E-mail:** info@ardwellestate.co.uk

BLAIRQUHAN CASTLE
Maybole, Ayrshire, Scotland KA19 7LZ
Tel: 01655 770239

BRODICK CASTLE ♨
Isle Of Arran KA27 8HY
Tel: 0131 243 9300

CAERLAVEROCK CASTLE ♨
Glencaple, Dumfries DG1 4RU
Tel: 01387 770244

DRUMLANRIG CASTLE ⛓ℹ
Thornhill, Dumfriesshire, Scotland DG3 4AQ
Tel: 01848 331555

SORN CASTLE ⛓ℹ
Sorn, Mauchline, Ayrshire KA5 6HR
Tel: 01290 551476 **E-mail:** info@sorncastle.com

THREAVE CASTLE ♨
Dumfries and Galloway DG7 1TJ
Tel: 07711 223 101

Sorn Castle

ABERDOUR CASTLE ♨
Aberdour Castle, Aberdour KY3 0SL
Tel: 01383 860519

ARBROATH ABBEY ♨
Arbroath, Tayside DD11 1EG
Tel: 01241 878756

ARBUTHNOTT HOUSE & GARDEN
Arbuthnott, Laurencekirk AB30 1PA
Tel: 01561 361226

CLUNY HOUSE
Aberfeldy PH15 2JT
E-mail: wmattingley@btinternet.com

DUNNINALD, CASTLE AND GARDENS ⛓ℹ
Montrose, Angus DD10 9TD
Tel: 01674 672031 **E-mail:** visitorinformation@dunninald.com

EDZELL CASTLE ♨
Perthshire DD9 7UE
Tel: 01356 648 631

HOUSE OF PITMUIES GARDENS ⛓ℹ
Guthrie, By Forfar, Angus DD8 2SN
Tel: 01241 828245

HUNTINGTOWER CASTLE ♨
Perth PH1 3JL
Tel: 01738 627 231

KELLIE CASTLE & GARDEN ♚
Pittenweem, Fife KY10 2RF
Tel: 0844 493 2184 **E-mail:** information@nts.org.uk

ST ANDREW'S CASTLE ♨
St Andrews, Fife KY16 9AR
Tel: 01334 477196

ARDCHATTAN PRIORY GARDENS ⛓ℹ
Connel, Argyll, Scotland PA37 1RQ
Tel: 01796 481355

ARDENCRAIG GARDENS
Ardencraig, Rothesay, Isle Of Bute,
West Highlands PA20 9ZE

ATTADALE GARDENS
Attadale Gardens, Strathcarron, Wester Ross IV54 8YX
Tel: 01520 722217 **E-mail:** info@attadale.com

DOUNE CASTLE ♨
Doune Castle, Doune FK16 6EA
Tel: 01786 841742

KISIMUL CASTLE ♨
Castlebay, Isle of Barra HS9 5UZ

STIRLING CASTLE ♨
Stirling FK8 1EJ
Tel: 01786 450 000 **E-mail:** hs.explorer@scotland.gsi.gov.uk

Abbotsford, Roxburghshire

Fonmon Castle, Glamorgan
©VISITBRITAIN / JOANNA HENDERSON

©VISITBRITAIN/ LEE BEEL

Gwydir Castle, Llanwrst

South Wales
Mid Wales
North Wales

Wales

North Wales

Mid Wales

South Wales

A tiny country that packs in so much variety. You know about its famous castles, but make sure you explore its smaller manor houses and its wealth of heritage gardens.

New Entries for 2016:
• Cornwall House
• Treowen

FONMON CASTLE 🏰Ⓕ
FONMON, BARRY, VALE OF GLAMORGAN CF62 3ZN
www.fonmoncastle.com

Just 25 minutes from Cardiff and the M4, Fonmon is one of few medieval castles still lived in as a home, since being built c1200, it has only changed hands once. Visitors are welcomed by an experienced guide and the 45 minute tour walks through the fascinating history of the Castle, its families, architecture and interiors. The Fonmon gardens are an attraction in their own right for enthusiasts and amateurs alike and visitors are free to wander and explore. Available as an exclusive wedding and party venue, corporate and team building location, visitor attraction and host for product launches and filming.
Location: Map 2:L2. OS Ref ST047 681. 15miles W of Cardiff, 1miles W of Cardiff airport. **Owner:** Sir Brooke Boothby Bt **Contact:** Casey Govier

Tel: 01446 710206 **E-mail:** Fonmon_Castle@msn.com
Open: Public opening: 1 Apr- 30 Sep on Tue & Wed afternoons for individuals, families & small groups. Midday-5pm, no need to book. Tours at 2pm, 3pm & 4pm & last 45 mins, last entrance to gardens at 4pm. Groups 20+ welcome by appointment throughout the year. Varied hospitality options with very popular Afternoon Teas. **Admission:** Entry and tour of the Castle priced at £6.00, Children free. Access to garden and grounds is free.
Key facts: ⓘ Conferences. 🅣 By arrangement. ♿ Suitable. WCs. 🅕 Guided Tour obligatory. 🅟 Ample free parking for cars and coaches. 🖼 🐕 Guide dogs only. 🏛 Licensed for Civil Ceremonies for up to 110 people.

LLANCAIACH FAWR MANOR
GELLIGAER ROAD, NELSON, TREHARRIS, CAERPHILLY COUNTY BOROUGH CF46 6ER
www.llancaiachfawr.co.uk

This superbly restored gentry manor house is no ordinary heritage attraction. History here is tangible. The costumed servants of the house are living and working in 1645 and allow you to share and engage in their world. Fires crackle, candles flicker and the sounds and smells of domestic life make your visit a memorable experience of the past. It takes a moment to attune your ear to the unfamiliar speech within the Manor itself, but within seconds of your warm welcome you become immersed in the time of the Civil Wars and the cares and concerns of ordinary people living in extraordinary times. Visitor Centre provides modern amenities and also caters for conferences, weddings and family functions.
Location: Map 2:M1. OS Ref ST114 967. S side of B4254, 1m N of A472 at Nelson. **Owner:** Caerphilly County Borough Council
Contact: Reception **Tel:** 01443 412248
E-mail: llancaiachfawr@caerphilly.gov.uk

Open: 10am-5pm Tue to Sun and BH Mons all year round. Last entry to the Manor 4pm Closed 24 Dec-1 Jan inclusive.
Admission: Adults £7.95, Concessions £6.50, Child £6.50, Family £22.00 (2 adults + 3 children). Group discounts available (20+).
Key facts: ⓘ No photography indoors. 🛍 Boutique gift shop. 🍴 🅣 ♿ Accessible WCs. Lift for access to upper floors. 🍽 Licensed. 10am-4pm. Hot & cold drinks, sandwiches cakes & snacks, hot food between 12pm & 2pm. 🍴 Licensed. Sunday lunches & private functions. 🅕 Costumed 17th Century servants lead tours. Approx 1.5 hours 🅟 90 free spaces. Disabled spaces close to visitor cente entrance. 🖼 Tours, activities, trails & workshops at primary, secondary & tertiary levels focussing on active & sensory learning. 🐕 In grounds only. Not in walled gardens. 🏛 The Parlour, Great Hall, Mansell Hall & Conservatory Restaurant are licensed for civil ceremonies. 🎗

ABERGLASNEY GARDENS
Llangathen, Carmarthenshire SA32 8QH
www.aberglasney.org

Aberglasney is one of Wales' finest gardens - a renowned plantsman's paradise of more than 10 acres with a unique Elizabethan cloister garden at its heart. The gardens and the fully restored ground floor of Aberglasney's grade II* listed mansion are open 364 days a year. Exhibitions and events held throughout the year. **Location:** Map 5:F10. OS Ref SN579 221. Aberglasney is 12 miles east of Carmarthen and 4 miles west of Llandeilo on the A40 at Broad Oak
Owner: Aberglasney Restoration Trust (Private Charitable Trust).
Contact: Booking Department **Tel/Fax:** 01558 668998
E-mail: info@aberglasney.org
Open: All year: daily (except Christmas Day). Apr-Oct: 10am-6pm, last entry 5pm. Nov-Mar: 10.30am-4pm.
Admission: Adult £8.00, Child £4.00, Conc. £8.00, Booked groups (10+) Adult £6.80. **Key facts:** ⊡ Free entry. ⊡ Free entry. ⊡ Contact for info. ⊡ Mostly suitable. ⊡ Licensed. ⊡ Pre-booked for groups. ⊡ Free parking, also large coach park. ⊡ ⊡ Guide dogs only. ⊡ Self-Catering Holiday Cottage on site, please contact to book or go to www.aberglasney.org. ⊡ Closed on Christmas Day. ⊡

ABERCAMLAIS HOUSE
Abercamlais, Brecon, Powys LD3 8EY
Splendid Grade I mansion dating from middle ages, altered extensively in early 18th Century with 19th Century additions, in extensive grounds beside the river Usk. Still in same family ownership and occupation since medieval times. Exceptional octagonal pigeon house, formerly a privy.
Location: Map 6:I10. OS Ref SN965 290. 5m W of Brecon on A40.
Owner: Mrs S Ballance **Contact:** Francis Chester-Master
Tel: 01982 553 248 **Fax:** 01982 553 154
E-mail: admin@chester-master.co.uk
Website: www.abercamlais.com
Open: Apr-Oct: by appointment.
Admission: Adult £5.00, Child Free.
Key facts: ⊡ No photography in house. ⊡ ⊡ Obligatory. ⊡ ⊡ Dogs on leads only.

CRESSELLY ⊡
Kilgetty, Pembrokeshire SA68 0SP

Home of the Allen family for 250 years. The house is of 1770 with matching wings of 1869 and contains good plasterwork and fittings of both periods. The Allens are of particular interest for their close association with the Wedgwood family of Etruria and a long tradition of foxhunting.
Location: Map 5:C11. OS Ref SN065 065. W of the A4075.
Owner/Contact: H D R Harrison-Allen Esq MFH
E-mail: hha@cresselly.com
Website: www.cresselly.com
Open: May 3-16 inclusive and Aug 1-14 inclusive. Guided tours only, on the hour. Coaches at other times by arrangement.
Admission: Adult £4.00, no children under 12.
Key facts: ⊡ Ground floor only. ⊡ Obligatory. ⊡ Coaches by arrangement. ⊡ ⊡ ⊡

Sunken Garden at Aberglasney

SOUTH WALES

LLANDAFF CATHEDRAL
Llandaff Cathedral Green, Cardiff CF5 2LA

Discover Llandaff Cathedral, a holy place of peace and tranquillity, art, architecture and music with a very warm welcome. Over 1500 yrs of history, standing on one of the oldest Christian sites in Britain. Works include Epstein, Piper, Pace, Rossetti, William Morris, Goscombe John, Frank Roper and Burne Jones. Services daily, some sung by the Cathedral Choir. Details on the Cathedral website: www.llandaffcathedral.org.uk.
Location: Map 2:L2. OS Ref ST155 397. At Cardiff Castle, drive West and cross River Taff; turn right into Cathedral Road (A4119) and follow signs to Llandaff.
Owner: Representative body of the Church In Wales **Contact:** Cathedral Office
Tel: 02920 564554 **E-mail:** office@llandaffcathedral.org.uk
Website: www.llandaffcathedral.org.uk
Open: Every week day 9am-6pm; Sun 7am-6pm.
Admission: Free. Donations gratefully received.
Key facts: ▦ ▣ ⴲ By arrangement. ᴘ Nearby. ▣ ▨ Guide dogs only. ▲ ❊ ▨

LLANVIHANGEL COURT ▥
Nr Abergavenny, Monmouthshire NP7 8DH

Grade I Tudor Manor. The home in the 17th Century of the Arnolds who built the imposing terraces and stone steps leading to the house. The interior has a fine hall, unusual yew staircase and many 17th Century moulded plaster ceilings. Delightful grounds. 17th Century features, notably Grade I stables.
Location: Map 6:K11. OS Ref SO325 205. 4m N of Abergavenny on A465.
Owner/Contact: Julia Johnson
Tel: 01873 890217
E-mail: jclarejohnson@googlemail.com
Website: www.llanvihangelcourt.com
Open: 1 May-13 May & 14 Aug-25 Aug. Inclusive, daily 2.30-5.30pm. Last tour 5pm.
Admission: Entry and guide, Adult £8.00, Child/Conc. £5.00.
Key facts: ⓘ No inside photography. ▣ Partial. ⴲ Obligatory. ᴘ Limited, no coaches. ▨ Dogs on leads only. ▲

CASTELL COCH ✚
Tongwynlais, Cardiff CF15 7JS

A fairytale castle in the woods, Castell Coch embodies a glorious Victorian dream of the Middle Ages. The castle is a by-product of a vivid Victorian imagination, assisted by untold wealth. **Location:** Map 2:L1. OS Ref ST131 826.
Tel: 029 2081 0101 **Website:** www.cadw.wales.gov.uk
Open: Please see website for up-to-date opening and admission details.

CORNWALL HOUSE ▥⊚
58 Monnow Street, Monmouth NP25 3EN

Town house, Georgian street façade, walled garden. **Location:** Map 6:L11. OS Ref SO506 127. Half way down main shopping street, set back from street. Please use centre door. **Tel:** 01600 712031 **E-mail:** jane2harvey@ tiscali.co.uk **Open:** 24-28 Mar, 30 Apr-2 May, 28-30 May, 6,13,20 & 27 Jul, 3,10,17,24, 27-29,31 Aug, 10-11 Sep, 2-5 pm. **Admission:** Adult £4.00, Concessions £2.00.

DYFFRYN GARDENS ⚘
St Nicholas, Vale of Glamorgan CF5 6SU

Grade I listed gardens featuring a collection of formal lawns, intimate garden rooms an extensive arboretum and reinstated glasshouse.
Location: Map 2:L2. OS Ref ST094 717. **Tel:** 02920 593328
E-mail: dyffryn@nationaltrust.org.uk
Website: www.nationaltrust.org.uk/dyffryngardens
Open: Please see website for up-to-date opening and admission details.

RAGLAN CASTLE ✚
Raglan, Monmouthshire NP15 2BT

Undoubtedly the finest late medieval fortress-palace in Britain, begun in the 1430s by Sir William ap Thomas who built the mighty 'Yellow Tower'.
Location: Map 6:K12. OS Ref SO415 084. **Tel:** 01291 690228
Website: www.cadw.wales.gov.uk **Open:** Please visit www.cadw.wales.gov.uk for opening times and admission details.

TINTERN ABBEY ✚
Tintern, Monmouthshire NP16 6SE

Tintern is the best-preserved abbey in Wales and ranks among Britain's most beautiful historic sites. The great Gothic abbey church stands almost complete to roof level. **Location:** Map 6:L12. OS Ref SO533 000.
Tel: 01291 689251 **Website:** www.cadw.wales.gov.uk **Open:** Please visit www.cadw.wales.gov.uk for opening times and admission prices.

TREBINSHWN
Llangasty, Nr Brecon, Powys LD3 7PX

16th Century mid-sized manor house. Extensively rebuilt 1780. Fine courtyard and walled garden. **Location:** Map 6:I10. OS Ref SO136 242. 1½m NW of Bwlch.
Tel: 01874 730653 **Fax:** 01874 730843
E-mail: liza.watson@trebinshunhouse.co.uk
Open: Easter-31 Aug: Mon-Tue, 10am-4.30pm. **Admission:** Free.

TREDEGAR HOUSE & PARK ⚘
Newport, South Wales NP10 8YW

Tredegar House is one of the most significant late 17th Century houses in Wales, if not the whole of the British Isles. **Location:** Map 2:M1. OS Ref ST290 852.
Tel: 01633 815880 **E-mail:** tredegar@nationaltrust.org.uk
Website: www.nationaltrust.org.uk/tredegarhouse
Open: Please see website for up-to-date opening and admission details.

TREOWEN ▥⊚
Wonastow, Monmouth NP25 4DL

The most important early 17th Century gentry house in the county. Particularly fine open well staircase. **Location:** Map 6:K11. OS Ref SO461 111. 3m WSW of Monmouth. **Tel:** 01600 712031 **E-mail:** john.wheelock@treowen.co.uk
Website: www.treowen.co.uk **Open:** May to Aug Fri 10am-4pm. Also Sat & Sun 9-10 & 16-17 Apr, 7-8 & 14-15 May and 10-11 Sep 2-5pm.
Admission: £6.00. Free to HHA Friends on Fridays only.

USK CASTLE ▥
Monmouth Rd, Usk, Monmouthshire NP5 1SD

Best kept secret, romantic ruins overlooking Usk. **Location:** Map 6:K12. OS Ref SO3701SE. Off Monmouth Road in Usk. **Tel:** 01291 672563
E-mail: info@uskcastle.com **Website:** www.uskcastle.com
Open: Castle open: All year, see website. House Open: May (not Mons), 2-5pm and BHs. Guided tours only. **Admission:** £7.00; Gardens £4.00.

Dyffryn Gardens

Register for news and special offers at **www.hudsonsheritage.com**

Powis Castle & Garden

GREGYNOG 🏛
Tregynon, Nr Newtown, Powys SY16 3PW
www.gregynog.org

Once a landed estate, now a vibrant conference centre, wedding venue and tourist destination. Set amidst 750 acres, Wales' newest National Nature Reserve and SSSI site offers 56 bedrooms and peace and tranquility. We pride ourselves on the quality of our home-produced locally sourced food from an extensive menu choice put together by our Chef. Grade 1 listed gardens, historic oak panelled rooms, an extensive library and a fine collection of furniture add to the unique ambience.
Location: Map 6:I6. OS Ref SO 084974. From the A483 follow the brown sign (Gregynog) or Bettws Cedewain. From Bettws follow Tregynon & look for large sign at end of drive. **Owner:** Gregynog **Contact:** enquiries@gregynog.org
Tel: 01686 650224 **E-mail:** enquiries@gregynog.org **Open:** Estate: every day. Café: please see website. **Admission:** Gardens Adult £3.00, Child £1.00.
Key facts: ℹ️ 📷 Open daily from 9am. 🌷 Plants for sale are on display in the Courtyard. 🎁 Bespoke packages tailored to your requirements. 🛍 Shop/Café/ some trails around the Hall. 🍽 Open (except in winter) from 11am. Menu on website. 🎫 Regular & various tours available - see website. 🅿️ Safe accessible parking. £2.50 charge. 🏫 School visits welcomed - and to our Forest School. 💒 💍 🏠 4 of the historic rooms are licensed. ❄️ Estate/grounds open all year. ♿

THE JUDGE'S LODGING
Broad Street, Presteigne, Powys LD8 2AD

Explore the fascinating world of the Victorian judges, their servants and felonious guests at this award-winning, totally hands-on historic house. Through sumptuous judge's apartments and the gas-lit servants' quarters below, follow an 'eavesdropping' audio tour featuring actor Robert Hardy. Damp cells, vast courtroom and new interactive local history rooms included.
Location: Map 6:K8. OS Ref SO314 644. In town centre, off A44 and A4113. Within easy reach from Herefordshire, Shropshire and mid-Wales.
Owner: Powys County Council **Contact:** Gabrielle Rivers **Tel:** 01544 260650
E-mail: info@judgeslodging.org.uk **Website:** www.judgeslodging.org.uk
Open: 1 Mar-31 Oct: Tues-Sun, 10am-5pm. 1 Nov-31 Nov: Wed-Sun, 10am-4pm, 1 Dec-22 Dec: Sat-Sun 10am-4pm. Open BH Mons.
Admission: Adult £7.95, Child £3.95, Conc. £6.95, Family £21.50. Groups (10-80): Adult £7.50, Conc. £6.50, Schools £4.95.
Key facts: ℹ️ 📷 🎁 🛍 Partial.
🎫 By arrangement. 🔊 🅿️ In town. 🏫 💍 Guide dogs only. 🏠 ♿

The Judge's Lodging

POWIS CASTLE & GARDEN 🌿
Welshpool, Powys SY21 8RF

Once a stark medieval fortress, Powis Castle has been transformed over 400 years into an extravagant family home with an exceptional collection of art, sculpture and furniture collected from Europe, India and the Orient. Outside you can enjoy the delights of a world famous garden with dramatic 17th Century terraces, lavish herbaceous borders and breath taking panoramic views. Visit our website for details of exciting events and our free daily talks and tours.
Location: Map 6:J6. 1 mile south of Welshpool. Signed from A483.
Info line: 01938 551944 **E-mail:** powiscastle@nationaltrust.org.uk
Website: www.nationaltrust.org.uk/powis-castle
Open: Mar-Dec. Peak times: Castle: 28 Mar-30 Sep 11am-5pm. Garden: 28 Mar-30 Sep 10am-6pm. **Admission:** Castle & Garden (Gift Aided): Adult £13.40, Child £6.70, Family (2 adults, 3 children) £33.50. See website for further details.
Key facts: ℹ️ No indoor photography. Photo Copyright NTPL/Andrew Butler. 📷
🌷 🛍 Partial. 🍽 🍴 Licensed. 🎫 🅿️ 🐕 Courtyard only. 🏠 ❄️ Closed 25 Dec. ♿

HAFOD ESTATE
Pontrhyd-y-groes, Ystrad Meurig, Ceredigion SY25 6DX

Ten miles of restored walks, the epitome of the Picturesque and Sublime. Set in 500 acres of wood and parkland featuring cascades, bridges and wonderful views.
Location: Map 5:G8. OS Ref SN768 736. 15 miles E of Aberystwyth, free car park.
Tel: 01974 282568 **E-mail:** trust@hafod.org **Website:** www.hafod.org
Open: All year - daylight hours. **Admission:** Free.

ISCOYD PARK
NR WHITCHURCH, SHROPSHIRE SY13 3AT
www.iscoydpark.com

A red brick Georgian house in an idyllic 18th Century parkland setting situated on the Welsh side of the Shropshire/Welsh border. After extensive refurbishment of the house and gardens we are now open for Weddings, parties, photography and film shoots, conferencing and corporate events of all kinds.

The house is only let on an exclusive basis meaning there is never more than one event occurring at any time. We offer a wide range of B&B and self-catering accommodation, The Secret Spa and beautiful gardens all within the context of a family home.

Location: Map 6:L4. OS Ref SJ504 421. 2m W of Whitchurch off A525.
Owner: Mr P C Godsal
Contact: Mr P L Godsal
Tel: 01948 780785
E-mail: info@iscoydpark.com
Open: House visits by written appointment.
Key facts: Private dinners and weddings a speciality. WCs. Licensed. Obligatory. Limited for coaches. Licensed. Open All Year.

DOLBELYDR
Trefnant, Denbighshire LL16 5AG
www.landmarktrust.org.uk

Set in a timeless, quiet valley this 16th Century gentry house has many of its original features, including a first floor solar open to the roof beams. It also has good claim to be the birthplace of the modern Welsh language.
Location: Map 6:I2. OS Ref SJ027 698.
Owner: The Landmark Trust
Tel: 01628 825925
E-mail: bookings@landmarktrust.org.uk
Open: Self-catering accommodation. Open days on 8 days per year. Other visits by appointment.
Admission: Free on open days and visits by appointment.
Key facts: There is an open plan kitchen and dining area in front of a huge inglenook fireplace.

GWYDIR CASTLE
Llanrwst, Conwy LL26 0PN
www.gwydircastle.co.uk

Gwydir Castle is situated in the beautiful Conwy Valley and is set within a Grade I listed, 10 acre garden. Built by the illustrious Wynn family c1500, Gwydir is a fine example of a Tudor courtyard house, incorporating re-used medieval material from the dissolved Abbey of Maenan. Further additions date from c1600 and c1828. The important 1640s panelled Dining Room has now been reinstated, following its repatriation from the New York Metropolitan Museum.
Location: Map 5:H3. OS Ref SH795 610. ½m W of Llanrwst on B5106.
Owner/Contact: Mr & Mrs Welford
Tel: 01492 641687 **E-mail:** info@gwydircastle.co.uk
Open: 1 Apr-31 Oct: daily, 10am-4pm. Closed Mons & Sats (except BH weekends). Limited openings at other times. Please telephone for details.
Admission: Adult £6.00, Child £3.00, Concessions £5.50. Group discount 10%.
Key facts: Partial. By arrangement. By arrangement. 2 doubles.

COCHWILLAN OLD HALL
Halfway Bridge, Bangor, Gwynedd LL57 3AZ

A fine example of medieval architecture with the present house dating from 1450. It is thought to have been built by William Gryffydd who fought for Henry VII at Bosworth. Once owned in the 17th Century by John Williams who became Archbishop of York. The house was restored from a barn in 1971.

Location: Map 5:G2. OS Ref OS Ref. SH606 695. 3 ½ m SE of Bangor. 1m SE of Talybont off A55.

Owner: R C H Douglas Pennant

Contact: Mark & Christopher Chenery

Tel: 01248 355139

E-mail: risboro@hotmail.co.uk

Open: By appointment.

Admission: Please email or telephone for details.

Bodnant Garden

FFERM
Pontblyddyn, Mold, Flintshire CH7 4HN

17th Century farmhouse. Viewing is limited to 7 persons at any one time. Open by appointment. No toilets or refreshments.

Location: Map 6:J3. OS Ref SJ279 603. Access from A541 in Pontblyddyn, 3½m SE of Mold.

Owner: Dr M.C. Jones-Mortimer Will Trust

Contact: Dr Miranda Dechazal

Tel: 01352 770161

Open: 2nd Wed in every month, 2-5pm. Open by appointment.

Admission: £5.00.

Key facts: ⌘ ✳

WERN ISAF
Penmaen Park, Llanfairfechan, Conwy LL33 0RN

This Arts and Crafts house was built in 1900 by the architect H L North as his family home and contains much of the original furniture and William Morris fabrics. Situated in a woodland garden with extensive views over the Menai Straits and Conwy Bay.

Location: Map 5:G2. OS Ref SH685 753. Off A55 midway between Bangor and Conwy.

Owner/Contact: Mrs P J Phillips

Tel: 01248 680437

Open: 1-15 Mar and 1-15 May: daily 1-3pm, excluding Weds.

Admission: Free.

HARTSHEATH 🏠ⓔ
Pontblyddyn, Mold, Flintshire CH7 4HP

18th and 19th Century house set in parkland. Viewing is limited to 7 persons at any one time. Open by appointment. No toilets or refreshments.

Location: Map 6:J3. OS Ref SJ287 602. Access from A5104, 3.5m SE of Mold between Pontblyddyn and Penyffordd.

Owner: Dr M.C. Jones-Mortimer Will Trust

Contact: Dr Miranda Dechazal

Tel/Fax: 01352 770204

Open: 1st, 3rd & 5th Wed in every month, 2-5pm. Open by appointment.

Admission: £5.00.

Key facts: ⌘ ✳

BODNANT GARDEN 🌿
Tal-Y-Cafn, Colwyn Bay LL28 5RE

One of the finest gardens in the country not only for its magnificent collections of rhododendrons, camellias and magnolias but also for its idyllic setting above the River Conwy. **Location:** Map 5:H2. OS Ref SH801 723. 8 miles S of Llandudno.

Tel: 01492 650460 **E-mail:** bodnantgarden@nationaltrust.org.uk

Website: www.nationaltrust.org.uk/bodnant-garden

Open: Please see website for opening times and admission prices.

CAERNARFON CASTLE ✚
Castle Ditch, Caernarfon LL55 2AY

The most famous and perhaps the most impressive castle in Wales, built by Edward I. Distinguished by polygonal towers and colour-banded stone.

Location: Map 5:F3. OS Ref SH477 626. **Tel:** 01286 677617

Website: www.cadw.wales.gov.uk **Open:** Please visit www.cadw.wales.gov.uk for up-to-date opening times and admission prices.

PLAS BRONDANW GARDENS, CAFFI & SHOP
Plas Brondanw, Llanfrothen, Gwynedd LL48 6SW

Italianate gardens with topiary.

Location: Map 5:G4. OS Ref SH618 423. 3m N of Penrhyndeudraeth off A4085, on Croesor Road.

Owner: Trustees of the Clough Williams-Ellis Foundation.

Tel: 01766 772772 / 01743 239236.

E-mail: enquiries@plasbrondanw.com

Website: www.plasbrondanw.com

Open: Mar-Sep daily, 10.00am-5.00pm.
Coaches accepted, please book.

Admission: Adult £4.00, Children under 12 £1.00.

Key facts: 🏛 ♿ 🍴 🍷 🎁 🅿 🏔 ⌘ 🔊

ERDDIG 🌿
Wrexham LL13 0YT

Widely acclaimed as one of Britain's finest historic houses, Erddig is a fascinating yet unpretentious early 18th Century country house.

Location: Map 6:K3. OS Ref SJ326 482. **Tel:** 01978 355314

E-mail: erddig@nationaltrust.org.uk **Website:** www.nationaltrust.org.uk/erddig

Open: Please see website for up-to-date opening and admission details.

PLAS MAWR ✚
High Street, Conwy LL32 8DE

The best-preserved Elizabethan town house in Britain, Plas Mawr reflects the status of its builder Robert Wynn. **Location:** Map 5:H2. OS Ref SH781 776.

Tel: 01492 580167 **Website:** www.cadw.wales.gov.uk

Open: Please visit www.cadw.wales.gov.uk for up-to-date opening times and admission prices.

ABERYSTWYTH CASTLE
Aberystwyth, Ceredigion SY23 2AG
Tel: 01970 612125

GLANSEVERN HALL GARDENS
Glansevern, Berriew, Welshpool, Powys SY21 8AH
Tel: 01686 640644 **E-mail:** glansevern@yahoo.co.uk

LLANERCHAERON ❧
Ciliau Aeron, Nr Aberaeron, Ceredigion SA48 8DG
Tel: 01545 570200 **E-mail:** llanerchaeron@nationaltrust.org.uk

THE HALL AT ABBEY-CWM-HIR
Nr Llandrindod Wells, Powys LD1 6PH
Tel: 01597 851727 **E-mail:** info@abbeycwmhir.com

TREWERN HALL
Trewern, Welshpool, Powys SY21 8DT
Tel: 01938 570243

ABERCONWY HOUSE ❧
Castle Street, Conwy LL32 8AY
Tel: 01492 592246 **E-mail:** aberconwyhouse@nationaltrust.org.uk

BEAUMARIS CASTLE ✚
Beaumaris, Anglesey LL58 8AP
Tel: 01248 810361

BODRHYDDAN HALL ▦ⓔ
Bodrhyddan, Rhuddlan, Rhyl, Denbighshire LL18 5SB
Tel: 01745 590414

CHIRK CASTLE ❧
Chirk LL14 5AF
Tel: 01691 777701 **E-mail:** chirkcastle@nationaltrust.org.uk

CONWY CASTLE ✚
Conwy LL32 8AY
Tel: 01492 592358

HARLECH CASTLE ✚
Castle Square, Harlech LL46 2YH
Tel: 01766 780552

PENRHYN CASTLE ❧
Bangor, Gwynedd LL57 4HN
Tel: 01248 353084 **E-mail:** penrhyncastle@nationaltrust.org.uk

PLAS NEWYDD
Hill Street, Llangollen, Denbighshire LL20 8AW
Tel: 01978 862834 **E-mail:** heritage@denbighshire.gov.uk

PLAS NEWYDD HOUSE & GARDENS ❧
Llanfairpwll, Anglesey LL61 6DQ
Tel: 01248 714795 **E-mail:** plasnewydd@nationaltrust.org.uk

PORTMEIRION
Minffordd, Penrhyndeudraeth, Gwynedd LL48 6ER
Tel: 01766 772311 **E-mail:** enquiries@portmeirion-village.com

RHUDDLAN CASTLE ✚
Castle Street, Rhuddlan, Rhyl LL18 5AD
Tel: 01745 590777

TOWER
Nercwys Road, Mold, Flintshire CH7 4EW
Tel: 01352 700220 **E-mail:** enquiries@towerwales.co.uk

ABERDEUNANT ❧
Taliaris, Llandeilo, Carmarthenshire SA19 6DL
Tel: 01588 650177 **E-mail:** aberdeunant@nationaltrust.org.uk

CAERPHILLY CASTLE ✚
Caerphilly CF83 1JD
Tel: 029 2088 3143

CHEPSTOW CASTLE ✚
Chepstow, Monmouthshire NP16 5EY
Tel: 01291 624065

KIDWELLY CASTLE ✚
Kidwelly, Carmarthenshire SA17 5BQ
Tel: 01554 890104

LAUGHARNE CASTLE ✚
King Street, Laugharne, Carmarthenshire SA33 4SA
Tel: 01994 427906

MARGAM COUNTRY PARK & CASTLE
Margam, Port Talbot, West Glamorgan SA13 2TJ
Tel: 01639 881635 **E-mail:** margampark@npt.gov.uk

NATIONAL BOTANIC GARDEN OF WALES
Llanarthne, Carmarthenshire SA32 8HG
Tel: 01558 667149 **E-mail:** info@gardenofwales.org.uk

PEMBROKE CASTLE
Pembroke SA71 4LA
Tel: 01646 681510 **E-mail:** info@pembrokecastle.co.uk

PICTON CASTLE & WOODLAND GARDENS ▦ⓔ
The Rhos, Nr Haverfordwest, Pembrokeshire SA62 4AS
Tel: 01437 751326 **E-mail:** info@pictoncastle.co.uk

ST FAGANS: NATIONAL HISTORY MUSEUM
Cardiff CF5 6XB
Tel: 029 2057 3500

STRADEY CASTLE ▦ⓔ
Llanelli, Carmarthenshire, Wales SA15 4PL
Tel: 01554 774 626 **E-mail:** info@stradeycastle.com

TRETOWER COURT & CASTLE ✚
Tretower, Crickhowell NP8 1RD
Tel: 01874 730279

TUDOR MERCHANT'S HOUSE ❧
Quay Hill, Tenby, Pembrokeshire SA70 7BX
Tel: 01834 842279 **E-mail:** tudormerchantshouse@nationaltrust.org.uk

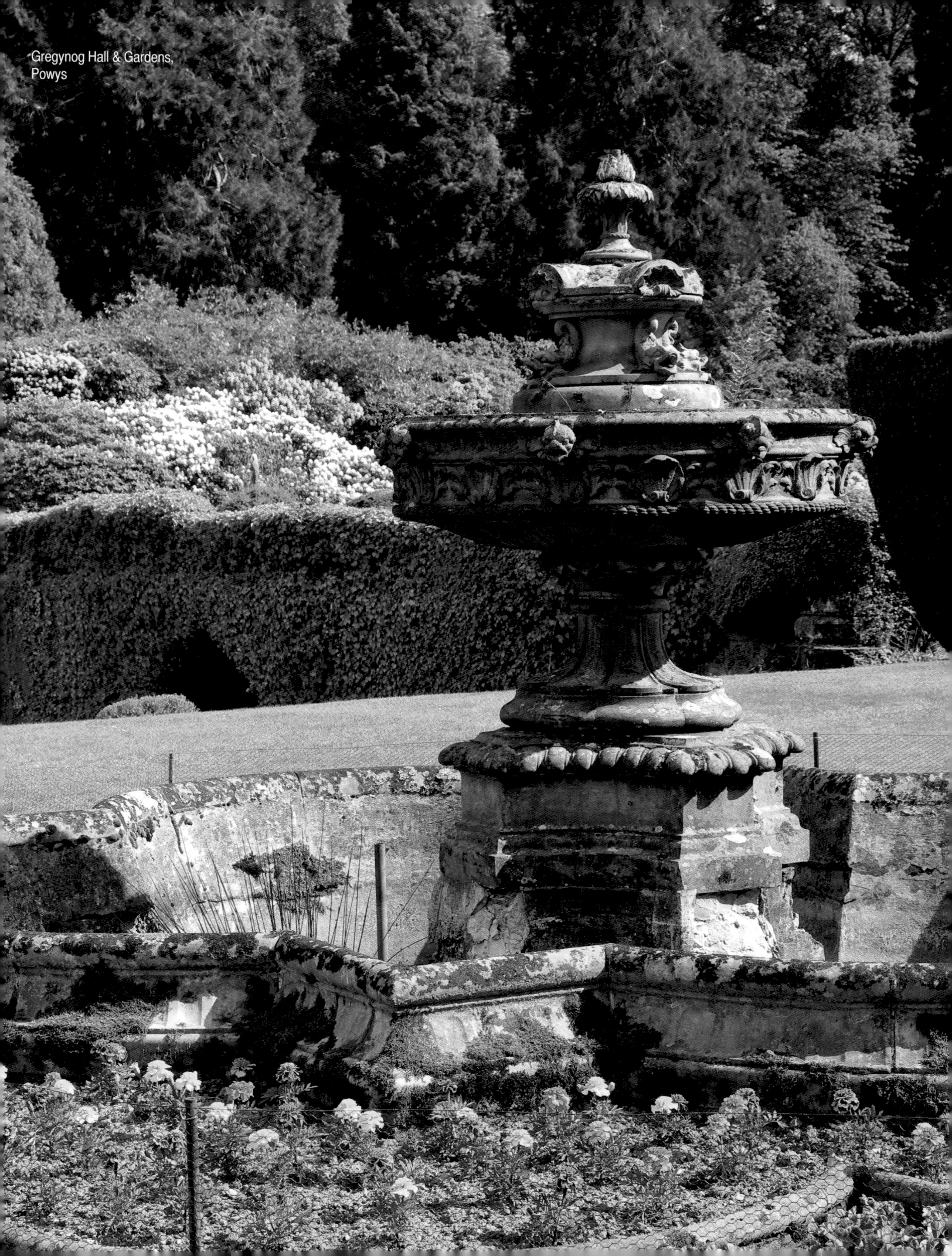
Gregynog Hall & Gardens,
Powys

Castle Ward, County Down

©NATIONAL TRUST IMAGES

Antrim
Armagh
Down
Fermanagh
Londonderry
Tyrone

Northern Ireland

Perfect for a weekend or a longer trip from the mainland, Northern Ireland's castles, houses and gardens have so much to tell us of the rich and distinctive history of the province.

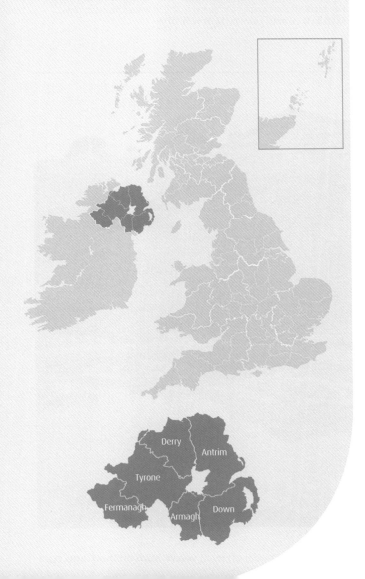

ANTRIM CASTLE GARDENS AND CLOTWORTHY HOUSE

RANDALSTOWN ROAD, ANTRIM BT41 4LH

www.antrimandnewtownabbey.gov.uk/antrimcastlegardens

Antrim Castle Gardens and Clotworthy House is a hidden gem waiting to be explored, these 400 year old Gardens have been transformed into a unique living museum and must see attraction.

Few historic gardens in Northern Ireland offer such evolutionary garden design characteristics with layer upon layer of design features and planting added over the centuries, including the magnificent 17th Century Anglo Dutch style canals, ponds and avenues that are unique in Northern Ireland.

Antrim Castle Gardens offers a breathtaking walk into history, but also much more. While you are here why not stay for a coffee or lunch in the Garden Coffee Shop, browse the visitor shop and have a look round the Garden Heritage Exhibition and Art Gallery.

Location: Map 18:N4. OS Ref J186 850. Outside Antrim town centre off A26 on A6. Follow Brown Signs for Antrim Castle Gardens.
Owner: Antrim and Newtownabbey Borough Council
Contact: Samuel Hyndman - Garden Heritage Development Officer
Tel: 028 9448 1338
E-mail: culture@antrimandnewtwonabbey.gov.uk
Open: All year: Mon, Wed and Fri 9.30am-5pm. Tue and Thu 9.30am–9.30pm. Sat and Sun 10am-5pm.
Admission: Free entry. Free guided group tours by arrangement only.
Key facts: Photographic shoots and filming by written permission only. WCs. Licensed.

BALLYWALTER PARK

Ballywalter, Newtownards, Co Down BT22 2PP

www.ballywalterpark.com

Ballywalter Park was built in the Italianate Palazzo style, by Sir Charles Lanyon for Andrew Mulholland. A Gentleman's wing was added in 1870 for Andrew's son, John Mulholland, later 1st Baron Dunleath. The house has a fine collection of original furniture and paintings, complemented by contemporary pieces.
Location: Map 18:P4. OS Ref J610 723. Off A2 on unclassified road, 1 km S of Ballywalter village. **Owner:** The Lord and Lady Dunleath **Contact:** Mrs Sharon Graham, The Estate Office **Tel:** 028 4275 8264 **Fax:** 028 4275 8818
E-mail: enq@dunleath-estates.co.uk
Open: By prior appointment only; please contact The Estate Office.
Admission: House or Gardens: £9.50. House & Gardens: £17.00. Groups (max 50): £9.50. Refreshments by arrangement.
Key facts: No photography indoors. The house is available for corporate & incentive events, lunches & dinners. Lunches & dinners can be booked by prior arrangement. Obligatory. Guide dogs only. Twelve en suite bedrooms available for group tours & corporate events. By appointment only. €

Mount Stewart

DOWN CATHEDRAL
Cathedral Office, English Street, Downpatrick
County Down BT30 6AB
www.downcathedral.org

Built in 1183 as a Benedictine monastery, Down Cathedral is now a Cathedral of the Church of Ireland. Prominent and majestic, the cathedral is believed to have the grave of St Patrick in its grounds. There is also wonderful stained glass and a pulpit and organ of highest quality.
Location: Map 18:O6. OS Ref SB583 989.
Located in Downpatrick, in the heart of English Street. Follow brown signs.
Owner: Church of Ireland **Contact:** Joy Wilkinson
Tel: 028 4461 4922 **Fax:** 028 4461 4456 **E-mail:** info@downcathedral.org
Open: All year round. Mon-Sat: 9.30am-4.00pm. Sun: 2-4pm.
Admission: Donations. Guided tours by arrangement.
Key facts: ⬛ ⬛ ⬛ By arrangement. 🅿 Limited for cars and coaches. ⬛ 🐕 Guide dogs only. ⬛

HILLSBOROUGH CASTLE
Hillsborough BT26 6AG
www.hrp.org.uk/hillsborough

The late Georgian mansion was built in the 1770s and is a working royal residence, functioning as the official residence of the Royal Family when they are in Northern Ireland, and it has been the home of the Secretary of State since the 1970s. A tour of the house will guide you through the elegant State Rooms, still in use today, including the majestic Throne Room. Don't miss 98 acres of stunning gardens.
Location: Map 18:N5.
Owner: Historic Royal Palaces
Tel: 028 9268 1300
E-mail: hillsboroughcastle@hrp.org.uk
Open: Apr-Sep: House open specific days for guided tours. Year round: Gardens open 10:00am-5:00pm. Visit website or call for details before visiting.
Admission: See website. House by guided tour only, must book in advance.
Key facts: ⬛ Weddings, receptions, conferences. ⬛ 🅿 No parking onsite. ⬛ ⬛

BARONS COURT ⬛
Newtownstewart, Omagh, Co Tyrone BT78 4EZ
The home of the Duke and Duchess of Abercorn, Barons Court was built between 1779 and 1782, and subsequently extensively remodelled by John Soane (1791), William and Richard Morrison (1819-1841), Sir Albert Richardson (1947-49) and David Hicks (1975-76).
Location: Map 18:M3. OS Ref H236 382. 5km SW of Newtownstewart.
Contact: The Agent
Tel: 028 8166 1683 **Fax:** 028 8166 2059
E-mail: info@barons-court.com **Website:** www.barons-court.com
Open: By appointment only.
Admission: Tour of House and/or Gardens £11.00pp. Tour inc. tea/coffee/scones £15.00pp. Groups max. 50.
Key facts: ⬛ No photography. ⬛ The Carriage Room in the Stable Yard. ⬛ Partial. ⬛ By arrangement. 🅿 ⬛ ⬛ Holiday cottages, 4 star rated by Northern Ireland Tourist Board. ⬛ €

CASTLE COOLE ⬛
Enniskillen, Co Fermanagh BT74 6JY
Surrounded by its stunning landscape park on the edge of Enniskillen, this majestic 18th Century home of the Earls of Belmore, designed by James Wyatt, was created to impress. **Location:** Map 18:I5. OS Ref H245 436. On A4, 1½m from Enniskillen. **Tel:** 028 6632 2690 **E-mail:** castlecoole@nationaltrust.org.uk
Website: www.nationaltrust.org.uk/castle-coole
Open: Please see website for up-to-date opening times and admission prices.

CASTLE WARD HOUSE & DEMESNE ⬛
Strangford, Downpatrick, Co Down BT30 7LS
Situated in a stunning location within an 820 acre walled demesne overlooking Strangford Lough. **Location:** Map 18:P6. OS Ref J573 498. On A25, 7m from Downpatrick and 1½m from Strangford. **Tel:** 028 4488 1204
E-mail: castleward@nationaltrust.org.uk
Website: www.nationaltrust.org.uk/castle-ward
Open: Please see website for opening times and admission prices.

KILLYLEAGH CASTLE ⬛
Killyleagh, Downpatrick, Co Down BT30 9QA
Oldest occupied castle in Ireland. Self-catering towers available, sleeps 4-9. Swimming pool and tennis court available by arrangement. Access to garden.
Location: Map 18:O5/6. OS Ref J523 529. **Tel:** 028 4482 8261 **E-mail:** gawnrh@gmail.com **Website:** www.killyleaghcastle.com **Open:** By arrangement.
Admission: Groups (30-50) by arrangement. Around £2.50 pp.

MOUNT STEWART ⬛
Newtonards, Co Down BT22 2AD
Home of the Londonderry family since the early 18th Century, Mount Stewart was Lord Castlereagh's house and played host to many prominent political figures.
Location: Map 18:P5. OS Ref J556 703. **Tel:** 028 4278 8387
E-mail: mountstewart@nationaltrust.org.uk **Website:** www.nationaltrust.org.uk/mount-stewart **Open:** Please see website for most up-to-date details.

Barons Court Estate

ANTRIM ROUND TOWER
16 High Street, Antrim, County Antrim BT41 4AN
Tel: 028 94428331

ARTHUR ANCESTRAL HOME
Cullybackey, County Antrim BT42 1AB
Tel: 028 2563 8494 **E-mail:** devel.leisure@ballymena.gov.uk

BELFAST CASTLE
Cave Hill, Antrim Road, Belfast BT15 5GR
Tel: 028 9077 6925

BENVARDEN GARDEN
Benvarden, Dervock, County Antrim BT53 6NN
Tel: 028 20741331

BOTANIC GARDENS
Stransmillis Road, Belfast BT7 1LP
Tel: 028 9031 4762

CARRICKFERGUS CASTLE
Marine Highway, Carrickfergus, County Antrim BT38 7BG
Tel: 028 9335 1273

CATHEDRAL OF CHRIST CHURCH, LISBURN
24 Castle Street, Lisburn BT28 1RG
Tel: 028 9260 2400 **E-mail:** sam@lisburncathedral.org

DUNLUCE CASTLE
87 Dunluce Road, Portrush, County Antrim BT57 8UY
Tel: 028 20731938

GLENARM CASTLE WALLED GARDEN
2 Castle Lane, Glenarm, Larne, County Antrim BT44 0BQ
Tel: 028 28841305

MONTALTO HOUSE
5 Craigaboney Road, Bushmills, County Antrim BT57 8XD
Tel: 028 2073 1257 **E-mail:** montaltohouse@btconnect.com

SENTRY HILL
Ballycraigy Road, Newtownabbey BT36 5SY
Tel: 028 90340000

ST. ANNE'S CATHEDRAL
Donegall Street, Belfast BT12 2HB
Tel: 028 9032 8332

ST. PETER'S CATHEDRAL
St Peters Square, Falls Road, Belfast BT12 4BU
Tel: 028 9032 7573

ARDRESS HOUSE ⁂
64 Ardress Road, Portadown, Co Armagh BT62 1SQ
Tel: 028 8778 4753 **E-mail:** ardress@nationaltrust.org.uk

BENBURB CASTLE
Servite Priory, Main Street, Benburb, Co, Tyrone BT71 7JZ
Tel: 028 37548241 **E-mail:** servitepriory@btinternet.com

DERRYMORE ⁂
Bessbrook, Newry, Co Armagh BT35 7EF
Tel: 028 8778 4753 **E-mail:** derrymore@nationaltrust.org.uk

GILFORD CASTLE ESTATE
Banbridge Road, Gilford BT63 6DT
Tel: 028 40623322 **E-mail:** gilford@irishfieldsports.com

AUDLEYS CASTLE
Strangford, County Down UK
Tel: 028 9054 3034

BANGOR ABBEY
Bangor, County Down BT20 4JF
Tel: 028 91271200

BANGOR CASTLE
Bangor, County Down BT20 4BN
Tel: 028 91270371

CLOUGH CASTLE
Clough Village, Downpatrick, County Down UK
Tel: 028 9054 3034

DUNDRUM CASTLE
Dundrum Village, Newcastle, County Down BT33 0QX
Tel: 028 9054 3034

GREENCASTLE ROYAL CASTLE
Cranfield Point, Kilkeel, County Down UK
Tel: 028 90543037

GREY ABBEY
9-11 Church Street, Greyabbey, County Down BT22 2NQ
Tel: 028 9054 6552

GREY POINT FORT
Crawfordsburn Country Park, Helens Bay, Co. Down BT19 1LE
Tel: 028 91853621

HELENS TOWER
Clandeboye Estate, Bangor BT19 1RN
Tel: 028 91852817

INCH ABBEY
Downpatrick, County Down UK
Tel: 028 9181 1491

KILCLIEF CASTLE
Strangford, County Down UK
Tel: 028 9054 3034

MAHEE CASTLE
Mahee Island, Comber, Newtownards BT23 6EP
Tel: 028 91826846

MOVILLA ABBEY
63 Movilla Road, Newtownards BT23 8EZ
Tel: 028 9181 0787

NEWRY CATHEDRAL
38 Hill Street, Newry, County Down BT34 1AT
Tel: 028 3026 2586

PORTAFERRY CASTLE
Castle Street, Portaferry, County Down BT22 1NZ
Tel: 028 90543033

QUOILE CASTLE
Downpatrick, County Down BT30 7JB
Tel: 028 9054 3034

RINGHADDY CASTLE
Killyleagh, County Down UK
Tel: 028 90543037

ROWALLANE GARDEN 🌱
Ballynahinch, Co Down BT24 7LH
Tel: 028 9751 0721 **E-mail:** rowallane@nationaltrust.org.uk

SKETRICK CASTLE
Whiterock, County Down BT23 6QA
Tel: 028 4278 8387

STRANGFORD CASTLE
Strangford, County Down UK
Tel: 028 9054 3034

THE PRIORY
Newtownards, County Down UK
Tel: 028 90543037

CROM ESTATE 🌱
Newtownbutler, County Fermanagh BT92 8AP
Tel: 028 6773 8118

ENNISKILLEN CASTLE 🌱
Castle Barracks, Enniskillen, County Fermanagh BT74 7HL
Tel: 028 6632 5000 **E-mail:** castle@fermanagh.gov.uk

FLORENCE COURT 🌱
Enniskillen, Co Fermanagh BT92 1DB
Tel: 028 6634 8249 **E-mail:** florencecourt@nationaltrust.org.uk

BELLAGHY BAWN
Castle Street, Bellaghy, County Londonderry BT45 8LA
Tel: 028 7938 6812

DUNGIVEN CASTLE
Main Street, Dungiven, Co Londonderry BT47 4LF
Tel: 028 7774 2428 **E-mail:** enquiries@dungivencastle.com

DUNGIVEN PRIORY AND O CAHANS TOMB
Dungiven, County Londonderry UK
Tel: 028 777 22074

KINGS FORT
7 Connell Street, Limavady, Co Londonderry BT49 0HA
Tel: 028 77760304 **E-mail:** tourism@limavady.gov.uk

MOUNTSANDAL FORT
Mountsandal Road, Coleraine, Co Londonderry BT52 1PE
Tel: 027 7034 4723 **E-mail:** coleraine@nitic.net

PREHEN HOUSE
Prehen Road, Londonderry BT47 2PB
Tel: 028 7131 2829 **E-mail:** colinpeck@yahoo.com

ROUGH FORT
Limavady TIC, 7 Connell Street, Limavady BT49 0HA
Tel: 028 7084 8728

SAINT COLUMBS CATHEDRAL
London Street, Derry, County Londonderry BT48 6RQ
Tel: 028 71267313 **E-mail:** stcolumbs@ic24.net

SAMPSONS TOWER
Limavady TIC, 7 Connell Street, Limavady BT49 0HA
Tel: 028 7776 0307

SPRINGHILL HOUSE 🌱
20 Springhill Road, Moneymore, Co Londonderry BT45 7NQ
Tel: 028 8674 8210 **E-mail:** springhill@nationaltrust.org.uk

THE GUILDHALL
Guildhall Square, Londonderry BT48 6DQ
Tel: 028 7137 7335

CASTLEDERG CASTLE
Castle Park, Castlederg, County Tyrone BT81 7AS
Tel: 028 7138 2204

HARRY AVERYS CASTLE
Old Castle Road, Newtownstewart BT82 8DY
Tel: 028 7138 2204

KILLYMOON CASTLE
Killymoon Road, Cookstown, County Tyrone UK
Tel: 028 86763514

NEWTOWNSTEWART CASTLE
Townhall Street, Newtownstewart BT78 4AX
Tel: 028 6862 1588 **E-mail:** nieainfo@doeni.gov.uk

OMAGH GAOL
Old Derry Road, Omagh, County Tyrone UK
Tel: 028 82247 831 **E-mail:** omagh.tic@btconnect.com

SAINT MACARTAN'S CATHEDRAL
Clogher, County Tyrone BT76 0AD
Tel: 028 0478 1220

SIR JOHN DAVIES CASTLE
Castlederg, County Tyrone BT81 7AS
Tel: 028 7138 2204

THE ARGORY 🌱
Moy, Dungannon, Co Tyrone BT71 6NA
Tel: 028 8778 4753 **E-mail:** argory@nationaltrust.org.uk

THE KEEP OR GOVERNORS RESIDENCE
Off Old Derry Road, Omagh, County Tyrone UK
Tel: 028 82247831 **E-mail:** omagh.tic@btconnect.com

TULLYHOGUE FORT
B162, Cookstown, County Tyrone, Northern Ireland UK
Tel: 028 86766727

Visit **www.hudsonsheritage.com** for special events and wedding venues

Opening Arrangements at places grant-aided by Historic England

Historic England is the public body that looks after England's historic environment. Each year they give grants to historic buildings in need in return for public access. Check here for details of opening times for many of the places recently in receipt of grants.

H Denotes opening for Heritage Open Days in September www.heritageopendays.org.uk.

Please note that parking and wheelchair access may be limited and toilets for people with disabilities are not always available. If you are travelling from afar or have special requirements, please check in advance. More details are available on www.historicengland.org.uk

Mark Dion's art installation enlivens Porthmeor Studios, St Ives, Cornwall TR26 1NG.
Lofts & cellars for the pilchard fishing industry used as artists' studios since the 1880s.
Telephone: 01736 339339
Open: By appointment.

LONDON

**Benjamin Franklins House,
36 Craven Street, London WC2N 5NF**
A 1730s terraced house the site retains a majority of original features and is the world's only remaining home of Benjamin Franklin.
Location: Behind Charing Cross station. Rail: Charing Cross. Tube: Charing Cross. Bus: 6, 9, 11, 13, 15, 23, 77a , 91 and 176
Recipient: Friends of Benjamin Franklin House
Telephone: 020 7839 2006
Contact: Ms Sally James
Email: info@benjaminfranklinhouse.org
Website: www.benjaminfranklinhouse.org
Open: Mon, Wed-Sun, 10.30am-5.30pm. Tours and Historical Experience shows running at specific times.
Admission Adult: £7.00 **Child:** Free
H

**Bromley Hall, Gillender Street,
Tower Hamlets, London E14 6RN**
A rare surviving 15th Century house and one of the oldest brick built houses in London.
Location: East side of A12. Rail: Devons Road. Tube: Bromley-by-Bow. Bus: 108.
Recipient: Leaside Regeneration
Telephone: 0845 262 0846
Contact: Mr David Black
Email: dblack@leasideplanning.co.uk
Open: By prior appointment.
P & H

The Charles Dickens Museum, 48 & 49 Doughty Street, London WC1N 2LX
Dating from c1807-9 Charles Dickens wrote Oliver Twist and Nicholas Nickleby whilst living there. Includes manuscripts, rare editions, personal items and paintings.
Location: East Bloomsbury on accessible road with parking. Rail: Kings Cross/St Pancras 1m., Farringdon 1m., Euston 1m. Bus: 7, 17, 19, 38, 45, 46, 55, 243. Tube: Russell Square, Chancery Lane, Holborn, or Kings Cross St Pancras.
Recipient: The Charles Dickens Museum
Telephone: 020 7405 2127
Contact: Mr Robert Moye
Email: info@dickensmuseum.com
Website: www.dickensmuseum.com
Open: All year, Mon-Sun, 10am-5pm. Temporary closures are advertised on website. Closed 25, 26 Dec and 1 Jan.
Admission Adult: £8.00 **Child:** £4.00
&

Headstone Manor, Pinner View, Harrow, London HA2 6PX
Grade I listed timber framed manor house, surrounded by a water filled moat and original residence of Archbishops of Canterbury until the Reformation.
Location: Access via Pinner View. Rail: Headstone Lane 1m. Bus: H9, H10 & H14.
Recipient: London Borough of Harrow
Telephone: 020 8863 6720
Contact: Ms Jo Saunders
Email: harrow.museum@harrow.gov.uk
Website: www.harrow.gov.uk/museum, www.harrowmuseum.org.uk
Open: Open most of year and for historic talks and school visits. Small Barn closed until 2017. Check website for details.
Admission Adult: £3.00 for tours
Child: Free
P & H

Red House, Red House Lane, Bexleyheath DA6 8JF
Strongly influenced by gothic medieval architecture and constructed with an emphasis on natural materials. Unaltered interior with numerous original features including wall paintings and stained glass.
Location: Follow A221 Bexleyheath from A2. Rail: Bexleyheath 0.75m.
Recipient: The National Trust
Telephone: 020 8303 6359
Contact: Mr James Breslin
Email: redhouse@nationaltrust.org.uk
Website: www.nationaltrust.org.uk
Open: Feb-Nov, Wed-Sun, Nov-Dec, Fri-Sun and all BH Mons, 11am-5pm. Pre booked guided tours tel: 020 8304 9878.
Admission Adult: £8.00 **Child:** £4.00
P &

Strawberry Hill, Waldegrave Road, Twickenham, London TW1 4SX
Georgian house and a fine example of gothic revival architecture and interior decoration including extraordinary rooms, towers and battlements.
Location: 268 Waldegrave Road, Twickenham A309. Rail: Strawberry Hill ¼m. Bus: 33, R68
Recipient: Strawberry Hill Trust
Telephone: 020 8744 1241
Contact: Mr Nicholas Smith
Email: nicholas.smith@strawberryhillhouse.org.uk
Website: www.strawberryhillhouse.org.uk
Open: Mar-Nov, Mons, Tues, Weds, Sats and Suns, Weekdays 2pm-6pm, Weekends 12pm-6pm. Guided tours available.
Admission Adult: £12 **Child:** Under 16 free
P &

Opening Arrangements at places grant-aided by Historic England

Painshill Grotto, Surrey

SOUTH EAST

Basildon Park, Lower Basildon, Reading, Berkshire RG8 9NR
Designed in the 18th Century and set in 400 acres of parkland the site include rich interiors with fine plasterwork, small flower garden, pleasure ground and woodland walks.
Location: Between Pangbourne and Streatley. Rail: Pangbourne 2½m., Goring and Streatley 3m. Bus: 132
Recipient: The National Trust
Telephone: 01491 672382
Contact: Ms Amanda Beard
Email: basildonpark@nationaltrust.org.uk
Website: www.nationaltrust.org.uk
Open: Daily, 10am-5pm, closes at dusk if earlier. Closed 24 and 25 Dec
Admission Adult: £14.00 (House and Grounds) **Child:** £7.00 (House and Grounds)
P ♿ H

Bletchley Park Mansion, Wilton Avenue, Milton Keynes, Buckinghamshire MK3 6BN
Victorian and Edwardian mansion, the estate was taken over in WWII and used for substantially developing the UK's code breaking centre.
Location: In central Bletchley, access from Sherwood Drive. Rail: Bletchley
Recipient: Bletchley Park Trust
Telephone: 01908 640404
Contact: Mr Iain Standen
Email: istanden@bletchleypark.org.uk
Website: www.bletchleypark.org.uk
Open: Mar-Oct, 9.30am-5pm (last admission 4pm). Nov-Feb, 9.30am-4pm (last admissinon 3pm. Closed 24, 25, 26 Dec &1 Jan.
Admission Adult: £16.75 **Child:** £10.00 under 12s free
P ♿ H

Brambletye House Ruins, Brambletye Lane, Forest Row, East Sussex RH18 5EH
Ruins of a house built in 1631 and destroyed during the civil wars by Cromwellian troops.
Location: Off A22, private road where double white lines end. 2m. from East Grinstead.
Recipient: Mrs Anne Crawford
Telephone: 01342 826646
Contact: Mrs Anne Crawford
Email: annecrawford111@gmail.com
Open: Reasonable times by appointment.

Chantry House, St Mary the Virgin, Hart Street, Henley on Thames, Oxfordshire RG9 2AR
14th-15th Century three storey timber framed building with exposed interior timbering and early leaded glazing.
Location: Adjacent to churchyard on Hart Street. Rail: Henley on Thames 0.3m.
Recipient: PCC of St Mary the Virgin
Telephone: 01491 577340
Contact: Parish Secretary
Email: office.hwr@lineone.net
Website: www.stmaryshenley.org.uk
Open: May-Sept, Suns, 2.00-5.00pm. At other times by prior appointment.
♿

Cobham Hall and Dairy, Cobham, Kent DA12 3BL
Gothic-style dairy in grounds of Cobham Hall, built by James Wyatt c1790.
Location: Adj. to A2, 8m.from M25 jct.2. Rail: Sole Street, Meopham.
Recipient: Cobham Hall Heritage Trust
Telephone: 01474 823371
Contact: Mrs J Brace
Email: enquiries@cobhamhall.com or BraceJ@cobhamhall.com
Open: Specific dates only, site is independent school for girls. Please check website for details.
Admission Adult: £5.50 **Child:** £4.50
P ♿

The Durdans Riding School, Chalk Lane, Epsom and Ewell, Surrey KT18 7AX
An indoor riding school built in 1881, Lord Rosebery bred three Derby winners; Lados, Cicero and St Visto here.
Location: Follow Chalk Lane from Epsom Racecourse, through double doors on left. Rail: Epsom 4m.
Telephone: 07930 915243
Contact: Mr Philip Buckman
Email: philip@psbconsultancy.co.uk
Website: www.thedurdansliverystables.co.uk
Open: By prior appointment.
P ♿ H

Firle Place, Lewes, East Sussex BN8 6LP
A grade I listed mansion the exterior dates mainly from 18th Century, but the western half was built in the early 16th Century, probably by Sir John Gage who was Constable of the Tower in Henry VIII's reign (d. 1557).
Location: 4m. E of Lewes, signposted on A27. Rail: Glynde Station 1m. Bus: Route 125
Recipient: Trustees of the Firle Estate Settlement
Telephone: 01273 858307
Contact: Mr Josh Feakins
Email: josh@firle.com
Website: www.firle.com
Open: Apr, Jun-Sept and May BH, Specific days, 1pm-4.30pm, check website for details
Admission Adult: £8.50 **Child:** £4.00
P ♿

Great Dixter House and Gardens, Northiam, nr. Rye, East Sussex TN31 6PH
Original medieval hall house built c1450 comprising three rooms, the Great Hall, Parlour and Solar.
Location: Off A268 in Northiam. Rail: Rye 7m.
Recipient: Ms O Eller
Telephone: 01797 252878 ext 3
Contact: Mr Perry Rodriguez
Email: office@greatdixter.co.uk
Website: www.greatdixter.co.uk
Open: Mar-Oct, Tues-Sun and BHs, 2pm-5pm. Gardens open from 11am.
Admission Adult: £10 (House and Garden) **Child:** £3.50 (House and Garden)
P ♿

Hall Barn Estate, Beaconsfield, Buckinghamshire HP9 2SG
Garden buildings situated in landscaped garden laid out in 1680s including gothic temple, classical temple and stone obelisk.
Location: 300yds S. of Beaconsfield Church. Rail: Beaconsfield 1½m. Bus: local services to Beaconsfield
Recipient: Hall Barn Trustees Ltd
Telephone: 01494 673 020
Contact: Estate Office
Email: giles.paddison@hallbarnestate.co.uk
Open: By prior appointment or written arrangement with Mr Farncombe, Hall Barn, Windsor End, Beaconsfield, Buckinghamshire HP9 2SG.
P ♿

Hardham Priory, London Road, Hardham, Chichester, West Sussex RH20 1LD
Ruins of an Augustinian monastery founded in the mid-13th Century and dissolved in 1534 with interesting Chapter House ruins.
Location: Rail: Pulborough 2m.
Telephone: 07881 788556
Contact: Mr John Rowell
Email: johnny.g.rowell@gmail.com
Open: Jun, specific dates, 10am to 4pm. Check website for details.
P ♿

The Hermitage, Carshalton House, Carshalton, Surrey SM5 3PS

One of three garden follies in an historic landscape, The Hermitage has a stone façade and is designed in a classical manner.
Location: A232 between Sutton and Croydon, off Pound Street.
Rail: Carshalton. Bus: 27, 157
Recipient: Carshalton Water Tower and Historic Garden Trust
Telephone: 020 8669 1546
Contact: c/o Jean Knight
Email: irvineknight@btinternet.com
Website: www.carshaltonwatertower.co.uk
Open: Apr-Sept, 1st and 3rd Sun of each month, 2.30pm-5pm. Tours available by arrangement. Please see website for details.
Admission Adult: £3.00 (also includes Water Tower entry) **Child:** Free

Temple of Diana, Highclere Castle and Park, Highclere, Newbury, Hampshire RG20 9RN

Early Victorian mansion rebuilt by Sir Charles Barry in 1842, surrounded by 'Capability' Brown parkland.
Location: 5m. S of Newbury off A34.
Rail: Newbury 5m.
Recipient: Executors of the 7th Earl of Carnarvon & Lord Carnarvon
Telephone: 01223 368771
Contact: Mr Alec Tompson
Email: alec.tompson@carterjonas.co.uk
Website: www.highclerecastle.co.uk
Open: View from car on exiting on Castle open days or on foot from permissive footpath. Please see website for details.
Admission Adult: £20 (Castle, Exhibition and Gardens) **Child:** £12.50 (Castle, Exhibition and Gardens)

Homeside, 7 Church Road, Oare, Kent ME13 0QA

Site including historic painted wallpaper dating from 1836 located in the current kitchen.
Telephone: 07977 531952
Contact: Mr Pierre Haincourt
Open: Jul, specific dates. Check website for details

Ightham Mote, Ivy Hatch, Sevenoaks, Kent TN15 0NT

Moated manor house covering nearly 700 years of history from medieval times to 1960s including a Tudor Chapel, Billiards Room and Drawing Room.

Location: 6m. E of Sevenoaks, off A25, 2½m. S of Ightham off A227. Rail: Borough Green and Wrotham 3½m. Bus: 222 ½m., 404 ¾m.
Recipient: The National Trust
Telephone: 01732 810378 exn 100
Contact: Property Manager
Email: ighthammote@nationaltrust.org.uk
Website: www.nationaltrust.org.uk
Open: All year except 24 and 25 Dec, daily, specific times. Estate open all year dawn-dusk.
Admission Adult: £12.00 **Child:** £6.00

Italianate Greenhouse, King George VI Memorial Park, Ramsgate, Kent CT11 8BD

Early 19th Century glasshouse curved in design to maximise heat and light, attached to former East Cliff Lodge outbuilding and stable block courtyards.
Location: Accessed by Montefiore Avenue. Rail: Dumpton Park ½m.
Recipient: Thanet District Council
Telephone: 01843 853839
Contact: Mr Phil Dadds
Email: phil@phildadds.co.uk
Website: www.thanet.gov.uk/pdf/greenhouse_lowres.pdf
Apr-Sept, Mon-Fri, 9am-5pm.
At other times by prior appointment, tel: 01843 853839

Knole, Sevenoaks, Kent TN15 0RP

The largest private house in England and a fine example of late medieval architecture the Cartoon Gallery contains six large copies of Raphael's cartoons.
Location: Off A22 at Sevenoaks High Street. Rail: Sevenoaks 1.5m.
Recipient: The National Trust
Telephone: 01732 462100
Contact: Steven Dedman
The Property Manager
Email: knole@nationaltrust.org.uk
Website: www.nationaltrust.org.uk/knole
Open: House: Mar-Nov; Tues-Sun, 12-4pm. Garden: Apr-Sept; Tues only 11am-4pm. Check website for details
Admission Adult: £11.50 **Child:** £5.75

Painshill Park, Portsmouth Road, Cobham, Surrey KT11 1JE

158 acres of restored, 18th Century landscape garden with follies, a Serpentine lake, ruined Abbey, Turkish Tent and recently restored crystal grotto.

Location: 200m. E. of A245/A307 roundabout. Rail: Cobham 2m. Walton on Thames or Weybridge. Bus: 408, 515 and 515A.
Recipient: Painshill Park Trust Ltd
Telephone: 01932 868113
Contact: Mr Michael Gove
Email: info@painshill.co.uk
Website: www.painshill.co.uk
Open: Mar-Oct: 10.30am-6pm, Nov-Feb: 10.30am-4pm . Closed 25 and 26 Dec. Guided tours by prior appointment at additional cost.
Admission Adult: £7.70 **Child:** £4.20

Provender, Provender Lane, Norton, Faversham, Kent ME13 0ST

A grade II* listed timber framed country house dating from 14th Century, restored using traditional methods of craftsmanship and historic materials.
Location: S off A2 between Faversham and Sittingbourne. Rail: Teynham 2m., Faversham and Sittingbourne.
Recipient: Princess Olga Romanoff
Telephone: 07583 859790-bookings
Contact: Princess Olga Romanoff
Email: olgaromanoff@aol.com
Website: www.provenderhouse.co.uk
May-Oct, tours on 1st and last Sun and first Tues of the month and BHs. Open all year for pre-booked group tours (minimum 15).
Admission Adult: £11.00 **Child:** £9.50

Stowe House, Buckingham, Buckinghamshire MK18 5EH

Mansion built in 1680 and surrounded by important 18th Century gardens and one of the most complete neo-classical estates in Europe.
Location: 3m. NW of Buckingham. Rail: Milton Keynes 15m. Bus: X5
Recipient: The Stowe House Preservation Trust
Telephone: 01280 818002
Contact: Ms Ruth Peters
Email: rpeters@stowe.co.uk
Website: www.stowehouse.org
Open: Throughout the year. Please see website for details or information line tel:01280 818166.
Admission Adult: £5.75 **Child:** free

Coldharbour Mill, Devon

Stowe Landscape Gardens, New Inn Farm, Buckingham, Buckinghamshire MK18 5EQ
Extensive and complex pleasure grounds and park around a country mansion, the park and gardens contain over 30 buildings, many of great architectural importance.
Location: 3m. NW of Buckingham off A422. Rail: Bicester North 9m., Milton Keynes Central 14m. or Aylesbury 20m. Bus: X5, 32, 66 3m.
Recipient: The National Trust
Telephone: 01280 822850
Contact: Property Manager
Email: stowe@nationaltrust.org.uk
Website: www.nationaltrust.org.uk
Open: Parkland: Open daily all year, dawn till dusk. Closed 25 December. See website for details and café and shop opening times
Admission Adult: £11.00 **Child:** £5.50
P & H

Watts Gallery, Down Lane, Compton, Guildford, Surrey GU3 1DH
Gallery and house built 1903-4 to contain the paintings and sculptures of George Frederick Watts.
Location: B3000 from A3, onto Down Lane. Rail: Guildford 2½m. Bus: 46
Recipient: The Watts Gallery
Telephone: 01483 810235
Contact: Ms Perdita Hunt
Email: director@wattsgallery.org.uk
Website: www.wattsgallery.org.uk
Open: Tues-Sun and BHs, 11am-5pm.
Admission Adult: £7.50 **Child:** free
P & H

Westenhanger Castle and Barns, Westenhanger, Kent CT21 4HX
Complex of 14th Century castle and 16th Century barns visited by Queen Elizabeth I. Now mostly ruinous, many features remain including Tudor fireplaces and dovecote tower.
Location: From M20 follow signs for Folkestone racecourse & take horsebox entrance. Rail: Westenhanger ¼m. Bus: Nearest bus stop Newing Green.
Recipient: G Forge Ltd
Telephone: 01227 738451
Contact: Mr Graham Forge
Email: grahamforge@btinternet.com
Website: www.westenhangercastle.co.uk
Open: Group tours and weddings by appointment.
P &

SOUTH WEST

Castle House, Taunton Castle, Castle Green, Taunton, Somerset TA1 4AA
15th Century lodging house, built by the Bishops of Winchester.
Location: Centre of Taunton in Castle Green. Rail: Taunton 1m.
Bus: Coach station adjacent
Recipient: Somerset Building Preservation Trust
Telephone: 01823 337363
Contact: Mr Chris Sidaway
Email: chrismsidaway@btconnect.com
Website: www.castlehousetaunton.org.uk
Open: Please see website for opening details.
& H

Cotehele, St Dominick, Saltash, Cornwall PL12 6TA
Built mainly between 1485-1627 the granite and slate-stone walls contain chambers adorned with tapestries, original furniture and armour.
Location: 1m. W of Calstock by steep footpath. Rail: Calstock 1¼m. Bus: 79
Recipient: The National Trust
Telephone: 01579 351346
Contact: General Manager, National Trust
Email: cotehele@nationaltrust.org.uk
Website: www.nationaltrust.org.uk
Open: House: Mar-Nov, daily, 11am-4.30pm. Garden: daily all year 10am-dusk.
Admission Adult: £10.50 (House, Garden & Mill), £6.50 **Child:** £5.50 (House, Garden & Mill)
P & H

Forde Abbey, Chard, Somerset TA20 4LU
Cistercian monastery founded in 1140 and dissolved in 1539 the monks quarters were converted in 1640 into an Italian style palazzo with plaster ceilings and Mortlake tapestries.
Location: 4m. SE of Chard off B3167. Rail: Crewkerne 7m.
Recipient: Trustees of the Roper Settlement
Telephone: 01460 220231
Contact: Mrs Clay
Email: info@fordeabbey.co.uk
Website: www.fordeabbey.co.uk
Open: Gardens: daily, 10am-4.30pm. House: Apr-Oct, Tues-Fri, Sun and BHs, 12pm-4pm.
Admission Adult: £11.00 **Child:** Free
P &

Manor Farm House, Meare, Glastonbury, Somerset BA6 9SP
14th Century summer residence of The Abbots of Glastonbury, now a farmhouse. The interior has a former open hall with large stone hooded fireplace.
Location: B3151 on E side of church. Rail: Castle Cary 12m. Bus: 668
Recipient: Mr Look
Telephone: 01458 860242
Contact: Mr Robyn Look
Email: robynlook@yahoo.co.uk
Open: Apr, May, Jul, Aug, specific dates, 9am-5pm. Wall paintings by prior appointment. Please see website for details.
P

Mapperton House, Beaminster, Dorset DT8 3NR
Grade I listed manor house, Elizabethan in origin, enlarged in late 1660s including the manor, church, stables, dovecote and outbuildings.
Location: Approach via B3163. Rail: Crewkerne 7m. Dorchester 17m.
Recipient: The Earl & Countess of Sandwich
Telephone: 01308 862645
Contact: Lord Sandwich
Email: office@mapperton.com
Website: www.mapperton.com
Open: House: May, Jul-Aug, Mon-Fri, 2pm-4.30pm. Gardens: Mar-Oct. Contact property or check website for details. Other times by prior appointment.
Admission Adult: £6.00 (Garden), £6.00 (House) **Child:** £3 (Garden, under 18). Free (Garden, under 5).
P & H

Old Duchy Palace, Quay Street, Lostwithiel, Cornwall PL22 0BS
Previously the administrative centre for the Duchy of Cornwall from 1878 it was a Freemasons' temple, becoming redundant in 2008.
Location: On A390 halfway between Liskeard and St Austell, turn left to Quay Street. Rail: Lostwithiel
Recipient: The Prince's Regeneration Trust
Telephone: 0203 262 0560
Contact: Dr Paul Gardner
Email: paul.gardner@princes-regeneration.org
Website: www.princes-regeneration.org/projects/old-d
Open: Ground floor, daily during trading hours, 10am-5pm. Most of the building is accessible apart from the upper second floor.

Powderham Castle, Kenton, Devon EX6 8JQ

Pseudo medieval gothic tower built 1717-1774 in the deer park of Powderham Castle, modelled on the Shrub Hill Belvedere at Windsor.

Location: 6m. SW of Exeter, 4m. miles from M5 jct.30, A379 in Kenton Village. Rail: Starcross station 2m. Bus: 2. Ferry: Exeter to Starcross

Recipient: The Earl of Devon Estate

Telephone: 01626 890243

Contact: The Estate Office

Email: castle@powderham.co.uk

Website: www.powderham.co.uk

Open: March-Oct, Sunday-Friday, 11am-4.30pm. Access to Belvedere Tower (exterior only) by paid admission. Check website or telephone before visiting

Admission Adult: £11.00 (includes guided tour) **Child:** £8.00 (4-16, includes guided tour)

P

Prior Park College, Ralph Allen Drive, Bath, Somerset BA2 5AH

Built in the mid-18th Century the site is part of the additions to adapt the property as a Catholic seminary for Bishop Baines.

Location: S. of Bath near top of Ralph Allen Drive. Rail: Bath Spa. Bus: 2, 4.

Recipient: Governors of Prior Park College

Telephone: 01584 016 040

Contact: Ms G Mead

Email: gmead@thepriorfoundation.com

Website: www.priorpark.co.uk

Open: Jul, specific dates, 10.30am-4pm. Group tours during school holidays, otherwise by prior appointment.

P ♿

The Red House, Painswick Rococo Gardens, Painswick, Gloucestershire GL6 6TH

Principal folly building within landscaped garden, displaying many of the classic attributes of the Rococo period.

Location: On B4073 ½ mile outside Painswick. Rail: Stroud 4m. Bus: 61 ½m.

Recipient: Painswick Rococo Garden Trust

Telephone: 01452 813204

Contact: Mr Paul Moir

Email: info@rococogarden.co.uk

Website: www.rococogarden.org.uk

Open: Jan-Oct, daily, 11am-5pm.

Admission Adult: £7.00 **Child:** £3.30

P ♿

Saltram House, Plympton, Plymouth, Devon PL7 1UH

George II mansion, complete with its original contents and state rooms worked on by Robert Adam, set in a landscaped park.

Location: 3½m. E of Plymouth centre between A38 and A379. Rail: Plymouth 3½m. Bus: 19/A/B, 20-2 or 51 ¾m.

Telephone: 01752 333500

Contact: Carol Murrin

Email: saltram@nationaltrust.org.uk

Website: www.nationaltrust.org.uk

Open: House: Feb-Dec, daily, 11am-4:30pm until 1 Nov, 11am-3.30pm Nov-Feb. Please see website for details. Special events, tours throughout, timed house tickets.

Admission Adult: £11.40 **Child:** £5,80

P ♿ H

Tyntesfield, Wraxall, Bristol BS48 1NX

Large country house built in 1813 the house has survived with almost all its Victorian fittings and still retains much of its original hot-air heating and ventilation system.

Location: On B3128. Rail: Nailsea and Backwell 2m. Bus: frequent services from Bristol

Recipient: The National Trust

Telephone: 01275 461900

Contact: The Property Manager

Email: tyntesfield@nationaltrust.org.uk

Website: www.nationaltrust.org.uk

Open: Please see website

Admission Adult: £15.30 **Child:** £7.70

P ♿ H

The Walronds, 6 Fore Street, Cullompton, Devon EX15 1JL

Built between 1602 and 1605 the site has a panelled hall with a large fireplace with decorated plaster overmantel and a parlour with a decorated plaster ceiling.

Location: Leave M5 Jct. 28 following Cullompton. Rail: Tiverton Parkway 5m. Bus: 1, 1A

Recipient: Cullompton Walronds Preservation Trust

Telephone: 01884 33394

Contact: Colonel Michael Woodcock

Email: michaelwoodcock46@yahoo.com

Website: www.walronds.com

Sept, specific dates, 10am-4pm. Please check website for details.

♿ H

EAST OF ENGLAND

173 High Street, Berkhamsted, Hertfordshire HP4 3HB

13th Century timber framed building, thought to be one of the oldest shops in England.

Location: High Street in Berkhamsted opp. Old Town Hall. Rail: Berkhamsted.

Recipient: Mr B Norman

Email: barrie@landfind.co.uk

Open: By prior appointment, tel: 01442 879996

♿

Bawdsey Manor, Ferry Road, Suffolk IP12 3BH

Enjoying a magnificent position at the mouth of the River Deben, the Estate was bought by the MOD in 1936 to provide facilities for the development of Radar.

Location: B1083 to Melton, Sutton, Bawdsey village, then to Bawdsey Quay.

Recipient: Niels Toettcher

Telephone: 01394 412395

Contact: Mr Niels Toettcher

Email: ann@skola.co.uk

Website: www.bawdseymanor.co.uk

Open: By prior appointment only

Admission Adult: £5.00 **Child:** £5.00 (open days free)

P

Clare Castle, Clare, Suffolk CO10 8HG

Remains of a 13th Century shell-keep, the north bailey contained the earliest foundation of Augustinian friars in England (1090).

Location: S. of Clare, two minutes walk from centre.

Recipient: Suffolk County Council

Telephone: 01284 757088

Contact: Mr David Robertson-Parks Department

Email: clerk@clare-uk.com

Website: www.stedmundsbury.gov.uk

Open: All year during daylight hours.

♿

Glasshouse, Hoveton Hall, Hoveton, Norwich NR12 8RJ

Glasshouse dated to early 19th Century it is constructed of predominately cast iron with brick wall and bothies behind and set amongst 15 acres of informal gardens.

Location: 150m NW of Hoveton Hall, 9m. N of Norwich on A1151. Rail: Hoveton, Wroxham 1m.

Recipient: A E Buxton

Telephone: 01603 782798

Contact: Mr A E Buxton

Email: andrew-buxton@tiscali.co.uk

Website: www.hovetonhallestates.co.uk

Open: May-June, Mon-Fri, 10.30am-4.30pm.

Admission: £7.50 for access to the gardens which include the glasshouse.

P

Holkham Hall Glasshouse, Norfolk

Holkham Hall Vinery, Wells-next-the-Sea, Norfolk NR23 1AB
Range of six late 19th Century Glasshouses repaired to include early and late peach houses, a muscat house, fig house and early and late vineries.
Location: B1105 from A149 Fakenham to Wells. Rail: King's Lynn. Bus: Hunstanton to Cromer.
Recipient: Coke Estates Ltd
Telephone: 01328 710227
Contact: Ms Celia Deeley
Email: enquiries@holkham.co.uk
Website: www.holkham.co.uk
Open: Mar-Oct, 10am-5pm, other times by appointment.
Admission Adult: £2.50 **Child:** £1.00 (age 5-16)

Knebworth House, Knebworth, nr. Stevenage, Hertfordshire SG1 2AX
Originally a Tudor manor house, rebuilt in gothic style in 1843 containing rooms in various styles including a Jacobean banqueting hall. Set in 250 acres of parkland with 28 acres of formal gardens.
Location: Jct7 A1(M) at Stevenage South. Rail: Stevenage.
Recipient: Knebworth House Education & Preservation Trust
Telephone: 01438 812661
Contact: Mrs Julie Loughlin
Email: info@knebworthhouse.com
Website: www.knebworthhouse.com
Open: Mar-Sept, please see website for details
Admission Adult: £12.50 (£11.50 group)
Child: £12.00 (£11.00 group)

Mettingham Castle House, Mettingham, Bungay, Suffolk NR35 1TH
Ruins of a moated fortified manor house and a late 14th-15th Century monastic college primarily including the flint gatehouse, barbican and curtain wall.
Location: 1m. SW of Bungay, follow sign to Annis Hill, then Lodge Road. Rail: Beccles Suffolk 6m.
Recipient: Jenny Gormley
Telephone: 01986 895669
Contact: Ms Jenny Gormley
Email: jenny.gormley@virgin.net
Open: Specific dates by appointment only.

Moggerhanger House, Moggerhanger, Bedfordshire MK44 3RW
Country House including 18th Century core, refurbished by Sir John Soane -1790 -99 and set in 33 acres of parkland.
Location: Signposted from A603 in Moggerhanger. Rail: Sandy 3m. Bus: M3
Recipient: Harvest Vision Ltd
Telephone: 01767 641007
Contact: Mrs Tracy Purser
Email: enquiries@moggerhangerpark.com
Website: www.moggerhangerpark.com
Open: Jun-Sept, daily, guided tours Sun and Wed at 2.30pm. Grounds open throughout year. 10am-5pm. Check website for specific dates.
Admission Adult: £5.00 **Child:** Free

Old Warden Park, Old Warden, nr. Biggleswade, Bedfordshire SG18 9EA
Built in 1872 in a Jacobean design it still houses original Gillow furniture, oak panelling, carvings and a collection of 18th Century paintings.
Location: 2m. off A1 at Biggleswade, follow Shuttleworth College and Old Warden. Rail: Biggleswade 4m.
Recipient: The Shuttleworth Trust
Telephone: 01767 627972
Contact: Ms Amanda Done
Email: amanda.Done@shuttleworth.org
Website: www.shuttleworth.org
Open: Exterior of building May-Sept, daily, 9am-5pm. Access to the interior by appointment. Call prior to visiting tel: 01767 627972

Queen Annes Summerhouse, Old Warden Bedfordshire SG18 9HQ
Standing on the Shuttleworth estate, the building is a foursquare folly of the early 18th Century featuring exceptionally fine brickwork of the period.
Location: 4m. W of Biggleswade. Access by foot from Old Warden village. Rail: Biggleswade 4m.
Recipient: The Landmark Trust
Telephone: 01628 825920
Contact: Ms Victoria O'Keefe
Email: vokeefe@landmarktrust.org.uk
Website: www.landmarktrust.org.uk
Open: Exterior: All reasonable times. Interior: specific dates and times by prior appointment.

The Shell House, Hatfield Forest, Takeley, Nr Bishops Stortford, Essex CM22 6NE
Rare garden house/folly, c1759, constructed of knapped and boulder flints, shells, glass fragments and brickwork with a low pitched pantile pediment gabled roof.
Location: Signposted from B1256. Rail: Stanstead Airport 3m. Bus: 307 ½m.
Recipient: The National Trust
Telephone: 01279 870678
Contact: Mrs Nicky Daniel
Email: hatfieldforest@nationaltrust.org.uk
Website: www.nationaltrust.org.uk
Open: Sats and Suns, 10am-4.30pm.

Somerleyton Hall and Gardens, Somerleyton, Lowestoft, Suffolk NR32 5QQ
Early Victorian stately home, built in Anglo-Italian style containing fine furnishings, paintings, ornate carved stonework. Set in twelve acres of historic gardens.
Location: B1074 5m NW of Lowestoft. Rail: Somerleyton
Recipient: The Rt Hon Lord Somerleyton GCVO
Telephone: 01502 730213
Contact: Ms Clare Durrant
Email: clare@somerleyton.co.uk
Website: www.somerleyton.co.uk
Open: Apr – Sept, Tues, Thurs & Sun, 10am-5pm plus Weds from 15 Jul-9 Sept. Hall tours are available 11.30am-3.30pm.
Admission Adult: £10.95 (Hall & Gardens
Child: £5.95 (Hall & Gardens)

South Elmham Hall, St. Cross, Harleston, Norfolk IP20 0PY
Ruined gatehouse, possibly 14th Century situated on a designated walk to adjacent ruined minster.
Location: A143 SW of Bungay, signed from B1062 at Homerfield Halesworth
Recipient: John Sanderson
Telephone: 07958793298
Contact: Mr John Sanderson
Email: info@southelmham.co.uk
Website: www.batemansbarn.co.uk
Open: Any reasonable time. Gatehouse is included on tours of South Elmham Hall, May-Sept: Thurs and Suns at 2pm and 3pm.

Arnos Vale Cemetery, Bristol
45 acre burial ground with restored lodges
Telephone: 0117 971 9117
Open: Daily, at least 10am to 4pm

The Tower,
Dilham Hall, Dilham, Norfolk NR28 9PN
Remains of a tower, said to be part of gatehouse dating from 15th Century, the tower stands to almost the original height of two storeys with a parapet above.
Location: A1151 from North Walsham.
Rail: North Walsham 5m.
Recipient: Bindwell Ltd
Telephone: 01692 536777
Contact: Mr Alistair Paterson
Open: By prior appointment.
Ⓗ

EAST MIDLANDS

Belvoir Castle Riding Ring,
Grantham, Leicestershire NG32 1PD
Grade II* listed circular exercise ring for horses constructed of colour washed brick, timber superstructure and slate roof over curved rafters.
Location: Between villages Knipton, Woolsthorpe-by-Belvoir and Redmile.
Recipient: Trustees of Frances, Duchess of Rutland's 2000 Settlement
Telephone: 01904 756301
Contact: Mr A R Harle
Email: andrew.harle@smithsgore.co.uk
Website: www.belvoircastle.com
Open: Apr-Jun, specific dates, exterior viewed when gardens are open. Access at other times by prior appointment only
Admission Adult: £15.00 (Castle and Gardens), £8.00 (Gardens) - charge to view ring included in fee. £2.50 at other times
Child: £8.00 (Castle & Gardens), £5.00 (Gardens) - charge to view ring included. £2.50 at other times.
Ⓟ ♿

Casterne Hall,
Ilam, Ashbourne, Derbyshire DE6 2BA
Manor house rebuilt in 1730, with a classic Georgian front and incorporating a 17th Century and medieval back.
Location: Towards Stanshope take left hand turn signposted 'Casterne'.
Rail: Uttoxeter 13m.
Recipient: Mr Charles Hurt
Telephone: 01335 310 489
Contact: Mr Charles Hurt
Email: mail@casterne.co.uk
Website: www.casterne.co.uk
Open: May-Jul, specific dates, Tours at 3pm weekdays only.
Admission Adult: £6.50 **Child:** Free
Ⓟ ♿

Hardwick Hall, Doe Lea,
Chesterfield, Derbyshire S44 5QJ
Late 16th Century 'prodigy house' designed for Bess of Hardwick containing an outstanding collection of 16th Century furniture, tapestries and needlework.
Location: Just off J29 of M1, 9½m. SE of Chesterfield. Rail: Chesterfield 8m. Bus: Chesterfield train and bus stations.
Recipient: The National Trust
Telephone: 01246 858400 or 858430
Contact: Denise Edwards
Email: hardwickhall@nationaltrust.org.uk
Website: www.nationaltrust.org.uk
Open: Feb-Nov, Wed-Sun and BH Mons, 12pm-4.30pm. Nov-Dec, Wed-Sun, 10.30am-3.30pm. Park, garden, shop and restaurant 9am-6pm all year, closed 25 Dec.
Admission Adult: £12.60 (Hall and Garden) **Child:** £6.30 (Hall and Gardens)
Ⓟ ♿ Ⓗ

King John's Palace Ruins, Kings Clipstone,
Nottinghamshire NG21 9BJ
Three standing walls of 12th Century ruin of King John's Palace; outstanding views overlooking Sherwood Forest.
Location: B6030 from Mansfield on entrance to Old Kings Clipstone.
Recipient: Michelle Bradley
Telephone: 01623 823559
Contact: Ms Michelle Bradley
Email: mabradley@talltalk.net
Website: www.mercian-as.co.uk
Open: Aug, specific dates. At other times by prior appointment.
♿

Melbourne Hall,
Melbourne, Derbyshire DE73 8EN
Small detached hexagonal garden building within Melbourne Hall Gardens.
Location: Off Church Sq. via Church St/ Blackwell Lane. Rail: Derby 7m. Bus: 61
Recipient: Trustees of the Melbourne Trust Fund
Telephone: 01530 410859
Contact: Mr William Gagie
Email: william.gagie@fishergerman.co.uk
Website: www.melbournehall.com
Open: By appointment only. Please see website for details
Admission Adult: £4.50 **Child:** £3.50
Ⓟ ♿

HEART OF ENGLAND

119-123 Upper Spon Street, Coventry,
West Midlands CV1 3BQ
Late medieval terrace of houses, the site is one of few timber framed structures in Coventry to survive in situ. No.122 restored as a medieval weavers cottage.
Location: Jct.7 from Coventry ring road.
Rail: Coventry 1m. Bus: 6, 6a, 10 and 18.
Recipient: Spon End Building Preservation Trust
Telephone: 024 7625 7117
Contact: Ms Debbie Rowley
Email: info@sebpt.org.uk or deb.be@hotmail.co.uk
Website: www.theweavershouse.org
Open: Apr-Sept, every 2nd wkend, 11am-4pm and specific open days. School and group visits by prior appointment.
♿ Ⓗ

Astley Castle, Astley,
North Warwickshire CV10 7QD
In continuous occupation since the Saxon period, the site includes the moated castle, gateway and curtain walls, lake, church and pleasure gardens.
Location: Nuthurst Lane, then follow parking signs. Rail: Nuneaton.
Recipient: The Landmark Trust
Telephone: 01628 825920
Contact: Ms Victoria O'Keeffe
Email: vokeeffe@landmarktrust.org.uk
Website: www.landmarktrust.org.uk
Open: May, Jun, Sept, specific dates. At other times by appointment only. Access to moated site (exterior) from 10am-4pm on specific dates. Check website for details.
Admission: Free
♿

Baginton Castle Remains, Church Road,
Baginton, Warwickshire CV8 3AR
13th Century castle ruin including buried remains of a Saxon settlement, the ruins of Bagot's Castle and 18th Century gazebo and remains of a WWII tank testing site.
Location: Nr. Jct. with A45, B4115. Follow signs to Baginton. Rail: Coventry 4m. Bus: 529
Recipient: David Hewer, The Custodian
Telephone: 07714 673450 / 07786 438711
Contact: Mr David Hewer
Email: david.hewer@yahoo.co.uk
Website: www.bagotscastle.org.uk
Open: Apr-Oct, weekends including BHs, 12pm-5pm. All year by appointment.
Admission Adult: £4.00 **Child:** £2.00 (Under 5s free)
Ⓟ ♿ Ⓗ

Bayley Lane Medieval Undercroft, 38 and 39 Bayley Lane, Jordan Well, Coventry, West Midlands CV1 5QP
Late medieval stone-vaulted undercroft, originally positioned to the rear of numbers 38 and 39 Bayley Lane. Now under Herbert Art Gallery.
Location: Opp. Coventry Cathedral. Rail: Coventry. Bus: Earl St or Little Park St.
Recipient: Coventry City Council
Telephone: 024 7623 7538
Contact: Mr David Bancroft
Email: david.bancroft@culturecoventry.com
Website: www.theherbert.org
Open: Daily, Mon-Sat, 10am-4pm. Sun 12pm-4pm.
Admission: Free
H

Castle House, Castle Square, Ludlow, Shropshire SY8 1AY
Grade II* listed house within Ludlow Castle, interior includes decorative plaster ceilings and pendants, fireplaces with fireback and imported panelling.
Location: A456 west of Birmingham, A49 from Hereford. Rail: Ludlow 0.4m. Bus: 435, 292, 492.
Recipient: Powys Castle Estate
Telephone: 01938 552554
Contact: Mr Tom Till
Email: info@ludlowcastle.com
Website: www.ludlowcastle.com
Open: Open as part of Ludlow Castle. Closed 25 Dec. Please check website for details.
♿

Chillington Hall, Codsall Wood, nr. Wolverhampton, Staffordshire WV8 1RE
House by Sir John Soane with earlier wing by Francis Smith (1724) with extensive grounds with gardens landscaped by 'Capability' Brown.
Location: A5 via Brewood or M54(J2) via Coven/Brewood. Rail: Codsall. Bus: Brewood or Codsall
Recipient: Mr J W Giffard
Telephone: 01902 850236
Contact: Mr J W Giffard
Email: info@chillingtonhall.co.uk
Website: www.chillingtonhall.co.uk
Open: Apr-Aug, 2pm-4pm, specific days only, check website for details
Admission Adult: £8.00 **Child:** £4.00
P ♿

Hagley Hall, Hagley Lane, Hagley, Worcestershire DY9 9LG
Great Palladian House built in 1760 and situated in Grade I listed parkland including fine interior plasterwork.
Location: Off A456, just outside Stourbridge. Rail: Hagley 1m.
Recipient: The Executors of 11th Viscount Cobham
Telephone: 01562 882 5823
Contact: Lord Cobham
Email: cobham@hagleyhall.com
Website: www.hagleyhall.com
Open: Jan-Mar, Guided Tours 1.30pm-4.30pm (last tour 3.30pm).
Admission Adult: £10.00 **Child:** £3.50 (under 14)
P ♿

Hanbury Hall, School Road, Hanbury, Droitwich, Worcestershire WR9 7EA
Built in 1701, containing painted ceilings, orangery, ice house and Moorish gazebos. The re-created 18th Century garden is surrounded by parkland and has a parterre, fruit garden and bowling green.
Location: Follow brown signs from A38 to B4090. Rail: Droitwich Spa 4m. Bus: 142/4 2½m.
Recipient: National Trust
Telephone: 01527 821214
Contact: General Manager
Email: hanburyhall@nationaltrust.org.uk
Website: www.nationaltrust.org.uk
Open: Jan-Feb and Nov-Dec (except 29 Jan, 24 and 25 Dec), house admission by guided tour. Admission by timed ticket on busy days. Check website for details
Admission Adult: £11.10 (House, Garden & Park), £7.50 (Garden, Park & Winter House), £5.20 (Winter Garden & Park)
P ♿ H

Hopton Castle Tower Keep, Hopton Castle, Craven Arms, Shropshire SY7 0QF
14th Century tower house, in 1644 it was the scene of a civil war siege held by 31 Roundheads, only 3 of whom survived.
Location: B4367 to Hopton Heath. Rail: Hopton Heath 1¼m., Craven Arms 7m.
Recipient: Hopton Castle Preservation Trust
Telephone: 01547 530 696
Contact: Mr P. Marquis
Email: p.m.marquis@bham.ac.uk
Website: www.hoptoncastle.org.uk
Open: Daily during daylight hours.
P

Old Grammar School, 81 Kings Norton Green, Birmingham, West Midlands B38 8RU
Early 15th Century house, probably the priests' house for St Nicholas Church, includes half-timbered first floor with faint remnants of Tudor decoration.
Location: A441 towards Birmingham city centre then turn left into The Green. Rail: Kings Norton. Bus: 18, 45, 49, 84, 145 and 146.
Recipient: Kings Norton PCC
Telephone: 0121 458 3289
Contact: Mrs Judy Ash
Email: info@saintnicolasplace.co.uk
Website: www.saintnicolasplace.co.uk
Open: Tues-Sat 10am to 3pm.
♿ H

Stoneleigh Abbey, Kenilworth, Warwickshire CV8 2LF
16th Century house built on site and incorporating remains of Cistercian Abbey founded in 1155. Also has restored Regency riding stables, 19th Century conservatory and landscaped riverside gardens.
Location: B4115 to Ashow off A452. Rail: Leamington Spa or Warwick Parkway.
Recipient: Stoneleigh Abbey Preservation Trust (1996) Ltd
Telephone: 01926 858535
Contact: The Estate Office
Email: enquire@stoneleighabbey.org
Website: www.stoneleighabbey.org
Open: Weekdays and Suns, 11.30am-2.30pm, check website for details
Admission Adult: £8.50
Child: £3.50 (age 5-15)
P ♿

The Summerhouse, Homme House, Much Marcle, Ledbury, Herefordshire HR8 2NJ
Late 17th Century summerhouse or banqueting house. An important and little altered early example of a gothic garden building.
Location: A449 between Ledbury and Ross on Wye. Rail: Ledbury 6m.
Recipient: Jocelyn D Finnigan
Telephone: 01531 660 419
Contact: Mrs Jocelyn D Finnigan
Email: jocelyn@hommehouse.co.uk
Website: www.hommehouse.co.uk
Open: By prior appointment. No access at weekends.
P H

Main Street Haworth, Yorkshire

Whittington Castle, Castle Street, Whittington, Oswestry, Shropshire SY11 4DF
One of a chain of fortresses along the English and Welsh border, the moated ruin consists of a bridge, gatehouse, towers and water frontage.
Location: 2m. E of Oswestry on A495
Rail: Gobowen 2m. Bus: D70
Recipient: Whittington Castle Preservation Trust
Telephone: 01691 662 500
Contact: Sue Ellis
Email: info@whittingtoncastle.co.uk
Website: www.whittingtoncastle.co.uk
Open: Castle: Mar-Oct, Wed-Sun, 10am-4pm, Nov-Feb, Thurs-Sun, 10am-4pm. Grounds: Free access all year.

P ⅃ H

Wilton Castle, Bridstow, nr. Ross on Wye, Herefordshire HR9 6AD
12th Century castle; a dry moat surrounds restored curtain walls which include three fortified accommodation towers.
Location: Between Wilton Bridge and Wilton roundabout on A40. Rail: Hereford 16m. and Gloucester 16m. Bus: routes 37, 38 and 32.
Recipient: Mr & Mrs A K Parslow
Telephone: 07836 386317 or 01989 565759
Contact: A K Parslow
Email: sue@wiltoncastle.co.uk
Website: www.wiltoncastle.co.uk
Open: Apr-May, specific dates, 12pm-5pm, every Weds and Sun afternoon in Jun, Jul and Aug. Check website for details.
Admission Adult: £5.00 **Child:** £2.00 (Under 11s Free)

P ⅃

YORKSHIRE

Beningbrough Hall, Gallery and Garden, Beningbrough, North Yorkshire YO30 1DD
Country house containing an impressive Baroque interior exhibiting over one hundred 18th Century portraits, fine woodcarving and other ornate decoration, a Victorian laundry and walled garden.
Location: 8m. NW of York, signposted from A19. Rail: York 10m. Bus: 31/A/X.
Recipient: The National Trust
Telephone: 01904 472027
Contact: Property Manager
Email: jane.whitehead@nationaltrust.org.uk
Website: www.nationaltrust.org.uk
Open: House: Feb-Nov, Tues-Sun, 11am-5pm, Jul-Aug, daily, 11am-5pm. Also BHs. Please check website for details.
Admission Adult: £11.00 (House and Grounds) **Child:** £5.50 (House and Grounds)

P ⅃ H

Bramham Park, Wetherby, West Yorkshire LS23 6LR
Early 19th Century Queen Anne house set in an early 18th Century landscape.
Location: 5m. S of Wetherby off A1(M).
Rail: Garforth 8m. Bus: 770
Recipient: Mr G. C. N. Lane Fox
Telephone: 01937 846000
Contact: Estate office
Email: NLF@bramhampark.co.uk
Website: www.bramhampark.co.uk
Open: Weekdays by appointment
Admission Adult: £4.00 **Child:** £2.00 (age 6-16) 5 & under Free

P ⅃

Castle Howard, York, North Yorkshire YO60 7DA
Large stately home dating from the beginning of the 18th Century and designed by Sir John Vanbrugh situated in 10,000 acres of landscaped grounds.
Location: 15m. N of York on A64. Rail: Malton 6m. or York 15m. Bus: Yorkshire Coachline.
Recipient: The Hon. Simon Howard, Castle Howard Estate Ltd
Telephone: 01653 64821
Contact: Visitor Services
Email: house@castlehoward.co.uk
Website: www.castlehoward.co.uk
Open: Mar-Dec, Daily, 11am-4pm (grounds from 10am), Nov-mid Mar, grounds open most days but telephone before visiting. Access to interior of Temple of the Four Winds by prior appointment.
Admission Adult: £15.00 **Child:** £7.50

P ⅃

The Medieval Rectory, Church Farm, Adlingfleet, Goole, East Riding DN14 8JB
A rare example of a medieval secular building, it was built from stones taken from an older church before being converted into an agricultural barn in the 18th Century.
Location: Centre of Adlingfleet village, 50m S of church on main road. Rail: Goole 9m. Bus: 360, 361
Recipient: Mr & Mrs Harding
Telephone: 01724 798575
Contact: Mr & Mrs Harding
Email: hardingsadlingfleet@yahoo.co.uk
Open: By prior appointment.

H

Hovingham Hall, Hovingham, York, North Yorkshire YO62 4LU
A unique c1760 Palladian house entered through an enormous Riding School and includes vaulted ceilings on the ground floor and a collection of pictures and furniture.
Location: 18m. N of York on Malton/Helmsley B1257. Rail: Malton 8m. Bus: Malton to Hovingham
Recipient: Sir William Worsley
Telephone: 01653 628771
Contact: Mrs Joanne Kelsey
Email: office@hovingham.co.uk
Website: www.hovingham.co.uk
Open: Jun, 12.30-4.30pm. Check website for details
Admission Adult: £9.50 **Child:** £4.00

P ⅃

Norton Conyers, Wath, Ripon, North Yorkshire HG4 5EQ
Medieval house with surviving traces of Norman and probably Anglo Saxon construction including family pictures, furniture and costumes.
Location: 4m. N of Ripon. Rail: Thirsk 10m. Bus: occasional weekday services.
Recipient: Sir James Graham Bt.
Telephone: 01765 640333
Contact: Sir James Graham Bt.
Email: norton.conyers@btinternet.com
Open: Garden: Jun-Aug, Mons, Thurs and BH Sun and Mon, 10am-4pm. House: Mainly closed due to major repair work, open to prior appointment only on specific dates.
Admission: Entry to Gardens is free, charge is made on charity open days. At other times, donations are welcome.

P ⅃ H

Ripley Castle, Ripley, Harrogate, North Yorkshire HG3 3AY
Large house with three storey mid 16th Century tower built for Sir William Ingilby.
Location: 4m. N of Harrogate off A61 in Ripley village. Rail: Harrogate 4m. Bus: 36A
Recipient: Sir Thomas Ingilby Bt.
Telephone: 01423 770152
Email: enquiries@ripleycastle.co.uk
Website: www.ripleycastle.co.uk
Open: Castle: Mar, Oct and Nov, weekends, Apr-Sept, daily, by guided tour only. Jan, Feb and Dec, group booked tours only. Gardens and parkland: open throughout the year. Please see website for details.
Admission Adult: £9.00; Gardens: £6.00 **Child:** £5.50 (age 5 -16)

P ⅃

The Ruin, Hackfall, Harrogate, North Yorkshire HG4 3DE

Folly, built c1750, standing in the remains of the 18th Century garden at Hackfall. It is a small pavilion above a steep wooded gorge.

Recipient: The Landmark Trust

Telephone: 01628 825920

Contact: Mrs Victoria O'Keeffe

Email: vokeeffe@landmarktrust.org.uk

Website: www.landmarktrust.org.uk

Open: By appointment only. Visitors will be asked to write to confirm the details of their visit. Access at other times will be round the perimeter of The Ruin to the west. Please see website for details.

P H

Shandy Hall,
Coxwold, North Yorkshire YO61 4AD

Country house, originally built in 1450, now an accredited museum to promote the life and writings of the author Laurence Sterne.

Location: A19 N of York, signposted Coxwold. Rail: Thirsk 7m. Bus: service by Stephensons and Hutchinson's

Recipient: Laurence Sterne Trust

Telephone: 01347 868465

Contact: Mr Patrick Wildgust

Email: shandyhall@dsl.pipex.com

Website: www.laurencesternetrust.org.uk

Open: May-Sept, Weds and Suns, 2.30pm-4.30pm. Wall painting tours available at specific times. Other times by appointment

Admission Adult: £4.50 **Child:** £1.00

P ♿ H

Thorpe Prebend House, High St. Agnesgate, Ripon, North Yorkshire HG4 1QR

Late medieval house with 17th Century alterations restored to form a heritage interpretation centre in 2004.

Location: South of Cathedral precinct. Rail: Thirsk 9m., Harrogate 15m. Bus: 36

Recipient: Chapter of Ripon Cathedral

Telephone: 01765 603462

Contact: Ms Julia Barker

Email: juliabarker@riponcathedral.org.uk

Website: www.riponcathedral.org.uk

Open: April-Oct, daily except Suns, 10.30am- 4pm. Occasionally closed for special events, please telephone before visiting.

Admission Adult: £2.00 **Child:** £1.00

P ♿

Wentworth Castle Gardens and Stainborough Park, Lowe Lane, Stainborough, Barnsley, South Yorkshire S75 3ET

500 acres of parkland and a 60 acre pleasure garden containing 26 listed buildings and monuments. The gardens are home to the National Plant collections of rhododendrons, camellias and magnolias.

Location: 2m. from M1 Jct. 37 in Stainborough, near Barnsley. Rail: Dodworth 1m., Barnsley Interchange 4m. Bus: 23, 24

Recipient: Wentworth Castle and Stainborough Park Heritage Trust

Telephone: 01226 776040

Contact: Ms Claire Herring

Email: heritagetrust@wentworthcastle.org

Website: www.wentworthcastle.org

Open: Parkland: all year, daily, Gardens: Apr-Sept, 10am-5pm, daily, Oct-Mar, check website for details. Closed 25 Dec.

Admission Adult: £6.50 **Child:** £3.25

P ♿

NORTH WEST

Adlington Hall, Mill Lane, Adlington, Macclesfield, Cheshire SK10 4LF

Manor house built around a medieval hunting lodge, the Great Hall houses a 17th Century organ, once played by Handel.

Location: 5m. N of Macclesfield off A523. Rail: Adlington ½m and Wilmslow or Macclesfield 5m.

Recipient: Mrs C J C Legh

Telephone: 01625 829206

Contact: Mrs Camilla J C Legh

Email: camilla@adlingtonhall.com

Website: www.adlingtonhall.com

Open: Private group tours available on request, contact 0191 2413 986.

Admission Adult: £9 (House and Garden), £6 (Garden only) and students £5 (House and Garden), free (Garden only)

P ♿

Brackenhill Tower, Carlisle, Cumbria CA6 5TU

14th Century Pele Tower and 16th Century Jacobean cottage with Victorian extension.

Location: 3m. E of Longtown on minor road. Rail: Carlisle 12m.

Recipient: Lightning Protection Services

Telephone: 01461 800323

Contact: Mr Andrew Ritchie

Email: Andy@lightningconductor.co.uk

Website: www.brackenhilltower.co.uk

Open: By prior appointment

Admission Adult: £5.00 **Child:** £2.50

P ♿ H

Browsholme Hall,
nr. Clitheroe, Lancashire BB7 3DE

Built in 1507, the house contains a collection of oak furniture, portraits and stained glass.

Location: 5m. NW of Clitheroe, 1m. from Bashall Eaves. Rail: Clitheroe 4m.

Recipient: Mr R R Parker

Telephone: 01254 826719

Contact: Mr Robert Parker

Email: robert@browsholme.com

Website: www.browsholme.com

Open: May-Sept, Wed, June-Sept, 1st Sun of the month, Spring and Aug BHs. Gardens and Tearoom 11am-4.30pm. Hall tours from 1pm. Booked parties welcome at other times by appointment. Check website for details.

Admission Adult: £8.00 **Child:** Under 10, Free

P ♿

Dacre Hall, Lanercost, Brampton, Cumbria CA8 2HQ

Part of the cloister of Lanercost Priory founded in 1168, contains unique remnants of 16th Century murals in the 'grotesque' style.

Location: 2m. NE of Brampton. Rail: Brampton 3m. Bus: 685 1½m.

Recipient: Lanercost Hall Committee

Telephone: 01697 741811

Contact: Mr G Sheridan

Email: gerry.sheridan16@btinternet.com

Open: Apr-Oct, Weekends and BHs, 10am-4pm. Check before travelling if Hall is closed for private hire.

P

Elizabeth Gaskell's House, 84 Plymouth Grove, Manchester M13 9LW

Detached regency style villa; the writer Elizabeth Gaskell wrote all but the first of her books whilst living here.

Location: A6 Stockport Road then A5184 Plymouth Grove. Rail: Manchester Piccadilly 1½m. Bus: 192, 197 and 157.

Recipient: Manchester Historic Buildings Trust

Telephone: 01663 744233

Contact: Janet Allan

Email: janetrallan@googlemail.com

Website: www.elizabethgaskellhouse.co.uk

Open: Wed, Thurs, Sun, 11am-5pm.

Admission Adult: £4.95 **Child:** Free

P ♿ H

Elizabeth Gaskell's House, Manchester

Isel Hall, Cockermouth, Cumbria CA13 0QG

An Elizabethan range with a fortified Pele Tower; the interior of hall has Tudor panelling with traces of contemporary painting and contains furniture, paintings and textiles.
Location: Signposted from A595 3½m. from Cockermouth. Rail: Penrith 35m.
Recipient: Miss Mary Burkett
Telephone: 01900 826127
Contact: Mr Esme Lowe
Email: ecelowe@gmail.com
Website: www.visitcumbria.com
Open: Mar-Oct, Mons including BHs, 1:30pm-4:30pm. Groups at other times by prior appointment.
Admission Adult: £6 **Child:** £3
P ♿ H

Lowther Castle, Penrith, Cumbria CA10 2HG

Country house built as a sham castle, now a ruin without roof.
Location: A6 to Askham and Lowther.
Recipient: Lowther Castle
Telephone: 01931 712577
Contact: Mr Ken Gribben
Email: ken.gribben@lowther.co.uk
Open: Open throughout year, check website or contact for dates and times.
Admission Adult: £8 **Child:** Free
P ♿

Lyme Park, Disley, Stockport, Cheshire SK12 2NX

Early 18th Century hunting tower within the 1400 acre medieval deer park of Lyme Park.
Location: Bus: 1,10,11,21,22,30,31,36,38, 71,72,80,81,87,88,100.
Recipient: Mr John Darlington
Telephone: 01663 762023
Contact: National Trust Regional Director
Email: lymepark@nationaltrust.org.uk
Website: www.nationaltrust.org.uk
Open: House and Garden: February-October, daily excpt Weds and Thurs, 11am-5pm, Park: open all year, 8am-6pm.
Admission Adult: £9.50 **Child:** £4.95
P ♿

Rydal Hall Mawson Gardens, Rydal, Ambleside, Cumbria LA22 9LX

Formal Italianate gardens designed in 1911 and set in 34 acres including an informal woodland garden, 17th Century summerhouse, fine herbaceous planting, orchard and apiary.
Location: Just off A591, 2m. N of Ambleside. Rail: Windermere 5m. Bus: 555/599
Recipient: Church of England/Carlisle Diocesan Board of Finance
Telephone: 01539 432050
Contact: Mr Jonathon Green
Email: mail@rydalhall.org
Website: www.rydalhall.org
Open: Daily, dawn-dusk.
P ♿

Samlesbury Hall, Preston New Road, Samlesbury, Preston, Lancashire PR5 0UP

Built in 1325, the hall is a black and white timbered manor house set in extensive grounds.
Location: A677 towards Blackburn, 3m. on left. Rail: Preston 4m. Bus: 59.
Recipient: Samlesbury Hall Trust
Telephone: 01254 812010/01254 812229
Contact: Ms Sharon Jones
Email: enquiries@samlesburyhall.co.uk
Website: www.samlesburyhall.co.uk
Open: Daily except Sat, 11am-4.30pm. Open BHs. For Christmas closing times please contact the Hall.
Admission Adult: £3.00 **Child:** £1.00 (4 to 16 years)
P ♿ H

Scarisbrick Hall, Southport Road, Ormskirk, Lancashire LA40 9RQ

Country house with some of the finest examples of Victorian Gothic architecture and 100 foot tower.
Location: On Southport Road.
Recipient: Scarisbrick Hall Ltd
Telephone: 07764 885003
Contact: Mr Greg Aylmer
Email: greg@scarisbrick-hall.co.uk
Open: Specific dates and times. Check website for details. Tickets booked prior to event.
Admission Adult: £5.00 **Child:** £5.00
P ♿

Staircase House, 30/31 Market Place, Stockport, Cheshire SK1 1ES

Timber framed town house dating from 1460 with early panelled rooms and an important 17th Century caged newel staircase.
Location: Stockport town centre, 5 mins from M60. Rail: Stockport ½m. Bus: 10 mins from bus station
Recipient: Stockport Metropolitan Borough Council
Telephone: 0161 474 2390
Contact: Mr Phil Catling
Email: philip.catling@stockport.gov.uk
Website: www.stockport.gov.uk/ staircasehouse
Open: Daily, Tues-Fri, 1pm-5pm, Sat, 10am-5pm, Sun, 11am-5pm, BHs, 11am-5pm. Closed 25, 26 Dec and 1 Jan
Admission Adult: £4.75 **Child:** Free up to 16
P ♿

NORTH EAST

Bowes Museum, Newgate, Barnard Castle, Durham DL12 8NP

French style chateau, built between 1869-c1885 housing a collection of European fine and decorative arts with a programme of exhibitions and special events.
Location: Close to A66. Rail: Darlington 18m. Bus: No.75 and No.76
Recipient: Bowes Museum
Telephone: 01833 690606
Contact: Mr Richard Welsby
Email: richard.welsby@thebowesmuseum.org.uk
Website: www.thebowesmuseum.org.uk
Open: All year apart from 25, 26 Dec and 1 Jan, 10am- 5pm
Admission Adult: £9.50 (includes donation)
Child: Free to under 16s (as part of family visit)
P ♿

Cockle Park Farm Pele Tower, Morpeth, Northumberland NE61 3EB

Early 16th Century tower house, the tower is thought to have been built c.1520 and in the 19th Century became the centre of the Duke of Portland's experimental farm.
Location: 2m. N of Morpeth follow signs. Rail: Morpeth 3.5m.
Telephone: 01670790227
Contact: Mr David Watson
Email: david.watson1@ncl.ac.uk
Website: www.ncl.ac.uk/afrd/business/ cockle/index.htm
Open: Mar, Apr, May, Aug, specific dates. All visitors to contact Cockle Park Farm tel: 07894 560071 or email prior to visiting.
P ♿

Cragside, Rothbury, Morpeth, Northumberland NE65 7PX

High Victorian mansion with original furniture and fittings including stained glass and earliest wallpapers. Built for Lord Armstrong who installed the world's first hydro-electric lighting.

Location: 13m. SW of Alnwick, follow B6341, entrance 1m. N of Rothbury. Rail: Morpeth 16m. Bus: Very limited service
Recipient: The National Trust
Telephone: 01669 622001
Contact: National Trust, Cragside
Email: john.obrien@nationaltrust.org.uk
Website: www.nationaltrust.org.uk
Open: Please see website
Admission Adult: £16.50 (House, Garden & Woodland) **Child:** £8.30 (House, Garden & Woodland) ages 5-17
P ♿ H

Gibside Chapel, Orangery and Stables, Gibside, nr. Rowlands Gill, Burnopfield, Tyne and Wear NE16 6BG
Palladian chapel completed 1812. Site includes stables and orangery situated south-west of Gibside Hall.
Location: On B6314 between Burnopfield and Rowlands Gill. Rail: Blaydon 4m., Newcastle-upon-Tyne 6m. Bus: 45, 46/A, 611-3 and 621
Recipient: The National Trust
Telephone: 01207 541 820
Contact: Visitor Services Manager
Email: gibside@nationaltrust.org.uk
Website: www.nationaltrust.org.uk
Open: Check website for dates and times.
Admission Adult: £7.95 **Child:** £4.10
P ♿ H

Middridge Grange Farm, Shildon Road, Newton Aycliffe, Darlington DL4 2QE
Dating back to 1578 the interior still has some fine bolection panelled walls with cornices and doors dating from the 17th Century.
Location: Off A6072 on roundabout leading to Redworth Road. Rail: Shildon 1-2m. Bus: 1B
Recipient: Messrs J & E Scott
Telephone: 07984407176
Contact: Mr Edward Scott
Email: fordtw15@btinternet.com
Open: All year, Mon-Fri, 9am-5pm by prior appointment. Visits outside these times to be discussed with owner.
P ♿

Netherwitton Hall, Morpeth, Northumberland NE61 4NW
Mansion house built c1685 access is available to main ground floor rooms and external elevations.
Location: 8m. W of Morpeth, just before entering village. Rail: Morpeth
Recipient: Mr J H T Trevelyan

Telephone: 01670 772 249
Contact: Mr J H T Trevelyan
Email: john@netherwitton.com
Open: Prior appointment at least 24hrs in advance. Tours available on specific dates. Groups at other times by prior arrangement.
Admission Adult: £5.00 **Child:** £1.00
P ♿

Raby Castle, Staindrop, Darlington, Durham DL2 3AH
Medieval castle, built in the 14th Century. Contains collections of art, fine furniture and highly decorated interiors. Also deer park, gardens and carriage collection.
Location: A67 to Barnard Castle. Rail: Darlington 14m. Bus: 75 or 6 1m.
Recipient: Lord Barnard TD
Telephone: 01833 660888/660202
Contact: Ms Clare Owen
Email: admin@rabycastle.com
Website: www.rabycastle.com
Open: Easter Weekend, Sat-Mon, May, Jun and Sept, Sun-Wed, Jul-Aug, Daily except Sat. Castle 1pm-4.30pm. Garden and Park 11am-5pm. Check website for details.
Admission Adult: £10.00 (Castle, Park & Gardens) **Child:** £4.50 age 5-15 (Castle, Park & Gardens)
P ♿

Rock Hall, Rock, Northumberland NE66 3SB
Manor house with parts dating back to 13th Century or early 14th Century set in five acres of grounds.
Location: 5m. N of Alnwick. Rail: Alnmouth 8m.
Recipient: Rock Hall School Charitable Trust
Telephone: 01665 579228
Contact: Rock Settled Estate
Email: carltuer@yahoo.co.uk
Open: Access to the exterior and grounds all year. Access to interior by appointment only.
P ♿

Sallyport Tower, Tower Street, Newcastle upon Tyne NE1 2HY
Tower forming the Lesser Gateway in Newcastle's medieval town wall with Company of Ships' Carpenters' meeting hall above.
Location: Tower Street, Newcastle upon Tyne. Rail and Metro: Newcastle Central Station 1m.
Recipient: Newcastle City Council

Telephone: 0191 2778992
Contact: Ms Donna Alderson
Email: donna.alderson@newcastle.gov.uk
Open: Visits by appointment. Tower open for exhibitions held in the Radcliffe Gallery. Please check website, www.radcliffegallery.co.uk
H

Stephens Hall, Lead Road, Ryton, Tyne & Wear NE40 4JE
Stone manor house built in early 15th Century, interior has arch centred doorways and fragments of contemporary wall paintings.
Location: 8m. W of Gateshead on B6315, south of Greenside Village. Rail: Blaydon
Recipient: Mr B Armstrong
Telephone: 0191 413 6030
Contact: Mr B Armstrong
Email: brian1965@hotmail.com
Open: By prior appointment.
P ♿ H

Molineux Hotel, Birmingham
Restored 1720 house, now Birmingham City Council Archives
Telephone: 01902 555637
Open: Tues, Wed & Thurs, 10am- 4pm (7pm on Weds)

SIGNPOST

RECOMMENDING THE UK'S FINEST HOTELS SINCE 1935

Motoring conditions may have changed since the founder of Signpost first took to the road in 1935, but inspectors' standards are still the same. Inspected annually, Signpost features the UK's Premier hotels who possess that something special – style, comfort, warmth of welcome, cuisine, location – which really make them worth the visit. Here are Signpost's recommendations, by region, of fantastic places to stay while you are visiting Britain's historic sites. A wonderful combination.

www.signpost.co.uk

LONDON

The Mayflower Hotel & Apartment
26-28 Trebovir Road
Earls Court
London SW5 9NJ
Tel: 0207 370 0991

New Linden Hotel
59 Leinster Square
London W2 4PS
Tel: 0207 221 4321

San Domenico House
29-31 Draycott Place
Chelsea
London SW3 2SH
Tel: 0207 581 5757

Searcys Roof Garden Rooms
30 Pavilion Road
London SW1X 0HJ
Tel: 0207 584 4921

Twenty Nevern Square Hotel
20 Nevern Square
London SW5 9PD
Tel: 0207 565 9555

SOUTH EAST

Chase Lodge Hotel
10 Park Road
Hampton Wick
Kingston Upon Thames
Surrey KT1 4AS
Tel: 020 8943 1862

Cottage Lodge Hotel
Sway Road
Brockenhurst
New Forest
Hampshire SO42 7SH
Tel: 01590 622296

Deans Place Hotel
Seaford Road
Alfriston
East Sussex BN26 5TW
Tel: 01323 870248

Drakes Hotel
44 Marine Parade
Brighton
East Sussex BN2 1PE
Tel: 01273 696934

Hotel Una
55-56 Regency Square
Brighton
East Sussex BN1 2FF
Tel: 01273 820464

Mill House Hotel & Restaurant
Station Road
Kingham
Oxfordshire OX7 6UH
Tel: 01608 658188

The Millsteam Hotel
Bosham Lane
Bosham
Chichester
West Sussex PO18 8HL
Tel: 01243 573234

Montagu Arms Hotel
Palace Lane
Beaulieu
Hampshire SO42 7ZL
Tel: 01590 612324

PowderMills Hotel
Powder Mill Lane
Battle
East Sussex TN33 0SP
Tel: 01424 775511

The Priory Bay Hotel
Priory Drive
Seaview
Isle of Wight PO34 5BU
Tel: 01983 613146

The White Horse Hotel
Market Place
Romsey
Hampshire SO51 8ZJ
Tel: 01794 512431

SOUTH WEST

Alexandra Hotel
Pound Street
Lyme Regis
Dorset DT7 3HZ
Tel: 01297 442010

The Berry Head Hotel
Berry Head
Brixham
Devon TQ5 9AJ
Tel: 01803 853225

Bridge House Hotel
Prout Bridge
Beaminster
Dorset DT8 3AY
Tel: 01308 862200

The Cottage Hotel
Hope Cove
Salcombe
Devon TQ7 3HJ
Tel: 01548 561555

The Dart Marina Hotel
Sandquay Road
Dartmouth
Devon TQ6 9PH
Tel: 01803 832580

The Feather's
Market St
Woodstock
Oxfordshire OX20 1SY
Tel: 01993 812 291

Grasmere House Hotel
70 Harnham Road
Salisbury
Wiltshire SP2 8JN
Tel: 01722 338388

Hannafore Point Hotel
Marine Drive
West Looe
Cornwall PL13 2DG
Tel: 01503 263273

Ilsington Country House Hotel
Ilsington Village
Nr Newton Abbot
Devon TQ13 9RR
Tel: 01364 661452

The Inn at Fossebridge
Fossebridge
Cheltenham
Gloucestershire GL54 3JS
Tel: 01285 720721

Langdon Court Country House Hotel
Down Thomas
Plymouth
Devon PL9 0DY
Tel: 01752 862358

The Lord's of The Manor
Upper Slaughter
Gloucestershire GL54 2JD
Tel: 01451 820243

The Lordleaze Hotel
Henderson Drive
Forton Road
Chard
Somerset TA20 2HW
Tel: 01460 61066

The Manor Hotel
Beach Road
West Bexington
Bridport
Dorset DT2 9DF
Tel: 01308 897 660

The Moorings Hotel
Gorey Pier
St Martin
Jersey JE3 6EW
Tel: 01534 853633

Mortons House Hotel
45 East Street
Corfe Castle
Wareham
Dorset BH20 5EE
Tel: 01929 480988

The Pear Tree at Purton
Church End
Purton
Swindon
Wiltshire SN5 4ED
Tel: 01793 772100

Plantation House Hotel & Restaurant
Totnes Road
Ermington
Ivybridge
Devon PL21 9NS
Tel: 01548 831100

Plumber Manor
Sturminster Newton
Dorset DT10 2AF
Tel: 01258 472507

EAST OF ENGLAND

Broom Hall Country Hotel
Richmond Road
Saham Toney
Thetford
Norfolk IP25 7EX
Tel: 01953 882125

Hintlesham Hall Hotel
Hintlesham
Ipswich
Suffolk IP8 3NS
Tel: 01473 652334

The Hoste
The Green
Burnham Market
King's Lynn
Norfolk PE31 8HD
Tel: 01328 738777

Hotel Felix
Whitehouse Lane
Huntingdon Road
Cambridge
Cambridgeshire CB3 0LX
Tel: 01223 277977

Maison Talbooth
Stratford Road
Dedham
Colchester
Essex CO7 6HW
Tel: 01206 322367

milsoms Kesgrave Hall
Hall Road
Kesgrave
Ipswich
Suffolk IP5 2PU
Tel: 01473 333741

The Norfolk Mead Hotel
Church Loke
Coltishall
Norwich
Norfolk NR12 7DN
Tel: 01603 737531

The Pier at Harwich
Hall Road
Kesgrave
Ipswich
Suffolk IP5 2PU
Tel: 01255 241212

The Victoria Inn,
Holkham
Park Road
Holkham
Wells-next-the-Sea
Norfolk NR23 1RG
Tel: 01328 711008

Wentworth Hotel
Wentworth Road
Aldeburgh
Suffolk IP15 5BD
Tel: 01728 452312

EAST MIDLANDS

Barnsdale Lodge Hotel
The Avenue, Rutland
Water
Exton LE15 8AH
Tel: 01572 724678

Biggin Hall Hotel
Biggin by Hartington
Buxton
Derbyshire SK17 0DH
Tel: 01298 84451

The Cavendish Hotel
Church Lane
Baslow
Derbyshire DE45 1SP
Tel: 01246 582311

The Dower House
01526 352 588
Manor Estate
Woodhall Spa
Lincolnshire LN10 6PY
Tel: 01526 352 588

East Bridgford Hill
Kirk Hill
East Bridgford
Nottinghamshire
NG13 8PE
Tel: 01949 20232

Langar Hall
Langar
Nottingham NG13 9HG
Tel: 01949 860559

**Losehill House
Hotel & Spa**
Edale Road
Hope
Hope Valley
Derbyshire S33 6RF
Tel: 01433 621219

The Manners Arms
Croxton Road
Knipton
Vale of Belvoir
Leicestershire NG32 1PE
Tel: 01476 879 222

Rushton Hall
Desborough Road
Rushton
Kettering
Northamptonshire
NN14 1RR
Tel: 01536 713001

**Washingborough Hall
Hotel**
Church Hill
Washingborough
Lincoln LN4 1BE
Tel: 01522 790340

**Whittlebury Hall
Hotel & Spa**
Whittlebury Hall
Whittlebury
NN12 8QH
Tel: 01327 850489

HEART OF ENGLAND

Castle House
Castle Street
Hereford
Herefordshire
HR1 2NW
Tel: 01432 356321

The Chase Hotel
Gloucester Road
Ross-on-Wye
Herefordshie HR9 5LH
Tel: 01989 763161

Cottage in the Wood
Holywell Road
Malvern Wells
Malvern WR14 4LG
Tel: 01684 577459

Eckington Manor
Manor Farm
Manor Road
Eckington
Nr. Pershore
Worcestershire
WR10 3BJ
Tel: 01386 751600

Soulton Hall
Soulton
Wem
Shropshire SY4 5RS
Tel: 01939 232786

YORKSHIRE & THE HUMBER

The Blue Bell Inn
Main Street
Weaverthorpe
YO17 8EX
Tel: 01944 738204

**The Coniston Hotel
& Country Estate**
Coniston Cold
Skipton
North Yorkshire
BD23 4EA
Tel: 01756 748080

**The Feversham Arms
Hotel & Verbena Spa**
8 High Street
Helmsley
York
North Yorkshire
YO62 5AG
Tel: 01439 770766

Lastingham Grange
Country House Hotel
High Street
Lastingham
North Yorkshire
YO62 6TH
Tel: 01751 417345

Sportsmans Arms Hotel
Wath-in-Nidderdale
Near Pateley Bridge
North Yorkshire
HG3 5PP
Tel: 01423 711306

The Traddock
Austwick
Nr Settle
North Yorkshire LA2 8BY
Tel: 01524 251224

NORTH WEST

Aynsome Manor Hotel
Cartmel
Grange-over-Sands
Cumbria LA11 6HH
Tel: 015395 36653

**Borrowdale Gates
Country House Hotel**
Grange-in-Borrowdale
Keswick
Cumbria CA12 5UQ
Tel: 017687 77204

**Gilpin Hotel &
Lake House**
Crook Road
Windermere
Cumbria LA23 3NE
Tel: 015394 88818

Holbeck Ghyll Country
House Hotel
Holbeck Lane
Windermere
Cumbria LA23 1LU
Tel: 015394 32375

**Lovelady Shield
Country House Hotel**
Nenthead Road
Alston
Cumbria CA9 3LF
Tel: 01434 381203

The Pheasant
Bassenthwaite Lake
Cockermouth
Cumbria CA13 9YE
Tel: 017687 76234

NORTH EAST

Waren House Hotel
Waren Mill
Northumberland
NE70 7EE
Tel: 01668 214581

SCOTLAND

Atholl Palace Hotel
Pitlochry
Perthshire
Scotland PH16 5LY
Tel: 01796 472400

**Blackaddie Country
House Hotel**
Blackaddie Road
Sanquhar
Dumfries and Galloway
Scotland DG4 6JJ
Tel: 01659 50270

Coul House Hotel
Contin
By Strathpeffer
Ross-shire
Scotland IV14 9ES
Tel: 01997 421487

Craigadam House
Crocketford
Kirkpatrick Durham,
Castle Douglas
Dumfries and Galloway
Scotland DG7 3HU
Tel: 01556 650233

Eddrachilles Hotel
Badcall Bay
Scourie
The Highlands
Scotland IV27 4TH
Tel: 01971 502080

**The Four Seasons
Hotel**
St Fillans
Perthshire
Scotland PH6 2NF
Tel: 01764 685333

**Roman Camp Country
House & Restaurant**
Main Street
Callander
Perthshire
Scotland FK17 8BG
Tel: 01877 330003

Viewfield House
Portree
Isle of Skye
Scotland IV51 9EU
Tel: 01478 612217

WALES

**Crug-Glas
Country House**
Abereiddy Rd
Solva
Haverfordwest
Pembrokeshire
SA62 6XX
Tel: 01348 831302

**The Falcondale
Hotel & Restaurant**
Falcondale Drive
Lampeter
Ceredigion SA48 7RX
Tel: 01570 422 910

**Ffin y Parc
Country House**
Betws Road
Llanrwst
Conwy LL26 0PT
Tel: 01492 642070

**Lake Vyrnwy
Hotel & Spa**
Lake Vyrnwy
Llanwddyn
Powys SY10 0LY
Tel: 01691 870692

Llys Meddyg
East Street
Newport
Pembrokeshire
SA42 0SY
Tel: 01239 820008

**Miskin Manor Country
Hotel**
Miskin
Nr Cardiff
Rhondda Cynon Taff
CF72 8ND
Tel: 01443 224204

Nanteos Mansion
Rhydyfelin
Aberystwyth
Ceredigion SY23 4LU
Tel: 01970 600522

Palé Hall Hotel
Pale Estate
Llandderfel
Bala
Gwynedd LL23 7PS
Tel: 01678 530285

**Penally Abbey
Country House**
Penally
Pembrokeshire SA70 7PY
Tel: 01834 843033

Trefeddian Hotel
Aberdyfi
Gwynedd LL35 0SB
Tel: 01654 767 213

**Tre-Ysgawen Hall Hotel
& Spa**
Capel Coch
Llangefni
Isle of Anglesey
LL77 7UR
Tel: 01248 750750

Warpool Court Hotel
St Davids
Pembrokeshire
SA62 6BN
Tel: 01437 720300

**Wolfscastle
Country Hotel**
Wolfscastle
Haverfordwest
Pembrokeshire
SA62 5LZ
Tel: 01437 741225

The Norfolk Mead Hotel, Norfolk

Gardens at Sherborne Castle, Dorset

Quick Guides

Plant Sales

Places where you can buy plants,
which may be rare or unusual

Haddon Hall, Derbyshire

Leeds Castle, Kent

Accommodation

Places where you can stay overnight, from grand apartments to cottages or glamping

355

Open All Year

Places or their grounds which are open during the winter season as well

Skipton Castle, North Yorkshire

ENGLAND

Aberglasney Garden, Dyfed

Civil Weddings

Places you can book for your wedding ceremony

Mount Stuart, Isle of Bute

ENGLAND

Capesthorne Hall, Cheshire

Private Hire

Places you can hire for private parties, wedding receptions, corporate functions and events

Beaulieu Palace House, Hampshire
©SAMANTHA COOK PHOTOGRAPHY

ENGLAND

Iscoyd Park, Wrexham

HEART OF ENGLAND

YORKSHIRE & THE HUMBER

NORTH WEST

NORTH EAST

SCOTLAND

WALES

SOUTH WALES

MID WALES

NORTH WALES

NORTHERN IRELAND

Guided Tours

Places that offer informative guided tours

Castle Howard, North Yorkshire

Dogs Welcome

Places where dogs are welcome

Floors Castle, Scottish Borders

ENGLAND

Dogs Welcome

Castle Howard, York

©VISITBRITAIN IMAGE

In the Movies

Places you may recognise from TV or the movies.

Chavenage House, Gloucestershire

Highclere Castle, Hampshire

Special Events

Heritage places that stage special events from festivals and fairs to concerts, fireworks and car rallies. Here we list just some of the larger regular events.

For more, go to www.hudsonsheritage.com/whatson

Arundel Castle, Sussex

JANUARY

2- 28 Feb (Sats & Suns)

Osborne House, Isle of Wight
Tales of the Empress of India

18

Great Dixter House & Gardens, Sussex
Behind the Scenes at Great Dixter

24

Capesthorne Hall, Cheshire
Wedding Fair

25

Great Dixter House & Gardens, Sussex
Getting the Garden Ready study day with Fergus Garrett

29

Leeds Castle, Kent
The Below Stairs Tour - A Servant's Life

30- 6 Feb

Great Dixter House & Gardens, Sussex
Symposium: The Art of Gardening

FEBRUARY

11

Osborne House, Isle of Wight
Conservation in Action: The Durbar Wing (Members only)

13-19

Leeds Castle, Kent
Half term Activities

15

Great Dixter House & Gardens, Sussex
Behind the Scenes at Great Dixter

15-19

Audley End, Essex
Victorian Games Galore!

15-19

Dover Castle, Kent
The Fairytale Castle

15-19

Osborne House, Isle of Wight
Victorian Fun and Games

16- 2 May

Blenheim Palace, Oxfordshire
Celebrating 'Capability' Brown Exhibition

20-21

Chatsworth, Derbyshire
Chatsworth Wedding Fair

20-21

Great Dixter House & Gardens, Sussex
Winter Opening Weekend

22

Great Dixter House & Gardens, Sussex
Succession Planting in the Mixed Border

25

Chiswick House & Gardens, London
Camellia Show

25-26

Dover Castle, Kent
The Great Tower Sleepover

MARCH

2

Capesthorne Hall, Cheshire
Capesthorne's Little Theatre -
Lady Connie & The Suffragettes

9

Great Dixter House & Gardens, Sussex
The Art & Craft of Gardening
(Term 1 starts)

14

Great Dixter House & Gardens, Sussex
Behind the Scenes at Great Dixter

18

Caerhays Castle and Garden, Cornwall
Magnolia Mania Lecture

19- 10 Apr

Burghley House, Lincolnshire
South Gardens Opening

19-20

Great Dixter House & Gardens, Sussex
Winter Opening Weekend

19

Hatfield House, Hertfordshire
Vintage, Antiques & Collectors Market

20

Hatfield House, Hertfordshire
Farmers Market

20

Hampton Court Palace, Surrey
Half Marathon 2016

21

Great Dixter House & Gardens, Sussex
Succession Planting in the Mixed Border

25-28

Audley End, Essex
Easter Adventure Quest

25-28

Blenheim Palace, Oxfordshire
Easter Weekend

25-28

Dover Castle, Kent
Children's Festival

25-28

Holkham Hall, Norfolk
Easter Fun at Holkham

25-28

Osborne House, Isle of Wight
Osborne Easter Fun

26-28

Arundel Castle, Sussex
Normans and Crusaders

28- Easter Mon

Chenies Manor House, Buckinghamshire
Children's egg races, egg spotting, magician, plants for sale

APRIL

2-3

Arundel Castle, Sussex
Life in a Medieval Castle

2-3

Great Dixter House & Gardens, Sussex
Great Dixter Spring Plant Fair

2

Woburn Abbey, Bedfordshire
Spring Gardening Skills

8

Caerhays Castle and Garden, Cornwall
Centurion Rhododendrons Lecture

11

Great Dixter House & Gardens, Sussex
Nursery Propagation Day

16

Hatfield House, Hertfordshire
Vintage, Antiques & Collectors Market

17

Arundel Castle, Sussex
MG Owner's Club Gathering

18

Great Dixter House & Gardens, Sussex
Behind the Scenes at Great Dixter

21-24

Blenheim Palace, Oxfordshire
CADA Antiques Fair

22

Capesthorne Hall, Cheshire
Starlight Walk

24

Beaulieu, Hampshire
Boatjumble

25

Great Dixter House & Gardens, Sussex
Good Planting

29 -2 May

Penshurst Place & Gardens, Kent
Weald of Kent Craft & Design Show

30- 2 May

Blenheim Palace, Oxfordshire
Spring Jousting Tournament

30- 1 May

Capesthorne Hall, Cheshire
Craft, Gift & Food Fair

30- 2 May

Holkham Hall, Norfolk
Pedal Norfolk Cycling Festival

MAY

2

Chenies Manor House, Buckinghamshire
Tulip Festival

8

Arundel Castle, Sussex
British Motorcycle Owners Club, Sussex Branch

13

Caerhays Castle and Garden, Cornwall
Popular Rhododendrons Lecture

13-15

Chatsworth, Derbyshire
Dodson & Horrell Chatsworth
International Horse Trials

14

Woburn Abbey, Bedfordshire
Kitchen Gardening

15

Arundel Castle, Sussex
Healey & Austin Healey Cars

16

Great Dixter House & Gardens, Sussex
Good Planting

21

Holkham Hall, Norfolk
Chamber Music Concert - Angela Hewitt

21-22

Beaulieu, Hampshire
Spring Autojumble

21- 12 Jun

Leeds Castle, Kent
The Chelsea Fringe at Leeds Castle

23

Great Dixter House & Gardens, Sussex
Behind the Scenes at Great Dixter

28-30

Arundel Castle, Sussex
Castle Siege

28-30

Blenheim Palace, Oxfordshire
The Bleheim Palace Food Festival

28-30

Leeds Castle, Kent
The Grand Medieval Joust

29-30

Beaulieu, Hampshire
Truckmania

29-30

Capesthorne Hall, Cheshire
Classic Car Show

Sundays

Bocconoc, Cornwall
Garden Open Days

JUNE

1-30

Leeds Castle, Kent
The Embroiderers' Guild Display

1-7

Penshurst Place & Gardens, Kent
Glorious Gardens Week

2

Arundel Castle, Sussex
Living History Day

5

Holkham Hall, Norfolk
Open Farm Sunday

10

Holkham Hall, Norfolk
Chamber Music Concert - Louis Schwizgebel

13

Great Dixter House & Gardens, Sussex
Meadow Gardening

18-19

Arundel Castle, Sussex
Medieval Tournament

19

Beaulieu, Hampshire
Hot Rod and Custom Drive In Day

20

Great Dixter House & Gardens, Sussex
Behind the Scenes at Great Dixter

23-26 (tbc)

Goodwood House, Sussex
Festival of Speed

24-28

Chatsworth, Derbyshire
Florabundance Flower Festival

25-26

Leeds Castle, Kent
Leeds Castle Triathlon

25-26

Woburn Abbey, Bedfordshire
Woburn Abbey Garden Show 2016

JULY

2-9

Great Dixter House & Gardens, Sussex
Symposium: The Art of Gardening

5-10

Hampton Court Palace, Surrey
Hampton Court Palace Flower Show

9-10

Arundel Castle, Sussex
Norman Knights Tournament

Skipton Castle, Yorkshire

9

Burghley House, Lincolnshire
Battle Proms Concert

9

Leeds Castle, Kent
Classical Concert

10

Arundel Castle, Sussex
Classic Cars Gathering

11

Great Dixter House & Gardens, Sussex
Succession Planting in the Mixed Border

13

Great Dixter House & Gardens, Sussex
The Art & Craft of Gardening
(Term 2 starts)

17

Chenies Manor House, Buckinghamshire
Plant and Garden Fair

18

Great Dixter House & Gardens, Sussex
Behind the Scenes at Great Dixter

24

Capesthorne Hall, Cheshire
Classic Car Show

26-31

Arundel Castle, Sussex
Jousting and Medieval Tournament Week

29-31

Bocconoc, Cornwall
Steam Fair

29-30

Holkham Hall, Norfolk
Diva Opera

AUGUST

2

Arundel Castle, Sussex
Living History Day

3

Holkham Hall, Norfolk
Outdoor Theatre

5-7

Capesthorne Hall, Cheshire
Rewind Festival 2016

10

Holkham Hall, Norfolk
Outdoor Theatre

15

Great Dixter House & Gardens, Sussex
Behind the Scenes at Great Dixter

17

Holkham Hall, Norfolk
Outdoor Theatre

20-21

Arundel Castle, Sussex
Medieval Tournament

21

Beaulieu, Hampshire
Supercar Showdown

24

Holkham Hall, Norfolk
Outdoor Theatre

27-29

Arundel Castle, Sussex
History in Action (Multi-period)

29- BH Mon

Chenies Manor House, Buckinghamshire
Dhalia Festival

31

Holkham Hall, Norfolk
Outdoor Theatre

SEPTEMBER

TBC

Beaulieu, Hampshire
International Autojumble

1-4

Burghley House, Lincolnshire
The Burghley Horse Trials

2-4

Chatsworth, Derbyshire
Chatsworth Country Fair

3-10

Great Dixter House & Gardens, Sussex
Symposium: The Art of Gardening

2nd Wk/d (Fri-Sun)

Penshurst Place & Gardens, Kent
Weald of Kent Craft & Design Show

9-11

Goodwood House, Sussex
Goodwood Revival Meeting

9-11

Leeds Castle, Kent
Leeds Castle Food Festival

11

Chiddingstone Castle, Kent
Country Fair

12

Great Dixter House & Gardens, Sussex
Nursery Propagation Day

17

Great Dixter House & Gardens, Sussex
The Christopher Lloyd Lecture

19

Great Dixter House & Gardens, Sussex
Exotic Gardening

23-25

Chatsworth, Derbyshire
The Chatsworth Festival - Art Out Loud

23

Holkham Hall, Norfolk
Chamber Music Concert - Sarah Jane Lewis,
Gareth Brynmor John and Simon Lepper

24

Capesthorne Hall, Cheshire
Born Survivor (physical endurance challenge)

24-28

Leeds Castle, Kent
Festival of Flowers

25

Arundel Castle, Sussex
Pirates & Smugglers Day

25

Great Dixter House & Gardens, Sussex
Dachshund Fun Show

26

Great Dixter House & Gardens, Sussex
Behind the Scenes at Great Dixter

OCTOBER

1-9

Burghley House, Lincolnshire
Burghley Flower Festival

1-2

Great Dixter House & Gardens, Sussex
Great Dixter Autumn Plant Fair

17

Great Dixter House & Gardens, Sussex
Behind the Scenes at Great Dixter

24

Great Dixter House & Gardens, Sussex
Integrating and Using Bulbs

26-27

Arundel Castle, Sussex
Normans & Crusaders in The Keep

26-27

Chenies Manor House, Buckinghamshire
Spooks and Surprises

NOVEMBER

1

Great Dixter House & Gardens, Sussex
Symposium: The Art of Gardening

9

Great Dixter House & Gardens, Sussex
The Art & Craft of Gardening (Term 3 starts)

14

Great Dixter House & Gardens, Sussex
Behind the Scenes at Great Dixter

DECEMBER

3

Holkham Hall, Norfolk
Chamber Music Concert - Gothic Choir

4

Holkham Hall, Norfolk
Chamber Music Concert - The Navarro
String Quartet

7-9

Holkham Hall, Norfolk
Christmas Candlelight Tours of Holkham Hall

12

Great Dixter House & Gardens, Sussex
Behind the Scenes at Great Dixter

14-16

Holkham Hall, Norfolk
Christmas Candlelight Tours of Holkham Hall

TBC

Chiddingstone Castle, Kent
Christmas Fair

Maps

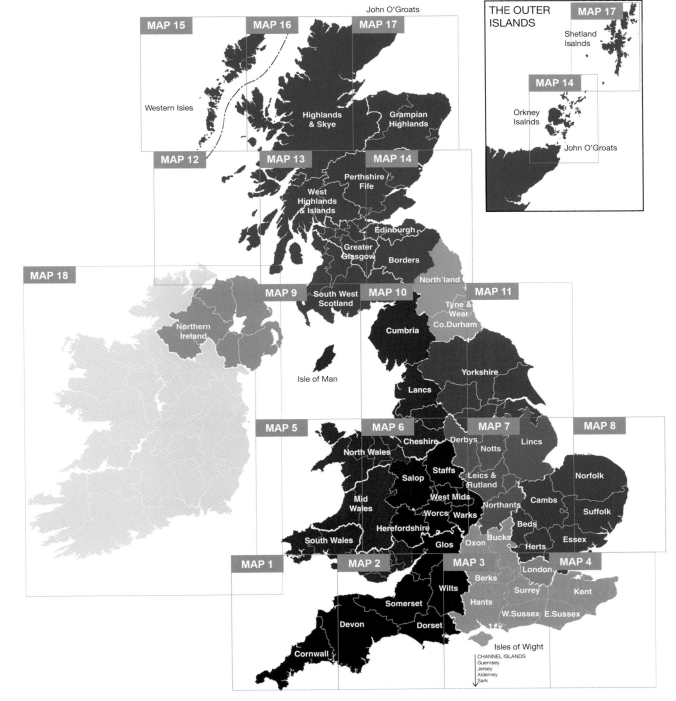

MAP 15

MAP 16

MAP 17

John O'Groats

Western Isles

Highlands & Skye

Grampian Highlands

MAP 12

MAP 13

MAP 14

West Highlands & Islands

Perthshire / Fife

Edinburgh

Greater Glasgow

Borders

MAP 18

MAP 9

South West Scotland

MAP 10

North'land

MAP 11

Tyne & Wear Co.Durham

Northern Ireland

Cumbria

Yorkshire

Isle of Man

Lancs

MAP 5

MAP 6

MAP 7

MAP 8

Cheshire

Derbys

Lincs

North Wales

Notts

Salop

Staffs

Leics & Rutland

Norfolk

Mid Wales

West Mids

Northants

Cambs

Worcs

Warks

Suffolk

Herefordshire

Beds

South Wales

Glos

Oxon

Bucks

Herts

Essex

MAP 1

MAP 2

MAP 3

London

MAP 4

Wilts

Berks

Surrey

Kent

Somerset

Hants

W.Sussex

E.Sussex

Devon

Dorset

Cornwall

Isles of Wight

CHANNEL ISLANDS
Guernsey
Jersey
Alderney
Sark

THE OUTER ISLANDS

MAP 17

Shetland Isalnds

MAP 14

Orkney Isalnds

John O'Groats

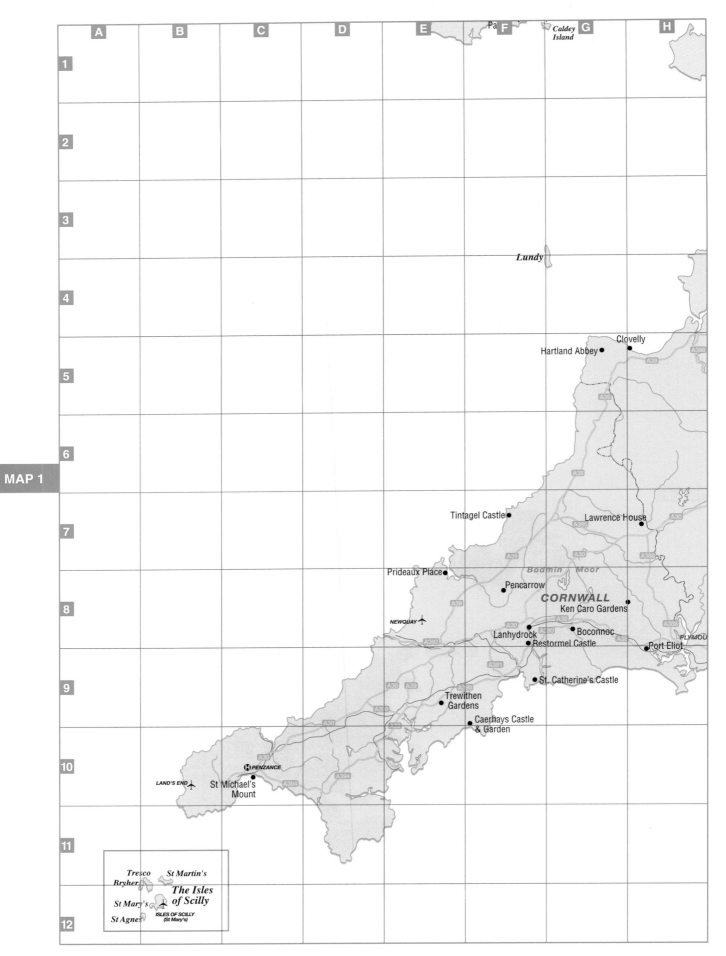

MAP 1

A B C D E F G H

1
2
3
4
5
6
7
8
9
10
11
12

Pa
Caldey Island

Lundy

Clovelly
Hartland Abbey •
A39
A386

A39

Tintagel Castle •
Lawrence House •
A395
A30

Bodmin Moor
A39
A30
A388

Prideaux Place •
Pencarrow •
CORNWALL
Ken Caro Gardens •
NEWQUAY
A392
A30
A38
Lanhydrock •
Boconnoc •
Restormel Castle •
Port Eliot •
PLYMOU
A391
St. Catherine's Castle •

Trewithen Gardens •
A30

Caerhays Castle & Garden •

PENZANCE
A30
LAND'S END
St Michael's Mount
A394

Tresco
Bryher St Martin's
The Isles of Scilly
St Mary's
St Agnes
ISLES OF SCILLY (St Mary's)

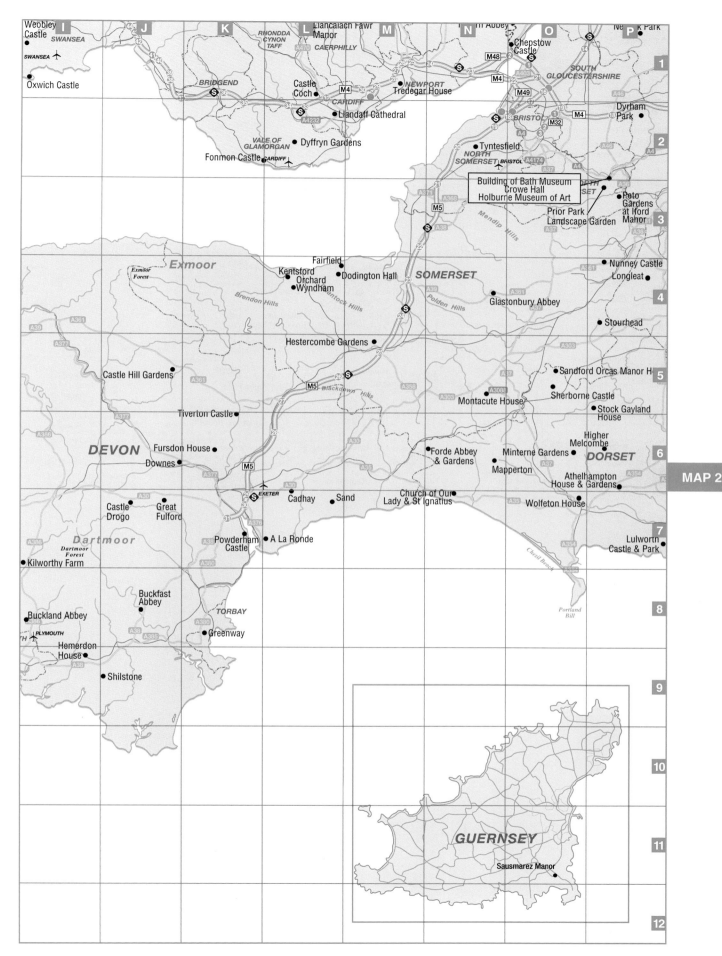

MAP 2

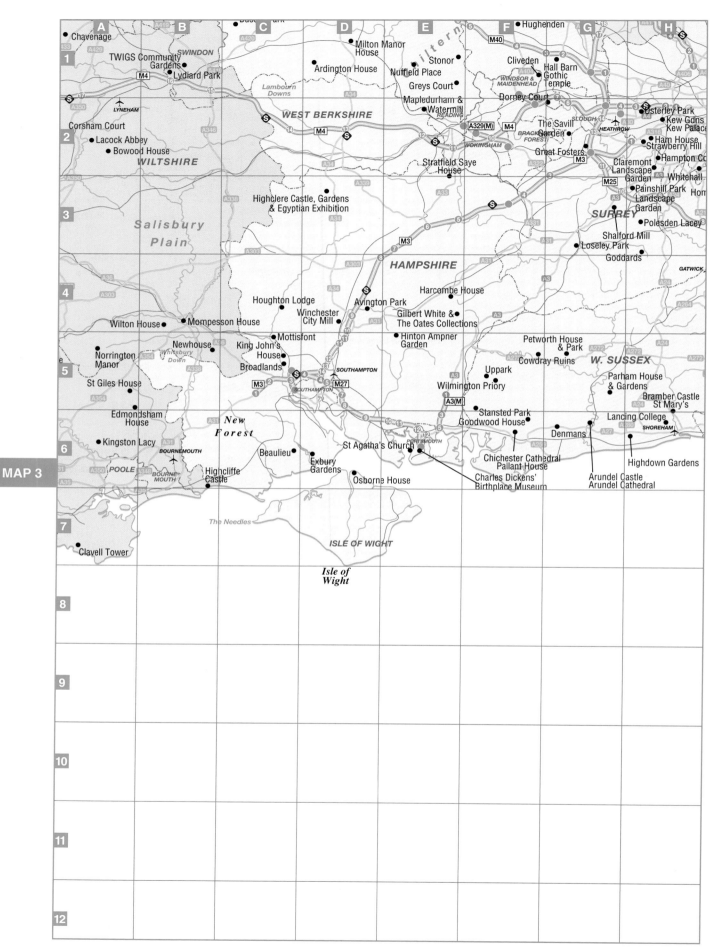

MAP 3

A   B   C   D   E   F   G   H

1 Chavenage
TWIGS Community Gardens
Lydiard Park
SWINDON
Milton Manor House
Ardington House
Lambourn Downs
Stonor
Nuffield Place
Greys Court
Hughenden
Cliveden
Hall Barn
Gothic Temple
WINDSOR & MAIDENHEAD

2 Corsham Court
Lacock Abbey
Bowood House
WILTSHIRE
WEST BERKSHIRE
Mapledurham & Watermill
READING
Dorney Court
Stratfield Saye House
A329(M)
Wokingham
BRACKNELL FOREST
The Savill Garden
Great Fosters
SLOUGH
HEATHROW
Osterley Park
Kew Gdns
Kew Palace
Ham House
Strawberry Hill
Hampton Co
Claremont Landscape Garden
Whitehall
Hom
Painshill Park Landscape Garden
M25
SURREY

3 Salisbury Plain
Highclere Castle, Gardens & Egyptian Exhibition
HAMPSHIRE
M3
Shalford Mill
Loseley Park
Goddards
Polesden Lacey
GATWICK

4 Houghton Lodge
Wilton House
Mompesson House
Winchester City Mill
Avington Park
Harcombe House
Gilbert White & The Oates Collections
Hinton Ampner Garden

5 Norrington Manor
Whitsbury Down
King John's House
Mottisfont
Broadlands
St Giles House
M3
SOUTHAMPTON
M27
Wilmington Priory
A3(M)
Petworth House & Park
Cowdray Ruins
Uppark
W. SUSSEX
Parham House & Gardens
Bramber Castle
St Mary's

6 Edmondsham House
Kingston Lacy
New Forest
BOURNEMOUTH
POOLE
BOURNEMOUTH
Beaulieu
Exbury Gardens
St Agatha's Church
Stansted Park
Goodwood House
Denmans
Chichester Cathedral
Pallant House
Charles Dickens' Birthplace Museum
Lancing College
SHOREHAM
Arundel Castle
Arundel Cathedral
Highdown Gardens

7 Highcliffe Castle
The Needles
Osborne House
ISLE OF WIGHT
Clavell Tower
Isle of Wight

8

9

10

11

12

GREATER

National Maritime Museum
Queen's House
Royal Observatory
LONDON
Eltham Palace
Wernher Collection
at Ranger's House

Carew Manor
Lullingstone Roman Villa
Little Holland
House
of Charles Darwin

Quebec
House
Titsey Place
Emmetts
Garden
Squerryes Court
Chartwell

St John's
Jerusalem
Nurstead Court
Owletts
Cobham Hall
Cobham Wood & Mausoleum

Knole
Riverhill Himalayan Gardens
Ightham Mote

Restoration House
Isle of Sheppey

Boughton Monchelsea Place
Stoneacre
Leeds
Castle

Chart Gunpowder Mills
Mount Ephraim Gardens

North Downs

Belmont

KENT

Powell-Cotton Museum,
Quex House & Gardens
The Grange

Goodnestone
Park Gardens
Walmer Castle
& Gardens

Dover Castle &
Secret Wartime
Tunnels

MEDWAY
THURROCK
SOUTHEND
SOUTHEND
Foulness
Island
Foulness Point

Hever Castle
Sackville College
High
Beeches
Gardens
Standen
Nymans
Borde Hill
Sheffield
Park Garden

Chiddingstone Castle
Penshurst Place
Hammerwood Park

Clinton Lodge Gardens
EAST SUSSEX

Bodiam Castle
Bateman's
1066
Battle of
Hastings

Sissinghurst Castle
Garden

Great Dixter
House &
Gardens

Romney
Marsh
Walland Marsh
Dungeness

CHANNEL
TUNNEL
TERMINAL
LONDON/ASHFORD

Glynde Place
Firle Place
The Royal Pavilion
BRIGHTON
& HOVE
Charleston
Wilmington Priory

MAP 4

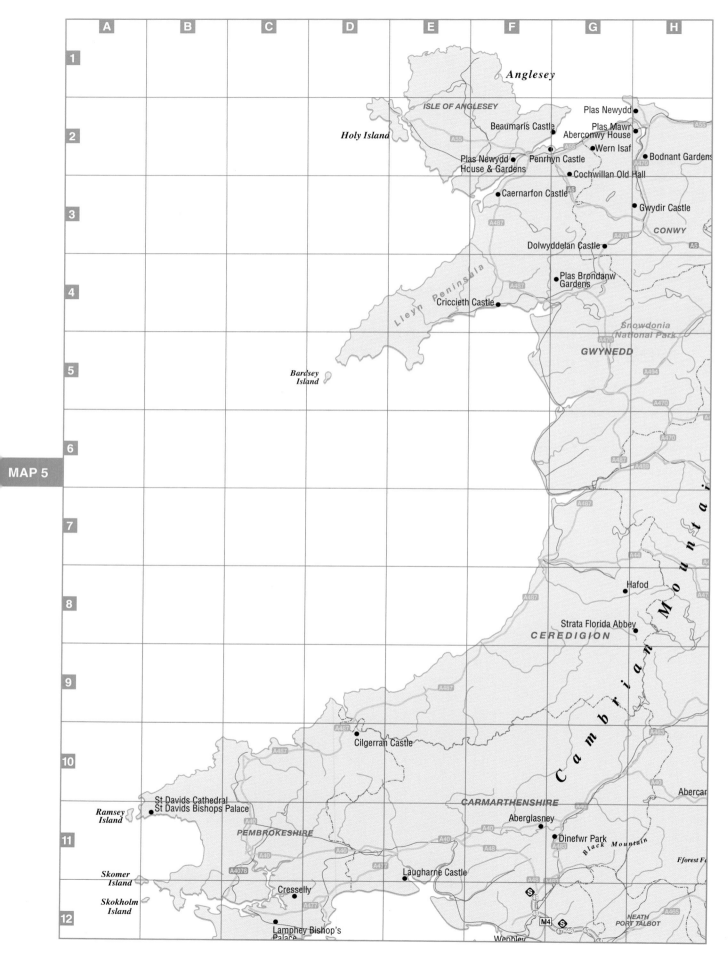

MAP 5

Anglesey

ISLE OF ANGLESEY

Holy Island

Plas Newydd
Beaumaris Castle
Plas Mawr
Aberconwy House
Wern Isaf
Bodnant Gardens
Plas Newydd
House & Gardens
Penrhyn Castle
Cochwillan Old Hall
Caernarfon Castle
Gwydir Castle

CONWY

Dolwyddelan Castle

Plas Brondanw
Gardens

Lleyn Peninsula

Criccieth Castle

Snowdonia
National Park

GWYNEDD

Bardsey
Island

Hafod

Strata Florida Abbey

CEREDIGION

Cambrian Mountains

Cilgerran Castle

CARMARTHENSHIRE

Abercar

St Davids Cathedral
St Davids Bishops Palace

Ramsey
Island

Aberglasney

PEMBROKESHIRE

Dinefwr Park

Black Mountain

Fforest F

Skomer
Island

Laugharne Castle

Cresselly

Skokholm
Island

M4

NEATH
PORT TALBOT

Lamphey Bishop's
Palace

Weobley

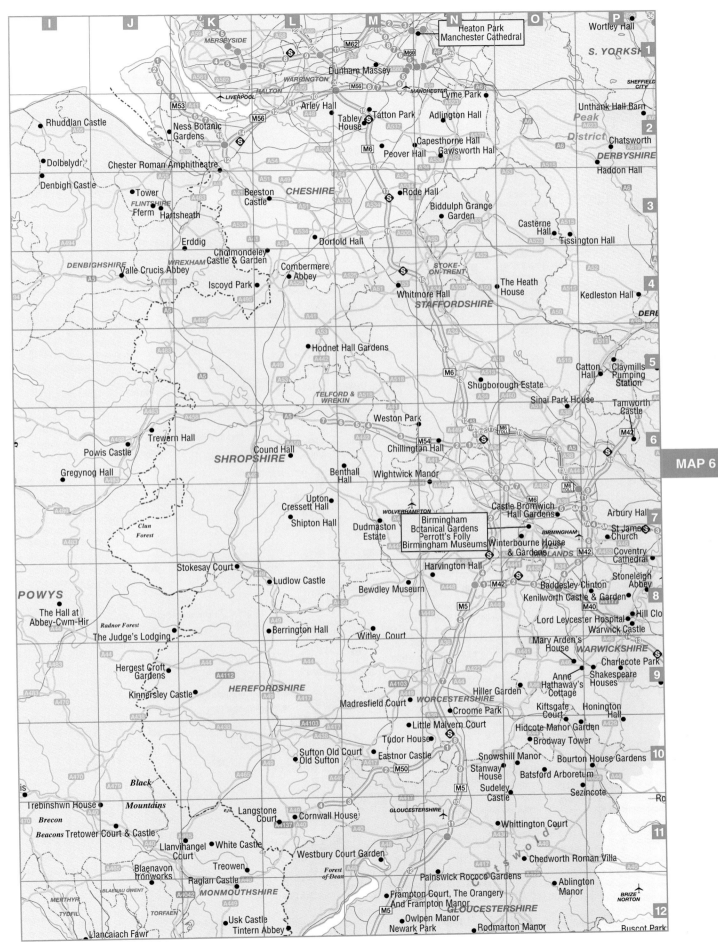

MAP 6

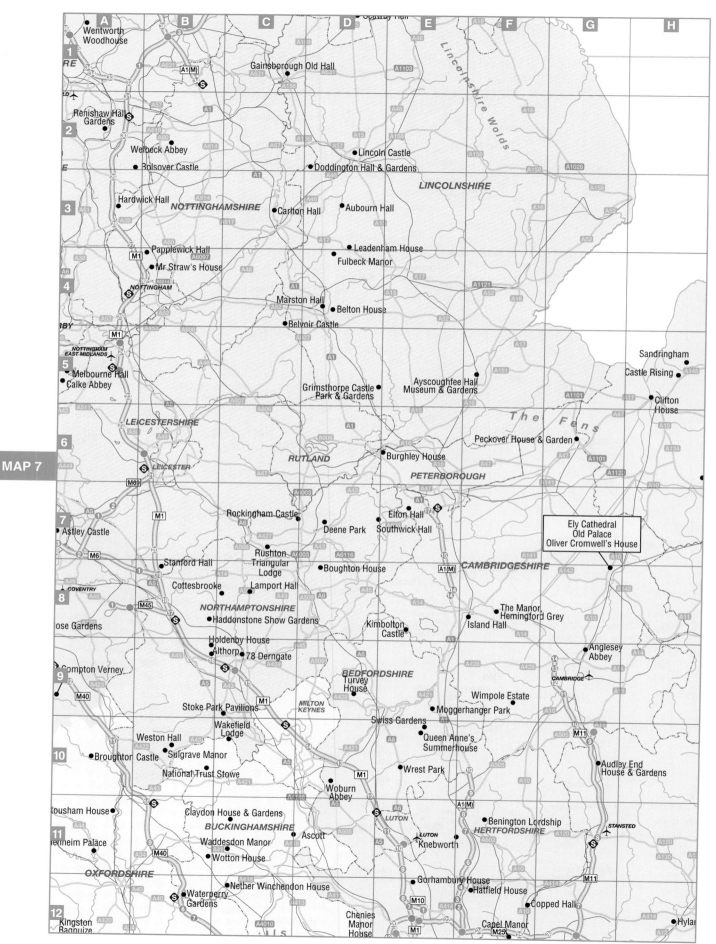

MAP 7

A B C D E F G H

Wentworth Woodhouse
Gainsborough Old Hall
Lincolnshire Wolds
Renishaw Hall Gardens
Welbeck Abbey
Lincoln Castle
Bolsover Castle
Doddington Hall & Gardens
LINCOLNSHIRE
Hardwick Hall
NOTTINGHAMSHIRE
Carlton Hall
Aubourn Hall
Papplewick Hall
Leadenham House
Mr Straw's House
Fulbeck Manor
NOTTINGHAM
Marston Hall
Belton House
Belvoir Castle
NOTTINGHAM EAST MIDLANDS
Sandringham
Melbourne Hall
Castle Rising
Calke Abbey
Clifton House
Grimsthorpe Castle Park & Gardens
Ayscoughfee Hall Museum & Gardens
LEICESTERSHIRE
The Fens
Peckover House & Garden
LEICESTER
RUTLAND
Burghley House
PETERBOROUGH
Rockingham Castle
Elton Hall
Ely Cathedral Old Palace Oliver Cromwell's House
Astley Castle
Deene Park
Southwick Hall
CAMBRIDGESHIRE
Rushton Triangular Lodge
Boughton House
Stanford Hall
Cottesbrooke
Lamport Hall
The Manor, Hemingford Grey
COVENTRY
NORTHAMPTONSHIRE
Haddonstone Show Gardens
Kimbolton Castle
Island Hall
ose Gardens
Holdenby House
Anglesey Abbey
Althorp
78 Derngate
Compton Verney
CAMBRIDGE
BEDFORDSHIRE
Turvey House
Wimpole Estate
Stoke Park Pavilions
Moggerhanger Park
MILTON KEYNES
Swiss Gardens
Wakefield Lodge
Weston Hall
Queen Anne's Summerhouse
Broughton Castle
Sulgrave Manor
Audley End House & Gardens
National Trust Stowe
Wrest Park
ousham House
Woburn Abbey
Claydon House & Gardens
BUCKINGHAMSHIRE
Ascott
Benington Lordship
STANSTED
enheim Palace
Waddesdon Manor
LUTON
HERTFORDSHIRE
Wotton House
Knebworth
OXFORDSHIRE
Nether Winchendon House
Gorhambury House
Copped Hall
Waterperry Gardens
Hatfield House
Kingston Bagpuize
Chenies Manor House
Capel Manor
Hyla

378
Register for news and special offers at www.hudsonsheritage.com

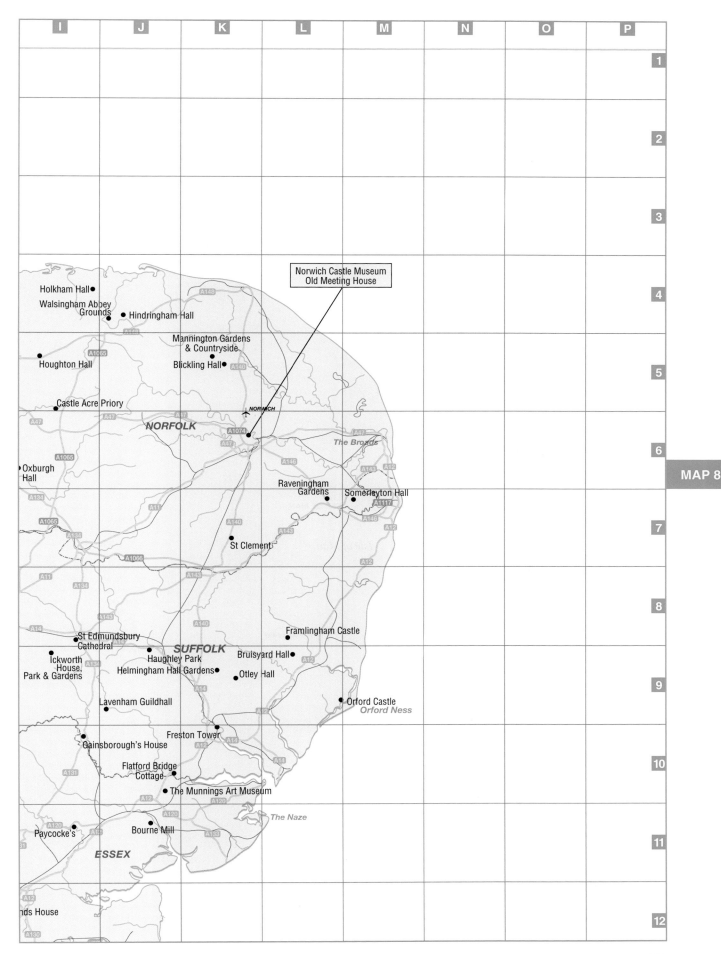

Norwich Castle Museum
Old Meeting House

Holkham Hall

Walsingham Abbey
Grounds

Hindringham Hall

Mannington Gardens
& Countryside

Houghton Hall

Blickling Hall

Castle Acre Priory

NORWICH

NORFOLK

The Broads

Oxburgh
Hall

Raveningham
Gardens

Somerleyton Hall

St Clement

Framlingham Castle

St Edmundsbury
Cathedral

SUFFOLK

Bruisyard Hall

Ickworth
House,
Park & Gardens

Haughley Park

Helmingham Hall Gardens

Otley Hall

Lavenham Guildhall

Orford Castle

Orford Ness

Freston Tower

Gainsborough's House

Flatford Bridge
Cottage

The Munnings Art Museum

The Naze

Paycocke's

Bourne Mill

ESSEX

nds House

MAP 8

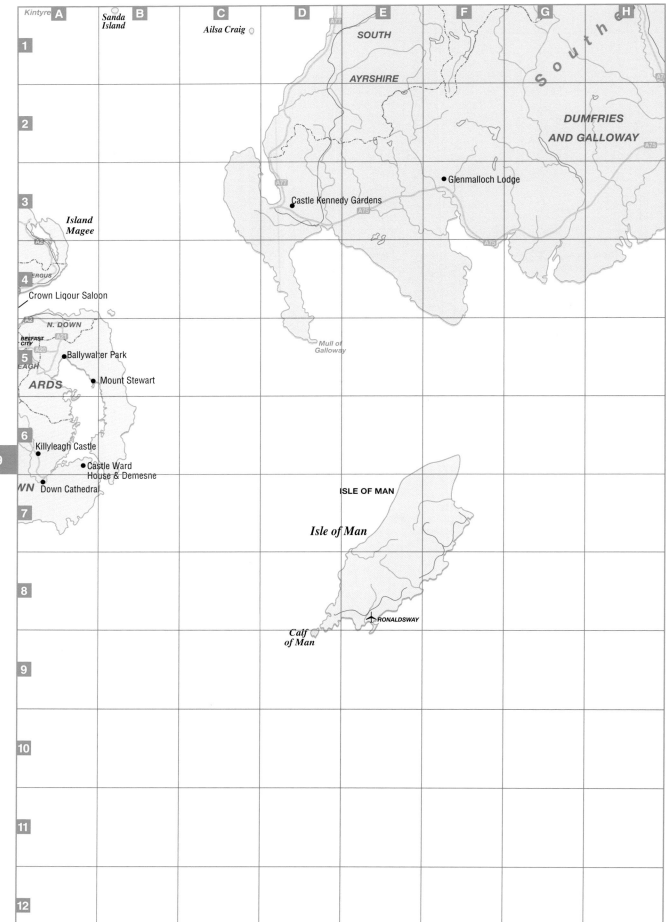

MAP 9

	A	B	C	D	E	F	G	H

Kintyre

Sanda Island

Ailsa Craig

SOUTH

AYRSHIRE

S o u t h

DUMFRIES

AND GALLOWAY

Glenmalloch Lodge

Island Magee

Castle Kennedy Gardens

Crown Liqour Saloon

N. DOWN

BELFAST CITY

Ballywalter Park

EAGH

ARDS

Mount Stewart

Killyleagh Castle

Castle Ward House & Demesne

Down Cathedral

Mull of Galloway

ISLE OF MAN

Isle of Man

RONALDSWAY

Calf of Man

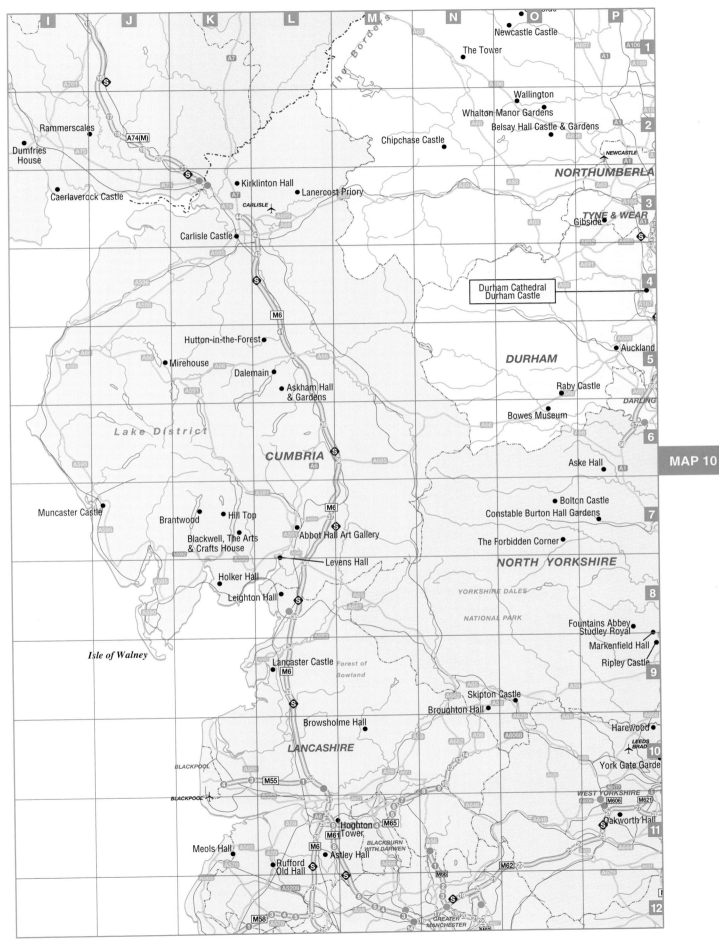

MAP 10

Isle of Walney

Lake District

CUMBRIA

NORTHUMBERLA

TYNE & WEAR

DURHAM

NORTH YORKSHIRE

YORKSHIRE DALES

NATIONAL PARK

LANCASHIRE

Forest of Bowland

BLACKPOOL

BLACKBURN WITH DARWEN

GREATER MANCHESTER

WEST YORKSHIRE

Newcastle Castle
The Tower
Wallington
Whalton Manor Gardens
Belsay Hall Castle & Gardens
NEWCASTLE
Chipchase Castle
Gibside
Durham Cathedral
Durham Castle
Auckland
Raby Castle
Bowes Museum
DARLING
Aske Hall
Bolton Castle
Constable Burton Hall Gardens
The Forbidden Corner
Fountains Abbey
Studley Royal
Markenfield Hall
Ripley Castle
Harewood
LEEDS BRAD
York Gate Garde
Oakworth Hall
Skipton Castle
Broughton Hall
Browsholme Hall
Lancaster Castle
Hoghton Tower
Astley Hall
Rufford Old Hall
Meols Hall
Levens Hall
Blackwell, The Arts & Crafts House
Holker Hall
Leighton Hall
Abbot Hall Art Gallery
Hill Top
Brantwood
Muncaster Castle
Askham Hall & Gardens
Dalemain
Mirehouse
Hutton-in-the-Forest
Carlisle Castle
CARLISLE
Kirklinton Hall
Lanercost Priory
Caerlaverock Castle
Dumfries House
Rammerscales

The Borders

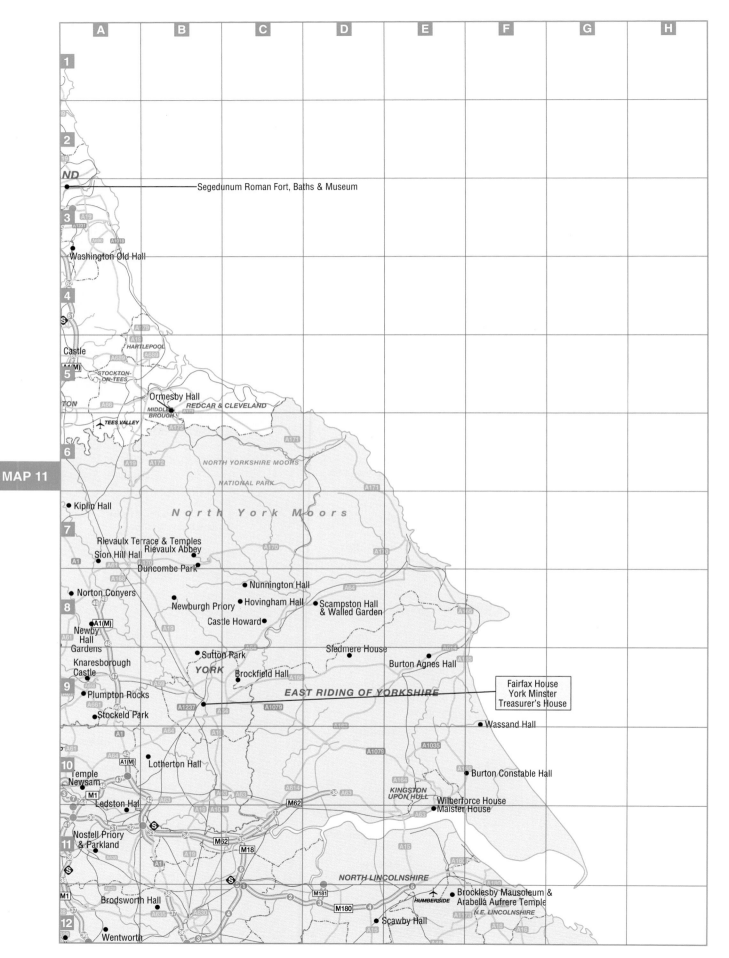

MAP 11

Segedunum Roman Fort, Baths & Museum

Washington Old Hall

HARTLEPOOL

Castle

STOCKTON-ON-TEES

Ormesby Hall

REDCAR & CLEVELAND

MIDDLESBROUGH

TEES VALLEY

NORTH YORKSHIRE MOORS

NATIONAL PARK

North York Moors

Kiplin Hall

Rievaulx Terrace & Temples
Rievaulx Abbey
Sion Hill Hall
Duncombe Park

Nunnington Hall

Norton Conyers

Newburgh Priory   Hovingham Hall

Scampston Hall
& Walled Garden

Newby
Hall
Gardens

Castle Howard

Sutton Park

Sledmere House

Knaresborough
Castle

YORK

Brockfield Hall

Burton Agnes Hall

Plumpton Rocks

EAST RIDING OF YORKSHIRE

Fairfax House
York Minster
Treasurer's House

Stockeld Park

Wassand Hall

Lotherton Hall

Temple
Newsam

Burton Constable Hall

KINGSTON
UPON HULL

Ledston Hall

Wilberforce House
Maister House

Nostell Priory
& Parkland

M62

M18

NORTH LINCOLNSHIRE

Brodsworth Hall

M180

HUMBERSIDE

Brocklesby Mausoleum &
Arabella Aufrere Temple

N.E. LINCOLNSHIRE

Scawby Hall

Wentworth

Register for news and special offers at www.hudsonsheritage.com

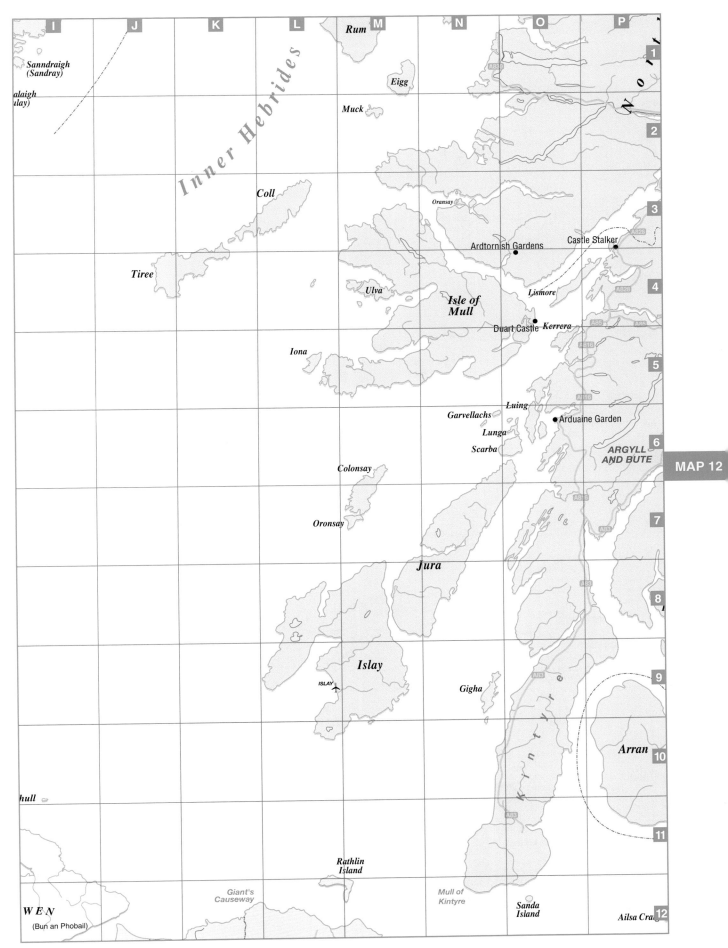

Inner Hebrides

Rum

Eigg

Muck

I J K L M N O P

1

2

Coll

Oransay

Ardtornish Gardens

Castle Stalker

3

Tiree

Ulva

Isle of
Mull

Lismore

4

Duart Castle Kerrera

Iona

5

Luing

Garvellachs

Arduaine Garden

Lunga

Scarba

6

ARGYLL
AND BUTE

MAP 12

Colonsay

7

Oronsay

Jura

8

Islay

9

ISLAY

Gigha

Arran

10

hull

11

Rathlin
Island

Giant's
Causeway

Mull of
Kintyre

Sanda
Island

Ailsa Craig

12

W E N

(Bun an Phobail)

Sanndraigh
(Sandray)

alaigh
lay)

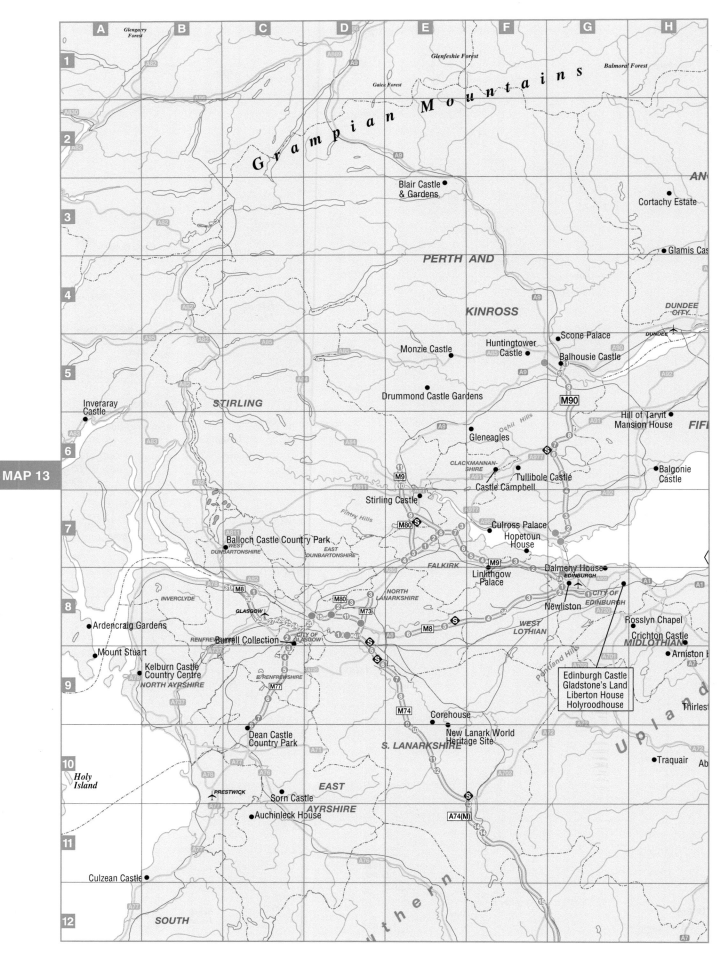

MAP 13

Glengarry Forest

Glenfeshie Forest

Balmoral Forest

Grampian Mountains

Gaick Forest

Blair Castle & Gardens

Cortachy Estate

Glamis Cas

PERTH AND

KINROSS

ANⓇ

DUNDEE CITY

Monzie Castle

Huntingtower Castle

Scone Palace

Balhousie Castle

DUNDEE

Inveraray Castle

STIRLING

Drummond Castle Gardens

M90

Gleneagles

Oschil Hills

Hill of Tarvit Mansion House

FIFI

CLACKMANNAN-SHIRE

Tullibole Castle

Balgonie Castle

M9

Castle Campbell

Stirling Castle

Culross Palace

Balloch Castle Country Park

M80

Hopetoun House

WEST DUNBARTONSHIRE

EAST DUNBARTONSHIRE

FALKIRK

M9

Linlithgow Palace

Dalmeny House

EDINBURGH

Newliston

CITY OF EDINBURGH

INVERCLYDE

NORTH LANARKSHIRE

M80

M73

GLASGOW

M8

WEST LOTHIAN

Rosslyn Chapel

Ardencraig Gardens

Burrell Collection

CITY OF GLASGOW

M8

Crichton Castle

MIDLOTHIAN

Mount Stuart

RENFREWSHIRE

Arniston H

Kelburn Castle Country Centre

E. RENFREWSHIRE

Pentland Hills

Edinburgh Castle
Gladstone's Land
Liberton House
Holyroodhouse

NORTH AYRSHIRE

M77

Thirles

Dean Castle Country Park

Corehouse

M74

Traquair

Ab

Holy Island

New Lanark World Heritage Site

S. LANARKSHIRE

PRESTWICK

EAST AYRSHIRE

Sorn Castle

Auchinleck House

Upland

A74(M)

Culzean Castle

SOUTH

uthern

Register for news and special offers at www.hudsonsheritage.com

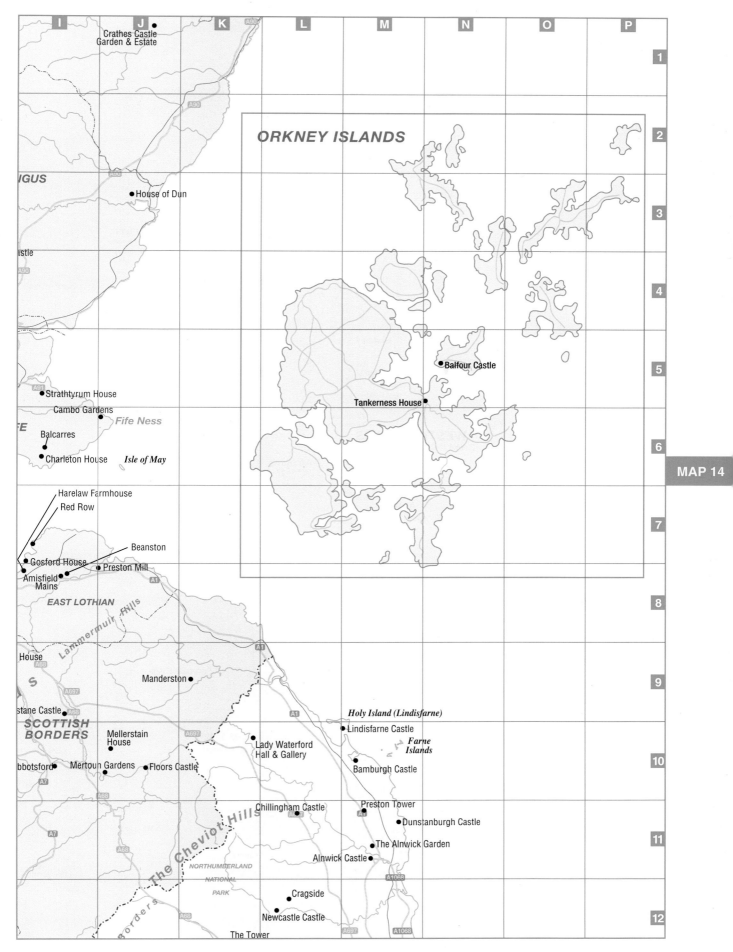

ORKNEY ISLANDS

Crathes Castle Garden & Estate

IGUS

House of Dun

Balfour Castle

Tankerness House

MAP 14

Strathtyrum House

Cambo Gardens

Fife Ness

FE

Balcarres

Charleton House

Isle of May

Harelaw Farmhouse

Red Row

Beanston

Gosford House

Preston Mill

Amisfield Mains

EAST LOTHIAN

Lammermuir Hills

House

Manderston

SCOTTISH BORDERS

Holy Island (Lindisfarne)

Lindisfarne Castle

Farne Islands

Mellerstain House

Lady Waterford Hall & Gallery

Bamburgh Castle

bbotsford

Mertoun Gardens

Floors Castle

Chillingham Castle

Preston Tower

Dunstanburgh Castle

The Alnwick Garden

Alnwick Castle

The Cheviot Hills

NORTHUMBERLAND

NATIONAL PARK

Cragside

Newcastle Castle

The Tower

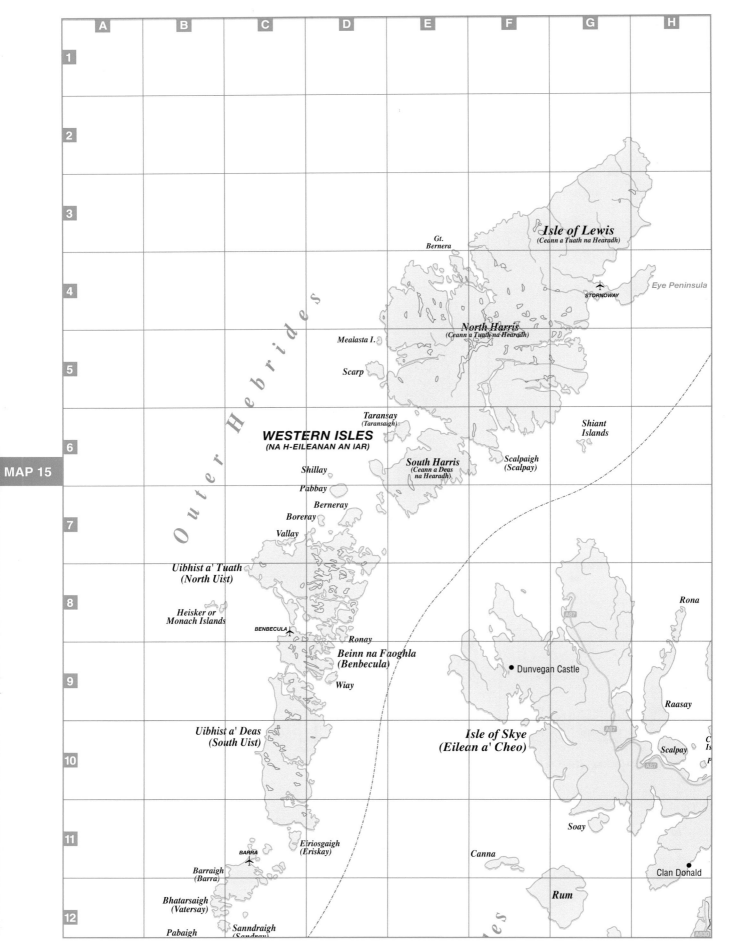

MAP 15

Isle of Lewis
(Ceann a Tuath na Hearadh)

Gt.
Bernera

STORNOWAY

Eye Peninsula

North Harris
(Ceann a Tuath na Hearadh)

Mealasta I.

Scarp

Taransay
(Taransaigh)

WESTERN ISLES
(NA H-EILEANAN AN IAR)

Shiant
Islands

South Harris
(Ceann a Deas
na Hearadh)

Scalpaigh
(Scalpay)

Shillay

Pabbay

Berneray

Boreray

Vallay

Outer Hebrides

Uibhist a' Tuath
(North Uist)

Heisker or
Monach Islands

BENBECULA

Ronay

Beinn na Faoghla
(Benbecula)

Wiay

Rona

Dunvegan Castle

Raasay

Uibhist a' Deas
(South Uist)

Isle of Skye
(Eilean a' Cheo)

Scalpay

C
Is

P

Soay

Eiriosgaigh
(Eriskay)

BARRA

Canna

Clan Donald

Barraigh
(Barra)

Rum

Bhatarsaigh
(Vatersay)

Pabaigh

Sanndraigh
(Sandray)

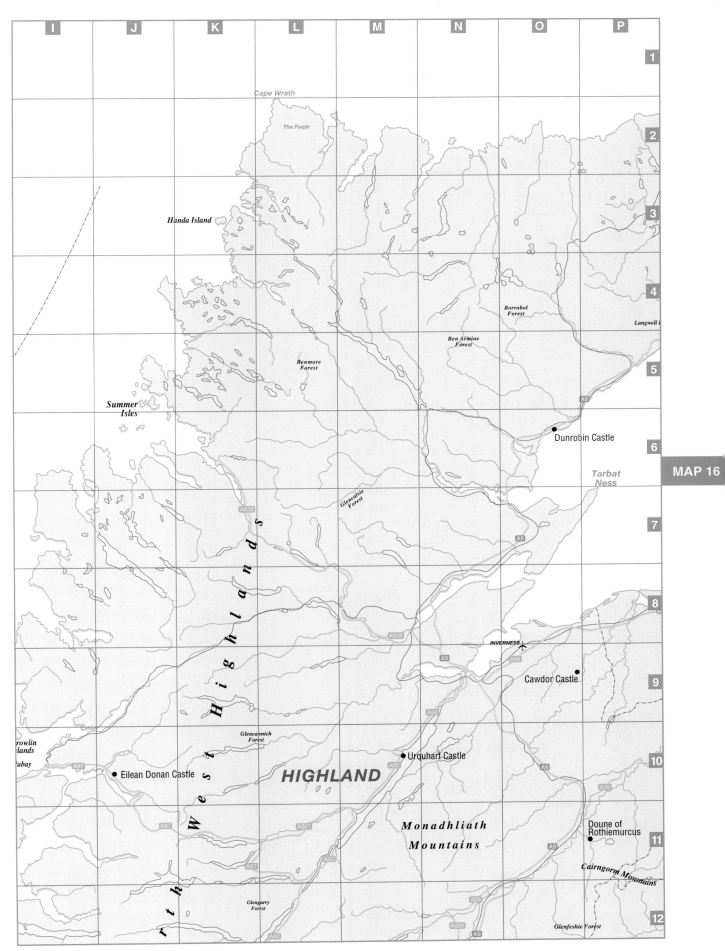

MAP 16

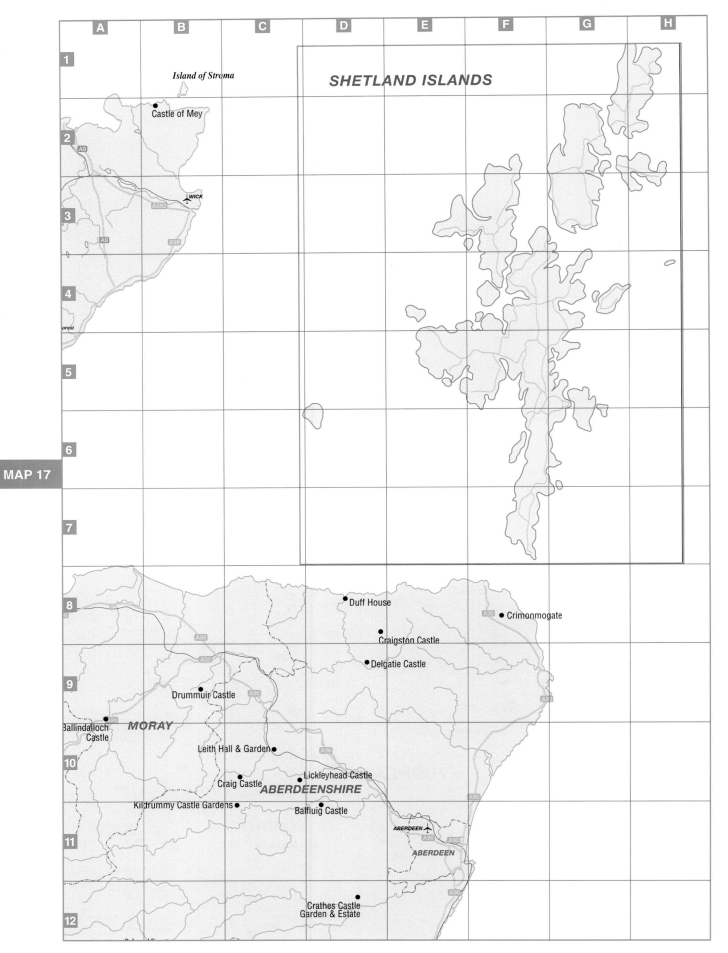

Island of Stroma

Castle of Mey

WICK

SHETLAND ISLANDS

MAP 17

Duff House

Crimonmogate

Craigston Castle

Delgatie Castle

Drummuir Castle

Ballindalloch
Castle

MORAY

Leith Hall & Garden

Lickleyhead Castle

Craig Castle

ABERDEENSHIRE

Kildrummy Castle Gardens

Balfluig Castle

ABERDEEN

ABERDEEN

Crathes Castle
Garden & Estate

388   Register for news and special offers at www.hudsonsheritage.com

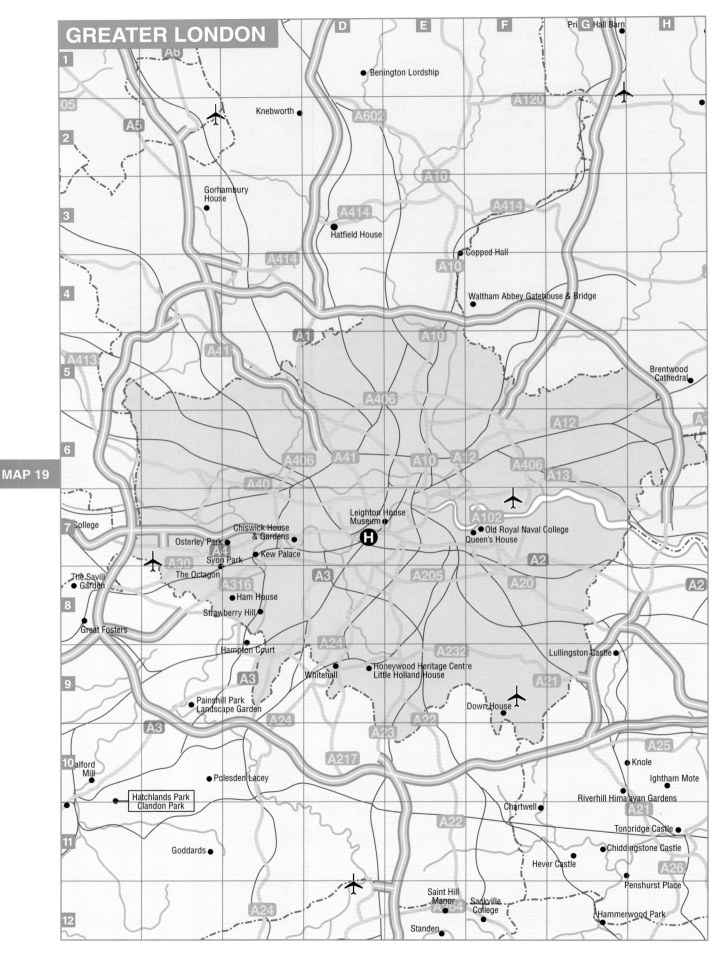

GREATER LONDON

MAP 19

Benington Lordship

Knebworth

Gorhambury House

Hatfield House

Copped Hall

Waltham Abbey Gatehouse & Bridge

Brentwood Cathedral

Pri... Hall Barn

College

Leighton House Museum

Old Royal Naval College
Queen's House

Chiswick House & Gardens

Osterley Park

Kew Palace

Syon Park

The Octagon

The Savill Garden

Ham House

Strawberry Hill

Great Fosters

Hampton Court

Lullingstone Castle

Whitehall

Honeywood Heritage Centre
Little Holland House

Down House

Painshill Park Landscape Garden

...alford Mill

Polesden Lacey

Knole

Ightham Mote

Hatchlands Park
Clandon Park

Riverhill Himalayan Gardens

Chartwell

Tonbridge Castle

Goddards

Chiddingstone Castle

Hever Castle

Penshurst Place

Saint Hill Manor

Sackville College

Hammerwood Park

Standen

Register for news and special offers at www.hudsonsheritage.com

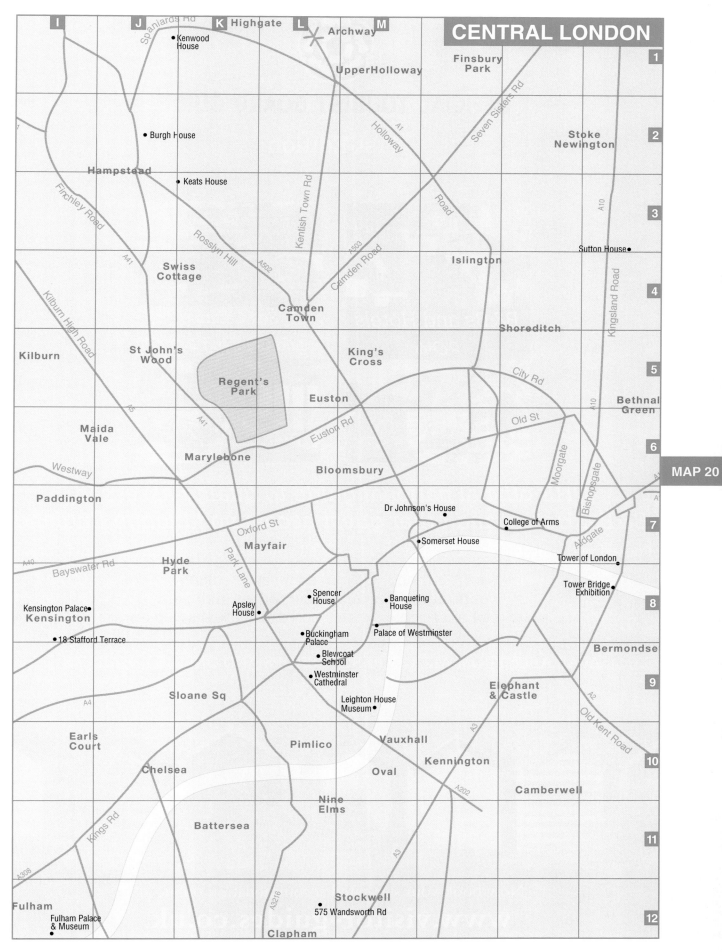

CENTRAL LONDON

Index

Places listed by name in alphabetical order

Hartland Abbey, Devon

Index

Athelhampton House, Dorset

©EDWIN REMSBERG

Kiplin Hall, Yorkshire

Whalton Manor, Northumberland